PUBLIC ORDER LAW

PUBLIC ORDER LAW

Richard Card LLB, LLM, FRSA
Professor of Law and Chairman of the School of Law
De Montfort University, Leicester

JORDANS

2000

Published by
Jordan Publishing Limited
21 St Thomas Street
Bristol BS1 6JS

British Library Cataloguing-in-Publication Data
A catalogue record for this book is available from the British Library.

ISBN 0 85308 595 1

Typeset by Mendip Communications Ltd, Frome, Somerset
Printed by MPG Books Ltd, Bodmin, Cornwall

PREFACE

Public disorder of various kinds is never far from the public eye. As has been the habit in modern times, Parliament has responded with legislation on a number of occasions, particularly in the last 15 years, to deal with perceived needs. The apparent inexorable march of public order law must now be reconciled with the provisions of the Human Rights Act 1998, and the Convention rights to which it applies, which will come into force soon after this book is published. Although at the time of writing the coming into force of the substantive parts of the 1998 Act is over seven months away, this book is written on the basis that that Act is in full force. Chapter 1 contains a basic outline of the Human Rights Act 1998 and of its impact on English law and the English legal system. Readers who are already familiar with these matters may safely skip this part of the text.

Some chapters in this book build on work previously published under my name, particularly *Public Order – The New Law*, published by Butterworths in 1987. As a perusal of the text shows, however, the law has not stood still – nor has my interpretation – since my original writing, so that the text in the relevant part of this book is often significantly different from my previous work.

In writing this book, I have tried to bear in mind the needs not only of the legal profession, but also of the magistracy, of members of police forces, of law students and of others who may read it.

For reasons of economy of space, all references to Acts of Parliament and subordinate legislation are to those instruments as amended and without reference to the amending legislation.

My thanks go to Stephen Honey and Mollie Dickenson of Jordans who, as always, have provided splendid assistance at all stages. Above all, I must thank my wife, Rachel, for her contribution to the preparation of this book, as research assistant, word processor and proof-reader. For all this help, I am grateful. For the imperfections which remain, I am solely responsible.

I have tried to summarise and explain the law as it was on 1 November 1999, although I have been able to include at proof stage some changes up to 1 February 2000.

RICHARD CARD
February 2000

CONTENTS

Preface		v
Table of Cases		xix
Table of Statutes		xxxix
Table of Statutory Instruments, By-laws and Codes of Practice		li
Table of EU and Foreign Legislation		lv
Table of Treaties and Conventions		lvii
Table of Abbreviations		lix
Further Reading		lxi

Chapter 1	**INTRODUCTION**	1
	GENERAL POINTS	1
	Role of the police	3
	Impact of public order law	5
	Trial and punishment	6
	EUROPEAN CONVENTION ON HUMAN RIGHTS AND HUMAN RIGHTS ACT 1998	7
	Impact of the Act	8
	Statutory interpretation	8
	Declaration of incompatibility	9
	Unlawful actions	10
	The Convention rights	11
	Application of Convention rights	15
	Prescribed by law/in accordance with the law	16
	Interference for a legitimate aim	16
	Necessary in a democratic society	17
	Proportionality	17
	Margin of appreciation	17
	Non-discriminatory	19

Chapter 2	**PREVENTIVE POWERS**	21
	INTRODUCTION	21
	COMMON LAW POWERS TO DEAL WITH OR PREVENT A BREACH OF THE PEACE	21
	Breach of the peace	21
	Definition	22
	Arrest without warrant	25
	Other powers	30
	Detention without arrest	31
	Entry to deal with or prevent a breach of the peace	32
	Remaining on premises to deal with or prevent a breach of the peace	34
	Prohibiting a meeting to prevent a breach of the peace	35
	Use of reasonable force to prevent a breach of the peace	37

Exercise of powers by private citizen   38
Reasonably apprehended breaches of the peace   38
Against whom can the preventive powers be exercised?   39
BINDING OVER TO KEEP THE PEACE OR TO BE OF
GOOD BEHAVIOUR   43
Statutory complaint procedure   48
Binding over outside the statutory complaint procedure:
binding over at the court's own motion   51
Against whom can a binding-over order be made?   52
When can an order be made?   53
Binding-over order   56
Refusal to enter into a recognisance   58
Appeal against order   59
Breach of binding-over order   60
Law Commission report   61
ANTI-SOCIAL BEHAVIOUR ORDERS   63
Rationale and background   63
The conditions for making an order   65
Who can apply for an order?   65
The requirements for an order   66
Anti-social manner   67
Reasonable acts disregarded   70
The effect of anti-social behaviour   71
Necessity for the order   72
'Further anti-social acts'   72
Applications in respect of juveniles   72
Procedure   73
Proof   73
The order   74
Appeals   76
Variation or discharge   77
Breach of the order   77
Evaluation   78

Chapter 3   MAJOR PUBLIC ORDER OFFENCES   81
INTRODUCTION   81
RIOT   83
Prohibited conduct   84
Use of unlawful violence   84
Unlawful violence   85
Violence   85
Unlawful   87
Twelve or more persons present together   88
Use or threat of unlawful violence   89
In pursuance of a common purpose   91
Conduct such as would cause fear   92
Mental element   93
Alternative bases for conviction   95
Prosecution, trial and punishment   96
Riot (Damages) Act 1886   97
'Riot' etc in other statutes   97
VIOLENT DISORDER   98
Prohibited conduct   99

An individual accused may be guilty if he uses or
threatens violence 100
Only three persons (including the accused) who are
present together are required to use or threaten
unlawful violence 100
Neither the accused nor the other participants are
required to use or threaten unlawful violence for a
common purpose 101
Mental element 101
Acquittal of all but one or two 101
Alternative bases for conviction 103
Prosecution, trial and punishment 104
AFFRAY 104
Prohibited conduct 105
Use or threat of unlawful violence towards another 106
Conduct such as would cause a person of reasonable
firmness present at the scene to fear for his personal
safety 109
Mental element 111
Alternative bases for conviction 112
Prosecution, trial and punishment 112
Arrest without warrant 113
GENERAL 114
Duplicity 114
Alternative verdicts 115
Trials on indictment 115
Summary trials 118

**Chapter 4 THREATENING, ABUSIVE, INSULTING OR
DISORDERLY CONDUCT AND RELATED OFFENCES 119**
INTRODUCTION 119
FEAR OR PROVOCATION OF VIOLENCE 119
Prohibited conduct 120
Threatening, abusive or insulting 120
Using words or behaviour 122
Distribution or display of any writing etc 122
Towards another ... or to another 123
Public or private place 125
The exception 125
Mental element 126
Prosecution, trial and punishment 131
Police powers 131
1986 ACT: SECTIONS 4A AND 5 132
INTENTIONALLY CAUSING HARASSMENT, ALARM OR
DISTRESS 133
Prohibited conduct 133
Threatening, abusive, insulting or disorderly 133
Conduct need not be towards or to another 135
Causing harassment, alarm or distress 135
Public or private place 137

Mental element   138
Defences   140
Trial and punishment   146
Arrest   146
CONDUCT LIKELY TO CAUSE HARASSMENT, ALARM
OR DISTRESS   146
    Prohibited conduct   147
        Harassment, alarm or distress likely   148
        Public or private places   151
    Mental element   151
    Defences   152
    Trial and punishment   153
    Arrest   153
    Conclusions   155
RACIALLY-AGGRAVATED PUBLIC ORDER OFFENCES   158
    When is an offence racially aggravated?   161
        Definition of racial group   161
        Racial aggravation   165
            Demonstration of hostility based on victim's
            membership etc of a racial group   166
            Motivation by hostility towards members of a racial
            group based on their membership of that group   168
    The offences   169
        Trial and punishment   170
        Alternative verdicts   170
        Arrest   171
        Why not offences of racially-aggravated riot, violent
        disorder or affray?   171
PROTECTION FROM HARASSMENT ACT 1997   172
    Prohibition of harassment   173
    Civil remedy   174
        Breach of injunction   175
    Offences   176
        Offence of harassment   176
        Putting people in fear of violence   176
        Restraining orders   177
    Racially-aggravated harassment   178
        Trial, punishment and arrest   178
        Alternative verdicts   179
            Trials on indictment   179
            Summary trials   179
PROVOCATION TO BREACH OF THE PEACE BY A
PUBLIC PLAY   180
RELATED OFFENCES   182

Chapter 5   **INCITING RACIAL HATRED**   **183**
INTRODUCTION   183
RACIAL HATRED   184
    Racial hatred intended or likely   186
    Racial harassment not enough   188

Threatening, abusive or insulting 188
THE OFFENCES 189
Use of words or behaviour or display of written material 189
Prohibited conduct 189
In a public or private place 189
Words, behaviour or display 190
Mental element 191
Prosecution, trial, punishment and arrest 191
Publishing or distributing 192
Prohibited conduct 192
Publication or distribution 192
To the public or a section of it 193
Written material 194
Mental element 194
Prosecution, trial, punishment and arrest 194
Recordings 194
Mental element 195
Prosecution, trial and punishment 196
Possession of racially inflammatory material 196
Mental element 197
Prosecution, trial and punishment 198
Entry and search 198
Public plays 198
Mental element 199
Prosecution, trial and punishment 200
Inclusion in programme service 200
Prosecution, trial and punishment 201
GENERAL POINTS ABOUT THE OFFENCES 201
Offences by corporations 201
Parliamentary and court reports 202
Prosecutions 203
Duplicity 205
Trial and punishment 205
Forfeiture 205
European Convention on Human Rights 207
Other racist offences 208

Chapter 6 PROCESSIONS AND ASSEMBLIES 209
INTRODUCTION 209
THE LAW ON PUBLIC PROCESSIONS 210
'Public procession' 210
Advance notice 212
When must notice be given? 213
Exempt processions 215
Who must give notice and to whom? 216
Delivery 216
Contents of the notice 218
Offences 218
Defences 220

Arrest	221
Imposing conditions on public processions	221
Who can impose conditions?	221
The grounds	223
Serious public disorder/serious damage	223
Serious disruption	224
Intimidation	225
The conditions	226
Procedural matters	227
Offences	227
European Convention on Human Rights	230
Prohibition of processions	231
The procedure	231
Notice of bans	233
Terms of a ban	233
Offences	235
European Convention on Human Rights	235
THE LAW ON PUBLIC ASSEMBLIES	236
Imposing conditions on public assemblies	237
What is a 'public assembly' under s 14?	237
Who can impose conditions, and when, and on whom?	238
Conditions that may be imposed	239
Offences	242
Prohibition of trespassory assemblies	243
The grounds for prohibition	243
Type of assembly	244
Lack of permission or excess of permission or right	245
Serious disruption or significant damage	245
The procedure	247
Terms of a ban	248
Offences	248
European Convention on Human Rights	251
Power to stop people proceeding to banned assembly	252
GENERAL	252
Arrest without warrant	252
Delegation of chief officer's powers	253
Challenging a condition or ban	254
No appeal against merits	254
Judicial review	254
REGULATION OF ROUTES ETC	257
DISORDERLY CONDUCT AT MEETINGS	259
Disorderly conduct at an election meeting	260
Chapter 7 COLLECTIVE TRESPASS OR NUISANCE ON LAND	**263**
INTRODUCTION	263
FAILURE TO LEAVE OR RE-ENTRY TO LAND AFTER POLICE DIRECTION TO LEAVE	263
Direction to leave etc	264
Two or more trespassers	265

Present with the common purpose of residing   268
Request to leave   269
Damage, threats etc or possession of vehicles   269
The making of the direction   272
Offences   275
Prohibited conduct   275
Mental element   278
Defences   278
Trial and punishment   279
Arrest   279
Seizure   280
Retention and disposal   280
Need   283
AGGRAVATED TRESPASS   284
The offence   285
Prohibited conduct   285
Mental element   289
Prevention of evil – a defence?   292
Trial, punishment and arrest   292
Direction to leave land   292
The power   292
The direction   293
Offences   296
Trial and punishment   297
Police powers   297
Concluding points   298
POWERS IN RELATION TO RAVES   300
What is a 'rave' for the purposes of the Act?   301
100 or more   302
Trespass unnecessary   302
The place   302
Spontaneous gatherings   303
Amplified music   303
During the night   303
Serious distress   304
Duration of a rave   304
Direction to leave   305
Who can direct?   305
The grounds   305
The direction   305
Offences   307
Arrest   307
Human rights   308
Power to stop persons proceeding   308
Entry and seizure   309
Entry   309
Seizure   309
Forfeiture of sound equipment on conviction   310
Determining claims   311
Other points   312

UNAUTHORISED VEHICULAR CAMPERS   312
  Abolition of local authority duty to provide sites for
    gypsies   312
  Other changes   314
  Directing unauthorised vehicular campers to leave   314
    Unauthorised vehicular campers   314
  The direction   317
    Notice   318
  Offences   319
    Defences   320
    Trial and punishment   320
  Order for removal   320
  Human rights   321
SQUATTERS   322
  Interim possession order   323
  Trespassing during currency of interim possession order
    or re-entering as trespasser thereafter   327
    Mental element   328
    Trial, punishment and arrest   329
  Interim possession order: false or misleading statements   329
    False or misleading statements to obtain an order   329
    Prohibited conduct   330
    Mental element   330
    False or misleading statements to resist an order   331
    Trial, punishment and arrest   331
ENTERING AND REMAINING ON PROPERTY   332
  Violence for securing entry   332
    Prohibited conduct   332
    Mental element   333
    Without lawful authority   333
    Displaced residential occupier and protected
      intending occupier   334
    Power of arrest   336
  Adverse occupation of residential premises   336
    Prohibited conduct   336
    Mental element   337
    Defences   337
  Other offences   338

Chapter 8   FOOTBALL HOOLIGANISM   339
            INTRODUCTION   339
            SPORTING EVENTS (CONTROL OF ALCOHOL ETC)
            ACT 1985   341
              Alcohol on coaches, trains etc   341
                Vehicles specified   341
                Designated sporting event   343
                  Sporting event ... designated ... by the Secretary
                    of State   343
                  Designated sporting event ... Part V of the Criminal
                    Justice (Scotland) Act 1980   344

Causing or permitting carriage of alcohol on a
vehicle 344
Possession of alcohol on a vehicle 345
Being drunk on a vehicle 347
A gap 347
Police powers 347
Alcohol, containers, fireworks etc at designated sports
grounds 348
Designated sports ground 348
Period of designated sporting event 348
Possession of alcohol etc at designated ground 349
Possession of fireworks etc 351
Being drunk at designated ground 352
General police powers under the 1985 Act 352
FOOTBALL (OFFENCES) ACT 1991 353
Throwing objects 354
Chanting 355
Pitch invasion 355
Arrest, trial and punishment 356
DOMESTIC FOOTBALL BANNING ORDERS (DFBOs) 356
Offences to which s 31 applies 358
Giving notice of order etc 362
Photographs 362
Duration of order 363
Appeal against order 364
Application for termination of order 364
Breach of order 365
INTERNATIONAL FOOTBALL BANNING ORDERS
(IFBOs) 365
When can an international football banning order be
made? 366
Effect of an IFBO 368
Giving notice of order etc 369
Duration of order 370
Reporting procedure 371
Appeal against order 373
Application for termination of order 373
Breach of order 373
Arrest 375
FOOTBALL TICKET TOUTING 375
Prohibited conduct 376
Sale etc of ticket by unauthorised person 376
For designated football match 377
Place of commission 377
Mental element 378
Arrest, trial and punishment 378

Chapter 9 **MISCELLANEOUS PUBLIC ORDER OFFENCES** 381
PROHIBITION OF POLITICAL UNIFORMS AND QUASI-
MILITARY ORGANISATIONS 381

Prohibition of political uniforms   381
A related offence   384
Prohibition of quasi-military organisations   385
Unlawful Drilling Act 1819   387
DRUNK AND DISORDERLY   388
TOWN POLICE CLAUSES ACT 1847, s 28   389
METROPOLITAN POLICE ACT 1839, s 54   391
BOMB HOAXES   392
Placing or dispatching an article   392
Messages known or believed to be false   393
Trial, punishment and arrest   394
DISTURBANCE IN CHURCH, CERTIFIED PLACE OF
WORSHIP OR BURIAL-GROUND   394
First part of s 2   395
Second part of s 2   396
Trial, punishment and arrest   397
Related offences   397
Reform   398
LABOUR RELATIONS: INTIMIDATION   399
Prohibited conduct   399
Using violence to or intimidating the other person or
his wife or children, or injuring his property   400
Persistently following the other person from place
to place   401
Hiding any tools, clothes or other property owned or
used by the other person or depriving him or
hindering him in the use thereof   401
Watching or besetting the house or other place where
the other person resides, works or carries on business
or happens to be, or the approach to any such house
or place   401
Following the other person with two or more persons
in a disorderly manner through a street or road   402
General requirement: 'wrongfully'   402
Mental element   403
Without legal authority   404
Trial, punishment and arrest   406
ASSAULTING, WILFULLY OBSTRUCTING OR
RESISTING A CONSTABLE IN THE EXECUTION OF HIS
DUTY   406
In the execution of his duty   407
Assaulting a constable in the execution of his duty   411
Prohibited conduct   412
Mental element   412
Wilful obstruction   413
Obstruction   413
Wilful   414
Resistance   416
Arrest   416
Related offences   417

OBSTRUCTION OF THE HIGHWAY 418
  Highways Act 1980, s 137 418
    Prohibited conduct 418
    Mental element 420
    Without lawful authority or excuse 421
    General 424
    Trial, punishment and powers 425
  Obstruction under Town Police Clauses Act 1847 and
  Metropolitan Police Act 1839 425
  Obstruction of highway: common law offence 426
PUBLIC NUISANCE 426
BY-LAWS UNDER LOCAL GOVERNMENT ACT 1972, s 235 429
  Offences against local authority by-laws 430

Index **433**

TABLE OF CASES

References are to paragraph numbers.

A v UK (1972) 42 CD 35, ECommHR   4.38

Abrahams v Cavey [1968] 1 QB 479; [1967] 3 All ER 179; [1967] 3 WLR 1229, DC   9.31

Absalom v Martin [1974] RTR 145; [1973] Crim LR 752, DC   9.86

Adsett v K & L Steelfounders and Engineers Ltd [1953] 1 All ER 97n, [1953] 1 WLR 137; 97 SJ 49   6.9

Agnew v Munrow (1891) 28 Sc LR 335; (1891) 18 R (J) 22, High Ct of Justiciary   9.39, 9.45

Albert v Lavin [1982] AC 546; [1981] 3 All ER 878; [1981] 3 WLR 955, HL   2.7, 2.11, 2.12, 2.19, 2.21

Allen v Ireland [1984] 1 WLR 903; (1984) 79 Cr App R 206; [1984] Crim LR 500, DC   3.12

Allied Amusements v Reaney (1936) 3 WWR 129   9.45

Amin v Nottingham City Council (1999) *The Times*, 2 December, CA   1.11

Andrews v Andrews [1908] 2 KB 567   8.32

Andrews v Chapman (1853) 3 Car & Kir 286   5.52

Ansell v Police [1979] 2 NZLR 53, NZCA   4.71

Armstrong, Re (1992) unreported, NIQBD   6.30

Armstrong v Moon (1894) 13 NZLR 517, NZSC   9.19

Arrowsmith v Jenkins [1963] 2 QB 561; [1963] 2 All ER 210; [1963] 2 WLR 856, DC   9.75, 9.76, 9.78

Associated Provincial Picture Houses Ltd v Wednesbury Corpn [1948] 1 KB 223; [1947] 2 All ER 680; 177 LT 641, CA   1.26, 2.48, 6.97

Atkin v DPP (1989) 89 Cr App R 199; [1989] Crim LR 581; (1989) 153 JP 383, DC   2.68, 4.8, 4.10, 7.19

Attorney-General v Beynon [1970] Ch 1; [1969] 2 All ER 263; [1969] 2 WLR 1447   7.97

Attorney-General v Ernest Augustus of Hanover [1957] AC 436; [1957] 1 All ER 49; [1957] 2 WLR 1   9.12

Attorney-General v O'Brien (1936) 70 ITLR 101   9.42

Attorney-General v PYA Quarries Ltd [1957] 2 QB 169; [1957] 2 WLR 770; *sub nom* Attorney-General (on the relation of Glamorgan County Council and Pontardawe RDC) v PYA Quarries Ltd [1957] 1 All ER 894, CA   9.92–9.95

Attorney-General of Hong Kong v Lee Kwong-Kut [1993] AC 951; [1993] 3 All ER 939; [1993] 3 WLR 329, PC   4.38

Attorney-General of Hong Kong v Tse Hung-lit [1986] AC 876; [1986] 3 All ER 173; [1986] 3 WLR 320, PC   8.11

Attorney-General's Reference (No 3 of 1983) [1985] QB 242; [1985] 1 All ER 501; [1985] 2 WLR 253, CA   3.5, 3.57

Austria v Italy (1963) 6 YB 740, ECommHR   2.52, 2.80

Backer v Secretary of State for the Environment [1983] 2 All ER 1021; [1983] 1 WLR 1485; (1983) 46 P&CR 357   7.20

Ball v Ward (1875) 40 JP 213; 33 LT 170, DC   9.89

Bamping v Barnes [1958] Crim LR 186; 225 LT 241, DC   2.27, 2.41

Barrett v Enfield LBC [1999] 3 All ER 193; [1999] 3 WLR 79; [1999] 2 FLR 426,
    CA   1.11
Bastable v Little [1907] 1 KB 59; 76 LJKB 77; 96 LT 115, DC   9.66
Bater v Bater [1951] P 35; [1950] 2 All ER 458; 66 TLR (Pt 2) 589   2.80
Beard v UK (1998) 25 EHRR CD 28, ECommHR   7.110
Beatty v Gillbanks (1882) 9 QBD 308; (1882) 13 Cox CC 138; [1881–5] All ER Rep
    559, DC   2.22, 2.23, 2.49, 6.106
Beckford v R [1987] 3 All ER 425, PC   3.31
Belgian Linguistic Case (1968) Ser A, no 6; 1 EHRR 252, ECtHR   1.27
Bennett v Bale [1986] Crim LR 404, DC   9.66
Bentley v Brudzinski (1982) 75 Cr App R 217; [1982] Crim LR 825, DC   9.58
Bent's Brewery Co v Hogan [1945] 2 All ER 570   9.47
Beseley v Clarkson (1861) 3 Lev 37   7.8
Betts v Stevens [1910] 1 KB 1; 79 LJKB 17; 73 JP 486, DC   9.66
Bewglass v Blair 1888 15 R (Ct of Sess) 45   2.3
Bishop of St Albans v Fillingham [1906] P 163; 22 TLR 293   9.33
Blackburn v Bowering [1994] 3 All ER 380; [1994] 1 WLR 1324; [1995] Crim LR
    38, DC   9.64
Boddington v British Transport Police [1999] 2 AC 143; [1998] 2 All ER 203;
    [1998] 2 WLR 639, HL   6.95, 9.101
Boxer v Snelling [1972] RTR 472; [1972] Crim LR 441; 116 SJ 564, DC   7.20
Bracey v Read [1963] Ch 88; [1962] 3 All ER 472; [1962] 3 WLR 1194   8.32
Brickley v Police (1988) (July) Legal Action 21, Crown Ct   6.39
British Broadcasting Corporation v Hearn [1978] 1 All ER 111; [1978] 1 WLR
    1004; [1977] ICR 685, CA   9.47
Brooks v Nottinghamshire Police [1984] Crim LR 677, Crown Ct   2.40
Broome v DPP [1974] AC 587; [1974] 1 All ER 314; [1974] 2 WLR 58, HL   9.47, 9.76
Brownsea Haven Properties Ltd v Poole Corpn [1958] Ch 574; [1958] 1 All ER
    205; [1958] 2 WLR 137, CA   6.102
Brutus v Cozens [1973] AC 854; [1972] 2 All ER 1297; [1972] 3 WLR 521, HL   3.15, 4.5,
                                                                      4.28, 5.14, 7.129, 9.6, 9.42
Bryan v Mott (1975) 62 Cr App R 71, DC   2.90, 7.30, 8.56
Bryan v Robinson [1960] 2 All ER 173, [1960] 1 WLR 506; 124 JP 310, DC   4.5
Buckley v UK (1996) 1996-IV RJD 1271; (1997) 23 EHRR 101; [1996] JPL 1018;
    (1996) *The Times*, 9 October, ECtHR   1.25, 7.110
Bullock v Turnbull [1952] 2 Lloyd's Rep 303, DC   9.78
Burden v Rigler [1911] 1 KB 337; 80 LJKB 100; 75 JP 36, DC   6.106
Burnett and Hallamshire Fuel Ltd v Sheffield Telegraph and Star Ltd [1960] 2 All
    ER 157; [1960] 1 WLR 502; 104 SJ 388   5.52
Burton v DPP (1998) unreported, DC   9.66

Capon v DPP (1998) *The Independent*, 23 March, DC   7.29, 7.30, 7.56, 7.61, 7.62
Carter v Secretary of State for the Environment [1994] 1 WLR 1212; 92 LGR 473;
    [1994] 29 EG 124, CA   7.20
Castorina v Chief Constable of Surrey (1988) 138 NLJ 180, CA   3.68
Chambers v DPP [1995] Crim LR 896; [1995] COD 321, DC   4.24, 4.28
Chapman v DPP (1989) 89 Cr App R 190; [1988] Crim LR 843; (1989) 153 JP 27,
    DC   9.51
Chapman v Hall (1988) 89 Cr App R 190, DC   3.68
Chappell v DPP (1988) 89 Cr App R 82, DC   4.7, 4.10, 4.25, 4.32, 4.44
Chappell v UK (1987) 53 D&R 241; 10 EHRR 510, ECommHR   6.89
Charnock v Court [1899] 2 Ch 35; 68 LJ Ch 550; 63 JP 546, High Ct   9.42

Charter v Race Relations Board [1973] AC 868; [1973] 1 All ER 512; [1973] 2
WLR 299, HL   5.24
Cheesman v DPP [1992] QB 83; [1991] 3 All ER 54; [1991] 2 WLR 1105, DC   9.19
Chief Constable of Avon and Somerset Constabulary v Singh [1988] RTR 107, DC   8.56
Chief Constable of Norfolk v Clayton [1983] 2 AC 473; [1983]1 All ER 984;
[1983] 2 All ER 462, HL   3.74, 4.3
Chief Constable of Surrey Constabulary v Ridley and Steel [1985] Crim LR 725,
DC   2.48
Choudhury v UK (1991) 12 HRLJ 172, ECommHR   5.5
Christians against Racism and Fascism v UK (1978) 21 D&R 138, ECommHR   6.50, 6.53,
7.66
Clarkson v Stewart (1894) 32 SLR 4, Ct of Sess   9.38
Cobb v DPP (1992) 156 JP 746; (1992) 156 JPN 330, DC   3.54
Coffin v Smith (1980) 71 81 Cr App R 221, DC   9.52, 9.53, 9.54
Collins v Wilcock [1984] 3 All ER 374; [1984] 1 WLR 1172; (1984) 79 Cr App R
229, DC   9.58
Commission for Racial Equality v Dutton [1989] QB 783; [1989] 1 All ER 306;
[1989] 2 WLR 17, CA   4.71, 5.5
Commissioner of Police of the Metropolis v Caldwell [1982] AC 341; [1981] 1 All
ER 961; [1981] 2 WLR 509, HL   7.124
Congreve v Home Office [1976] QB 629; [1976] 1 All ER 697; [1976] 2 WLR 291,
CA   6.96
Conlan v Oxford (1983) 5 Cr App R (S) 237; (1984) 148 JP 97; (1984) 79 Cr App
R 157, DC   2.48
Conway v Wade [1909] AC 506, HL   9.47
Cope v Barber (1872) LR 7 CP 393; 36 JP 439; 41 LJ 137, DC   9.33
Cooper v Metropolitan Police Comr (1985) 82 Cr App R 238, DC   9.76, 9.82
Cotterill v Penn [1936] 1 KB 53, DC   9.78
Crafter v Kelly [1941] SASR 237, Sth Aust FC   8.21
Cummings v DPP [1999] COD 288; (1999) 143 SJLB 112; [1999] EHLR Dig 455,
DC   8.63
Cundy v Le Cocq (1884) 13 QBD 207; 53 LJMC 125; 48 JP 599, DC   7.118
Curlett v M'Kechnie 1938 JC 176   9.65
Curran v Treleavan [1891] 2 QB 545; 61 LJMC 9; 55 JP 485, CCR   9.39

Dallison v Caffery [1964] 1 QB 348; [1964] 2 All ER 610; [1964] 3 WLR 385, CA   3.68
Davey v Towle [1973] RTR 328; [1973] Crim LR 360, DC   6.39
Davies v Griffiths [1937] 2 All ER 671, DC   2.3
Davis v Lisle [1936] 2 All ER 213, DC   9.58
Dawkins v Crown Suppliers (PSB) Ltd [1993] ICR 517; [1993] IRLR 284; (1993)
The Times, 4 February, CA   4.71
Despard v Wilcox (1910) 102 LT 103, DC   6.101
Dew v DPP (1920) LJKB 1166, DC   5.21
DH Edmonds Ltd v East Sussex Police Authority (1988) *The Times*, 15 July, CA   3.39
Dibble v Ingleton [1972] 1 QB 480; [1972] 1 All ER 275; [1972] 2 WLR 163, DC   9.66
Dickins v Gill [1896] 2 QB 310, DC   8.21
Dino Services Ltd v Prudential Assurance Co Ltd [1989] 1 All ER 422; [1989] 1
Lloyd's Rep 379; 1989 Fin LR 316, CA   3.15, 7.129
Donnelly v Jackman [1970] 1 All ER 987; [1970] 1 WLR 562; 54 Cr App R 229, DC
9.58
DPP v Baillie [1995] Crim LR 426, DC   6.38, 6.61, 6.66, 6.68
DPP v Barnard (1999) 96 (42) LSG 40; (1999) 143 SJLB 256; (1999) *The Times*, 9
November, DC   7.44
DPP v Clarke [1994] Crim LR 58, DC   4.61

DPP v Clarke; Lewis; O'Connell and O'Keefe (1992) 94 Cr App R 359; [1992]
    Crim LR 60; [1992] COD 103, DC   3.29, 4.5, 4.11, 4.27, 4.34, 4.36, 4.38, 4.54, 5.18
DPP v Cotcher [1993] COD 181; (1992) *The Times*, 29 December, DC   3.58
DPP v Fellowes (1993) 157 JP 936; [1993] Crim LR 523; (1993) *The Times*, 1
    February, DC   8.63
DPP v Fidler [1992] 1 WLR 91; (1992) 94 Cr App R 286; [1992] Crim LR 62, DC   4.61,
    9.37, 9.45
DPP v Gormley (1992) unreported, DC   3.58
DPP v Hamandishe (1999) 5 Archbold News 3, DC   9.66
DPP v Hawkins [1988] 3 All ER 537, DC   9.59
DPP v Johnson [1995] 4 All ER 53; [1995] 1 WLR 728; [1995] RTR 53, DC   9.12
DPP v Jones (Margaret) [1999] 2 AC 240; [1999] 2 All ER 257; [1999] 2 WLR 625,
    HL   6.85–6.89
DPP v Kitching [1990] Crim LR 394; [1990] COD 149; (1990) 154 JP 293, DC   9.17
DPP v London Borough of Merton (1998) unreported, DC   4.71
DPP v London Borough of Merton (1999) unreported, DC   4.71
DPP v Majewski [1976] 2 WLR 623; [1976] 2 All ER 142; 62 Cr App R 262, HL   3.30,
    4.35
DPP v Moseley [1999] TLR 466; (1999) *The Times*, 23 June; (1999) *The Independent*,
    21 June, DC   4.91
DPP v Orum [1989] 1 WLR 88; (1989) 88 Cr App R 261; [1988] Crim LR 848,
    DC   2.4, 4.49, 4.51, 4.58
DPP v Roffey [1959] Crim LR 283; (1959) 123 JP 241, DC   6.57
DPP v Schildkamp [1971] AC 1; [1969] 3 All ER 1640; [1970] 2 WLR 279, HL   7.97,
    9.12
DPP v Speede; R v Liverpool JJ, ex parte Collins; R v Liverpool JJ, ex parte Santos
    [1998] 2 Cr App R 108, DC   2.30, 2.31, 2.41
DPP v Taylor; DPP v Little [1992] QB 645; [1992] 1 All ER 299; [1992] 2 WLR
    460, DC   9.61
DPP v Todd [1996] Crim LR 344; [1996] COD 111; (1995) *The Independent*, 5 May,
    DC   9.37
DPP v Whalley [1991] Crim LR; [1991] RTR 161; (1992) 156 JP 661, DC   8.56
DPP v Whyte [1972] AC 849; [1972] 3 All ER 12; [1972] 3 WLR 410, HL   5.12
Dumbell v Roberts [1944] 1 All ER 326, CA   3.68
Duncan v Jones [1936] 1 KB 218; [1935] All ER Rep 710; 99 JP 399, DC 2.16, 2.17, 2.21,
    2.22, 6.106
Duport Steels v Sirs [1980] 1 All ER 529; [1980] 1 WLR 142; [1980] ICR 161, HL   9.47
Dwyer v Mansfield [1946] KB 437; [1946] 2 All ER 247; [1947] LJR 894   9.82, 9.95

Eaton v Cobb [1950] 1 All ER 1016; 114 JP 271; 48 LGR 528, DC   9.78
Edwards v DPP (1993) 97 Cr App R 301, DC   9.59
Edwards v DPP (1996) unreported, DC   2.4, 4.14
Elsey v Smith (Procurator Fiscal) [1983] IRLR 292, High Ct of Justiciary   9.43
Engel v Netherlands (1976) Ser A, no 22; 1 EHRR 647, ECtHR   2.52
England v Secretary of State for Social Services (1982) FLR 222   2.75
Evans v Dell [1937] 1 All ER 349; 156 LT 240; 101 JP 149, DC   8.11
Evans v Hughes [1972] 3 All ER 412; [1972] 1 WLR 1452; 56 Cr App R 813, DC   2.90,
    7.30, 8.56
Everett v Ribbands [1952] 2 QB 198; [1952] 1 All ER 823; [1952] 1 TLR 933, CA   2.29,
    2.33, 2.40, 2.41
Ewart v Rogers (1985) unreported, DC   4.5
Express Newspapers Ltd v McShane [1980] AC 672; [1980] 1 All ER 65; [1980] 2
    WLR 89, HL   9.47
Ezelin v France (1991) Ser A, no 202; 14 EHRR 362, ECtHR   7.66

Fabbri v Morris [1947] 1 All ER 315; (1947) 176 LT 172; 63 TLR 34, DC   9.76, 9.82

Fagan v Metropolitan Police Comr [1969] 1 QB 439; [1968] 3 All ER 442; [1968]
    3 WLR 1120, DC   9.61
Fay v DPP [1998] COD 339, DC   9.17
Ferguson v Carnochan 1889 16 R (Ct of Sess) 93   2.3
Field v Receiver of Metropolitan Police [1907] 2 KB 853, DC   3.2
Fisher v Bell [1961] 1 QB 394; [1960] 3 All ER 731; [1960] 3 WLR 919, DC   8.61
Flockhart v Robertson *see* Flockhart v Robinson
Flockhart v Robinson [1950] 2 KB 498; 48 LQR 454; *sub nom* Flockhart v
    Robertson [1950] 1 All ER 1091, DC   6.6, 6.38
Foulkes v Chief Constable of the Merseyside Police [1998] 3 All ER 705; [1998] 2
    FLR 789; [1998] Fam Law 661, CA   2.7, 2.21
Fowler v Kibble [1922] 1 Ch 487, CA   9.41, 9.44
Foy v Chief Constable of Kent (1984) unreported, DC   2.17
Friedl v Austria (1995) 21 EHRR 83, ECommHR   6.89
Fuller v Fuller [1973] 2 All ER 650; [1973] 1 WLR 730; 117 SJ 224, CA   2.75
Furniss v Cambridge Daily News Ltd (1907) 23 TLR 705   5.52

G v Chief Superintendent of Police, Stroud (1988) 86 Cr App R 92; [1987] Crim
    LR 269, DC   2.4, 2.20, 3.68
G v FRG (1989) 60 D&R 256, ECommHR   6.89, 7.66
G & E v Norway Applications no 9278/81, 9415/81 (1981) 35 D&R 30,
    ECommHR   7.110
Gage v Jones [1983] RTR 508, DC   6.92
Galletly v Laird 1953 SC(J) 16; 1953 SLT 67   9.19
Galt (Procurator Fiscal) v Philp [1984] IRLR 156; (1984) 134 New LJ 257, High Ct
    of Justiciary   9.42, 9.44
Gammon (Hong Kong) Ltd v A-G of Hong Kong [1985] AC 1; [1984] 2 All ER
    503; [1984] 3 WLR 437, PC   7.118, 8.64
Gatland v Metropolitan Police Comr [1968] 2 QB 279; [1968] 2 All ER 100;
    [1968] 2 WLR 1263, DC   8.57, 9.79
Gayford v Chouler [1898] 1 QB 316; 67 LJQB 404; 62 JP 165, DC   6.77
Gelberg v Miller [1961] 1 All ER 291; [1961] 1 WLR 153; 125 JP 123, DC   9.69
Gibson v Dalton [1980] RTR 410, DC   4.59
Gibson v Lawson [1891] 2 QB 545; 61 LJMC 9; 55 JP 485, DC   9.39
Gillingham Borough Council v Medway (Chatham) Dock Co Ltd [1993] QB 343;
    [1992] 3 All ER 923; [1992] 3 WLR 449, CA   9.95
Glasgow College of Art v A-G (1848) 1 HL Cas 800   9.33
Glimmerveen v Netherlands (1978) 18 D&R 187; 4 EHRR 260, ECommHR   4.60
Goldsmith v Deakin (1933) 150 LT 157; [1933] All ER Rep 102; 98 JP 4, DC   8.11
Goodlad v Chief Constable of South Yorkshire [1979] Crim LR 51, Crown Ct   2.44
Gouriet v Union of Post Office Workers [1978] AC 435; [1977] 3 All ER 70;
    [1977] 3 WLR 300, HL   5.55
Green v DPP [1991] Crim LR 784; (1991) 155 JP 816; (1991) 155 JPN 474, DC   9.67
Green v Moore [1982] QB 1044; [1982] 1 All ER 428; [1982] 2 WLR 671, DC   9.66
Grey v Pearson (1857) 6 HL Cas 61; [1843–60] All ER Rep 21; 26 LJ Ch 473   7.24
Grieve v Macleod [1967] Crim LR 424; 1967 SLT 70; 1967 SC(J) 32, High Ct of
    Justiciary   8.21
Groom v DPP [1991] Crim LR 713; [1991] COD 362, DC   4.59
Gwynedd County Council v Jones [1986] ICR 833; (1986) 83 LS Gaz 3836, EAT   4.73,
     4.75

H and Others (Minors) (Sexual Abuse: Standard of Proof), Re [1996] AC 563;
  [1996] 2 WLR 8; [1996] 1 All ER 1, HL   4.16
Halford v Brooks [1992] PIQR P175; (1991) *The Times*, 3 October; (1991) *The*
  Independent, 1 October   2.80
Handyside v UK (1976) Ser A, no 24; 1 EHRR 737, ECtHR   1.23, 1.24, 1.25, 5.13, 5.60
Hardy v O'Flynn (1948) IR 343   9.38
Harrison v Duke of Rutland [1893] 1 QB 142; [1891–4] All ER Rep 514; 57 JP
  278, CA   6.85, 9.72
Hashman v UK (1999) *The Times*, 1 December, ECtHR   2.27, 2.34, 2.52, 2.83
Health Computing v Meek [1980] ICR 24; [1980] IRLR 437   9.47
Heinl v Jyske Bank (Gibraltar) Ltd [1999] TLR 661; (1999) *The Times*, 28
  September, CA   2.80
Hendry v Ferguson 1883 10 R (Ct of Sess) 63   2.3
Henry Bates v UK Application no 26280/95, ECommHR   4.38
Herrington v DPP (1992) unreported, DC   4.38
Hey v Moorhouse (1839) 6 Bing NC 52   7.9
Hibberd v DPP [1997] CLYB 1251, DC   7.46
Hickman v Maisey [1900] 1 QB 752; 69 LJQB 511; 82 LT 321, CA   6.85, 9.72
Hickman v O'Dwyer [1979] Crim LR 309, DC   2.18
Hill v Baxter [1958] 1 QB 277; [1958] 1 All ER 193; [1958] 2 WLR 76   6.39
Hillen & Pettigrew v ICI (Alkali) Ltd [1936] AC 65, HL   7.9
Hills v Ellis [1983] QB 680; [1983] 1 All ER 667; [1983] 2 WLR 234, DC   4.79, 9.67
Hinchcliffe v Sheldon [1955] 3 All ER 406; [1955] 1 WLR 1207; 120 JP 797, DC   9.66,
                                                                                      9.67
Hirst v Chief Constable of West Yorkshire (1987) 85 Cr App R 143; [1987] Crim
  LR 330; (1987) 151 JP 304, DC   8.57, 9.75, 9.76, 9.78, 9.79, 9.80, 9.81, 9.82, 9.85
Hoffman v Thomas [1974] 2 All ER 233; [1974] 1 WLR 374; [1974] Crim LR 122,
  DC   9.54
Homer v Cadman (1886) 50 JP 454, DC   9.75
Hoogstraten v Goward [1967] Crim LR 590; 111 SJ 581, DC   9.19
Hornal v Neuberger Products Ltd [1957] 1 QB 247; [1956] 3 All ER 970; [1956] 3
  WLR 1034   2.80
Howley v Oxford (1985) 81 Cr App R 246; [1985] Crim LR 724; (1985) 149 JP
  363, DC   2.48
Hubbard v Pitt [1976] QB 142; [1975] 3 All ER 1; [1975] 3 WLR 201, CA   9.85
Huckerby v Elliott [1970] 1 All ER 189; (1969) 113 SJ 1001, DC   5.50
Hudson v Chief Constable of Avon and Somerset Constabulary [1976] Crim LR
  451, DC   4.5
Hughes v Holley (1988) 86 Cr App R 130; [1987] Crim LR 253; (1987) 151 JP
  233, DC   2.26, 2.27, 2.33, 2.35, 2.41
Humphries v Connor (1864) 17 Ir CLR 1   2.12, 2.18, 2.21, 4.7
Huntingdon Life Sciences Ltd v Curtin (1997) *The Times*, 11 December, QBD   4.91
Hyam v DPP [1975] AC 55; [1974] 2 All ER 41; [1974] 2 WLR 607   4.35

I v DPP [2000] Crim LR 45, DC   3.7, 3.21, 3.54, 3.55
Invicta Plastics Ltd v Clare [1976] RTR 251; [1976] Crim LR 131; (1975) 120 SJ
  62, DC   6.41
IRC v Rossminster Ltd *see* R v IRC ex parte Rossminster Ltd
Islington BC v Panico [1973] 3 All ER 485; [1973] 1 WLR 1166; [1973] Crim LR
  536, DC   4.38

J Lyons & Co Ltd v Wilkins [1896] 1 Ch 811; 65 LJ Ch 601; 60 JP 325, CA   9.44

J Lyons & Co Ltd v Wilkins [1899] 1 Ch 255; 68 LJ Ch 146; 63 JP 339, CA   9.44, 9.45

Jacobs v London County Council [1950] AC 361; [1950] 1 All ER 737; 66 TLR (Pt
   1) 659, HL   9.93

Jaggard v Dickinson [1981] QB 527; [1980] 3 All ER 716; [1981] 2 WLR 118, DC   8.57,
                                                                                                 9.79

Jersild v Denmark (1994) Ser A, no 298; 19 EHRR 1; (1994) *The Times*, 20
   October, ECtHR   5.60

John Calder (Publications) Ltd v Powell [1965] 1 QB 509; [1965] 1 All ER 159;
   [1965] 2 WLR 138, DC   9.19

Johnson v Phillips [1975] 3 All ER 682; [1976] 1 WLR 65; [1976] RTR 170, DC   9.54,
                                                                                            9.57, 9.67

Johnson v Whitehouse [1984] RTR 38, DC   3.68

Jones v Bescoby (1987) unreported, DC   9.82

Jones v Sherwood [1942] 1 KB 127; 111 LJKB 95; 106 JP 65, DC   9.61

Jordan v Burgoyne [1963] 2 QB 744; [1963] 2 All ER 225; [1963] 2 WLR 1045,
   DC   4.16, 4.102

Jordan v Gibbon (1863) 8 LT 391   2.4

Joyce v Hertfordshire Constabulary (1985) 80 Cr App R 298, DC   2.6

Judge v Bennett (1887) 52 JP 247; 36 WR 103; 4 TLR 75   9.39

JW Dwyer Ltd v Metropolitan Police District Receiver [1967] 2 QB 970; [1967] 2
   All ER 1051; [1967] 3 WLR 731, DC   3.38

Kamara v DPP [1974] AC 104; [1973] 2 All ER 1242; [1973] 3 WLR 198   3.4

Kaufman v Belgium (1986) 50 D&R 98, ECommHR   2.52

Kavanagh v Hiscock [1974] QB 600; [1974] 2 All ER 177; [1974] 2 WLR 421, DC   9.67,
                                                                                            9.88

Kelleher v DPP (1994) unreported, DC   4.5, 4.11

Kenlin v Gardiner [1967] 2 QB 510; [1966] 3 All ER 931; [1967] 2 WLR 291, DC   9.58,
                                                                                            9.63, 9.64

Kennedy v Cowie [1891] 1 QB 771, DC   9.40

Kent County Council v Holland (1997) 161 JP 558; [1996] COD 469; [1996]
   EGCS 135, DC   9.75, 9.77

Kent v Metropolitan Police Commissioner (1981) *The Times*, 15 May, CA   6.6, 6.50, 6.51,
                                                                                            6.97

Kerr v DPP (1994) 158 JP 1048; [1995] Crim LR 394; (1994) 158 JPN 653, DC   9.51, 9.56

Khawaja v Secretary of State for the Home Department [1984] AC 74; [1983] 1 All
   ER 765; [1983] WLR 321   2.80

King v Hodges [1974] Crim LR 424, DC   2.18

Knox v Anderton (1983) 76 Cr App R 156; [1983] Crim LR 114; (1983) 147 JP
   340, DC   8.63, 9.17

Krumpa v DPP [1989] Crim LR 295; (1988) *The Times*, 31 December, DC   7.26, 7.60

Kruse v Johnson [1898] 2 QB 91; 62 JP 469; 67 LJQB 782, DC   9.101

Kwasi-Poku v DPP [1993] Crim LR 705, DC   4.36

Lamb v DPP (1989) 154 JP 381; (1990) 154 JPN 172, DC   2.15

Lanham v Rickwood (1984) 148 JP 737; (1984) 81 LS Gaz 1915; (1984) 148 JPN
   733, DC   9.17

Lansbury v Riley [1914] 3 KB 229; 77 JP 440; 83 LJKB 1226, DC   2.25, 2.26, 2.35, 2.40

Large v Mainprize [1989] Crim LR 213; [1989] COD 249, DC   7.124

Lawrence v Same [1968] 2 QB 93; [1968] 1 All ER 1191; [1968] 2 WLR 1062, DC   3.74,
                                                                                             4.3

Lawrenson v Oxford [1982] Crim LR 185, DC   6.5

LC v Criminal Injuries Compensation Board (1999) *The Times*, 3 June, Ct of Sess
   (OH)   3.15

Ledger v DPP [1991] Crim LR 439, DC 9.58, 9.67
Lee v Nursery Furnishings Ltd [1945] 1 All ER 387 6.9
Lewin v Bland [1985] RTR 171; (1984) 148 JP 69, DC 4.102
Lewis v Cattle [1938] 2 KB 454; [1938] 2 All ER 638; 107 LJKB 429, DC 9.50
Lewis v Chief Constable of Greater Manchester (1991) *The Independent*, 23
    October, CA 2.4
Lewis v Cox [1985] QB 509; [1984] 3 All ER 672; [1984] 3 WLR 875; (1984) 80 Cr
    App R 1, DC 9.66, 9.67
Lewis v DPP (1995) unreported, DC 4.5, 4.36, 4.37, 4.43
Lewis v Levy (1858) EB&E 537 5.52
Lewis, ex parte (1888) 21 QBD 191; 52 JP 773; 57 LJMC 108, DC 6.85, 9.74
Lingens v Austria (1981) 26 D&R 171, ECommHR 4.38
Lister v Morgan [1978] Crim LR 292, Crown Ct 2.44
Lister v Perryman (1870) LR 4 HL 521, HL 3.68
Loade v DPP [1990] 1 QB 1052; [1990] 1 All ER 36; [1989] 3 WLR 1281, DC 4.13, 4.17
Lockyer v Gibb [1967] 2 QB 243; [1966] 2 All ER 653; [1966] 3 WLR 84, DC 5.34, 8.12
Lodge v DPP (1988) *The Times*, 26 October, DC 4.29, 4.47
Loizidou v Turkey (1995) Ser A, no 310; 20 EHRR 99, ECtHR 1.19
London Borough of Ealing v Race Relations Board [1972] AC 342; [1972] 1 All
    ER 105; [1972] 2 WLR 71, HL 4.68, 4.70
Lowdens v Keaveney [1903] 2 IR 82, Ir DC 9.83
Lucy v DPP (1997) 73 P&CR D25, DC 7.50
Ludlow v Burgess [1971] Crim LR 238, DC 9.54
Luisi and Carbone v Ministero del Tesero (Cases 286/82, 26/83) [1984] ECR 377;
    [1985] 3 CMLR 52, ECJ 8.47
Lunt v DPP [1993] Crim LR 534; [1993] COD 430, DC 9.66, 9.67

Maidstone Borough Council v Mortimer [1980] 3 All ER 552; (1982) 43 P&CR 67;
    [1981] JPL 112, DC 9.78
Malik v Bartram Personnel Group (1990) 4343/90 unreported, ET 4.71
Mallows v Harris [1979] Crim LR 320; [1979] RTR 404, DC 8.57, 9.79
Malone v UK (1985) Ser A, no 82; 7 EHRR 14, ECtHR 1.21
Mandla v Dowell Lee [1983] 2 AC 548; [1983] 1 All ER 106; [1983] 2 WLR 620,
    HL 4.71, 4.75
Marsh v Arscott (1982) 75 Cr App R 211; [1982] Crim LR 827, DC 2.6
Masterson v Holder [1986] 3 All ER 39; [1986] 1 WLR 1017; (1986) 83 Cr App R
    302, DC 4.5, 4.8
Mats Jacobsson v Sweden (1990) Ser A, no 180; 13 EHRR 79, ECtHR 7.34
Matthews v King [1934] 1 KB 505; [1933] All ER Rep 942; 97 JP 345, DC 9.30, 9.33, 9.35
McArdle v Egan (1933) 150 LT 412, CA 3.68, 6.28
McArdle v Wallace [1967] Crim LR 467, DC 9.58
McBean v Parker (1983) 147 JP 205, DC 2.4, 2.6
McBride v Turnock [1964] Crim LR 456; 108 SJ 336, DC 9.64
McCarrick v Oxford [1982] Crim LR 750; [1983] RTR 117, CA 3.68
McConnell v Chief Constable of Greater Manchester Police [1990] 1 All ER 423;
    [1990] 1 WLR 364; (1990) 91 Cr App R 88, CA 2.5, 4.19
McGowan v Chief Constable of Kingston-upon-Hull [1968] Crim LR 34; 117 New
    LJ 1138, DC 2.13, 2.15
McLeod v Commissioner of Police for the Metropolis [1994] 4 All ER 34; (1994)
    The Independent, 21 February, CA 2.14, 2.17
McLeod v UK [1998] 2 FLR 1048; 5 BHRC 364; [1998] HRCD 878, ECtHR 2.14
McLeod (or Houston) v Buchanan [1940] 2 All ER 179; 1940 SC (HL) 17; 1940
    SLT 232, HL 8.11
Mepstead v DPP [1996] Crim LR 111; [1996] COD 13; (1996) 160 JPN 448, DC 9.58

Miller v Minister of Pensions [1947] 2 All ER 372; [1947] WN 241; [1948] LJR
   203   2.73, 4.38, 4.91, 7.114
Minister of Health v Bellotti [1944] 1 All ER 238   7.9
Mohammed-Holgate v Duke [1984] AC 437; [1984] 1 All ER 1054; [1984] 2 WLR
   660, HL   6.97
Moore v Green [1983] 1 All ER 663, DC   9.67
Morphitis v Salmon [1990] Crim LR 48; (1990) 154 JP 365; (1990) 154 JPN 186,
   DC   6.77
Morrow v DPP [1994] Crim LR 58, DC   4.1, 4.36, 4.37, 4.55
Moss v McLachlan [1985] IRLR 76; (1985) 149 JP 167; (1985) 149 JPN 149, DC   2.17,
                    7.35
Mouncer v Mouncer [1972] 1 All ER 289; [1972] 1 WLR 321; (1971) 116 SJ 78   2.75
Muller v Switzerland (1991) Ser A, no 133; 13 EHRR 212, ECtHR   4.62
Murphy, Re [1991] 5 NIJB 88   6.30
Myers v Garrett [1972] Crim LR 232, DC   9.21

Nagy v Weston [1965] 1 All ER 78; [1965] 1 WLR 280; 129 JP 104, DC   8.57, 9.76, 9.79,
                  9.81, 9.82, 9.86
Nakkuda Ali v MF De S Jayaratne [1951] AC 66; 66 TLR (Pt 2) 214; 66 LQR 422,
   PC   3.68, 6.28
Nash v Finlay (1901) 85 LT 682; 62 JP 183; 18 TLR 92, DC   9.101
Neal v Evans [1976] RTR 333, DC   9.66
Neale v E (A Minor) (1983) 80 Cr App R 20, DC   9.17
Needham v DPP (1994) unreported, DC   6.100
Neizer v Rhodes (1995) SCCR 799, High Ct of Justiciary   7.16
Nelder v DPP [1998] TLR 375; (1998) *The Times*, 8 June; (1998) *The Independent*,
   8 June, DC   7.38, 7.47, 7.50
Neville v Mavroghenis [1984] Crim LR 42, DC   7.118
Newell v Cross; Newell v Cook [1936] 2 KB 632; [1936] 2 All ER 203; 100 JP 371,
   DC   8.11
News Group Newspapers Ltd v Society of Graphical and Allied Trades '82 (No 2)
   [1987] ICR 181   9.39
Nicol v DPP (1996) 160 JP 155, DC   2.23, 2.26, 2.32, 2.33
Northern Joint Police Board v Power [1997] IRLR 610, EAT   4.71
Norton v Lees (1921) 85 JPN 500; on appeal 87 JPN 675, DC   9.83
NWL Ltd v Woods [1979] 3 All ER 614; [1979] 1 WLR 1294; [1979] ICR 867, HL   9.47

O'Hara v Chief Constable of the Royal Ulster Constabulary [1997] AC 286; [1997]
   1 All ER 129; [1997] 2 WLR 1, HL   3.68
O'Kelly v Harvey (1883) 15 Cox CC 435   2.22
O'Moran v DPP [1975] QB 864; [1975] 1 All ER 473; [1975] 2 WLR 413, DC   9.4, 9.5,
                   9.7
Ostler v Elliott [1980] Crim LR 584, DC   9.67

Padfield v Minister of Agriculture, Fisheries and Food [1968] AC 997; [1968] 1 All
   ER 694; [1968] 2 WLR 924, HL   6.96
Pankhurst v Jarvis (1910) 101 LT 946; 74 JP 64; 26 TLR 118, DC   6.101
Papworth v Coventry [1967] 2 All ER 41; [1967] 1 WLR 663; 111 SJ 316, DC   6.101,
                   6.103
Parkin v Norman [1983] QB 92; [1982] 2 All ER 583; [1982] 3 WLR 523, DC   2.4, 4.5,
                  4.16, 5.14

Partridge v Crittenden [1968] 2 All ER 421; [1968] 1 WLR 1204; (1968) 132 JP
    367, DC   8.61
Pedro v Diss [1981] 2 All ER 59; (1980) 72 Cr App R 193, DC   9.54, 9.63
Pendragon v UK (No 2) (1998) Application no 31416/96, ECommHR   6.89
Pepper (Inspector of Taxes) v Hart [1993] AC 593; [1993] 1 All ER 42; [1992] 3
    WLR 1032, HL   2.53
Percy v DPP [1995] 3 All ER 124; [1995] 1 WLR 1382; [1995] Crim LR 714, DC   2.4,
    2.29, 2.32, 2.33, 2.34, 2.40, 2.41, 2.50
Percy v Hall [1997] QB 924; [1996] 4 All ER 523; [1996] 3 WLR 573, CA   9.101
Pham Hoang v France (1992) Ser A, no 243; 16 EHRR 53, ECtHR   4.38
Pharmaceutical Society of Great Britain v Storkwain Ltd [1986] 2 All ER 635;
    [1986] 1 WLR 903; (1986) 83 Cr App R 359, HL   7.118
Piddington v Bates [1960] 3 All ER 660; [1961] 1 WLR 162; 105 SJ 110, DC   2.17, 2.20
Pitcher v Lockett [1966] Crim LR 283; 64 LGR 477; [1966] CLY 5559, DC   9.82
Platform 'Artze fur das Leben' v Austria (1988) Ser A, no 139; 13 EHRR 20;
    (1988) *The Times*, 30 June, ECtHR   6.53
Plowden v DPP [1991] Crim LR 850, DC   9.60
Police v Reid (Lorna) [1987] Crim LR 702, Mag Ct   6.32
Polychronakis v Richards & Jerrom Ltd [1998] Env LR 347; [1998] JPL 588;
    (1997) *The Times*, 19 November, DC   8.57
Postermobile plc v Brent LBC (1997) *The Times*, 8 December, DC   6.16
Powell v Kempton Park Racecourse Co [1899] AC 143   9.12
Powell v May [1946] KB 330; [1946] 1 All ER 444; 110 JP 157, DC   9.101
Practice Direction (Majority Verdicts) [1970] 2 All ER 215   3.49
Practice Direction (Crown Court: Allocation of Business) (No 3) (2000) *The*
    Times, 18 January   1.9
Practice Note (QBD) (Mode of Trial: Guidelines) [1990] 3 All ER 979; [1990] 1
    WLR 1439; (1991) 92 Cr App R 142   3.50, 3.66
Pugh v Pigden (1987) 151 JP 644; (1987) 151 JPN 510, DC   9.80

R v Afzal [1993] Crim LR 791, CA   4.14
R v Ahlers [1915] 1 KB 616; 84 LJKB 901; 79 JP 255, CCA   4.35, 7.51
R v Allan [1963] 2 All ER 897, CCA   3.12
R v Ambrose (1973) 57 Cr App R 538, CA   4.5
R v Anderson [1971] 3 All ER 1152, CA   9.19
R v Anderson [1995] Crim LR 430, CA   3.17
R v Ashton-Rickhardt [1978] 1 All ER 173; [1978] 1 WLR 37; (1977) SJ 774, CA   8.12
R v Atakpu [1994] QB 69; [1993] 4 All ER 215; [1993] 3 WLR 812, CA   4.77
R v Atkinson (1988) 10 Cr App R (S) 740, CA   2.45
R v Aubrey-Fletcher, ex parte Thompson [1969] 2 All ER 846; [1967] Crim LR
    368, DC   2.32, 2.37, 2.39–2.41, 2.43, 2.49
R v Ayu [1958] 3 All ER 636; [1958] 1 WLR 1264; 43 Cr App R 31, CCA   2.44
R v Baker (1911) 7 Cr App R 89, CCA   9.39
R v Ball [1911] AC 47; 103 LT 738; 75 JP 180, HL   4.79
R v Ball (1990) 90 Cr App R 378; [1989] Crim LR 579, CA   4.26, 4.47, 4.49, 4.51
R v Banks [1916] 2 KB 621; [1916–17] All ER Rep 356; 85 LJKB 1657, CCA   6.28
R v Beaconsfield Justices, ex parte Stubbings (1987) 85 LGR 821; (1987) P&CR
    327; (1988) 152 JP 17   7.97
R v Biffen [1966] Crim LR 111, CCA   2.39
R v Birdwood [1995] 6 Archbold News 2, CA   5.10
R v Bishirigian [1936] 1 All ER 586   7.122
R v Boal [1992] QB 591; [1992] 3 All ER 177; [1992] 2 WLR 890, CA   5.50
R v Bolton JJ, ex parte Graeme (1986) 158 JP 129; (1986) 150 JPN 271, DC   2.29
R v Bonsall [1985] Crim LR 550, Crown Ct   9.39, 9.45, 9.47

R v Boyesen [1982] AC 768; [1982] 2 All ER 161; [1982] 2 WLR 882, HL   8.12
R v Bradish [1990] 1 QB 981; [1990] 1 All ER 460; [1990] 2 WLR 223, CA   8.12
R v Breckenridge (1984) 79 Cr App R 244; [1984] Crim LR 174, CA   7.124
R v Briggs [1977] 1 All ER 475, [1977] 1 WLR 605; (1976) 63 Cr App R 215, CA   7.124
R v Brightling [1991] Crim LR 364, CA   9.64
R v Britton [1967] 2 QB 51; [1967] 1 All ER 486; [1967] 2 WLR 537, CA   4.7, 5.23, 5.24
R v Brown (1841) Car & M 314   2.19
R v Brown (1976) 64 Cr App R 231, CA   2.12
R v Buddo (1983) 4 Cr App R (S) 268; [1982] Crim LR 837, DC   7.90
R v Burns (1886) 16 Cox CC 355; (1886) 2 TLR 510   5.1
R v Buswell [1972] 1 All ER 75; [1972] 1 WLR 64; 116 SJ 36, CA   8.12
R v Cain [1976] QB 496; [1975] 2 All ER 900; [1975] 3 WLR 131, CA   3.34, 5.53
R v Caird (1970) 54 Cr App R 499; [1970] Crim LR 656   3.2
R v Carr-Briant [1943] KB 607; [1943] 2 All ER 156; 112 LJKB 581, CCA   4.38
R v Carson (1991) 21 Cr App R 236; [1990] Crim LR 729; (1990) 154 JP 794, CA   3.71
R v Caunt (1947) unreported; *noted* 64 LQR 203   5.1
R v Central Criminal Court, ex parte Boulding [1984] QB 813; [1984] 1 All ER
    766; [1984] 2 WLR 321, DC   2.45, 2.49
R v Chief Constable of Devon and Cornwall, ex parte Central Electricity
    Generating Board [1982] QB 458; [1981] 3 All ER 826; [1981] 3 WLR 967,
    CA   2.4, 2.5, 2.6, 2.20
R v Chief Constable of Sussex, ex parte International Trader's Ferry Ltd [1999] 1
    All ER 129; [1998] 3 WLR 1260; [1999] 1 CMLR 1320, HL   1.26, 2.21, 6.97
R v Chief Metropolitan Stipendiary Magistrate, ex parte Choudhury [1991] QB
    429; [1990] 1 WLR 986; (1990) 91 Cr App R 393, DC   5.1
R v Clarke (No 2) [1963] 3 All ER 884; [1963] 3 WLR 1067; 107 SJ 983, CCA   9.95
R v Clarkson; R v Carroll; R v Dodd [1971] 3 All ER 344; [1971] 1 WLR 1402; 55
    Cr App R 445, Cts-Martial App Ct   3.12
R v Clerkenwell Metropolitan Stipendiary Magistrate, ex parte Hooper; *sub nom*
    R v Clerkenwell Justices, ex parte Hooper [1998] 4 All ER 193; [1998] 1 WLR
    800; (1998) 162 JPN 243, DC   2.40, 2.46
R v Collins (1839) 9 C&P 456; 3 State Tr NS 1149   5.1
R v Collins [1973] QB 100; [1972] 2 All ER 1105; [1972] 3 WLR 243, CA   7.29, 7.53
R v Collison (1980) 71 Cr App R 249; [1980] Crim LR 591, CA   3.73
R v Commissioner of Police of the Metropolis, ex parte Blackburn (No 1) [1968]
    2 QB 118; [1968] 2 WLR 893; *sub nom* R v Metropolitan Police Comr, ex parte
    Blackburn (No 1) [1968] 1 All ER 763, CA   2.61, 6.97, 6.99
R v Commissioner of Police of the Metropolis, ex parte Blackburn (No 3) [1973]
    1 All ER 324; [1973] Crim LR 185, CA   6.97
R v Coney (1882) 8 QBD 534; 51 LJMC 66; 46 JP 404, CCR   3.12
R v Constantza [1997] 2 Cr App R 492; [1997] Crim LR 576; (1997) *The Times*,
    31 March, CA   4.14
R v Conway; R v Burkes [1994] Crim LR 826, CA   8.12
R v County of London Quarter Sessions Appeals Committee, ex parte
    Metropolitan Police Comr [1948] 1 KB 670; [1948] 1 All ER 72; [1948] LJR
    472, DC   2.3
R v Courtie [1984] AC 463; [1984] 1 All ER 740; [1984] 2 WLR 330, HL   4.66
R v Cousins [1982] QB 526; [1982] 2 All ER 115; [1982] 2 WLR 621   3.21
R v Coventry Magistrates' Court, ex parte CPS (1996) 160 JP 741; [1996] Crim LR
    723; [1996] COD 348, DC   2.30
R v Crown Court at Lincoln, ex parte Jude [1997] 3 All ER 737; (1997) 161 JP
    589; (1997) 161 JPN 838, QBD   2.36, 2.39, 2.43, 2.45, 2.47
R v Crown Court at Swindon, ex parte Pawittar Singh [1984] 1 All ER 941; [1984]
    1 WLR 449; (1984) 79 Cr App R 137, DC   2.37, 2.38

R v Cugullere [1961] 2 All ER 343; [1961] 1 WLR 858; 45 Cr App R 108, CCA   8.12
R v Croydon JJ, ex parte Dean [1993] QB 769; [1993] 3 All ER 129; [1993] 3 WLR
    198, (1994) 98 Cr App R 76, DC   6.16
R v Davies (1990) unreported, CA   3.7
R v Davison [1992] Crim LR 31, CA   3.14, 3.52, 3.53, 3.57, 3.58, 3.61, 3.65
R v Denbigh Justices, ex parte Williams [1974] QB 759; [1974] 2 All ER 1052;
    [1974] 3 WLR 45, DC   8.34
R v Densu [1998] 1 Cr App R 400; [1998] Crim LR 345; 162 JP 55, DC   8.56
R v Dixon [1993] Crim LR 579, CA   3.55
R v Downey [1970] Crim LR 287; [1970] RTR 257, CA   7.30, 8.56
R v DPP, ex parte C [1995] 1 Cr App R 136; [1994] COD 375; (1995) 159 JP 227,
    DC   2.61
R v DPP, ex parte Kebeline [1999] 4 All ER 801; [1999] 3 WLR 972; (1999) 11
    Admin LR 1026, HL   1.11, 1.26, 4.38
R v DPP, ex parte Panayiotou [1997] COD 83, DC   2.61
R v DPP, ex parte Treadaway (1997) *The Times*, 31 October, DC   2.61
R v Durham Justices, ex parte Laurent [1945] KB 33; [1944] 2 All ER 530; 114
    LJKB 125, DC   2.50
R v Edgar (1913) 9 Cr App R 13; (1913) 109 LT 416; 77 JP 356, CCA   2.44
R v Edwards (Llewellyn); R v Roberts (1978) 67 Cr App R 228; [1978] Crim LR
    564; (1978) 122 SJ 177, CA   8.63
R v Fairbanks [1986] 1 WLR 1202; (1986) 83 Cr App R 251; [1986] RTR 309, CA   3.73
R v Farrant [1973] Crim LR 240, Crown Ct   9.31
R v Felixstowe JJ, ex parte Baldwin *see* R v Ipswich Crown Court, ex parte Baldwin
    (note)
R v Fellows [1997] 2 All ER 548; [1997] 1 Cr App R 244; [1997] Crim LR 524, CA   5.21,
                                                                            5.29, 5.33
R v Fennell [1971] QB 428; [1970] 3 All ER 215; [1970] 3 WLR 513, CA   9.64
R v Finch (1963) 47 Cr App R 58; (1962) 106 SJ 961, CCA   2.50
R v Fleming [1989] Crim LR 658; (1989) 153 JP 517; (1989) 153 JPN 530, CA   3.46–3.48,
                                                                                   3.71
R v Forbes and Webb (1865) 10 Cox CC 362   9.64
R v Forest Justices, ex parte Hartman [1991] Crim LR 641, DC   7.139
R v Forsyth (Elizabeth) [1997] 2 Cr App R 299; [1997] Crim LR 581; (1997) *The
    Times*, 8 April, CA   3.68, 6.28
R v Gaston (1981) 73 Cr App R 164, CA   3.13
R v Geddes [1996] Crim LR 894; (1996) 160 JP 697; (1996) 160 JPN 730, CA   7.52
R v Gilbert (1974) unreported, CA   2.50
R v Gittins [1982] Crim LR 584; [1982] RTR 363, DC   9.78
R v Gullefer [1990] 3 All ER 882; [1990] 1 WLR 1063, CA   7.52
R v Hale (1978) 68 Cr App R 415; [1978] Crim LR 596, CA   4.77
R v Harrison [1938] 3 All ER 134; 159 LT 95; 26 Cr App R 166, CCA   6.28
R v Hazell [1985] Crim LR 513; [1985] RTR 369; (1985) 82 LS Gaz 2081, CA   3.73
R v Henderson (1984) unreported, CA   6.77, 7.18
R v Hendon JJ, ex parte Gorchein [1974] 1 All ER 168; [1973] 1 WLR 1502;
    [1973] Crim LR 754, DC   2.38, 2.39, 2.43
R v Hendrickson [1977] Crim LR 356, CA   6.41
R v Highbury Corner Stipendiary Magistrates' Court, ex parte Di Matteo [1992] 1
    All ER 102; [1991] 1 WLR 1374; (1991) 92 Cr App R 263, DC   7.90
R v Horseferry Road Metropolitan Stipendiary Magistrates' Court, ex parte
    Siadatan [1991] 1 QB 280; [1991] 1 All ER 324; [1990] 3 WLR 1006, DC   4.13, 4.14

R v Houlden (1994) 99 Cr App R 244, CA   3.49
R v Howell [1982] QB 416; [1981] 3 All ER 383; [1981] 3 WLR 501, CA   2.4, 2.6,
                                                            2.7–2.9, 2.17, 2.21, 4.20
R v Hunt [1978] Crim LR 697, CA   5.59
R v Hunt (Richard) [1987] AC 352; [1987] 1 All ER 1; [1986] 3 WLR 1115, HL   4.38
R v Hussain [1981] 2 All ER 287; [1981] 1 WLR 416; (1980) 42 Cr App R 143, CA   8.12
R v Ilminster JJ, ex parte Hamilton (1983) *The Times*, 23 June, DC   2.49
R v IRC, ex parte Rossminster Ltd [1980] AC 952; [1980] 2 WLR 1; *sub nom* IRC v
    Rossminster Ltd [1980] 1 All ER 80, HL   3.68, 6.28
R v Inner London Crown Court, ex parte Benjamin (1987) 85 Cr App R 267;
    [1987] Crim LR 417, DC   2.38, 2.39, 2.41, 2.49
R v Ipswich Crown Court, ex parte Baldwin (note) [1981] 1 All ER 596; *sub nom*
    R v Felixstowe JJ, ex parte Baldwin (1980) 72 Cr App R 131; [1981] Crim LR
    242, DC   2.49
R v Ipswich Crown Court, ex parte Eris (1989) *The Times*, 23 February, DC   2.42
R v Jefferson [1994] 1 All ER 270; (1994) 99 Cr App R 13; [1993] Crim LR 880,
    CA   3.9, 3.12, 3.13, 3.25, 3.29, 3.35, 3.40, 3.53, 4.11
R v Johnson [1997] 1 WLR 367; [1996] 2 Cr App R 434; [1996] Crim LR 828, CA   9.94
R v Jones (1812) 3 Camp 230   9.95
R v Jones (1974) 59 Cr App R 120, CA   3.70, 9.39
R v Jones (Terence Michael) [1995] QB 235; [1995] 3 All ER 139; [1995] 2 WLR
    64, CA   9.80
R v Jordan and Tyndall [1963] Crim LR 124, CCA   9.12
R v Keeton [1995] 2 Cr App R 241; (1994) *The Times*, 21 July, CA   3.49
R v Keighley JJ, ex parte Stoyles [1976] Crim LR 573, DC   2.43
R v Kelbie (Peter) [1996] Crim LR 802, CA   2.9
R v Kelt [1977] 3 All ER 1099; [1977] 1 WLR 1365; (1977) Cr App R 556, CA   7.97
R v Key (1992) unreported, CA   3.56
R v Khan [1995] Crim LR 78, CA   3.17
R v Khan [1997] AC 558; [1996] 3 All ER 289; [1996] 3 WLR 162, HL   1.11
R v Kimber [1983] 3 All ER 442; [1983] 1 WLR 1118; (1984) 77 Cr App R 225, DC
                                                                                         9.61
R v Kingston-upon-Thames Crown Court, ex parte Guarino [1986] Crim LR 325,
    DC   2.38
R v Krause (1902) 18 TLR 238   6.41
R v Lacey (1996) unreported, CA   3.47
R v Lawrence [1982] AC 510; [1981] 1 All ER 974; [1981] 2 WLR 524, HL   7.124
R v Lemon; R v Gay News [1979] AC 617; [1979] 1 All ER 898; [1979] 2 WLR 281,
    HL   5.5, 9.19
R v Lennard [1973] 2 All ER 831; [1973] 1 WLR 483; [1973] RTR 252, CA   8.56
R v Lewis (1988) 87 Cr App R 270, CA   8.12
R v Lincoln Crown Court, ex parte Jones [1990] COD 15; (1989) *The Times*,
    16 June, DC   2.38
R v Lincolnshire County Coucil, ex parte Atkinson; *sub nom* R v Wealden District
    Council, ex parte Wales; R v Wealdon District Council, ex parte Stratford
    (1995) 8 Admin LR 529; [1995] NPC 135; [1995] EGCS 145, DC   7.101, 7.103
R v Liverpool JJ, ex parte Collins; Same, ex parte Santos *see* DPP v Speede;
    R v Liverpool JJ, ex parte Collins; R v Liverpool JJ, ex parte Santos
R v Lloyd (1802) 4 Esp 200   9.94
R v Lobell [1957] 1 QB 547; [1957] 1 All ER 734; [1957] 2 WLR 524, CCA   4.37
R v Lockley [1995] Crim LR 656; (1995) *The Times*, 27 June; (1995) *The
    Independent*, 15 June, CA   4.77
R v Londonderry JJ (1891) 28 LR Ir 440, Ir QBDC   2.22
R v Long (1888) 52 JP 630; 59 LT 33; 16 Cox CC 442, DC   9.89

R v Lord Kylsant [1932] 1 KB 442   7.122

R v Madden [1975] 3 All ER 155; [1975] 1 WLR 1379; [1975] Crim LR 582, CA   9.24, 9.92–9.94

R v Mahroof (1989) 88 Cr App R 317, CA   3.47, 3.48

R v Maidstone Crown Court, ex parte Clark [1995] 3 All ER 513; [1995] 1 WLR 831; [1995] 2 Cr App R 617, DC   2.29

R v Maidstone Crown Court, ex parte Gill [1987] 1 All ER 129; [1986] 1 WLR 1405; [1986] Crim LR 737, DC   5.58

R v Mallett [1978] 3 All ER 10; [1978] 1 WLR 820; (1978) 67 Cr App R 239, CA   7.123

R v Mandair [1995] 1 AC 208; [1994] 2 All ER 715; [1994] 2 WLR 700, HL   3.9

R v Manchester Stipendiary Magistrate, ex parte Hill; R v Dartford Justices, ex parte Dhesi; R v Edmonton Justices, ex parte Hughes [1983] AC 328; [1982] 3 WLR 331; (1982) 75 Cr App R 346, HL   2.30

R v Marlow JJ, ex parte O'Sullivan [1984] QB 381; [1983] 3 All ER 578; [1984] 2 WLR 107, DC   2.32, 2.50

R v Marsden (1868) LR 1 CCR 131; 37 LJMC 80; 32 JP 436, CCR   2.9

R v Martindale [1986] 3 All ER 25; [1986] 1 WLR 1042; (1987) 84 Cr App R 31, CA   8.12

R v Marylebone Metropolitan Stipendiary Magistrate, ex parte Okunnu (1988) 87 Cr App R 295; (1987) *The Times*, 4 November, DC   2.40

R v Maxwell and Clanchy (1909) 2 Cr App R 26; (1909) 73 JP 176, CCA   9.64

R v McCalla (1988) 87 Cr App R 372; (1988) 152 JP 481; (1988) 152 JPN 494, CA   8.12

R v McCarthy, Holland and O'Dwyer [1903] 2 IR 146   9.39

R v McGuigan; R v Cameron [1991] Crim LR 719, CA   3.43, 3.46

R v McGregor [1945] 2 All ER 180; 115 LJKB 100; 30 Cr App R 155, CCA   2.50

R v McKenzie [1892] 2 QB 519; 61 LJMC 181; 56 JP 712, DC   9.43, 9.45

R v McNamara (James) (1988) 87 Cr App R 246, CA   8.12

R v McVitie [1960] 2 QB 483; [1960] 2 All ER 498; [1960] 3 WLR 99, CCA   3.13

R v Meredith (1993) unreported, CA   3.20, 3.28, 3.43

R v Metropolitan Police Comr, ex parte Blackburn (No 1) *see* R v Commissioner of Police of the Metropolis, ex parte Blackburn (No 1)

R v Metropolitan Police Comr, ex parte Lewisham Borough Council (1977) unreported   6.99

R v Middlesex Crown Court, ex parte Khan (1997) 161 JP 240; (1997) 161 JPN 212; [1997] COD 186, DC   2.38, 2.41

R v Mohan [1976] QB 1; [1975] 2 All ER 193; [1975] 2 WLR 859, CA   4.35

R v Morpeth Ward JJ, ex parte Ward, Jenks, Hughes, Joseland (1992) 95 Cr App R 215; [1992] Crim LR 497; (1992) 156 JPN 442, DC   2.23, 2.29, 2.33, 2.49

R v Morris [1951] 1 KB 394; [1950] 2 All ER 965; 34 Cr App R 210, CCA   9.91, 9.92

R v Most (1881) 7 QBD 244; 50 LJMC 113; 45 JP 696, CCR   6.41

R v North Curry (Inhabitants) (1825) 4 B&C 953   7.99

R v North London Metropolitan Magistrate, ex parte Haywood [1973] 3 All ER 50; [1973] 1 WLR 965, DC   2.40, 2.43

R v Notman [1994] Crim LR 518, CA   3.72

R v Nottingham Crown Court, ex parte Brace (1989) 154 JP 161, [1990] COD 127, DC   2.45

R v Oakwell [1978] 1 All ER 1223; [1978] 1 WLR 32; (1977) 66 Cr App R 174, CA   4.5

R v O'Boyle [1973] RTR 445, CA   8.57

R v O'Brien [1993] Crim LR 70; (1992) 156 JP 925; (1992) 156 JPN 538, CA   3.72

R v Owens (1986) unreported, CA   5.11

R v Owino [1996] 2 Cr App R 128; [1995] Crim LR 743, CA   3.31

R v Pawlicki [1992] 3 All ER 902; [1992] 1 WLR 827; (1992) 95 Cr App R 246, CA   8.12

R v Pearce (1981) 72 Cr App R 295; [1981] Crim LR 639, CA   3.34, 5.54

R v Perrins [1995] Crim LR 432, CA   3.72

R v Phillips [1991] 3 NZLR 175   4.38

R v Pine (1934) 24 Cr App R 10, CCA   2.50

R v Podger [1979] Crim LR 524, Crown Ct   2.9

R v Prebble (1858) 1 F&F 325   9.52

R v Presdee (1927) 20 Cr App R 95, CCA   9.17

R v Preston Crown Court, ex parte Pamplin [1981] Crim LR 338; (1981) 125 SJ
240, DC   2.38, 2.49

R v Pulham [1995] Crim LR 296, CA   3.56

R v Radio Authority, ex parte Bull [1997] 2 All ER 561; [1997] 3 WLR 1094;
[1997] COD 382, CA; [1995] 4 All ER 481; [1995] 3 WLR 572; (1995) 145
NLJ Rep 1297, DC   9.6

R v Ramsell (Celia Rosemary) (1999) unreported, CA   2.7, 2.21

R v Randall (RP) (1987) 8 Cr App R (S) 433; [1987] Crim LR 254, CA; (1987) 8
Cr App R (S) 433, DC   2.44, 2.49

R v Reading Crown Court, ex parte Hutchinson; Same v Devizes Justices, ex parte
Lee; Same v Same, ex parte DPP [1988] QB 384; [1988] 1 All ER 333; [1987]
3 WLR 1062, DC   9.101

R v Reid [1973] 3 All ER 1020; [1973] 1 WLR 1283; [1973] RTR 536, CA   7.30, 8.56

R v Riches (1989) unreported, CA   3.53

R v Roberts (1995) unreported, CA   3.72

R v Robinson [1993] Crim LR 581, CA   3.55

R v Rothwell [1993] Crim LR 626, CA   3.17, 3.56

R v Roxburgh (1871) 12 Cox CC 8   9.52

R v Russell (1984) 81 Cr App R 315; [1984] Crim LR 231, CA   8.12

R v Sanchez [1996] Crim LR 572; (1996) 160 JP 321; (1996) *The Times*, 6 March,
CA   3.52, 3.58, 3.61

R v Sandbach JJ, ex parte Williams [1935] 2 KB 192; [1935] All ER Rep 680; 99 JP
251, DC   2.27, 2.41

R v Satnam; R v Kewal (1984) 78 Cr App R 149; [1985] Crim LR 236, CA   7.124

R v Saunders [1988] AC 148; [1987] 2 All ER 973; [1987] 3 WLR 355, HL   3.73

R v Savage (1985) 5 Cr App R (S) 216, CA   5.59

R v Scarrow (1968) 52 Cr App R 591, CA   3.5

R v Secretary of State for Education and Science, ex parte Avon County Council
(No 2) [1991] 1 QB 558; [1991] 1 All ER 282; [1991] 2 WLR 702, CA   6.98

R v Secretary of State for the Home Department, ex parte Brind [1991] 1 AC 696;
[1991] 1 All ER 720; [1991] 2 WLR 588, HL   1.26

R v Secretary of State for the Home Department, ex parte Simms [1999] QB 349;
[1998] 2 All ER 491; [1998] 3 WLR 1169, CA   1.11

R v Sharp [1957] 1 All ER 577; [1957] Crim LR 821, CCA   2.36, 2.39

R v Sharpe (1857) Dears & B 160; 26 LJMC 47; 21 JP 86, CCR   4.79

R v Sheppard [1981] AC 394; [1980] 3 All ER 899; [1980] 3 WLR 960, HL   9.78

R v Sherlock (1866) LR 1 CCR 20; 5 LJMC 92; 30 JP 85   2.19

R v Shorrock [1994] QB 279; [1993] 3 All ER 917; [1993] 3 WLR 698, CA   7.67, 9.93,
9.96

R v Smith [1997] 1 Cr App R 14; [1996] Crim LR 893, CA   3.52, 3.64

R v Solicitor-General, ex parte Taylor [1996] 1 FLR 206; [1996] COD 61; (1995)
The Times, 14 August, DC   5.55

R v South Hams District Council, ex parte Gibb [1995] QB 158; [1994] 4 All ER
1012; [1994] 3 WLR 1151, CA   7.93

R v South Molton JJ, ex parte Ankerson [1988] 3 All ER 989; (1988) 152 JP 644;
(1988) 132 SJ 1431, DC   2.41, 2.43, 2.44, 2.45, 2.47

R v South West London Magistrates' Court, ex parte Brown [1974] Crim LR 313;
(1974) Fam Law 158, DC   2.40, 2.41

R v Stanley [1965] 2 QB 327; [1965] 1 All ER 1035; [1965] 2 WLR 917, CCA   9.19

R v Stanley and Knight [1993] Crim LR 618, CA　　　　　　　　　　　　　　　3.72
R v Steele [1980] Crim LR 689, CA　　　　　　　　　　　　　　　　　　　　8.12
R v Stephenson [1979] QB 695; [1979] 2 All ER 1198; [1979] 3 WLR 193, CA　　　7.124
R v Stewart [1896] 1 QB 300; 65 LJMC 83; 60 JP 356, DC　　　　　　　　　　9.101
R v Thornley (1981) 72 Cr App R 302; [1981] Crim LR 637, CA　　　　　　　　9.58
R v Tolson (1889) 23 QBD 168; [1886–90] All ER Rep 26; 54 JP 4, CCR　　　　9.67
R v Turpin [1990] Crim LR 514, CA　　　　　　　　　　　　　　　　　　　3.48
R v Tyler (Patrick John); Same v Frost (Perry Peter); Same v Hester (Andrew);
　　　Same v Hammett (1992) 96 Cr App R 332; [1993] Crim LR 60; (1992) 156
　　　JPN 762, CA　　　　　　　　　　　　　　　　　　　　　　　　　3.9, 3.13
R v Va Kun Hau [1990] Crim LR 518, CA　　　　　　　　　　　　　　　3.72, 4.10
R v Vann [1996] Crim LR 52, CA　　　　　　　　　　　　　　　　　　　　8.12
R v Venna [1976] QB 421; [1975] 3 All ER 788; [1975] 3 WLR 737, CA　　　　　9.61
R v Walker (1854) Dears CC 358; 23 LJMC 123; 18 JP 281, CCR　　　　　　　2.9
R v Walker (1989) 90 Cr App R 226, CA　　　　　　　　　　　　　　　　4.35
R v Wall (1907) 21 Cox CC 401　　　　　　　　　　　　　　　　　　9.40, 9.42
R v Waller [1991] Crim LR 381, CA　　　　　　　　　　　　　　　　　　　8.12
R v Waterfield [1964] 1 QB 164; [1963] 3 All ER 659; [1963] 3 WLR 946, CCA　　9.53,
　　　　　　　　　　　　　　　　　　　　　　　　　　　　　　　9.54, 9.58
R v Waters (1963) 47 Cr App R 149; (1963) 107 SJ 275, CCA　　　　　　　6.5, 8.63
R v Waugh (1976) *The Times*, 1 October, Crown Ct　　　　　　　　　　　　2.19
R v Wealden District Council, ex parte Wales; R v Wealdon District Council, ex
　　　parte Stratford *see* R v Lincolnshire County Coucil, ex parte Atkinson
R v Webb (1995) *The Times*, 19 June; (1995) *The Independent*, 26 June; (1995)
　　　92(27) LS Gaz 31, CA　　　　　　　　　　　　　　　　　　　　　9.28
R v West London Coroner's Court, ex parte Gray; Same v Same, ex parte Duncan
　　　[1988] QB 467; [1987] 2 All ER 129; [1987] 2 WLR 1020, DC　　　　　　2.80
R v West London Magistrates' Court, ex parte Small (1998) unreported　　　　7.21
R v Whitehouse (2000) 97(1) LSG 22; [1999] TLR 863; *The Times* (1999),
　　　December 10, CA　　　　　　　　　　　　　　　　　　　　　　　4.16
R v Whiteley (1991) 93 Cr App R 25; [1991] Crim LR 436; [1993] FSR 168, CA　　6.77
R v Wilkins [1907] 2 KB 380; 71 JP 327; 76 LJKB 722, DC　　　　　2.38, 2.40, 2.43
R v Williams (1891) 55 JP 406, DC　　　　　　　　　　　　　　　　　　9.89
R v Williams [1982] 3 All ER 1092; [1982] 1 WLR 1398; (1982) 75 Cr App R 378,
　　　CA　　　　　　　　　　　　　　　　　　　　　　　　　　　　2.49
R v Williams [1987] 3 All ER 411; (1984) 78 Cr App R 276; [1984] Crim LR 163,
　　　CA　　　　　　　　　　　　　　　　　　　　　　　　　　　　3.31
R v Williams (Clarence Ivor) (1987) 84 Cr App R 299; [1987] Crim LR 198, CA　　4.79
R v Wilson (Rupert) [1997] 1 All ER 119; [1997] 1 WLR 1247; (1996) 93 (35)
　　　LSG 33, CA　　　　　　　　　　　　　　　　　　　　　　　　5.50
R v Wilson; R v Jenkins [1984] AC 242; [1983] 3 All ER 448; [1983] 3 WLR 686,
　　　HL　　　　　　　　　　　　　　　　　　　　　　　　　　　　3.73
R v Wiltshire Constabulary, ex parte Taylor (1992) unreported, DC　　　　　　7.21
R v Woking JJ, ex parte Gossage [1973] 1 QB 448; [1973] 2 All ER 621; [1973] 2
　　　WLR 529, DC　　　　　　　　　　　　　　　　　　　　　2.38, 2.43
R v Wolverhampton MBC, ex parte Dunne [1997] 29 HLR 745; [1997] COD 210;
　　　(1997) *The Times*, 2 January, DC　　　　　　　　　　　　　7.101, 7.107
R v Woollin (Stephen Leslie) [1999] 1 AC 82; [1998] 3 WLR 382; [1998] 4 All ER
　　　103, HL　　　　　　　　　　　　　　　　　　　　　　　　4.35, 7.51
R v Woodrow (1959) 43 Cr App R 105, CCA　　　　　　　　　　　　　　　3.70
R v Worton (1990) 154 JP 201; [1990] Crim LR 124, CA　　　　　　　　　　3.48
R v Younis [1965] Crim LR 305, CCA　　　　　　　　　　　　　　　　　2.36
Race Relations Board v Applin [1973] 2 All ER 1190, CA　　　　　　　　　　6.41
Ransom v Burgess (1927) 137 LT 530; [1927] All ER Rep 667; 91 JP 133, DC　　5.21

Rassemblement Jurassien, Unité Jurassienne v Switzerland (1979) 17 D&R 93,
 ECommHR   6.9, 6.42, 6.89
Rayware Ltd v Transport and General Workers Union [1989] 3 All ER 583; [1989]
 1 WLR 675; [1989] ICR 457, CA   9.47
Read v Perrett (1876) 1 Ex D 349; 41 JP 135, DC   9.19, 9.76
Redbridge LBC v Jacques [1971] 1 All ER 260; [1970] 1 WLR 1604; [1971] RTR
 56, DC   9.80
Redford v Birley (1822) 1 State Tr NS 1071   3.3
Redmond-Bate v DPP (1999) 163 JP 789; 7 BHRC 375; (1999) Crim LR 998, DC   1.11,
                                                    2.7, 2.22, 2.23, 3.68
Reed v Wastie [1972] Crim LR 221; (1972) *The Times*, 10 February, DC   9.88
Reynolds v GH Austin & Sons Ltd [1951] 1 All ER 606, DC   8.11
Rice v Connolly [1966] 2 QB 414; [1966] 2 All ER 649; [1966] 3 WLR 17, DC 9.54, 9.66,
                                                                     9.67
Richards v West [1980] RTR 215, DC   6.92
Ricketts v Cox (1981) 74 Cr App R 298; [1982] Crim LR 184, DC   9.67
Riley v DPP (1989) 91 Cr App R 14; [1990] Crim LR 422; [1990] COD 152, DC 9.51
Robson v Hallett [1967] 2 QB 939; [1967] 2 All ER 407; [1967] 3 WLR 28, DC 2.5, 2.13,
                                                                2.15, 9.58
Rookes v Barnard [1964] AC 1129; [1964] 1 All ER 367; [1964] 2 WLR 269, HL 9.39
Roper v Taylor's Central Garages (Exeter) Ltd [1951] 2 TLR 284; [1951] WN 383,
 DC   6.37, 7.124, 8.11
Ross v Moss [1965] 2 QB 396; [1965] 3 All ER 145; [1965] 3 WLR 416, DC   6.37
Rukwira v DPP [1993] Crim LR 882; (1994) 158 JP 65; (1993) 137 JPN 709, DC   4.10

Salabiaku v France (1988) Ser A, no 141-A; 13 EHRR 379, ECtHR   4.38
Sandy v Martin [1974] Crim LR 258; [1974] RTR 263, DC   6.5, 8.63
Scarfe v Wood [1969] Crim LR 265; (1969) 113 SJ 143, DC   9.75
Scott v Howard [1912] VLR 189   9.98
Searle v Randolph [1972] Crim LR 779, DC   8.12
Secretary of State for Education and Science v Tameside Metropolitan Borough
 Council [1977] AC 1014; [1976] 3 All ER 665; [1976] 3 WLR 641, HL   6.96
Seekings v Clarke (1961) 59 LGR 268; (1961) 105 SJ 181, DC   9.75, 9.77
Seide v Gillette Industries Ltd [1980] IRLR 427, EAT   4.71
Shaaben Bin Hussien v Chong Fook Kam [1970] AC 492; [1969] 3 All ER 1626;
 [1970] 2 WLR 441, PC   3.68
Shah v Swallow [1984] 2 All ER 528; [1984] 1 WLR 886; (1984) 79 Cr App R 162,
 HL   7.25
Shaw v Hamilton [1982] 2 All ER 718; [1982] 1 WLR 1308; (1982) 4 Cr App R (S)
 80, DC   2.40, 2.49
Sheldon v Bromfield JJ [1964] 2 QB 573; [1964] 2 All ER 131; [1964] 2 WLR
 1066, DC   2.38, 2.39, 2.43
Sherras v de Rutzen [1895] 1 QB 918; [1895–9] All ER Rep 1167; 59 JP 440, DC   7.118
Shropshire CC v Wynne [1998] COD 40; (1997) 96 LGR 689; (1997) *The Times*, 22
 July, DC   7.107
Silver v UK (1983) Ser A, no 61; 5 EHRR 347, ECtHR   1.21, 1.23, 1.24
Simcock v Rhodes (1977) 66 Cr App R 192; [1977] Crim LR 751, DC   4.5
Simmons v Pizzey [1979] AC 37; [1977] 2 All ER 423; [1977] 3 WLR 1, HL   2.75
Smith v Thomasson (1891) 16 Cox CC 740; (1891) 62 LT 68; 54 JP 596, DC   9.40
Sodeman v R [1936] 2 All ER 1138; 80 SJ 532; 55 CLR 192, PC   4.38
Somerset v Hart (1884) 12 QBD 360; 53 LJMC 77; 48 JP 327, DC   5.50
Sparks v Worthington [1986] RTR 64, DC   6.39
Steel v UK (1999) 28 EHRR 603; 5 BHRC 339; [1998] Crim LR 893, ECtHR   1.19, 1.21,
                              2.3, 2.10, 2.14, 2.23, 2.27, 2.52, 2.80

Sunday Times v UK (1979) Ser A, no 49; 2 EHRR 245, ECtHR   1.21, 7.61
Sutton v Commissioner of Metropolitan Police (1998) unreported, CA   2.4
Swallow v London County Council [1916] 1 KB 224; [1914–15] All ER Rep 403;
    85 LJKB 234, DC   9.70
Swanston v DPP (1997) 161 JP 203; [1997] COD 180; (1997) 161 JPN 212, DC   3.54, 4.8,
                                                                              4.13
Sweet v Parsley [1970] AC 132; [1969] 1 All ER 347; [1969] 2 WLR 470, HL   7.118, 8.64

Taylor v Baldwin [1976] Crim LR 137; [1976] RTR 265, DC   6.92
Taylor v DPP [1973] AC 964; [1973] 2 All ER 1108; [1973] 3 WLR 140, HL   3.5, 3.59
Tesco Supermarkets Ltd v Nattrass [1972] AC 153; [1971] 2 All ER 127; [1971] 2
    WLR 1166, HL   5.49
Thomas v National Union of Mineworkers (South Wales Area) [1986] Ch 20;
    [1985] 2 All ER 1; [1985] 2 WLR 1081   9.39, 9.44
Thomas v Sawkins [1935] 2 KB 249; [1935] All ER Rep 655; 104 LJKB 572, DC   2.13,
                                                                              2.14
Thorne v British Broadcasting Corporation [1967] 2 All ER 1225; [1967] 1 WLR
    1104; 111 SJ 478, CA   5.55
Torbay Borough Council v Cross (1995) 159 JP 682, DC   9.77
Tudor Grange Holdings Ltd v Citibank NA [1992] Ch 53; [1991] 4 All ER 1;
    [1991] 3 WLR 750   9.12
Turner v Sullivan (1862) 6 LT 130   5.52
Tynan v Balmer [1967] 1 QB 91; [1966] 2 All ER 133; [1966] 2 WLR 1181, DC   9.47,
                                                                              9.67

Valentine v DPP [1997] COD 339, DC   2.68, 4.14
Vallancey v Fletcher [1897] 1 QB 265; 61 JP 183; 66 LJQB 297, DC   9.30, 9.31
Veator v G *see* Veater v Glennon
Veater v Glennon [1981] 1 WLR 567; (1981) 72 Cr App R 331; *sub nom* Veator v G
    [1981] 2 All ER 304, DC   2.26, 2.29, 2.47, 2.48
Vehicle Inspectorate v Nuttall [1999] 3 All ER 833; [1999] 1 WLR 629; [1999]
    IRLR 656, HL   8.11
Verrier v DPP [1967] 2 AC 195; [1966] 3 All ER 568; [1966] 3 WLR 924, HL   9.91, 9.92
Vigon v DPP [1998] Crim LR 289; (1998) 162 JP 115; (1998) 162 JPN 88, DC   4.6, 4.45,
                                                                              4.49

Waite v Taylor (1985) 149 JP 551; (1985) 82 LS Gaz 1092, DC   9.75, 9.82
Wallwork v Giles [1970] RTR 117; (1969) 114 SJ 36, DC   6.92
Walsh v Barlow [1985] 1 WLR 90; [1984] 6 Cr App R (S) 286; (1985) 149 JP 65,
    DC   8.37
Waltham Forest LBC v Mills [1980] Crim LR 243; [1980] RTR 201; (1979) 78 LGR
    248, DC   9.82
Ward v Chief Constable of Avon & Somerset Constabulary (1986) *The Times*,
    26 June, CA   3.68
Ward Lock and Co Ltd v The Operative Printers' Assistants' Society (1906) 22
    TLR 327, CA   9.44
Warner v Metropolitan Police Comr [1969] 2 AC 256; [1968] 2 All ER 356; [1968]
    2 WLR 1303, HL   8.12
Wemhoff v FRG (1968) Ser A, no 7; 1 EHRR 55, ECtHR   1.19
Wershof v Metropolitan Police Comr [1978] 3 All ER 540; (1978) 68 Cr App R 82;
    [1978] Crim LR 424, DC   9.69

Westminster City Council v Croyalgrange Ltd [1986] 2 All ER 353; [1986] 1 WLR
   674; [1986] Crim LR 167, HL   6.37
Westminster Corpn v London and North Western Rly Co [1905] AC 426, HL   6.96
Westwood v Post Office [1974] AC 1; [1973] 3 All ER 184; [1973] 3 WLR 287, HL;
   reversing [1973] 1 QB 591; [1973] 1 All ER 283; [1973] 2 WLR 135, CA   7.8
Whitley v Stumbles [1930] AC 544, HL   8.32
Williams v DPP [1993] 3 All ER 365; [1992] 95 Cr App R 415; [1994] RTR 61, DC 9.17
Wills v Bowley [1983] AC 57; [1982] 2 All ER 654; [1982] 3 WLR 10, HL   2.7, 9.17
Willmott v Atack [1976] 3 All ER 794; [1976] 3 WLR 753; (1976) 63 Cr App R
   207, DC   9.67
Wilson v Renton (1909) 47 SLR 209, High Ct of Justiciary   9.38
Wilson v Skeock (1949) 113 JP 294; 93 SJ 389; [1949] WN 203, DC   2.5, 2.44
Winder v DPP (1996) 160 JP 713; (1996) 160 JPN 786; (1996) *The Times*,
   14 August, DC   7.52, 7.66
Winn v DPP (1992) 156 JP 881; (1992) 156 JPN 554; (1992) 142 NLJ 527, DC 4.13, 4.17
Wisconsin v Mitchell 124 L Ed 2d 436 (1993)   4.65
Wise v Dunning [1902] 1 KB 167; [1900–3] All ER Rep 727; 66 JP 212, DC 2.22, 2.23,
                                                                        2.33, 2.41
Wolverton UDC v Willis [1962] 1 All ER 243; [1962] 1 WLR 205; 126 JP 84, DC   9.76,
                                                                             9.77
Wood v Bowron (1867) LR 2 QB 21   9.39
Wood v Leadbetter (1845) 13 M&W 838   7.9
Wooding v Oxley (1839) 9 C&P 1   2.4
Woolley v Corbishley (1860) 24 JP 773, DC   9.19
Woolmington v DPP [1935] AC 462; [1935] All ER Rep 1; 104 LJKB 433, HL   4.38
Worth v Terington (1845) M&W 781; 14 LJ Ex 7, 133; 2 Dow & L 352   9.31

Young v Peck (1912) 29 TLR 31   9.47

TABLE OF STATUTES

References are to paragraph numbers.

Abortion Act 1967	4.37	Civil Aviation Act 1982	
Accessories and Abettors Act 1861		s 57	9.50
s 8	3.34, 5.53	Civil Evidence Act 1995	
Act of Union 1707	4.70	s 1	2.81
Ancient Monuments and		Commons Act 1899	
Archaeological Areas Act		s 1	9.99
1979	6.77, 7.13	s 10	9.99
		Commons Registration Act 1965	
		s 22	7.12
		(1)	7.12
British Nationality Act 1981	4.69	Conspiracy and Protection of	
British Transport Commission Act		Property Act 1875	
1949		s 7	9.37, 9.38
s 53	9.50	Contempt of Court Act 1981	
Broadcasting Act 1990		s 12	2.36, 2.48
s 201(1), (2)	5.15	s 14(1)	2.48
s 202(1)	5.45	Countryside Act 1968	
Burgh Police (Scotland) Act 1892	9.19	s 41	9.99
Burial Laws Amendment Act 1880		County Courts Act 1959	9.70
s 7	3.39, 9.35	Crime and Disorder Act 1998	1.2, 4.64,
			5.61, 7.21
		Part II	4.65, 4.72, 5.4
Caravan Sites Act 1968		s 1	2.53, 2.58, 2.61, 2.62, 2.63, 2.64,
Part II	7.93		2.65, 2.66, 2.68, 2.71, 2.72,
ss 6–12	7.93		2.74, 2.75, 2.78, 2.80, 2.81,
s 6	7.93		2.85, 2.91, 4.64, 7.115
s 10	7.95, 7.97	(1)	2.57, 2.59, 2.74, 2.82
ss 11, 12	7.95	(a)	2.62, 2.72, 2.74, 2.76
s 16	7.93	(b)	2.62, 2.63, 2.71, 2.76, 2.77,
Caravan Sites and Control of			2.83
Development Act 1960		(2)	2.59
s 24	7.94	(4)	2.57, 2.74
s 29(1)	7.20, 7.100	(5)	2.72, 2.73, 2.80, 2.89
Cemeteries Clauses Act 1847		(6)	2.83, 2.84
s 59	9.35	(7)	2.82
Children Act 1989		(8)	2.87
s 31	4.16	(10)	2.88, 2.89
Children and Young Persons Act		(11)	2.88
1933		(12)	2.57, 2.59
s 34A	2.79	s 4(1)–(3)	2.86
s 44	2.78	ss 5–7	2.59
City of London Police Act 1839		s 8	2.78
s 22	6.100	s 27	7.64
Civic Government (Scotland) Act		s 28	4.80
1982	6.48	(1)	4.67, 4.74, 4.82
		(a)	4.76–4.80

Crime and Disorder Act 1998 –
  cont
  s 28(1)(b)   4.76, 4.79, 4.80
      (2)   4.76, 4.78
      (3)   4.80
         (b)   4.77
      (4)   4.68, 4.69
  s 30   4.87
  s 31   3.40, 4.66, 4.82, 4.85, 4.86, 5.13,
                      5.19, 8.27, 8.35
      (1)   4.81
         (c)   4.82
      (4), (5)   4.83
      (6)   4.84, 4.85
      (7)   4.82
  s 32   4.99, 5.13
      (1)   4.97
         (a), (b)   4.98, 4.100
      (2), (3)   4.98
      (5), (6)   4.100
      (7)   4.99
  s 33   4.77
  s 82   4.65, 4.79, 4.87, 4.88
  s 84(2)   8.58
Criminal Appeal Act 1968
  s 9   8.40
      (1)   5.58
  s 10   8.35, 8.40
  s 11(1)   8.40
      (1A)   8.40
      (3)   8.40
  s 50   8.35
      (1)   5.58
Criminal Attempts Act 1981   1.9, 7.52,
                      7.118
  s 1   6.41, 7.117
      (4)   1.9, 6.41, 7.117
  s 2(2)   3.34, 5.53
  s 3   7.117
      (3)–(5)   7.117
Criminal Damage Act 1971   4.65, 6.77,
                      7.18, 7.124
  s 1   2.54
      (1)   3.17
  s 2   9.24
  s 3   8.22
  s 5(2)   3.17
  s 10(1), (2)   7.17
Criminal Justice Act 1967
  s 91   4.105, 6.105, 8.23, 9.17
      (1)   8.35, 9.17
      (4)   9.17
Criminal Justice Act 1972
  s 34   9.17

Criminal Justice Act 1982
  s 1(1)   2.48
  s 9(1)(c)   2.48
      (5)   2.48
  s 17(1)(a)   2.48
  s 37   1.9
  s 74   1.9
Criminal Justice Act 1988   5.59
  Part V   1.9
  s 52   9.100
Criminal Justice and Public Order
    Act 1994   1.2, 4.64, 7.3, 7.73, 7.101,
                      7.112
  Part V   1.2, 1.6, 1.8, 6.92, 7.1, 7.21, 7.23
  s 51(2)   4.79
  s 60   7.64
      (4A)   7.64
      (8)   7.64
  s 61   6.70, 6.77, 7.3–7.6, 7.8, 7.9, 7.12,
                  7.13, 7.17–7.18, 7.20–7.23,
                  7.28, 7.32, 7.33, 7.35–7.37,
                  7.41, 7.42, 7.43, 7.55, 7.60,
                  7.62, 7.63, 7.80, 7.82, 7.83,
                  7.88, 7.95, 7.99, 7.105, 7.118,
                      7.137
      (1)   7.5, 7.7, 7.10, 7.12, 7.21, 7.23–
                  7.25, 7.26, 7.28, 7.33
      (2)   7.21
      (3)   7.23
         (b)   7.83
      (4)   7.25, 7.29, 7.31, 7.62, 7.83,
                      7.104
         (a)   7.25–7.28, 7.30
         (b)   7.25, 7.27, 7.29
      (5)   7.23, 7.32
      (6)   7.30
      (7)   7.12
         (b)   7.16
      (8)   7.16
         (b)   7.12
      (9)   7.8, 7.12, 7.13–7.20, 7.43
  s 62   7.3, 7.33, 7.35, 7.88
      (1)   7.89
  s 63   1.5, 7.6, 7.23, 7.60, 7.67–7.70, 7.76,
                  7.81–7.83, 7.85–7.87, 7.88,
                  7.89, 7.90, 7.118, 7.137
      (1)   7.68, 7.77, 7.86
         (a)   7.79
         (b)   7.75
      (2)   7.80–7.82, 7.87
      (3)–(5)   7.82
      (6)   7.83
         (b)   7.83
      (7)   7.83

Criminal Justice and Public Order
  Act 1994 – *cont*
  s 63(8)   7.84, 7.87
    (9)   7.69
    (10)   7.72, 7.82
  s 64   7.67–7.69, 7.88
    (1)–(3)   7.87
    (4)   7.87–7.90
    (5), (6)   7.88
  s 65   7.67–7.69, 7.82, 7.86
    (1)–(6)   7.86
  s 66   5.58, 7.68
    (1)   7.90–7.92
    (2), (3)   7.90
    (4)   7.90, 7.91
    (5)   7.91, 7.92
    (7), (8)   7.91
    (10)   7.92
    (13)   7.90
  s 67   7.34
    (1)   7.34, 7.89
    (2)   7.89
    (4)   7.34
    (6)–(8)   7.34
    (9)   7.89
  s 68   7.37, 7.39, 7.42, 7.43, 7.44, 7.46,
       7.51, 7.52, 7.57, 7.59, 7.61,
       7.62, 7.63, 7.65, 7.66, 7.137
    (1)   7.38, 7.44, 7.49–7.52
    (2)   7.46
    (3), (4)   7.55
    (5)   7.43
  s 69   1.5, 6.70, 7.5, 7.6, 7.23, 7.29, 7.30,
       7.37, 7.50, 7.56, 7.59, 7.61,
       7.62, 7.65, 7.66, 7.80, 7.82,
       7.118
    (1)   7.56, 7.59, 7.61, 7.62
    (2)   7.60
    (3)   7.62, 7.63
    (4)   7.62
    (5)   7.64
    (6)   7.57
  ss 70, 71   6.69
  ss 72–74   7.127
  s 75   7.122, 7.124, 7.126, 8.52
    (1)   7.121, 7.125, 7.126
    (2)   7.125, 7.126
    (3)   7.126
    (4)   7.122
  s 76   7.116–7.118, 7.120, 7.137
    (1)   7.116
    (2)   7.116–7.119
    (3)   7.116
    (4)   7.117–7.119

  s 76(5)   7.119
    (6)   7.116, 7.117
    (7)   7.120
  s 77   7.4, 7.14, 7.21, 7.95–7.97, 7.99,
       7.100, 7.103, 7.105, 7.107,
       7.110, 7.118
    (1)   7.97, 7.98, 7.101, 7.104
    (2)   7.98, 7.103
    (3)   7.26, 7.104, 7.106
    (4)   7.102, 7.104
    (5)   7.105
    (6)   7.96, 7.97, 7.99, 7.100, 7.102
    (7)   7.96
  s 78   7.14, 7.95, 7.101, 7.106, 7.107,
       7.110
    (1)   7.107
    (2), (3)   7.108
    (4)   7.109
    (5), (6)   7.107
  s 79   7.95, 7.110
    (2)–(4)   7.103
  s 80(1)   7.94
  s 154   4.22
  s 166   8.2, 8.35, 8.59–8.66
    (1)   8.60, 8.61, 8.63
    (2)(a), (b)   8.61
    (c)   8.62
    (3), (4)   8.65
    (5)   8.66
    (6)–(8)   8.59
  s 172(5)   8.59
  Sch 10, para 53   7.120
Criminal Justice (Scotland) Act
  1980
  Part V   8.7, 8.9
Criminal Law Act 1967
  s 3   1.2, 2.12, 4.37, 7.134, 8.21, 9.88
    (1)   4.37, 9.59
  s 5(2)   9.24
  s 6(1)(b)   3.72
    (2)   3.73
    (3)   3.71, 3.73, 4.84, 4.100
Criminal Law Act 1977
  Part II   6.92, 7.127, 7.133, 7.135
  s 4(1)   1.9
    (3)   3.34, 5.53
  s 6   7.13, 7.99, 7.111, 7.112, 7.120, 7.130,
       7.134, 7.135
    (1)   7.128, 7.131, 7.134
    (1A)   7.134
    (2)   7.132
    (4)   7.129
    (5)   7.127
    (6)   7.135

Criminal Law Act 1977 – *cont*
s 7   7.13, 7.111, 7.112, 7.115, 7.120,
                 7.130, 7.134, 7.136, 7.137
    (1)   7.136
    (2), (3)   7.139
    (4)   7.136
    (5)   7.127
    (6)   7.136
s 8   7.120
s 9   7.140
    (1)   7.140
    (3)   7.140
    (5)–(7)   7.140
s 10   7.120, 9.70, 9.71
    (1)–(4)   9.70
    (5)   9.71
s 12   7.114, 7.127
    (1)(a)   7.114
       (b)   7.127
    (2)   7.114
    (3)–(7)   7.133
    (8)   7.127, 9.70
s 12A   7.133
    (2)–(5)   7.133
    (6)   7.133
       (d)   7.136
    (7), (8)   7.133
    (9)   7.139
       (b)   7.136
    (10)   7.133
s 31(2), (3)   9.100
s 51   9.24, 9.25, 9.27–9.29
    (1)   9.25, 9.26
    (2), (3)   9.26, 9.28
    (4)   9.29
Sch 1   6.105
Criminal Law (Consolidation)
    (Scotland) Act 1995
Part II   8.7
Cycle Tracks Act 1984   7.14

Dangerous Dogs Act 1991
s 1   4.38
s 5(5)   4.38

Ecclesiastical Courts Jurisdiction
    Act 1860
s 2   3.39, 4.105, 9.21, 9.30–9.36
s 3   9.34
Environmental Protection Act
    1990   7.67
s 79   2.54, 7.73

s 80   2.54, 7.73, 7.82
ss 81, 82   2.54, 7.73
Explosive Substances Act 1883   3.34
s 2   9.25, 9.27
s 3   9.25
Explosives Act 1875
s 80   9.19

Family Law Act 1996   2.75
s 42   2.75
s 45   2.75
Fire Safety and Safety of Places of
    Sport Act 1987   8.3
Firearms Act 1968
s 5   8.22
s 19   9.80
Football (Offences) Act 1991   1.2, 7.55,
                      8.2, 8.25–8.29, 8.35
s 1(1)   8.25, 8.62
    (2)   8.25
s 2   5.8, 8.26
s 3   8.27
    (1)   8.27
    (2)(a), (b)   8.27
s 4   7.42, 8.28
s 5(2)   8.29
Football (Offences and Disorder)
    Act 1999   8.2, 8.4, 8.14, 8.27, 8.30,
                           8.35, 8.44, 8.45
s 10   8.62
Football Spectators Act 1989   1.2, 8.2
Part I   8.3, 8.35, 8.62
Part II   5.57, 8.35, 8.44, 8.48, 8.62
s 1(8)   8.35
    (8A)   8.35
s 2   8.43
    (1)   8.35
ss 2–7   8.3
s 5(7)   8.35
ss 8–13   8.3
s 14   8.45
    (1)–(3)   8.44
    (4)   8.47
    (6)   8.35
    (7)   8.48
    (9)   8.35, 8.44, 8.48, 8.49
s 15   8.45–8.47, 8.53
    (1), (2)   8.45
    (2A)   8.45
    (3)   8.45
    (5)   8.47
    (5A)–(5C)   8.47
ss 16–21   8.47

Football Spectators Act 1989 – *cont*
s 16(1)   8.49
    (1A), (1B)   8.49
    (2), (3)   8.47
    (3A)   8.47
    (4)   8.55, 8.58
    (5)   8.55
s 17   8.54
    (1)   8.54
s 18   8.48
    (1)   8.48
    (2)   8.54
    (3), (4)   8.48
s 19(2)   8.50
    (3)   8.44, 8.47, 8.50, 8.51
        (a)   8.50
        (b)   8.44, 8.50
    (4)–(7)   8.50
    (8)   8.44
s 20(1)–(9)   8.51
    (10), (11)   8.52
s 21   8.50, 8.51
s 22   8.45–8.47, 8.53
    (1)   8.46
    (1A)   8.46
    (2)–(5)   8.46
    (5A)   8.46
    (6)   8.46
    (7)   8.53
    (8)   8.47
    (9)–(11)   8.46
s 23   8.45
    (1)–(4)   8.35
s 25(1)   8.48, 8.54
s 27(2)   8.43
    (5)   8.43
Sch 1   8.35, 8.45, 8.46, 9.17
Forgery and Counterfeiting Act
    1981   8.59

Government of Wales Act 1998
s 22(1)   9.97
Greater London Authority Act
    1999   6.47

Highways Act 1835
s 72   9.78
Highways Act 1980   7.14, 8.59
s 35(6)   9.99
s 137   6.1, 6.88, 7.14, 7.43, 9.47, 9.73–
                                       9.89, 9.91
    (1)   9.73, 9.87

s 143   7.14
s 161   9.19
s 328(1), (2)   9.74
s 329(1)   7.14
Housing Act 1985   7.133
Part III   2.55
Housing Act 1996   2.55
Part VII   2.55
s 152   2.55
    (2), (3)   2.55
Human Rights Act 1998   1.3, 1.5, 1.7,
            1.10–1.27, 2.10, 2.85, 4.5, 6.9,
                            6.42, 6.97, 7.61
s 1   1.17
s 2(1)   1.18
s 3   1.14
    (1)   4.38
    (2)(b), (c)   1.12
ss 4, 5   1.15
s 6   9.102
    (1)   1.16, 9.102
    (2), (3)   1.16
    (6)   1.16
ss 7–9   1.16
s 10   1.15
s 19   1.11, 1.14
Sch 1   1.12, 1.17

Interpretation Act 1978
s 5   1.9, 4.7, 5.20, 6.9, 6.26, 6.46, 7.27,
                                       8.41, 9.15
s 6   6.32, 7.45, 7.60, 7.78, 7.98, 7.107,
                                              9.19
s 7   6.13
s 8   6.83, 7.86
Sch 1   1.9, 4.7, 5.20, 6.9, 6.26, 6.46, 7.27,
                                       8.41, 9.15

Juries Act 1974
s 17   3.49
Justices of the Peace Act 1361   2.3, 2.25,
                    2.32, 2.35, 2.36, 2.37, 2.38
Justices of the Peace Act 1968
s 1(7)   2.36–2.39, 2.44, 2.48

Law of Libel Amendment Act 1888
s 3   5.52
Law Officers Act 1997
s 1   5.53
Legal Aid Act 1988   2.29
Part III   2.91
s 19(5)   2.29

Licensing Act 1872
  s 12   8.23, 8.35
Licensing Act 1964
  s 188   3.39
  s 201   8.10
Limitation Act 1986
  s 2   4.92
  s 11   4.92
Local Government Act 1933
  s 251   9.97
Local Government Act 1963
  s 76   9.21
  Sch 12   7.69
Local Government Act 1972
  s 1(1)   6.45
    (3), (4)   6.45
  s 20(1)   6.45
    (3)   6.45
  s 214   9.35
  s 222   9.92
  s 235   9.97, 9.98, 9.100, 9.101
    (1)–(3)   9.97
  s 236   9.97
  ss 237, 238   9.100
  s 262   6.7
  s 272(2)   9.97
  Sch 1, Pt I   6.45
  Sch 4, Pts I, II   6.45
  Sch 14
    para 23   9.18, 9.19
    para 26   9.18, 9.19
Local Government Finance Act
  1988
  Sch 5, paras 3–8   7.13
Local Government (Miscellaneous
  Provisions) Act 1982   6.66
  Sch 1   7.69
Local Government, Planning and
  Land Act 1980
  s 70   7.93, 7.94
Local Government (Wales) Act
  1994
  Sch 1   9.97
London Government Act 1963
  Sch 12   7.69

Magistrates' Courts Act 1980
  s 17(1)   9.35, 9.92
  s 31   2.48
  s 32   1.9
  s 45(3)   6.41
  s 51   2.29, 2.30
  s 52   2.29

  s 53   2.29
    (2)   2.32
  s 54   2.29
  s 55   2.29, 2.79
    (2)–(4)   2.31
  ss 56, 57   2.29
  s 63(2)   8.41
  s 98   2.32
  s 101   4.38, 7.69, 8.57, 9.46, 9.79
  s 108   8.35, 8.40
    (3)   5.58, 7.92
  s 111   2.49, 2.86, 8.40
  s 115   2.22–2.24, 2.26, 2.27–2.35, 2.39–
                 2.41, 2.44, 2.48, 2.52
    (1)   2.28, 2.29, 2.34
    (3)   2.48
  s 120(2), (3)   2.50
  s 123   2.30
  s 127(1)   4.94
  s 141   8.36, 8.48
  s 143(1)   1.9
  Sch 1   9.35, 9.92
Magistrates' Courts (Appeals from
  Binding Over Orders) Act
  1956
  s 1   2.49
    (2)(a)   2.49
Malicious Communications Act
  1988   4.32
Metropolitan Police Act 1839   1.3, 6.2,
                        9.89
  s 52   6.100, 6.101
  s 54   2.4, 4.105, 9.21, 9.22, 9.23, 9.90
    para 6   9.90
    para 9   6.35, 6.100, 6.101
    para 13   4.8
  s 60   9.76
Ministry of Defence Police Act
  1987
  s 1   9.50

National Heritage Act 1983   6.77
National Parks and Access to
  Countryside Act 1949
  s 90   9.99
Night Poaching Act 1828   7.76
  s 12   7.76
Noise Act 1996   2.54, 7.73

Obscene Publications Act 1959
  s 1(1)   9.19
  s 2   5.12

Offences Against the Person Act
  1861   4.65
  s 20   3.40
  s 36   9.35, 9.36
  s 47   3.40

Parades (Northern Ireland) Act
  1998   6.30
Parks Regulations Act 1872   6.3
Places of Worship Registration Act
  1855   9.30, 9.32
Police Act 1996
  s 1(2)   6.12
  s 30(1)–(3)   9.50
  s 57   8.48
  s 89   9.50, 9.55, 9.57, 9.69
    (1)   9.50, 9.61, 9.62, 9.64, 9.67, 9.68,
                                            9.69
    (2)   9.50, 9.69
    (3)   9.50
  s 101   6.26
  Sch 1   6.12
Police and Criminal Evidence Act
  1984   7.23
  Part IV   8.37
  s 2   8.15
  s 4   9.80
  ss 15, 16   5.39
  s 17   1.2, 3.68, 4.18, 4.40, 4.86, 5.27,
               7.120, 7.135, 9.9, 9.71
    (1)   7.136
    (2)   4.18
    (4)   4.18
    (5)   2.13, 2.14
    (6)   2.2, 2.13, 2.14
  s 24   1.2, 7.126
    (1)   1.2, 2.88, 3.35, 3.50, 3.68, 4.93,
               4.95, 4.96, 4.98, 9.29
    (2)   1.2, 2.88, 4.94, 4.98, 5.27, 7.55,
               7.64, 8.29, 8.42, 8.58, 8.65
    (7)   8.58
  s 25   1.2, 2.4, 2.9, 3.68, 4.57, 4.60, 5.19,
               6.24, 6.92, 6.107, 6.110, 7.32,
               7.35, 7.55, 7.64, 7.84, 7.106,
               7.120, 9.15, 9.20, 9.34, 9.59,
               9.69, 9.88
    (1)–(3)   4.18
    (6)   2.2
  s 26   9.17
    (2)   7.135, 9.71
  s 27   8.37
  s 28   2.9, 8.37, 9.59
    (3)   2.9

s 30   8.37
s 32   2.9, 8.66
  (1)   8.37
  (2)(a)   8.37
s 54   2.9, 8.37
s 56   2.9, 8.37
s 58   2.9, 8.37
s 78   4.79
s 117   1.2
Sch 2   7.135, 9.71
Police (Property) Act 1897   7.64
Post Office Act 1953
  s 11   9.19
Post Office (Protection) Act 1884
  s 6   8.21
Powers of Criminal Courts Act
  1973
  s 12(4)   5.59
  s 43   5.59, 7.64
    (1A)   7.90
Prevention of Corruption Act 1906
                                           4.38
Prevention of Corruption Act 1916
                                           4.38
Prevention of Crime Act 1953
  s 1   8.22, 8.26, 8.57
    (1)   8.21
Prevention of Terrorism
  (Temporary Provisions) Act
  1989
  s 2   9.11
  s 3   9.10
    (1)   9.4, 9.10
    (3)   9.10
  s 16A   4.38
    (3)   4.38
  s 19(1)   9.10
  Sch 1   9.10
Private Places of Entertainment
  (Licensing) Act 1967   7.69
Property Misdescriptions Act 1991
  s 3   7.121
  Sch   7.121
Prosecution of Offences Act 1985
  s 1(6)   3.34
  s 3(2)(c)   2.29
  s 25   3.34, 5.53
Protection from Harassment Act
  1997   2.55, 2.56, 4.65, 4.89–4.101,
                                           5.13
  s 1   4.89, 4.94
    (1)   4.90, 4.91
    (2)   4.90
    (3)   4.91

Protection from Harassment Act
  1997 – *cont*
s 1(3)(c)   4.91
s 2   2.54, 2.66, 4.20, 4.92, 4.95, 4.96,
                        4.97, 4.98, 4.100
  (1)–(3)   4.94
s 3   4.92, 7.115
  (1), (2)   4.92
  (3)–(9)   4.93
s 4   4.20, 4.95, 4.96, 4.97, 4.100
  (1)–(5)   4.95
s 5   4.96, 4.99
  (1)–(6)   4.96
s 6   4.92
s 7(2)   4.90
  (3), (4)   4.90, 4.95
s 12   4.89
Protection of Badgers Act 1992
s 2   7.46
Public Health Act 1875
s 171   9.18
Public Health Acts Amendment
  Act 1907
s 81   9.19
Public Meeting Act 1908   4.105
s 1   6.105, 6.108–6.110
  (1), (2)   6.105, 6.107
  (3)   6.107, 6.110
Public Order Act 1936   1.3, 1.5, 4.102, 6.3,
                        6.43, 6.92, 9.1, 9.4
s 1   6.106, 9.2, 9.3, 9.5, 9.6, 9.8, 9.9,
                           9.12, 9.17
  (1)   9.2, 9.6
  (2)   9.8
s 2   9.12, 9.13, 9.15
  (1)   9.6, 9.11, 9.13, 9.14
    (a), (b)   9.12
  (2), (3)   9.14
  (4)   9.11
  (5)   9.15
s 3   6.2, 6.44, 6.50, 6.92
  (1)   6.2, 6.99
  (2)   6.2
  (3)   6.2, 6.8
  (6)   9.11
s 5   2.9, 4.1, 4.5, 4.8, 4.16, 5.1
s 7(2)   9.8
  (3)   2.9, 9.8
s 9   6.106
  (1)   9.3, 9.10
  (3)   9.2
Public Order Act 1986   1.2, 1.3, 1.5, 1.7,
            2.11, 2.21, 3.11, 3.31, 3.34,
        3.74, 4.65, 6.2, 6.8, 6.10, 6.30,
        6.55, 7.5, 8.25, 8.59, 9.98

Part I   3.1, 3.11, 3.24, 3.39, 4.20, 5.16,
                    5.19, 8.26, 8.28, 9.31
Part II   5.19, 6.4, 6.18, 6.100, 8.63, 9.85
Part III   4.64, 5.1–5.5, 5.7–5.9, 5.11,
             5.13, 5.14, 5.17–5.19, 5.49–
        5.53, 5.56, 5.57, 5.60, 8.35
Part IV   5.57, 8.2, 8.30
s 1   3.7, 3.15, 3.21, 3.31, 3.38, 3.39, 3.69,
                        5.56, 9.31
  (1)   3.9, 3.35
  (2)   3.22, 3.43
  (3)   3.25
  (4)   3.28
  (5)   3.11
  (6)   3.35
s 2   3.7, 3.15, 3.17, 3.21, 3.40, 3.47, 3.69,
                         5.56
  (1)   3.40, 3.41
  (2)   3.43
  (3), (4)   3.41
  (5)   3.50
s 3   3.7, 3.15, 3.53, 3.54, 3.57, 3.69, 5.19,
                         5.56
  (1)   3.51, 3.58, 3.60
  (2)   3.60, 3.63
  (3)   3.21, 3.55
  (4)   3.61
  (5)   3.53
  (6)   3.68
  (7)   3.66, 3.67
s 4   1.6, 2.9, 2.21, 2.51, 2.66, 2.68, 3.10,
  3.15, 3.47, 3.52, 3.54, 3.55, 3.65, 3.71,
  3.72, 4.1, 4.3, 4.4, 4.6–4.10, 4.11, 4.14,
  4.16–4.20, 4.25, 4.26, 4.32, 4.34, 4.39,
  4.40, 4.43, 4.45, 4.46, 4.47, 4.51, 4.52,
  4.53, 4.56, 4.66, 4.77, 4.81, 4.83–4.85,
  4.87, 4.102, 5.8, 5.13, 5.14, 5.16, 5.18,
    5.19, 5.56, 5.57, 6.104, 7.19, 7.35,
      8.27, 9.4, 9.30, 9.36, 9.37, 9.67
  (1)   4.2, 4.13, 4.17
  (2)   4.9, 4.10, 4.32
  (3)   3.68, 4.18, 4.19
  (4)   4.3, 4.17
ss 4–5   2.54, 2.68, 4.89, 4.91, 4.94
s 4A   1.6, 2.4, 2.51, 2.54, 2.66, 2.68, 2.72,
    3.40, 4.1, 4.7, 4.8, 4.20–4.22, 4.25,
  4.27, 4.31–4.35, 4.38, 4.39, 4.40, 4.42,
  4.43, 4.45, 4.46, 4.53, 4.56, 4.64, 4.66,
  4.77, 4.81, 4.83, 4.84, 4.87, 4.89, 4.91,
  4.94, 4.102, 5.8, 5.13, 5.14, 5.16, 5.18,
    5.19, 5.57, 6.104, 6.105, 7.35, 8.27,
      9.4, 9.17, 9.30, 9.36, 9.37, 9.67
s 4A(1)   4.35
  (2)   4.32

Public Order Act 1986 – *cont*

s 4A(3)	4.36, 4.38, 4.55
(a), (b)	4.36, 4.38
(4)	4.40
(5)	4.39
s 5	1.5, 1.6, 1.8, 2.4, 2.21, 2.51, 2.53, 2.54, 2.66, 2.68, 2.69, 2.72, 2.88, 3.40, 4.1, 4.3, 4.5, 4.7, 4.8, 4.11, 4.20, 4.22, 4.27, 4.28, 4.32, 4.34, 4.36, 4.37, 4.39, 4.42–4.45, 4.47–4.57, 4.61, 4.62, 4.66, 4.77, 4.81, 4.83, 4.87, 4.102, 5.8, 5.13, 5.14, 5.16, 5.18, 5.56, 5.57, 6.104, 6.105, 7.35, 7.39, 8.27, 8.35, 9.4, 9.17, 9.30, 9.36, 9.37, 9.45, 9.67
(1)	4.24, 4.41, 4.49, 4.51, 4.58
(2)	4.32, 4.53
(3)	4.38, 4.55
(a)	4.46, 4.54, 4.55
(b)	4.55
(c)	4.36, 4.55
(4)	4.57–4.59, 7.61
(a)	4.59
(5)	4.57
(6)	4.56
s 6(1)	3.19, 3.29, 3.30
(2)	3.43, 3.45, 3.63
(3)	4.11, 4.34, 4.54
(4)	3.29, 4.11, 4.34, 4.54
(5)	3.30, 3.45, 3.63, 4.12, 4.35, 4.54
(6)	3.30, 3.45, 3.63, 4.12
(7)	3.19, 3.45
s 7	4.85
(1)	3.34
(2)	3.69, 4.17, 4.39, 4.56, 4.81
(3)	3.71, 3.73, 4.17
(4)	3.71, 4.17
s 8	3.14, 3.15, 3.16, 3.29, 3.54, 4.10, 4.13, 5.16
s 9(1)	3.7
s 10	3.39
(1)	3.38
(3), (4)	3.39
ss 11–16	6.4
s 11	6.5–6.7, 6.9, 6.10, 6.16, 6.18, 6.21, 6.24, 6.35, 6.37, 6.38, 6.46, 6.91, 6.92
(1)	6.9, 6.11, 6.17
(2)	6.10
(3)	6.17
(4)(a), (b)	6.12
(5)	6.13
(6)	6.13, 6.14
(7)	6.18
(b)	6.18
s 11(8)	6.19, 6.21, 6.23
(9)	6.22, 6.23
(10)	6.18
ss 12–14	6.20, 6.101
s 12	5.19, 6.17, 6.22, 6.25, 6.26, 6.28, 6.32, 6.33, 6.37–6.40, 6.45, 6.52, 6.56, 6.60, 6.62, 6.67, 6.76, 6.91–6.93, 6.95, 6.97, 6.98, 7.50, 9.84
(1)	6.28, 6.30, 6.33, 6.62
(2)	6.26, 6.27
(a), (b)	6.26, 6.35
(3)	6.35
(4)	6.37
(5)	6.39
(6)	6.41
(7)	6.92
(8)	6.37
(9)	6.39, 6.41
s 13	5.2, 5.19, 6.17, 6.25, 6.26, 6.34, 6.43, 6.45, 6.46, 6.50–6.53, 6.71, 6.77, 6.78, 6.80, 6.91– 6.93, 6.95, 6.97, 6.98, 9.83
(1)	6.45, 6.46, 6.50
(2)	6.46
(4)	6.45, 6.47, 6.50
(5)	6.50
(6)	6.46
(7)–(13)	6.52
s 14	5.19, 6.26, 6.28, 6.39, 6.56–6.58, 6.66–6.68, 6.72, 6.73, 6.76, 6.77, 6.91–6.93, 6.95, 6.97, 6.98, 7.50, 7.72, 9.84
(1)	6.60–6.63
(2), (3)	6.60
(4)–(6)	6.68
(7)	6.92
(8)–(10)	6.68
s 14A	5.2, 5.19, 6.26, 6.46, 6.69–6.72, 6.74, 6.76–6.78, 6.81–6.87, 6.89–6.93, 6.95, 6.97, 6.98, 7.14
(1)	6.71, 6.78
(a)	6.74
(2)(a), (b)	6.78
(4)	6.71, 6.79
(5)	6.82
(6)	6.83
(7), (8)	6.81
(9)	6.72–6.74
s 14B	6.69, 6.84
(1)–(3)	6.84
(4)	6.92
(5)–(7)	6.84

Public Order Act 1986 – _cont_

s 14C	6.69, 6.90, 6.92, 7.86
(1)–(5)	6.90
s 15	6.26, 6.27, 6.93
s 16	6.5, 6.6, 6.57, 6.58, 6.61, 6.68
(a), (b)	6.5
s 17	5.4
ss 17–29	5.1
s 18	3.40, 5.15–5.19, 5.22, 5.25, 5.26, 5.41, 5.52, 5.54, 5.57, 5.58
(1)	5.15
(2)	5.16
(3)	5.19
(4)	5.16
(5)	5.18
(6)	5.15
s 19	4.7, 4.25, 5.10, 5.22, 5.23, 5.25–5.28, 5.31, 5.36, 5.54, 5.56–5.58
(1)	5.20
(2)	5.26
(3)	5.21
s 20	4.102, 5.41, 5.42, 5.54, 5.58
(1)	5.40
(2)	4.102, 5.8, 5.43
(3)	5.42
(4)	5.41
(5)	5.40
(6)	5.42
s 21	5.17, 5.28, 5.30, 5.54, 5.58
(1), (2)	5.29
(3)	5.31
(4)	5.30
s 22	5.15, 5.30, 5.47, 5.54
(1)	5.45
(2), (3)	5.46
(4), (5)	5.8, 5.47
(6)	5.46
s 23	5.10, 5.35, 5.36, 5.39, 5.54, 5.57, 5.58
(1), (2)	5.33
(3)	5.35, 5.36
s 24	5.39
(1)	5.39
(3), (4)	5.39
s 25	5.58, 5.59
(1)	5.58, 5.59
(2)	5.59
s 26(1)	5.52
(2)	5.52
s 27	5.53
(1)	5.53
(2)	5.56
(3)	5.57

s 28	5.20, 5.51
(1), (2)	5.50
s 29	5.15, 5.17, 5.25, 5.33, 5.45
s 30	8.30, 8.34
(1)	8.32
(2), (3)	8.34
(4)	8.33, 8.34
s 31	8.30, 8.32, 8.35
(1)–(3)	8.35
s 32(1), (2)	8.39
(3)	8.42
s 33	8.43
(1)–(6)	8.41
s 34	8.37
(1)	8.36
(2)	8.41, 8.43
s 35	8.37
(1), (2)	8.37
(3)	8.36, 8.37
(4)	8.37
s 36	8.31
s 37(1)–(3)	8.31
s 39	1.5, 7.2, 7.3, 7.9, 7.26, 7.60
s 40(3)	6.7
(4)	2.2, 6.55
Sch 1	8.6, 8.21, 8.35
Sch 3	6.7
Public Order (Amendment) Act 1996	4.57
Public Passenger Vehicles Act 1981	8.6
s 1(1)	8.6
s 81	8.10
Public Processions (Northern Ireland) Act 1998	
s 6	6.13
s 8	6.13, 6.26
s 11	6.48
Race Relations Act 1965	5.1
s 6	5.1, 5.55
Race Relations Act 1968	
s 1	4.70
s 12	5.24
Race Relations Act 1976	4.70, 4.71
Railways Act 1993	
s 132	9.50
Representation of the People Act 1983	4.105
s 97	6.109, 6.110
(1)	6.109, 6.110
(2)	6.109
(3)	6.110
s 169	6.109
Sch 1, para 16	3.39

Riot (Damages) Act 1886	3.37, 3.38
s 1	3.38
Road Traffic Act 1988	7.14
ss 4, 5	8.35
s 34	7.35
s 35	9.55
(1)	9.55, 9.57
(2)	9.55
s 179	4.59
s 192	9.74
Road Traffic Offenders Act 1988	9.87
Sch 3	9.87
Safety of Sports Grounds Act 1975	8.3
s 1(1)	8.3, 8.25, 8.31, 8.35
s 12	8.3
Sexual Offences Act 1956	
s 30(2)	4.38
Sporting Events (Control of Alcohol etc) Act 1985	1.2, 8.2, 8.5–8.24, 8.30
s 1	8.5, 8.6, 8.10, 8.13, 8.15, 8.35
(1)	8.6, 8.10
(2)	8.10, 8.11
(3)	8.12
(4)	8.13
(5)	8.6
s 1A	8.5, 8.6, 8.10, 8.12, 8.13, 8.15
(1)	8.6
(2)	8.10, 8.11
(3)	8.12
(4)	8.13
(5)	8.6, 8.10
s 2	8.16, 8.18–8.20, 8.35
(1)	8.19, 8.21
(2)	8.23
(3)	8.20
s 2A	8.16, 8.18
(1)	8.21, 8.22
(2), (3)	8.21
s 5A	8.19
s 7(1)	8.24
(2)	8.15, 8.24
(3)	8.15
s 8(a)	8.11
(b)	8.12, 8.19
(c)	8.13, 8.23
s 9(2)	8.17
(3)	8.7
(4)	8.18
(6)	8.7
(7)	8.10
(8)	8.7, 8.17
Summary Jurisdiction Act 1879	
s 25	2.28, 2.35
Supreme Court Act 1981	
s 15	2.36
s 18(1)(a)	2.29
s 19	2.36
s 28	8.40
(3)	5.58
s 45	2.36
s 48	8.40
s 79	8.40
(3)	2.86
Theatres Act 1968	
s 6	4.102, 4.103, 4.104
(1), (2)	4.102
s 7(2)	4.102, 5.42
s 8	4.102
s 9	5.42
(1), (2)	4.102
s 10	4.103, 5.42
s 15	4.104, 5.42
s 16	4.102, 5.50
s 18	4.102, 5.40
(2)(c)	4.102
Theft Act 1968	8.59
s 10	4.65
s 12	7.104
s 12A	4.65
s 17	7.123
Town Police Clauses Act 1847	1.3, 6.2
s 3	9.19
s 21	6.102
s 28	2.4, 4.105, 6.102, 9.17, 9.18–9.23, 9.76, 9.89, 9.90
Trade Disputes Act 1906	2.17
Trade Union and Labour Relations (Consolidation) Act 1992	
s 204	9.47
s 207(1)	9.47
s 219	9.44
s 220	2.17, 6.59, 6.72, 9.47
(1)	9.47, 9.76
(2)–(4)	9.47
s 241	4.105, 7.50, 9.37–9.39, 9.41, 9.42, 9.44, 9.45, 9.47
(1)	9.37, 9.45, 9.48, 9.49
(a)	6.32, 7.50
(2)	9.48

Trade Union and Labour	
Relations (Consolidation) Act	
1992 – *cont*	
s 241(3)	9.49
s 242	1.9
s 244	9.47
s 246	9.47
Trafalgar Square Act 1844	6.3

Unlawful Drilling Act 1819	
ss 1, 2	9.16
s 7	9.16

Vagrancy Act 1824	7.106
s 4	7.99
Vehicles Excise and Registration	
Act 1994	8.10

Wildlife and Countryside Act 1981	6.77
ss 53, 54	7.14

TABLE OF STATUTORY INSTRUMENTS, BY-LAWS AND CODES OF PRACTICE

References are to paragraph numbers.

Air Navigation (No 2) Order 1995, SI 1995/1970   4.16

British Railways Board By-laws
    Art 3(A)   8.6

Civil Procedure Rules 1998, SI 1998/3132
    Sch 1 Rules of the Supreme Court 1965
        Ord 53, r 3(10)   6.98
        Ord 113   7.115, 9.70
          r 6   7.115
    Sch 2 County Court Rules 1981   7.116
        Ord 1, r 9(4)   7.114
        Ord 24   9.70
          Pt I   7.113–7.115
          Pt II   7.113
          r 4   7.115
          r 8   7.114
            (2)   7.114
          rr 9, 10   7.114
          r 11   7.116
            (1)–(3)   7.114
          r 12   7.114
            (5)   7.114
          r 13   7.114
            (3)   7.115
          r 14(2)–(4)   7.114
          r 15   7.114
Code of Practice for the Exercise by Police Officers of Statutory Powers of Stop
    and Search (Code A)   8.15, 8.24
    para 1.8   7.64
    para A1.6   8.24
    Notes for Guidance 1A, 1AA   7.64
    Notes for Guidance 1D   8.24
Code of Practice for the Searching of Premises by Police Officers and the
    Seizure of Property Found by Police Officers on Persons or Premises (Code
    B)   5.39
Code of Practice on Detention, Treatment and Questioning of Persons by Police
    Officers (Code C)   2.9, 8.37
Code of Practice for the Identification of Persons by Police Officers (Code D)   8.37
County Court Rules 1981 *see* Civil Procedure Rules 1998, Sch 2
Crime and Disorder Act 1998 (Commencement No 3 and Appointed Day)
    Order 1999, SI 1999/3263   2.57

Employment Code of Practice (Picketing) Order 1992, SI 1992/476   9.47

European Parliamentary Elections Regulations 1999, SI 1999/1214
  art 3(1)   6.109
  Sch 1   6.109

Football (Offences) (Designation of Football Matches) Order 1999, SI 1999/
  2462   8.25
Football Spectators (Corresponding Offences in France) Order 1998, SI 1998/
  1266   8.46
Football Spectators (Corresponding Offences in Italy) Order 1990, SI 1990/992   8.46
Football Spectators (Corresponding Offences in Norway) Order 1996, SI 1996/
  1634   8.46
Football Spectators (Corresponding Offences in Republic of Ireland) Order
  1996, SI 1996/1635   8.46
Football Spectators (Corresponding Offences in Scotland) Order 1990, SI 1990/
  993   8.46
Football Spectators (Corresponding Offences in Sweden) Order 1992, SI 1992/
  708   8.46
Football Spectators (Designation of Enforcing Authority) Order 1999, SI 1999/
  2459   8.48
Football Spectators (Designation of Football Matches in England and Wales)
  Order 1999, SI 1999/2461
    art 3   8.35
    Sch   8.35
Football Spectators (Designation of Football Matches outside England and
  Wales) Order 1990, SI 1990/732   8.44
Football Spectators (Seating) Order 1994, SI 1994/1666   8.3
Football Spectators (Seating) Order 1995, SI 1995/1706   8.3
Football Spectators (Seating) Order 1996, SI 1996/1706   8.3
Football Spectators (Seating) Order 1997, SI 1997/1677   8.3
Football Spectators (Seating) Order 1999, SI 1999/1926   8.3

Human Rights Act 1998 (Commencement) Order 1998, SI 1998/2882   1.11

Indictment Rules 1971, SI 1971/1253
  r 4(2)   3.69

Local Authorities Cemeteries Order 1977, SI 1977/204
  arts 18, 19   9.35
London Transport Executive Railways By-laws   8.6

Magistrates' Courts (Forms) Rules 1981, SI 1981/553   2.30
Magistrates' Courts Rules 1981, SI 1981/552
  r 4(2)   2.30
  r 12   7.25
    (1)   3.69
  r 14(1)   2.32
  r 100   4.13
Magistrates' Courts (Sex Offender and Anti-Social Behaviour Orders) Rules
  1998, SI 1998/2682   2.58, 2.84
  Sch 5   2.79
Motor Vehicles (Wearing of Seat Belts) Regulations 1993, SI 1993/176   6.6

National Assembly for Wales (Transfer of Functions) Order 1999, SI 1999/672   9.97

Police (Disposal of Sound Equipment) Regulations 1995, SI 1995/722   7.92
    reg 2(1), (2)   7.92
    regs 3, 4   7.92
Police (Property) Regulations 1997, SI 1997/1908   7.64
Police (Retention and Disposal of Items Seized under s 60 of the Criminal
    Justice and Public Order Act 1994) Regulations 1999, SI 1999/269
    reg 3   7.64
Police (Retention and Disposal of Vehicles) Regulations 1995, SI 1995/723
    reg 2(2)   7.34
    reg 3   7.34
      (1)   7.34
    reg 4(1)   7.34
      (3), (4)   7.34
    reg 5   7.34
      (1), (2)   7.34
    reg 6   7.34
      (1)–(5)   7.34
    reg 7(1), (2)   7.34
    reg 8(1)–(3)   7.34
    reg 9(1), (2)   7.34
Public Order Act 1986 (Commencement No 2) Order 1987, SI 1987/198   3.39
Public Order (Domestic Football Banning) Order 1999, SI 1999/2460   8.31, 8.36
Public Order (Northern Ireland) Order 1987, SI 1987/463 (NI 7)   5.7

Riot (Damages) Regulations 1921, SR&O 1921/1536   3.37
Royal and Other Parks and Gardens Regulations 1977, SI 1977/217   6.3
Rules of the Supreme Court 1965 *see* Civil Procedure Rules 1998, Sch 1

Sports Grounds and Sporting Events (Designation) Order 1985, SI 1985/1151   8.8, 8.17
Sports Grounds and Sporting Events (Designation) (Scotland) Order 1980,
    SI 1980/2030   8.9

Trafalgar Square Regulations 1952, SI 1952/776   6.3

TABLE OF EU AND FOREIGN LEGISLATION

References are to paragraph numbers.

EU Legislation

Council Directive 73/148 on the abolition of restrictions on movement and
 residence within the Community with regard to establishment and the
 provision of services   8.47

Foreign Legislation

Anti-Discrimination (Racial Vilification) Act 1989 (New South Wales) 5.8

Bill of Rights (Hong Kong)
 Art 11(1)   4.38

Bill of Rights Act 1990 (New Zealand)
 s 6   4.38

Criminal Code (Canada)
 s 281.2   5.7

New Penal Code (France)
 Arts 624–3 to 624–6   4.65

Summary Offences Act 1988 (New South Wales)
 Part 4   6.16

TABLE OF TREATIES AND CONVENTIONS

References are to paragraph numbers.

European Convention on the Protection of Human Rights and Fundamental
    Freedoms 1950   1.3, 1.5, 1.7, 1.10–1.27, 2.34, 2.44, 5.60, 6.4, 7.33, 9.98
    Art 2   1.17, 1.20
    Arts 3, 4   1.17
    Art 5   1.16, 1.17, 1.21, 2.3, 2.9, 2.10, 2.27, 2.51, 2.52, 7.61
        (1)   2.10, 2.27
            (b)   2.27
            (c)   2.10
    Art 6   1.17, 1.19, 2.3, 2.9, 2.51, 2.52, 2.80, 2.91, 7.34, 7.89
        (1)   2.52
        (2)   2.80, 4.38, 8.57, 9.46, 9.79
        (3)   2.52
    Art 7   1.17, 1.20
    Arts 8–11   1.20, 1.21, 2.85
    Art 8   1.17, 2.14, 5.16, 7.33–7.34, 7.36, 7.89, 7.110, 9.36, 9.85
        (2)   2.14, 7.110
    Art 9   1.17, 2.23, 4.62, 5.5
    Art 10   1.17, 1.21, 2.10, 2.23, 2.27, 2.51, 2.52, 4.5, 4.36, 4.62, 4.91, 5.13, 5.16, 5.60,
         6.42, 6.53, 6.56, 6.89, 6.90, 7.61, 7.62, 7.66, 9.85
        (1)   2.10, 2.27
        (2)   2.10, 2.27, 5.60, 6.42, 6.53, 6.89, 7.61, 7.62, 7.66
    Art 11   1.17, 2.51, 4.62, 4.79, 4.91, 6.9, 6.42, 6.53, 6.56, 6.89–6.90, 7.36, 7.66, 7.85–
         7.86, 7.110
        (2)   6.9, 6.42, 6.53, 6.77, 6.89, 7.61, 7.66, 7.85
    Art 12   1.17
    Art 14   1.17, 1.27, 6.89, 7.110
    Art 16   1.17
    Art 17   1.17, 5.60
    Art 18   1.17
    First Protocol
        Art 1   1.17, 7.33, 7.34, 7.89
        Art 2   1.17
        Art 3   1.17
    Fourth Protocol
        Art 2   6.90, 8.47
    Sixth Protocol
        Arts 1, 2   1.17

International Covenant on Civil and Political Rights 1966
    Art 12(1), (2)   8.47

Universal Declaration of Human Rights 1948   1.3

TABLE OF ABBREVIATIONS

1839 Act	Metropolitan Police Act 1839
1847 Act	Town Police Clauses Act 1847
1855 Act	Places of Worship Registration Act 1855
1860 Act	Ecclesiastical Courts Jurisdiction Act 1860
1861 Act	Offences Against the Person Act 1861
1875 Act	Conspiracy and Protection of Property Act 1875
1908 Act	Public Meeting Act 1908
1936 Act	Public Order Act 1936
1968 Act	Theatres Act 1968
1972 Act	Local Government Act 1972
1977 Act	Criminal Law Act 1977
1983 Act	Representation of the People Act 1983
1985 Act	Sporting Events (Control of Alcohol etc) Act 1985
1986 Act	Public Order Act 1986
1989 Act	Football Spectators Act 1989
1990 Act	Environmental Protection Act 1990
1991 Act	Football (Offences) Act 1991
1992 Act	Trade Union and Labour Relations (Consolidation) Act 1992
1994 Act	Criminal Justice and Public Order Act 1994
1997 Act	Protection from Harassment Act 1997
1998 Act	Crime and Disorder Act 1998
ASBO	anti-social behaviour order
DFBO	domestic football banning order
ECHR	European Convention on the Protection of Human Rights and Fundamental Freedoms
ECtHR	European Court of Human Rights
IFBO	international football banning order
PACE	Police and Criminal Evidence Act 1984
PIO	protected intending occupier

FURTHER READING

Archbold on Criminal Pleading, Evidence and Practice (Sweet & Maxwell, 2000)

Card, Cross and Jones *Criminal Law* 14th edn (Butterworths, 1998)

Law Commission *Binding Over: the Issues* Law Com Working Paper no 103 (1987)

Law Commission *Criminal Law: Offences Relating to Public Order Law* Law Com Report no 123 (1983)

Marston and Tain *Public Order Offences* (Sweet & Maxwell, 1995)

Report by Lord Justice Taylor *The Hillsborough Stadium Disaster: Report of Inquiry* (Cm 962, 1990)

Review of Public Order Law (Cmnd 9510, 1985)

ATH Smith *Offences against Public Order* (Sweet & Maxwell, 1987)

Smith and Hogan *Criminal Law* 9th edn (Butterworths, 1999)

Supperstone *Brownlie's Law of Public Order and National Security* 2nd edn (Butterworths, 1981)

Thornton *Public Order Law* (Blackstone Press, 1987)

Trespass and Protest: Policing under the Criminal Justice and Public Order Act 1994 (Home Office Research Study no 190, 1998)

Chapter 1

INTRODUCTION

GENERAL POINTS

1.1   This book is about public order law in England and Wales. It examines a range of criminal offences dealing with public order, as well as a few mechanisms under the civil law. '*Public* order law' is in a sense a misleading title in respect of a number of the provisions dealt with because they apply to private places as well as public ones.

   The choice of contents of this book is somewhat arbitrary because there are no clear boundaries to what constitutes public order law. In terms of offences, offences against the person, offences involving damage to property, weapons and firearms offences, and statutory nuisance offences can all disturb public order, but they are not included in this book because it cannot be said that their essential mischief (or one of their essential mischiefs) is the protection of public order; they are designed essentially to protect the person, property or the environment. Views may differ about where the line is drawn. Arguably, some of the firearms and weapons offences come closest to being public order offences. Constraints of space, and the fact that these offences are already dealt with fully in other modern works, resolved any doubts on the matter.

   Of the mechanisms of the civil law included in this book, the most important are the powers to prevent or deal with a breach of the peace, which remain at the heart of the policing of public disorder, and the power to bind over.

1.2   In modern times, Parliament has substantially increased the range and number of public order offences and powers. The Sporting Events (Control of Alcohol etc) Act 1985 created a number of alcohol-related offences aimed at curbing football hooliganism. The Public Order Act 1986, in addition to re-fashioning the offences of riot and affray, introduced new offences of violent disorder and of threatening, abusive or insulting words or behaviour, recast and extended offences involving incitement to racial hatred, introduced exclusion orders for convicted football hooligans, and introduced a new police power to direct those who had trespassed on open land to reside there to leave. The Football Spectators Act 1989 and Football (Offences) Act 1991 added further provisions to deal with football hooliganism. The Criminal Justice and Public Order Act 1994 heaped on even more public order provisions, particularly those in Part V of the Act relating to aggravated trespass, raves, unauthorised vehicular campers and squatters, as well as strengthening existing offences. Lastly, the Crime and Disorder Act 1998 introduced, inter alia, racially-aggravated public order offences and anti-social behaviour orders.

   This chronology shows that, as in other areas of criminal justice, the modern tendency is to throw more law at a problem in the hope that it will eliminate or reduce it, and will reduce the cost of policing,[1] whether it is the large-scale disorder of the 1980s, such as inner city riots and mass picketing, or the low-level disorder of the 1990s, such as disorderly conduct by groups on housing estates, or new forms of protest, eg by environmental or animal rights protesters, or mass trespasses by New Age Travellers. Likewise, Parliament has shown in the above public order legislation a remarkable willingness to add minor offences to the list of arrestable offences in s 24 of the Police and Criminal Evidence Act 1984 (PACE)[2] or to create special powers of arrest for others, quite contrary to the overall philosophy of PACE, which was to limit arrestable offences generally to the more serious types of offence and otherwise generally to permit arrest only under the general conditional power of arrest under s 25 of PACE.[2]

The problem with such knee-jerk reactions, just like those in other areas (eg the responses to joy-riding and dangerous dogs) is not only that they overlap with existing law to some extent, but that they respond to a narrow social harm with a widely drawn provision which impinges to an excessive extent on the rights and freedoms of another and is socially divisive.

The knee-jerk changes to the law just referred to were made partly as a result of public demand for tighter controls, whipped up by the tabloid press in particular. There is a danger that the freedoms of individuals are subjected to Mill's 'tyranny of the majority'.

---

1   The financial cost of policing disorder can be great. For example, the total cost of policing the Newbury bypass operation 'in financial years 1995/96 and 1997/98 [sic]' was estimated at £18m (£10.5m opportunity cost and £7.5m real costs): *Keeping the Peace: Policing Disorder* (HM Inspectorate of Constabulary, 1999).

2   By PACE, s 24(1), arrestable offences are defined as offences for which the sentence is fixed by law or for which a person (not previously convicted) may be sentenced to imprisonment for a term of five years. Section 24(2) declares to be arrestable offences certain other offences (initially quite a short list but subsequently added to) whose maximum sentence is less than five years' imprisonment.

Any person may arrest without warrant anyone who is (or whom he, with reasonable cause, suspects to be) in the act of committing an arrestable offence. Where an arrestable offence has actually been committed, any person may arrest without warrant anyone who is (or whom he, with reasonable cause, suspects to be) guilty of the offence.

Additionally, a *constable* may arrest without warrant:

(a)   where he suspects, with reasonable cause, that an arrestable offence has been committed, any person whom he suspects, with reasonable cause, to be guilty of it; or

(b)   any person who is (or whom he suspects, with reasonable cause, to be) about to commit an arrestable offence.

To effect an arrest under these powers a constable may enter, if need be by force, and search any place where the person to be arrested is, or is with reasonable cause suspected by the constable to be.

By PACE, s 17, a *constable* may enter and search any premises for the purpose of arresting a person for an arrestable offence whom he reasonably believes is on the premises. In relation to premises consisting of two or more separate dwellings, they are limited to powers to enter and search the communal parts of the premises and any dwelling where the person in question is reasonably believed to be. The power of search is only a power to search to the extent that is reasonably required for the purpose for which the power of entry is exercised.

PACE, s 25, provides that, in addition a *constable* who reasonably suspects that any offence which is not an arrestable offence has been, or is being, committed or attempted, may arrest without warrant any person whom he reasonably suspects of having committed or attempted, or of being in the course of committing or attempting, that offence. However, this power is exercisable only if it appears to the constable that service of a summons is impracticable or inappropriate because any of the 'general arrest conditions' is satisfied. These are:

(a)   that the suspect's name is unknown to, and unascertainable by, the constable;

(b)   that the constable has reasonable grounds for doubting whether the name furnished is the person's real name;

(c)   that the person has failed to furnish a satisfactory address for service, or that the constable has reasonable grounds for doubting whether the address furnished is so satisfactory;

(d) that the constable has reasonable grounds for believing that the arrest is necessary to prevent the suspect physically harming himself or another, suffering physical injury, causing loss of or damage to property, committing an offence to public decency (provided members of the public going about their normal business cannot reasonably be expected to avoid the person to be arrested), or causing an unlawful obstruction of the highway;

(e) that the constable has reasonable grounds for believing that arrest is necessary to protect a child or other vulnerable person from the suspect.

Reasonable force may be used to effect an arrest, entry or search under the above provisions (Criminal Law Act 1967, s 3; PACE, s 117).

1.3   The principal Act in the area of public order law, the Public Order Act 1986, did not codify the law. It left untouched the common law powers to prevent or deal with a breach of the peace, indeed it expressly preserved them, and the powers to bind over. In addition to the modern statutes referred to in para **1.2**, many other statutes contain public order provisions to a greater or lesser extent: for example, the Metropolitan Police Act 1839, the Town Police Clauses Act 1847, and the Public Order Act 1936. The result of all this is that our public order law lacks any coherent structure; indeed, there are substantial areas of duplication and overlap.[1]

As elsewhere in the criminal law, there is a need for public order law as a whole to be reviewed according to a coherent set of principles,[2] simplified and codified. The enactment of the Human Rights Act 1998[3] has increased the need for codification.[4] The case for it was well made by Lord Scarman at the beginning of his report into the Red Lion Square disorders in 1974:[5]

> 'There is a case, some would think a strong case, for codifying our law as to public order so as to ensure that the fundamental human rights set out in the UN Declaration of 1948 and the European Convention of 1950 are protected by statute ... [T]he real issue is ... whether our law confers upon those whose duty it is to maintain public order sufficient powers without endangering the right of peaceful protest.'

1   Card 'Disorder in public order law' in *Criminal Law: Essays in Honour of JC Smith* (Butterworths, 1987) p 204.
2   For such a review in respect of controls over processions and meetings, see Bevan 'Protest and public order' [1979] PL 163.
3   See para **1.11**.
4   See The Hon Mrs Justice Arden 'Criminal law at the crossroads: the impact on human rights from the Law Commission's perspective and the need for a code' [1999] Crim LR 439.
5   *Report on Red Lion Square Disorders of 16 June 1974* (Cmnd 5919, 1975). The disorders involved a violent assault on a police cordon leading to a riot.

Role of the police

1.4   The police, of course, play a pivotal role in public order law. As Lord Scarman said in his report on the Red Lion Square disorders about protest and disorder:

> 'The law requires of the citizen as the necessary condition for the exercise of his rights that he respects the rights of others, even though he may fundamentally disagree with them and totally disapprove of their policies.'

He added:

'Civilised living collapses – it is obvious – if public protest becomes violent protest or public order degenerates into the quietism imposed by a successful oppression. The fact that those who at any one time are concerned to secure the tranquillity of the streets are likely to be the majority must not lead us to deny the protesters their opportunity to march: the fact that the protesters are desperately sincere and are exercising a fundamental human right must not lead us to overlook the rights of the majority.'

The policing of this balance lies 'at the sharp end' with the police under their statutory and common law powers of intervention. The range of police powers dealt with in this book undoubtedly puts the police in a strong position in policing public order and often enables them to negotiate peaceful settlements to potentially disorderly situations, which never show up in the statistics.

1.5   In this respect, a facet of public order law which is open to criticism and has been on the increase is the number of offences which can occur due to disobedience to police orders made on the basis of judgments by the police, often about events which may occur in the future. This approach has its antecedents in the power of the police to take reasonable steps to prevent a breach of the peace, breach of which can result in a conviction for obstructing a constable in the execution of his duty. More specifically, the Public Order Act 1936 gave the police powers to impose conditions on public processions, and the Public Order Act 1986 gave them similar powers in relation to public assemblies, breach of which results in criminal liability. Section 39 of the 1986 Act added a power to direct trespassers on open land for the purpose of residing there to leave, breach being an offence. Sections 63 and 69 of the Criminal Justice and Public Order Act 1994 added similar powers and offences in respect of raves and aggravated trespass. A reasonably suspected failure to comply with one of these conditions or directions is also made a ground of arrest, as is failure to comply with a warning to stop threatening, abusive, insulting or disorderly words or behaviour under s 5 of the Public Order Act 1986.

Especially where the discretion given to the police is wide, this is a worrying trend. It raises a fundamental issue in respect of public order law, since police discretion as to when and how to act is inherent and essential to preserving public order. On the other hand, it is inconsistent with the tradition of individual liberty that a person should be obliged to take orders from a police officer except in the narrowest of circumstances.[1] These may be represented by the circumstances under which the police can give orders under their breach of the peace powers. These powers are not without their critics, but to go further is particularly open to criticism and to conflict with the European Convention on the Protection of Human Rights and Fundamental Freedoms (ECHR). The exercise of police discretion can often involve determining the balance between competing rights and freedoms and in practical terms is subject to little in the way of effective external control. Moreover, the police service tends to be imbued with a particular view, an orderly one, of society that can impact on others whose views are different. There is a clear danger that the police will appear to be partisan in any clash of points of view and to be a politically biassed part of the executive, even where the view which they are protecting is not one which they share. The nature of much of modern public order law, particularly the collective trespass and nuisance powers discussed in Chapter 7, places the police on one side in a clash of values. It would be naive today to consider a police officer simply as an impartial 'keeper of the peace', however genuinely individual officers attempt to be so.

The reality of individual freedom depends very much on the wise exercise by the police of their discretionary powers. It is regrettable that the exercise of that discretion is left unstructured by statute, although in some areas government guidance has been given.

Although judicial review is available, there are traditionally broad margins of exemption for the exercise of public discretion; there is a long-standing reluctance on the part of the court to overturn operational decisions by the police, although this should change as a result of the enactment of the Human Rights Act 1998.

---

1   Stone and Bonner 'The Public Order Act 1986: Steps in the wrong direction?' [1987] PL 202 at 211.

Impact of public order law

1.6   With some notable exceptions, such as violent disorder, affray and offences of threatening, abusive, insulting or disorderly words or behaviour, contrary to ss 4–5 of the Public Order Act 1986, prosecutions for the various public order offences are uncommon. That is not to say that the other provisions are without effect. They can have a formative effect on behaviour, although sometimes this is simply in the direction of sophisticated evasion of an offence, as in the case of publishing or distributing material intended or likely to stir up racial hatred. Alternatively, they can form the background to negotiation with the police which leads to arrangements in which they do not have to be invoked, as, for example, in the case of the provisions concerning the imposition of conditions on public processions and public assemblies. Lastly, the threat of arrest and prosecution can have a powerful deterrent effect and end demonstrations or collective trespasses or nuisance of the type dealt with in Part V of the Criminal Justice and Public Order Act 1994.

1.7   More than in most areas of criminal law, the law relating to public order often lacks precise definitions. This is particularly true, for example, of the non-criminal law relating to breach of the peace (where the cynic might say that the judges have deliberately left things vague so as to allow the law to develop pragmatically) and binding over,[1] but it is also true of a number of public order offences. Important terms like 'threatening', 'abusive' and 'insulting' are all left at large as a question of fact for an individual bench. The result has been that the courts have tended to apply a number of offences beyond their intended purpose and to the detriment of the rights and freedoms of others, particularly the rights to freedom of expression and freedom of association.

The 'bringing home' of the ECHR by the Human Rights Act 1998 described below will serve to clarify these rights and freedoms and to redress the imbalance which has developed between the rights of the individual and those of the State.

---

1   In the White Paper, *Review of Public Order Law* (Cmnd 9510, 1985) preceding the Public Order Act 1986, the then government rejected codification of these powers on the ground that 'there is advantage in the flexibility of common law powers which are defined and controlled by the courts; and the police have not sought codification and see no benefit in it': ibid, para 6.13.

1.8   There is a danger that some modern public order provisions tilt the balance too far in favour of a nuisance-free, orderly society at the expense of the freedoms of expression and association. Examples of these provisions are the offence of threatening, abusive, insulting or disorderly words or behaviour likely to cause harassment, alarm or distress, contrary to s 5 of the Public Order Act 1986, and the provisions relating to collective trespass and nuisance under Part V of the Criminal Justice and Public Order Act 1994. Quite a number of these provisions do not require any evidence to be given by a 'victim'. There is a practical reason for this in some cases, at least, viz that victims are liable to be vulnerable and reluctant to come and give evidence, but it gives an undesirable advantage to the prosecution.

There is also a danger in such cases of intruding too far into the proper preserve of the civil law – and beyond. There is also the danger of creating social outcasts, against whom the law is directed because they question property values, authority or conventional views or standards, by criminalising the lifestyle of people asserting their rights to family life, expression and association.

Trial and punishment

1.9   Most of the offences described in this book are summary ones, ie triable only in a magistrates' court. This fact, and the fact that the vast majority of public order offences are dealt with in magistrates' courts and most binding-over orders are made by them, means that magistrates' courts are the major players at the judicial stage of public order law enforcement. The available punishment for a summary offence includes a fine whose maximum is described by reference to 'the standard scale'.[1] When this book went to press the standard scale was as follows:

level 1	£200
level 2	£500
level 3	£1,000
level 4	£2,500
level 5	£5,000.[2]

It is not an offence, contrary to the Criminal Attempts Act 1981, to attempt to commit a summary offence,[3] but it is an offence to incite someone to commit, or to conspire to commit,[4] a summary offence.

Of the remaining offences in this book, all but riot and a couple of others, which are triable only on indictment and are Class 3 offences,[5] are triable either way and are Class 4 offences.[6] A fine imposed for an either-way offence on summary conviction must not exceed the 'statutory maximum',[7] currently £5,000.

---

1   The meaning of the standard scale is that given by the Criminal Justice Act 1982, s 37, and the Interpretation Act 1978, Sch 1.
2   The Home Secretary has power by order to change the amounts specified in the standard scale in the light of a change in the value of money: Magistrates' Courts Act 1980, s 143(1).
3   Criminal Attempts Act 1981, s 1(4).
4   Except for a conspiracy relating to a summary offence where the acts in pursuance of the agreement are to be done in contemplation or furtherance of a trade dispute (within the meaning of the Trade Union and Labour Relations (Consolidation) Act 1992) and the summary offence is not punishable with imprisonment: 1992 Act, s 242. A prosecution for conspiracy to commit a summary offence can be brought only by or with the consent of the Director of Public Prosecutions: Criminal Law Act 1977, s 4(1).

5   *Practice Direction (Crown Court: Allocation of Business) (No 3)* (2000) *The Times*, 18 January. A Class 3 offence may be tried by a High Court judge or, in accordance with general or particular directions given by a presiding judge, by a circuit judge or a recorder: ibid.

6   An 'offence triable either way' means an offence, other than an offence triable on indictment only by virtue of Part V of the Criminal Justice Act 1988 (which empowers the Crown Court to try a summary offence on indictment in certain cases if it is related to an indictable offence charged in the indictment), which, if committed by an adult, is triable either on indictment in the Crown Court or summarily in a magistrates' court: Interpretation Act 1978, s 5 and Sch 1. A Class 4 offence may be tried by a High Court judge, a circuit judge, a recorder or an assistant recorder. It will not be listed for trial by a High Court judge without the consent of that judge or of a presiding judge: *Practice Direction (Crown Court: Allocation of Business) (No 3)* (2000) *The Times*, 18 January.

7   The 'statutory maximum' is the prescribed sum within the meaning of s 32 of the Magistrates' Courts Act 1980 (Criminal Justice Act 1982, s 74), which is the maximum fine which can be imposed on a summary conviction for an offence triable either way. The Home Secretary has power to change this sum by order in the light of a change in the value of money: Magistrates' Courts Act 1980, s 143(1).

EUROPEAN CONVENTION ON HUMAN RIGHTS AND HUMAN RIGHTS ACT 1998

1.10 Many of the offences and powers discussed in this book have considerable implications for the legitimate freedom of the individual. Some, such as offences relating to incitement to racial hatred, offences of threatening, abusive or insulting words or behaviour in general, and the provisions about aggravated trespass and powers to control public processions or assemblies, impinge on freedom of expression. Some, such as the various offences of collective trespass and nuisance, and the powers to control public processions and assemblies, impact on freedom of association. Some of the provisions about collective trespass or nuisance also have implications for the freedom to a private life, to home and to a family. The relentless march of public order law, in the last part of the twentieth century in particular, has appeared to reduce individual freedom with each step. These freedoms, like others, inevitably come into conflict with other competing rights and interests. Maintaining the correct level and balance of individual rights and freedoms is basic to the needs of a democratic society. The provisions described below are of crucial importance in achieving this end. Not least, they provide some protection against knee-jerk changes to the law of the type referred to in para **1.2**.

1.11 Hitherto, the rights guaranteed under the ECHR and the Protocols to it to which the UK is a party have not had any legal effect in the domestic law of England and Wales (or other parts of the UK), although it had become established that a court might have regard to the Convention.[1] The Human Rights Act 1998, the principal provisions of which are expected to come into force on 2 October 2000,[2] changes this approach radically and will have a fundamental impact on public order law, as in other areas of law.

1   *R v Khan* [1996] 3 All ER 289, HL.

2   The only provision of the Act referred to in this book in force at the time of writing is s 19 (see para **1.14**), which came into force on 24 November 1998: Human Rights Act 1998 (Commencement) Order 1998, SI 1998/2882.

The ECHR and decisions of the European Court of Human Rights began to feature prominently in some appellate decisions in advance of the commencement date of the main provisions of the Human Rights Act 1998: see, for example, *DPP, ex parte Kebeline* [1999] 4 All ER 801, HL; see para **4.38**; *Redmond-Bate v DPP* (1999) *The Times*, 28 July, DC; see para **2.23**; *Barrett v Enfield LBC* [1999] 3 All ER 193, CA; *R v Secretary of State for the Home Department, ex parte Simms* [1999] QB 349, CA; *Amin v Nottingham City Council* (1999) *The Times*, 2 December, CA.

Impact of the Act[1]

1.12 The Human Rights Act 1998 'brings home' those Convention rights set out in Sch 1 to the Act. Essentially what this means is that remedies will be available in courts and tribunals (hereafter simply 'courts') in England and Wales in respect of the Convention rights. This has not been achieved by the incorporation of the Convention rights into English law. Parliamentary sovereignty has been retained. Our domestic courts have not been given a power to strike down or disapply an inconsistent Act of Parliament (primary legislation),[2] but the effect of the main provisions in the Act comes close to permitting disapplication without disturbing Parliamentary sovereignty. On the other hand, subordinate legislation incompatible with a Convention right can be quashed unless (leaving aside the possibility of revocation) primary legislation prevents removal of the incompatibility,[3] which it normally will in the case of the subordinate legislation of England and Wales.

1   See Lord Woolf 'Bringing home the European Convention on Human Rights' [1997] Denning LJ 1; Lord Steyn 'Incorporation and devolution' [1998] EHRLR 153; Duffy and Stanley [1998] *Current Law Statutes: Human Rights Act 1998*; Emmerson 'The Human Rights Bill: its effect on criminal proceedings' [1998] 2 Archbold News 6.
2   Human Rights Act 1998, s 3(2)(b).
3   Ibid, s 3(2)(c).

1.13 The Human Rights Act 1998 gives the judges a new role:

–   Primary legislation and subordinate legislation must, so far as possible, be read and given effect to in a way which is compatible with the Convention rights, and this means even if there is contrary authority on the question.
–   If an appellate court is unable to interpret primary legislation so as to make it compatible with a Convention right, it may (and presumably will feel obliged to do so) make a declaration of incompatibility. It can also make such a declaration in such a circumstance in respect of secondary legislation where primary legislation prevents removal of the incompatibility.
–   It is unlawful for a public authority, such as a court, local authority or police officer to act in a manner incompatible with a Convention right.

Statutory interpretation

1.14 Acts of Parliament and subordinate legislation must, so far as possible, be read and given effect to in a way which is compatible with the Convention rights,[1] and this means even if there is contrary authority on the question. The courts, where necessary, will prefer a strained but possible interpretation which is consistent with Convention rights to one more consistent with the statutory words themselves. Where necessary to correct a defect in terms of ambiguity or omission the courts will be able to insert words into a statute to give effect to a Convention right. This is radically different from conventional techniques of statutory interpretation. There are, however, limits, as indicated by 'as far as possible'. A court cannot construe a statute in a way which Parliament could not conceivably have intended. Perverse interpretation or extensive redrafting is not permissible. In the rare case where the mismatch between Convention rights and the statute is this great, the court will have to make a declaration of incompatibility.

This strong interpretative provision is the lynchpin of the Human Rights Act 1998. As the White Paper preceding the Act said:

> 'This goes far beyond the present rule which enables the courts to take the Convention into account in resolving any ambiguity in a legislative provision. The courts will be required to interpret legislation so as to uphold the Convention rights unless the legislation itself is so clearly incompatible with the Convention that it is impossible to do so.'

The Act clearly has a major impact on the doctrine of precedent. As a result of the present provision the Crown Court may be obliged to ignore a decision of a superior court on the meaning of a statute in order to give effect to a Convention right.

A Minister of the Crown in charge of a Bill in Parliament must, before Second Reading, make a written statement about the compatibility of the Bill with the Convention rights.[2] In practice, such a statement is printed on the face of a Bill. This will reinforce, in Acts subject to this process, the presumption that Parliament did not intend to infringe Convention rights and be a further encouragement to the courts to imply safeguards or to interpret restrictively unduly broad provisions.

---

1   Human Rights Act 1998, s 3. See Lord Lester of Herne Hill 'The art of the possible – interpreting statutes under the Human Rights Act' [1998] EHRLR 665; Lord Steyn 'Incorporation and devolution' [1998] EHRLR 153 at 155.

2   Ibid, s 19.

Declaration of incompatibility

1.15 If a magistrates' court or the Crown court is unable to interpret a statutory provision compatibly with a Convention right, it will have to proceed as normal. The issue of incompatibility can then be raised on appeal. The High Court, Court of Appeal and House of Lords, if satisfied that a provision of primary legislation is incompatible with a Convention right, may then (and presumably will feel obliged to do so) make a declaration of incompatibility.[1] They may also make such a declaration in respect of a provision of subordinate legislation that is so incompatible if satisfied that (disregarding the possibility of revocation) the primary legislation prevents removal of that incompatibility.[1]

If a court is considering whether to make a declaration of incompatibility, the Crown is entitled to notice of this and to be joined as party to the proceedings.[2] If a declaration of incompatibility is made, the Government and Parliament are not required to take remedial action, although almost certainly they will. A fast-track route for doing so via a ministerial order is provided by s 10 of the Human Rights Act 1998.

---

1   Human Rights Act 1998, s 4.

2   Ibid, s 5.

Unlawful actions

1.16 It is unlawful for a public authority, such as a court, local authority or police officer to act[1] in a manner incompatible with a Convention right, unless:

(a) as the result of one or more provisions of primary legislation, the authority could not have acted differently; or

(b) in the case of one or more provisions of, or made under, primary legislation which cannot be read or given effect in a way which is compatible with the Convention rights, the authority was acting so as to give effect to or enforce those provisions.[2]

Parliament (other than the House of Lords in its judicial capacity) is not a 'public authority' in the present context, nor is someone exercising functions in connection with proceedings in Parliament.[3]

The effect of this is to render it unlawful for a public authority, for example, to make subordinate legislation incompatible with a Convention right, or to commit a physical act incompatible with such a right, or to fail to amend pre-Act subordinate legislation so as to make it compatible with a Convention right, or for a court to give a judgment which is incompatible with such a right (instead, it is bound to overrule an inconsistent judicial precedent). This is a way in which Convention rights can take precedence over common law rules and those in subordinate legislation.

Only a victim (actual or potential) may bring legal proceedings (including those for judicial review) against the public authority, or rely on the Convention rights in any legal proceedings.[4] The 'victim-rule' is in line with the requirement for a claim to the European Court of Human Rights but it means that pressure groups, like Liberty, are unable to bring test cases in their own names. Legal proceedings in respect of a judicial act may only be brought by an appeal or on application for judicial review.

In relation to any act (or proposed act) of a public authority which the court finds is (or would be) unlawful, it may grant such relief or remedy (including compensatory damages) or make such order, within its powers, as it considers just and appropriate within the terms of the Act.[5] Under this, a court would have power, for example, to recognise a new defence or to allow a submission of no case to answer on the basis of an incompatible Convention right. Likewise, an appeal court could quash a conviction on the basis of such a right, or on an application for judicial review a court could grant certiorari to quash an incompatible executive decision (eg by the police in relation to imposing a condition on a procession).

In respect of a judicial act done in good faith, damages may not be awarded otherwise than to compensate a person for arrest or detention in contravention of Art 5 of ECHR.[6]

---

1   'act' includes a failure to act: Human Rights Act 1998, s 6(6).
2   Ibid, s 6(1)–(3).
3   Ibid, s 6(3).
4   Ibid, s 7.
5   Ibid, s 8.
6   Ibid, s 9.

The Convention rights

1.17 The Convention rights are specified by s 1 of the Human Rights Act 1998 and are set out in Sch 1 to that Act. They are:

(a) Arts 2–12 and 14 of the Convention;
(b) Arts 1–3 of the First Protocol; and
(c) Arts 1 and 2 of the Sixth Protocol;

as read with Arts 16–18 of the Convention.

These Articles have effect for the purposes of the 1998 Act subject to designated derogations and reservations which are not material in the context of public order law.

The Articles listed are, in essence, the substantive rights guaranteed under those parts of the Convention which the UK has signed and ratified. Those rights which are specifically of relevance to public order law are extracted in full in the edited version of Sch 1 set out below:

'THE ARTICLES

PART I

THE CONVENTION

Rights and freedoms

Article 2

Right to life

[…]

Article 3

Prohibition of torture

[…]

Article 4

Prohibition of slavery and forced labour

[…]

Article 5

Right to liberty and security

1. Everyone has the right to liberty and security of person. No one shall be deprived of his liberty save in the following cases and in accordance with a procedure prescribed by law:

(a) the lawful detention of a person after conviction by a competent court;
(b) the lawful arrest or detention of a person for non-compliance with the lawful order of a court or in order to secure the fulfilment of any obligation prescribed by law;

(c) the lawful arrest or detention of a person effected for the purpose of bringing him before the competent legal authority on reasonable suspicion of having committed an offence or when it is reasonably considered necessary to prevent his committing an offence or fleeing after having done so;

(d) the detention of a minor by lawful order for the purpose of educational supervision or his lawful detention for the purpose of bringing him before the competent legal authority;

(e) the lawful detention of persons for the prevention of the spreading of infectious diseases, of persons of unsound mind, alcoholics or drug addicts or vagrants;

(f) [...]

2. [...]

3. Everyone arrested or detained in accordance with the provisions of paragraph 1(c) of this Article shall be brought promptly before a judge or other officer authorised by law to exercise judicial power and shall be entitled to trial within a reasonable time or to release pending trial. Release may be conditioned by guarantees to appear for trial.

4. [...]

5. [...]

Article 6

Right to a fair trial

1. In the determination of his civil rights and obligations or of any criminal charge against him, everyone is entitled to a fair and public hearing within a reasonable time by an independent and impartial tribunal established by law. Judgment shall be pronounced publicly but the press and public may be excluded from all or part of the trial in the interest of morals, public order or national security in a democratic society, where the interests of juveniles or the protection of the private life of the parties so require, or to the extent strictly necessary in the opinion of the court in special circumstances where publicity would prejudice the interests of justice.

2. Everyone charged with a criminal offence shall be presumed innocent until proved guilty according to law.

3. [...]

Article 7

No punishment without law

1. No one shall be held guilty of any criminal offence on account of any act or omission which did not constitute a criminal offence under national or international law at the time when it was committed. Nor shall a heavier penalty be imposed than the one that was applicable at the time the criminal offence was committed.

2. [...]

Article 8

Right to respect for private and family life

1. Everyone has the right to respect for his private and family life, his home and his correspondence.

2. There shall be no interference by a public authority with the exercise of this right except such as is in accordance with the law and is necessary in a democratic society in the interests of national security, public safety or the economic well-being of the country, for the prevention of disorder or crime, for the protection of health or morals, or for the protection of the rights and freedoms of others.

Article 9

Freedom of thought, conscience and religion

1. Everyone has the right to freedom of thought, conscience and religion; this right includes freedom to change his religion or belief and freedom, either alone or in community with others and in public or private, to manifest his religion or belief, in worship, teaching, practice and observance.

2. Freedom to manifest one's religion or beliefs shall be subject only to such limitations as are prescribed by law and are necessary in a democratic society in the interests of public safety, for the protection of public order, health or morals, or for the protection of the rights and freedoms of others.

Article 10

Freedom of expression

1. Everyone has the right to freedom of expression. This right shall include freedom to hold opinions and to receive and impart information and ideas without interference by public authority and regardless of frontiers. This Article shall not prevent States from requiring the licensing of broadcasting, television or cinema enterprises.

2. The exercise of these freedoms, since it carries with it duties and responsibilities, may be subject to such formalities, conditions, restrictions or penalties as are prescribed by law and are necessary in a democratic society, in the interests of national security, territorial integrity or public safety, for the prevention of disorder or crime, for the protection of health or morals, for the protection of the reputation or rights of others, for preventing the disclosure of information received in confidence, or for maintaining the authority and impartiality of the judiciary.

Article 11

Freedom of assembly and association

1. Everyone has the right to freedom of peaceful assembly and to freedom of association with others, including the right to form and to join trade unions for the protection of his interests.

2. No restrictions shall be placed on the exercise of these rights other than such as are prescribed by law and are necessary in a democratic society in the interests of national security or public safety, for the prevention of disorder or crime, for the protection of health or morals or for the protection of the rights and freedoms of others. This Article shall not prevent the imposition of lawful restrictions on the exercise of these rights by members of the armed forces, of the police or of the administration of the State.

Article 12

Right to marry

[...]

Article 14

Prohibition of discrimination

The enjoyment of the rights and freedoms set forth in this Convention shall be secured without discrimination on any ground such as sex, race, colour, language, religion, political or other opinion, national or social origin, association with a national minority, property, birth or other status.

Article 16

Restrictions on political activity of aliens

Nothing in Articles 10, 11 and 14 shall be regarded as preventing the High Contracting Parties from imposing restrictions on the political activity of aliens.

Article 17

Prohibition of abuse of rights

Nothing in this Convention may be interpreted as implying for any State, group or person any right to engage in any activity or perform any act aimed at the destruction of any of the rights and freedoms set forth herein or at their limitation to a greater extent than is provided for in the Convention.

Article 18

Limitation on use of restrictions on rights

The restrictions permitted under this Convention to the said rights and freedoms shall not be applied for any purpose other than those for which they have been prescribed.

PART II

THE FIRST PROTOCOL

Article 1

Protection of property

Every natural or legal person is entitled to the peaceful enjoyment of his possessions. No one shall be deprived of his possessions except in the public interest and subject to the conditions provided for by law and by the general principles of international law.

The preceding provisions shall not, however, in any way impair the right of a State to enforce such laws as it deems necessary to control the use of property in accordance with the general interest or to secure the payment of taxes or other contributions or penalties.

Article 2

Right to education

[…]

Article 3

Right to free elections

[…]

PART III

THE SIXTH PROTOCOL

Article 1

Abolition of the death penalty

[…]

Article 2

Death penalty in time of war

[...]'

Most of the Convention rights are specific to a particular issue. Articles 14 and 16–18, however, are more general, in that they relate to the exercise of the specific rights as a whole (or a group of them).

Application of Convention rights

1.18 Section 2(1) of the Human Rights Act 1998 provides that in determining a question which has arisen in connection with a Convention right, a court must *take into account* the case law of[1] the European Court of Human Rights and the European Commission of Human Rights[2] (which were effectively merged in 1998 in a restructured European Court of Human Rights) and the Committee of Ministers.[3] The Court and Commission have produced a well-developed jurisprudence about the ECHR and its Protocols. The terms of s 2(1) make it clear that these decisions are not binding; they are to be taken into account along with other relevant decisions, such as those of the Privy Council or of courts in constitutional cases elsewhere in the common law world. The right of individual petition to the European Court of Human Rights remains, however, and a failure by an English court to apply a decision of that Court could lead to an application to it.

What follows is an attempt to give a basic understanding of the structure of the Convention and its key concepts, concentrating on the Convention rights relevant to this book.

1   The order in which the three bodies are referred to represents the descending level of their authority as sources.
2   The Commission decides on the admissibility of applications (ie complaints of a breach of the ECHR).
3   In respect of Member States' responses to applications.

1.19 A starting point is to note that the European Court of Human Rights has often emphasised the importance of a broad approach to interpretation, according full weight to the object and purpose of the ECHR, rather than a narrower, more literal approach, in order to make the rights accorded by the ECHR effective.[1]

In addition, the European Court of Human Rights has on occasions given a term in the ECHR a meaning which is different from, and independent of, its meaning under a domestic law. For example, a breach of the peace is not an offence and cannot result in a criminal charge under English law but the Court has held that someone who appears in binding-over proceedings in respect of such a breach (technically civil proceedings in English law) appears on a 'criminal charge' for the purposes of Art 6 (right to a fair trial), on the ground of the consequences and general nature of the proceedings.[2]

1   See *Wemhoff v FRG* (1968) Ser A, no 7; 1 EHRR 55, ECtHR; *Loizidou v Turkey* (1995) Ser A, no 310; 20 EHRR 99, ECtHR.
2   *Steel v UK* (1999) 28 EHRR 603.

1.20 A few Convention rights are absolute, permitting no interference. Of the specific rights potentially relevant to public order law, Art 7 (no punishment without law) is the only example. Some Convention rights are strong rights from which derogation is strictly limited. For example, although a State may derogate from a non-absolute Convention right in time of war or grave public emergency, it may not derogate from Art 2 (right to life) except in respect of 'lawful acts of war'. However, in general, the Convention rights follow the model of stating a right and then permitting interference with it if it can be justified on the basis of some legitimate interest.

Common to the analysis of a problem allegedly involving any of the Convention rights is the requirement that there must have been an interference with that right. In answering this, it must be borne in mind that the ECHR is construed broadly so as to give it practical effect. The case law of the Court and Commission helps in many areas in this task of interpretation. Where there is an interference with an absolute right that is the end of the matter in terms of whether there has been a breach of the ECHR.

Where some interference has been shown with a specific right where interference can be justified, that justification typically (see Arts 8–11) requires the following criteria to be satisfied:

–   the interference must be 'prescribed by law' or 'in accordance with the law';
–   any interference must have a legitimate aim;
–   the interference must be 'necessary in a democratic society' in the interests of a legitimate aim;
–   the interference must not be discriminatory.

Prescribed by law/in accordance with the law

1.21 'Lawfulness' means more than merely 'authorised' by law. The European Court of Human Rights has held that, in addition, for a rule to be 'prescribed by law' or 'in accordance with the law', it must satisfy the following:

(a)   *accessibility*, ie the law must be adequately accessible: the citizen must be able to have adequate information, in the circumstances, on the legal rules applicable in a given case;
(b)   *foreseeability*, ie the law under which action is taken must be formulated with sufficient degree of precision to enable the citizen to regulate his conduct: he must be able, if need be with appropriate advice, to foresee, to a degree that is reasonable in the circumstances, the consequences which a given action may entail.[1]

---

1   *Sunday Times v UK* (1979) Ser A, no 49; 2 EHRR 245, ECtHR (a case concerned with 'prescribed by law' in Art 10). 'Prescribed by law'/'in accordance with the law'/'lawful' in Arts 5 and 8–11 are to be read in the same way: ibid, para 48; *Silver v UK* (1983) Ser A, no 61; 5 EHRR 347, para 85; *Malone v UK* (1985) Ser A, no 82; 7 EHRR 14, para 66; *Steel v UK* (1999) 28 EHRR 603, para 54.

Interference for a legitimate aim

1.22 The legitimate aim of the interference must be one of the aims specified as a potential justification in the article concerned, such as the prevention of crime or disorder, or the protection of the rights and freedoms of others.

Necessary in a democratic society

1.23 The reference to a 'democratic society' means that regard must be had not only to the legitimate aim which the interference was intended to protect, but also to the importance of the freedom in question in such a society. It is not enough that the interference is simply reasonable or desirable; there must be a 'pressing social need' for it, although it need not be indispensable.[1] According to the jurisprudence of the European Court, whether an interference is 'necessary in a democratic society' involves the application of two principles:

(a) 'proportionality', and
(b) the 'margin of appreciation'.

---

1   *Handyside v UK* (1976) Ser A, no 24; 1 EHRR 737, para 49, ECtHR; *Silver v UK* (1983) Ser A, no 61; 5 EHRR 347, para 85.

Proportionality

1.24 'Proportionality' requires that the interference be 'proportionate to the legitimate aim pursued'.[1] It is intended to ensure that a fair balance is struck between the relevant right of the individual and the legitimate aim(s) which the interference sought to protect.

---

1   *Handyside v UK* (1976) Ser A, no 24; 1 EHRR 737, para 49, ECtHR; *Silver v UK* (1983) Ser A, no 61; 5 EHRR 347, para 85.

Margin of appreciation

1.25 The idea behind the 'margin of appreciation' employed by the European Court of Human Rights is that the public authorities in a State are better able than the European Court to evaluate local needs and conditions[1] and therefore better able to determine what the interests of the democratic society require in their society, and that it is therefore for them to make the initial assessment of the 'necessity' for an interference, subject to review by the European Court. Thus, the 'margin of appreciation' provides an area of discretion to public authorities in a State. The degree of latitude accorded is, however, not uniform in respect of each legitimate aim. It varies according to the nature and importance of the right interfered with, the context, and the degree to which practice varies among States party to the Convention.[1]

The margin of appreciation involves the European Court in affording a certain amount of deference to national authorities. It recognises that the Convention does not need to be applied uniformly by all States, but may be applied variably according to local needs and conditions. The margin of appreciation is a corollary of the view articulated by that Court that the machinery of protection under the ECHR is subsidiary to the national system protecting human rights,[2] and it accounts for the reluctance of the Court to substitute its judgment for theirs.

---

1   See for example *Buckley v UK* RJD (1996) 1996-IV 1271; 23 EHRR 101, ECtHR.
2   *Handyside v UK* (1976) Ser A, no 24; 1 EHRR 737, paras 48 and 50.

1.26 It is uncertain to what extent, if at all, English courts will apply the European Court of Human Rights' concept of margin of appreciation when reviewing the conduct of public authorities under the Human Rights Act 1998 in respect of an interference with a Convention right. As indicated above, the European Court regards that concept as defining the relationship between a supranational court and public authorities in a State. There is therefore no reason for any English court to apply the margin of appreciation (as that concept is applied by the European Court). Indeed, given that an English court will be closer to the society in which the interference occurs, and therefore better able to assess its interests, there is much less reason for it to defer to the same extent to such an assessment by a public authority via a margin of appreciation. To do so would potentially frustrate the purpose of bringing the ECHR home.

The European Court's concept of the margin of appreciation is like the well-known English public law concept of *Wednesbury* unreasonableness[1] applied in judicial review proceedings. Both concepts recognise that the 'decision-maker' reviewed may be better placed to assess the needs of society and to make a choice between considerations and that there is a legitimate area of discretion left to decision-makers which is primarily for them and with which the courts ought not to be too ready to interfere. However, the *Wednesbury* principle (that an executive decision, or the like, which is not ultra vires will only be overturned if it is perverse, or so unreasonable that no reasonable decision-maker could have made it)[2] leaves a wider area of discretion free from interference than even the broadest application of the margin of appreciation. This is too deferential a standard for the judicial review of decisions affecting Convention rights.[3] On the other hand, it cannot be ignored that an English court, when reviewing the compatibility with a Convention right of legislation or executive action will have to decide questions involving issues of balance between the competing interests of the rights of the individual and the needs of society. Although its task will be to decide this issue of judgment for itself, having regard to the principle of proportionality, which is fundamentally different from, and stricter than, the principle of *Wednesbury* unreasonableness,[4] the court in applying that principle may defer (to a limited extent) to the opinion of the national authority (Parliament or an executive body or person) whose act or decision is alleged to be incompatible. The extent (if any) of the deference (ie of the area of judgment) will depend on various factors.[5] In *R v DPP, ex parte Kebeline*,[6] Lord Hope said:

> 'It will be easier for such an area of judgment to be recognised where the Convention itself requires a balance to be struck, much less so where the right is stated in terms which are unqualified. It will be easier for it to be recognised where the issues involve questions of social or economic policy, much less so where the rights are of high constitutional importance or are of a kind where the courts are especially well placed to assess the need for protection.'

Thus, the English courts will apply a 'margin of appreciation' in determining an alleged breach of a Convention right but it will not be the same as – it will be narrower than – that applied by the European Court.

---

1   *Associated Provincial Picture Houses Ltd v Wednesbury Corpn* [1947] 2 All ER 680, CA; see para
     6.97. This has also been described as a 'margin of appreciation': *R v Chief Constable of Sussex,
     ex parte International Trader's Ferry Ltd* [1999] 1 All ER 129, HL.

2   Hitherto, an English court has not been able judicially to review the exercise of an administrative discretion on the basis that the discretion had to be exercised in conformity with the ECHR: *R v Secretary of State for the Home Department, ex parte Brind* [1991] 1 All ER 720, HL.

3   Lord Steyn 'Incorporation and devolution – a few reflections on the changing scene' [1998] EHRLR 153 at 155.

4   *R v Secretary of State for the Home Department, ex parte Brind* above at 735 and 737–739, per Lords Ackner and Lowry.

5   Pannick 'Principles of interpretation of Convention rights under the Human Rights Act and the discretionary area of judgment' [1998] PL 545 at 549–551; Lester and Pannick (eds) *Human Rights Law and Practice* (Butterworths, 1999) p 74. Also see Singh et al 'Is there a role for the "margin of appreciation" after the Human Rights Act?' [1999] EHRLR 15; and Fenwick 'The right to protest, the Human Rights Act and the margin of appreciation' (1999) 62 MLR 491.

6   [1999] 4 All ER 801 at 844.

Non-discriminatory

1.27 Article 14 of the ECHR prohibits discrimination in the enjoyment of the rights and freedoms guaranteed by the Convention. Consequently, Art 14 is relevant whenever it is necessary to justify an interference with a Convention right. Discrimination is established contrary to Art 14 where a distinction in treatment has 'no reasonable and objective justification'.[1]

1   *Belgian Linguistic Case (No 2)* (1968) Ser A, no 6; 1 EHRR 252, para 10.

Chapter 2

PREVENTIVE POWERS

INTRODUCTION

2.1   Preventive powers are of considerable importance in public order law. The following are dealt with in this chapter:

– the common law powers to deal with or prevent a breach of the peace;
– the common law and statutory binding-over powers;
– the statutory power to make an anti-social behaviour order.

Other preventive powers provided by legislation are described elsewhere in this book, in particular in Chapters 6 (Processions and assemblies) and 7 (Collective trespass or nuisance on land).

COMMON LAW POWERS TO DEAL WITH OR PREVENT A BREACH OF THE PEACE

2.2   These common law powers have not been supplanted by the law enforcement powers set out in PACE nor by the Public Order Act 1986.[1] If it had been otherwise, there would have been a significant gap in police powers in respect of actual or apprehended public disorder, particularly in respect of preventive powers, which would have had to be filled by legislation. The attraction (for some) of retaining the common law powers is that they are capable of development in a way which a statutory power is not.

---

1   See PACE, ss 25(6) and 17(6) and 1986 Act, s 40(4).

Breach of the peace

2.3   In Scotland, a breach of the peace is an offence in itself.[1] In England and Wales the creation of a breach of the peace is not an offence in itself, nor is conduct likely to lead to a breach of the peace,[2] although they are so regarded for the purposes of Arts 5 and 6[3] of the ECHR because coercive penalties like arrest, detention and imprisonment attach to them.[4] On the other hand, the creation or apprehension of a breach of the peace is a 'trigger' for the exercise of the powers discussed below. Moreover, it may also involve the commission of one of a range of public order offences (particularly those of assaulting, wilfully obstructing or resisting a constable in the execution of his duty) or a number of other offences. In addition, a breach of the peace can lead to a binding-over order.

---

1   *Hendry v Ferguson* (1883) 10 R (Ct of Sess) 63; *Bewglass v Blair* (1888) 15 R (Ct of Sess) 45; *Ferguson v Carnochan* (1889) 16 R (Ct of Sess) 93.
2   Glanville Williams 'Arrest for breach of the peace' [1954] Crim LR 578 at 583, citing *Davies v Griffiths* [1937] 2 All ER 671, DC; cf *Brownlie's Law of Public Order and National Security* (1981) p 1, where the view is taken that creating a breach of the peace is 'probably' not an offence.

R v County of London Quarter Sessions Appeals Committee, ex parte Metropolitan Police Comr [1948] 1
All ER 72, DC, is often cited as an authority that there is no offence of breach of the peace,
but all that the majority of the Divisional Court said was that the Justices of the Peace Act
1361 (the statutory binding-over provision referred to in para **2.25**) did not create an offence
of breach of the peace.
3   Because 'breach of the peace' is an offence for the purposes of Arts 5 and 6, a person
       arrested for breach of the peace has all the rights provided by those Articles.
4   *Steel v UK* (1999) 28 EHRR 603, ECtHR.

Definition

2.4   Although the concept of breach of the peace dates back to the infancy of the
common law, the judges have been reluctant to give it a precise definition. In *R v
Howell*,[1] the Court of Appeal said:

> 'A comprehensive definition of the term "breach of the peace" has very rarely been
> formulated so far as we have been able . . . to discover from cases which go back as far as
> the eighteenth century. The older cases are . . . not a sure guide to what the term is
> understood to mean today, since keeping the peace in this country in the latter half of
> the twentieth century presents formidable problems which bear on the evolving
> process of the development of this branch of the common law. Nevertheless, even in
> these days when affrays, riotous behaviour and other disturbances happen all too
> frequently, we cannot accept that there can be a breach of the peace unless there has
> been *an act done or threatened to be done which either actually harms a person, or in his presence
> his property, or is likely to cause such harm, or which puts someone in fear of such harm being
> done.* There is nothing more likely to arouse resentment and anger in him, and a
> desire to take instant revenge, than attacks or threatened attacks on a person's body or
> property . . . We are emboldened to say that there is a breach of the peace *whenever
> harm is actually done or is likely to be done to a person or in his presence to his property or a person
> is in fear of being so harmed through an assault, an affray, a riot, an unlawful assembly or other
> disturbance.*'

There is a potential conflict between the two passages italicised. Was the
reference to assault, affray etc in the second passage intended simply to exemplify
the types of conduct which can suffice or which were thought to cover all forms of
violent action, or was it intended to limit the relevant types of violent conduct? If
the answer is the latter, the two definitions conflict and it is then unclear whether
that limit applies to all forms of harm or only feared harm.[2] Reference to the cases
in which the definition in *Howell* has been applied (see below) shows a fairly even
split between those in which the first passage has been relied on and those in
which the second has been relied on. It is submitted, in any event, that the
reference to 'or other disturbance' at the end of the second passage favours the
former interpretation.

The Court of Appeal in *Howell* emphasised that, as had been held in previous
cases,[3] a disturbance which does not relate to violence (ie mere noise and
disturbance) cannot in itself constitute a breach of the peace. It may, however,
provide the basis on which a constable or anyone else may reasonably apprehend
that a breach of the peace may be imminent, in which case the common law
powers to prevent such a breach can be exercised.[4] In addition, it may constitute
an offence under s 54 of the Metropolitan Police Act 1839 or s 28 of the Town
Police Clauses Act 1847[5] or under ss 4A or 5 of the Public Order Act 1986.[6]

Lord Denning MR defined 'breach of the peace' in wider terms than those in
Howell in *R v Chief Constable of Devon and Cornwall, ex parte Central Electricity
Generating Board*, which was concerned with whether those protesting at the

possible siting of a nuclear power station by the unlawful obstruction of the Board's right to enter and survey land were thereby committing a breach of the peace. Lord Denning said:[7]

> 'There is a breach of the peace whenever a person who is lawfully carrying out his work is unlawfully and physically prevented by another from doing it ... If anyone unlawfully and physically obstructs the worker, by lying down or chaining himself to a ring or the like, he is guilty of a breach of the peace.'

This view, not shared by Lord Denning's two colleagues in the Court of Appeal, Lawton and Templeman LJJ, diluted the emphasis on violence in the definition in *Howell*, which was cited to the Court of Appeal but not referred to in the judgments. The reason is that, while physical obstruction may involve actual or threatened violence, lying down, chaining oneself to a ring or other types of passive physical obstruction cannot in themselves do so, although they may give rise to a reasonable apprehension that somebody else will use or threaten violence.

The definition in *Howell* was applied by the Divisional Court in *Parkin v Norman*,[8] *McBean v Parker*,[9] *G v Chief Superintendent of Police, Stroud*,[10] and *DPP v Orum*.[11] It was confidently regarded as representing the relevant law. However, a more restrictive approach was adopted by the Court of Appeal in *Lewis v Chief Constable of Greater Manchester*.[12] Farquharson LJ referred to passages in *Howell* 'which appear to say that an act constituting a threat of violence or which puts a person in fear of violence is itself a breach of the peace within the definition of that offence.' His Lordship continued: 'The act which puts someone in fear of violence taking place entitles a police officer or a member of the public to detain the actor but it is not in itself a breach of the peace, for the violence has not yet occurred'.

More recently, the definition of breach of the peace in *Howell* was applied by the Divisional Court in *Percy v DPP*[13] and *Edwards v DPP*,[14] and by the Court of Appeal in *Sutton v Commissioner of Metropolitan Police*,[15] although *Lewis v Chief Constable of Greater Manchester* does not appear to have been cited in these cases. The Divisional Court in *Percy v DPP* doubted Lord Denning's dictum in *Chief Constable of Devon and Cornwall* and pointed out that it was implicit in the judgments of Lawton and Templeman LJJ that they thought violence or a threat of violence was necessary.

Howell can now be regarded as representing the law.

1　[1981] 3 All ER 383 at 388–389 (italics added).

2　This point is made by Nicholson and Reid 'Arrest for breach of the peace and the European Convention on Human Rights' [1996] Crim LR 764 at 767.

3　*Wooding v Oxley* (1839) 9 C&P 1 (disturbance by noise at a public meeting not a breach of the peace); *Jordan v Gibbon* (1863) 8 LT 391 (disturbance caused by quarrel between spouses not a breach of the peace unless violence or threatened violence). The point was confirmed in *Lewis v Chief Constable of Greater Manchester* (1991) *The Independent*, 23 October, CA (loud music and screaming not a breach of the peace).

4　*G v Chief Superintendent of Police, Stroud* (1988) 86 Cr App R 92, DC.

5　See paras **9.18–9.23**. The general conditional power of arrest under PACE, s 25 would be available in such a case.

6　See paras **4.20–4.62**. Note the specific powers of arrest for these offences, as well as the general conditional power of arrest.

7　[1981] 3 All ER 826 at 832.

8　[1982] 2 All ER 583, DC (first passage in *R v Howell*).

9　(1983) 147 JP 205, DC (second passage in *R v Howell*).

10　(1988) 86 Cr App R 92, DC (first passage in *R v Howell*).

11   [1989] 1 WLR 88, DC (second passage in *R v Howell*).
12   (1991) *The Independent*, 23 October, CA.
13   [1995] 3 All ER 124, DC (first passage in *R v Howell*).
14   (1996) unreported, DC (second passage in *R v Howell*).
15   (1998) unreported, CA (first passage in *R v Howell*).

2.5   A breach of the peace can occur on private premises, even in a dwelling, and can do so even if the only people likely to be affected by the conduct are on the premises. This had been assumed by statements in three cases: *Wilson v Skeock*,[1] *Robson v Hallett*[2] and *R v Chief Constable of Devon and Cornwall, ex parte Central Electricity Generating Board*,[3] but it was only in *McConnell v Chief Constable of Greater Manchester Police*[4] that the point was established.

In *McConnell*, a store manager asked M to leave, but he refused. A police officer took M outside the store, but M tried to re-enter. Thereupon the officer arrested him on suspicion that he was guilty of conduct whereby a breach of the peace might be occasioned or that, if he allowed him to re-enter, such a breach might occur. M sued the Chief Constable on the ground that his arrest and subsequent detention were unlawful. The trial judge made a preliminary ruling that a breach of the peace could take place on private premises. Dismissing M's appeal against it, the Court of Appeal agreed with that preliminary ruling. It also rejected M's alternative contention that there could not be a breach of the peace on private premises unless there was some disturbance that could affect members of the public, or at least one other person, outside the premises themselves. As Glidewell LJ pointed out, this would lead to the unsatisfactory distinction between an abusive altercation between two people in an isolated house and a similar altercation between the same two people in a terrace house with thin walls and neighbours who could hear everything that was going on. However, as members of the Court of Appeal recognised, conduct at a public gathering may more readily result in a breach of the peace than the same conduct in a private place between two people.

1   (1949) 113 JP 294 at 296, per Lord Goddard CJ.
2   [1967] 2 All ER 407 at 413 and 414, per Lord Parker CJ and Diplock LJ.
3   [1981] 3 All ER 826 at 832 and 838, per Lord Denning MR and Templeman LJ.
4   [1990] 1 All ER 423, CA.

2.6   In *McBean v Parker*,[1] the Divisional Court held that, for the purposes of the definition of 'breach of the peace' in *R v Howell*, 'harm' 'must be unlawful harm'; consequently harm resulting from the use of reasonable force to resist an unlawful police search did not constitute a breach of the peace.

This can be contrasted with a statement by Lord Denning MR in *R v Chief Constable of Devon and Cornwall, ex parte Central Electricity Generating Board* which appeared to suggest that there could be a breach of the peace even where the conduct concerned is lawful. Lord Denning said:[2] 'in deciding whether there is a breach of the peace ... the law does not go into the rights and wrongs of the matter, or whether it is justified by self-help or not'. The other two members of the Court of Appeal did not express a view on this point.

It is submitted that Lord Denning's view cannot be supported. It cannot be the case that if the only harm (or threat of harm) results from lawful conduct there is a breach of the peace, with the consequent trigger for the powers described later. It can hardly be the law, for example, that a person who causes harm to another (or threatens to do so) by the use of reasonable force to make a valid 'citizen's arrest' of X or to eject, X, a trespasser, thereby creates a breach of the peace. To extend the law in this way would be insupportable.

The issue is not a major one because in many cases where harm is caused (or threatened) lawfully by a person there will also be someone else involved and if that person causes or threatens harm against the other it will inevitably be unlawful harm and there will be a breach of the peace. Once there is a breach of the peace, or a likelihood of an imminent breach of the peace, the powers described below are operative. An example of this is *Marsh v Arscott.*[3] D was found in an intoxicated state in a car on his private property by three police officers. D repeatedly asked the officers to leave and eventually became aggressive. Holding that there had been a breach of the peace, McCullough J said:[4]

> '... the police officers, having been told to leave, were acting unlawfully in remaining. If the defendant was using no more force than was reasonably necessary to evict them he was acting lawfully, and in arresting him the police were acting unlawfully. This violent incident amounted to a breach of the peace but it was one for which the police officers were responsible and not the defendant himself. ... Suppose ... that the defendant's threats and use of force towards the police had been unlawful, once again there would have been a breach of the peace. Thus, regardless of who was acting lawfully and who was acting unlawfully there was at the time of the incident a breach of the peace.'

---

1   (1983) 147 JP 205 at 208.
2   [1981] 3 All ER 826 at 833.
3   (1982) 75 Cr App R 211, DC.
4   Ibid, at 215. Also see *Joyce v Hertfordshire Constabulary* (1985) 80 Cr App Rep 298 at 303.

Arrest without warrant

2.7   This is the most significant power in relation to a breach of the peace. The person arrested may be charged with an offence involved in the breach or in respect of his resistance to, or obstruction of, the arrest, or may be subjected to binding-over proceedings (whether or not any offence has been committed) or may simply be released. The case law was reviewed by the Court of Appeal in *R v Howell.* The court clarified an area of law which had previously been uncertain.[1] It concluded:[2]

> 'We entertain no doubt that a constable has a power of arrest where there is reasonable apprehension of imminent danger of a breach of the peace; so for that matter has the ordinary citizen ... We hold that there is power of arrest for breach of the peace where (1) a breach of the peace is committed in the presence of the person making the arrest, or (2) the arrestor reasonably believes[3] that such a breach will be committed in the immediate future by the person arrested although he has not yet committed any breach, or (3) where a breach has been committed and it is reasonably believed[3] that a renewal of it is threatened.'

It appears from this formulation that if someone makes an arrest in the mistaken belief that a breach *is* being committed in his presence, he will be liable for wrongful arrest even though his mistake was reasonable. Admittedly, in *Wills v Bowley,*[4] the House of Lords construed a statutory power (now repealed) to arrest 'any person who within his view commits any such offence' as not being confined to cases where the offence had in fact been committed, but as extending to cases where the constable believed on reasonable grounds derived wholly from his own observation that an offence had been committed within his sight (a formula which could have been particularly appropriate here). However, the juxtaposition and express reference to reasonable grounds in (2) and (3) in the above passage seems to preclude the implication of such words in (1).

The drafting of heads (2) and (3) is open to criticism in that (2) refers to a requirement of 'immediacy' whereas (3) does not for no apparent reason. Following the Court of Appeal's decision in the civil case of *Foulkes v Chief Constable of the Merseyside Police*,[5] it is now established that, as indicated by the opening words of the above quotation from *Howell*, where no breach of the peace has taken place in the presence of the arrestor but an arrest is made because of a fear of a future breach, such apprehended breach must be 'about to occur or be imminent'. The use of 'imminent' in the alternative to 'about to occur' (and not as an explanation of that term) suggested that 'imminent' might bear a different, wider meaning in the present context. The Court of Appeal did not, however, appear to perceive a difference between the two terms nor to regard them as different in meaning from 'immediate' in the Court of Appeal's statement in *Howell* quoted above. In this, it was not out of line with *Howell*; elsewhere in that decision the Court of Appeal appears to have regarded 'immediate' and 'imminent' as synonymous in the present context. In *R v Ramsell*,[6] the Court of Appeal, relying on *Howell*, stated the test in terms of 'imminent' which, it said, meant in the present context 'about to take place', and could encompass the situation where a constable feared that a person would leave her house and go a little way down a road and around a corner to the house of a person she had assaulted shortly before, and there assault him again.

On the above basis, there is no distinction between (2) and (3), which the Court of Appeal also considered to involve a reasonable belief that a breaching of the peace was imminent, save that (3) requires a breach of the peace to *have been committed* and (2) does not, a pointless distinction.

In *Foulkes v Chief Constable of the Merseyside Police*, F was locked out of his jointly owned matrimonial home after a family argument. He called the police and an officer spoke to members of his family. F was advised to leave the immediate vicinity for a short while until tempers had abated, but refused to do so and insisted that he wished to re-enter his home. A police officer then arrested F as he feared that if F were to remain outside the home or managed to re-enter an argument or violence would occur occasioning a breach of the peace. F brought proceedings against the Chief Constable for wrongful arrest and false imprisonment. The Court of Appeal held that, although the police officer had believed on reasonable grounds that the arrest was necessary to prevent a breach of the peace, this was not enough to entitle the officer to arrest F.

Having referred to the extract from *Howell*, quoted above, Beldam LJ, with whom Schiemann and Thorpe LJJ agreed, said:[7]

'In *Albert v Lavin*[8] Lord Diplock referred to a well-established principle:

"... every citizen in whose presence a breach of the peace is being, or reasonably appears to be about to be, committed has the right to take reasonable steps to make the person who is breaking or threatening to break the peace refrain from doing so; and those reasonable steps in appropriate cases will include detaining him against his will."

In my view, the words used by Lord Diplock and in the other authorities show that where no breach of the peace has taken place in his presence but a constable exercises his power of arrest because he fears a further breach, such apprehended breach must be about to occur or be imminent. In the present case PC McNamara acted with the best of intentions. He had tried persuasion but the plaintiff refused to be persuaded or to accept the sensible guidance he had been given but in my judgment that was not a sufficient basis to conclude that a breach of the peace was about to occur or was imminent. There must, I consider, be a sufficiently real and present threat to the peace to justify the extreme step of depriving of his liberty a citizen who is not at the time acting unlawfully. The factors identified by the recorder in the present case do not in my judgment measure up to a sufficiently serious or imminent threat to the peace to justify arrest. Accordingly I would hold that PC McNamara, though acting honestly and from the best of motives, did not in fact have reasonable grounds for the arrest.'

---

1   See Glanville Williams 'Arrest for breach of the peace' [1954] Crim LR 578.
2   [1981] 3 All ER 383 at 388.
3   As elsewhere in the law of arrest, the test of reasonableness is objective in the sense that it is for a court to decide whether, in the light of what the constable knew and perceived at the time, it is satisfied that it was reasonable to fear an imminent breach of the peace; reasonable belief is evaluated without the qualification of hindsight: *Redmond-Bate v DPP* (1999) *The Times*, 28 July, DC. Also see para **6.28**.
4   [1982] 2 All ER 654, HL.
5   [1998] 3 All ER 705, CA.
6   *R v Ramsell* (1999) unreported, CA.
7   [1998] 3 All ER 705 at 711.
8   [1981] 3 All ER 878 at 880.

2.8   An oddity with the formulation in *R v Howell* set out at the start of para **2.7** results from the inclusion in the definition of 'breach of the peace' of putting someone in fear of harm. The formulation above gives a power to arrest for an apprehended breach of the peace, a term which itself refers to apprehension of harm. As Professor Glanville Williams put it, the draftsmanship in *Howell*:

'is open to criticism in being repetitive to the point of creating an infinite regress ... [T]here is power of arrest for an apprehended apprehended apprehended ... ad infinitum breach. It would have been better to define a breach of the peace as an actual breach, while asserting the power to arrest and to bind over for an apprehended breach.'[1]

---

1   'Dealing with breaches of the peace' (1982) 146 JPN 199 at 200.

2.9   There is some old authority to support a power of arrest *immediately after* a breach of the peace, even though a threat of renewal is not reasonably apprehended.[1] This authority is not, however, strong because it seems that in each case the breach of the peace was continuing or its imminent renewal was reasonably apprehended at the time of the arrest.[2] This authority can be contrasted with many statements to the effect that once a breach of the peace has occurred and a threat of renewal is not reasonably apprehended there is no power of arrest.[1] This view was taken by Professor Smith in a commentary in the Criminal Law Review,[3] which was endorsed by the Court of Appeal in *R v Howell*, although the point did not arise for consideration in that case. Of course, if the breach of the peace has involved the commission of an offence, there may be an arrest for that offence if the conditional power of arrest under s 25 of PACE, or some other power, is available.

There is an indication in two Victorian cases that there can be an arrest for a breach of the peace which has been concluded, and whose imminent renewal is not reasonably apprehended, if there has been a continued (or fresh) pursuit of the breaker of the peace.[4] There is sense in this; if it was not possible to arrest a person who had committed a breach of the peace at the time of the breach and he ran away pursued by a police officer, he could not be arrested 100 yards down the street. Arguably, 'a breach of the peace is committed' in head (1) of the formulation in *Howell* can be regarded as extending to cover an arrest for a concluded breach committed in the arrestor's presence if it was immediately followed by a continued pursuit culminating very soon afterwards in that arrest.[4] The argument would be more difficult to make if the phrase had been 'is being committed'. Nevertheless, if, as appears to be the case from the authorities, the breach of the peace powers are essentially preventive, in terms of preventing a continuance or an anticipated breach, a power of arrest even immediately after the event is hard to explain.

The requirements of s 28 of PACE as to the information to be given on arrest apply to an arrest for breach of the peace. The statement 'I am arresting you for a breach of the peace' suffices for the purposes of s 28(3), regardless of whether the arrest is for a past, present or apprehended breach of the peace.[5] Section 32 of PACE (search upon arrest) also applies to an arrest for breach of the peace; as does s 54 (search at a police station), and ss 56 and 58 (right to have someone informed of arrest and access to legal advice). In addition, the Code of Practice on Detention (Code C) applies.

Because breach of the peace has been held to be a criminal offence for the purposes of Arts 5 and 6 of the ECHR,[6] the provisions of those Articles apply to someone arrested for breach of the peace.

---

1   The authorities were reviewed by Glanville Williams in 'Arrest for breach of the peace' [1954] Crim LR 578 at 586–587.
2   See the commentary to *R v Kelbie* [1996] Crim LR 802, CA.
3   *R v Podger* [1979] Crim LR 524, Crown Ct. *Podger* was overruled in *R v Howell* above. Also see the commentary to *R v Kelbie* above.
4   *R v Walker* (1854) Dears CC 358; *R v Marsden* (1868) LR 1 CCR 131.
5   In *R v Howell* [1981] 3 All ER at 386–387, the Court of Appeal expressed the tentative view that such words would *also* serve to constitute a lawful arrest under s 7(3) of the Public Order Act 1936 for committing an offence under s 5 of that Act, because 'a breach of the peace is involved in both offences'. These provisions have been replaced by s 4 of the Public Order Act 1986 but the point would seem equally applicable to the offence, and power of arrest for it, under s 4 because that offence also involves a breach of the peace (although that term does not appear in the section).
6   See para **2.3**.

2.10 The law relating to arrest for breach of the peace, and its application in three separate incidents, was reviewed by the European Court of Human Rights in *Steel v UK*[1] in 1998. In all three incidents the applicants were arrested for breach of the peace and detained for several hours.

The applications to the Court were based principally on alleged breaches of Arts 5(1) and 10(1) of the Convention. Article 5(1) provides that no one is to be deprived of liberty, save in specified circumstances and in accordance with a procedure prescribed by law; one of these circumstances (Art 5(1)(c)) is lawful arrest for the purpose of bringing someone before a court on reasonable suspicion that the person has committed an offence or when it is reasonably necessary to prevent him committing an offence. Article 10(1) provides the right to freedom of expression, which (by Art 10(2)) can be restricted if the restriction is prescribed by law and is necessary in a democratic society for, inter alia, the prevention of disorder or crime or for the protection of the rights of others.

The facts of the first of the three incidents in *Steel v UK* were that S was arrested while attending a demonstration against a grouse shoot after she walked in front of a member of the shoot, thereby preventing him firing. She was 'charged' (inter alia) with causing a breach of the peace and was detained for 44 hours before being brought before a court. At her trial, the complaint of a breach of the peace was found proved. She appealed unsuccessfully to the Crown Court, which ordered her to agree to be bound over for 12 months. S refused and was committed to prison for 28 days.

In the second incident, L was arrested when, as part of an anti-motorway-construction protest, she stood in front of a JCB digger. She was 'charged' with conduct likely to cause a breach of the peace and detained for 18 hours before being brought before a court. At her trial, she was found to have committed a breach of the peace. She, too, refused to agree to be bound over; she was committed to prison for seven days.

The third incident involved three applicants, C, P and N. They were all arrested as they handed out leaflets and held up barriers protesting against arms sales at the 'Fighter Helicopter II' Conference in London. They were detained for seven hours. Proceedings against them were subsequently dropped.

All five persons applied to the European Court of Human Rights, contending that their arrests and pre-trial detention had not been 'prescribed by law' as required by Art 5(1) and had amounted to disproportionate interferences with their right to freedom of expression in breach of Art 10.

The Court stated that it was satisfied that the concept of breach of the peace had been clarified by the English courts over the last two decades to the extent that it was sufficiently clear for the purposes of the Convention that a breach of the peace was only committed when an individual caused harm, or appeared likely to cause harm, to persons or property or acted in a manner the natural consequences of which would be to provoke others to violence.[2] It was also clear that English law allowed a person to be arrested if he caused a breach of the peace or was reasonably feared to be likely to cause one. Thus, the breach of the peace doctrine satisfied the requirement of sufficient precision inherent in 'lawful' and 'prescribed by law' in Art 5(1).[3]

Turning to the question whether in each incident the arrest and pre-trial detention of each applicant had complied with English law, the Court stated that the national courts which dealt with S and L had found that each had caused or been likely to cause a breach of the peace and, having reviewed the evidence, it found no reason to doubt that their arrest and pre-trial detention had complied with English law. In the case of N, P and C, on the other hand, their protest had been entirely peaceful and did not involve any behaviour capable of justifying the police in fearing that a breach of the peace was likely. For that reason, the Court stated, in the absence of any national decision on the question, it found that the arrest and pre-trial detention of N, P and C had not been lawful in terms of either English law or of Art 5(1). The Court concluded that there had been no violation of Art 5(1) in respect of S or L (two judges dissented in respect of S), but that there had been in respect of N, P and C.

In terms of the alleged violation of Art 10(1) in respect of the arrest and pre-trial detention of the five applicants, the Court answered the question of whether the restrictions (ie the arrests and pre-trial detention) on the applicants' freedom of expression were 'necessary in a democratic society for the prevention of disorder or crime' by concluding in respect of S (by a majority of five to four) and unanimously in respect of L that, having regard to the dangers inherent in their chosen form of protest, the risk of disorder arising from their conduct and the likelihood of their resuming their protest, the restrictions were 'not disproportionate' to the danger sought to be averted. Therefore there had not been a breach of Art 10(1). On the other hand, given that the requirement under Art 10(2) that any interference with the exercise of freedom of expression be 'prescribed by law' was similar to that under Art 5(1) that a deprivation of liberty be 'lawful', it followed from the Court's finding in relation to Art 5(1), with respect to N, P and C, that there had also been breach of Art 10. In any case, the arrest and detention of N, P and C had been disproportionate to the aim of preventing disorder or of protection of the rights of others.[4]

Thus, the common law power to arrest for a breach of the peace has effectively been found by the European Court to comply with Arts 5 and 10, although failure to comply with it in its application in respect of N, P and C constituted violations. However, its conclusions about breach of the peace and the power of arrest were influenced by its doctrine of the margin of appreciation. An English court taking a more rigorous approach under the Human Rights Act 1998 might disagree with those conclusions.

---

1   (1999) 28 EHRR 603, ECtHR.
2   The last alternative is a reference to powers relating to breach of the peace, not part of the
     definition of that term.
3   Para **1.21**.
4   N, P and C were awarded £500 each by the Court in respect of compensation for non-
     pecuniary damage, together with legal costs and expenses.

Other powers

2.11 In *Albert v Lavin*,[1] Lord Diplock, with whom the other Law Lords agreed, acknowledged that the powers to deal with present or apprehended breaches of the peace are not limited to arrest without warrant. He said:[2]

> '... every citizen in whose presence a breach of the peace is being, or reasonably
> appears to be about to be, committed has the right to take reasonable steps to make
> the person who is breaking or threatening to break the peace refrain from doing so;
> and those reasonable steps in appropriate cases will include detaining him against his
> will. At common law this is not only the right of every citizen, it is also his duty,
> although, except in the case of a citizen who is a constable, it is a duty of imperfect
> obligation.'

Lord Diplock's statement that: 'Every citizen in whose presence a breach of the peace ... reasonably appears to be about to be committed ...' more naturally seems to mean that the apprehension must be of a breach in that citizen's presence, rather than meaning that it must be based on facts occurring in that citizen's presence regardless of whether the apprehended breach is to occur in his presence.

Examples of the application of these wider preventive powers to take reasonable steps for the specified purpose are set out in the following paragraphs. The open-endedness of, and expandability of, these powers is a cause for complaint, although this was the very reason why the then Government decided against codifying them when the Public Order Act 1986 was being put together.[3]

---

1   [1981] 3 All ER 878, HL.
2   Ibid at 880.
3   *Review of Public Order Law* (Cmnd 9510, 1985) para 6.13.

Detention without arrest

2.12 Arrest is a method of beginning the criminal process or binding-over process. Although every arrest involves a deprivation of liberty, not every deprivation of liberty involves an arrest,[1] because a person may be restrained and detained temporarily solely to prevent a continuing or apprehended breach of the peace, ie without an arrest.[2] This was established by the House of Lords in *Albert v Lavin*, referred to above. Albert caused a disturbance in a bus queue by queue-jumping. Lavin, an off-duty police officer in plain clothes, restrained him. A struggle between the two men ensued. During it, Lavin told Albert that he was a police officer. In his excited state, Albert unreasonably disbelieved this. He continued to hit Lavin and was arrested for assaulting a constable in the execution of his duty. He was convicted and appealed to the Divisional Court. That court dismissed Albert's appeal, holding that it was not a defence to a charge of assault that Albert honestly but mistakenly believed that his actions were justified as reasonable self-defence if there were no reasonable grounds for his belief. Dismissing Albert's appeal to it, the House of Lords dealt with the case in another way. It held that the issue of mistake did not arise.

As indicated in the quotation from Lord Diplock's statement in *Albert v Lavin* set out in para **2.11**, his Lordship stated that the reasonable steps which every citizen in whose presence a breach of the peace is being, or reasonably appears to be about to be, committed may take include detaining against his will the person breaking or threatening to break the peace. His Lordship, with whom the other Law Lords agreed, followed this statement by saying:

> 'On the findings of the magistrates in the stated case this well-established exception was plainly applicable to the instant case ... Even if Albert's belief that Lavin was a private citizen and not a constable had been correct, it would not have made his resistance to Lavin's restraint of him lawful.'[3]

It will be noted that, according to Lord Diplock's statement and, unlike the power of arrest for breach of the peace,[4] only the person breaking, or threatening to break the peace may be detained. This limitation is open to doubt in the light of the fact that other applications of the general power to take steps to deal with actual or threatened breaches of the peace have been held to extend to action against someone other than such a person.[5]

---

1   *R v Brown* (1976) 64 Cr App R 231, CA.
2   Just as reasonable force may be used to prevent the commission of an offence: Criminal Law Act 1967, s 3.
3   [1981] 3 All ER 878 at 880.

4   See para **2.7**.
5   See *Humphries v Connor* (1864) 17 Ir CLR 1; see para **2.18**.

Entry to deal with or prevent a breach of the peace

2.13 Although s 17(5) of PACE abolished the general common law powers of a constable to enter premises without a warrant, s 17(6) expressly preserved any power of entry to deal with or prevent a breach of the peace.

It was held in *Robson v Hallett*,[1] that where a breach of the peace actually occurs on private premises a constable is entitled to enter them and remain for the purposes of stopping it. This decision was not surprising in the light of that in *Thomas v Sawkins*.[2] T was the convener of a meeting on private premises held to protest against a Bill then before Parliament and to advocate the removal of a chief constable. The public were invited to attend the meeting without charge. S, a police officer, attended the meeting with another officer. They both refused to leave when requested by T who laid his hand on the other officer, which was then removed by S. The officers remained on the premises. No breach of the peace occurred at the meeting. The Divisional Court upheld the dismissal of an information against S for common assault. It held that T and S were lawfully on the premises because the magistrates had found that the constables had reasonable grounds for believing that if they were not present at the meeting there would be sedition and other incitements to violence and a breach of the peace would occur, that they were entitled to enter and remain on the premises throughout the meeting and that consequently S did not unlawfully apply force to (ie commit a common assault against) T.

Thomas v Sawkins was not justified by the earlier authorities and has been heavily criticised.[3] Nevertheless, the Divisional Court in *McGowan v Chief Constable of Kingston-upon-Hull*[4] held that police officers had been acting in the execution of their duty in entering a house because they suspected a danger of a breach of the peace, a decision presumably based on *Thomas v Sawkins* although it is not mentioned in the report.

1   [1967] 2 All ER 407, DC. It had been accepted by early in the twentieth century that the
     police had power to enter meetings on private premises if they had reason to believe that a
     breach of the peace was actually taking place: see the report of the *Departmental Committee on
     the Duties of the Police with Respect to the Preservation of Order at Public Meetings* (Cd 4673, 1909)
     p 6. The view was taken there that there was no 'breach of the peace power' to enter premises
     to prevent an anticipated breach of the peace, ibid.
2   [1935] 2 KB 249, DC.
3   Goodhart '*Thomas v Sawkins*: a constitutional innovation' (1936–38) 6 CLJ 22; Feldman *Civil
     Liberties and Human Rights in England and Wales* (Clarendon Press, 1993) pp 832–835.
4   [1968] Crim LR 34, DC.

2.14 The grounds for the Divisional Court's decision in *Thomas v Sawkins* were uncertain. Lord Hewart CJ held that a constable had the right to enter and remain on private premises when he had reasonable grounds for believing that an offence was imminent or was likely to be committed; he did not limit this to an offence involving a breach of the peace. Avory J's view was that, where a constable had reasonable grounds to believe that, if he was not present, seditious speeches would be made and/or that a breach of the peace would take place, he was entitled to enter and remain on the premises to prevent any such offence or a breach of the peace. In a brief judgment, Lawrence J, the third judge, stated that the court's decision proceeded on the particular facts of the case and that a constable was 'entitled to commit a trespass' in the preservation of the peace. The balance of the judgments would seem to recognise a power of entry to deal with apprehended breaches of the peace. To the extent that it also recognised a power of entry to deal with an apprehended offence (whether any offence or sedition alone), it was overturned by s 17(5) of PACE.

A second point of uncertainty with the decision in *Thomas v Sawkins* was whether the power of entry to private premises was limited to public meetings on private premises or extended to private premises in general. Statements in support of both propositions can be found in the judgments of Lord Hewart CJ and Avory J. This uncertainty was resolved by the Court of Appeal in *McLeod v Commissioner of Police for the Metropolis.*[1]

In *McLeod*, an ex-husband, accompanied by his brother and sister, a solicitor's clerk and two police officers, went to his ex-wife's house. She had failed to comply with a court order to deliver up certain goods to the husband's solicitor. The wife was not at home but the ex-husband and his brother and sister entered the house without the permission of the elderly lady who answered the door, and so did the two officers (although it appears that they did not stay there long). One of the civil actions brought by the ex-wife was against the Commissioner for trespass and breach of duty. The police argued that they had been entitled to enter the house in order to prevent a breach of the peace, which they had reasonably believed was likely to result from the ex-husband's attempt to recover his property.

The issue for decision was the circumstances, if any, in which the police officers could enter a private house to prevent a breach of the peace, and (if there was such a right) whether they applied on the facts. The Court of Appeal held that the power of entering and remaining to deal with an apprehended breach of the peace extended to any type of premises and did not depend on the nature of any invitation offered to the public; in respect of private premises, it was not limited to public meetings. Delivering the Court of Appeal's judgment, Neill LJ said:[2]

'... I am satisfied that Parliament in s 17(6) [of PACE] has now recognised that there is a power to enter premises to prevent a breach of the peace as a form of preventive justice. I can see no satisfactory basis for restricting that power to particular classes of premises such as those where public meetings are held. If the police reasonably believe that a breach of the peace is likely to take place on private premises, they have power to enter those premises to prevent it. The apprehension must, of course, be genuine and it must relate to the near future ...

It seems to me it is important that when exercising his power to prevent a breach of the peace a police officer should act with great care and discretion; this will be particularly important where the exercise of his power involves entering on private premises contrary to the wishes of the owners or occupiers. The officer must satisfy himself that there is a real and imminent risk of a breach of the peace, because, if the matter has to be tested in court thereafter there may be scrutiny not only of his belief at the time but also of the grounds for his belief.

It may be necessary in some future case to consider how far in advance of a possible breach of the peace the right to enter arises. It will depend on the facts of the case, and on the nature and scale of the apprehended breach.'

The Court of Appeal decided on the facts that there had been a genuine, reasonable belief that there was a real and imminent risk of a breach of the peace and that therefore the police officers had been entitled to enter the house to prevent it.

It is arguable that s 17(6) of PACE does not support the Court of Appeal's conclusion,[3] and that, since the concept of a 'public assembly' is recognised in other areas of public order law, that concept could have provided a 'satisfactory basis' for restricting the power of entry in *Thomas v Sawkins.*

It was also arguable that the outcome of *McLeod v Commissioner of Police for the Metropolis* offended the right to respect for private life and home under Art 8 of the ECHR. An interference with this right by a public authority, such as the police, can be justified under Art 8(2) if it is in accordance with the law and is necessary in a democratic society in, inter alia, the prevention of disorder or crime, but it was argued that:

> 'In terms of the ECHR, the power may be insufficiently defined to be "in accordance with the law", does not self-evidently respond to a pressing social need, and may be disproportionate to its purpose in cases where such a need exists.'[3]

When the European Court of Human Rights[4] heard an application by the ex-wife that there had been a violation of Art 8 it did not, however, find that the power was in breach of that provision, although it did hold, in contradiction of the trial judge and the Court of Appeal, that the police officers' belief that there was a real possibility of a threat to the peace was not founded on reasonable grounds.

The European Court, in line with the approach taken by it a few days later in *Steel v UK*,[5] concluded that there was sufficient certainty about the common law power of the police to deal with breaches of the peace in general and to enter premises to deal with them in particular and that the power could properly be said to be 'in accordance with the law'. It also concluded that entry to premises was a legitimate aim for the purposes of Art 8(2), viz the prevention of disorder or crime. Turning to the facts of the particular case, the European Court considered whether the power as exercised was 'necessary in a democratic society'. By a majority of seven to two, it concluded that 'upon being informed that the [ex-wife] was not present, the police officers should not have entered her house, as it should have been clear to them that there was little or no risk of disorder or crime occurring', and that therefore 'the means employed by the police officers were disproportionate to the legitimate aim pursued. Accordingly there has been a violation of the Convention'.

It must be noted that the European Court's conclusion was based on the facts at the time of the incident. It was not concerned with hypotheticals, such as whether the police would have been justified in entering if the ex-wife had returned while the ex-husband was in the house.

---

1   [1994] 4 All ER 553, CA.
2   Ibid, at 560.
3   See Feldman 'Interference in the home and anticipated breach of the peace' (1995) 111 LQR 562.
4   *McLeod v UK* [1998] 2 FLR 1048, ECtHR.
5   See para **2.10**.

Remaining on premises to deal with or prevent a breach of the peace

2.15 Even if he has entered premises as a trespasser, or even if, although he entered as a licensee, his licence has been revoked, a constable may remain on the premises to deal with it if he reasonably apprehends an actual or threatened breach of the peace. He is not required to leave the premises and then lawfully to re-enter them.[1]

1　*Robson v Hallett* [1967] 2 All ER 407 at 414, per Diplock LJ; *McGowan v Chief Constable of Kingston-upon-Hull* [1968] Crim LR 34, DC; *Lamb v DPP* (1989) 154 JP 381, DC.

Prohibiting a meeting to prevent a breach of the peace

2.16 In *Duncan v Jones*,[1] it was held that, in the discharge of his duty to prevent breaches of the peace, a constable may forbid the holding of a meeting if he reasonably apprehends a breach of the peace. In this case, about 30 people, including D, collected near a training centre for the unemployed with a view to holding a meeting which had been advertised. Some 14 months previously, a meeting addressed by D had been held in the same place and had been followed by a disturbance in the centre. A constable, whom it was found as a fact reasonably apprehended a breach of the peace, forbade D to hold the meeting outside the centre but said it could be held 175 yards away in another street. D said 'I'm going to hold it' and started to address the people, whereupon she was arrested. She was convicted of obstructing a constable in the execution of his duty. On appeal, the question for the Divisional Court was whether the constable had been acting in the execution of his duty. The Divisional Court answered 'yes' because it had been found as a fact that the constable reasonably apprehended a breach of the peace. Humphreys J said:[2]

> 'It does not require authority to emphasize the statement that it is the duty of a police officer to prevent apprehended breaches of the peace. Here it is found as a fact that the respondent reasonably apprehended a breach of the peace. It then, as is rightly expressed in the case, became his duty to prevent anything which in his view would cause that breach of the peace. While he was taking steps to do so he was wilfully obstructed by the appellant. I can conceive no clearer case within the statutes than that.'

As explained in para **2.23**, *Duncan v Jones* does not permit someone to be prohibited from holding a meeting, in order to prevent a breach of the peace, where the anticipated violence is a wholly unreasonable reaction by other people.

1　[1936] 1 KB 218, DC. For criticism, see ECS Wade 'Police powers and public meetings' (1937) 6 CLJ 175; Daintith 'Disobeying a policeman: a fresh look at *Duncan v Jones*' [1966] PL 248; *Brownlie's Law of Public Order and National Security* (1981) pp 111–115.
2　[1936] 1 KB 218 at 223.

2.17 *Duncan v Jones* was developed by the Divisional Court in *Piddington v Bates*.[1] According to this decision, if it appears:

(a) that facts existed from which a constable could reasonably have apprehended a breach of the peace, as a real (as opposed to remote) possibility; and
(b) he did so apprehend,

the constable is under a duty to take such steps as he reasonably thinks are necessary to prevent it.

In *Piddington v Bates*, 18 men arrived to picket a printer's works where a third of the normal workforce were working. B, a chief inspector, told P that two pickets at each of the two entrances was sufficient. P refused to comply and pushed past B to join two pickets. B arrested him. P was convicted of obstructing B in the execution of his duty. The Divisional Court dismissed P's appeal against conviction. On the basis of the facts found by the magistrate, the requirements set out above were satisfied. Thus, notwithstanding what is now s 220 of the Trade Union and Labour Relations (Consolidation) Act 1992,[2] which makes it lawful for a person to picket at or near his place of work in contemplation or furtherance of a trade dispute, a constable can limit the number of pickets if he reasonably considers that necessary to prevent the real possibility of a breach of the peace.

An apparent distinction between the formulation of the power dealt with in *Piddington v Bates* and the power to arrest for a breach of the peace defined in *R v Howell* is that, in relation to the power to arrest for an anticipated breach of the peace where the person arrested has not already committed a breach of the peace, the arrestor must reasonably believe that a breach will be committed in the 'immediate' future by the person arrested, whereas in *Piddington v Bates* it was held that the power currently under discussion required the police officer to anticipate a real, and not remote, possibility of a breach of the peace. In *Moss v McLachlan*,[3] the Divisional Court denied that there was any conflict between the two cases in respect of the issue of immediacy. Skinner J, delivering the judgment of the court, said:

> 'The possibility of a breach must be real to justify any preventive action. The imminence or immediacy of the threat to the peace determines what action is reasonable. If the police feared that a convoy of cars travelling towards a working coal field bearing banners and broadcasting, by sight or sound, hostility or threats towards working miners might cause a violent episode, they would be justified in halting the convoy to inquire into its destination and purpose. If, on stopping the vehicles, the police were satisfied that there was a real possibility of the occupants causing a breach of the peace one and a half miles away, a journey of less than five minutes by car, then in our judgment it would be their duty to prevent the convoy from proceeding further and they have the power to do so.
>
> If and in so far as there may be any differences between the two approaches (and we do not believe there is), we respectfully prefer that in *Piddington v Bates*.'[4]

As indicated in para **2.7**, 'immediate' in respect of the relevant power of arrest has been interpreted to mean 'imminent' (ie about to take place). It would seem that what is required is at least a real possibility that a breach of the peace is imminent.[5]

The decision in *Moss v McLachlan* shows the extent of the present power. During a national miners' strike, a number of police officers were stationed at a motorway junction within five miles of four collieries. Their object was to stop and turn back cars carrying people who appeared to be striking miners en route to a mass picket at one of the collieries. M was in a convoy of cars carrying 60–80 men who were clearly identifiable as striking miners. The officers told the men that they apprehended a breach of the peace if they continued, and that if they did so they would be arrested. After a short delay, 40 of the men tried to force their way through police lines and were arrested on the grounds that the police apprehended a breach of the peace at one of the four collieries. M and three others were convicted of obstructing a constable in the execution of his duty and appealed unsuccessfully to the Divisional Court on the ground that the officers had not been acting in the execution of their duty. The magistrates had found that the police feared on reasonable grounds that there would be breach of the peace if there was a mass demonstration at whichever of the collieries M and his colleagues chose to congregate and the Divisional Court held that there was ample evidence to support that finding. It held that, on the facts found, a breach of the peace was not only a real possibility, but also, because of the proximity of the collieries and the availability of cars, imminent, immediate and not remote.

During the same strike the police attempted to stop miners and other apparent supporters of the strike from crossing the Thames via the Dartford Tunnel en route to collieries in the north of England. They purported to be exercising their 'breach of the peace' powers but, despite the fact that the action was approved by the courts,[6] it is difficult to see how they could reasonably have apprehended the real possibility of an imminent breach of the peace.

---

1   [1960] 3 All ER 660, DC. Strangely, the Court did not refer to *Duncan v Jones* in its decision. The case was, however, cited to it: see [1961] 1 WLR 162 at 168.
2   At the time a differently worded provision was contained in the Trade Disputes Act 1906.
3   (1984) 149 JP 167, DC. For critical comment, see Newbold 'Picketing miners and the courts' [1985] PL 30.
4   (1984) 149 JP 167 at 171.
5   In *McLeod v Commissioner of Police for the Metropolis*, para **2.14**, the Court of Appeal spoke of a 'real and imminent risk' of a breach of the peace occurring.
6   *Foy v Chief Constable of Kent* (1984) unreported, DC.

Use of reasonable force to prevent a breach of the peace

2.18 In *King v Hodges*,[1] a police officer was called to a disturbance at a probation hostel to assist in the removal of an inmate to another part of the premises. The officer, in the belief that there would be a breach of the peace, gently put his arm under one of the inmate's elbows in order to guide her to the door. The inmate then assaulted him. Dismissing her appeal against conviction for assaulting a constable in the execution of his duty, the Divisional Court held that, as a general rule, a police officer reasonably believing that a breach of the peace was about to take place was entitled to take such steps, including the use of reasonable force to prevent it which appeared to him to be proper. When he took the inmate by the arm the officer had reasonable grounds for suspecting a breach of the peace and he was acting reasonably in attempting to prevent such a breach. Therefore, even though he had not attempted to arrest the inmate when assaulted, he had been acting in the execution of his duty at that time.

Within this category can also be placed the use of reasonable force to seize items, such as flags and banners, intended or likely to lead to a breach of the peace. In the Irish case of *Humphries v Connor*,[2] where a police officer removed from H's lapel an orange lily after she had refused to do so, the facts alleged were as follows. The lily symbolised a particular political persuasion and was 'calculated [ie likely] ... to provoke animosity' among a crowd of opponents of that persuasion. Indeed, a number of people were provoked by it; they caused considerable noise and disturbance and threatened H with personal violence. The Court of Queen's Bench in Ireland held that, on the assumption that the facts alleged were true, the officer was not liable for assault; his action was justified because he had reasonable grounds to anticipate a breach of the peace by the crowd. It would appear from this decision that no intention to provoke a breach of the peace is required on the part of the object of the power before the present power can be exercised against him. Whether conduct of the present type is justified depends on who is the source of the threat to the peace (see para **2.23**); it could be that if the same facts as in *Humphries v Connor* occurred today the decision on them would be different.

In circumstances such as those just outlined, a police officer has power to require that property be handed over to him.

1   [1974] Crim LR 424, DC. Compare with *Hickman v O'Dwyer* [1979] Crim LR 309, DC (police
     officer physically tried to 'move on' a youth lying on a bench; no reason to apprehend breach
     of the peace; youth entitled to resist).
2   (1864) 17 Ir CLR 1.

Exercise of powers by private citizen

2.19 Although the cases referred to above have involved conduct by police
officers, and the courts' statements of law have generally been in terms of such
officers, it must not be forgotten that the powers to act in relation to breaches of
the peace referred to are vested in private citizens as well.

Indeed, the common law imposes on all citizens alike a duty to suppress
actual and apprehended breaches of the peace. A modern statement to this effect
is contained in the dictum of Lord Diplock in *Albert v Lavin* quoted in para **2.11**. As
his lordship acknowledged, in the case of a private citizen the duty is one of
imperfect obligation. However, it was held in *R v Brown*[1] that it is a common law
offence for a private citizen to fail to assist a police officer to restore the peace
when requested by the latter to do so. There must be a reasonable necessity for the
officer to request assistance, and neither physical impossibility nor lawful excuse
for the failure[2] (although what constitutes a 'lawful excuse' is unclear). A modern
example of the offence is provided by *R v Waugh*,[3] where a ticket collector was
convicted of it when he failed to come to the assistance of a policewoman
struggling with a thief. Although *Brown* was concerned with an actual breach of the
peace, it is submitted that it would also be an offence, subject to the same
principles, to fail to assist a police officer in preventing an imminent breach of the
peace.

1   (1841) Car & M 314. Compare *R v Sherlock* (1866) LR 1 CCR 20.
2   (1841) Car & M 314.
3   A Crown Court case reported in *The Times* of 1 October 1976.

Reasonably apprehended breaches of the peace

2.20 At a number of points in this chapter, reference has been made to the power
to take steps to prevent reasonably apprehended breaches of the peace. Some
attention has already been given to the degree of risk which must be apprehended
but, in the light of its importance, the point merits further treatment.

We have seen in para **2.17** that the imminent breach of the peace must be
reasonably apprehended as a real, and not remote, possibility by the police officer
(or other person exercising the power).[1] It must be stressed that the officer etc
must actually so apprehend and that he must also have reasonable grounds for
that apprehension. A statement by him that he expected a breach of the peace will
not suffice.[2] However, in assessing the reasonableness of an alleged apprehension
that there was a real possibility of a breach of the peace, allowance must be made
for the circumstances in which a spur-of-the-moment decision has to be made in
an emergency.[3]

1   A similar statement was made in *R v Chief Constable of Devon and Cornwall, ex parte Central
     Electricity Generating Board* [1981] 3 All ER 826 at 837 by Lawton LJ who spoke of 'a real and
     imminent risk' of a breach of the peace occurring.

2   *Piddington v Bates* [1960] 3 All ER 660, DC.

3   *G v Chief Superintendent of Police, Stroud* (1988) 86 Cr App R 92, DC.

Against whom can the preventive powers be exercised?

2.21 Although the power of arrest and the other preventive powers will normally be exercised against a person or persons who commits a breach of the peace or reasonably appears to be about to do so, they can in some cases be exercised against someone who is not committing, or about to commit, the breach of the peace in issue. While the general statement by Lord Diplock in *Albert v Lavin*, cited in para **2.7**, is in terms of taking reasonable steps against the person committing or threatening to commit the breach, and there is a similar statement in respect of a threatened breach in *R v Howell*, a case such as *Duncan v Jones*, referred to in para **2.16**, shows that the taking of such steps against someone whose conduct is liable to result in or provoke a breach of the peace by others has been approved.

In 1998, the Court of Appeal in *Foulkes v Chief Constable of the Merseyside Police*,[1] re-affirmed that a person whose conduct is lawful but is liable to result in or provoke a breach of the peace by others may be arrested, although this would only occur in exceptional circumstances. Beldam LJ, with whom Schiemann and Thorpe LJJ agreed, said:[2]

> 'I would accept [the] submission that the common law power of a police constable to arrest where no actual breach of the peace has taken place but where he apprehends that such a breach may be caused by apparently lawful conduct is exceptional. Many of the instances in which such a power has been upheld in the past are, as a result of the enactment of the Public Order Act 1986, unlikely to give rise to difficulty since for offences under that Act, and particularly under ss 4 and 5, statutory powers of arrest without warrant are conferred on a constable.
>
> In the circumstances of this case, although I am prepared to accept that a constable may exceptionally have power to arrest a person whose behaviour is lawful but provocative, it is a power which ought to be exercised by him only in the clearest of circumstances and when he is satisfied on reasonable grounds that a breach of the peace is imminent.'

A protection against abuse in such a case is that the steps taken must be reasonable steps; if the steps taken are unnecessary or excessive the person taking them is not protected by the breach of the peace power and, depending on what has been done, may be civilly liable.[3]

Cases like *Duncan v Jones* raise the question of the propriety of taking action against somebody acting lawfully, and not against his opponents who are threatening to act violently. In addition, as has been well expressed in a modern work: 'The risk of creating a "heckler's veto" is apparent'.[4]

1   [1998] 3 All ER 705, CA. Also see *R v Chief Constable of Sussex, ex parte International Trader's Ferry Ltd* [1999] 1 All ER 129, HL; and *R v Ramsell* (1999) unreported, CA.

2   *Foulkes v Chief Constable of Merseyside Police* [1998] 3 All ER 705 at 711.

3   This point was recognised by O'Brien J in *Humphries v Connor* (1864) 17 Ir CLR 1.

4   ATH Smith *Offences against Public Order* (1987) p 13.

2.22 When can breach of the peace powers be exercised against someone acting lawfully on the basis of a reasonable apprehension of a real risk of an imminent violent response by that person's opponents? A similar question can confront magistrates in binding-over proceedings under s 115 of the Magistrates' Courts Act 1980, described later in this chapter.

The answer, according to Sedley LJ, with whom Collins J agreed, in *Redmond-Bate v DPP*[1] depends on where the threat of violence is coming from, because it is there that the preventive action must be taken.

A classic illustration of this is provided by *Beatty v Gillbanks*[2] where it was held that a person may be held responsible for a threat to the peace if he intended to produce the disturbance of the peace (as opposed to knowing it might result from his conduct) or if it was a natural result of his conduct. The Salvation Army held regular processions through Weston-super-Mare. Another group, called the Skeleton Army, was organised to impede its passage. Clashes took place and breaches of the peace occurred on several occasions. One day, a Salvation Army procession, surrounded by a mob, was stopped by the police. A police sergeant told Beatty, who was in charge of the procession, that he must disperse the procession at once. Beatty refused to comply and, with two others who also persisted in leading the procession on, was arrested. All three were subsequently bound over to keep the peace on the basis that they had committed the now-repealed offence of unlawful assembly, although the justices found as a fact that none of the three were guilty of an overt act of violence and had submitted quietly to their arrest. The justices also found that the assembling of the Salvation Army in Weston was calculated to cause a breach of the peace and lead to mob violence.

On appeal to the Divisional Court, the questions of law were whether, on the facts found by the magistrates, there had been an unlawful assembly and whether the binding-over order was valid. The Divisional Court answered 'no' to both questions.

Field J stated that for an assembly to be unlawful it had to be tumultuous and against the peace. He continued:[3]

'[T]here was nothing so far as the appellants were concerned to show that their conduct was in the least degree "tumultuous" or "against the peace". All that they did was to assemble together to walk through the town, ... [A]s regards the appellants themselves, there was no disturbance of the peace, and ... their conduct was quiet and peaceable. But then it is argued that, as in fact their line of conduct was the same as had on previous similar occasions led to tumultuous and riotous proceedings with stone-throwing and fighting, ..., and as on the present occasion like results would in all probability be produced, therefore the appellants, being well aware of the likelihood of such results again occurring, were guilty of the offence charged against them. Now, without doubt, as a general rule it must be taken that every person intends what are the natural and necessary consequences of his own acts, and if in the present case it had been their intention, or if it had been the natural and necessary consequence of their acts, to produce the disturbance of the peace which occurred, then the appellants would have been responsible for it, and the magistrates would have been right in binding them over to keep the peace. But the evidence as set forth in the case shows that, so far from that being the case, the acts and conduct of the appellants caused nothing of the kind, but, on the contrary, that the disturbance that did take place was caused entirely by the unlawful and unjustifiable interference of the Skeleton Army, ..., and that but for the opposition and molestation offered to the Salvationists by these other persons, no disturbance of any kind would have taken place. ... The present decision of the justices, however, amounts to this, that a man may be punished for acting lawfully if he knows that his doing so may induce another man to act unlawfully – a proposition without any authority whatever to support it.'

Cave J limited himself to basing his decision on the absence of an intention on the part of the appellants to meet force with force. He did not address the 'natural consequence' point made by Field J.

Beatty v Gillbanks was distinguished in *Wise v Dunning*.[4] W was a Protestant lecturer who held meetings in Liverpool. At these meetings, he used language and gestures which were insulting to Catholics, and some breaches of the peace by his opponents occurred. It was W's declared intention to hold further meetings, and he was arrested, brought before a magistrate and bound over to keep the peace. The Divisional Court upheld the order on the ground (per Darling and Channell JJ) that breaches of the peace were the 'natural consequence' of W's conduct, despite the fact that, as a general rule, an unlawful act could not be regarded as being the natural consequence of a lawful though provocative act.

Darling J said:[5]

'... Counsel for the appellant contended that the natural consequence must be taken to be the legal acts which are a consequence. I do not think so. The natural consequence of such conduct is illegality. I think that the natural consequence of this "crusader's" eloquence has been to produce illegal acts, and from his acts and conduct circumstances have arisen which justified the magistrate in binding him over to keep the peace and be of good behaviour ...'

Channell J stated[6] that while:

'the law does not as a rule regard an illegal act as being the natural consequence of a temptation which may be held out to commit it ... the cases with respect to apprehended breaches of the peace show that the law does regard the infirmity of human temper to the extent of considering that a breach of the peace, although an illegal act, may be the natural consequence of insulting or abusive language or conduct.'

In *Redmond-Bate v DPP*,[7] Sedley LJ thought that the facts of *Duncan v Jones*[8] provided a 'sharper example' than *Wise v Dunning* of a case where the defendant's conduct was 'calculated to provoke ... violent reaction'.

---

1   [1999] 3 WLR 175, DC.
2   (1882) 13 Cox CC 138, DC. Followed in *R v Londonderry JJ* (1891) 28 LR Ir 440, Ir QBDC (another Salvationist case where the facts were similar). Compare *O'Kelly v Harvey* (1883) 15 Cox CC 435.
3   (1882) 13 Cox CC 138, at 145–147.
4   [1902] 1 KB 167, DC.
5   Ibid, at 179.
6   Ibid, at 179–180.
7   (1999) *The Times*, 28 July, DC. This is a brief report; reliance has been placed on the transcript. The case is discussed by Foster 'Freedom of speech and breach of the peace' (1999) 149 NLJ 1398.
8   [1936] 1 KB 218, DC; see para **2.16**.

2.23 As was held by the Divisional Court in *Nicol v DPP*,[1] violence is not a natural consequence of what a person does unless his conduct clearly interferes with the rights of others so as to make a violent reaction not wholly unreasonable. Only if this is satisfied can it be said that that person is responsible for a threat of violence or, to put it another way, the source of it.

In judging the source of a threat to the peace (ie where the threat of violence was coming from) assistance can be derived from *Nicol v DPP*. The defendants, concerned about cruelty to animals, had obstructed an angling competition by, inter alia, blowing horns. No violence was used or threatened by the defendants but, in spite of police requests to desist, the defendants continued until they were arrested. They were bound over under s 115 of the Magistrates' Courts Act 1980 and appealed unsuccessfully to the Divisional Court. Simon Brown LJ, with whom Scott Baker J agreed, explained the case law as follows:

> 'Before a court can properly find that the natural consequence of lawful conduct by a defendant would, if persisted in, be to provoke another to violence, it should, it seems to me, be satisfied that in all the circumstances it is the defendant who is acting unreasonably rather than the other person ...[A]s it seems to me, some clear interference at least with the rights of others ... is bound to characterise any conduct of which it can properly be said that it would naturally provoke violence in others.
>
> Putting it another way, the Court would surely not find a s 115 complaint proved if any violence likely to have been provoked on the part of others would be not merely unlawful but wholly unreasonable as, of course, it would be if the defendants' conduct was not merely lawful but such as in no material way interfered with the others' rights. A fortiori, if the defendant was properly exercising his own basic rights, whether of assembly, demonstration or free speech.'

The critical difference between the class of case where the defendant is responsible for the threat to the peace and those where somebody else is responsible for it is also shown by reference to *Redmond-Bate v DPP* as contrasted with *R v Morpeth Ward JJ, ex parte Ward*. In *Redmond-Bate*, D and two others were preaching on the steps of Wakefield Cathedral to passers-by in the street. In response to a complaint, PC T approached D and the other two preachers and warned them not to stop people. PC T later returned to find that a large crowd had gathered and that some of them were showing hostility towards the speakers. A gang of youths who had been chanting were moved on; others in the crowd were shouting 'bloody lock them up' and 'shut up'. Fearing a breach of the peace, PC T asked the speakers to stop preaching. They refused, whereupon he arrested them for a breach of the peace.

D was convicted of obstructing a constable in the execution of his duty. She appealed unsuccessfully to the Crown Court, and thence to the Divisional Court. The underlying issue on appeal to the Divisional Court was whether it was reasonable for PC T, in the light of what he perceived, to believe that D was about to cause a breach of the peace.

Applying *Nicol v DPP*, the Divisional Court allowed D's appeal. It held that the question for PC T was whether there was a threat of violence and, if so, from whom it was coming. If D and her companions were (like the preacher in *Wise v Dunning*) being so provocative that someone in the crowd, without behaving wholly unreasonably, might be moved to violence PC T was entitled to ask them to stop. On the other hand, if the threat of violence came from passers-by who were taking the opportunity to react so as to cause trouble (like the Skeleton Army in *Beatty v Gillbanks*), it was they and not D and her companions who should have been asked to stop and arrested if they did not.

On the facts, it concluded that PC T was not justified in apprehending an imminent breach of the peace, much less a breach of the peace for which D and the two other women were responsible. Consequently, PC T was not acting in the execution of his duty when he required the speakers to stop preaching. D was therefore not guilty of obstructing him in the execution of his duty when she refused to comply.

In reaching this decision, Sedley LJ considered the importance of Arts 9 and 10 of the ECHR. In doing so, he rejected the argument that there would not be a breach of the peace by a speaker provided that what he said was not offensive. Free speech, said Sedley LJ, included not only the inoffensive, but the irritating, the heretical, the unwelcome and the provocative provided it did not tend to provoke violence; freedom only to speak inoffensively was not worth having.

Nicol v DPP and *Redmond-Bate v DPP* can be contrasted with *Morpeth Ward JJ, ex parte Ward*.[2] There, animal rights protesters had disrupted a pheasant shoot by noisy and disorderly behaviour but without committing a breach of the peace (since there was no physical harm nor was anyone put in fear of being harmed). The Divisional Court refused to quash binding-over orders made under s 115. It held on the facts that, because provocative conduct likely to have the natural consequence of causing violence (even if only to the protesters) could be treated as conduct likely to cause a breach of the peace, it was impossible to say that the justices were perverse in finding a risk that the protesters were likely, unless bound over, to cause a risk of such a breach. Although the test of reasonableness was not referred to by the Divisional Court, it clearly could not have been said that it would have been perverse to conclude that the protesters' interference with the shooters' rights was an unreasonable interference with them.

Despite the fact that the test of reasonableness is a rather vague one, dependent on the viewpoint of the judiciary, the explanation given in *Nicol v DPP* and *Redmond-Bate v DPP* has much to commend it. However, the statements in those cases indicating that violent response to it cannot be a natural consequence of it, unless inter alia that conduct involves an interference with the rights of others, is liable to produce problems. It is unclear what the rights were which were interfered with in *Wise v Dunning* or in *Morpeth Ward JJ* unless 'right' simply means a 'privilege' (ie to do (or not to do) anything unless it is proscribed by law), eg not to listen to a preacher or to shoot, in which case this requirement seems meaningless.

Those who hoped that in *Steel v UK*[3] the European Court of Human Rights would take a strict approach to the case where the conduct of the individual concerned was likely to cause a breach of the peace were dismayed. The Court's approach was less strict than the English courts have become. It required only an interference with the rights of others and the risk of disorder in order for the test of proportionality to be satisfied; it did not add a requirement that the individual was acting unreasonably.

---

1   (1996) 160 JP 155, DC; discussed by Kerrigan 'Breach of the peace and binding over – continuing confusion' (1997) 2 J Civ Lib 30.
2   (1992) 95 Cr App R 215, DC.
3   See para **2.10**.

BINDING OVER TO KEEP THE PEACE OR TO BE OF GOOD BEHAVIOUR[1]

2.24 A person who comes before a magistrates' court, by whatever route, may be the subject of a binding-over order to keep the peace or to be of good behaviour, or both. Thus, such an order can be made against someone who has been arrested for an offence or for a breach of the peace or against a person who has been summonsed after the laying of an information or the making of a complaint.

It is an important aspect of the power to arrest for a breach of the peace that even if the arrestee is not subsequently charged with a criminal offence he may nevertheless be brought before the magistrates to be bound over to keep the peace under the powers described in para **2.29**.

Binding over to keep the peace or to be of good behaviour can be done either:

–   on a complaint under s 115 of the Magistrates' Courts Act 1980; or
–   by a court acting of its own motion.

The power to bind over to keep the peace or to be of good behaviour is not limited to magistrates' courts (although this is where it is usually exercised), since other courts can bind over of their own motion, as explained in para **2.36**.

A binding-over order requires that a person should enter into a recognisance[2] with or without a surety or sureties[3] to keep the peace or to be of good behaviour or both for a period on pain of forfeiture of the specified sum(s) if he fails to do so.

---

1   As to binding over generally, see Glanville Williams 'Preventive justice and the rule of law' (1953) 16 MLR 417; DGT Williams *Keeping the Peace: the Police and Public Order* (Hutchinson, 1967) ch 4; 'Suspended sentence at common law' [1963] PL 441; 'Protest and public order' [1970] CLJ 96 at 103–106; 'Preventive justice and the courts' [1977] Crim LR 703, especially at 706–709; *Brownlie's Law of Public Order and National Security* (1981) pp 312–315; Grunis 'Binding over to keep the peace and be of good behaviour in England and Canada' [1976] PL 16; Dodds 'The jurisdiction of magistrates to bind over' (1985) 149 JPN 259 and 278.

2   Ie an undertaking whereby he binds himself to pay a specified penalty if he breaks the terms of the binding-over order.

3   Ie a person who by recognisances guarantees to pay a specified sum in the event of a breach of the binding-over order.

2.25 The origins of the powers to bind over to keep the peace or be of good behaviour can be traced back to the tenth century, when laws were introduced which combined suretyship with self-policing. By the end of the twelfth century the enforcement of oaths of the peace was entrusted to knights assigned for the purpose. This was the origin of the office of conservators of the peace from which the office of justice of the peace developed in the fourteenth century. These conservators of the peace are understood to have exercised a common law power to bind people over to be of good behaviour if they were shown to be likely to endanger the public peace. Concerns about the behaviour of troops returning to England during a halt in the 100 Years War after a peace treaty in 1360 led to the enactment of the Justices of the Peace Act 1361, which put into statutory form the power of justices to take of people who came before them 'sufficient surety and mainprize of their good behaviour towards the King and his people'. Whatever the precise intent of the 1361 Act, Blackstone's influential summary of the law of binding over in 1769[1] stated that the law was founded both on the common law (the powers of the conservators of the peace) and on the 1361 statute, and that there could be under that law a binding over to keep the peace and a binding over to be of good behaviour.[2]

This view was endorsed by a number of cases in the nineteenth century,[3] and subsequently in a host of more modern cases.

1   Blackstone 4 *Commentaries* 251–253.
2   This historical account is derived from *Binding Over: The Issues* (Law Com, 1987), paras 2.1 and 2.2. For the historical origins, see Feldman 'The King, peace, the Royal prerogative and public order: the roots and early development of binding over powers' [1988] CLJ 101.
3   These cases are neatly summarised in *Lansbury v Riley* [1914] 3 KB 229 by Bray and Avory JJ.

2.26 Binding over involves an undertaking as to future conduct. It does not amount to a conviction for an offence, something which is often not appreciated by the general public. As Lord Kilmuir, the then Lord Chancellor, said in 1956:

> 'Whatever be the technical position, in the minds of innumerable people who read the report in a local newspaper there is the belief that the person who has been ordered to enter into recognisances, with or without sureties, to be of good behaviour or to keep the peace has been convicted; and even when there is more legal knowledge there is a general feeling that behind the order is a piece of discreditable conduct.'[1]

The powers to bind over to keep the peace or to be of good behaviour are exercisable 'not by reason of any offence having been committed, but as a measure of preventive justice';[2] indeed they do not depend on the actual or suspected commission of an offence.[3] Binding over is not a punishment, although where a court acts under its powers to bind over of its own motion, binding over to keep the peace or be of good behaviour may be used as a sentencing option against a convicted offender, as explained in para **2.39**.

As preventive powers, the binding-over powers are as significant as the powers described earlier in this chapter in respect of breach of the peace. Like those powers, they are anomalous and uncertain in definition. Their application is wide-ranging. They have been used, for example, to restrain political demonstrators from engaging in or repeating violence; to restrain someone from inciting others to break the peace, as in the famous case of *Lansbury v Riley*,[4] where a prominent MP who had incited suffragettes to militant action was bound over to be of good behaviour; to control the conduct of those involved in industrial action; to restrain the conduct of prostitutes and kerb-crawling motorists looking for them;[5] to restrain various types of disorderly conduct or indecent behaviour in public;[6] and to control neighbour disputes and domestic disputes.[6]

A research study commissioned by the Law Commission in 1983 showed that most binding-over orders were both to keep the peace and to be of good behaviour; only 12% were solely to keep the peace and 9% solely to be of good behaviour.[7]

1   HL Deb, vol 196, col 940.
2   *Veater v G* [1981] 2 All ER 304 at 307, per Lord Lane CJ. The powers to bind over to come up for judgment and to bind over a parent or guardian to take proper care of a child or young person are outside the scope of this book.
3   See, for example, *Hughes v Holley* (1988) 86 Cr App R 130 at 138, per Glidewell LJ; *Nicol v DPP* (1996) 160 JP 155, DC (both cases under the Magistrates' Courts Act 1980, s 115).
4   [1914] 3 KB 229, DC.
5   *Hughes v Holley* (1988) 86 Cr App R 130, DC.
6   Various examples are given in *Binding Over: The Issues* (Law Com, 1987) para 5.2.
7   Ibid, para 4.4.

2.27 Central to the powers to bind over under discussion here are the concepts of 'keeping the peace' and 'being of good behaviour'.

The vagueness of these terms has raised the issue of whether a binding-over order made under the present powers would be in violation of the ECHR on the ground that these terms are insufficiently precisely formulated to enable a citizen to regulate his conduct, so that the interference cannot be justified as 'lawful' or 'prescribed by law' as required (the requirement of foreseeability).[1]

As seen earlier in this chapter, 'breach of the peace' to which 'keeping the peace' is the opposite is a somewhat vague term, despite the attempts of the courts in recent years to give it more precision, attempts which somewhat surprisingly the European Court in *Steel v UK*[2] has held have made the elements of breach of the peace adequately defined and were sufficiently specific for the purposes of the requirement of foreseeability under Arts 5 and 10 of the ECHR.

In *Steel v UK*, referred to in para **2.10**, S and L were ordered to keep the peace and be of good behaviour for 12 months on recognisances of £100. They both refused to enter into recognisances and were committed to prison for 28 and seven days, respectively. S and L argued that their detention by the magistrates' court violated their rights under Art 5(1), because of the vagueness of the bind-over orders and the judicial immunity of the magistrates. With one dissentient, the European Court of Human Rights held that there had been no breach of Art 5(1) of the ECHR. Article 5(1) provides that no one is to be deprived of liberty save in specified circumstances, one of which (Art 5(1)(b)) is the lawful detention of a person for non-compliance with the lawful order of a court or in order to secure the fulfilment of any obligation prescribed by law. The question for the Court was whether the detentions of S and L were lawful within Art 5(1)(b), including whether English law was formulated with sufficient precision.

In this respect, the Court concluded that it was satisfied that S and L could reasonably have foreseen that, if they acted in a way whose natural consequence was to provoke others to violence, they might be bound over to keep the peace, and that if they refused to be bound over they might be imprisoned.

The Court also assessed whether the binding-over orders were specific enough for the purposes of Art 5(1)(b). Although it considered the orders to be expressed in rather vague and general terms, the term 'to be of good behaviour' being particularly imprecise, it considered that, given the context, it must have been sufficiently clear to the applicants that they were being asked to refrain from causing further, similar breaches of the peace in the next 12 months.

Having found no evidence of non-compliance with English law, the Court concluded (with the one dissentient) that there had been no violation of Art 5(1) in respect of S and L's imprisonment for refusing to be bound over.

In addition, the Court held (with four dissentients) that there had been no violation of the right to freedom of expression protected by Art 10(1), because the refusal of S and L to be bound over had legitimately been interpreted by the English courts as a statement of their intent to continue with their protest activities, which were attended by a risk of a breach of the peace despite their order requesting them not to do so. In those circumstances, bearing in mind not only the aim of deterrence but also the importance in a democratic society of maintaining the rule of law and the authority of the judiciary, the Court did not find the periods of committal to prison disproportionate.

'Good behaviour' is particularly uncertain in its definition. It includes keeping the peace, but it is wider than this since there can be a breach of good behaviour without a breach of the peace. Criminal behaviour can also be a breach of good behaviour without any breach of the peace being committed,[3] and so can conduct 'contra bonos mores'.[4] Conduct is contra bonos mores if it is 'contrary to the good way of life', in the words of Glidewell LJ in *Hughes v Holley*. He added:

> 'What is a good way of life is for the magistrates to decide ... contra bonos mores is conduct which has the property of being wrong rather than right in the judgment of the vast majority of contemporary fellow citizens.'[4]

The difficulty in saying with precision what conduct 'has the property of being wrong rather than right in the judgment of the vast majority of contemporary fellow citizens' causes obvious problems in anticipating what conduct will 'trigger' the making of a binding-over order and in terms of anticipating what kind of behaviour will be a breach of that order. In *Steel v UK*, the European Court of Human Rights noted that the term 'to be of good behaviour' was particularly imprecise and offered little guidance to the person bound over as to the type of conduct which would amount to a breach of the order.

The Court returned to this point in *Hashman v UK*.[5] In this case, no breach of the peace, actual or threatened, had been proved in binding-over proceedings under s 115 of the 1980 Act, so that – unlike *Steel v UK* – the issue of whether the concept of 'good behaviour' was too broad was central to the decision. In *Hashman v UK*, H1 and H2, two hunt saboteurs, had respectively blown a horn and shouted at hounds. They were bound over to keep the peace and be of good behaviour after it had been found that, although no breach of the peace had been proved, their behaviour had been contra bonos mores.

With one dissentient, the European Court of Human Rights held that the binding-over orders constituted a violation of Art 10 of the ECHR (freedom of expression) because behaviour contra bonos mores was so broad – indeed it was not described at all – that it did not comply with the requirement in Art 10(2) that any interference with freedom of expression must be 'prescribed by law'. The Court did not accept that it must have been evident to H1 and H2 what they were being ordered not to do for the period of their binding over. It noted that, while in *Steel v UK* the applicants had been found to have breached the peace, and the Court found that it was apparent that the bind-over related to similar behaviour, H1 and H2 had not broken the peace, and given the lack of precision of 'contra bonos mores', it could not be said that what they were being bound over not to do must have been apparent to them. Thus, the binding-over order to keep the peace and not to behave contra bonos mores did not comply with the 'prescribed by law' requirement in Art 10(2).

As a result of this case, a binding over made on the basis of actual and anticipated conduct contra bonos mores would be inconsistent with Art 10 (and no doubt Art 5) of the ECHR.

Because of the width of 'good behaviour', and the fact that the court cannot give specific guidance as to what is required in order to comply with a binding-over order,[6] even a binding-over order to be of good behaviour which is based on criminal conduct, and not conduct contra bonos mores, will fall foul of the ECHR because the person bound over will not be able to see what will constitute a breach of the order.

The easiest way out of the difficulties exposed in *Hashman* would be for Parliament to abolish binding-over to be of good behaviour and the concept of 'good behaviour'. This is also the preferable option. Should it be necessary for the courts to have power to bind someone over simply because his conduct is contra bonos mores? If his conduct is not 'good behaviour' because it is criminal there are other adequate ways of dealing with him.

Unless and until Parliament takes the necessary action, the courts should construe 'good behaviour' in a very narrow sense and permit specific guidance to be given to the person bound over. This would satisfy the requirement of foreseeability, at the expense of ignoring the judicial decisions which establish the definition found unacceptable in *Hashman*.

---

1   See para **1.21**.
2   (1999) 28 EHRR 603, ECtHR.
3   *R v Sandbach JJ, ex parte Williams* [1935] 2 KB 192, DC (obstruction of a constable acting in
    execution of duty by warning others of his approach); *Bamping v Barnes* [1958] Crim LR 186,
    DC (persistent breach of street by-law).
4   *Hughes v Holley* (1988) 86 Cr App R 130, DC ('kerb crawling', not an offence at the time).
5   (1999) *The Times*, 1 December, ECtHR.
6   Para **2.44**.

Statutory complaint procedure

2.28 Section 115(1) of the Magistrates' Courts Act 1980 provides a statutory procedure by which a person can be brought before a magistrates' court for the sole purpose of having him bound over.

The power under s 115(1) originated in the old commissions of the peace. It was codified by s 25 of the Summary Jurisdiction Act 1879 and is now restated by s 115 with minor alterations. The power is vested in a magistrates' court composed of at least two justices and not by an individual justice of the peace.

2.29 Section 115(1) of the 1980 Act provides:

> 'The power of a magistrates' court on the complaint of any person to adjudge any other person to enter into a recognizance, with or without sureties, to keep the peace or to be of good behaviour towards the complainant shall be exercised by order on complaint.'

The complaint may be brought by an individual citizen or it may be brought by a police officer. The Crown Prosecution Service is obliged to take over the conduct of all binding-over proceedings instituted on behalf of a police force.[1]

If it is wished to have somebody bound over to keep the peace or to be of good behaviour in circumstances where it is not alleged that that person has committed an offence, the appropriate procedure is to proceed by way of complaint under s 115.[2]

Proceedings by way of complaint are within the civil jurisdiction of a magistrates' court. Sections 51–57 of the 1980 Act govern that jurisdiction and the procedure to be followed. However, although the proceedings under s 115 are technically civil, and a binding-over order is not a conviction, in reality they bear 'many of the characteristics of a criminal proceeding'.[3] In *R v Bolton JJ, ex parte Graeme*,[4] the Divisional Court held that the procedure under s 115 is 'a criminal cause or matter' for the purposes of s 18(1)(a) of the Supreme Court Act 1981 (restrictions on appeals from the High Court to the Court of Appeal) because it may result in imprisonment and it has integrally been treated as part of the criminal jurisdiction of magistrates' courts. In addition, proceedings under s 115 are 'criminal proceedings' for the purposes of the Legal Aid Act 1988.[5]

---

1   Prosecution of Offences Act 1985, s 3(2)(c).
2   *R v Morpeth Ward JJ, ex parte Ward* (1992) 95 Cr App R 215 at 220, per Brooke J.
3   *Everett v Ribbands* [1952] 1 All ER 823 at 826, per Denning LJ. Without deciding the point, the Divisional Court in *Veater v G* [1981] 2 All ER 304 at 308 and in *Percy v DPP* [1995] 3 All ER 124 at 134 was inclined to label the proceedings criminal.
4   (1986) 158 JP 129, DC.
5   Legal Aid Act 1988, s 19(5). An application to forfeit a recognisance does not give rise to criminal proceedings for these purposes: *R v Maidstone Crown Court, ex parte Clark* [1995] 2 Cr App R 617, DC.

2.30 A complaint is normally made in writing or on oath, but this is not essential; it may simply be made orally.[1]

When a complaint is lodged under s 115, a summons may be issued to the person named in it requiring him to appear before a magistrates' court acting for the petty sessions area and answer the complaint.[2] This enables the respondent to give evidence and to cross-examine before an order is made. However, the jurisdiction of a magistrates' court to hear a complaint does not depend upon a summons being issued.[3] Thus, the procedure under s 115 can be used against a person who has been arrested for an offence or breach of the peace and whose appearance before the court is ensured by his arrest and detention in custody or release on police bail,[4] rather than by a summons. In this type of case, a complaint may well not have been lodged before the person's appearance before the magistrates' court. The Divisional Court has held that a notice or record of charge served by the police on the person and forwarded to the justices' clerk and before the court (or read out to it) can be construed as a written (or oral) complaint.[4] The validity of that document as a complaint is not affected by its non-compliance with the form of complaint prescribed by the Magistrates' Courts (Forms) Rules 1981 (form 98);[5] defects can be cured under s 123 of the Magistrates' Courts Act 1980.[6] The substance of the complaint and the complainant must, however, be sufficiently identified.[5]

---

1   Magistrates' Courts Rules 1981, r 4(2).
2   Magistrates' Courts Act 1980, s 51.
3   *R v Manchester Stipendiary Magistrate, ex parte Hill* [1983] AC 328 at 335, per Lord Roskill; *Coventry Magistrates' Court, ex parte CPS* (1996) 160 JP 741, DC.
4   As in *R v Coventry Magistrates' Court, ex parte CPS* above; *DPP v Speede* [1998] 2 Cr App R 108, DC.
5   *Coventry Magistrates' Court, ex parte CPS* above.
6   As pointed out in *DPP v Speede* above at 118.

2.31 Although the purpose of s 115 was to provide a means of bringing a person before a magistrates' court so that he can be heard, a magistrates' court may hear the case in the absence of a defendant to a complaint, instead of adjourning the hearing. Alternatively, having substantiated the complaint by hearing the complainant briefly, it may issue a warrant for the respondent's arrest. It may not, however, hear the case in the absence of the defendant or issue an arrest warrant unless satisfied that a summons was served on him within a reasonable time before the hearing or unless the defendant has appeared on a previous occasion to answer the complaint. If the court proceeds to hear the complaint in the absence of the defendant, and finds the case proved, it cannot take the matter further in the defendant's absence because he needs to be present when the binding-over order is made.[1] To secure that presence, the court will have to adjourn and the defendant will have to be given notice of the adjourned hearing. If he fails to attend that hearing, an arrest warrant may be issued if the court is satisfied that he had adequate notice of the time and place of that hearing.[2]

---

1   See para **2.47**.
2   Magistrates' Courts Act 1980, s 55(2)–(4); *R v Liverpool JJ, ex parte Collins; same, ex parte Santos* [1998] 2 Cr App R 108, DC.

2.32 A binding-over order cannot be made under s 115 unless the complaint is strictly proved by sworn,[1] admissible evidence beyond reasonable doubt[2] (the criminal standard of proof may be noted) after a full hearing of the complaint, ie after the case has been fully heard.[3] However, during the course of proceedings under s 115, the magistrates' court may decide to bind over the respondent, or the complainant or a witness, under their common law powers or their powers under the 1361 Act dealt with in paras **2.35–2.43**.[4] This can happen, for example, where the defendant makes an admission to a complaint without evidence being heard.

---

1   Magistrates' Courts Act 1980, ss 53(2) and 98; Magistrates' Courts Rules 1981, r 14(1).
2   *Percy v DPP* [1995] 3 All ER 124, DC; *Nicol v DPP* (1996) 160 JP 155, DC.
3   See *R v Aubrey-Fletcher, ex parte Thompson* [1969] 2 All ER 846, DC. An order made after an agreement to enter into a recognisance under s 115, no evidence being called, was accepted without comment by the Divisional Court in *R v Marlow JJ, ex parte O'Sullivan* [1983] 3 All ER 578. The lack of evidence was not, however, raised on appeal.
4   It is not certain whether they can do so on grounds other than those stated in the complaint.

2.33 A magistrates' court can make a binding-over order under s 115 only if it is satisfied beyond reasonable doubt that one of two criteria are satisfied.

The first criterion is that the defendant is 'guilty' (not using that word in its strict sense) of the past conduct alleged against him in the complaint and that there is a real risk that he may in the future repeat his conduct and commit a breach of the peace[1] or may provoke others to do so as a natural consequence of his future conduct.[2] It need not be proved that the past conduct alleged in the complaint constituted an 'actual' breach of the peace, it may simply consist of conduct which is likely to cause such an 'actual' breach; as pointed out in para **2.4**, a 'breach of the peace' covers acts or threats giving rise to a likelihood of violence or of a fear of violence. Thus, the proof required for a binding over under s 115 may relate simply to risk. This is shown by *R v Morpeth Ward JJ, ex parte Ward*,[3] referred to in para **2.23**. However, if the defendant's conduct does not give rise to any likelihood of violence or a fear of violence he cannot be bound over. In *Percy v DPP*,[4] a bind-over of a woman who kept climbing over a perimeter fence into a military base was quashed because there was no likelihood that trained security personnel would be provoked to violence by her conduct. There was no threat to the peace at all.

The second alternative criterion for an order under s 115, at the time of writing, is that the defendant has committed an offence or acted contra bonos mores,[5] and that there is a real risk that he might repeat that conduct.[6]

1   Breach of the peace bears the same meaning as in respect of the preventive powers of the
     police etc (para **2.4**): *Percy v DPP* [1995] 3 All ER 124, DC. In *Everett v Ribbands* [1952] 1 All
     ER 873, CA, breach of the peace for the purposes of binding over was equated, obiter, with
     any breach of the law. This was disapproved in *Percy v DPP*.
2   See *Wise v Dunning* [1902] 1 KB 167, DC; *R v Morpeth Ward JJ, ex parte Ward* (1992) 95 Cr App
     R 215, DC; *Nicol v DPP* (1996) 160 JP 155, DC; see paras **2.21–2.23**.
3   (1992) 95 Cr App R 215, DC.
4   [1995] 3 All ER 124, DC.
5   See para **2.27**.
6   *Hughes v Holley* (1988) 86 Cr App R 130, DC.

2.34 The wording of s 115(1) suggests that an order to be of good behaviour
under it may require the person bound over to be of good behaviour only with
respect to the complainant, as opposed to being of good behaviour in general.
Where an order to keep the peace could not be made on the evidence, this would
be a major limitation on s 115(1) because often the nominal complainant is a
police officer with no personal interest in the matter. As the binding-over order in
Hashman v UK (para **2.27**) exemplifies, it is common for courts to bind defendants
over under s 115 to be of good behaviour in general. In *Percy v DPP*,[1] the Divisional
Court, without adverting to the wording of s 115(1), saw no problem with an order
under s 115(1) that Percy be bound over 'in the sum of £100 to keep the peace and
be of good behaviour, particularly towards Mr Williams-Brown [the complainant],
for a period of 12 months', except that it thought the reference to Mr
Williams-Brown was inappropriate. This is a matter clearly in need of judicial
resolution. The limitation of a binding-over order to be of good behaviour to
specified victims would go some way to resolving the problems in respect of the
ECHR outlined in para **2.27**.

1   [1995] 3 All ER 124, DC.

Binding over outside the statutory complaint procedure: binding over at the court's own motion

2.35 Section 25 of the Summary Jurisdiction Act 1879, now s 115 of the 1980 Act,
did not codify the entire law of binding over to keep the peace or to be of good
behaviour. Section 115 was intended to provide a means of bringing before the
magistrates' court a person with a view to his being bound over. The personal
powers vested in justices at common law and under the 1361 Act to bind over
someone *already* before the court survive. They are exercisable of the justices' own
motion, ie no complaint or information is required.

The powers at common law and under the 1361 Act appear to be identical in
scope. The 1361 Act empowers justices 'to take of all of them that be [not][1] of
good fame, where they shall be found, sufficient surety and mainprize of their
good behaviour towards the King and his people . . . to the intent that . . . the peace
be not blemished . . .'.

1   This word, which does not appear in the first edition of the Act, has been inserted in all
     translations of the law French text of the Act on the ground that this must have been the
     intention of Parliament. See *Hughes v Holley* (1988) 86 Cr App R 130 at 137, per Glidewell LJ.
     In *Lansbury v Riley* [1913] 3 KB 229, the Divisional Court held that in the light of the judicial
     decisions on the construction of the Act it was too late to question its accepted meaning.

2.36 Section 1(7) of the Justices of the Peace Act 1968 confirms the power of any court of record, such as the Crown Court,[1] with a criminal jurisdiction to make an order of its own motion binding over a person to keep the peace or to be of good behaviour.[2] Section 1(7) provides:

> 'It is hereby declared that any court of record having a criminal jurisdiction has, as ancillary to that jurisdiction, the power to bind over to keep the peace, and power to bind over to be of good behaviour, a person who or whose case is before the court by requiring him to enter into his own recognisances or to find sureties or both …'

Quite apart from this provision, judges of the High Court and Court of Appeal are justices for the peace for every county in England and Wales and can exercise the personal binding-over powers of justices referred to above.[3]

---

1   By the Supreme Court Act 1981, ss 45, 19 and 15 respectively, the Crown Court, High Court and Court of Appeal are courts of record. Magistrates' courts are generally not regarded as courts of record, despite their limited power to punish contempt of court under s 12 of the Contempt of Court Act 1981. See, for example, Ingman *The Legal Process* 7th edn (Blackstone Press, 1998) p 1. The point is, however, of no importance here in the light of their common law powers and the Justices of the Peace Act 1361.
2   The power derives from the 1361 Act: *R v Crown Court at Lincoln, ex parte Jude* [1997] 3 All ER 737 at 739, per Auld J.
3   *R v Sharp* [1957] 1 All ER 577, CCA; *R v Younis* [1965] Crim LR 305.

2.37 An order at the court's own motion can be made at any stage of proceedings before the court if it emerges in evidence that there is a likelihood of the breach of the peace.[1]

---

1   *R v Aubrey-Fletcher, ex parte Thompson* [1969] 2 All ER 846, DC (1361 Act); *R v Crown Court at Swindon, ex parte Pawittar Singh* [1984] 1 All ER 941, DC (Justices of the Peace Act 1968, s 1(7)). See, further, paras **2.40** and **2.41**.

Against whom can a binding-over order be made?

2.38 A binding-over order at the court's own motion can be made against any one or more of the following participants in proceedings on the basis of facts which emerge in those proceedings:

– a complainant or prosecutor;[1]
– a defendant to a complaint;
– an accused;[2] or
– a witness.[3]

However, an order cannot be made under s 1(7) of the Justices of the Peace Act 1968 against a person who has given a witness statement but who has not been called upon to give evidence, as where the Crown has offered no evidence, because he is not 'a person *who* or whose case is *before the court*'.[4] This limitation does not seem to arise – certainly it does not on its wording – in respect of the power of magistrates to bind over under the 1361 Act. Binding over a witness is a 'serious step' which 'should only be taken where facts are proved by evidence before the court which indicate the likelihood that the peace will not be kept … Such cases will be exceedingly rare.'[5]

Although a binding-over order can be made against a prosecutor, this should only occur in exceptional circumstances where the accused has pleaded guilty.[6]

Similar caution must be exercised before an accused who has been acquitted on the merits of the offences with which he has been charged is bound over. It has been said that in such a case it is 'particularly important' that the court is satisfied beyond reasonable doubt that he poses 'a potential threat to other people and is a man of violence. Belief that [he] might pose such a threat is not enough.'[7] It was added that it is exceedingly rare that it is appropriate to bind over an accused who has been acquitted on the merits.[7]

1   See, eg, *R v Wilkins* [1907] 2 KB 380, DC; *R v Hendon JJ, ex parte Gorchein* [1974] 1 All ER 168, DC.
2   *R v Woking JJ, ex parte Gossage* [1973] 2 All ER 621, DC; *R v Inner London Crown Court, ex parte Benjamin* [1987] Crim LR 417, DC (acquitted accused).
3   *Sheldon v Bromfield JJ* [1964] 2 All ER 131, DC.
4   *R v Crown Court at Swindon, ex parte Pawittar Singh* [1984] 1 All ER 941, DC (victim of assault, not party to proceedings and not called as witness against accused who pleaded guilty); *R v Kingston-upon-Thames Crown Court, ex parte Guarino* [1986] Crim LR 325, DC (person subject to unconditional witness summons but not required to give evidence); *R v Lincoln Crown Court, ex parte Jones* [1990] COD 15.
5   *R v Crown Court at Swindon, ex parte Pawittar Singh* above at 943, per Stephen Brown LJ.
6   *R v Preston Crown Court, ex parte Pamplin* [1981] Crim LR 338, DC.
7   *R v Middlesex Crown Court, ex parte Khan* (1997) 161 JP 240, DC.

When can an order be made?

2.39 An order under the present powers can be made at any stage of criminal proceedings for an offence: for example, on acquittal[1] or conviction,[2] on adjournment,[3] or on discontinuance of the prosecution case,[4] or when an appeal is allowed and a conviction quashed.[5]

A binding over ordered against an accused after conviction may be ordered in addition to a penalty for the offence, such as a fine or compensation order. It is uncertain whether a binding-over order imposed on a convicted accused can be the sole order imposed by the court, or whether some additional penalty, even if nominal, must be imposed. The better view is that it can be the sole order[6] even in the case of an order under s 1(7) of the Justices of the Peace Act 1968. The reference in that provision to the bind-over being 'ancillary' to the court's criminal jurisdiction may mean that the Court should determine the penalty for the offence before the ancillary power of binding over is considered. However, *Blackstone's Criminal Practice*[7] states that there is evidence that bind-overs are sometimes made on sentence without any additional penalty.

Although the powers of justices in a magistrates' court to bind over of their own motion are normally exercised in criminal proceedings, they may also be used in the course of proceedings under s 115 of the Magistrates' Courts Act 1980 or other civil proceedings brought before them.

1   See, eg, *Sheldon v Bromfield JJ* [1964] 2 All ER 131, DC (both acquitted accused and number of witnesses bound over); *R v Inner London Crown Court, ex parte Benjamin* (1987) 85 Cr App R 267, DC.
2   See, eg, *R v Hendon JJ, ex parte Gorchein* [1974] 1 All ER 168, DC (both convicted accused and private prosecutor bound over).
3   See, eg, *R v Aubrey-Fletcher, ex parte Thompson* [1969] 2 All ER 846, DC.
4   See, eg, *R v Crown Court at Lincoln, ex parte Jude* [1997] 3 All ER 737, DC.

5   *R v Sharp* [1957] 1 All ER 577, CCA; *R v Biffen* [1966] Crim LR 111, CCA provides an example
     of this.
6   The matter is discussed in *Binding Over: The Issues* (Law Com, 1987) para 2.20.
7   1999 edn, para E15.3

2.40 The threat to the peace or not to be of good behaviour perceived by the
court must be disclosed by the evidence before it.[1] In *R v Aubrey-Fletcher, ex parte
Thompson*, Edmund-Davies LJ, as he then was, said in relation to the former type of
threat:[2] 'there must emerge during the course of a hearing, which need not be a
completed hearing, material[3] from which it may fairly be deduced that there is at
least a risk of a breach of the peace in the future.'[4] The degree of risk was
described, obiter, by the Divisional Court in *Percy v DPP*[5] as a 'real risk, not a mere
possibility', the same degree of risk as under s 115.

That material must be admissible evidence.[6] There is authority that, if the
facts are contested, the evidence must be sworn evidence,[7] although this has also
been denied.[8]

If there is no admissible evidence from which the court could apprehend a
breach of the peace, an offence or conduct contra bonos mores, consent by a
person to being bound over does not confer jurisdiction to make a binding-over
order; it simply relieves the court of the duty to allow that person an opportunity to
show cause why a binding over should not be made.[9]

1   *R v Aubrey-Fletcher, ex parte Thompson* [1969] 2 All ER 846, DC; *R v South West London
     Magistrates' Court, ex parte Brown* [1974] Crim LR 313, DC.
2   [1969] 2 All ER 846 at 848. In *Shaw v Hamilton* [1982] 2 All ER 718 at 719, Donaldson LJ said:
     'A bind-over order is a preventive order, but it has to be justified by existing evidence'.
3   When someone causes a disturbance in the face of the court which suggests a breach of the
     peace is imminent, the court may bind that person over without the need to hear evidence: *R
     v North London Metropolitan Magistrate, ex parte Haywood* [1973] 3 All ER 50, DC; *R v Clerkenwell
     Metropolitan Stipendiary Magistrate, ex parte Hooper* [1998] 4 All ER 193, DC.
4   No particular person needs to be threatened: *R v Wilkins* [1901] 2 KB 380, DC; *Lansbury v
     Riley* [1914] 3 KB 229, DC.
5   [1995] 3 All ER 124, DC.
6   *Brooks v Nottinghamshire Police* [1984] Crim LR 677, Crown Court in its appellate capacity.
     Thus, the word of a prosecuting advocate or of a police officer with no personal knowledge of
     the facts will not do: *Everett v Ribbands* [1952] 1 All ER 823.
7   *Shaw v Hamilton* [1982] 2 All ER 718, DC; *Brooks v Nottinghamshire Police*, above.
8   *R v South West London Magistrates' Court, ex parte Brown*, above.
9   Ibid; *R v Marylebone Metropolitan Stipendiary Magistrate, ex parte Okunnu* (1988) 87 Cr App R
     295, DC.

2.41 In order for a court to bind over of its own motion, there is no need (in
contrast to a case dealt with under s 115 of the 1980 Act) for the matters
complained of to be proved.[1] On the other hand, in *Percy v DPP*[2] the Divisional
Court held, obiter, that, before a court can bind over of its own motion, it must be
proved that there is a real risk of a breach of the peace[3] in the future. That risk of a
breach of the peace may be that the person concerned may commit a breach of
the peace or that he may behave in a way whose natural conseqence[4] is to bring
about a breach.[5] The Divisional Court in *Percy v DPP* added that the standard of
proof in this respect was beyond reasonable doubt, just as it is in proceedings
under s 115 of the 1980 Act.[6] There is no difference, it seems, between the 'real
risk' required under s 115 and the requisite degree of risk under the 'own motion'
power.

Likewise, a person cannot be bound over to be of good behaviour unless (at the time of writing) it is proved, beyond reasonable doubt (it appears), that there is a real risk that he may in the future commit an offence[7] or act contra bonos mores.[8]

---

1   *R v Aubrey-Fletcher, ex parte Thompson* [1969] 2 All ER 846 at 848.
2   [1995] 3 All ER 124 at 134. These views were repeated in *DPP v Speede* [1998] 2 Cr App R 108 at 115, per Hooper J.
3   Breach of the peace bears the meaning given in para **2.4**: *Percy v DPP* [1995] 3 All ER 124, DC. In *Everett v Ribbands* [1952] 1 All ER 823, CA, breach of the peace for the purposes of binding over was equated, obiter, with any breach of the law. This was disapproved in *Percy v DPP*.
4   See paras **2.21–2.23**.
5   *Wise v Dunning* [1902] 1 KB 167, DC; *R v Aubrey-Fletcher, ex parte Thompson* [1969] 2 All ER 846, DC; *R v South West London Magistrates' Court, ex parte Brown* [1974] Crim LR 313, DC; *R v Inner London Crown Court, ex parte Benjamin* (1987) 85 Cr App R 267, DC.
6   *R v Middlesex Crown Court, ex parte Khan* (1997) 161 JP 240, DC.
7   *R v Sandbach JJ, ex parte Williams* [1935] 2 KB 192, DC; *Bamping v Barnes* [1958] Crim LR 186, DC.
8   *Hughes v Holley* (1988) 86 Cr App R 130, DC. The statement in *R v South Molton JJ, ex parte Ankerson* [1988] 3 All ER 989, DC, that before a binding-over order to be of good behaviour is made there must be material justifying the conclusion that there is a risk of a breach of the peace, has not been made in other cases and directly conflicts with the contrary statement in *R v Sandbach JJ* above, to which the Divisional Court did not refer. *R v Sandbach JJ* represents the better view.

2.42 A court is not entitled to bind an accused over to be of good behaviour simply on the ground that he has used his criminal trial as a vehicle for airing his views. This was held by the Divisional Court in *R v Ipswich Crown Court, ex parte Eris*,[1] where, after E had been acquitted of possessing a hacksaw blade with intent to cause damage to Sizewell Nuclear Power Station, the judge had imposed a binding-over order for three years not because of any future breach of the peace apprehended but to punish the accused who (in his opinion) had used the court as a platform to publicise his views on nuclear issues. The correct course, said the Court, was to exercise judicial control during the trial and, if necessary, use the contempt of court procedure.

---

1   (1989) *The Times*, 23 February, DC.

2.43 Subject to what is said below, if the court is minded to bind over a person it must warn him, give its reasons and give him an opportunity to be heard.[1] Failure to do so can result in the binding over being quashed by certiorari on an application for judicial review on grounds of breach of natural justice.[1]

It is not strictly necessary to warn an acquitted or convicted accused who comes into court knowing and prepared to meet the nature of the case against him,[2] although it has been said in relation to an acquitted person, that it would be 'courteous and perhaps wise to do so',[3] so that he can address the court on the matter. Failure to do so, however, is not a breach of natural justice.

Where a person shows by his behaviour in the face of the court that a breach of the peace is imminent, natural justice does not require him to be given a warning or the chance to make representations before being bound over.[4]

However, the rules about the opportunity to make representations as to the size of the recognisance and about surety, referred to in paras **2.45–2.46**, apply even in these cases.

---

1   *R v Wilkins* [1907] 2 KB 380, DC (complainant); *Sheldon v Bromfield JJ* [1964] 2 All ER 131, DC (prosecution witnesses); *R v Aubrey-Fletcher, ex parte Thompson* [1969] 2 All ER 846 at 847, per Lord Parker CJ (binding over on adjournment); *R v Hendon JJ, ex parte Gorchein* [1974] 1 All ER 168, DC (person complainant and witness); *R v Keighley JJ, ex parte Stoyles* [1976] Crim LR 573, DC; *R v South Molton JJ, ex parte Ankerson* [1988] 3 All ER 989, DC (binding over accused prior to determination of matter).

2   *R v Woking JJ, ex parte Gossage* [1973] 2 All ER 621, DC (acquitted accused); *R v Hendon JJ, ex parte Gorchein* above, at 170, per Lord Widgery CJ; *R v Crown Court at Lincoln, ex parte Jude* [1997] 3 All ER 737 at 740, per Auld J (acquitted or convicted accused). An accused in respect of whom the Crown Court proposes to direct the indictment to remain on the file is in much 'the same category as a convicted or acquitted accused, provided the judge knows enough about the circumstances to enable him to form a judgment about the need for a binding-over order': *Crown Court at Lincoln, ex parte Jude*, ibid.

3   *R v Woking JJ, ex parte Gossage*, above, at 623, per Lord Widgery CJ.

4   *R v North London Metropolitan Magistrate, ex parte Haywood* [1973] 3 All ER 50, DC.

Binding-over order

2.44 There does not appear to be any limit on the duration of a binding-over order. In *R v Edgar*,[1] however, the Court of Criminal Appeal said:

> 'Objection is taken in the case to the fact that the defendant has been ordered to enter into a recognisance for an indefinite period. It is not necessary to decide whether there is a power to order a recognisance to be entered into for life; we do not decide that there is no such power. It seems, however, that in all cases it has been the practice to limit the time for recognisance, and in no case has an indefinite time been inserted in the order. The court thinks it is better, whether there is power to leave the time indefinite or not, that the usual practice should be followed, and a time inserted.'

Commenting on this in *R v South Molton JJ, ex parte Ankerson*,[2] where a number of accused had been bound over to be of good behaviour, pending the fixing of a date for committal proceedings, no finite period being specified on the grounds of their 'misbehaviour' in court, McCowan J said: 'I would not myself seek to make a general pronouncement on this matter, but certainly I would say that it was not appropriate to bind over until the date of committal. There ought to have been a finite date expressed in this case.'

There is no limit on the sum specified in the recognisance of the person bound over or of a surety, but this – like the duration of an order – is subject to an overall requirement of reasonableness.

Strangely, the wording of s 1(7) of the Justices of the Peace Act 1968[3] seems to permit a person to be bound over under it without entering into a personal recognisance, if there is a surety or sureties, although it seems that in practice this does not occur.

It is not possible to include specific conditions in a bind-over order to keep the peace or to be of good behaviour.[4] Thus, the appellate courts have declared invalid conditions directing the person bound to keep away from a specified nightclub for 12 months;[5] forbidding the carrying of a firearm;[6] or forbidding the person bound over to teach or try to teach anyone under 18 for three years.[7] Thus, a binding-over order is made in general terms and cannot relate the required future conduct to the misconduct which led to the making of the order. The only exception is that, where the court acts of its own motion, a person can be bound over under the procedure to be of good behaviour to a named person[8] or to the world in general (or somewhere in between). The extent of a binding over to be of good behaviour under s 115 of the 1980 Act was dealt with in para **2.34**.

The effect of the inability of the courts to insert conditions in an order is that a person can only be given general guidance by the court as to how he can avoid forfeiture of his recognisance. As the Law Commission has pointed out:

> 'At least technically speaking, someone who is bound over to be of good behaviour will be in peril if he or she commits any further act which is deemed not to be "of good behaviour", even if it is an act very different in kind from the species of bad behaviour for which he or she was originally bound over.'[9]

The same point can be made about binding someone over to keep the peace. The availability of a power to insert conditions would go some way to resolving the problems in respect of the ECHR outlined in para **2.27**.

1 (1913) 9 Cr App R 13 at 14.
2 [1988] 3 All ER 989 at 992.
3 See para **2.36**.
4 *R v Ayu* [1958] 3 All ER 636, CCA; *Goodlad v Chief Constable of South Yorkshire* [1979] Crim LR 51, Crown Court in appellate capacity; *R v Randall* (1987) 8 Cr App R (S) 433, CA and DC.
5 *Lister v Morgan* [1978] Crim LR 292, Crown Court in appellate capacity.
6 *Goodlad v Chief Constable of South Yorkshire*, above.
7 *R v Randall*, above.
8 As was done in *Wilson v Skeock* (1949) 113 JP 494, DC.
9 *Binding Over* (Law Com Report 222, 1994) para 4.36.

2.45 Unless the amount of the recognisance is trivial, it is a denial of natural justice not to inquire into a person's means and give him a chance to make representations about its amount before fixing its level.[1] If this is not done, the binding-over order can be quashed by certiorari on an application for judicial review.[1] It was held in a case decided by the Divisional Court in 1997 that the sum of £500 was not so trivial an amount as to dispense with the need to ascertain the person's means.[2] Since 'triviality' must be relative to a person's means, it is submitted that it would be wise for a court always to inquire into a person's means before fixing the recognisance for his bind-over. Indeed, there is authority that a court should always do so.[3]

1 *R v Central Criminal Court, ex parte Boulding* [1984] 1 All ER 766, DC; *R v Atkinson* (1988) 10 Cr App Rep (S) 740, CA; *R v Nottingham Crown Court, ex parte Brace* (1989) 154 JP 161, DC.
2 *R v Crown Court at Lincoln, ex parte Jude* [1997] 3 All ER 737, DC.
3 In *R v South Molton JJ, ex parte Ankerson* [1988] 3 All ER 989 at 991, McCowan J stated: 'In my judgment an inquiry must be made into the means, however small the figure may appear to the justices to be'. Taylor LJ, as he then was, said 'before fixing the amount of the recognisance [the magistrates] should inquire as to the defendant's means': [1988] 3 All ER at 992.

2.46 A court is not obliged to require a surety or sureties. However, if a court is minded to require a surety or sureties it must give the person to be bound over the chance to make representations as to the availability and suitability of a surety, and as to the sum in which the surety will be bound.[1] The taking of sureties appears to be unusual.[2]

1   *R v Clerkenwell Metropolitan Stipendiary Magistrate, ex parte Hooper* [1998] 4 All ER 193, DC.
2   *Binding Over: The Issues* (Law Com, 1987) para 3.3.

Refusal to enter into a recognisance

2.47 A court clearly cannot force someone to be a surety, but nor can it force the person whom it orders to be bound over to enter into recognisances to do so.[1] This has sometimes been described as a requirement of consent as a pre-requisite to a binding-over order,[2] but this is not a strictly accurate description, as explained in *R v Crown Court at Lincoln, ex parte Jude*.[3] Thus, there is no need to ask the person concerned for his consent to the court's order, although he cannot be forced to comply with it.

1   For an acknowledgement of this, see *Veater v G* [1981] 2 All ER 304 at 309.
2   Ibid; *R v South Molton JJ, ex parte Ankerson* [1988] 3 All ER 989 at 991 and 992, per McCowan J and Taylor LJ.
3   [1997] 3 All ER 737, DC.

2.48 If the defendant in a case heard on complaint under s 115 of the 1980 Act refuses to enter into a binding-over recognisance or is unable or unwilling to find sureties, the magistrates can commit him to prison for a maximum of six months or until he sooner complies with the order.[1]

The same power is available to justices where they act of their own motion, except that there appears to be no maximum limit on the period of imprisonment which may be imposed. If the person refusing to consent to being bound over has been convicted of an offence in respect of which that order is made, the normal six-month limit on imprisonment under s 31 of the 1980 Act is inapplicable, because it only applies to imprisonment for an offence, whereas the power of imprisonment here is one for refusing to consent to a civil order. If a term of imprisonment is one which no reasonable bench could decide on, it could be challenged by an application for judicial review on the basis of the *Wednesbury* principle.

Committal to prison is the only sanction available to the magistrates where a person refuses to be bound over,[2] subject to the following rules about someone under 21 who refuses. It is certainly odd that it is always available for a refusal to consent to being bound over when the behaviour which triggers the binding over may not be an imprisonable offence and, indeed, may not be an offence at all.

There is no power of imprisonment or detention in respect of someone under 18.[3] However, this does not prevent a court binding over such a person who is prepared to enter into a recognisance.[2] If he is not, a magistrates' court may order such a person to attend an attendance centre instead.[4]

In the case of someone aged 18 or over but under 21 who refuses to enter into a recognisance, the power to commit to detention under s 9(1)(c) of the Criminal Justice Act 1982 is available, subject to the terms of s 9(5).[5] Section 9(1)(c) empowers a court to order those aged 18–20 to be detained for 'contempt of court or any kindred offences'. A refusal to enter into a recognisance vis-à-vis a magistrates' court is not a contempt of court for the purposes of that court's contempt jurisdiction under s 12 of the Contempt of Court Act 1981, but it is regarded as a 'kindred offence' in respect of a magistrates' court for this purpose,[5] a somewhat doubtful interpretation.

No specific provision is made by the Justices of the Peace Act 1968, s 1(7) or otherwise, in respect of a person who refuses to enter into a recognisance or to provide sureties on the order of the Crown Court or any other court of record. It would seem that the matter should be dealt with as a contempt of court,[6] in which case the maximum sentence of imprisonment is two years.[7] What was said above about those under 18 is equally applicable here.

---

1   Magistrates' Courts Act 1980, s 115(3) (complaint under s 115).
2   *Conlan v Oxford* (1984) 79 Cr App R 157, DC.
3   *Veater v G* [1981] 2 All ER 304, DC; *Conlan v Oxford*, above. The Criminal Justice Act 1982, s 1(1) prohibits imprisonment of someone under 18.
4   Criminal Justice Act 1982, s 17(1)(a). However, see Gibson 'Refusal to be bound over – a game of chess' (1984) 148 JPN 230 for doubts about the practicalities of this.
5   *Howley v Oxford* (1985) 81 Cr App Rep 246, DC; *Chief Constable of Surrey Constabulary v Ridley* [1985] Crim LR 725, DC.
6   *Archbold* (2000) para 5.272 suggests this may be the solution.
7   Contempt of Court Act 1981, s 14(1).

Appeal against order

2.49 A binding-over order is not a conviction for the purposes of the various provisions about appeal against conviction. However, if it is made in relation to an accused person who has been convicted, an appeal against it as an appeal against sentence is possible in the normal way.

In relation to an order by a magistrates' court, s 1 of the Magistrates' Courts (Appeals from Binding Over Orders) Act 1956 provides that where a person is bound over by a magistrates' court, he may appeal to the Crown Court. The appeal is by way of a re-hearing,[1] and, unless the appellant is prepared to admit the evidence which was before the magistrates, the facts justifying the making of the order must be strictly proved in the Crown Court by sworn evidence, which may be cross-examined.[1]

The operation of this provision is problematical where someone other than the defendant or accused has been bound over. Section 1(2)(a) states that the other party to the proceedings which were the occasion of the making of the order shall be the respondent to the appeal. Where the order is made in respect of a complainant/prosecutor or a witness, the other party (the defendant or accused) will have no interest in the appeal, and is most unlikely to attend its hearing to support an order which he did not ask the magistrates to make. This point was raised in Law Commission Working Paper *Binding Over: The Issues* where it was said:[2]

> 'It seems that in the past some Crown Court judges have been prepared to take account of a statement of what has happened before the magistrates, even without the magistrates being represented, provided all parties have seen and considered that statement, but other judges have not been prepared to accept this. Must, then, the magistrates appear in person to support the making of their order? The position has to some extent been clarified by the decision in *Preston Crown Court, ex parte Pamplin*,[3] which stated that the function of the justices is limited to appearing and assisting the court and in effect "to do the things which an amicus curiae could do if he appeared before the court", stating the surrounding circumstances in so far as they are not in dispute. According to Donaldson LJ in that case, however:
>
> "... [the justices] cannot be cross-examined as to any disputed matters of fact. In this case, ... the Crown Court was placed in a very difficult situation indeed in that there

was no-one appearing before them who could put contested facts before them. It may very well be that in those circumstances they should have allowed the appeal ..."

The consequence may be that if, on an appeal by a prosecutor who has been bound over, the original defendant does not appear in order to put contested facts before the court, the Crown Court will be obliged to allow the appeal, even though the making of the order was quite justified. Lack of enthusiasm on the part of parties being required to argue an appeal surely does not make for properly conducted proceedings.'

A binding-over order made by a magistrates' court may also be questioned on an appeal by case stated to the High Court on the ground that it is wrong in law or in excess of jurisdiction.[4]

It remains the position that, leaving aside an appeal against sentence if a binding-over order is made on conviction,[5] there is no right of appeal against a binding-over order made by the Crown Court.[6] Given the consequences of such an order there ought always to be a right of appeal on its merits.

A binding-over order made in excess of jurisdiction, breach of natural justice or some other judicially renewable ground by a magistrates' court or by the Crown Court[7] may be challenged on an application for judicial review and quashed by an order of certiorari.[8] Normally, an appeal by case stated from a magistrates' court is a more appropriate mode of challenge on a point of law than an application for judicial review, where both are available, because the case stated will identify any facts critical to the resolution of the issue.[9]

---

1   *Shaw v Hamilton* [1982] 2 All ER 718, DC.
2   Law Com WP No 103 (1987), para 3.6.
3   [1981] Crim LR 338, DC.
4   Magistrates' Courts Act 1980, s 111. For an example, see *Beatty v Gillbanks* (1882) 9 QBD 308, DC.
5   Per *R v Inner London Crown Court, ex parte Benjamin* (1987) 85 Cr App R 267, DC, relying on *R v Williams* [1982] 3 All ER 1092, CA (a case concerned with binding over to come up for judgment).
6   *R v Randall* (1986) 8 Cr App R (S) 433, DC and CA; *R v Inner London Crown Court, ex parte Benjamin*, above.
7   Binding over by the Crown Court as a court of trial is not part of the jurisdiction of the Crown Court 'in matters relating to trial on indictment': *R v Inner London Crown Court, ex parte Benjamin* above; *R v Randall* above.
8   See, eg, *R v Aubrey-Fletcher, ex parte Thompson* [1969] 2 All ER 846, DC; *R v Ilminster JJ, ex parte Hamilton* (1983) *The Times*, 23 June, DC; *R v Central Criminal Court, ex parte Boulding* [1984] 1 All ER 766, DC; *R v Morpeth Ward JJ, ex parte Ward* (1992) 95 Cr App R 215, DC.
9   *R v Ipswich Crown Court, ex parte Baldwin (note)* [1981] 1 All ER 596, *sub nom Felixstowe JJ, ex parte Baldwin* (1980) 72 Cr App Rep 131, DC; *R v Morpeth Ward JJ, ex parte Ward*, above.

Breach of binding-over order

2.50   A breach of the recognisance must be properly proved.[1] In *R v Marlow JJ, ex parte O'Sullivan*,[2] the Divisional Court held that, as proceedings for breach are civil proceedings, the civil standard of proof (ie on the balance of probabilities) applies. This represents the current state of the law, although it was doubted, obiter, by the Divisional Court in *Percy v DPP*,[3] on the ground that the rule fails to reflect the implications of the broken recognisance being enforceable in the same way as a fine, with the consequent power of imprisonment in default. The inconsistency of approach between standards of proof at the order-making and enforcement stages is puzzling, to say the least.

Where a person bound over by a magistrates' court is proved to have failed to comply with the terms of the binding over, a magistrates' court for the petty sessions area may declare the recognisance to be forfeited and adjudge each person bound thereby, whether as principal or as surety, to pay the sum in which he is respectively bound,[4] in whole or part.[5] The magistrates' court must not declare a recognisance forfeited except by order made on complaint;[4] it cannot act of its own motion. A magistrates' court does not have power to order imprisonment for breach of a recognisance, although imprisonment can be imposed if the sum forfeited is not duly paid or recovered.

Likewise, the Crown Court may order forfeiture in whole or part of a recognisance (whether of the person bound or a surety) where a binding-over order made by it has been broken. It cannot impose a term of imprisonment or any other sanction although imprisonment can be imposed if the sum forfeited is not duly paid or recovered.[6]

This inability to imprison someone for breach of a recognisance can be contrasted with the power to imprison if a person refuses to enter into a recognisance in the first instance. The law is certainly anomalous in this area.

Before a court makes a determination about forfeiture, the person(s) concerned should be told about the nature of the breach alleged and given a chance to present evidence, call witnesses or give an explanation.[7]

There is no right of appeal against an adjudication of forfeiture of a recognisance.[8] However, an aggrieved person could apply for judicial review to have the adjudication quashed by certiorari on the ground that it was in excess of jurisdiction, in breach of natural justice etc.

---

1   *R v Pine* (1934) 24 Cr App R 10, CCA.
2   [1983] 3 All ER 578, DC.
3   [1995] 3 All ER 124 at 134.
4   Magistrates' Courts Act 1980, s 120(2).
5   Ibid, s 120(3).
6   *R v Finch* (1963) 47 Cr App R 58, CCA; *R v Gilbert* (1974) unreported, CA.
7   *R v McGregor* [1945] 2 All ER 180.
8   *R v Durham JJ, ex parte Laurent* [1945] KB 33, DC.

Law Commission report

2.51 In 1994, the Law Commission published a report, *Binding Over*,[1] which contained considerable adverse criticism of the law in this area. It firmly recommended that the powers of binding over described above should be abolished without replacement. It did so despite the fact that the majority of those consulted were in favour of the retention of those powers (notwithstanding the objections of principle identified) because of their practical advantages, such as the ability of a court to defuse a situation without conferring the stigma of a conviction, the saving of court time and money, and the additional sentencing option.

Considerations which weighed with the Commission included:

(a) a criminal sanction was now available for many forms of anti-social behaviour for which previously only binding over was available (such as the Public Order Act 1986, ss 4–5, dealt with in Chapter 4 and, outside public order law,

statutory offences dealing with malicious telephone calls, poison pen letters and kerb-crawling);
(b) the 'own motion' procedure was unsatisfactory, eg in relation to who could be subject to it;
(c) the vagueness of some of the law, eg the concept of 'good behaviour';
(d) there had been modern developments in police cautioning and diverting anti-social offenders from the courts;
(e) it was impracticable to design a satisfactory new form of judicial warning system.

The Law Commission's conclusion in favour of abolition was strengthened by the conclusion that in many material respects the practice relating to binding over would breach the ECHR in terms of the certainty and ascertainability of a citizen's obligations, the limitation on arrest and detention (Art 5), the requirements of a fair trial (Art 6) and the right to freedoms of expression and assembly (Arts 10 and 11).

---

1   Law Com No 222.

2.52 Although the decision in *Steel v UK*[1] did not find a binding-over order based on a breach of the peace to contravene Art 5 or Art 10 of the ECHR, this was a decision on the facts and does not contradict the Law Commission's recommendations.[2] The decision in *Hashman v UK*[1] in respect of binding-over orders based on conduct contra bonos mores means that the whole issue of 'good behaviour' in binding-over law adds urgency to the need to reform the law.

A point of interest arising from *Steel v UK* is that the European Court held, for the purposes of Art 6 (right to a fair trial on 'criminal charge'),[3] that binding-over proceedings are criminal in nature. It would seem that the procedure under s 115 of the 1980 Act meets the requirements of Art 6.[4] On the other hand, there must be doubts about whether the 'own motion' procedure does in terms of the principle of 'equality of arms' inherent in the right to a fair trial under Art 6(1), which requires that a party has a reasonable opportunity of presenting his case to the court under conditions which do not place him at a substantial disadvantage vis-à-vis his opponent (the court in this instance),[5] and which is reinforced by the specific guarantees in Art 6(3). Of these, the right to be informed promptly of the nature and cause of the accusation and the right to have adequate time for the preparation of a defence are particularly relevant. Under Art 6, proof of a criminal charge does not require proof beyond reasonable doubt.[6] In this respect, the requirements of English law certainly seem to exceed those of the ECHR.[7]

---

1   See para **2.27**.
2   See Ashworth [1998] Crim LR 893 at 896.
3   In *Engel v The Netherlands* (1976) Ser A, no 22; 1 EHRR 647, ECtHR, it was held that 'criminal charge' in Art 6 has an autonomous character, ie it cannot be interpreted merely by reference to the domestic law of an individual State.
4   See Mead 'Human Rights Act – a panacea for public protest' (1999) 4 J Civ Lib 7.
5   *Kaufman v Belgium* (1986) 50 D&R 98, ECommHR.
6   *Austria v Italy* (1963) 6 YB 740, ECommHR.
7   In *Steel v UK* Application No 24838/94, the European Commission considered that it was not a breach of Art 6 to apply the civil standard of proof.

ANTI-SOCIAL BEHAVIOUR ORDERS

2.53 Section 1 of the Crime and Disorder Act 1998 gave magistrates' courts the power to make an anti-social behaviour order (ASBO) to deal with public disorder, harassment, nuisance and other kinds of anti-social behaviour. The power is discussed here in the context of public order.[1] Examples in that context are persistent unruly behaviour by a small group of individuals on a housing estate, who may cause minor damage to property, and persistent abusive behaviour towards elderly people or other vulnerable people causing them alarm and distress.[2] This is the same type of conduct as that at which s 5 of the Public Order Act 1986 is aimed.

An ASBO is made in civil proceedings. It is akin to an injunction. It prohibits the defendant from doing anything described in the order. Breach of an ASBO without reasonable excuse is an offence. A criminal sanction for breach of a civil order is unusual, although not unique.[3]

To assist in the operation of the rules on ASBOs, the Government issued in 1999 non-statutory guidance.[2] Although it is not technically binding, the Guidance is intended for use by all involved with ASBOs; a failure to do so might form part of an application for judicial review.[4] In any event, the spirit of the guidance was set out by ministers during the House of Commons Committee stage of the Bill, and thus forms part of the statutory intent for the purposes of any *Pepper v Hart* argument.[5]

When this book went to press, very few orders had been made, only ten in the first six months of the operation of s 1,[6] although there were indications that they were likely to become more common.

---

1   For a discussion of ASBOs in all contexts, see Card and Ward *The Crime and Disorder Act 1998 – A Practitioner's Guide* (Jordans, 1998) ch 5.
2   *Anti-Social Behaviour Orders – Guidance* (Home Office, 1999), hereafter *Guidance*.
3   For other examples, see paras **4.93** and **7.116**.
4   See para **2.61**.
5   *Pepper (Inspector of Taxes) v Hart* [1993] 1 All ER 42, HL.
6   HC Deb, vol 340, col 549.

Rationale and background

2.54 The purpose of the ASBO is to provide a civil remedy to prevent the repetition of anti-social conduct. Many, although not all, anti-social acts amount to criminal offences, for example, under ss 4–5 of the Public Order Act 1986,[1] s 1 of the Criminal Damage Act 1971, ss 79–82 of the Environmental Protection Act 1990, the Noise Act 1996 or s 2 of the Protection from Harassment Act 1997.[1] Common law powers relating to breaches of the peace may be applicable; in particular, the binding-over powers of a magistrates' court are relevant. Like a binding-over order, an ASBO seeks to regulate future conduct.

ASBOs are not intended for private inter-neighbour disputes. They are intended to deal with criminal activity which, for one reason or another, cannot be proven to the criminal standard (but see para **2.80**), or where criminal proceedings are inappropriate, and with sub-criminal activity.[2] The Guidance states that:

'As a general rule, an application for an [ASBO] should be made either when other methods to prevent further misbehaviour have failed or when such methods have been considered but have been deemed either to be inappropriate in the circumstances or to be less effective than an order.'[3]

---

1   See Chapter 4.
2   *Guidance* para 2.6.
3   Ibid, para 3.13.

2.55 The ASBO provisions supplement civil proceedings under the Housing Act 1996 and the Protection from Harassment Act 1997, as well as prosecutions for offences of the type just mentioned.

Section 152 of the Housing Act 1996 gives the High Court or a county court, on an application by a local authority, the power to grant an injunction prohibiting a person in respect of residential premises to which s 152 applies,[1] from:

(a) engaging in or threatening to engage in conduct causing or likely to cause a nuisance or annoyance to a person residing in, visiting or otherwise engaging in a lawful activity in such premises or in the locality of such premises;

(b) using or threatening to use such premises for immoral or illegal purposes; or

(c) entering such premises or being found in the locality of any such premises.

This provision was introduced to combat the menace and nuisance caused by young persons, often in gangs, on local authority estates. Although the scope of a s 152 application might appear to be wide, the court has to be satisfied that the respondent has used, or threatened to use, violence against a person mentioned in (a), and that there is a significant risk of harm to that person or a person of that description if the injunction is not granted.[2] Conduct which might found a s 152 application will almost always amount to anti-social behaviour. However, an ASBO goes further in that it is not subject to the limitations and preconditions set out above. It is also not confined to conduct in, or in the locality of, local authority housing.

---

1   Housing Act 1996, s 152, applies to residential premises which are dwelling-houses held under secure or introductory tenancies from the local authority, or accommodation provided under Part VII of the 1996 Act, or Part III of the Housing Act 1985 (homelessness): 1996 Act, s 152(2).
2   1996 Act, s 152(3).

2.56 The Protection from Harassment Act 1997, dealt with in paras **4.89–4.96**, gives individuals the protection of the criminal or civil law in respect of a course of conduct which causes harassment. The 1997 Act was prompted by public concern about the harassment of individuals, but its provisions are not limited to such situations. They can apply where harassment is aimed at a community. A civil action under the 1997 Act for damages or an injunction requires a claimant or claimants to pursue it, and this may depend on the availability of the financial resources, private or through the legal aid scheme.

The conditions for making an order

2.57 By s 1(4) of the 1998 Act, the conditions for the making of an ASBO are the two conditions set out in s 1(1):

'(a) that the person has acted, since the commencement date [1 April 1999[1]], in an anti-social manner, that is to say, in a manner that caused or was likely to cause harassment, alarm or distress to one or more persons not of the same household as himself; and

(b) that such an order is necessary to protect persons in the local government area in which the harassment, alarm or distress was caused or was likely to be caused from further anti-social acts by him.'

In England and Wales, 'local government area' means a district or London borough, the City of London, the Isle of Wight and the Isles of Scilly; in Wales it means a county or county borough.[2]

---

1 Crime and Disorder Act 1998 (Commencement No 3 and Appointed Day) Order 1999 (SI 1999/3263).
2 1998 Act, s 1(12).

2.58 An application under s 1 is made by a complaint to the magistrates' court whose commission area includes the place where it is alleged that the harassment, alarm or distress was caused or was likely to be caused. Where there is more than one such area, there is no reason why an application cannot be made to the court for any one of such areas, nor does the Act prohibit multiple applications being made to different magistrates' courts. An application under s 1 must be made in writing in the form specified in the Magistrates' Courts (Sex Offender and Anti-social Behaviour Orders) Rules 1998.[1]

---

1 SI 1998/2682.

Who can apply for an order?

2.59 An application for an ASBO cannot be made by an individual, but only by a relevant authority, represented by an authorised advocate employed or instructed by it. Such an application may be made by a relevant authority if it appears to it that the conditions set out in para **2.57** are fulfilled with respect to a person aged 10 or over. 'Relevant authority' means the council for the relevant 'local government area' defined in para **2.57** *or* the chief officer of police for the police[1] area any part of which lies within the relevant local government area.[2] As can be seen, an application for an ASBO can be made by one relevant authority. However, one relevant authority 'shall not make an application' without consulting each other relevant authority.[3] Thus, a local authority must consult the relevant chief officer(s) of police, and a chief officer of police must consult the local authority and any other relevant chief officer. Which agency takes the lead will be a matter to be discussed and agreed locally within the framework of the statutory partnership to prevent crime created by ss 5–7 of the 1998 Act.[4] Implicit in the above framework is the fact that a court which is being asked to make an order should expect to have the view of all the relevant authorities before deciding whether or not to make an order, and is entitled to know what the result of the consultation was. A court is entitled to decline to make an order until it is told what the views of all the relevant authorities are.

---

1 See para **6.26** fn 1.
2 1998 Act, s 1(1) and (12).
3 Ibid, s 1(2).
4 *Community Safety Orders: A Consultation Paper* (Home Office, 1997) para 1.

2.60 What happens if a relevant authority entitled to make an application does not consult the other (or others) is unclear. Despite the view taken by the Government in its Consultation Paper[1] that a court would be able to grant an order on the application of one authority if satisfied that it would be right to do so, even if the observations of another authority are not available or the support of another authority is not forthcoming, it is submitted that the requirement to consult is mandatory. This conclusion is reached not only because the words 'shall not' are indicative of a mandatory requirement, but also on the more pragmatic ground that, otherwise, the person who is the subject of the proposed application would be at risk of different approaches by the two agencies. It also appears to have become the intent of the Government by the time that the legislation reached the Committee stage in the House of Commons.[2]

The relevant authorities are not required to agree before an application is made, but a failure to do so may weaken the case in court.

---

1 *Community Safety Orders: A Consultation Paper* (Home Office, 1997) para 6.
2 See Alun Michael, MP, Minister of State, Home Office, Report of HC Standing Committee B, col 58 (1998).

2.61 If an individual wants an ASBO made, he will make representations to a relevant authority (ie the local authority or police). If neither of those authorities decides to seek a s 1 order, the individual is left to seek his own remedy against the troublemaker(s), or, possibly, may seek to challenge the decision not to proceed by an application for judicial review. Whether an application for an ASBO is made is a matter of executive discretion, and not subject to appeal. It may be likened to the decision to commence the prosecution process. For that reason, the decision not to seek an order may, potentially, be subject to an application for judicial review.[1]

---

1 A decision of the police not to prosecute or of the CPS to discontinue a prosecution is judicially reviewable on a limited basis: *R v Metropolitan Police Comr, ex parte Blackburn* [1968] 1 All ER 763, CA; *R v DPP, ex parte C* [1995] 1 Cr App R 136, DC; *R v DPP, ex parte Panayiotou* [1997] COD 83, DC; *R v DPP, ex parte Treadaway* (1997) *The Times*, 31 October, DC.

The requirements for an order

2.62 The applicant must show not only (per s 1(1)(a)) that the defendant has, since the commencement of s 1 (1 April 1999), acted in an anti-social manner (as defined by the Act), but also (per s 1(1)(b)) that such an order is necessary to protect persons in the local government area where the harassment, alarm or distress was caused, or likely to be caused, from further anti-social acts by him.

'Acting in an anti-social manner' means acting in a manner that causes, or is likely to cause, harassment, alarm or distress to one or more persons not of the same household as the person engaging in the act or acts. If that is not the case, no order can be made. Pre-commencement acts cannot be cited in aggregation with post-commencement acts to establish anti-social behaviour. By this means, retrospectivity is avoided. Although a court cannot take the pre-commencement conduct into account in determining whether the threshold condition for the making of an order has been satisfied, it can take that pre-commencement conduct into account in determining whether, on the merits of the case, an order should be made. It is clearly important for a court to know that conduct is not isolated, but is conduct that has continued for some months.

2.63 'Acting' in an anti-social manner encompasses not only a course of conduct but also single acts. There is nothing in s 1 to prevent a court from making an order on the basis of one act which meets the threshold condition. This may be because only one act can be proved or, less likely, because only one act occurred. A court should be slow to make an order based on a single act, given that the rationale of the provisions is to prevent on-going anti-social behaviour. Section 1(1)(b) makes it clear that an order must be necessary to protect persons in the local government area from further anti-social acts by him. The main test is whether there is a pattern of 'behaviour' over a period of time that cannot be dealt with easily or adequately through the prosecution of those concerned for a single 'snapshot' or criminal event.[1]

---

1   *Guidance* para 3.10.

2.64 A question of fundamental importance is: what is an 'act'? This term is defined by the *Shorter Oxford English Dictionary* as including 'thing done, a deed, the process of doing something', and in its normal sense suggests a positive act. Omissions are not 'acts', and to apply 'act' in the context of s 1 in this way may lead to its scope being somewhat more limited than might have been supposed. Examples of 'acts' in the present context are the shouting of racist abuse, throwing stones at windows on an estate and the daubing of slogans. On the other hand, simply failing to prevent or stop an anti-social situation or anti-social behaviour by others, is an omission to act, and not an act.

Often an act and refusal (ie failure) to act go hand-in-hand. The youth engaging in loutish behaviour who refuses to stop is both acting and refusing to act. Suppose, however, that a householder whose children are continually abusing local old people on the estate and causing distress regularly fails to take any action. There is no 'act' in any ordinary sense of the term by the householder (as opposed to the children). Unless 'act' is given an unusual meaning, an ASBO cannot be made against the householder or anyone else who has failed to intervene to prevent or stop an anti-social situation. In the above example, the children, if aged 10 or over, could of course be made subject to an ASBO.

Anti-social manner

2.65 As part of the conditions for an ASBO the defendant must be proved to have acted in an anti-social manner, ie 'in a manner that caused, or was likely to cause harassment, alarm or distress to one or more persons not of the same household as himself'. The term, 'anti-social manner' is characterised by breadth and vagueness, and could be open to objection on the basis that it will catch conduct which is unorthodox or unusual, eccentric or bizarre, but which, nevertheless, is conduct which ought not to be the subject of the legal process. However, the limitation of the term to conduct causing, or likely to cause, harassment, alarm or distress must be emphasised.

The effect of all this is that the use of the term 'anti-social' in s 1 has no real significance other than to mark, in judgmental terms through the label 'anti-social', the objectionable nature of such conduct, measured by the effects of the conduct rather than the conduct itself.

2.66 Perfectly lawful conduct may cause harassment, alarm or distress, and be a trigger for an ASBO, although often the behaviour will also be such as to constitute an offence, eg under ss 4, 4A or 5 of the Public Order Act 1986 or s 2 of the Protection from Harassment Act 1997, or to give rise to the powers of the police to deal with an actual or apprehended breach of the peace. Alun Michael, MP, the then Minister of State, Home Office, stated, during the passage of the Act, that it was intended that the orders be used in respect of criminal or 'sub-criminal' activity,[1] not for 'run of the mill civil disputes between neighbours', petty intolerance, minor one-off disorderly acts or the penalising of the eccentric. Where the relevant behaviour is criminal, the ASBO should be used if criminal procedures might not be appropriate or might not prevent anti-social behaviour. The term 'sub-criminal' activity was not defined by the Minister, and is a term with which lawyers may feel unhappy: either behaviour is criminal, or it is not. However, the examples given indicate the sort of lawful behaviour which, it is envisaged, might fall within the scope of s 1 of the 1998 Act: arguments with neighbours, peppered with threats; persistent loud noise at anti-social hours; the posting of excrement through the letter-box of a neighbour who dared to complain; the dumping of refuse all over the place, perhaps in neighbours' gardens; abusive language and intimidating behaviour; and the intimidation and bullying of neighbours' children on the way to and from school.

---

1   Report of HC Standing Committee B, col 47 (1998).

2.67 As in other criminal offences where they appear, the meaning of 'harassment', 'alarm' and 'distress' would seem to be a question of fact for the magistrates' court to decide, according to the ordinary and natural meaning of those terms.[1]

---

1   See paras **4.28–4.30**.

2.68 Conduct which falls within the ambit of public order offences, particularly s 5 of the 1986 Act,[1] will often, although not always, be within the ambit of an ASBO. The individual who shouts threats or abuse, throws stones or daubs slogans on an individual's house may well be guilty of an offence under s 5 and within the ambit of these provisions.

There are differences. Under ss 4–5 of the 1986 Act, there needs to be threatening, abusive or insulting behaviour, or disorderly conduct. There is no such requirement in s 1. Section 5 of the 1986 Act requires the conduct, or display, to be within the sight or hearing of a person likely to be caused harassment, alarm or distress. No such limitation exists in respect of s 1 of the 1998 Act. Thus, while dropping a threatening letter through a letter box of an intended recipient's house has been held not to be a s 5 offence,[2] it would be conduct which potentially falls within s 1. Further, an offence under s 4 of the 1986 Act must involve the 'use towards another' of threatening or abusive words or behaviour, meaning that the person at whom the behaviour was aimed must have been present to perceive it.[3] It is also concerned with conduct intended, or likely, to cause fear of (or to provoke) immediate unlawful violence.[4] These are not requirements for the purposes of s 1.

There is nothing to prevent the making of an ASBO in respect of a person who has already been prosecuted for a criminal offence based on the conduct that is relied upon to satisfy the threshold condition. The rules against double jeopardy do not prevent this. Making an ASBO in such a case can be justified on the ground that the purposes of the two processes are different. A criminal prosecution is designed to punish an individual for his conduct. By contrast, the purpose of the s 1 order is to take legal action to seek a civil order to prevent the repetition of conduct of a certain type, which has specified consequences.

1   See para **4.41**.
2   See para **4.44**.
3   See *Atkin v DPP* (1989) 89 Cr App R 199, DC; see para **4.8**.
4   See *Valentine v DPP* [1997] COD 339, DC; see para **4.13**.

2.69 Anti-social behaviour is defined by reference to its consequences or likely consequences. The nature of the conduct itself is irrelevant; it is its consequences or likely consequences that matter. The defendant must have acted in a manner that caused or was likely to cause 'harassment', 'alarm' or 'distress'. No intent or other state of mind need be proved, simply a causal link between the defendant's behaviour and one of these consequences or an objective likelihood[1] of such a consequence. As under s 5 of the Public Order Act 1986,[2] a victim of the conduct who was likely to be caused harassment etc need not be identified and the court can evaluate the likely effect of conduct without evidence from a victim (who may be reluctant to come forward), relying on the evidence of others, such as a police officer or council official, who have observed the behaviour. While the reasons for this may be understandable, it weakens the protection against the inappropriate application of the power to make an ASBO.

1   See para **4.15**.
2   See para **4.50**.

2.70 As a condition to the making of an order, the actual or likely harassment, alarm or distress need not be serious. Nevertheless, the seriousness of such harassment, alarm or distress will clearly be a relevant factor when the relevant authority decides whether or not to make an application, or when a magistrates' court decides whether or not an order should be made. In addition, the less serious the conduct the easier it may be to prove that it was reasonable; see para **2.72** below.

2.71 The harassment, alarm or distress, or likelihood of it, can be to one person or more than one person not of the same household[1] as the person against whom the order is sought. As mentioned in para **2.68**, a 'victim' does not have to be present, nor does the behaviour have to be within his sight or hearing. Because there need be only one 'victim', an order could be made, for example, where an old lady living alone on a housing estate is the subject of abuse or bullying. Likewise, an ASBO could be made where a black person, who is the only non-white in the area, suffers racial taunts and abuse. Of course, in some circumstances, the fact that there is only one person who suffers, or is likely to suffer, harassment etc, may be relevant to the question of the reasonableness[2] of the conduct of the defendant, but, as the above examples show, that is by no means inevitably so.

Although s 1 of the 1998 Act is aimed at conduct which is both anti-social and anti-community, and the fact that an application cannot be made by an individual but has to be made by a local authority or chief constable provides some means of ensuring the fulfilment of this aim, there is nothing in s 1 which adds 'anti-community' to the conditions for the making of an ASBO. Arguably, the wording of s 1(1)(b)[3] extends the operation of the order to cases where actual or likely harassment is to one neighbour in a neighbour-dispute. Section 1 does not confine its operation to anti-social acts committed in a public place: so to confine it would remove from its operation cases such as where a group of youths gather in the garden of one of their number to shout racial abuse and taunts at a black neighbour. By contrast, domestic violence victims are not likely to be covered by s 1.[4]

---

1   For the meaning of this term, see para **2.75**.
2   See para **2.72**.
3   See para **2.76**.
4   See para **2.75**.

Reasonable acts disregarded

2.72 Section 1(5) of the 1998 Act states that, in determining whether the condition in s 1(1)(a) is fulfilled, 'the court shall disregard any act of the defendant which he shows was reasonable in the circumstances'. The reasonableness of an act would seem to depend on its nature, purpose, circumstances and consequences (actual or likely), and not simply on its nature and circumstances. Clearly, the intention of s 1(5) is to take outside the scope of the condition in s 1(1)(a) behaviour which conforms to the normal standards of give-and-take of everyday life.

To regard s 1(5) as providing a 'defence', like the defences of reasonable conduct in ss 4A and 5 of the Public Order Act 1986[1] would, strictly speaking, be inaccurate. It requires a court to disregard certain conduct in determining whether one of the conditions for the making of a s 1 order is satisfied.

---

1   See paras **4.36** and **4.55**.

2.73 It is the reasonableness of the defendant's act or acts that has to be judged, not the reasonableness of the reaction, or likely reaction, of persons in the locality. However, such reaction may have a bearing on the reasonableness or otherwise of the defendant's conduct.

Section 1(5) clearly places the burden of establishing reasonableness on the respondent. The standard of proof will be the balance of probabilities.[1]

---

1   See *Miller v Minister of Pensions* [1947] 2 All ER 372.

2.74 Reasonableness is an important concept in keeping the use of s 1 of the 1998 Act within the boundaries of what Parliament intended. The scope of the wording of s 1(1) potentially goes far beyond the general intent of the legislation. That wording could clearly apply not only to the obvious anti-social types of behaviour commonly found on housing estates, but also to the activities of protesters, anti-hunt and road protest groups and the like. Because of the width of s 1(1), the disregard of reasonable conduct in determining whether the condition in s 1(1)(a) is fulfilled will be crucial, as will the exercise of discretion at both the application stage (by the police or local authority) and by the court, if an application is in fact made. The scope of s 1 can be limited by the courts themselves. The granting of an order is discretionary, not mandatory, even if the threshold conditions are satisfied: the court 'may' make an order.[1] It is open to the courts to refuse to grant applications that fall within the terms of s 1 but which appear to be neighbour rather than community disputes, or which do not appear deserving of intervention by way of a s 1 order. It should also be borne in mind that courts will find it extremely difficult to distinguish between neighbour disputes which have an 'anti-community' element and those which do not.

This discretion provides some safeguards. It is a matter of regret, and against normal principle, for safeguards against the misuse of powers to be dependent on executive or judicial discretion and not on clear legal preconditions and safeguards.[2]

---

1   1998 Act, s 1(4).
2   See para **2.91**.

The effect of anti-social behaviour

2.75 The scope of s 1 is limited to acts of anti-social behaviour which cause harassment, etc, or which are likely to do so, to one or more persons not of the same household. 'Household' is not defined by the Act and will, generally, be a question of fact and degree,[1] although there may be some cases where the only conclusion, as a matter of law, that a court can reach is that persons are part of the same household. It is not intended that s 1 should operate in cases of domestic incidents, disputes or violence. Thus, if violence or threatened violence occurs between man and wife, or unmarried partners, while they are living together, the appropriate remedies are those available under the Family Law Act 1996; this may be so even where the spouses or partners have temporarily separated. However, if violence or threatened violence occurs between a couple who are no longer of the same household (as is clearly the case where they are formally separated, whether by court order or otherwise) the potential arises for the grant of an order under s 1. Of course, in that situation a court will have to have regard to the appropriateness of the order being sought, bearing in mind the potential for an application for a non-molestation order under s 42 or s 45 of the 1996 Act. Further, unlike such orders, an ASBO can be sought only by the relevant local authority or chief constable. This provides a filter which enables what are basically individual, not community, disputes to be weeded out. However, circumstances can be envisaged where the conduct of a separated or divorced spouse was such as to give rise to distress or alarm in the community.

---

1   People can be in separate households even though they are living under the same roof, as in the case of an estranged couple who live completely separate and independent lives, neither performing services for the other qua spouse or partner: *Mouncer v Mouncer* [1972] 1 All ER 289; *Fuller v Fuller* [1973] 2 All ER 650, CA. Also see *Simmons v Pizzey* [1977] 2 All ER 423, HL; *England v Secretary of State for Social Services* (1982) FLR 222.

Necessity for the order

2.76 Section 1(1)(b) of the 1998 Act provides the second condition to be satisfied, namely that the court must be satisfied that an ASBO is necessary to protect persons in the local government area in which the harassment, alarm or distress was caused or was likely to be caused from further anti-social acts by him.[1]

---

1   Ie anti-social acts as defined by s 1(1)(a).

'Further anti-social acts'

2.77 In terms of the phrase 'further anti-social acts', it is an open question whether what has to be shown is the risk of conduct of the same kind as has been proved against the defendant, or simply the risk of further anti-social behaviour. A court will be expected to have regard to the defendant's past behaviour in determining whether s 1(1)(b) is satisfied and it would be an unusual case if, having had such regard, a court could decide that an order was necessary to protect against a different type of anti-social behaviour but not against conduct of the same type.

Applications in respect of juveniles

2.78 An ASBO can be made against a juvenile, the minimum age being 10. Proceedings will be by a magistrates' court, not a youth court. Proceedings against 10–12-year-olds are unlikely except where the child's behaviour is part of anti-social behaviour by a family or group including older people. In the case of juveniles aged 12–17, it is envisaged that applications will be made more routinely, especially if other methods to prevent anti-social behaviour have failed.[1] There is no legal obligation, in the case of a young offender, to consult a youth offending team, but the relevant team will have a significant role in the processes of consultation prior to decisions as to whether an application for an order should be made.

Section 1 does not make it explicit, but appears, theoretically, to permit an application in respect of a defendant who is 10 at the date of application in respect of anti-social acts when he was only nine. That, seemingly unfair conclusion is mitigated by the fact that the use of the powers against juveniles is intended to be exceptional.

Where a juvenile is involved, the court is required by s 44 of the Children and Young Persons Act 1933 to have regard to the welfare of the child. Although the 1998 Act does not say so specifically, there is nothing to prevent a court which is considering making an order from asking for reports on that child or young person, although the need to take prompt action to prevent recurrence of anti-social acts will also need to be borne in mind. It should also be noted that the power to make a parenting order under s 8 of the 1998 Act arises where a court makes an anti-social behaviour order against a child or young person.

---

1   *Guidance* paras 2.1 and 5.8.

Procedure

2.79 An ASBO can be made in the absence of a defendant, provided it can be proved that he has been served with a summons.[1] The proceedings will usually be in public, and may be so even in cases involving children or young persons. It is intended that a court should, generally, deal with the case on first hearing. Schedule 5 to the Magistrates' Courts (Sex Offender and Anti-social Behaviour Orders) Rules 1998[2] includes in the prescribed form of summons issued on application for an ASBO a note to the effect that (if the defendant fails to appear) the court may issue a warrant for his arrest or proceed in his absence, and that if an ASBO is made against him and, without reasonable excuse, he breaks it he is liable on conviction to imprisonment for up to five years or to a fine, or both.

If a child or young person is the defendant, a court may require a parent or guardian to attend.[3]

1   Magistrates' Courts Act 1980, s 55.
2   SI 1998/2682.
3   Children and Young Persons Act 1933, s 34A.

Proof

2.80 The burden of proof is on the applicant for the order, save in respect of any matters as to the reasonableness of any act which arise under s 1(5).[1] The key question is whether the conditions in s 1 are satisfied. Only then can the court go on to consider whether there is a need to make an order and, if so, what it should contain. The Government intended that, because the proceedings are civil proceedings, they should attract the civil standard of proof, namely the balance of probabilities. It should, however, be clearly noted that it is wrong to regard the law of evidence as providing distinct and separate standards. The standard of proof on the claimant or applicant in a civil case varies according to the seriousness of what has to be proved. Although dicta exist to suggest that a civil court never adopts the criminal standard even where allegations of a criminal nature are being made,[2] case law suggests that allegations of crime or other similar serious allegations have to be proved to the criminal standard of beyond reasonable doubt.[3] In *Khawaja v Secretary of State for the Home Department*[4] Lord Scarman said that, in the context of an application for habeas corpus (where the liberty of the individual is at stake), the difference between the criminal and civil standards was 'largely a matter of words'. Findings by coroners' courts of suicide and of unlawful killing have each been held to require proof beyond reasonable doubt.[5] So too in civil cases where the allegation is one of murder[6] or child abuse. Of course, allegations of anti-social acts do not fall into the same league of seriousness. Nevertheless, the consequences of the making of an order are that if breach of a requirement is shown, the defendant may be convicted of a criminal offence, and subjected to substantial penalties, without any opportunity at his criminal trial to demonstrate that his conduct was reasonable. For this reason, there is a strong argument that the courts should apply a higher standard of proof than 51% in respect of the threshold conditions,[7] perhaps, even, beyond reasonable doubt (as in binding-over proceedings).[8] If the court has particular concerns one would certainly expect it to apply a higher standard than a mere balance of probabilities. Moreover, there can be no doubt that, like binding-over proceedings,[9] ASBO proceedings are a 'criminal matter' for the purposes of Art 6 of the ECHR. Although the presumption of innocence in Art 6(2) does not require proof beyond reasonable doubt, the court must base its judgment on 'direct or indirect evidence sufficiently strong in the eyes of the law to establish [the defendant's] guilt'.[10]

---

1   See para **2.72**.
2   *Bater v Bater* [1951] P 35 at 37, per Denning LJ (as he then was).
3   See *Hornal v Neuberger Products Ltd* [1956] 3 All ER 970.
4   [1983] 1 All ER 765 at 783.
5   See *R v West London Coroner's Court, ex parte Gray* [1987] 2 All ER 129, DC.
6   *Halford v Brooks* (1991) *The Times*, 3 October.
7   In *Heinl v Jyske Bank (Gibraltar) Ltd* [1999] TLR 661, Colman J held that, to establish a claim in equity to make good loss against a person as constructive trustee based on his alleged dishonesty, the standard of proof of dishonesty, although not beyond reasonable doubt, had to involve a high level of probability.
8   See para **2.33**.
9   *Steel v UK* (1999) EHRR 603, ECtHR.
10 *Austria v Italy* (1963) 6 YB 740, ECommHR.

2.81 Clearly, the conditions must be proved by admissible evidence, although (as said in para **2.69**) that need not be evidence from the 'victim' (if the 'likely to cause' approach is taken).

As these are civil proceedings, the provisions of the Civil Evidence Act 1995 relating to the admissibility of hearsay evidence apply. The court can hear testimony, whether orally or on paper, which satisfies the relevant conditions for admissibility and establishes the threshold conditions. In cases where there is likelihood of victimisation or reprisals, it may be that it is inappropriate for the identity of the complainant to be disclosed as part of the application. However, the power to withhold the identity of a complainant, where the application is based upon actual harassment, alarm or distress, is doubtful. In such circumstances, the applicant may wish to rely instead on the 'likely to cause' approach permitted by s 1.

The order

2.82 If the conditions in s 1(1) of the 1998 Act are satisfied, a court may make an order. It is not obliged to do so. An order has effect for a period of not less than two years specified in the order or until further order.[1] The Guidance recommends that an order for a finite period be made whenever possible.[2] The order comes into force on the date on which it is made. The Guidance recommends that in all cases it should be served on the defendant and that (if he is a juvenile) a copy should be given to his parent or guardian and (in any event) to the police, local authority and any other relevant organisations.[3]

---

1   1998 Act, s 1(7).
2   *Guidance* para 6.11.
3   Ibid, paras 6.18 and 6.19.

2.83 If an order is made, it prohibits the defendant from doing anything prescribed in it. Section 1(6) of the 1998 Act states that the prohibitions which may be imposed by an ASBO are those necessary for the purpose of protecting from further anti-social acts by the defendant:

(a) persons in the local government area; and
(b) persons in any adjoining[1] local government area specified in the application for the order.

It is important that the prohibitions in an ASBO are reasonably precise. Otherwise an ASBO could be open to the objections found in *Hashman v UK*[2] in respect of a binding-over order to be of good behaviour.

It will be noted that the word used in (b) is 'adjoining', which, given its ordinary meaning, means 'contiguous'.[3] Thus if defendant A, who lives in one local government area, shouts racial abuse and taunts at Family X who live across the street and the local authority boundary runs through the middle of the street, the court can make an order prohibiting future such conduct in either local government area, provided the applicant specifies the area in the application. It would seem odd for a court not to have such a power if the applicant does not specify the adjoining local government area, but no doubt such points could be dealt with by an amendment to the application.

As in s 1(1)(b) of the 1998 Act, the reference to 'further anti-social acts' by the defendant in s 1(6) is ambiguous. Does it refer to such acts of the same kind as have been proved against the defendant or simply further anti-social acts of any kind or what? In most cases the point is academic because a court could not properly impose prohibitions to prevent anti-social acts of a type of which there is no evidence of risk.

---

1   A relevant authority must not specify an adjoining local government area in an ASBO application without consulting the council for that area and each chief officer of police any part of whose area lies within that area: 1998 Act, s 1(6).
2   See para **2.27**.
3   'Adjoining' in the present context does not pose the same problems of definition as in aggravated trespass: see para **7.45**.

2.84 There appears to be no limit to what may be included in the order, subject to compliance with the terms of s 1(6). No guidance is given by the Act as to what the word 'necessary' actually means in s 1(6). On one interpretation, a prohibition is not 'necessary' if the conduct can be prevented by other means. Thus, for example, a child might be brought under control by a parenting order. In one sense, therefore, prohibitions in an anti-social order are not 'necessary' unless there is no alternative. It is submitted that this is too narrow an approach. The purpose of the word 'necessary' is to limit the scope of any prohibition to the context which justifies the making of the order, and to prevent the imposition of prohibitions which are not directly related to that anti-social conduct. If it is not so related, it is not 'necessary'. A provision is 'necessary' if it is needed. A prohibition is needed even though there are alternative ways of achieving the protection sought. Thus, a binding-over order may provide an appropriate sanction for repetition of anti-social conduct, but the potential to make such an order does not prevent a court making an anti-social behaviour order.

The requirement that a prohibition be 'necessary' means that it must be restricted to prohibiting the kind of behaviour that led to the order being sought. Care is required in drafting the order, otherwise it can easily be circumvented by carrying out similar behaviour to that prohibited, but which is not specifically prohibited. Prohibitions should be specific as to time and place so that it is readily apparent what does or does not constitute a breach. They should contain a prohibition on inciting others to commit specified anti-social acts within the meaning of the Act.[1]

The order must contain a warning that breach of it is punishable with imprisonment for up to five years or a fine, or both.[2]

---

1   *Guidance* para 6.10.
2   Magistrates' Courts (Sex Offender and Anti-social Behaviour Orders) Rules 1998, SI 1998/2682.

2.85 The order can only contain prohibitions. There is no power to impose requirements to perform positive obligations.

Whatever the prohibitions imposed, they must be reasonable.[1] Further, to the extent that they interfere with a Convention right under the Human Rights Act 1998 (Arts 8–11 of the ECHR), they will need to be proportionate to the legitimate aim being pursued.[1] Extreme orders, such as requiring a defendant not to visit property at which he lives, or not to go to a particular housing estate or street, are Draconian in effect and would need the highest level of justification. A court will need to consider the effect of the proposed prohibition, and balance the effect of that prohibition on the defendant against the seriousness of the anti-social behaviour and the capacity to prevent its occurrence by other means. Arguably, a court should consider, and take into account, the range of different powers and orders which might appropriately be used or sought to prevent the anti-social behaviour, and the overall intention of Parliament that s 1 is primarily designed to prevent 'anti-community' behaviour and not a means to achieve a private law remedy through public law process.

---

1   An order is judicially reviewable if this requirement is not met.

Appeals

2.86 An appeal against the making of an ASBO is to the Crown Court.[1] There is no appeal to the Crown Court against the refusal to make an order, but since there are no restrictions on the relevant authority making repeat applications, there is no obstacle to a fresh application being made in such circumstances, provided this does not amount to an abuse of process.

On appeal against an ASBO, the Crown Court may make such orders as may be necessary to give effect to its determination of the appeal, and may make such incidental or consequential orders as appear to it to be just.[2] It can therefore remit the case to the magistrates' court for rehearing. Alternatively, it may make a new ASBO against the appellant and impose such prohibitions as are necessary for the purpose of protecting persons in the local government area from further anti-social acts. Such an order will be deemed to be made by the magistrates' court from which the appeal to the Crown Court came.[3]

An appeal against the making of, or refusal to make, an ASBO by a magistrates' court (or against the decisions of the Crown Court on appeal) may be made by case stated to the High Court, but only on the ground that it is wrong in law or in excess of jurisdiction.[4] Alternatively, such a decision can be challenged by an application for judicial review in an appropriate case.

---

1   1998 Act, s 4(1). Appeal is by re-hearing: Supreme Court Act 1981, s 79(3).
2   1998 Act, s 4(2).
3   Ibid, s 4(3).
4   Magistrates' Courts Act 1980, s 111.

Variation or discharge

2.87 Section 1(8) of the 1998 Act states that the applicant or the defendant may apply by complaint to the court which made an ASBO for it to be varied or discharged. Except with the consent of both parties, no such order can be discharged before the end of the period of two years beginning with the date of service of the order. An order can always be varied without the agreement of both parties.

Breach of the order

2.88 Breach of the order is a criminal offence. Prosecutions are conducted by the CPS, like other prosecutions. By s 1(10) of the 1998 Act if, without reasonable excuse, a person does anything which he is prohibited from doing by an ASBO, he commits an either-way offence and is liable:

(a) on summary conviction, to imprisonment for a term not exceeding six months or to a fine not exceeding the statutory maximum, or to both; or
(b) on conviction on indictment, to imprisonment for a term not exceeding five years or to a fine, or to both.

A conditional discharge may not be ordered.[1]

By virtue of its maximum sentence, an offence under s 1(10) is an arrestable offence under s 24(1) of PACE. Compared with other offences discussed in this book, it seems quite excessive that the present offence is triable either way and punishable as it is. Comparison with the maximum for an offence under s 5 of the Public Order Act 1986 is instructive in this regard. It is most unlikely that breach of an ASBO would be tried in the Crown Court or, if so, would ever be punished anywhere near the maximum term of imprisonment. That maximum is probably simply a 'dodge' to bring into play police powers in respect of an arrestable offence. If it was necessary to make this offence an arrestable one, why wasn't the normal route chosen of adding it to the list of arrestable offences in s 24(2) of PACE?

If the accused is a child or young person, summary trial of the charge will be in the youth court, unlike the application for the making of the order (which is dealt with by a magistrates' court).

---

1   1998 Act, s 1(11).

2.89 The burden of proving the offence is, of course, on the prosecution, beyond reasonable doubt. Clearly, an evidential burden of establishing reasonable excuse is placed on the accused, but on whom is the legal burden? Unlike some statutory provisions, no express burden of proof is placed on the accused. The fact that the accused is in a better position to know and explain why he acted might suggest that he bears the burden of proof. However, the balance of authority[1] suggests that this is no more than an evidential burden and that once it is satisfied the burden is on the prosecution to prove the absence of reasonable excuse beyond reasonable doubt. On this basis, the burden in respect of reasonable excuse under s 1(10) differs from that in respect of reasonableness under s 1(5). Against that, however, the wording of s 1(5) specifically allocates the burden of proof. The failure to do so in s 1(10) seems to confirm that the accused does not have the burden of proving a reasonable excuse.

---

1   See para **8.57**.

2.90 Reasonable excuse should not be found simply because no harassment, alarm or distress was created, or likely to be created by the breach of the order. The reasonable excuse must relate to the conduct in breach of the prohibition, not the effect of that breach. In other contexts, it has been held that whether there is a reasonable excuse depends on whether a reasonable man would think the excuse reasonable in the circumstances,[1] but that as a matter of law there are limitations as to what a reasonable man thinks.[2] This is likely to be the approach taken by the courts in relation to the present provision.

---

1   *Bryan v Mott* (1975) 62 Cr App R 71, DC.
2   Ibid; *Evans v Hughes* [1972] 3 All ER 412, DC.

Evaluation

2.91 Few people would disagree with the objective of preventing the lives of a community, or part of it, being ruined by the anti-social behaviour of others. Whether the solution contained in s 1 is appropriate is more open to argument. Quite extensive offences and powers existed before 1998, but the powers created in 1998 might be justified in terms of protection from future acts.

   Nevertheless, s 1 is open to criticism. While ASBO proceedings in themselves are civil, the effect of s 1 is to extend the operation of the criminal law without the controls that apply to criminal charges, in terms of the burden of proof (subject to what is said in para **2.80**) and the admissibility of evidence. This is bad enough when the anti-social behaviour proven would constitute a criminal offence, but it is even worse when that behaviour is 'sub-criminal', particularly when the effect of an order is to restrict the liberty of its subject, who may be as young as 10, for two years or more.

   In addition, in the event of criminal proceedings for an alleged breach of an ASBO, the accused is unable to challenge its terms and is liable to conviction and punishment for its breach, even though the contravening conduct may not be criminal in itself.[1]

   As there can be no doubt that, despite their civil status under English law, ASBO proceedings are criminal for the purposes of the ECHR under the jurisprudence of the European Court of Human Rights,[2] the standards expected under Art 6 of the ECHR apply.[3] It is not entirely certain that an allegation of a breach of Art 6 of the ECHR would fail.

1   Cooper (1998) (February) Legal Action 24.
2   See para **2.80**.
3   Advice and assistance are available to defendants under the duty solicitor arrangements and defendants can apply for assistance by way of representation under Part III of the Legal Aid Act 1988.

Chapter 3

MAJOR PUBLIC ORDER OFFENCES

INTRODUCTION

3.1   The major public order offences are provided by Part I of the Public Order Act 1986: riot, affray and violent disorder. Part I also provides less serious offences, involving threatening, abusive or insulting behaviour, which are discussed in the next chapter.

   The major public order offences in the 1986 Act replaced the common law misdemeanours of riot, rout, affray and unlawful assembly. They were triable only on indictment and the maximum punishment for them was a fine and imprisonment at the discretion of the court.

3.2   There were five elements necessary to constitute the common law offence of *riot*:

(a)   there had to be three or more persons present;
(b)   who had a common purpose; and
(c)   had begun to execute such purpose;
(d)   intending to help one another by force if necessary against any person who might oppose them in the execution of their common purpose; and
(e)   they had to display such violence as to alarm at least one person of reasonable firmness and courage.[1]

Any person who participated in a riot could be convicted of perpetrating the offence.[2]

---

1   *Field v Receiver of Metropolitan Police* [1907] 2 KB 853, DC.
2   *R v Caird* (1970) 54 Cr App R 499 at 504.

3.3   Where three or more persons who were assembled together with an intention to do something which, if executed, would have amounted to riot actually moved towards the execution of their common purpose, they were guilty of *rout*.[1] In other words, rout was similar to riot without the execution of the common purpose.

---

1   *Redford v Birley* (1822) 1 State Tr NS 1071 at 1211, 1214.

3.4   Where three or more persons were gathered together for the common purpose of committing an offence involving the use of violence, or of achieving a lawful or unlawful object in such a way as to lead to the apprehension by reasonable persons of a breach of the peace as a natural and probable result of their conduct, they were guilty of *unlawful assembly*.[1] This offence was described in *Kamara v DPP*[2] as 'only an inchoate riot', in that the elements of riot were present except that the common purpose had not yet been carried out. The dividing line between unlawful assembly and riot (the commencement of the execution of the purpose), and a fortiori rout, was in many cases a slight one.

1   Hawkins *Pleas of the Crown* 8th edn (1795), vol I, ch 28; Stephen *Digest* 9th edn (1950), Art 90,
     and *History of the Criminal Law* (1883), vol II, p 385.
2   [1973] 2 All ER 1242 at 1248, per Lord Hailsham.

3.5   If one or more persons unlawfully participated in a fight or in violence on a
person who did not retaliate, or unlawfully displayed force (which included the
carrying or brandishing of weapons), in such a way that a bystander of reasonably
firm character might reasonably be expected to be terrified, they were guilty of the
common law offence of *affray*.[1]

1   See, in particular, Hawkins *Pleas of the Crown* 8th edn (1795), vol I, ch 28; Blackstone 4
     Commentaries 1st edn (1769), vol IV, p 145; *R v Scarrow* (1968) 52 Cr App R 591, CA; *Taylor v
     DPP* [1973] 2 All ER 1108, HL; *A-G's Reference (No 3 of 1983)* [1985] 1 All ER 501, CA.

3.6   The Law Commission recommended in 1983[1] that the four common law
offences be abolished and that the offences of riot, unlawful assembly and affray
be replaced by statutory offences. It took the view that the offence of rout was
obsolete and recommended that it should be abolished and not be replaced,
which came as no surprise. The Commission considered that its task was to restate
the common law in a modern statutory form, rather than attempt any radical
restructuring. One of its reasons was that there was general acceptance of the need
for major offences to deal with serious public disorder. Its other reason was that it
should move with caution in a sphere so closely related to the freedom of the
individual. These were not strong reasons for abstaining from a thorough-going
review. The result of the Commission's approach was that, overall, its recommendations sought to retain 'for the greater part the principal features of the
structure and application of the common law offences', while eliminating certain
uncertainties and anomalies.[2]

1   *Criminal Law: Offences Relating to Public Order Law* (Law Com Report no 123, 1983).
2   Ibid, para 2.2.

3.7   Sections 1–3 of the 1986 Act contain in substance (and in descending order
of gravity) the three offences (riot, violent disorder and affray) recommended by
the Commission, while s 9(1) abolished the four common law offences.[1] Although
the Court of Appeal has stated that the citation of cases dealing with the
requirements of the above common law offences is unlikely to be helpful and may
be potentially misleading when considering the three offences under the 1986
Act, on the ground that it was clear from s 9(1) of the 1986 Act that the statutory
offences are different,[2] the Divisional Court has subsequently looked at case law
on common law affray on a point where the Act mirrored the common law.[3] It did
so, however, with the warning that that case law should be approached with care.
Presumably, it would have taken the same view about reference to case law on
common law riot.

1   It is arguable that the abolition of the common law offence of affray did not abolish the
     obsolescent (if not obsolete) form of that offence of unlawfully carrying or brandishing
     weapons in such a way that a bystander of reasonably firm character might reasonably be
     expected to be terrified. Sometimes it was treated as an independent offence rather than a
     version of common law affray, in which case it would not be affected by the abolition of
     common law affray by s 9(1).

2   *R v Davies* (1990) unreported, CA, a case concerned with affray contrary to the 1986 Act, s 3.
3   *I v DPP* [2000] Crim LR 45, DC. This point is not made in the brief report but appears in the transcript.

3.8   It is questionable whether there would be a significant gap in the law if the three offences did not exist. The Law Commission thought that there would be, despite the range of offences against the person or against property which are available to be charged. It appears to have rested this view very much on the ground that there was a seriousness in these offences quite separate from any individual offence against the person or property which may take place during their commission because they involve 'group offending', which can cause particular fear in ordinary members of the public and increased difficulties for the police. As we shall see, however, only one person need actually be involved in using or threatening violence for an affray, and only three for violent disorder. Moreover, although in all three offences the conduct must be such as would cause a hypothetical person present at the scene to fear for his personal safety, no one person need have been present or put in fear. Are these separate offences necessary when there are other simpler offences available with adequate maximum penalties to reflect the gravity of its commission in context?

Another argument favoured by the Law Commission for these offences was that, in situations of public disorder, precise identification of who does what to whom may not be possible, although it is clear that the participants have engaged in fighting or violence, or aiding and abetting others in this. There may not be sufficient evidence to charge an offence against the person and, while less serious cases could be dealt with by minor public order offences, the Law Commission thought that there would be a significant gap in the law if an offence such as riot, violent disorder or affray could not be charged in cases of serious public disorder.[1] Unfortunately, the drafting of these three offences, especially the last two, means that they are not limited to such cases.

---

1   See, for example, Report no 123 (1983), para 3.5.

RIOT

3.9   Section 1(1) of the 1986 Act provides that:

> 'Where 12 or more persons who are present together use or threaten unlawful violence for a common purpose and the conduct of them (taken together) is such as would cause a person of reasonable firmness present at the scene to fear for his personal safety, each of the persons using unlawful violence for the common purpose is guilty of riot.'

Section 1(1) falls into two parts:

> 'The first specifies the context, namely "Where 12 or more persons who are present together use or threaten unlawful violence for a common purpose ..." The context of the offence thus provides, as an alternative to the use of unlawful violence, a threat of such violence. The second part of the section specifies the actual offence, namely "each of the persons using unlawful violence for the common purpose is guilty of riot". The offence, so described, thus does not include the threat of unlawful violence as an alternative to its use.'[1]

1   *R v Jefferson* [1994] 1 All ER 270 at 275, referring to *R v Tyler* (1992) 96 Cr App R 332, CA.
     Also see *R v Mandair* [1994] 2 All ER 715 at 731, per Lord Mustill, also referring to *R v Tyler*.

Prohibited conduct

3.10 What is required is that an accused uses unlawful violence in the following
circumstances:

(a) that 12 or more persons (including the accused) who are present together
     use or threaten unlawful violence for a common purpose; and
(b) that their conduct (taken together) is such as would cause a person of
     reasonable firmness present at the scene to fear for his personal safety; and
(c) that the accused's use of unlawful violence was for the common purpose.

Where there is doubt about whether there were 12 people present and/or
whether 12 people present used or threatened violence and/or whether they did
so pursuant to a common purpose, a charge of violent disorder or affray or
threatening, abusive or insulting behaviour, contrary to s 4, may be appropriate,
depending on the circumstances.

3.11 Despite the title of the 1986 Act, riot (like the other offences under Part I of
the Act) may be committed in private as well as in public places.[1] Thus, a riot can
take place at factory premises, in a club, in a college, or in someone's home. The
apparent justification is that conduct involving violence in a private place can
threaten public order,[2] although clearly it will not always do so. Moreover, given
that the conduct covered by the offence may start in a public place and then 'spill
over' into a private one, the elements of riot being wholly fulfilled when the
private place has been reached, and vice versa, it would be unfortunate if the
offence of riot was excluded by reason of the fact that part of the conduct was not
in a public place. Moreover, cases have occurred of gang fights wholly on private
premises in circumstances where it would have been difficult to bring charges
involving offences against the person due to the absence of witnesses.

1   Public Order Act 1986, s 1(5).
2   Law Com Report no 123 (1983) paras 3.34, 5.34 and 6.26.

Use of unlawful violence

3.12 A person does not perpetrate the offence of riot merely by threatening
unlawful violence; he must actually use violence in the prescribed circumstances.
If 12 or more people simply threaten violence for a common purpose in a
frightening way, but none of them *uses* violence, riot is *not* committed. On the
other hand, if one of those 12 or more people then actually uses violence for the
common purpose, the offence of riot is perpetrated by him. However, where one
or more people actually use violence for the common purpose, those who merely
threaten violence for the common purpose can be convicted as accomplices to
riot if, with the appropriate mens rea for a secondary party, they encourage the use
of violence by another[1] (like anyone else who does so). Thus, the apparent
distinction between liability for riot and liability for violent disorder, which can be
perpetrated by a threat of violence, is not a real one. In fact, the boundaries of
liability for riot, as with many other offences, are wide, since someone who incites
the use of mob violence can be convicted, as an accomplice to riot, notwithstand-

ing that he is not present at the time if someone uses such violence. In addition, although mere presence as a bystander is insufficient, mere non-accidental presence, such as deliberate presence as a spectator, may be evidence from which encouragement of the perpetrator coupled with an intention to do so (the two main elements of secondary liability) can be inferred.[2] As one commentator has put it, 'anybody who fails to dissociate himself effectively and rapidly when a riot develops will run the risk of conviction'.[3]

Of course, if all the participants had agreed not to go beyond threats of violence in furtherance of their common purpose, but one of them quite unexpectedly uses violence in furtherance of it, the others will not be guilty as accomplices, although he will be guilty of perpetrating riot.

Whether or not they are guilty as accomplices to riot, those who merely threaten violence can be convicted of a perpetration of a lesser offence, such as violent disorder.

---

1   *R v Jefferson* [1994] 1 All ER 270, CA.
2   *R v Coney* (1882) 8 QBD 534; *R v Allan* [1963] 2 All ER 897, CCA; *R v Clarkson* [1971] 3 All ER 344, C-MAC; *Allen v Ireland* [1984] 1 WLR 903, DC.
3   ATH Smith 'Public order law: the Government proposals' [1985] PL 533.

3.13 An indictment for riot alleging that the accused used or threatened unlawful violence will be defective, although the judge may allow the prosecution to amend it so as to exclude the words 'or threatened'. This was held in *R v Tyler*,[1] where Farquharson LJ said:

> 'The statement of offence clearly and accurately referred to riot. The particulars disclosed the correct offence but widened its ambit to include "threaten" as well as the "use" of violence. In our judgment, that is not in the same category as alleging an offence which does not exist, as in *Gaston*.[2] It gives an imperfect description of one that does. In those circumstances, the defect is capable of amendment on the basis laid down in *McVitie*.'[3]

Tyler was applied by the Court of Appeal in *R v Jefferson*,[4] where an indictment was badly framed for the same reason. It was plain from the way in which the Crown had argued its case and from the judge's direction to the jury that a threat of violence alone would not suffice to constitute the offence of riot. As a result, the Court of Appeal dismissed appeals against convictions for riot, even though the indictment had not been amended.

---

1   (1992) 96 Cr App R 332 at 336.
2   (1981) 73 Cr App R 164, CA.
3   [1960] 2 All ER 498, CCA.
4   [1994] 1 All ER 270, CA.

Unlawful violence

Violence

3.14 '"Violence" means any violent conduct'.[1] It is not limited to violent conduct towards a person or persons since it includes violent conduct towards property (for example, smashing shop windows or overturning cars).[1] Nor is it limited to conduct causing or intended to cause personal injury or damage to property,[1] since it 'includes any other violent conduct (for example, throwing at or towards a person a missile of a kind capable of causing injury which does not hit or falls short)'.[1] Thus, there can be violence even though conduct which could have harmed a person or property did not actually do so and was not intended to do so. In fact, the wording of s 8 of the 1986 Act suggests that violence does not have to be used against either a person or property (although this will be so in the vast majority of cases). What is required is conduct carried out in a way which can be described as violent. Swinging a knife at someone[2] or firing a gun in his direction[3] is violence under the definition in s 8, even though he is not hit. In short, the emphasis is on the nature of the conduct, and its associated risks, and not on its consequences. This is sensible; it may often be difficult to prove that particular conduct by a particular person caused injury or damage in a group situation, as where a mob hurl stones in the direction of others.

---

1   1986 Act, s 8.
2   See *R v Davison* [1992] Crim LR 31, CA; see para **3.52**.
3   Law Com Report no 123 (1983) para 3.53.

3.15 Notwithstanding the definition and the single example given in s 8, our understanding of 'violence' is not greatly assisted by it, since that term is defined by reference to violent conduct. This must win a prize for circuity of definition! 'Violent conduct' is the crucial term in s 8. We know that 'violence' includes violent conduct towards persons or property and that it is not restricted to conduct causing or intended to cause injury or damage, but includes other violent conduct (the example given being missile throwing). But what is 'violent conduct'? The Act does not say. It is submitted that 'violence' and 'violent' are not being used in an unusual sense but in their ordinary sense. On this basis, as with some other terms in the 1986 Act[1] (and elsewhere), it is for the tribunal deciding the case (the jury in the case of riot) to consider as a matter of fact whether in all the circumstances what has occurred constitutes violent conduct according to the ordinary usage of the English language.[2] For example, it would be for them to decide whether, if charged with riot, a dozen football supporters pushing or shoving at a chairman of a football club outside the ground in an effort to secure his resignation were using violent conduct and therefore 'violence'.

Support for this approach can be found in *Dino Services Ltd v Prudential Assurance Co Ltd*, a Court of Appeal decision concerned with the interpretation of 'violent' in an insurance policy. Kerr LJ, with whom the other two Lords Justice agreed, said:

> 'The word "violent" is an ordinary English word, which here appears in a common commercial document. It seems to me that there is no reason why its meaning should be in any way different from what any ordinary person would understand. At first sight I therefore conclude that there should be no need to resort either to a dictionary, or to authorities, to interpret this word. On that basis I would take the ordinary meaning of the word "violent" in this context to be that it is intended to convey that (sic) the use of *some* force to effect entry, which may be minimal, such as the turning of a key in a lock or the turning of a door handle, *if accentuated or accompanied by some physical act which can properly be described as violent in its nature or character.* An obvious picture that springs to mind is the breaking down of a door or the forcing open of a window, which would be acts of violence directed to the fabric of the premises to effect entry. Or there might be violence to a person, such as knocking down someone who seeks to prevent entry.'[3]

Even if it could be viewed as 'violent conduct', trivial conduct would be unlikely to satisfy another requirement, viz that the violence be such as would cause a person

of reasonable firmness present at the scene to fear for his personal safety.[4]
'Violence' is a strong word and should not be watered down.

---

1   See para **4.5**.
2   *Brutus v Cozens* [1972] 2 All ER 1297, HL. See, further, para **4.5**.
3   [1989] 1 All ER 422 at 426. In *LC v Criminal Injuries Compensation Board* (1999) *The Times*, 3
    June, Outer House of the Court of Session, Lord MacFadyen stated that 'crime of violence' in
    the CICB scheme did not constitute a term of art. The words were ordinary words of the
    English language, and had to be given their ordinary sense as such.
4   There is, however, no such requirement in respect of the offence under the 1986 Act, s 4,
    dealt with in the next chapter, which could mean that violence that would not suffice on a
    charge under ss 1–3 could suffice under s 4.

3.16 The dividing line (which is crucial for riot) between the *use* and the *threat* of
violence is a fine one. Suppose that a group of supporters of one football club
throw missiles at supporters of the other. This is the *use* of violence, as s 8 indicates.
On the other hand, if one group merely advances on another group, shouting
'Bastards. Kill the bastards' and waving their fists in the air, this is not the *use* of
violence but merely the *threat* of it. Consequently, if the police intervene before
any more is done, the offence of riot will not be committed. There can, however,
be a fine line between the use and the threat of violence. For example, swinging a
knife at someone can be the use of violence, but holding it while shouting out:
'Die, Die', is only a threat.

Unlawful
3.17 The requirement that the violence be unlawful excludes from riot violence
which is justified by law (for example, under the common law rules relating to the
use of reasonable force in self-defence or in the defence of another or of property
or to prevent or terminate a breach of the peace, or unlawful imprisonment, or a
trespass, or under the statutory provisions relating to the use of such force in the
prevention of crime or the effecting of a lawful arrest).[1] Thus, it will not be a riot
for 12 or more security guards to use force to fight off would-be bullion robbers, or
to prevent protesters from conducting a sit-in, provided the force used is
reasonable.

As in other offences where one of these public or private defences is raised, a
judge must leave the issue to the jury with a direction on it,[2] indicating that it is for
the prosecution to disprove an element of the defence set out in his direction.[3]

The use of reasonable violence against property in order to defend property
is not violence justified by law. The rules about self-defence etc do not apply to the
use of force to damage or destroy *property* to defend other property. While s 5(2) of
the Criminal Damage Act 1971 provides that a person charged with simple
criminal damage under s 1(1) of that Act may have the defence of 'lawful excuse'
to that charge if he destroys or damages property in order to protect other
property, s 5(2) is limited to that offence and, in any event, it does not justify (ie
render lawful) the damage etc or force used to achieve it. The same is true in
respect of a case where a defence of duress is available.

---

1   This was confirmed in *R v Rothwell* [1993] Crim LR 626, CA (a case concerned with 'unlawful
    violence' in the 1986 Act, s 2). It is for the prosecution to prove that the violence was
    unlawful, but only if there is evidence (which will normally be adduced by the accused)
    raising self-defence or the like as an issue: ibid.
2   The comments made in the latter part of para **3.56** apply mutatis mutandis here.

3   *R v Khan* [1995] Crim LR 78, CA; *R v Anderson* [1995] Crim LR 430, CA (both cases
      concerned 'unlawful violence' in affray).

Twelve or more persons present together

3.18 Riot is unlikely to be prosecuted unless a large crowd, well in excess of 12,[1] is
involved in violence or threatening violence (assuming at least one of them
actually uses violence). In such a case, it will not be necessary to provide evidence
of the precise number involved.

On the other hand, difficulties may be experienced where the group is
around a dozen in number; in these cases, evidence of a headcount of those using
or threatening violence will be necessary. Likewise, difficulties may be experienced, and head count evidence will be necessary, where those alleged to be
involved in a riot form part of a larger, peaceful assembly (such as a crowd at a
football match). How, in a very large crowd, with all the noise that even a peaceful
crowd can generate, will the police be able to pick out, and later prove, the
minimum of 12 people using violence or uttering threats etc? In practice, riot may
often be very hard, if not impossible, to prove, and this may be one of the reasons
why it is not charged on many occasions.[2]

1   The Law Commission's selection of 12 as the minimum number was arbitrary, although the
      Commission thought that a number substantially less would not adequately have reflected the
      purpose or seriousness of the offence: see Law Com Report no 123 (1983) paras 6.13–6.16.
2   See para **3.40**.

3.19 Whilst the 12 or more persons (including the accused) must be using or
threatening unlawful violence for a purpose common to them, it is not necessary
that they should each be criminally responsible. Consequently, it is irrelevant that
some (or even all but one) are under the age of criminal responsibility or
criminally insane or acting under duress. In addition, it is irrelevant that some (or
even all but one) lack the mental state (viz an intent to use violence or awareness
that conduct may be violent) required by s 6(1) of the 1986 Act of a perpetrator of
riot.[1] The one or more who is not lacking in criminal responsibility or the relevant
mental state can nevertheless be convicted of riot if he *uses* violence for the
common purpose and those who lack criminal responsibility or the relevant mens
rea can be counted in determining whether or not there are '12 or more persons
using or threatening violence for a common purpose', although they cannot be
convicted as accomplices. This is of obvious importance when not all the
participants are apprehended or before the court, so that their age (in the case of
mobs including children) or state of mind cannot be proved.

Since the violence used or threatened must be unlawful, riot will not be
committed if some of 12 people present together using or threatening violence
for a common purpose are acting in self-defence or under some other
circumstance legally justifying the violence. A difficulty with this is that in a mêlée
some people may be using force to defend themselves from others in the mêlée or
to prevent others committing a criminal offence, in which case it may not be easy
to prove the use or threat of unlawful violence by 12 or more people, a point which
is also relevant to the offence of violent disorder. There is case law relating to these
points in respect of the offence of violent disorder. It is dealt with in paras
3.46–3.48; what is said there is equally applicable here mutatis mutandis.

Although the prosecution must prove that at least 12 people were present
together, threatening or using unlawful violence, in pursuance of a common

purpose, it is not, of course, necessary that at least 12 people appear or are brought before the court. There can be a conviction of riot of a single participant who has used unlawful violence etc.

---

1   1986 Act, s 6(7). The same applies mutatis mutandis in the case of violent disorder: ibid.

3.20 'Present together' does not mean that the 12 or more people should form a cohesive group or be acting in concert. Nor need they be present pursuant to an agreement to come together; consequently, they may be 'present together' by accident. The nature of the phrase is limited by the word 'together' and by the requirement of common purpose.[1] It is submitted that what is required is that the presence of any one individual in a particular place should be proximate physically and contemporaneous to that of at least 11 others at the time of the use of violence. Twelve youths individually (or in small groups) roaming the streets of Leicester at night for the common purpose of terrorising innocent pedestrians cannot constitute a riot, whereas if they are behaving in the same way in the Town Hall Square they can.[2] Of course, presence together can be a continuing happening, and riot can be a continuing offence (as discussed in para **3.22**). Provided that 12 or more were present together at the time of the accused's use of violence, it is irrelevant that people have been leaving or joining the crowd or that its numbers have fallen below 12 before or afterwards.

---

1   See para **3.24**.
2   See *R v Meredith* (1993) unreported, CA, a violent disorder case; see para **3.43**.

Use or threat of unlawful violence

3.21 What was said above about 'use' and 'unlawful violence' applies equally here. If, during public disorder, the residents of a street use or threaten reasonable violence[1] for the common purpose of defending themselves or their property from attack, their use or threat of violence does not constitute a riot because their violence is not unlawful. It is submitted that a threat must be of violence by the person uttering it. It cannot have been Parliament's intention that riot is committed where one person uses violence after the 11 or more others with him have uttered threats that he will.

Threats of violence may be by gestures alone (eg brandishing a weapon) or by words alone or by a combination of both (eg waving a car-jack accompanied by words such as 'I'll get you with this'). Indeed, in *I v DPP*,[2] an affray case, the Divisional Court held that an aura of menace derived from conduct and/or appearance can amount to a threat of violence, for example a pointed display of a weapon or the visible possession of a petrol bomb by a member of a gang. There can be no doubt that this is equally true for riot and violent disorder, as is the statement by Auld LJ in that case that similar conduct by a number of people acting together may amount to a threat of violence when the same conduct by an individual acting on his own would not.[3]

Confirmation that words alone will suffice for riot (in the present context) and for violent disorder can be found in s 3(3) of the 1986 Act, which states that words alone will not suffice for affray and thereby implies that it will for offences under s 1 and s 2 (violent disorder). Although, in the case of words, they will normally be spoken, there seems no reason why it will not do if the threat is communicated by words on placards or banners or leaflets or badges if the other conditions for riot are satisfied.[4]

In contrast, it is submitted that *mere presence* in a group whose common purpose is to threaten or use violence cannot be taken to be threatening violence, although it may give rise to an inference of aiding and abetting others who are using violence (and, if there are 12 or more using or threatening violence, result in liability for riot as an accomplice).

It is submitted that a threat of violence must be explicit. One reason why a *peaceful* mass picket (or other crowd) at a time of tension cannot provide the context for a riot is that there is no express threat of violence by its members. Therefore if one 'idiot' uses violence, riot is not committed.

1   A threat of violence of a particular degree may be reasonable, although the actual use of that degree might not be: *R v Cousins* [1982] 2 All ER 115 at 117.
2   [2000] Crim LR 45, DC; para **3.55**.
3   This point appears only in the transcript.
4   Compare the view expressed by Thornton *Public Order Law* (1987) p 11:
       'In an early draft of the Public Order Bill references to "words" were to include the distribution or display of any writing, sign or other visible representation, presumably such as leaflets, placards, banners, posters and even badges. But this reference to "words" has been deleted from the final draft, therefore it must be given its ordinary meaning, which in this context ought to be no less than the spoken word or clearly visible written words.' *Sed quaere.*

3.22 Section 1(2) of the 1986 Act provides that it is immaterial whether or not the 12 or more use or threaten violence simultaneously. Equally, it is immaterial whether or not *any* of the others used or threatened violence at the time of the use of violence by the accused which is in issue. This is, of course, consistent with the notion that the conduct of those other than each individual accused forms a continuing context in which he acts, but it does weaken the notion of the offence as one of group disorder. A requirement of simultaneity would make the offence very difficult to prove.[1] As a result of s 1(2), provided someone uses violence, riot can be committed in a series of connected incidents where only one, two or three people are using or threatening violence at the same time for the common purpose.[2] Provided that 12 or more persons who use or threaten violence are present *together* throughout and that the violence is used or threatened by 12 or more for a common purpose, the offence of riot can be committed. Thus, it covers the situation where violence is used or threatened in one part of a crowd, then dies away, only to break out in another part at a later time. Nevertheless, it has to be admitted that in such cases of sporadic violence it will be more difficult to prove that the participants are present together for a common purpose.

Not only is there no requirement of simultaneity but there is in fact no maximum period which applies between the threats or uses of violence by individuals or which limits overall the time in which such threats or uses by 12 persons must occur. Obviously, the greater time gap between the threats or violence of individuals the greater will be the difficulty of proving that 12 or more were *together* using or threatening violence for a common purpose, so that the matter is probably self-regulating.

1   Law Com Report no 123 (1983) para 6.21.
2   McFarlane 'Public order – reform against a dark background' (1986) 83 LS Gaz 278.

3.23 The width of 'use or threaten violence' means that hostility or a commotion is not required for a riot (although it may colour conduct which would not otherwise be threatening), nor is any noise or disturbance to the neighbourhood or even to neighbours. A good humoured and quiet crowd of 12 or more can, therefore, commit a riot if the various requirements are fulfilled.

The linking of threats of violence with use of violence, coupled with the fact that both must be such as (taken together) would cause a person of reasonable firmness present at the scene to fear for his personal safety, suggests that the threats must be of immediate violence, as opposed to violence to take place in the non-immediate future.

In pursuance of a common purpose

3.24 The use or threat of violence by the 12 or more present together must be for a purpose common to them (or at least to 12 of them). Members of a mob may have different purposes. If so, riot will be proved if 12 of them used or threatened violence (at least one of them using violence) in order to achieve a common purpose which they shared.

The question is not whether the 12 or more used violence and were present for a common purpose, but whether they threatened or used violence for a common purpose. This commonality of purpose highlights the essential concept of riot and its seriousness, viz a body of people who by weight of numbers are intent on achieving their purpose,[1] distinguishing it from violent disorder and the other offences under Part I of the 1986 Act. The nature of the purpose is irrelevant,[2] the common purpose need not be violence and it need not be an unlawful purpose (although no doubt it will normally be so). A mob of football supporters who violently demand the reinstatement of the club manager who has been wrongfully dismissed would act for a common lawful purpose.

---

1   Law Com Report no 123 (1983) para 6.23.
2   The 1986 Act does not impose any limitation on the nature of the common purpose. Thus, although technically the widespread use of violence for a common political purpose may well constitute treason by levying war, it will also be a riot (and it is the latter which is likely to be charged in modern peacetime society).

3.25 'Purpose' in this context does not mean motive (ie a person's reason for acting as he does). The individual motives of participants in a riot, which may be various (since some may join in to express a grievance against a particular body, some to take the chance to indulge in looting, and some simply because they are carried away by mob hysteria), are irrelevant. If they are engaged in seeking to achieve something in common, eg attacking the shop premises of Asian traders, they will be acting in pursuance of a common purpose. Moreover, it is submitted that the element of common purpose does not mean that there must be proof of some prior agreement upon the action to be taken or even that the violence is threatened or used in any way in concert.[1]

In the absence of admissions, it will not be easy in many cases to prove a common purpose, or that violence used or threatened was directed to it, which may be another reason why riot is not charged on many occasions. In most instances, it will have to be proved as a matter of inference from the conduct of the 12 or more, and s 1(3) of the 1986 Act expressly provides that such an inference may be drawn. Thus, for example, if a mob are attacking the police or resisting their efforts to restore order, or are trying to occupy a police station, the common purpose (eg a 'show of force against the police') may be identified accordingly and specified in such terms in the indictment.[2] Section 1(3) does not limit the drawing of inferences to inferences from the conduct of various individuals that is similar in nature. Thus, inferences can be drawn from the fact that some are gathering stones, others pulling up pavements, others brandishing weapons and others shouting abuse against the subject of an alleged riot.

It is preferable for the common purpose to be specified in the indictment, but, if it is not, a conviction will be upheld if the prosecution case has clearly identified the common purpose and the judge's direction has been in terms of the need for the jury to be in no reasonable doubt that the purpose was proved.[3]

1   Just as no prior agreement is required for those involved to be 'present together' (see para **3.20**).
2   Law Com Report no 123 (1983) para 6.24.
3   *R v Jefferson* [1994] 1 All ER 270, CA.

Conduct such as would cause fear

3.26 The question is not whether the conduct of an individual accused would cause fear but whether the conduct of the '12 or more present together ...' *taken together* is such as would cause a person of reasonable firmness present at the scene to *fear* for his personal safety. It is not necessary that that conduct must be such as, taken together, would cause terror (ie a state of being extremely frightened[1]).

1   *Shorter Oxford English Dictionary.*

3.27 The requirement that conduct be such as would cause a person of reasonable firmness present at the scene to fear for his personal safety also applies to violent disorder and affray. It has been elucidated in a number of cases on affray; see paras **3.57–3.58**. It is a question for the jury to determine the reaction of a person of reasonable firmness. Such a person is hypothetical and objectively assessed (so that that person is not invested with any vulnerability to fear on the part of those, eg children or the aged, who were or might have been present).[1] The conduct of the 12 or more must be such as *would* (as opposed simply to 'might') cause a person (ie a third party bystander) of reasonable firmness present at the scene to fear for his *personal* safety (as opposed to fear for someone else, possibly not present); it does not matter whether it actually caused fear to a person present at the scene or even might have. The point has not yet been decided but, presumably, the fear in question must be fear for *immediate* personal safety.

Although not necessary for proof of an element of the offence, evidence from a bystander of the actual impact on him of the conduct of the 12 or more can be important in establishing its potential impact on the hypothetical bystander of reasonable firmness. Its importance will, of course, vary depending on the age, characteristics etc of the witness.

Other relevant criteria can relate to the use of weapons, the number of participants and the language (spoken or written) used by them. Evidence as to the location of the conduct of the 12 or more may be important. Conduct which would not have any great impact in alarming any reasonable person in an open space may have considerably more potential impact in a confined space.

---

1   Compare Thornton *Public Order Law* (1987) p 13.

3.28 No person of reasonable firmness need actually be, or be likely to be, present at the scene;[1] in fact, no one else (besides the 12 or more) need be present or likely to be present at the scene. Where the conduct occurs on private premises, this 'stretches' the nature of the offence as a public order one. No doubt the case where there are no bystanders will be exceptional; where it occurs, proof of the riot may be particularly difficult.

The Act does not define what is meant by 'presence at the scene', but, as in affray, it refers to being near enough to the disturbance to have been in real danger of becoming involved in it,[2] or, perhaps, being within sight or earshot of the violence.[2]

The hypothetical bystander test represents the gravamen of riot (and of violent disorder and affray as well). It is the capacity to put in fear a notional bystander of reasonable firmness which marks out the conduct involved in the three offences as offences against public order. If bystanders had to be present and caused fear, the success of a prosecution would depend on their presence and on their fortitude. This would lead to variable results, depending on the temerity or timidity of who happened to be present.

---

1   1986 Act, s 1(4).
2   See para **3.57**. In *R v Meredith* (1993) unreported, CA, see para **3.43**, where a number of fights broke out in a nightclub car park, the accused's fight being some 70 metres from another fight, the Court of Appeal held (in respect of violent disorder) that it was open to the jury to conclude that the concept of 'the scene' was wide enough to include the various parts of the car park where the separate fights occurred.

Mental element

3.29 To be guilty of perpetrating riot, the accused must, of course, share the common purpose. In addition, s 6(1) of the 1986 Act states that 'a person is guilty of riot only if he intends[1] to use violence or is aware that his conduct may be violent'. The word 'aware' imports a concept similar to subjective recklessness,[2] except that it does not include the element of the unreasonableness of the risk of violence resulting.

According to the provisions of s 6(1) read with the definition of 'violence' in s 8, it need not be proved that the accused intended, or was aware of the risk, that his conduct would cause injury or damage. It has been suggested, however, that a person will not have been aware that his conduct might be violent if he was unaware of any risk that it would cause injury or damage, although in fact it did give rise to such a risk or did actually cause injury or damage.[3] If this is correct, proof of the offence will often be difficult. The wording of s 8, referred to in para **3.14**, seems to preclude such an interpretation, in which case the requirement in s 6(1) does not add up to much because it is hard to see how, unless he is an automaton or a person in some other impaired mental state, a person who has used violence will be unaware of the nature of his conduct.

---

1   'Only if he intends' does not exclude the operation of the law relating to complicity: *R v Jefferson* [1994] 1 All ER 270, CA.

2   For confirmation that 'awareness' in s 6 imputes a subjective awareness on the part of the
     accused, see *DPP v Clarke* (1992) 94 Cr App R 359, DC, a case on s 6(4).
3   Smith and Hogan *Criminal Law* (1999) p 744.

3.30 A case where a person is particularly likely to be able to say, truthfully, that he was unaware that his conduct was violent is where he was intoxicated. Since the mental element for riot includes a concept akin to subjective recklessness, the accused may be convicted of it if he was suffering from *self-induced* intoxication at the time of committing the prohibited conduct, even though because of his intoxication he did not intend to use violence and was not aware that his conduct might be violent.[1] However, lest the concept of 'awareness' should be construed by a court as meaning that the present type of mens rea was to be classified as an offence of specific intent (in which case evidence of its absence due to self-induced intoxication would generally be relevant),[1] s 6(5) of the 1986 Act makes the matter clear by providing that, for the purposes of s 6(1), a person whose awareness is impaired by intoxication shall be taken to be aware of that of which he would be aware if not intoxicated, unless he proves[2] either that his intoxication was not self-induced (as where his drink has been 'laced') or that it was caused solely by the taking or administration of a substance in the course of medical treatment. 'Intoxication' here means any intoxication, whether caused by drink, drugs or other means (eg glue), or by a combination of means.[3] If one or other of these things is proved, this does not necessarily mean that the accused is not guilty of riot, but merely that he is not guilty unless it is proved that he actually intended to use violence or was aware that his conduct might be violent.

It is regrettably increasingly common for modern criminal statutes to place a burden of proof on the accused, an issue discussed in para **4.38**. The present instance was justified by the Law Commission on the ground that the means of proving it would be peculiarly within the accused's knowledge.[4]

The mental element required to be proved against an alleged accomplice is governed by the common law. In addition, s 6(5) has no application to an alleged accomplice. It follows that evidence of self-induced (voluntary) intoxication in support of a claim of lack of mens rea by someone accused as an accomplice to riot can only be left to the jury if the offence of riot is one of specific intent as to the element of violence; there can be no doubt that it is not.

Section 6(1) and (5) has, of course, no application in respect of any of the 12 who are not charged before the court at all. As stated in para **3.19**, no state of mind at all needs to be proved in respect of such a person.

On the other hand, if a participant of any kind lacked the common purpose on account of his self-induced intoxication, he would be entitled to be acquitted if charged and would not count in calculating the necessary 12 participants. Thus, this part of the mens rea is a specific intent. An accused can successfully say that he was too drunk to have a purpose or to be aware of the existence and/or purpose of others with whom he is accused of rioting. This latter point would also be true in respect of a participant who has not been charged. This would not affect liability for violent disorder which does not require a common purpose.

4   Law Com Report no 123 (1983) para 3.54. Section 6(5) would be repealed by the draft Criminal Law Bill if it was enacted, on the ground that to place on the accused the burden of proof in this respect would be inconsistent with the general principles relating to intoxication set out in the draft Code: *Legislating the Criminal Code: Intoxication and Criminal Liability* Law Com Report no 229 (1995).

3.31 The 1986 Act does not expressly require that an accused should have any mental element as to the unlawfulness of the violence used by him or used or threatened by the others, nor as to the requirement that the violence used by him or used or threatened by others must be such as would cause a person of reasonable firmness present at the scene to fear for his personal safety. In respect of the former point, it would seem that the only relevant material element is that the issue of unlawfulness must be judged on the facts as the accused believed them to be.[1] On this basis, a group of 12 or more, who intentionally use violence in the circumstances outlined in s 1 in the mistaken belief that they must do so to save another's life or property, will be guilty of riot unless their violence is reasonable on the facts as they believe them. Unless a mental element is implied in respect of the latter requirement, the situation will be that, if 12 or more use violence to demolish a fence for a bonfire to celebrate England's victory in the World Cup, being unaware that this would cause a person of reasonable firmness present at the scene to fear for his personal safety, they are guilty of riot.

1   *R v Williams* [1987] 3 All ER 411, CA; *Beckford v R* [1987] 3 All ER 425, PC; *R v Owino* [1996] 2 Cr App R 128, CA.

3.32 As with other offences, an accused's mens rea can be proved by admissions made by him or by evidence of prior planning or agreement, and from evidence of the accused's conduct before, during or after the time of the offence.

Alternative bases for conviction

3.33 A public order incident may spread over a period of time and at different places, involving changing participants. As group offences, riot and violent disorder may more easily be proved if the prosecution relies on evidence of a sequence of events to show, in riot for example, presence together and commonality of purpose. It may be that the sequence forms one unbroken, continuous incident. In such a case, as indicated above, the jury can convict even though the essential elements of the offence occurred at different times and places in the incident. However, where an allegation of riot consists of more than one separate incident, eg one in the High Street and another in London Road, soon afterwards, the jury must be sure either unanimously or by a majority that at least one of those incidents was proved and that the incident (or one of the incidents) proved amounted to a riot.[1]

1   There is case law to this effect in relation to violent disorder and affray (see paras **3.49** and **3.64**); it is equally applicable to riot.

Prosecution, trial and punishment

3.34 A prosecution for an offence of riot may not be instituted except by or with the consent of the Director of Public Prosecutions;[1] the same applies to incitement to riot[1] and to charges of conspiracy to riot, attempt to riot and of aiding, abetting, counselling or procuring a riot.[2] The Law Commission regarded it as desirable to have this check on private prosecutions for riot because charges of riot may raise sensitive 'political' issues (in a broad sense) and there may be cases where there is every justification for deciding in the public interest that the offence should not be charged – a decision best taken by the Director of Public Prosecutions (or a Crown Prosecutor).[3] The same arguments may be made about serious cases of violent disorder, but the Director's consent is not required for the institution of a prosecution for that offence or for affray (although his advice may well be sought in practice).

The Director's consent to the prosecution may be expressed in general terms; there is no need to specify the section under which the prosecution should proceed, as opposed to the Act. In *R v Cain*,[4] the Court held that the Attorney-General's consent to a prosecution under the Explosive Substances Act 1883 expressed in the following terms was sufficient: 'In pursuance of my powers under the above-named Act I hereby consent to the prosecution of [the accused] of [address] for an offence or offences contrary to the provisions of the said Act'. A consent in the above form to a prosecution for riot does not provide consent to a prosecution for conspiracy to commit riot, or for attempted riot, because conspiracy and attempt are not offences under the Public Order Act 1986.[5]

The requirement for the Director to institute, or consent to, a prosecution for riot does not prevent an arrest without warrant, or the issue or execution of a warrant for the arrest of a person for riot etc, or the remand in custody or on bail of a person charged with riot etc.[6]

---

1   1986 Act, s 7(1).
2   See, respectively, the Criminal Law Act 1977, s 4(3); Criminal Attempts Act 1981, s 2(2);
     Accessories and Abettors Act 1861, s 8.
3   Every Crown Prosecutor has all the powers of the DPP as to the institution of proceedings but
     must exercise them under the direction of the DPP: Prosecution of Offences Act 1985, s 1(6).
4   [1976] QB 496, CA.
5   *R v Pearce* (1981) 72 Cr App R 295, CA.
6   Prosecution of Offences Act 1985, s 25.

3.35 Riot is triable only on indictment. The indictment should reflect the two parts of the 1986 Act, s 1(1), described in para **3.9**, first stating the statutory context and second the commission, within that context, of the offence as defined.[1]

The maximum punishment is 10 years' imprisonment or an unlimited fine, or both.[2] By virtue of its maximum punishment, riot is an arrestable offence under s 24(1) of PACE. The maximum imprisonment is high compared with that for riot in other common law jurisdictions, where the maximum is normally in the range of two to three years.[3]

---

1   *R v Jefferson* [1994] 1 All ER 270, CA.
2   1986 Act, s 1(6).
3   Law Com Report no 123 (1983) Appendix B.

3.36 The question of alternative verdicts is dealt with in para **3.73**.

Riot (Damages) Act 1886

3.37 This Act provides for compensation to be paid out of the police fund for the area, in respect of damage done by rioters to a house, shop or building, or any property therein, in England and Wales, whether or not the rioters have been prosecuted, and whether or not there has been any default or negligence on the part of the police, the police authority or the local authority.[1] The range of property covered by the Act must be noted; damage to motor vehicles in the open air is not covered, for example.

1   For the procedure relating to a claim, see the Riot (Damages) Regulations 1921, SR&O 1921/1536.

3.38 In order that the recovery of compensation may be had under the 1886 Act, the damage must have been caused by 'persons riotously and tumultuously assembled together'. Section 10(1) of the 1986 Act provides that henceforth 'riotously' in the 1886 Act is to be construed in accordance with s 1 of the 1986 Act.

'Tumultuously' adds an extra dimension to the provisions of the 1886 Act; it requires that the rioters were in such numbers and in such state of agitated commotion, and were generally so acting, that the forces of law and order should have been well aware of the threat and should have taken steps to prevent the rioters causing damage.[1] Generally, but not necessarily, the riot should be accompanied by noise.[1] Thus, where people who entered a shop and robbed its owner committed a riot by virtue of their method but without attracting the attention of passers-by, it was held that they did not do so 'tumultuously', with the result that the compensation provisions of the 1886 Act did not apply.[2] The same has been held in relation to a smash and grab robbery by three or four people (at a time when the minimum number for a riot was three).[1]

Although the raising of the threshold for a 'riot' technically limited the operation of the 1886 Act, the change was not as great as it may seem because of the meaning given to 'tumultuously'.

Compensation is available under the Act, even though no one has been charged with riot and regardless of whether any offence has been charged. However, in the event of a dispute with the authority, the onus lies on a claimant to show that the offence of riot has been committed (and that the other requirements of s 1 of the 1886 Act have been fulfilled).

1   *D H Edmonds Ltd v East Sussex Police Authority* (1988) *The Times*, 15 July, CA.
2   *J W Dwyer Ltd v Metropolitan Police District Receiver* [1967] 2 All ER 1051, DC.

'Riot' etc in other statutes

3.39 Section 10(3) of the 1986 Act provides that 'riot' and cognate expressions in any Act in force before the coming into force of that section[1] are to be construed in accordance with s 1 if they would previously have been construed in accordance with the common law offence of riot.

This would seem to amend the definition of 'riot' or riotous, in the following Acts, since those terms would previously have been construed in accordance with the common law offence of riot:

(a) Ecclesiastical Courts Jurisdiction Act 1860, s 2 (provision penalising any person guilty of 'riotous, violent or indecent behaviour' in places belonging to the Church of England and various other places of worship);[2]

(b) Burial Laws Amendment Act 1880, s 7 (provision penalising any person guilty of 'riotous, violent or indecent behaviour' at any burial under the terms of the Act, ie burials without the rites of the Church of England);[3]

(c) Licensing Act 1964, s 188 (provision for licensed premises to be closed on the order of the justices in or near the place where 'a riot or tumult' happens or is expected to happen);

(d) Representation of the People Act 1983, Sch 1, para 16 (provision for the adjournment of nominations on any day interrupted or obstructed by 'riot or open violence').

On the other hand, unless a different intention appears, nothing in Part I of the 1986 Act affects the meaning of 'riot' or any cognate expression in any enactment in force before s 10 came into force[3] if that expression would not previously have been construed in accordance with the common law offence of riot.[4] This was intended to apply to 'riotous behaviour' in certain local Acts. In addition, unless a different intention appears, nothing in Part I affects the meaning of 'riot' or any cognate expression in any instrument, eg a by-law, taking effect before s 10 came into force.

---

1   1 April 1987: Public Order Act 1986 (Commencement No 2) Order 1987, SI 1987/198.
2   See paras **9.30–9.34**.
3   See paras **9.35**.
4   1986 Act, s 10(4).

VIOLENT DISORDER

3.40 Section 2(1) of the 1986 Act provides that:

> 'Where 3 or more persons who are present together use or threaten unlawful violence and the conduct of them (taken together) is such as would cause a person of reasonable firmness present at the scene to fear for his personal safety, each of the persons using or threatening unlawful violence is guilty of violent disorder.'

Violent disorder was intended to be the usual offence charged in respect of serious breaches of public order by groups, riot being intended to be charged only in the most serious cases.[1] This intention seems to have been fulfilled. In the 11-year period 1987–1997 the average annual number of convictions or cautions for riot was 14 and for violent disorder 1448.[2] Research on the use of charges under s 2 also serves to show that violent disorder is the offence charged in more serious cases. In a survey of 470 public order cases taken from police records at five police stations in two police areas in 1988, 80% of which involved charges of minor public order offences, 6% of the cases led to charges of violent disorder and none to charges of riot.[3]

Because violent disorder can be committed by words alone, it can be charged against groups of demonstrators of all kinds who use or simply threaten violence. Thus, for example, if a racist march or static demonstration takes place in the centre of an immigrant community, accompanied by threats of immediate violence that would make a person of reasonable firmness fear for his personal safety, the offence is committed. However, violent disorder is not limited to serious public disorder. If three or more gather outside a dance hall using or threatening violence against others, they (or any one of them) can be convicted of violent disorder if they are acting collectively and their conduct (taken together) is sufficiently frightening to be liable to affect a person of reasonable firmness. Others who assist or encourage a perpetrator of violent disorder to commit that offence can be convicted of it as accomplices in accordance with the ordinary principles of secondary participation.[4] On the other hand, if three or more 'merely' make taunts of a racist nature highly offensive to the local inhabitants, they do not commit violent disorder although they may give rise to an offence under s 4A (see para **4.21**), s 5 (see para **4.41**) or s 18 of the 1986 Act (see para **5.15**) or s 31 of the Crime and Disorder Act 1998 (see para **4.81**).

The research referred to above[3] indicates that, whatever the extent of its technical application, violent disorder tends to be charged in the more serious type of case, usually involving quite a number of people and mostly involving fights between groups of youths which sometimes resulted in fairly serious injuries. According to one custody officer anything premeditated or planned would lead to a charge of violent disorder, as opposed to affray, if sufficient numbers were involved. A charge of violent disorder would also be used as an alternative to a charge of assault occasioning bodily harm or inflicting grievous bodily harm, contrary to s 47 or s 20 of the Offences Against the Person Act 1861, if there was doubt about the sufficiency of the evidence of such an offence.

1   Home Secretary, HC Deb, vol 89, col 795 (1986).
2   *Criminal Statistics: England and Wales 1997* (Cm 4162, 1998). There were no cautions for riot
     in 1997; the figures for violent disorder in that year show a 4:1 ratio for convictions:cautions.
3   Newburn et al 'Policing the streets' (1990) 29 *Home Office Research Bulletin* 10.
4   Affirmed in *R v Jefferson* [1994] 1 All ER 270, CA.

Prohibited conduct

3.41 Section 2(1) of the 1986 Act requires an individual accused to use or threaten unlawful violence in the following circumstances:

(a) that three or more people (including the accused) present together use or threaten unlawful violence;
(b) that the conduct of them (taken together) is such as would cause a person (ie a third party bystander) of reasonable firmness present at the scene to fear for his personal safety. No person of reasonable firmness need actually be, or be likely to be, present at the scene.[1]

As in the case of riot and affray, and for the same reason (see para **3.11**), violent disorder may be committed in private as well as in public places.[2]

The prohibited conduct for this offence is substantially the same as for that of riot (and the comments made when discussing the identical elements in riot[3] are equally applicable here) with the following exceptions.

1   1986 Act, s 2(3).
2   Ibid, s 2(4).
3   See paras **3.12–3.17**, **3.20–3.23**, and **3.26–3.28** mutatis mutandis.

An individual accused may be guilty if he uses or threatens violence

3.42 For the reason given in para **3.21**, a threat of violence must be of violence by the threatener and not of violence by someone else. Because of the need for three or more people present together *actually* to use or threaten violence, a group of people who decide to commit an offence by the use of violence or to achieve some other object by violence are not thereby guilty of violent disorder. Thus, if 10 football supporters together in a pub agree to attack a rival group when they get to the football ground, but they are arrested en route, they cannot be convicted of violent disorder (nor could they have been convicted of riot if their number had exceeded 12). The obvious offence to charge in such a case is conspiracy to commit violent disorder or conspiracy to commit riot, as the case may be.

Only three persons (including the accused) who are present together are required to use or threaten unlawful violence

3.43 This can be compared with the minimum of 12 for riot. It will be noted that the minimum number (three) accords with the common law requirement in regard to riot and unlawful assembly. It is immaterial whether or not the three or more use or threaten unlawful violence simultaneously.[1] This exclusion of simultaneity corresponds to that provided for the offence of riot by s 1(2) of the 1986 Act. However, it is submitted that it is less defensible here since, while it would be unrealistic to expect 12 or more people to use or threaten violence, the same cannot be said when only three are involved. If three individuals who are present together threaten violence at different points of time (and possibly in different places as they move around) it cannot really be said that this is a case of group disorder (the mischief of the offence), especially when, unlike riot, a common purpose need not be proved against them.

It is commonplace for a number of individual fights to break out outside licensed premises after closing time. In *R v Meredith*,[2] where fights broke out in a nightclub car park, an accused and another man being involved in a fight about 70 metres away from another fight, the Court of Appeal stated that a jury could find that there were three or more persons present together using unlawful violence.

While the three or more persons must be using or threatening unlawful violence (so that no offence is committed if all but one or two are using or threatening violence in self-defence), it is not necessary that they should be criminally responsible. Consequently (as in the case of riot), it is irrelevant that some (or even all but one) are under the age of criminal responsibility, criminally insane or acting under duress. Likewise, it is expressly provided that the determination of the number of persons who use or threaten violence is not affected by the fact that some lack the mens rea required for violent disorder under s 6(2) of the 1986 Act, although of course that offence cannot be committed unless at least one person has that mens rea.

It must be proved that three or more were using or threatening unlawful violence. Aiders and abettors cannot be counted in. Thus, violent disorder is not committed if X merely encourages Y and Z to use unlawful violence and no one else is involved in the use or threat of such violence.[3]

1   1986 Act, s 2(2).
2   (1993) unreported, CA.
3   *R v McGuigan* [1991] Crim LR 719, CA.

Neither the accused nor the other participants are required to use or threaten unlawful violence for a common purpose

3.44 Since violence need not be used, merely threatened, the offence may be committed by three pickets who shout out 'we will get the scabs', although whether the threat must be of immediate violence (so that no offence would be committed if the scabs were not then present) has, as in the case of riot,[1] yet to be decided.

1   See para **3.27**.

Mental element

3.45 A person is guilty of perpetrating violent disorder only if he intends to use or threaten violence or is aware that his conduct may be violent or threaten violence.[1] This requirement does not affect the determination of the number of persons who use or threaten violence.[2]

As in the case of riot, a person whose awareness is impaired by intoxication is to be taken to be aware of that of which he would be aware if not intoxicated, unless he shows either that his intoxication was not self-induced or that it was caused solely by the taking or administration of a substance in the course of medical treatment.[3]

1   1986 Act, s 6(2). See para **3.29**.
2   1986 Act, s 6(7).
3   Ibid, s 6(5). 'Intoxication' is defined by s 6(6); see para **3.30**.

Acquittal of all but one or two

3.46 Where the only persons against whom there is evidence of using or threatening violence are those named in the indictment and it is not proved that at least three of the accused were using or threatening unlawful violence, but it is proved that one or two were, the one or two cannot be convicted of violent disorder.[1] This was held by the Court of Appeal in *R v Fleming*,[2] where the Court held that the jury should be specifically directed to that effect. In *Fleming*, F, R, M and D were charged with violent disorder. The evidence did not indicate the involvement of anyone else in the conduct which formed the basis of the charge. The jury acquitted M and failed to agree in regard to D. They convicted F and R. Applying the above principles, the Court of Appeal allowed F and R's appeal against conviction, although it substituted a conviction for affray.[3] It held that, subject to the 'extremely rare' case where someone who uses or threatens unlawful violence lacks mens rea, is insane or under the age of criminal responsibility or has a defence of duress, an accused could not be convicted of violent disorder if only the accused were alleged to have been involved in the use or threatened use of unlawful violence and all but one or two were acquitted.

1   The same applies, of course, at a summary trial.
2   (1989) 153 JP 517, CA.
3   If a jury only finds the use or threat of violence to property, such a verdict is not possible: see
      para **3.54**. Also see *R v McGuigan* [1991] Crim LR 719, CA; see para **3.43** fn 3.

3.47 In *R v Fleming*, the Court of Appeal distinguished its decision in *R v Mahroof.*[1]
In *Mahroof*, it had held that there could be a conviction of only one or two persons
accused of violent disorder, despite the acquittal of other co-accused, if there was
evidence of the use or threat of unlawful violence by others who were not charged
before the court, provided that the defence had been properly informed of any
allegations which they would have to meet. In *Mahroof*, the indictment charged B,
M and S with violent disorder. There was evidence at the trial that two other men,
not before the court, had been present at the scene and had been involved in
using or threatening unlawful violence. The jury acquitted B and S, but convicted
M of violent disorder after the judge had indicated that such a course was open to
them. He had also told them to consider each accused separately, but at the same
time to bear in mind that they should convict only if they were satisfied that there
had been three persons using or threatening unlawful violence.

The judge certified the following question for the Court of Appeal:

> 'Where three defendants are indicted for an offence of violent disorder contrary to s 2
> of the Public Order Act 1986 and following unanimous verdicts of a jury that two of the
> defendants are not guilty of this charge, is the jury entitled in law to convict the
> remaining defendant of the offence provided the jury have been directed that they
> must be satisfied that the latter defendant is one of three or more persons who are
> present together using or threatening violence within the meaning of s 2 of the Public
> Order Act 1986?'

The Court of Appeal answered, '"Yes, subject to two important qualifications":
first of all, that there is evidence before the jury that there were three people
involved in the criminal behaviour, though not necessarily those named in the
indictment; secondly, that the defence are apprised of what it is they have to meet.'
The Court concluded that, although the first qualification had been met, the
second had not. It therefore allowed M's appeal against conviction for violent
disorder, although it substituted a conviction for an offence under s 4 of the 1986
Act.

In respect of the second qualification, the Court said that:

> 'The best way of alerting the defence, and we would say generally speaking the only
> way of alerting the defence to a situation such as this, is by putting it in the indictment.[2]
> ... If that had been done, there could be no question but that the defence were alerted
> to what it was they had to meet. Then if they wanted, they could have asked for
> particulars and the evidence of [the prosecution witness] as to these other two [men]
> would then have assumed the importance which it assumed before us and defence
> counsel could have made his plans accordingly.'[3]

The Court of Appeal allowed M's appeal because it was not certain that he should
or could have been so alerted by the way in which the case against him was
presented.

On the other hand, in *R v Lacey*,[4] where the indictment charged violent
disorder as committed by three accused, including D (who alone was convicted),
and no one else (ie it did not say 'and others'), an appeal against conviction was
dismissed; the defence was well aware from the prosecution opening, and the

committal statements, of the case being put and the evidence showed that more than three were involved in the offence.

1   (1989) 88 Cr App R 317, CA.
2   For example by adding 'and others' after the names of the accused in the indictment.
3   (1989) 88 Cr App R 317 at 321.
4   (1996) unreported, CA.

3.48 The nature of the direction which the judge should give to a jury in the present type of case was considered further by the Court of Appeal in *R v Worton*,[1] where there was evidence that a large number had participated in unlawful violence. Of the four persons charged with violent disorder, only three were tried and one of them was acquitted. Because there was evidence of participation by others, *R v Fleming* was distinguishable and the first qualification was satisfied. So, it was apparently held, was the second qualification in *R v Mahroof* because the defence had been alerted to the case they had to meet by the way the evidence was led of the participation of others.

Nevertheless, the Court of Appeal allowed an appeal against conviction for violent disorder, although it substituted a conviction for affray. It held that the judge had misdirected the jury by simply describing the offence of violent disorder in general terms. He had to go further 'and warn the jury specifically that if any of the three defendants should be acquitted of violent disorder, then they must necessarily acquit the other two, unless satisfied that some other person not charged was taking part in the violent disorder'.[2]

It is submitted that the Court's apparent satisfaction that the second qualification in *Mahroof* was satisfied is unfair to the defence. It certainly is in contradiction of the view taken in the quotation from *Mahroof* in para **3.47**. Is it fair that the second qualification should be fulfilled by evidence given at the trial, rather than information set out in advance of the trial?[3]

In *R v Turpin*,[4] the Court of Appeal held that it was not always necessary where three were in the dock for a judge to direct a jury to acquit all three if they acquitted one. In that case, the appellant had conceded that violent disorder had occurred, but contended that he had played no part in it and that others not charged were involved.

1   (1990) 154 JP 201, CA.
2   Ibid, at 204.
3   This point is made in *Blackstone's Criminal Practice* (Blackstone, 1999), para B.11.31.
4   [1990] Crim LR 514, CA.

Alternative bases for conviction

3.49 Where an allegation of violent disorder consists of more than one separate incident, eg one inside a nightclub and a separate one soon after outside it,[1] the jury must be sure either unanimously or by a majority[2] that at least one of those incidents was proved and that the incident (or one of the incidents) proved amounted to violent disorder.[3] It is a misdirection for the judge not to direct the jury in this respect.[3] There is, of course, no need for such a direction if, although the incident in question (eg outside a nightclub) was associated with another incident (eg inside the nightclub), the judge has made clear that they were only concerned with one incident (eg by telling them that they are only concerned with the incident outside the nightclub).[4]

---

1   Like riot and affray (paras **3.22** and **3.64**), an offence of violent disorder may well involve a continuous course of conduct.
2   In accordance with the Juries Act 1974, s 17; *Practice Direction (Majority Verdicts)* [1970] 2 All ER 215.
3   *R v Houlden* (1994) 99 Cr App R 244, CA.
4   *R v Keeton* [1995] 2 Cr App R 241, CA.

Prosecution, trial and punishment

3.50 Violent disorder is triable either way.[1] However, according to the *National Mode of Trial Guidelines*, it should generally be committed for trial.[2]

The maximum punishment is five years' imprisonment or an unlimited fine, or both, on conviction on indictment, or six months or a fine not exceeding the statutory maximum, or both, on summary conviction.[1] By virtue of the maximum term of imprisonment on conviction on indictment, violent disorder is an arrestable offence under s 24(1) of PACE.

The terms of the offence are such that the more restricted offence of riot (involving as it does a minimum of 12, not three, a common purpose and the use of violence) is not often charged. There are not many occasions where a prosecutor will consider that an offence is so deserving of a greater penalty than the maximum of five years for violent disorder that it merits all the added complications of a riot charge.

---

1   1986 Act, s 2(5).
2   *Practice Note* [1990] 3 All ER 979. The Mode of Trial Guidelines in the *Note* were revised and re-issued by the Criminal Justice Consultative Council, with the commendation of Lord Taylor CJ, in 1995. The revised version has not yet been reported but is to be found in *Archbold on Criminal Pleading, Evidence and Practice* (2000) and in Murphy *Blackstone's Criminal Practice* (Blackstone Press, 1999).

AFFRAY

3.51 Section 3(1) of the 1986 Act provides that:

'A person is guilty of affray if he uses or threatens unlawful violence towards another and his conduct is such as would cause a person of reasonable firmness present at the scene to fear for his personal safety.'

3.52 As will be seen, the definition of affray is a wide one. It has been said that:

'It typically involves a group of people who may well be shouting, struggling, threatening, waving weapons, throwing objects, exchanging and threatening blows and so on.'[1]

However, one reason why affray is a wide offence is that, unlike riot and violent disorder, the use or threat of unlawful violence by one person alone can suffice. A trivial common assault or battery will not involve an affray, but in a more serious assault or battery there may be evidence that a person of reasonable firmness present at the scene would have feared for his personal safety. If so, there would be evidence of the much more serious offence of affray. It would be immaterial that the context was a domestic dispute at home or some other context lacking a 'public element'. Nevertheless, the propriety of charging affray in such a context is open to doubt. Such incidents can hardly be said to give rise to the serious disturbance to public order which the Law Commission intended the offence to deal with. They are in reality simply offences against the person and should be charged as such.[2] The number of convictions and cautions a year,[3] however, suggests that inappropriate use, a 'downgrading', is being made of affray, as does research on the use of charges of that offence. The research into 470 public order cases in 1988 referred to in para **3.40** indicated that 14% of the sample were charged as affray, the vast majority of those incidents being generally relatively minor in nature. The research also showed that a charge of affray would also be used as an alternative to one of assault occasioning ABH or inflicting GBH if there was doubt about the sufficiency of the evidence of either of these offences.[4]

An example of a case satisfying the definition of affray, but which appears to fall well outside the Law Commission's perception of the mischief of affray, is *R v Davison*.[5] Police were called to an alleged domestic incident at D's flat. When one of the officers entered the flat, he saw D holding an 8 inch kitchen knife. He told D twice to put it down. D replied by 'swiping' the knife from right to left towards the officer, saying 'I'll have you'. The officer jumped over a settee and joined the rest of his colleagues. D then threw the knife out of a window and was arrested. Dismissing an appeal against a conviction for affray, the Court of Appeal rejected D's argument that there was no case to answer; there was evidence on which the jury could find that every element of the offence had been proved.

There is a good deal of overlap between affray and violent disorder. If three or more are involved in the use or threat of unlawful violence towards another (other than a threat by words alone) and the other elements of violent disorder are satisfied, this will ipso facto satisfy the requirements for the less serious offence of affray. Likewise, there is much overlap between affray and the offence under s 4 of the Public Order Act 1986, dealt with in the next chapter.

---

1   *R v Smith* [1997] 1 Cr App R 14 at 16.
2   Law Com Report no 123 (1983) para 3.38.
3   The annual average number of persons convicted or cautioned for affray in the period 1987–1997 was about 5,000 and growing (the number in 1997 was almost double that, of whom a fifth were cautioned).
4   Newburn et al 'Policing the streets' (1990) 29 *Home Office Research Bulletin* 10.
5   [1992] Crim LR 31, CA; compare *R v Sanchez* (1996) 160 JP 321, CA.

Prohibited conduct

3.53 As the Court of Appeal noted in *R v Davison*,[1] there are two limbs to affray:

(a) the accused must use or threaten unlawful violence towards another; and
(b) his conduct must be such as would cause a person of reasonable firmness present at the scene to fear for his personal safety.

Like riot and violent disorder, affray may be committed in private as well as in public places,[2] and the same comments and justifications concerning this apply as mentioned in the case of riot (para **3.11**). One result is that, if a fight breaks out between two people at a party in someone's home or at a private function at a discotheque, they can be guilty of affray if the terms of the offence are satisfied. In fact any assault, even a domestic one, whether accompanied by the use or threat of violence is an affray if it would cause a person of reasonable firmness present at the scene to fear for his personal safety. The 'public' element of the fight or violence is not an obvious one in such a case. Indeed, the definition of the offence under s 3 is such as to raise the question whether it can be classified as a public order offence at all.

Most of the elements of the prohibited conduct are common to riot and violent disorder, but a fundamental difference is that there is no requirement of the participation of others.[3] An affray can be constituted by the use or threat of such violence by one person alone; there need be no reciprocity. If there is, otherwise than in self-defence or the like, each participant may be convicted of affray. It has been argued that affray is an aggravated assault, although without clearly identified aggravating features.[4]

Someone who aids and abets another to commit an affray can be convicted of that offence as an accomplice.[5]

---

1   [1992] Crim LR 31, CA; see para **3.52**.
2   1986 Act, s 3(5).
3   This was confirmed in *R v Riches* (1989) unreported, CA. The court also pointed out that there was no need for the accused to contemplate or encourage any unlawful violence to others.
4   ATH Smith 'Metamorphosis of affray' (1986) 136 NLJ 521.
5   The principles of secondary liability apply to the offence under the 1986 Act, s 3: *R v Jefferson* [1994] 1 All ER 270, CA.

Use or threat of unlawful violence towards another[1]

3.54 Unlike the position in riot and violent disorder, 'violence' here does not include violent conduct towards property.[2] In *Cobb v DPP*,[3] an information alleging affray referred to the threat or use of violence 'by causing damage to property, fighting and assaulting' P. It was held that the reference to property damage and assault were unnecessary on a charge of affray and did not have to be proved by the prosecution, since those allegations were not essential elements of the offence. Indeed, said the Divisional Court, the reference to property damage was irrelevant. Because the violence must be used or threatened *towards* another, a public suicide attempt is not an affray even if the mode of the attempt would have made a person of reasonable firmness fear for his personal safety. On the other hand, provided force has been used or threatened towards another, it is irrelevant whether that other is a bystander or is a participant in a fight etc with the accused.

In the offence under s 4 of the 1986 Act, dealt with in the next chapter, where threatening words or behaviour must be used *towards another*, it has been held that the words or behaviour must be used in the physical presence of and in the direction of another person directly,[4] ie be directed towards that other person. Overall, 'towards another' has a similar meaning in s 3. In *I v DPP*,[5] which was concerned with a threat of violence, the Divisional Court held that affray requires the presence of a person threatened (ie not simply a hypothetical person). On the other hand, it held, a person threatened need not actually feel threatened. Nor, indeed, according to Hughes J, need the person threatened be aware of the threat;[6] it does not matter, for example, that his back was turned. The person threatened need not be identified. In addition, the Divisional Court held, a threat could be made generally in a populous place to all about, whether local residents, other members of the public at the scene or police officers called to the scene.

In *I v DPP*, whose facts are set out more fully in para **3.55**, the accused, members of a gang 'milling around' outside a residential block, had made a threat of unlawful violence by their visible possession of petrol bombs. The Divisional Court held that in the circumstances the magistrate had been entitled to conclude that the diffuse threat of violence, inherent in carrying the bombs, constituted a threat of violence towards anyone in the vicinity, including the police on arrival at the scene.

It would seem obvious that, as in s 4 of the 1986 Act, the accused's conduct cannot be 'towards another' unless it was 'directed at' (ie 'aimed at') another. There is nothing in the actual decision to gainsay this but an obiter dictum in the judgment of Hughes J seems to do so. He said that the people threatened 'in cases like the present' might include people able to see the events from the windows of the residential block. It is difficult to see how it could be said that the threat of violence in a case like *I v DPP* could be said to have been towards such people, since it would not have been aimed at them. If Hughes J was correct, 'towards another' would be deprived of any real meaning; any threat of unlawful violence per se would suffice.

---

1   See paras **3.12–3.17** and **3.21–3.23** mutatis mutandis.
2   1986 Act, s 8.
3   (1992) 156 JP 746, DC.
4   See para **4.8**.
5   [2000] Crim LR 45, DC. This is a brief report; reliance has been placed on the transcript.
6   This is at odds with the rule in s 4; see *Swanston v DPP*, para **4.8**.

3.55 Another important difference between affray and riot and violent disorder is that a threat of violence cannot be made by the use of words alone,[1] whether the words are uttered orally or displayed or distributed in writing, and however aggressively the words are expressed.[2] If a threat by words alone could suffice, the offence under s 4 of the 1986 Act (para **4.2**) would be redundant. There must be some conduct on the part of the accused, such as brandishing a knife or the visible possession of a weapon in circumstances amounting to a threat of unlawful violence, which is a threat of violence on the part of the threatener.[3] Of course, an affray can be committed where a threat of violence is made by a combination of words and gestures (such as shouting out 'I'll get you for that', while brandishing a weapon or even shaking a fist) as well as by gestures alone.

The obvious examples of threats are those made by gestures (eg brandishing a weapon) or by a combination of words and gestures (such as shouting out 'I'll get you for that', while brandishing a weapon or shaking a fist). However, as indicated in para **3.21**, conduct and/or the appearance giving rise to an aura of menace was held by the Divisional Court in *I v DPP*[4] to be capable of amounting to a threat of violence.

In *I v DPP*, the facts found by the magistrate were as follows. The police, responding to a call, approached a gang of 40 to 50 youths 'milling around' outside a residential block in East London. About eight or nine of the youths, including I, M and H, were carrying what appeared to be petrol bombs. None of them lit or brandished the bombs in a threatening way or threw them. One of the officers thought that there would be a disturbance, although there was no other gang or anyone other than the police present at the scene. On the arrival of the police the youths dispersed. I, M and H, and others, threw away their bombs. In that part of East London, street gangs were territorial and there was bad blood between the various gangs. The magistrate convicted I, M and H of affray. One of their questions on appeal to the Divisional Court was whether the mere possession of petrol bombs in the circumstances was capable of amounting to a threat of violence.

Dismissing the appeals, the Divisional Court held that there was no reason why an aura of menace derived from conduct and/or appearance could not amount to a threat of violence for the purposes of affray. However, what amounted to a threat was essentially a question of fact in each case. The visible carrying in public of petrol bombs by a large number of members of what was obviously an East London gang out for no good was clearly capable of constituting a threat of unlawful violence, regardless of the fact that the armed gang members were not yet throwing or brandishing their weapons. The Court stressed, however, that mere possession of a weapon without threatening circumstances was sufficient to constitute a threat of violence.

R v Dixon[5] is a borderline case. Two police officers pursuing D met him with his Alsatian-type dog which was running free. The dog was in an excitable state, barking, snarling and dashing about. The officers asked D to restrain it, but instead of doing so D kept on saying 'go on, go on'. The dog then ran forward and bit both officers. At D's trial for affray, the Crown's case rested on the events up to, but prior to, the biting of the officers. Dismissing D's appeal against conviction, the Court of Appeal held that the case was indistinguishable as a matter of law from that in which a man with a weapon, loaded or unloaded, uttered threats of violence. It was not a case of a threat by words alone. The Court emphasised that the dog had been in an excitable state and that the accused had used the dog in such a way as to use it as a weapon for the purpose of creating fear in the minds of the officers. The essence of the prosecution case could have been put shortly as 'setting the dog at the police officers'. It seems that it would have been different if the dog had been passive and unresponsive to D's words; there would only have been a threat by words alone since the dog could not be said to be used as a weapon to create fear. A fortiori, simply to say 'I'll set my dog on you' would not suffice for the purposes of affray.

As recognised by Auld LJ in *I v DPP*,[6] where a number of people are alleged to have been concerned together, their conduct should be considered together as well as individually. Similar conduct by a number of people acting together may amount to a threat of violence when the same conduct by an individual acting on his own may not.

---

1   1986 Act, s 3(3).

2   *R v Robinson* [1993] Crim LR 581, CA (adoption of an aggressive voice insufficient).

3   *R v Dixon* [1993] Crim LR 579, CA. The suggestion in the commentary that what occurred in *Dixon* amounted to the use (and not a mere threat) of violence is difficult to accept, and does not appear to have been the view of the court. The conduct in *Dixon* was treated by Auld LJ in *I v DPP* [2000] Crim LR 45, DC, as amounting to a threat of violence. This point does not appear in the brief report but does appear in the transcript.

4   [2000] Crim LR 45, DC.

5   [1993] Crim LR 579, CA.

6   [2000] Crim LR 45, DC. This point does not appear in the brief report; reliance has been placed on the transcript.

3.56 An affray, like riot and violent disorder, can only be committed if the violence is unlawful (see para **3.17**). Thus, a person who fights another in self-defence (or in effecting a lawful arrest or with some other private or public defence[1]) cannot be guilty of an affray,[2] although his assailant (or the person being arrested) can be if his use of violence would make a person of reasonable firmness fear for his personal safety.

As in other offences where a private or public defence is raised, a judge must leave the issue to the jury with a direction on that defence.[2] Where some other offence is also charged in respect of the same incident, eg unlawful wounding and/or assault occasioning actual bodily harm, and a private or public defence is raised as a justification in respect of all the offences charged in respect of that incident, the judge must direct the jury as to what would be the position on the affray charge if they acquitted on the other charge or charges.[3] This will involve the judge in a difficult task. Quite apart from this, to charge a number of offences in relation to the same incident is going to face the judge with the weighty burden of explaining to the jury the difference between an affray and the other offences.[4]

---

1   *R v Rothwell* [1993] Crim LR 626, CA.
2   *R v Pulham* [1995] Crim LR 296, CA; *R v Key* (1992) unreported, CA.
3   *R v Pulham* above.
4   See commentary to *R v Pulham*, above.

Conduct such as would cause a person of reasonable firmness present at the scene to fear for his personal safety

3.57 Section 3 does not explain what is meant by 'presence at the scene'. In the common law offence, the term was understood as referring to 'an innocent member of the public within sight or earshot' of the violence.[1] The Law Commission recognised that:

> '[T]here may be some degree of uncertainty as to what is meant by "presence", but we doubt whether it is possible or desirable to be more specific as to how far away from or how near to the disturbance the hypothetical person must be. Every case will to this extent depend on its circumstances, but we believe that a jury will sufficiently understand what is meant by "present at the scene", that is anyone who would have been in real danger of becoming involved in the disturbance.'[2]

To the extent that there is any difference between 'within sight and earshot' and the test at the end of the quotation, it would seem that the latter is the more appropriate in respect of the present requirement.

---

1   *A-G's Reference (No 3 of 1983)* [1985] 1 All ER 501, CA.
2   Law Com Report no 123 (1983) para 3.38. The Court of Appeal had regard to this
     explanation in *R v Davison* [1992] Crim LR 31.

3.58 As with the similar requirement in riot[1] and violent disorder, the question is whether a hypothetical bystander of reasonable firmness would have been caused to fear for his own[2] personal safety; it is not enough that he would have been put in fear as to the personal safety of a participant in a fight or someone else.[2]

In deciding whether the present requirement is satisfied, the jury or magistrates are entitled to take into account evidence of the circumstances such as whether the violence used was indiscriminate (or a threat generalised) or was focused between those directly involved, the nature of the place where the incident occurred,[3] whether or not anyone not involved was afraid,[4] and so on. In *DPP v Cotcher*,[5] where the accused had been involved in a fight in a pub, the Divisional Court dismissed the prosecutor's appeal against acquittals for affray, on the ground that in assessing whether a person of reasonable firmness present at the scene would have feared for his personal safety, the magistrates were entitled to take into account evidence as to the nature of the scene of the incident, as to the fact that the violence was clearly limited to those involved and as to the fact that the other people in the pub carried on as usual despite the fight and did not appear to be in fear for their own safety.

1   See para **3.27**. Presumably, the fear must be for immediate personal safety.
2   This point is clear from the words of s 3(1). It was recognised in *R v Davison* [1992] Crim LR 31, CA, and in *DPP v Cotcher* [1993] COD 181, DC.
3   A person of reasonable firmness might fear for his personal safety if violence was used or threatened in a confined space, but not if the same conduct occurred in an open space: *R v Sanchez* (1996) 160 JP 321, CA, see para **3.61**, approving the statement to this effect in Professor Sir John Smith's commentary to *R v Davison* above.
4   In *DPP v Gormley* (1992) unreported, the Divisional Court held that the magistrates had applied the law correctly in concluding on the evidence (including evidence from two women who had tried to intervene in the fight that they were not frightened, but simply annoyed) that a hypothetical bystander of reasonable firmness would not have feared for his personal safety.
5   [1993] COD 181, DC.

3.59 The common law offence referred to 'terror', but the Law Commission thought that 'fear' was a more suitable term for modern legislation. It considered that any distinction between the two words was marginal. This is questionable; 'affray' is derived from the French word 'effrayer' (to terrify) and, in *Taylor v DPP*,[1] Lord Hailsham said this about the common law offence: 'It is essential to stress that the degree of violence required to constitute the offence of affray must be such as to be calculated to terrify a person of reasonably firm character. This should not be watered down.' The transition from 'terror' (defined by the *Shorter Oxford English Dictionary* as, inter alia, 'state of being extremely frightened') to 'fear for personal safety' is surely a watering down.

1   [1975] 2 All ER 1108.

3.60 Although s 3(1) of the 1986 Act requires that an accused's conduct 'is such as would cause a person of reasonable firmness present at the scene to fear for his personal safety', s 3(2) of the 1986 Act provides that, where two or more people use or threaten the unlawful violence, it is the conduct of them taken together that must be considered for the purpose of ascertaining whether the conduct would have the required effect. It is not necessary that an individual accused's conduct on its own would have had this effect. It is enough that the conduct of all who used or threatened the unlawful violence would have done so, whether or not any of the others are also charged before the court.

3.61 As in the case of riot and violent disorder no one besides the participants (ie no bystander) need be present, or be likely to be present, at the scene, and it is expressly provided by s 3(4) of the 1986 Act that no person of reasonable firmness need actually be, or be likely to be, present at the scene.

Nevertheless, the offence of affray envisages at least three persons:

(a) the person using or threatening unlawful violence;
(b) a person towards whom the violence or threat is directed; and
(c) a person of reasonable firmness who need not actually be, or be likely to be, present at the scene.[1]

It is not enough that the victim of the violence or threat is put in fear for his personal safety[2] or that a reasonable person in *his* position would have been put in such fear.[3] The question is whether, if the hypothetical person of reasonable firmness had been present at the scene, he would have been caused fear for his personal safety.[1] In *R v Davison*, whose facts are set out in para **3.52**, the Court of Appeal held that the use of the knife was the sort of violence which, on a proper approach to the question, could cause the hypothetical bystander of reasonable firmness to fear for his personal safety. There had therefore been a case to answer. In answering it, it said, it was a matter for the jury to decide whether in fact that person would be under such a degree of fear.

R v Sanchez[4] provides an example of the importance of the present requirement. D lunged at her boyfriend with a knife in the car park of a block of flats during an altercation over another woman. P deflected D's arm and ran away. At D's trial for affray, the judge directed the jury that P was a person of reasonable firmness and that he was to be believed when he said that he was frightened by D's conduct. The judge did not direct the jury to consider the impact of D's conduct on a hypothetical bystander of reasonable firmness. Allowing D's appeal against conviction for affray, the Court of Appeal held that this was a misdirection. It stated that it was clear that, had the jury been properly directed, one could not be sure that they would have found that a bystander of reasonable firmness would have feared for his personal safety. The court noted that the violence which had taken place solely between D and P was personal to them, and also noted the location of the incident with every opportunity for a hypothetical bystander to distance himself from any danger. It might have been different if the events had happened in a small room.

---

1   *R v Sanchez* (1996) 160 JP 321, CA, approving the commentary of Professor Sir John Smith to *R v Davison* [1992] Crim LR 31, CA.
2   *R v Sanchez*, above.
3   *R v Davison*, above.
4   (1996) 160 JP 321, CA.

3.62 The rule that no bystander need actually be, or be likely to be, present at the scene is open to criticism in the case of private places, since where (as may be the case) there is little or no likelihood of members of the public being present or being alarmed, there seems to be little connection between the violence and the maintenance of *public* order. This is another reason why it is doubtful whether the offence should be included in a *public order* Act.

Mental element

3.63 A person is guilty of perpetrating affray only if he intends to use or threaten violence or is aware that his violence may be violent or threaten violence.[1] The same comments apply to this as apply to the mens rea for riot (see paras

3.29–3.32). Where the prosecution rely on s 3(2) of the 1986 Act (see para **3.60**), it will probably be necessary to show that the accused's awareness extended to the conduct of the other person(s) using or threatening unlawful violence.[2]

As in the case of riot, a person whose awareness is impaired by intoxication, whether by drink, drugs or other means (or a combination of these), should be taken to be aware of what he would have been aware of if not intoxicated, unless he proves that his intoxication was not self-induced or that it was caused solely by the taking or administration of a substance in the course of medical treatment.[3] Subject to concerns over the burden of proof, this is an eminently sensible provision given that affray is an appropriate offence to deal with serious fights outside pubs and clubs by those who have consumed too much alcohol.

1   1986 Act, s 6(2).
2   Smith and Hogan *Criminal Law* (1999) p 747.
3   1986 Act, s 6(5) and (6); see para **3.30**.

Alternative bases for conviction

3.64 The law is similar to that which applies to the offence of violent disorder, discussed in para **3.49**. Typically, the nature of the offence of affray involves a continuous course of conduct, as in the case of an indiscriminate mêlée, the criminal character of which depends on the general nature and effect of the conduct as a whole, and not on particular incidents and events which may take place during the course of it. Where the prosecution relies on such a continuous course of conduct, it is unnecessary for the prosecution to identify and prove particular incidents.[1]

On the other hand, different considerations may[2] apply where the conduct relied on by the prosecution is not continuous but falls into separate sequences of incidents, as where D becomes violent at a party in a house and attacks X and then goes outside the house and attacks Y. The reason is that the character of the conduct in each sequence and its effect on those present at the scene may be quite different. Unless the jury are directed that they must be satisfied[3] (or magistrates are satisfied) that the same sequence satisfies the requirements of affray, a conviction will be quashed, because there will not be the necessary verdict or finding that the ingredients of affray have been proved.

1   *R v Smith* [1997] 1 Cr App R 14, CA.
2   It is submitted that, although 'may' was used in *R v Smith*, above, at 17, the word 'would' would have been preferable by reference to the law applying to violent disorder.
3   Either unanimously or, where the majority verdict provisions are applicable, by the requisite majority.

Prosecution, trial and punishment

3.65 It is implicit in the gradation of offences in the Act that affray was meant to be reserved for serious cases involving the use or threat of violence, and this was certainly the intention of the Law Commission.[1] In less serious cases, prosecutors should charge an offence under s 4 of the Act or common assault. Nevertheless, there have been prosecutions for affray in less serious cases, such as *R v Davison*, referred to in para **3.52**.

1   Law Com Report no 123 (1983) para 3.5.

3.66 Affray is triable either way.[1] The *National Mode of Trial Guidelines*[2] provide that cases of affray should be tried summarily unless the magistrates' court conducting mode of trial proceedings considers that one or more of the following features is present in the case *and* that its sentencing powers are insufficient:

(a) organised violence or use of weapons;
(b) significant injury or substantial damage;
(c) the offence has clear racial motivation; or
(d) an attack upon police offices, prison officers, ambulancemen, firemen and the like.

This specific guidance is subject to the general guidance in the *Guidelines* that, where the case involves complex questions of fact or difficult questions of law, the court should consider committal for trial. An example of a case where there may be complex questions of fact would be one where the number of accused is substantial and the case against each is not a uniform one or where some (or all) are pleading self-defence.

1   1986 Act, s 3(7).
2   *Practice Note* [1990] 3 All ER 979; see para **3.50** fn 2.

3.67 The maximum punishment for affray is three years' imprisonment or an unlimited fine, or both, on conviction on indictment, or six months' imprisonment or a fine not exceeding the statutory maximum, or both, on summary conviction.[1]

1   1986 Act, s 3(7).

Arrest without warrant

3.68 The maximum punishment for affray is too low to qualify as an arrestable offence under s 24(1) of PACE. However, s 3(6) of the Public Order Act 1986 provides a much more limited statutory power of arrest: a constable may arrest without warrant anyone he reasonably suspects[1] *is committing* affray. The provisions of s 17 of PACE which empower a constable to enter and search premises to effect an arrest do not apply to an arrest for affray under the power given by s 3(6).[2]

Where the conduct has ceased, the only statutory power of arrest would be the conditional power of arrest under s 25 of PACE. This power would also be available in the case of the attempted use of violence or a threat thereof. Like the power of arrest under s 3(6) of the 1986 Act, the conditional power of arrest is limited to constables and depends on the constable having a reasonable suspicion that the person arrested has attempted or committed an affray; one of the general arrest conditions specified in s 25 must also be satisfied.

In addition to these statutory powers, it is inconceivable that an affray will not involve an actual or apprehended breach of the peace,[3] in which case there will be a common law power of arrest without warrant in the cases specified in paras **2.7–2.10**.

1   'Suspicion' is something less than belief: *Johnson v Whitehouse* [1984] RTR 38, DC; *R v Forsyth* [1997] 2 Cr App R 299, CA. 'Suspicion in its ordinary meaning is a state of conjecture or surmise when proof is lacking': *Shaaben Bin Hussien v Chong Fook Kam* [1969] 3 All ER 1626 at 1630, per Lord Devlin. A suspicion may be reasonable even though the material on which it is founded would not amount to a prima facie case for conviction of an offence: *Dumbell v Roberts* [1944] 1 All ER 326, CA; *Shaaben Bin Hussien v Chong Fook Kam*, above, or where it would not be admissible evidence, eg because it is hearsay: *McArdle v Egan* (1933) 150 LT 412, CA; *O'Hara v Chief Constable of the Royal Ulster Constabulary* [1997] 1 All ER 129, HL. Thus, the constable's suspicion need not be based on his own observations but could be based on what he has been told, or on information given to him anonymously. It is not necessary for him to prove what was known to his informant or that any of the facts on which he based his suspicion were in fact true. Whether such information provides reasonable grounds for the constable's suspicion depends on the source and context, viewed in the light of the surrounding circumstances: *O'Hara v Chief Constable of the Royal Ulster Constabulary* above. However, the mere fact that an arresting constable has been instructed by a superior officer to effect the arrest is not capable of amounting to reasonable grounds for the necessary suspicion: ibid.

    Where a constable has to make a spur of the moment decision in an emergency, this is a surrounding circumstance for which allowance must be made: *G v Chief Superintendent of Police, Stroud* (1988) 86 Cr App R 92, DC.

    The test of reason to suspect is a wholly objective test, ie 'would a reasonable person, in the light of what the constable knew at the time, have suspected . . .?' See *Lister v Perryman* (1870) LR 4 HL 521, HL; *McArdle v Egan* above; *Nakkuda Ali v M F De S Jayaratne* [1951] AC 66, PC; *Dallison v Caffery* [1964] 2 All ER 610, CA; *IRC v Rossminster Ltd* [1980] 1 All ER 80 at 84, 92, 103 and 104. Reasonableness of suspicion is evaluated without the qualification of hindsight: *Redmond-Bate v DPP* (1999) *The Times,* 28 July, DC. A constable who has formed a reasonable suspicion on the facts known to him is not obliged to discount all possible defences or seek complete proof before arresting the suspected person: *McCarrick v Oxford* [1983] RTR 117, CA; *Ward v Chief Constable of Avon & Somerset Constabulary* (1986) *The Times,* 26 June, CA. However, failure to follow an obvious course of verification may in exceptional circumstances be grounds for impugning the exercise of the power of arrest as a wrongful exercise of discretion: *Castorina v Chief Constable of Surrey* (1988) 138 NLJ 180, CA.

    The existence of the reasonable grounds and of the suspicion founded on them is ultimately a question of fact to be decided in the light of the circumstances disclosed by the evidence. It is not enough that the constable has reasonable grounds to suspect that the offence has been committed or attempted; he must actually suspect that thing: *Castorina v Chief Constable of Surrey*, above; *Chapman v Hall* (1988) 89 Cr App R 190, DC.

2   Compare the similar power of arrest under s 4(3), to which s 17 does apply; see para **4.18**.
3   See para **2.4**.

GENERAL

Duplicity

3.69 Section 7(2) of the 1986 Act provides that, for the purposes of the rules against duplicity,[1] each of ss 1–3 creates *one* offence. This ensures that a count in an indictment (or an information) charging, for example, an accused under s 3 (affray) with using *or* threatening violence in such a way as to cause a person of reasonable firmness to fear for his safety is not held to be bad for duplicity.

    Arguably, s 7(2) permits the prosecution to make broadly based and vague allegations which make it impossible for accused persons to know the charge to be met. If so, this could happen even if s 7(2) did not exist, since charges of using or threatening in indictments (or informations) for violent disorder or affray could still be brought simply by charging the use of violence under one count (or information) and the threat of violence under a second. Given that it is very likely that events of public disorder will give rise to indictments charging more than one offence, eg violent disorder and affray, the provisions in s 7(2) go some way to simplifying an indictment and making the task of judge and jury less complicated.

---

1   'Duplicity' means charging two offences in the same count of an indictment or in the same
     information (which is contrary to r 4(2) of the Indictment Rules 1971 and r 12(1) of the
     Magistrates' Courts Rules 1981, respectively).

3.70 The rule against duplicity also prohibits charging two (or more) *separate instances* of the same type of offence in the same count of an indictment or the same information. On the other hand, the rule is not infringed where the charge relates to a continuing offence as, for example, where there is evidence that the accused were milling around, uttering threats and fighting over a quarter of a mile for a number of hours. In such a case, a charge alleging a single offence of affray in 'divers streets' will not be bad for duplicity.[1] Of course, if the evidence shows that the violence or threat thereof had ceased and then recommenced, there would be a separate affray on the recommencement and a charge of an affray in different streets and at different times would be bad for duplicity.[2]

There can be no doubt that the above is equally applicable to riot and violent disorder. Unless the prosecution can prove that that conduct has formed one continuous sequence of occurrences in an unbroken run (at least on a prima facie basis), each separate occurrence should be charged separately. If it does not, either the count must be split by amendment for each offence or the prosecution must be directed to elect upon which offence the trial should proceed.[3]

---

1   *R v Woodrow* (1959) 43 Cr App R 105, CCA (common law affray).
2   *R v Jones* (1974) 59 Cr App R 120, CA (common law affray). See para **3.69**.
3   *Archbold on Criminal Pleading, Evidence and Practice* (2000) paras 1–140.

Alternative verdicts

Trials on indictment

3.71 Section 7(3) of the 1986 Act makes special provision for alternative verdicts where a trial takes place on indictment on a charge of violent disorder or affray.

Section 7(3) provides that if, at the trial on indictment of a person charged with violent disorder or affray, the jury find him not guilty of the offence charged, they may find him guilty of an offence under s 4 of the 1986 Act (threatening, abusive or insulting words or behaviour etc intended or likely to cause fear or to provoke violence), which is a summary offence and therefore not one in respect of which an alternative verdict can be returned under s 6(3) of the Criminal Law Act 1967.[1] The offence under s 4 was described by the Court of Appeal in *R v Fleming*[2] as being one step down the ladder of gravity from affray. Given that riot is committed only by the *use* of violence in specified circumstances, it is not surprising that s 7(3) does not apply on a charge of riot.

A jury can return an alternative verdict under s 7(3) only if it has returned a verdict of not guilty of violent disorder or affray, as the case may be, whether as a result of its own deliberations or following a direction from the judge to find the accused not guilty of that offence.[3]

Section 7(4) provides that, after a conviction for a s 4 offence under s 7(3), the Crown Court has the same powers and duties as a magistrates' court would have on convicting the accused of an offence under s 4.

---

1   See para **3.73**.
2   (1989) 153 JP 517 at 522.
3   *R v Carson* (1991) 21 Cr App R 236, CA.

3.72 Where the judge intends to leave the alternative of s 4 to the jury, he should give defence and prosecution counsel the chance to address him on that course of action[1] and then, if the alternative is to be left, to address the jury about it.[2] Failure to do the latter will result in an alternative conviction for a s 4 offence being quashed on appeal.[3] This safeguard is the answer to any complaint that the provision exposes an accused to the risk of conviction for an offence which has not been fully investigated during the trial (so that he has not had a chance to defend himself in relation to that offence) and which contains elements which may not have been part of the express allegations in the indictment. The judge should direct the jury about s 4 if it is left to them as an alternative.[4]

Unlike the offences of violent disorder and affray, an offence under s 4 cannot be committed where the incident occurs inside a dwelling and the victim is inside that dwelling or another dwelling. Thus, there cannot be an alternative conviction under s 4 in such a case.[5]

Where an accused is indicted for violent disorder or affray and pleads not guilty to that offence, he is at liberty to plead guilty to an offence under s 4 without it being necessary to empanel a jury.[6] The fact that the judge in such a case can accept the plea to the lesser offence without empanelling a jury, directing them to acquit of violent disorder or affray and thereafter inviting them to return a verdict of guilty under s 4, means that a great deal of unnecessary time and expense is avoided. Of course, the judge is not obliged to accept a plea of guilty under s 4 as an alternative to violent disorder or affray (to which the accused pleads not guilty). If the judge does not accept the plea, a jury will be empanelled to try the charge of violent disorder or affray, and the plea of guilty under s 4 is deemed to be withdrawn. As a result, if the accused is acquitted by the jury on the violent disorder or affray charge, the judge cannot direct the jury to convict the accused of the s 4 offence. There can only be a conviction of a s 4 offence in such a case if the jury has been fully directed on it or if there has been a formal admission of guilt *during* the trial (which is best effected by a plea of guilty in the jury's presence).[7]

---

1   *R v Stanley* [1993] Crim LR 618, CA.
2   *R v Perrins* [1995] Crim LR 432, CA.
3   Ibid; *R v Roberts* (1995) unreported, CA.
4   *R v Stanley*, above. The jury should only consider s 4 if it is unsure that violent disorder or
     affray (as the case may be) has been committed: ibid. Simply to read s 4 to the jury is not a
     proper direction. What must be done is to sort out from the words of the section those that
     are applicable in the case in question and either use only those words, or, perhaps better still,
     put them in the form of questions which the jury would have to answer if they were to find
     the essential ingredients of the offence proved: *R v Perrins*, above.
5   *R v Va Kun Hau* [1990] Crim LR 518, CA.
6   *R v O'Brien* (1992) 156 JP 925, CA, applying Criminal Law Act 1967, s 6(1)(b).
7   *R v Notman* [1994] Crim LR 518, CA.

3.73 The alternative verdict provisions in s 7(3) do not affect the general provision for alternative verdicts (at a trial on indictment) under s 6(3) of the Criminal Law Act 1967.[1]

An alternative verdict may only be returned under s 6(3) in relation to an offence within the jurisdiction of the court of trial. Section 6(3) of the Criminal Law Act 1967 provides that if the jury find the accused not guilty of the offence[2] specifically charged in the indictment, but the allegations in the indictment amount to or include (expressly or by implication) an allegation of another offence falling within the jurisdiction of the court of trial, the jury may find him guilty of that other offence or of an offence of which he could be found guilty on an indictment specifically charging that other offence.

In the consolidated appeals of *R v Wilson; R v Jenkins,*[3] the House of Lords held that s 6(3) envisaged four cases where a conviction of another offence than that charged in the indictment is permissible. These are where the allegation in the indictment:

(a) *expressly* amounts to an allegation of another offence;
(b) *impliedly* amounts to an allegation of another offence;
(c) *expressly* includes an allegation of another offence; and
(d) *impliedly* includes an allegation of another offence.

Provided one of these requirements is fulfilled, it is irrelevant that the other offence is not a necessary ingredient of the offence charged. Moreover, if the allegations in the indictment are *capable* of including (either expressly or impliedly) an allegation of another offence, the accused can be convicted of that other offence; the allegations need not necessarily involve the specific allegation of the other offence.

A count charging riot will expressly or impliedly include an allegation of violent disorder or affray, and a count charging violent disorder will expressly or impliedly include an allegation of affray. This is subject, in the case of an alternative verdict for affray, to the proviso that the allegations in the indictment do not specify only violence to property or only threats by words. It follows from the inclusion of an allegation of violent disorder or affray, as the case may be, in the above circumstances that alternative verdicts can be returned in these respects under s 6(3) of the 1967 Act if the jury are left with the possibility of returning an alternative verdict.

It may, however, be wiser to include alternative counts in the indictment if the prosecution wishes to put its case in the alternative. This is because a judge is not obliged to leave an alternative verdict under s 6(3) to the jury, and because the jury will always be able to see from the indictment the requisite elements and particulars of each offence charged against the accused.

As just indicated, and as in the case of leaving an alternative verdict under s 7(3) of the 1986 Act, a judge is not obliged to direct the jury about the option of convicting the accused of an alternative offence, where such a possibility is available in law. It is wrong to leave an alternative verdict to the jury if it does not arise on the evidence presented at the trial, but, if it has arisen and if directing the jury about it will not unnecessarily complicate the case, the judge should leave the alternative to them,[4] with a direction on the law relating to it.[4]

As with s 7(3) of the 1986 Act, whose case law reflects that in relation to s 6(3) of the 1967 Act, a judge who intends to leave an alternative verdict to the jury should warn defence and prosecution counsel beforehand and should give them the chance to make representations about that course of action[5] and, if it is to be left, to address the jury about the alternative verdict.[5]

---

1   1986 Act, s 7(3).

2   Except murder or treason. Because s 6(3) applies only if the jury find the accused not guilty of the offence specifically charged, a verdict of guilty of an alternative offence may not be returned under s 6(3) if the jury are unable to agree in respect of the offence charged: *R v Collison* (1980) 71 Cr App R 249, CA. In such a case, an alternative count can be added to the indictment if this causes no injustice: ibid. It seems that s 6(3) did not take away the common law power to return an alternative verdict of a lesser offence whose definition was necessarily included in that of the offence charged where the jury could not agree on the offence charged. In *R v Saunders* [1987] 2 All ER 973, the House of Lords took this view in relation to s 6(2) (alternative verdict for murder).

3   [1983] 3 All ER 448, HL.

4   *R v Fairbanks* [1986] 1 WLR 1202, CA.

5   *R v Hazell* [1985] RTR 369, CA.

Summary trials

3.74   There are no corresponding provisions for alternative findings of guilt in a summary trial, either in the 1986 Act or any other Act. It follows that a magistrates' court trying a charge of violent disorder or affray may not return an alternative finding of guilt. The court can reach a decision of guilty or not guilty only on the offence(s) charged in the information(s) before it.[1] Potential problems can be avoided if the prosecution lays two or more informations, charging different offences, since the magistrates may try the informations together without the accused's consent, provided the facts are sufficiently closely connected to justify this course and there is no risk of injustice to the accused by its adoption.[2] A justification for the absence of provision for alternative findings of guilt appears to be that an accused in a magistrates' court on a charge of one offence may not be prepared, without notice, to defend himself in relation to a different offence.[3] But, given the availability of legal aid etc, is there any real distinction between accused tried in the Crown Court and the accused in a magistrates' court? The point is one of general application, which should be dealt with in separate legislation.

---

1   *Lawrence v Same* [1968] 1 All ER 1191, DC.

2   *Chief Constable of Norfolk v Clayton* [1983] 1 All ER 984, HL.

3   Law Com Report no 123 (1983) para 7.11.

Chapter 4

THREATENING, ABUSIVE, INSULTING OR DISORDERLY CONDUCT AND RELATED OFFENCES

INTRODUCTION

4.1   This chapter is concerned principally with the offences provided by ss 4, 4A and 5 of the 1986 Act, which are less serious than those in the previous chapter. These offences replaced a number of statutory offences, the most important of which was that under s 5 of the Public Order Act 1936, which made it a summary offence for a person, in any public place or at any public meeting:

(a)   to use threatening, abusive or insulting words or behaviour; or
(b)   to distribute or display any writing, sign or visible representation which was threatening, abusive or insulting;

with intent to provoke a breach of the peace or whereby a breach of the peace was likely to be occasioned.

The offences under ss 4, 4A and 5 of the 1986 Act are described by their respective marginal notes as: 'fear or provocation of violence'; 'intentional harassment, alarm or distress'; and 'harassment, alarm or distress'. Although the language of the sections refers to the commission of the offences by a person, the offences, like any other, can be committed by a number of people as joint perpetrators.[1]

As will be seen, there is a good deal of overlap between all three offences, and especially between that under s 4A and the less serious one under s 5. The choice of charge is crucial. If the wrong offence is charged, and cannot be proved, the prosecution will fail entirely (unless another offence which can be proved is charged) because of the magistrates' inability to make an alternative finding of guilt.[2]

---

1   *Morrow v DPP* [1994] Crim LR 58, DC.
2   See para **4.3**.

FEAR OR PROVOCATION OF VIOLENCE

4.2   Section 4(1) of the Public Order Act 1986 provides that:

'A person is guilty of an offence if he:

(a)   uses towards another person threatening, abusive or insulting words or behaviour, or
(b)   distributes or displays to another person any writing, sign or other visible representation which is threatening, abusive or insulting,

with intent to cause that person to believe that immediate unlawful violence will be used against him or another by any person, or to provoke the immediate use of unlawful violence by that person or another, or whereby that person is likely to believe that such violence will be used or it is likely that such violence will be provoked.'

4.3   An offence under s 4 is triable summarily only,[1] although in some cases there may be an alternative conviction for it in the Crown Court on the trial on indictment of a charge of violent disorder or affray.[2] Where a magistrates' court finds an accused not guilty on a charge under s 4, it cannot find him guilty of some other offence (such as the lesser offence under s 5). As stated in para **3.74**, there is no general power to make an alternative finding of guilt in a magistrates' court,[3] nor does the 1986 Act provide one.

The maximum punishment is six months' imprisonment or a fine not exceeding level 5 on the standard scale, or both.[1]

---

1   1986 Act, s 4(4).
2   See para **3.71**.
3   *Lawrence v Same* [1968] 1 All ER 1191, DC. Potential problems which this incapacity can cause can be avoided if the prosecution lays two or more informations, charging different offences, since the magistrates may try them together without the accused's consent, if the facts are sufficiently closely connected and there is no risk of injustice to the accused in doing so: *Chief Constable of Norfolk v Clayton* [1983] 1 All ER 984, HL.

Prohibited conduct

4.4   Section 4 of the 1986 Act requires that the accused:

(a) uses towards another person threatening, abusive or insulting words or behaviour; or

(b) distributes or displays to another person any writing, sign or other visible representation which is threatening, abusive or insulting.

Threatening, abusive or insulting

4.5   It will be noted that only one of these three elements need be proved: the conduct need not be threatening, violent and abusive.

In *Brutus v Cozens*,[1] the House of Lords held that 'insulting' in s 5 of the Public Order Act 1936 was to be given its ordinary meaning and that the question whether words or behaviour were insulting was a question of fact, and not a question of law. The same approach has been adopted in relation to the 1986 Act.[2] It applies also to 'threatening' and 'abusive'.[2] Thus, the magistrates must decide as a question of fact whether the accused's conduct was threatening, abusive or insulting according to the ordinary meaning of those terms, and this is to be judged according to the impact which the conduct in its context[3] would have on a reasonable member of the public, and not by reference to the impact on a particular addressee. That 'threatening', 'abusive' or 'insulting' involve questions of fact means, as in the case of other terms which involve a question of fact, that it is difficult to say in advance what words or behaviour are covered and that different benches may take different views about essentially the same conduct. There is a risk in relation to such terms that a successful challenge could be brought for a contravention of Art 10 of the ECHR (right to freedom of expression) on the ground that, while this freedom can be restricted if the restriction is *prescribed by law* and necessary in a democratic society to prevent disorder or crime or for the protection of the rights and freedoms of others, the principle of foreseeability of the legal consequences of a course of action inherent in 'prescribed by law'[4] may be infringed. The impact of the Human Rights Act 1998 may well lead our courts to re-assess any tendency to leave the meaning of statutory words as questions of fact.

The fact that words such as 'threatening, abusive or insulting' involve a question of fact for the magistrates does not leave them with a completely free hand, since their decision on a question of fact can be overturned on appeal if no reasonable bench acquainted with the ordinary use of language could have reached that conclusion.[5] An appellate court will not interfere simply because it would have taken a different view.

In deciding whether or not a conclusion about the use of language was one that a reasonable bench could reach, the High Court is able to offer guidance as to the limits of a term. The distinction between doing this and positively defining a term (ie making its meaning a question of law) is shown in Lord Kilbrandon's speech in *Brutus v Cozens*:

> 'It would be unwise, in my opinion, to attempt to lay down any positive rules for the recognition of insulting behaviour as such, since the circumstances in which the application of the rules would be called for are almost infinitely variable; the most that can be done is to lay down limits in order to ensure that the statute is not interpreted more widely than its terms will bear.'[6]

The following limits appear from Divisional Court decisions in respect of 'threatening, abusive or insulting'.

Speech or behaviour is not threatening, abusive or insulting merely because it gives rise to a risk that immediate violence will be feared or provoked,[7] nor simply because it gives rise to annoyance,[7] anger, disgust or distress,[8] nor simply because it is vigorous, distasteful or unmannerly[9] or offensive or rude.[10] This is demonstrated by *Brutus v Cozens*, where the accused's activities in disrupting a tennis match at Wimbledon (by running on to No 2 court and distributing leaflets) caused anger among spectators, some of whom tried to hit him as he was removed. The House of Lords did not disturb the magistrates' finding that, albeit annoying and irritating, the accused's behaviour was not threatening, abusive or insulting. A decision which is, perhaps, questionable in the present respect is *Parkin v Norman*,[11] where the Divisional Court held that masturbation in a public convenience in the view of a stranger is capable of being insulting behaviour because he might be a heterosexual who would be insulted at being taken for a homosexual. Such conduct was certainly offensive, and it was certainly not threatening or abusive. Was it insulting in the ordinary sense of that term and in terms of its impact in its context on a reasonable person? In the *Shorter Oxford English Dictionary* 'offend the modesty or self-respect of' is included in the definition of 'insult'. Perhaps it was the offence to modesty which was the insult in *Parkin v Norman*.

For words to be 'insulting' there must be a human target which they strike, no matter whether they are intended to strike that target or not.[12] No doubt the same is true in respect of 'threatening' and 'abusive'. If conduct is threatening,[13] abusive or insulting, it does not matter whether or not anyone who witnessed it felt himself to be threatened, abused or insulted. It is the potentiality of the conduct to have this effect which is crucial. As McCullough J stated in *Parkin v Norman* in the context of the offence under s 5 of the 1936 Act:[14]

> 'What is required is conduct of a threatening, abusive or insulting character which is likely in the circumstances to occasion a breach of the peace. If the conduct in question is of this character it does not, in our judgment, matter whether anyone feels himself to have been threatened, abused or insulted. Insulting behaviour does not lose its insulting character simply because no one who witnessed it was insulted ...'

Words or visible representation can be abusive or insulting despite the fact that they are truthful. In *Lewis v DPP*,[15] a case under s 5, for example, protesters outside an abortion clinic had carried placards showing an aborted foetus in a pool of blood and entitled '21 weeks abortion'. The Divisional Court found no fault with the view of the court below that there had been abusive and insulting behaviour. Pill LJ stated:

> 'The point taken is that the photograph on the placard was an accurate representation of the result of the abortion, and that what is truthful cannot be abusive or insulting. … A patient (or … someone visiting … the clinic) may be abused or insulted in having the activities (lawful activities in this case) depicted in the way that they were on the placard.'

---

1   [1972] 2 All ER 1297, HL. See also *Simcock v Rhodes* (1977) 66 Cr App R 192, DC. Professor Elliott's view that the approach in *Brutus v Cozens* had remained ineffectual and come to an ignominious end ('*Brutus v Cozens* decline and fall' [1989] Crim LR 323) has not been borne out in relation to various offences against public order.

2   *Ewart v Rogers* (1985) unreported, DC ('threatening' in context of Public Order Act 1936, s 5); *DPP v Clarke* (1992) 94 Cr App R 359 at 366 ('abusive' in the context of the offence under the 1986 Act, s 5). There can be no doubt that these authorities are equally applicable to all offences discussed in this book where these terms appear.

3   Dickey 'Conduct likely to cause a breach of the peace' [1971] Crim LR 265 at 269–270.

4   See para **1.21**.

5   *Bryan v Robinson* [1960] 2 All ER 173, DC; *Brutus v Cozens* [1972] 2 All ER 1297 at 1298–1299, per Lord Reid; *Hudson v Chief Constable, Avon and Somerset Constabulary* [1976] Crim LR 451, DC.

6   [1972] 2 All ER 1297 at 1303.

7   *Brutus v Cozens* [1972] 2 All ER 1297, HL.

8   *Parkin v Norman* [1982] 2 All ER 583, DC.

9   *Brutus v Cozens*, above, at 1300, per Lord Reid.

10 *R v Ambrose* (1973) 57 Cr App R 538, CA.

11 *Parkin v Norman*, above. Also see *Masterson v Holder* [1986] 3 All ER 39, DC; see para **4.10**, which raises the same issue on the present point.

12 *Masterson v Holder*, above, at 43–44, per Glidewell LJ.

13 This word is not limited to threats of violence, since an actual act of violence, eg fighting, can be 'threatening': *R v Oakwell* [1978] 1 All ER 1223, CA

14 [1982] 2 All ER 583 at 587. The same view was taken in *Kelleher v DPP* (1994) unreported, DC, a case where the 1986 Act was in issue.

15 (1995) unreported, DC.

Using words or behaviour

4.6   The use of words or behaviour does not require any further explanation in the context of s 4. The decision in *Vigon v DPP*,[1] referred to in para **4.45** is most unlikely to have any application to s 4.

---

1   (1998) 162 JP 115, DC.

Distribution or display of any writing etc

4.7   'Distribute' and 'display' are not defined for the purposes of s 4 by the Act. Consequently, it seems that they bear their ordinary relevant meaning of 'deal out, spread about' and 'expose to view, make visible', 'show, exhibit',[1] respectively. The distribution or display of any writing,[2] sign or other visible representation which is threatening, abusive or insulting covers handing out leaflets (distribution) or posting a bill on a wall, writing graffiti on it, holding up a banner or placard, or even wearing a badge (which are all examples of 'display').[3] However, as we shall see in para **4.8**, there may be other reasons why an offence under s 4 (as opposed to ss 4A or 5) may not be committed in the case of graffiti and badges. In *R v Britton*,[4] which was concerned with an offence of inciting racial hatred, the Court of Appeal held that sticking a pamphlet on the front door of an MP's house constituted a distribution. It added, obiter, that if the pamphlets had been visible from the road there might also have been a display of the written material. In *Chappell v DPP*,[5] the Divisional Court agreed with the magistrates' court that the deposit of an insulting letter contained in an envelope through a letter box had not been a 'display' of insulting writing for the purposes of s 5, which does not include 'distribution' in the alternative. Unlike the offence under s 19 of the Public Order Act 1986, referred to in para **5.20**, distribution does not have to be to the public or a section of the public. In *Britton*, a case involving the predecessor to s 19, the distribution had only been to the MP's house; the accused's appeal against conviction was allowed on the ground that, although there had been a distribution, it had not been to the public or a section of the public.

It is submitted that the section does not catch wearing an orange lily[6] or some other non-representational symbol which is in the circumstances threatening, abusive or insulting, as where a Protestant deliberately wears an orange lily in a strongly Catholic district at the time of inter-religious strife. A non-representational symbol is certainly not writing or other visible representation (since it is the real thing). In a sense, an orange lily or other non-representational symbol is a sign but, applying the noscitur a sociis principle of interpretation, 'sign' is probably limited to representational signs, particularly as it is followed in the definition by 'or other visible representation'. A banner or badge displaying a picture of an orange lily would of course be a 'sign'. The point about the orange lily or the like may well be academic because it may be that the walking (ie behaviour) in its context could be viewed as threatening, abusive or insulting.

---

1   *Shorter Oxford English Dictionary.*
2   'Writing' includes typing, printing, lithography, photography and other modes of representing or reproducing words in a visible form, and expressions referring to writing are to be construed accordingly: Interpretation Act 1978, s 5 and Sch 1.
3   Neither the Act nor any other provision obliges the owner of property on which threatening, abusive or insulting material appears to remove it. If he does nothing, and allows it to remain on his property, it would seem unlikely that he can be said to 'display' it. On the other hand, there is certainly a 'display' where the owner of a car, which has been subjected to such graffiti while parked in his car-port, drives the car in public and parks it in a street.
4   [1967] 1 All ER 486, CA; see para **5.23**.
5   (1988) 89 Cr App R 82, DC.
6   As in *Humphries v Connor* (1864) 17 Ir CLR 1; see para **2.18**.

Towards another ... or to another

4.8   Section 4 requires that threatening, abusive or insulting words or behaviour must be used towards another person or that threatening etc written material be distributed or displayed to another.

In relation to the use of threatening, abusive or insulting words or behaviour, 'used towards another' means that the words or behaviour in question must be used 'in the [physical] presence of and in the direction of another person directly';[1] the latter phrase requires that the words or behaviour be directed towards that other person.[1] If this test is not satisfied, one must fall back on the offences under ss 4A and 5 of the 1986 Act if either is applicable on the facts; alternatively, a charge of affray may sometimes be available. If, for example, the 'other person' is out of earshot of threatening words, and they are conveyed to him by an intermediary, no offence is committed under s 4. In *Atkin v DPP*,[2] customs officers accompanied by a bailiff went to D's farm to recover outstanding VAT. The bailiff remained outside in a car while the officers entered the farmhouse. When they told D that the bailiff would have to enter to distrain his goods, he said that if the bailiff got out of the car he was a 'dead un'. An officer went out and told the bailiff of the threat and that there was a gun in the farmhouse. The Divisional Court held that an offence under s 4 had not been committed because D had not used the threatening words towards the bailiff since they had not been used in the presence of and in the direction of the bailiff directly; he was not in earshot and the words were not directed towards him. Although the victim must be present in order to perceive the threatening etc words or behaviour, it is not necessary for him to give evidence that he had perceived what has taken place. The magistrates can rely solely on evidence that he perceived it given by other witnesses, such as police officers, and infer from that evidence (eg as to the physical proximity between the accused and the victim) that the victim did perceive the words or behaviour in question.[3] Although the decision to this effect is undoubtedly correct, it is unsatisfactory (as far as the accused's rights are concerned) to dispense with the need for evidence from the alleged 'victim'. The other witnesses will usually be police officers. As a commentator has put it, 'As defence practitioners know all too well, it is easy for an officer to allege: "I saw a woman with a pram who feared for her safety." Easy to say, impossible to rebut.'[4]

As a result of the interpretation in *Atkin*, it would seem that if the facts in *Masterson v Holder*[5] recurred a conviction of an offence under s 4 would be unlikely, even if the other elements of the offence could be proved. In that case, the two accused men engaged in the early hours of the morning in overt homosexual behaviour in Oxford Street, London. They were seen by two couples who were passing by, although the two accused appeared not to notice that there were other people in the vicinity. Upholding convictions under s 54, para 13, of the Metropolitan Police Act 1839, which provided an offence in respect of words or behaviour almost identical to that under s 5 of the 1936 Act and which did not require the insulting behaviour to be used 'towards another', the Divisional Court held that an overt display of homosexual conduct in a public place might well be considered to be insulting, and the offence committed, even though the conduct was not deliberately aimed at a particular person or persons. Although a conviction under s 4 would seem unlikely on these facts, a prosecution under s 5 of the 1986 Act would stand a much greater chance of success because it does not require the accused's behaviour to be 'towards another'.

Because the presence of the accused and his victim is required, an offence under s 4 cannot be committed by telephone.

The insertion of 'to another' after 'distributes or displays' would equally seem to require that the written material be distributed or displayed directly to another and in his presence, rather than simply being distributed (eg by leaflets being left lying around in a shopping centre) or displayed (eg by sticking a poster on a wall in the middle of the night). This interpretation is supported by the absence of 'to another' in the corresponding offences under ss 4A and 5. If this is correct, it means that delivering a threatening leaflet through an office letter box cannot result in a conviction for an offence under s 4. By contrast, handing out abusive leaflets to people in the street or carrying an insulting banner during a demonstration clearly involves distributing or displaying written material to another.

---

1   *Atkin v DPP* (1989) 89 Cr App R 199, DC. The headnote to this report is inaccurate, although
     it does accord with the briefer report in (1989) *The Times*, 1 February.
2   (1989) 89 Cr App R 199, DC. See, further, **4.10**.
3   *Swanston v DPP* (1997) 161 JP 203, DC.
4   Enright (1997) 147 NLJ 635.
5   [1986] 3 All ER 39, DC.

Public or private place

4.9   With one exception, an offence under s 4 can be committed in private places such as factory premises, clubs or college premises, as well as in public places, such as football grounds, dance halls, public car parks and shopping precincts.[1] Thus, an offence can be committed by pickets who threaten working colleagues, whether the pickets are inside or outside factory premises, or by protesters who invade a military base, or by animal liberationists who enter laboratories (provided in each case that the various elements of s 4 are satisfied). The absence of a limit of the offence to public places or meetings corresponds to the absence of such a limit in respect of the major public order offences mentioned in the previous chapter.

---

1   1986 Act, s 4(2).

The exception

4.10   In order to exclude domestic disputes, s 4(2) of the 1986 Act provides:

> '. . . no offence [under s 4] is committed where the words or behaviour are used, or the writing, sign or other visible representation is distributed or displayed, by a person inside a dwelling and the other person [ie another person towards whom the words or behaviour are used or to whom the writing etc is distributed or displayed][1] is also inside that or another dwelling.'

Thus, to use threatening, abusive or insulting words towards someone else in the same house cannot be an offence under s 4, as in *Va Kun Hau*,[2] where the accused threatened a bailiff and a constable with a kitchen cleaver and then a kitchen knife in his own home (and had his conviction under s 4 quashed on appeal), and the same is true if such words are shouted to someone in the house next door or displayed so as to be visible only to him.[3] In *Atkin v DPP*,[4] referred to in para **4.8**, it could have been said that D's threatening words had been used towards the customs officers but, since they were in the farmhouse at the time, there was no offence under s 4 in respect of them. On the other hand, if such words are shouted in a house at someone in the street, at a next-door neighbour who is in his back garden or, even, at someone at the front door of the house in question, an offence under s 4 will be committed, provided that the other elements of the offence are satisfied.

For the purpose of s 4(2), 'dwelling' means 'any structure or part of a structure occupied as a person's home or as other living accommodation (whether the occupation is separate or shared with others) but does not include any part not so occupied',[5] such as a garage, a shop with accommodation over or the communal parts of a block of flats (eg communal landings).[6] Thus, if threatening words are shouted from a flat to a shop below, an offence under s 4 may be committed, and so may it if the words are shouted from the shop to the flat upstairs. 'Structure' here includes a tent, caravan, vehicle, vessel or other temporary or movable structure.[5]

A garden attached to a dwelling is not covered by the exception in s 4(2). Consequently, a couple quarrelling heatedly in their garden may fall foul of s 4.

---

1   *Atkin v DPP* (1989) 89 Cr App R 199, DC.
2   [1990] Crim LR 518, CA. The conviction had been returned as an alternative verdict on a charge of affray.
3   This was recognised in *Chappell v DPP* (1989) 89 Cr App R 82 at 89, per Potter J.
4   (1989) 89 Cr App R 199, DC.
5   1986 Act, s 8. The definition of 'dwelling' in s 8 answers a number of questions which might otherwise arise, but some points remain unanswered. Normally, there will be no difficulty in deciding whether or not a structure (or part) is someone's home, but what about a 'holiday home' (eg a country cottage) which is unoccupied at the material time because it is winter and the cottage is only used for accommodation during summer weekends? It is submitted that it would not be a person's home at the material time (although it would be if it was the subject of a squat). 'Other living accommodation' refers, presumably, to bedrooms in hotels, hostels or halls of residence. These are dwellings (even if occupation is shared) but not, it is submitted, the bar or dining room or staircases because they are not *occupied as living accommodation*, nor (for the same reason) communal toilets or the residents' lounge.
6   *Rukwira v DPP* [1993] Crim LR 882, DC (communal landing that was the means of access to a flat held not to be part of a dwelling, even though access to it was via an entry telephone system).

Mental element

4.11 It is submitted that the accused must intend to use the words or behaviour towards another (or to distribute or display the writing etc to another).

In addition, he must either intend the words, behaviour or writing etc to be threatening, abusive or insulting or be aware[1] that they or it may be.[2] The result of this requirement is that a person who uses words, intending to persuade his audience, without being aware that a court may find them to be threatening, abusive or insulting, is not guilty. The mere fact that the person towards whom threatening, abusive or insulting words or behaviour are used does not feel insulted does not prevent the attribution of the relevant intent to the accused.[3] In most cases, the proof of the present requirement will be derived from the nature of the threatening, insulting or abusive words or behaviour or writing etc in question, since the nature of that conduct will on its face sufficiently indicate the accused's intention or awareness.

---

1   'Awareness' is, of course, a subjective concept: *DPP v Clarke* (1992) 94 Cr App R 359, CA (a case concerning similar wording in the Public Order Act 1986, s 6(4) in respect of s 5). The defendant's state of mind must be judged in the light of the whole of the evidence (including, most particularly, the evidence of the accused, if he chooses to give it).
2   1986 Act, s 6(3). Section 6(3) provides that '[A] person is guilty of an offence under s 4 only if he intends his words or behaviour, or the writing' etc to have such an effect 'or is aware that it may ...', but this does not exclude the general common law principles relating to secondary liability as an accomplice: *R v Jefferson* [1994] 1 All ER 270, CA; para **3.29** fn 1. As with proof of mens rea generally, the prosecution has the burden of proving the necessary mens rea: *DPP v Clarke* above.
3   In *Kelleher v DPP* (1994) unreported, DC, D shouted threats at a man who was surrounded by policemen, and who, for that reason, could not be said to feel threatened. The Divisional Court held that this was irrelevant, and that it was clear from an analysis of D's state of mind at the material time that he had intended to make the man feel threatened.

4.12 A person whose awareness is impaired by intoxication must be taken to be aware of that of which he would be aware if not intoxicated, unless he proves[1] either that his intoxication was not self-induced or that it was caused solely by the taking or administration of a substance in the course of medical treatment.[2] For this purpose, 'intoxication' means any intoxication, whether caused by drink, drugs or other means, or by a combination of means.[3]

---

1 See para **3.30**.
2 1986 Act, s 6(5).
3 Ibid, s 6(6). The comments in para **3.30** are equally applicable here.

4.13 Section 4(1) of the 1986 Act requires that the accused's use of the words or behaviour towards another (hereafter described as 'an addressee'), or the accused's distribution or display to another ('an addressee') of the writing etc, must be intended by the accused or be likely (whether or not the accused realises this) either:

(a) to provoke the immediate use of unlawful violence by an addressee or another; or
(b) to cause an addressee[1] to believe that such violence (ie immediate unlawful violence)[2] will be used against him or another.

As was indicated in *Winn v DPP*,[3] an offence under s 4(1) can be committed in four ways:

– the accused must intend the person against whom the conduct is directed to believe that immediate unlawful violence will be used against him or another by any person; or
– the accused must intend to provoke the immediate use of unlawful violence by that person or another; or
– the accused must have used threatening, abusive or insulting words or behaviour by which a person against whom the conduct is directed is likely to believe that such violence will be used; or
– the accused must have used such words or behaviour by which it is likely that such violence will be provoked.

'Common to all four ways are the requirements that the accused must intend or be aware that his words or behaviour are or may be threatening, abusive or insulting, and must be directed to another person.'[3] The list above is equally applicable mutatis mutandis to a 'distribution or display' of writing etc.

'Violence' means any violent conduct.[4] It includes fear or provocation of violent conduct towards property as well as violent conduct towards persons, and it is not restricted to conduct causing or intended to cause injury or damage but includes any other violent conduct (such as throwing at or towards a person a missile of a kind capable of causing injury which does not hit or falls short). It is irrelevant whether or not a person is caused to apprehend immediate violence or provoked to immediate violence. As McCowan LJ put it in *Swanston v DPP*,[5] in relation to the variant of the s 4 offence involving an intent to cause a belief that immediate unlawful violence will be used, 'It is a vital component of the offence that it does not have to be shown that the other person believed: it has to be shown that the [accused] had the intention to cause that person to believe [that such violence will be used against him].' To require otherwise might place too great a restriction on powers of the police to intervene.

---

1   *Loade v DPP* [1990] 1 All ER 36, DC. An information charging a person with using 'towards another threatening, abusive or insulting words or behaviour whereby another person was likely to believe that immediate unlawful violence will be used against him or another' is defective because of the need for the relevant belief to be the belief of the person towards whom the threatening etc words or behaviour are used: *Loade v DPP*. However, such an information can be saved (as could one also omitting 'immediate' or in some other way defective) by the Magistrates' Courts Rules 1981, r 100 (which provides for an information to be sufficient if it describes the offence charged in ordinary language), provided it does not cause unfairness to the accused by misleading or confusing him or throwing doubt on the nature of the offence: ibid. See *Winn v DPP* (1992) 156 JP 881, DC.

2   *R v Horseferry Road Metropolitan Stipendiary Magistrates' Court, ex parte Siadatan* [1991] 1 All ER 324, DC.

3   (1992) 156 JP 881, DC.

4   1986 Act, s 8; see further, paras **3.14–3.15**.

5   (1997) 161 JP 203 at 205.

4.14 It will be noted, under (a), that it is not necessarily an addressee who must be intended or likely to be provoked to immediate violence. It is sufficient that someone else present, towards whom the threatening behaviour etc was not directed, was intended or likely to be provoked. Thus, if D shouts at a coloured person whom he knows cannot speak English, 'Paki bastard, go home', intending that this should provoke immediate violence on the part of a group of racists with him, the present offence is committed. Likewise, the offence is committed if Y shouts abuse at a policeman in circumstances where others, eg Y's associates, are likely to be provoked to violence. On the other hand, racist insults made in the presence only of a racist mob which are calculated to incite the mob to attack members of an immigrant community who live *elsewhere* in the town cannot be said to be likely to provoke *immediate* unlawful violence.

Under (b), fear of immediate violence intended or likely, the fear must be on the part of an addressee (although it need not be fear of violence against himself, nor of violence by the accused). Paragraph (b) is important where the victim of intimidatory conduct, eg a policeman or old lady, is unlikely to be provoked into violence by it and there is no one else around who is likely to be so provoked either. The intended or likely fear instilled in the addressee must be of immediate unlawful violence.

'Immediate' does not mean 'instantaneous'; a relatively short period of time may elapse between the conduct which is threatening, abusive or insulting and the unlawful violence. 'Immediate' connotes proximity in time and in causation; that it is likely that violence will result within a relatively short period of time and without any other intervening occurrence. All this was decided by the Divisional Court in *R v Horseferry Road Metropolitan Stipendiary Magistrates' Court, ex parte Siadatan*,[1] where it was held that it is not enough to satisfy the requirement of immediacy that conduct was likely to lead to violence at some unspecified time in the future. The liberal approach to 'immediate' taken in the above case, which would be a more appropriate definition of 'imminent' than of 'immediate', has been mirrored in respect of 'immediate unlawful violence' which must be feared for an assault.[2]

The elasticity of the concept of immediacy as a result of the above decision is shown by reference to *Valentine v DPP*.[3] A disturbance occurred outside Mr and Mrs P's house. Mrs P was upset and Mr P was called home from work. D then made threats to Mr and Mrs P that next time Mr P was on duty he would burn the house down. D was convicted of an offence under s 4 of the 1986 Act and appealed unsuccessfully to the Divisional Court, the question in the case stated being whether there was evidence before the magistrates on which they could convict D under s 4. D contended that the threats were conditional on Mr P not being at home but being at work and that the condition precedent of his absence amounted to the 'intervening occurrence' referred to in *Horseferry Road*. D therefore submitted that any fear was not going to be of violence which was immediate in the sense of a relatively short time interval. The Divisional Court dismissed this submission relying on the magistrates' 'critical conclusion' that Mr P could have returned to work to continue his night shift at any time thereby giving the defendant an opportunity to carry out the threat. The magistrates were entitled to come to this finding and on the basis of it there was a sufficient factual foundation for the conviction. Simon Brown LJ added that, if the magistrates had only found that Mrs P feared violence at some time after that night, eg 24 hours later at the earliest assuming Mr P was then on night duty, D could not properly have been convicted. As can be seen the Divisional Court paid scant regard to the words of *Horseferry Road* that 'immediate' connotes that it is likely that violence will result in a relatively short period of time *and without any other intervening occurrence.* The status of the words italicised must now be doubtful. It is certainly a liberal interpretation of 'fear of immediate' violence that it can embrace violence dependent on an intervening occurrence, especially where the court is unsure when that occurrence would take place.

If the violence which it is intended or likely to be provoked or feared is justified on grounds of self-defence, prevention of crime or other public or private defence, it will not be 'unlawful violence' for the purposes of this offence.[4] On the other hand, if it is not so justified, it is irrelevant that the accused's conduct is in response to unlawful conduct by the addressee.[5]

---

1   [1991] 1 All ER 324, DC. The decision on this point is criticised in the commentary in [1996] Crim LR 599.
2   *R v Constanza* [1997] 2 Cr App R 492, CA.
3   [1997] COD 339, DC.
4   *R v Afzal* [1993] Crim LR 791, CA.
5   In *Edwards v DPP* (1996) unreported, Newman J stated, obiter, that a threat of immediate unlawful violence directed to a constable in response to a request to hand over a baseball bat would be an offence under s 4 even if the request was unlawful. Pill J reserved the point.

4.15 Clearly, an intent to cause an addressee to believe that immediate unlawful violence will be used or to provoke the immediate use of unlawful violence is more difficult to prove than that the accused's conduct was likely to have that effect. However, it could be proved where the accused has urged others to attack constables or other sections of the community, or to damage their property. If an intent to cause fear or provoke violence is proved, it is irrelevant that in the circumstances fear or provocation of violence was unlikely, eg because the only person present was the addressee who was, unknown to the accused, a plain clothes policeman.

4.16 Because of the common difficulty in proving the specified intent, it will normally be preferable to allege the alternative requirement, viz that the use of the words or behaviour etc was likely to cause an addressee to believe that immediate unlawful violence will be used or to provoke the immediate use of unlawful violence. 'Likely' means 'probable', and not merely 'liable' (ie possible)[1] to cause the addressee to apprehend immediate violence or to provoke the immediate use of violence by him. No awareness of this likelihood is required on the part of the accused, the test of likelihood being objective (ie likelihood is assessed on the basis of what an ordinary person would think was likely). Likelihood is assessed on the circumstances as they actually are (and not as they are believed to be by the accused). Consequently, a person can be convicted even though he firmly, but wrongly, believed that his threats etc were not likely to cause fear or provoke violence.

It is submitted that, where a number of people are charged on the basis of their joint perpetration of threatening etc words or behaviour, the test of likelihood must be judged on the basis of their aggregate conduct, not their individual conduct.

In deciding whether unlawful violence was likely to be feared or provoked, the magistrates are not concerned with the reactions of a hypothetical person of reasonable firmness. Instead, they must look at the actual circumstances and the likely reactions of persons to whom the accused's conduct was addressed or, in the case of likely provocation of violence, of others who were present;[2] the reactions of a constable, an old lady and a skinhead may well vary. A constable is unlikely to respond to threatening, abusive or insulting conduct by using unlawful violence.[2] In *Parkin v Norman*,[2] for example, the Divisional Court held (in respect of the corresponding requirement in s 5 of the 1936 Act, that a breach of the peace must have been likely to be occasioned) that a constable to whom insulting behaviour had been addressed (homosexual advances by indecent gestures and masturbating directed towards him) would not have been likely to break the peace. Nevertheless, such conduct directed towards a constable will constitute an offence under s 4 of the 1986 Act if it is intended or likely to put him in fear of immediate unlawful violence or is intended to provoke him to such violence. If the conduct is so serious as to amount to a breach of the peace and make it likely that a constable to whom it is addressed will have to use violence in the exercise of his common law power to arrest for a breach of the peace, an offence under s 4 will not be committed because the violence likely to be provoked will not be unlawful.

Because 'likelihood' is assessed objectively on the basis of all the circumstances, a speaker must take his audience as he finds it. If he deliberately uses insulting words at a meeting, he is guilty of the present offence if they are likely to provoke the immediate use of violence by the particular audience he is addressing, even though he does not intend to provoke and even though his words would not be likely to cause a reasonable person so to react,[3] provided that he intended his words to be insulting or was aware that they might be.[4] Likewise, if an addressee is likely to be induced to believe that there will be immediate unlawful violence, although no reasonable person would have been led so to believe, the particular sensitivity of that addressee is no bar to proof of a s 4 offence. This can be contrasted with the rule that 'threatening, abusive or insulting' are assessed objectively, by reference to the impact of the words etc on a reasonable member of the public.[5]

1   *Parkin v Norman* [1982] 2 All ER 583 at 588, per McCullough J. This case was concerned with 'likely' in the Public Order Act 1936, s 5 (para **4.1**), a similar context to the 1986 Act, s 4. In other, rather different, contexts, 'likely' has been construed as not meaning 'probably' but as simply requiring a 'real risk, a risk which should not be ignored': *Re H and Others (Minors) (Sexual Abuse: Standard of Proof)* [1996] AC 563, HL (likelihood that child will suffer significant harm as a requirement for a care order under the Children Act 1989, s 31); *R v Whitehouse* (2000) 97 (1) LSG 22, CA (offence of recklessly or negligently acting in a manner likely to endanger aircraft, or person therein, contrary to the Air Navigation (No 2) Order 1995, SI 1995/1970).

2   *Parkin v Norman* [1982] 2 All ER 583, DC.

3   *Jordan v Burgoyne* [1963] 2 All ER 225, DC; discussed by DGT Williams 'Insulting words and public order' (1963) 26 MLR 425.

4   See para **4.11**.

5   See para **4.5**.

Prosecution, trial and punishment

4.17 Section 4(1) creates one offence.[1] This means that a charge that the accused has committed an offence under s 4 is not void for duplicity[2] if, for example, it charges 'threatening, abusive or insulting words or behaviour'.

A charge of an offence under s 4 must be formulated so that the way of committing the offence reflects the facts of the case; if the charge does not there may be an unjustifiable variance between it and the particulars alleged. More than one way of committing the offence may be included in the charge.[3]

An offence under s 4 is triable summarily only.[4] The maximum punishment is six months' imprisonment or a fine not exceeding level 5 on the standard scale, or both.[4] Where a person is on trial on indictment for violent disorder or affray, and the jury find him not guilty, they may, as an alternative, find him guilty of an offence under s 4.[5] In this case, the Crown Court has the same sentencing powers as a magistrates' court would have had on convicting the accused of an offence under s 4.[6]

1   1986 Act, s 7(2).

2   See paras **3.69–3.70**.

3   *Winn v DPP* (1992) 156 JP 881, DC; *Loade v DPP* [1990] 1 All ER 36, DC. Amendment of the charge is possible, if necessary: *Loade v DPP*. The reference to 'way of committing' is to that term as it is used in para **4.13**.

4   1986 Act, s 4(4).

5   Ibid, s 7(3).

6   Ibid, s 7(4).

Police powers

4.18 By s 4(3) of the 1986 Act, a constable may arrest without warrant anyone whom he reasonably suspects[1] *is committing* an offence under s 4. Where there are reasonable grounds for suspecting that the offence under s 4 *has been* committed by a particular individual, a constable may arrest him for that offence only if it appears to him that service of a summons is impracticable or inappropriate because one of the general arrest conditions specified in s 25(3) of PACE is satisfied.[2] Thus, a constable who sees a football supporter committing a s 4 offence on closed circuit television at a football ground cannot subsequently arrest him if the offence has ceased, unless one of the general arrest conditions is satisfied or the requirements for an arrest to prevent a breach of the peace are satisfied.

By s 17 of PACE, a constable may enter and search any premises for the purpose of arresting a person for an offence under s 4 of the 1986 Act. The powers to enter and search under s 17 are exercisable only if the constable has reasonable grounds for believing[3] that the person whom he is seeking is on the premises.[4] In relation to premises consisting of two or more separate dwellings, they are limited to powers to enter and search the communal parts of the premises and any dwelling where the constable has reasonable grounds for believing that the person in question may be.[4]

The power of search is a power to search only to the extent that is reasonably required for the purpose for which the power of entry is exercised.[5]

---

1   See para **3.68** fn 1.
2   PACE, s 25(1) and (2).
3   See para **6.28**.
4   PACE, s 17(2).
5   Ibid, s 17(4).

4.19   The power of arrest under s 4(3) covers virtually all cases where an arrest could be effected under the common law power of arrest in respect of a breach of the peace.[1] The common law power, however, is wider in that it not only entitles *anyone* to make an arrest in respect of reasonably *anticipated* imminent violence, but also because it permits the arrest of a person engaged in an incident where all concerned are in the same dwelling or adjoining dwellings (in which case an offence would not be committed under s 4 of the 1986 Act).[2]

---

1   See para **2.7**.
2   *McConnell v Chief Constable of Greater Manchester Police* [1990] 1 All ER 423, DC.

1986 ACT: SECTIONS 4A AND 5

4.20   Section 4 of the Public Order Act 1986 does not deal with the various kinds of anti-social behaviour which are prevalent, particularly in inner city areas, and which either cause or are likely to cause harassment, alarm or distress. Such conduct is a particular cause for concern when it is directed at a vulnerable person or at members of especially vulnerable groups. Such a person or persons may have a particular difficulty in dealing with the nuisance or escaping it and may be deterred from participating in everyday activities or even from leaving home. Behaviour of this type[1] is dealt with by ss 4A and 5 of the 1986 Act. By s 4A, an offence is committed where harassment, alarm or distress is actually caused and was intended to be caused by the accused. Section 5 deals with the case where it cannot be proved that harassment, alarm or distress was actually caused to anyone or it cannot be proved that this was intended by the accused, or both, but it can be proved that someone was likely to be caused harassment, alarm or distress. Riot is at the top of the range of public order offences in Part I of the 1986 Act; that under s 5 is at the bottom. Section 5 enables the police and the Crown Prosecution Service to deal with a wide range of situations involving a minor breach of public order.

Behaviour which satisfies the requirements of s 4 or s 4A of the 1986 Act may, in the case of s 4, satisfy the requirements of s 5 as well depending on the circumstances, and will almost inevitably do so in the case of s 4A. The converse is, of course, not the case.

Like an offence under s 4, and unlike offences under ss 2 and 4 of the Protection from Harassment Act 1997, described in paras **4.94–4.95**, offences under s 4A or s 5 can be committed by an isolated piece of conduct; persistence is not required.

Section 5 is the most contentious of offences in Part I of the 1986 Act because it criminalises behaviour previously regarded as too trivial to justify criminal liability, although the behaviour might have resulted in binding-over proceedings.

---

1   Such conduct is not a breach of the peace, according to the definition in *R v Howell* [1981] 3
     All ER 383, CA. See para **2.4**.

INTENTIONALLY CAUSING HARASSMENT, ALARM OR DISTRESS

4.21 Section 4A(1) of the Public Order Act 1986 provides that:

'A person is guilty of an offence if, with intent to cause a person harassment, alarm or distress, he –

(a) uses threatening, abusive or insulting words or behaviour, or disorderly behaviour, or

(b) displays any writing, sign or other visible representation which is threatening, abusive or insulting,

thereby causing that or another person harassment, alarm or distress.'

4.22 Section 154 of the Criminal Justice and Public Order Act 1994 added s 4A to the 1986 Act. Although s 4A was intended to address the problem of racial harassment, it is not limited to such conduct. It covers intentionally causing harassment, alarm or distress on whatever ground, be it racial (although here a more serious offence has since been introduced; see para **4.81**), sexual, religious or whatever. If harassment, alarm or distress is not intended and/or caused, but is likely to be caused, a prosecution under s 5 will have to be brought. Essentially, s 4A operates to increase the maximum penalty for what would otherwise have been only the non-imprisonable offence under s 5, in cases where an intent to cause harassment, alarm or distress can be proved.

Prohibited conduct

Threatening, abusive, insulting or disorderly

4.23 The accused must use threatening, abusive or insulting words or behaviour, or disorderly behaviour, or display any writing, sign or other visible representation which is threatening, abusive or insulting. It should be noted that only 'disorderly *behaviour*' will do. A person does not 'use' words or behaviour of the above types if he simply writes and/or delivers a letter to another, who opens it in his absence (see para **4.44**).

As indicated in para **4.5**, the words 'threatening, abusive or insulting' are ordinary English words and do not bear an unusual legal meaning. Instead, the magistrates must decide as a question of fact whether the accused's conduct was threatening, abusive or insulting in the ordinary meaning of those terms, and this is to be judged according to the impact which the conduct would have on reasonable members of the public. What is said in para **4.5** is equally applicable here.

4.24 A similar approach applies to 'disorderly behaviour', a term which does not require any element of violence, actual or threatened, or any threatening, abusive or insulting conduct. This was held in *Chambers v DPP*,[1] whose facts are set out in para **4.28**. The Divisional Court held that whether conduct was disorderly was a question of fact, and needed no further definition. Keene J stated:

> 'For my part, I can see no reason why one should conclude that the word "disorderly" is being used in some unusual or narrower sense than normal in the context of s 5(1) ... Whether behaviour on any occasion is characterised as disorderly is a question of fact for the trial court to determine. That decision can be upset if the trial court has misdirected itself or has reached a decision which no reasonable tribunal could properly reach.'

In judging whether conduct is 'disorderly' in the ordinary sense of that term the magistrates must assess it in the light of its circumstances. As has been pointed out: 'The conduct of a football crowd would be disorderly if it were to be repeated in a theatre during a performance'.[2] Even more so than 'insulting', disorderly is a term which is capable of being applied to a wide variety of conduct, including conduct which is simply irritating or annoying. However, the mental element requirements of the offence mean that criminal liability would be unlikely in such a case.

Despite the width of 'threatening, abusive, insulting or disorderly', there are instances of harassment which are caused by behaviour which does not clearly fall within any of those terms, for example, pushing excrement through a letter box, dumping a dead animal in a front garden, or the playing of loud music.

---

1   [1995] Crim LR 896, DC.
2   Marston and Tain *Public Order Offences* (1995) p 94.

4.25 The display of any writing, sign or other visible representation which is threatening, abusive or insulting covers writing graffiti on a wall,[1] holding up a banner or placard, or even wearing a badge, provided that a threat, abuse or insult is involved.

The discussion in para **4.7** about whether wearing a non-representational symbol which is in the circumstances threatening, abusive or insulting can constitute the display of any threatening, abusive or insulting *visible representation* is equally applicable here.

In relation to any threatening, abusive or insulting writing, sign or other visible representation, the offence is limited to displaying and (unlike an offence under s 4 of the 1986 Act) cannot also be committed by distribution. One result is that handing out threatening, abusive or insulting leaflets is not caught by s 4A,[2] unless the leaflets are so printed, and so held, that their contents can be said to be displayed in the sight of another. Another result is that a person who simply delivers a threatening, abusive or insulting letter, contained in an envelope, through someone's letter box does not commit an offence under s 4A since he does not display the threatening etc writing.[3] It is submitted that the same would be true if the thing delivered was a threatening etc leaflet, which the recipient displayed to himself when he picked it up.

1 What if someone else has written graffiti on X's property and X allows it to remain there? See para **4.7** fn 3.
2 If the leaflets are intended or likely to stir up racial hatred, an offence under the 1986 Act, s 19 would be committed.
3 *Chappell v DPP* (1989) 89 Cr App R 82, DC; also see para **4.32**.

Conduct need not be towards or to another

4.26 Another way in which the present offence is unlike that under s 4 of the 1986 Act is that the words or behaviour need not be used towards another person (nor need writing etc be displayed to another). It follows that words or behaviour need not be directed towards another,[1] nor need written material be distributed or displayed directly to another and in his presence.

1 This was recognised in respect of the identical terminology in s 5 in *R v Ball* (1990) 90 Cr App R 378, CA.

Causing harassment, alarm or distress

4.27 While the accused's conduct need not be directed towards another (and written material need not be displayed by him to another), there must be a victim in the sense that some other identified person is actually caused harassment, alarm or distress by that conduct. This is one of the ways in which an offence under s 4A of the 1986 Act differs from that under s 5, since the latter offence simply requires the accused's conduct to be in the hearing or sight of a person likely to be caused harassment, alarm or distress. It is submitted that where a number of individuals are charged under s 4A on the basis of being joint perpetrators in threatening etc words or behaviour, the issue of causation must be decided by looking at the effect of the aggregate conduct, and not of each individual's conduct.

Conduct may cause harassment, alarm or distress without being threatening, abusive or insulting, and vice versa.[1]

1 *DPP v Clarke* (1992) 94 Cr App R 359 at 366.

4.28 'Harassment, alarm or distress' are not defined by the 1986 Act. The three terms are somewhat vague, and 'harassment' and 'distress' in particular are capable of a liberal application by magistrates' courts. Since the three terms are ordinary words of the English language, and since the context does not show that they are being used in an unusual sense, it would seem that their meaning is a question of fact, not law, according to the House of Lords' decision in *Brutus v Cozens*.[1]

The *Shorter Oxford English Dictionary* defines 'harassment' in terms such as 'troubled by repeated attacks' and 'subjected to constant molestation'. Such definitions are, at least in one sense, unhelpful: the common statutory habit of grouping 'harassment' with 'alarm' and 'distress' suggests that harassment means something different from alarm or distress. It was held by the Divisional Court in *Chambers v DPP*,[2] a case concerned with an offence under s 5, that 'harassment' does not require any element of apprehension about one's personal safety (which would seem to accord with the ordinary usage of that term). In that case, D1 and D2 were road protesters who had disrupted progress on a highway construction site by getting in the way of the beam created by a surveyor's theodolite; they thus prevented him from using it properly and caused him inconvenience and annoyance. They were prosecuted for, and convicted of, an offence of disorderly conduct contrary to s 5 of the 1986 Act, the magistrates' court concluding that their conduct was not only disorderly but also caused harassment to the surveyor. There was no threat or fear of violence, but the surveyor was inconvenienced and annoyed by the appellants' behaviour. On appeal, they argued that an element of apprehension about one's personal safety was necessary in order to establish harassment. This argument was rejected by the Divisional Court, which dismissed the appeals. The conviction of D1 and D2 on the basis of conduct which caused inconvenience and annoyance shows the width of 'harassment'.

---

1   [1972] 2 All ER 1297, HL; see para **4.5**.
2   [1995] Crim LR 896, DC.

4.29 'Alarm' does not require proof that the victim of conduct was concerned about physical danger to himself; it may be alarm about the safety of an unconnected third person.[1] It is also clear that the alarm of an individual can be proved by the testimony of a person who witnessed the alarm.[1] The alarm has to be judged on the facts of each case on the standards which apply in the individual circumstances: if the person in fact was alarmed, the fact that others may be of stouter disposition is immaterial. The defendant must take the 'victim' as he finds him, and cannot successfully argue that his conduct should be judged by its effect, or likely effect, on a reasonable person. A constable is a person who can be alarmed, although whether he was alarmed is, again, a question of fact for the court to decide.

---

1   *Lodge v DPP* (1988) *The Times*, 26 October, DC ('alarm' in s 5).

4.30 The relevant definition of 'distress' in the *Shorter Oxford English Dictionary* is 'severe pressure of trouble or sorrow; anguish'. 'Distress' is probably the most subjective of the three terms. It can be caused by incidents like swearing or carrying a banner showing a dead foetus or other striking picture.

4.31 The need to identify someone who has been caused harassment, alarm or distress is liable to present problems in prosecuting an offence under s 4A. The reason is that it may be difficult to prove that a person has been caused harassment etc by the accused's conduct unless that person gives evidence to that effect. It would not, in itself, be enough simply to produce evidence that there was threatening, abusive or insulting behaviour by the accused and that thereafter someone was seen in a distressed state. On the other hand, the court could draw an inference that the distress was *caused* by the accused's behaviour without evidence from an alleged victim if the facts were cogent to this effect. Evidence of abuse aimed at a particular person who was observed immediately to burst into tears might be sufficient to persuade a court to infer that that distress was caused by the abuse. Thus, in some cases it may be possible to prove that the accused's conduct caused some other identifiable person harassment, alarm or distress without calling the victim as a witness. There are, however, obvious dangers if such evidence by a police officer is not submitted to rigorous scrutiny.

In many cases, however, there will be no observable harassment, alarm or distress after the incident. In such cases, a prosecution under s 4A will not succeed unless the alleged victim is called as a witness. This means that some (possibly many) cases falling within s 4A will not be prosecuted under that section because victims of harassment etc may well be reluctant to go to court and give evidence for fear of reprisals. The offence is intended to protect the vulnerable, and the vulnerable are most likely to be influenced by the fear of reprisals.

The offence is inadequate to deal with harassment etc for another reason. In some cases, such as graffiti on walls or chanting, there is no identifiable individual victim who is harassed, alarmed or distressed but, rather, an offence to a section of the public at large. In the case of graffiti a prosecution for criminal damage would be more appropriate if the wall belonged to someone other than the graffiti-writer.

Because the offence can be committed by an isolated piece of conduct, it goes a long way beyond the stereotype of harassment, which involves persistent conduct. A person who loses his temper over, say, a collision with another car and intentionally distresses the other driver by his insulting or abusive words could, for example, be convicted of an offence under s 4A. This type of case is far removed from the type of case which prompted the enactment of s 4A.

Public or private place
4.32 By s 4A(2) of the 1986 Act, an offence under s 4A can be committed in private places, as well as in public places, unless the words or behaviour are used, or the writing etc is displayed, by a person inside a dwelling and the person harassed, alarmed or distressed is inside that dwelling or any other dwelling. It will be remembered that there is a corresponding provision in relation to an offence under s 4, and the reader is referred to para **4.10** for an explanation of it.

As in the corresponding provision in s 4 and s 5, the exemption refers to the accused and the victim being inside a dwelling at the material time, not that the accused's threatening words etc should simply take effect inside a dwelling where the victim is. Consequently, a statement by Potter J, as he then was, in *Chappell v DPP*,[1] a pre-s 4A case, where an offence under s 5 was charged merits comment. In that case, a woman had received four anonymous letters through the letter box of her home. They were threatening and abusive and caused her alarm and harassment. D was alleged to have deposited them through the letter box. Potter J, with whom the other member of the Divisional Court agreed, held that what had occurred was not a display or use of the threatening words by the accused, as indicated elsewhere in this chapter. His Lordship also stated:

'Sections 4 and 5 each extend the ambit of the pre-existing corpus of public order offences, and, placed as they are within the Public Order Act 1986, they plainly contemplate offences with a requisite public element. They appear to be aimed at conduct giving rise to apprehension of violence or alarm in a public context, such as creation of disturbances on housing estates or at dance halls, shouting of abuse or obscenities at bus queues, and rowdy behaviour generally, for example when directed at the elderly, ethnic groups, or those living on housing estates.

Subsection (2) of each section, whilst providing that an offence may take place in a public or private place, makes clear the intention to exclude conduct taking place within a dwelling house and having its effect solely on another person within that dwelling or another dwelling. Thus, a person yelling or gesturing to persons in the street from the confines of his own house might commit an offence in relation to the persons in the street, but would not commit an offence vis-à-vis another person within his own house or a neighbouring house across the street.

Thus examined, it is plain that the delivery of a threatening or abusive letter to a person within his or her own home where he or she reads it and is alarmed or distressed by its contents, could not on any view be an offence within the ambit of the Act.'[2]

This conclusion is puzzling – the accused was not inside any dwelling at the time of his conduct, as required by the 'dwelling house' exemption – and must be wrong, although the decision on the 'use/display' point was clearly correct.

Conduct of the type in *Chappell v DPP* can amount to an offence under the Malicious Communications Act 1988. Alternatively, it might provide grounds for an anti-social behaviour order.

---

1   (1989) 89 Cr App R 82.
2   Ibid at 89.

4.33 Displaying an abusive poster in the front window of a house adjacent to the street is capable of being an offence under s 4A, whereas if the poster was displayed in a place where it could only be seen by a person in the house or in the house next door, an offence could not be committed under s 4A. Likewise, if someone makes a threatening telephone call from his living room to someone who receives it on a cordless telephone while in his garden, an offence can be committed under s 4A, although the caller would have a defence (see para **4.36**) if he could prove that he had no reason to believe that the recipient of his telephone call had taken his telephone into the garden. If the telephone call had actually been answered in the recipient's home, no offence under s 4A could be committed.

While the exclusion from s 4A of domestic disputes may be understandable, the way that the exception is drafted has the effect of excluding from the offence those who force a householder to admit them to his home, or who telephone from their home to the victim's home, and then intentionally harass him by abuse or the like. In these respects, and in respect of cases where the only victim is a neighbour in his own home, the width of the exception is regrettable, particularly since no other offence may have been committed.

Mental element

4.34 The accused must either intend his words or behaviour, or the writing etc, to be threatening, abusive or insulting or be aware[1] that they or it may be threatening, abusive or insulting, or (as the case may be) intend his conduct to be or be aware that it may be disorderly.[2] Although such a requirement is expressly made in respect of an offence under ss 4 or 5 of the 1986 Act by s 6(3) and (4) of that Act respectively, and no such requirement is expressly made in relation to an offence under s 4A, it is submitted that it would be consistent with the general principles of criminal liability to imply the same formulation here. Consequently, a person who gives no thought to the nature of his conduct, or who honestly believes that there is no risk of it being threatening etc, does not commit this offence.

It by no means follows from the mere fact that an accused intended that his conduct should cause harassment, alarm or distress that he intended that conduct to be threatening, abusive, insulting or disorderly or was aware that it might be so.[3]

---

1   See para **4.11**.

2   As with proof of mens rea generally, the prosecution has the burden of proving the necessary intent or awareness: *DPP v Clarke* (1992) 94 Cr App R 359, DC (a case on s 5 of the 1986 Act). Proof often depends on drawing proper inferences from the evidence.

3   *DPP v Clarke,* above, at 366.

4.35 The accused must also intend his threatening etc words or behaviour or his display of a threatening etc visible representation to cause a person harassment, alarm or distress;[1] it is irrelevant that the person who was actually caused the harassment etc was not the intended victim. Thus, the accused's conduct need not be aimed at, or directed towards, the particular victim. The need for an intent to harass to be proved by the prosecution is a significant limiting factor on the offence, particularly because its proof may be difficult in practice. However, given that the prohibited conduct can be satisfied if an unduly sensitive person is inadvertently caused distress by disorderly conduct, some sort of subjective state of mind does seem to be essential if the offence is not to be too wide, and to place the burden on the accused of disproving the intention would have been open to criticism. It would have been better if awareness as to the risk of causing harassment etc had been specified as an alternative to intention. The necessary intent here would seem to be limited to a purposive intention.[2]

The intent to cause harassment etc is undoubtedly a specific intent for the purposes of the law relating to the liability of those who are voluntarily intoxicated, so that an accused may rely on evidence of voluntary intoxication as evidence that he lacked that intent.[3] On the other hand, the mental element as to the nature of the accused's words, behaviour etc is not a specific intent so that the accused may not rely on voluntary intoxication as evidence of its absence and, if he does, he can be convicted without proof that he had the specified state of mind as to the nature of his words, behaviour etc.[4]

---

1   1986 Act, s 4A(1).

2   'Intention' was defined by the Court of Appeal in *R v Mohan* [1975] 2 All ER 193 as 'a decision to bring about, insofar as it lies within the accused's power, [a particular consequence], no matter whether the accused desired that consequence of his act or not'. As the court recognised, this can be described more briefly as the 'aim'. Alternatively, it can be described as the accused's 'purpose'. The definition in *Mohan* probably accords with most people's idea of what constitutes intention, as well as being the relevant meaning given by the dictionaries. As Lloyd LJ said in *R v Walker* (1989) 90 Cr App R 226, CA, 'It has never been suggested that a man does not intend what he is trying to achieve'. Provided that he has decided to bring about a particular consequence, insofar as it lies within his power, a person acts with intention in relation to it even though he believes he is unlikely to succeed in bringing it about. It follows, from the reference in the definition in *Mohan* to the fact that it is irrelevant that the accused did not desire a consequence which he had decided to bring about, that a person can be said to act with an intention to cause a particular consequence, even though it is not desired in itself, if it is the means (ie a condition precedent) to the achievement of a desired objective and he decides to cause that consequence, insofar as it lies within his power: Lord Hailsham in *Hyam v DPP* [1974] 2 All ER 41 at 51.

In most 'offences of intent', where it is not proved that the accused's aim or purpose was to bring about a prescribed result but it is proved that it was a virtually certain result of his conduct and that he foresaw it as a virtually certain result of his conduct, the jury or magistrates may find from proof of that foresight that he intended that result: *R v Woollin*

[1998] 4 All ER 103, HL. A finding of intention from foresight of virtual certainty is not possible in all offences of 'intention'; the nature of the offence or the context in which the word 'intention' appears in a definition of the offence may (as is submitted is so here) preclude the possibility of a finding of intention from proof that the requisite consequence was virtually certain to result from the accused's conduct and was foreseen by him as such, and limit 'intention' in that offence to a purposive intention (see, eg, *R v Ahlers* [1915] 1 KB 616).

3   *DPP v Majewski* [1976] 2 All ER 142, HL.

4   Ibid. Section 4A does not contain a provision corresponding to s 6(5) of the 1986 Act (para **4.12**).

Defences

4.36 Section 4A(3) of the 1986 Act provides two defences which also apply on a charge under s 5 of that Act. Section 4A(3)(a) provides a defence for an accused who alleges that he was inside a dwelling at the material time. It states that it is a defence for him to prove that he was inside a dwelling[1] and had no reason to believe[2] that the words or behaviour used, or the writing, sign or other visible representation displayed, would be heard or seen by a person outside that or any other dwelling. Because the test of 'no reason to believe' is an objective one, it is not enough that the accused did not think (or did not think there was any reason to believe) that his words or behaviour would be heard or seen by someone outside the dwelling where he was or any other dwelling.

Section 4A(3)(b) provides that it is a defence for an accused to prove that his conduct was reasonable. This has the potential to exempt behaviour falling within the offence on the ground that in its context a criminal conviction is inappropriate. The Act gives no guidance as to the meaning of 'reasonable conduct', but it was held in *DPP v Clarke*[3] that the question whether the accused's conduct was reasonable can be answered only by reference to objective standards of reasonableness, as assessed by the magistrates' court. In judging this, regard must be had to the context, ie all the circumstances indicating the reason for the accused's conduct.[4] Ultimately, the court is involved in a balancing exercise between the offensive behaviour and that context. The more serious the accused's behaviour, the stronger the contextual support must be. With the 'bringing home' of the ECHR, the courts are going to have to bear in mind the terms of Art 10 (freedom of expression) when dealing with cases involving protesters; indeed, they may recognise in such cases a presumption in favour of the freedom when considering the question of reasonableness.[5] However, the accused is not entitled to have his conduct judged only on the basis of his own moral stance or views. This was held by the Divisional Court in *Lewis v DPP*, another of the anti-abortion protester cases, referred to in para **4.5**. Keene J said:

> '[T]he Appellant does have a particular view about the desirability of abortion as a process. However, it cannot be right that a trial Court should have to adopt the same approach in judging this issue of reasonable conduct and view the matter entirely through the eyes of the defendant ... That would lead to situations where the more extreme were the opinions of a defendant, the more readily would his conduct be regarded as reasonable. That does not seem to me to be right, and it would be contrary to the approach adopted in *DPP v Clarke*.'

The Court left open what the position would be if the accused was labouring under a mistake as to the factual situation. It is submitted that he would be governed by the general principles of criminal liability whereby if on the facts as he *reasonably* believed them to be his conduct was reasonable he would have a defence.[6]

The defence under s 4A(3)(b) is unlikely to succeed in many cases. An example of a case where threatening conduct would no doubt be objectively reasonable would be a threat shouted at a pickpocket across a street to deter him. In *Kwasi-Poku v DPP*,[7] D, who had been trading unlawfully in an ice-cream van and had been wrongly informed by a constable that his van could be seized, replied 'You're not taking my fucking van' and pushed the constable. The Divisional Court held that to protest in such language in response to the constable's threat relating to a non-existent power could be reasonable conduct. It is implicit in this decision that a circumstance can be taken into account (eg that a threat was a false one) even though the accused is unaware of it at the time.

---

1   See para **4.10**.
2   See para **6.28**.
3   (1992) 94 Cr App R 359, DC (in respect of the corresponding defence under the 1986 Act, s 5(3)(c)). The statement of the Divisional Court in *Morrow v DPP* [1994] Crim LR 58, DC, a case involving disorderly behaviour by demonstrating outside an abortion clinic, that: 'All that was needed was the honest and genuine belief of the appellants [that crimes were being committed]' is suspect, since there seems to be no justification for it in the words of the provision.
4   *Morrow v DPP*, above (in respect of the corresponding defence under the 1986 Act, s 5(3)(c)).
5   See Lord Browne-Wilkinson 'The infiltration of a Bill of Rights' [1992] PL 405 at 408.
6   See Card, Cross and Jones *Criminal Law* (1998) paras 4.27–4.35.
7   [1993] Crim LR 705, DC in respect of the defence under s 5(3)(c).

4.37 Where the threatening conduct is aimed at preventing someone else peacefully exercising a lawful right it can hardly be described objectively as reasonable, a view taken in two cases involving prosecutions under s 5 against protesters outside abortion clinics: *Morrow v DPP*,[1] and *Lewis v DPP*.[2] In such a case, the clash between competing exercises of rights must be resolved in favour of those who are not exercising their right in a threatening, abusive, insulting or disorderly way. What if both sides are behaving in this way though? In *Morrow v DPP* the appellants, who had strong views about abortion, demonstrated outside an abortion clinic. They shouted slogans, waved banners and prevented staff and patients entering the clinic. Some patients became distressed as a result. The appellants were convicted of an offence contrary to s 5 of the 1986 Act in relation to the above conduct and appealed unsuccessfully against conviction to the Crown Court, and thence to the Divisional Court. There was no dispute that their conduct had been disorderly. The Crown Court was satisfied that the clinic functioned within the terms of the Abortion Act 1967, so that the abortions there were not illegal.

The appeal to the Divisional Court was based on two arguments relevant here:

(a) that the appellants had the defence of reasonable conduct; and
(b) that, since the appellants believed that there were illegal abortions being carried out at the clinic, their conduct was directed to the prevention of such crimes and therefore came within s 3(1) of the Criminal Law Act 1967 (a person may use reasonable force in the prevention of crime).

Dismissing the appeals, the Divisional Court held in relation to the alleged defence of reasonable conduct that, even allowing for the sincerity of the appellants' views, there was ample evidence that their conduct was not justified (ie was not reasonable). The same view was taken on similar facts involving anti-abortion clinic protesters in *Lewis v DPP*, whose facts are given in para **4.5**.

In relation to the second ground of appeal in *Morrow v DPP* referred to above, the Divisional Court held that, given the appellants' genuine belief that criminal acts were being committed, it had to decide if the force used was reasonable, and whether it was used in the prevention of crime. In the Court's view, a defence under s 3 of the 1967 Act was not apt where an aggressive demonstration was being held. The appellants were preventing others from exercising their lawful rights and were preventing all abortions taking place, whether lawful or not. The Crown Court was entitled to conclude that the prosecution had made out its case on this head.

This part of the decision does not rule out a successful defence being run under s 3 of the 1967 Act in an appropriate case. Where it might be available, it would be better to run that defence as well as, or instead of, the defence of reasonable conduct because the accused does not have to prove the s 3 defence. Instead, it is up to the prosecution to disprove it once evidence in support of it has been adduced.[3]

On the other hand, a person who knows that conduct is not criminal but believes that it should be, as where someone believes that the Abortion Act was invalid and that all abortionists should be in prison, cannot succeed with a defence under s 3 of the 1967 Act because he would not on the facts as he believed them be using force to prevent crime,[4] nor objectively could his conduct be described as reasonable.

---

1   [1994] Crim LR 58, DC.
2   (1995) unreported, DC.
3   *R v Lobell* [1957] 1 All ER 734, CCA.
4   This point is made in the commentary to *Morrow v DPP*.

4.38 Section 4A(3) states that an accused has a defence under s 4A(3)(a) or (b) if he proves one or other of the specified defences. Many other provisions in public order legislation expressly put the burden of proving a defence on the accused.[1] According to the ordinary principles of construction, such provisions have traditionally been interpreted as placing the persuasive burden, ie the burden of proof of the defence, on the accused, *proof being on the balance of probabilities*,[2] notwithstanding the rule in *Woolmington v DPP*.[3] Viscount Sankey LC, having stated in *Woolmington* that 'Throughout the web of English criminal law one golden thread is always to be seen, that it is the duty of the prosecution to prove the prisoner's guilt ...',[4] went on to note that it has always been possible for Parliament by way of a statutory exception to transfer the onus of proof of some matter to the accused. An exception of this type is known as a 'reverse onus provision'.

Unless the context is apparent and undisputed from the prosecution case, either on the evidence alone or after legal analysis of the legal status of what is described by prosecution witnesses, proof of the defence of reasonable conduct requires the accused to adduce and prove evidence of the circumstances relied on, as well as having to prove that in those circumstances his conduct was reasonable.[5] Given that the reasonableness of one's conduct and reason to believe the 'presence' of a 'victim' are specified as factors relevant to the culpability of conduct potentially caught by s 4A, it is unfortunate that the accused must prove his innocence in these respects. The requirement that he should do so is part of a regrettable trend to this effect in modern criminal legislation. Is it right to convict a person of the present offence when he has not been proved to have acted unreasonably or to have had reason to believe that a 'victim' might be 'present'?

Putting the burden of proving an issue on the accused is open to the grave objection that, assuming that the prosecution has discharged its burden of proof, a magistrates' court may have to convict the accused although it thinks it as likely as not that he had a defence or is otherwise not guilty. In its Eleventh Report,[6] the Criminal Law Revision Committee recommended a provision whose effect would be to place on the prosecution the burden of disproving any statutory defence, despite the fact that the statute placed the burden of proving the defence on the accused. In such a case, the accused would merely bear an 'evidential burden' in respect of that defence, ie a burden of adducing sufficient evidence (evidence raising a reasonable doubt) to support a defence, after which it would be for the prosecution to disprove it beyond reasonable doubt. It is this rule which already applies to many defences unless statute expressly or impliedly places the burden of proving a particular defence on the accused. Placing an evidential burden on the accused is not incompatible with Art 6(2) of the ECHR, which provides 'Everyone charged with a criminal offence shall be presumed innocent until proved guilty.' On the other hand, a statutory provision which places the burden of proof on the accused may be incompatible with Art 6(2).[7]

Most of the instances in this book where statute expressly requires the accused to prove a defence relate to a burden to disprove an essential element of the offence. An example is where the offence is defined as doing something in prescribed circumstances 'without lawful authority', proof whereof lies on the accused; the accused will have to prove such authority. Some, however, concern an exception or excuse which is not an essential element of the offence, but which an accused must establish to avoid conviction. There may be disputes about whether a 'defence' relates to an essential element of an offence or relates to an exception or excuse,[8] but the 'defences' referred to in paras **6.39**, **6.68** and **7.105** would seem to be of the latter type.

In *R v DPP, ex parte Kebeline*,[9] Lord Hope stated that the former type of provision is inconsistent with the presumption of innocence, but that the latter may or may not be depending on the circumstances. However, the jurisprudence of the European Court of Human Rights and of the European Commission of Human Rights shows that, even if a provision is *inconsistent* with Art 6(2), this will not inevitably lead to the conclusion that it is *incompatible* with Art 6(2). That jurisprudence shows that it is necessary to examine each case on its merits; there is no hard and fast rule about reverse onus provisions in general. One has to look at the particular provision and its justifications and whether it has resulted in injustice to the accused concerned.

In *Lingens v Austria*,[10] which concerned the defence of truth to a charge of criminal defamation, the burden of proof of which was cast on the accused, the Commission found that Art 6(2) had not been contravened because the general burden of proving all the other elements of the offence remained with the prosecution. It concluded that it would be unfair to impose on the prosecution the burden of proving a negative (ie that the statement was not true) and part of the purpose of the Austrian statute was to impose a standard of care on the makers of potentially defamatory statements not only to ensure such statements were true, but that they could be proved to be so. The reverse onus provision did not breach Art 6(2).

A similar approach has been taken in relation to an express rebuttable presumption in respect of an essential element of an offence that operates against the accused, the ability to rebut the presumption operating as a defence. They are not necessarily incompatible with Art 6(2). In *Salabiaku v France*,[11] where there was a presumption under the French Customs Code that a person bringing prohibited goods through customs was guilty of smuggling them, which was rebuttable by the defence that it was impossible for him to have known of the goods' nature, the European Court gave the following guidance:

> 'Presumptions of fact or of law operate in every legal system. Clearly, the Convention does not prohibit such presumptions in principle. It does, however, require the Contracting States to remain within certain limits in this respect as regards criminal law ... Article 6(2) does not therefore regard presumptions of fact or of law provided for in the criminal law with indifference. It requires States to confine them within reasonable limits which take into account the importance of what is at stake and maintain the rights of the defence.'[12]

In *A v UK*,[13] the Commission held that the presumption in s 30(2) of the Sexual Offences Act 1956 that a man who lives with a prostitute is presumed to be knowingly living on her immoral earnings for the purposes of the offence of living off immoral earnings did not infringe Art 6(2).

The guidance given in *Salabiaku* was applied in *Henry Bates v UK*.[14] Section 5(5) of the Dangerous Dogs Act 1991 provides that 'if in any proceedings it is alleged by the prosecution that a dog is one to which [s 1 of the Act] applies [eg a pit bull terrier], it shall be presumed that it is such a dog unless the contrary is shown by the accused by such evidence as the court considers sufficient'. The Commission, following the European Court of Human Rights' decisions in *Salabiaku* and *Pham Hoang v France*,[15] did not find a violation of Art 6(2) since there was the opportunity to disprove the presumption and the courts retained an area of assessment, albeit limited, where the matter was put in issue. The provision was of a type which fell within reasonable limits.

Salabiaku must be regarded as the leading case on reverse onus provisions and Art 6(2). As the quotation given above indicates, the Court was taking into account the principle of proportionality in considering the alleged infringement of Art 6(2). As Lord Hope said about *Salabiaku* in *Kebeline*, 'As a matter of general principle therefore a fair balance must be struck between the demands of the general interest of the community and the protection of the fundamental rights of the individual.'[16] The same approach was taken by the Privy Council in *A-G of Hong Kong v Lee Kwong-Kut*[17] in respect of the compatibility of reverse onus provisions with Art 11(1) of the Hong Kong Bill of Rights, which was in identical terms to Art 6(2) of the ECHR. In *Kebeline*, Lord Hope adopted counsel's suggestion that:

> 'in considering where the balance lies it may be useful to consider the following questions: (1) What does the prosecution have to prove in order to transfer the onus to the defence? (2) What is the burden on the accused – does it relate to something which is likely to be difficult for him to prove, or does it relate to something which is likely to be within his knowledge or (I would add) to which he readily has access? (3) What is the nature of the threat faced by society which the provision is designed to combat? It seems to me that these questions provide a convenient way of breaking

down the broad issue of balance into its essential components, and I would adopt them for the purpose of pursuing the argument as far as it is proper to go in the present case.'[18]

If an English court found that placing the burden of proof on the accused in respect of a particular defence would be incompatible with Art 6(2) it might be able to avoid making a declaration of incompatibility by construing 'prove' in the particular 'reverse onus provision' as merely placing an evidential burden on the accused, and not a persuasive one. It would be facilitated in doing so by s 3(1) of the 1998 Act (legislation to be construed, as far as possible, in a way compatible with Convention rights). As Lord Cooke pointed out in *Kebeline*:

> '[s 3(1)] . . . is a strong adjuration. It seems distinctly possible that it may require s 16A of [the Prevention of Terrorism (Temporary Provisions) Act 1989, the reverse onus provision in question] to be interpreted as imposing on the defendant an evidential, but not a persuasive (or ultimate), burden of proof. I agree that such is not the natural and ordinary meaning of s 16A(3). Yet for evidence that it is a *possible* meaning one could hardly ask for more than the opinion of Professor Glanville Williams in "The logic of 'Exceptions'"[19] that "unless the contrary is proved" can be taken, in relation to a defence, to mean "unless sufficient evidence is given to the contrary"; and that the statute may then be satisfied by "evidence that, if believed and on the most favourable view, could be taken by a reasonable jury to support the defence".
>
> I must not conceal that in New Zealand the Glanville Williams approach was not allowed to prevail in *Phillips*.[20] But, quite apart from the fact that the decision is of course not authoritative in England, s 6 of the New Zealand Bill of Rights Act 1990 is in terms different from s 3(1) of the Human Rights Act 1998. The United Kingdom subsection, read as a whole, conveys, I think, a rather more powerful message.'[21]

On the other hand, Lord Hobhouse in *Kebeline* was 'not presently persuaded that the approach taken by Professor Glanville Williams . . . is the right one. Similarly there are clearly arguable questions as to the breadth to be ascribed to the construction of statutes which will be required of the courts by s 3(1) [of the Human Rights Act].'[22]

---

1   See paras **3.30**, **4.55**, **4.91**, **4.95**, **5.16**, **5.26**, **5.31**, **5.43**, **5.46**, **5.47**, **6.20**, **6.39**, **6.68**, **7.30**, **7.62**, **7.83**, **7.105**, **7.139**, **7.140**, **8.21**, **8.26**, **8.28**, **9.13** and **9.70**.

2   *DPP v Clarke* (1992) 94 Cr App R 359, DC (in respect of the corresponding defences under the 1986 Act, s 5(3)). Also see *Sodeman v R* [1936] 2 All ER 1138, PC (defence of insanity); *R v Carr-Briant* [1943] 2 All ER 156, CCA (rebutting presumption of corrupt gift under Prevention of Corruption Acts 1906 and 1916); *Islington BC v Panico* [1973] 3 All ER 485, DC (Magistrates' Courts Act 1980, s 101). The accused will prove a defence on the balance of probabilities if the magistrates (or the jury in the Crown Court) are satisfied that it is more likely than not (or more probable than not) that the defence is made out: *Miller v Minister of Pensions* [1947] 2 All ER 372 at 373–374.

3   [1935] AC 462, HL.

4   Ibid, at 481.

5   See Cooper 'Public order review' (1994) *Legal Action* (February) 10–11.

6   Cmnd 4991 (1972), paras 137–142. The proposal is repeated in a much diluted form in the Law Commission's draft Criminal Code Bill (*A Criminal Code for England and Wales* (1989), Law Com no 177).

7   See Ashworth and Blake 'Presumption of innocence: English criminal law' [1996] Crim LR 306.

8   Guidance on this point may be obtained from *R v Hunt* [1987] 1 All ER 1, HL.

9   [1999] 4 All ER 801, HL.

10   (1981) 26 D&R 171, ECommHR.

11   (1988) Ser A, no 141-A; 13 EHRR 379, ECtHR.

12   13 EHRR at 388.

13   (1972) 42 CD 35, ECommHR.

14   Application no 26280/95, ECommHR.

15   (1992) Ser A, no 243; 16 EHRR 53, ECtHR.

16   [1999] 4 All ER at 847. Cf Lord Cooke in *Kebeline* [1999] 4 All ER at 837, who thought that to introduce 'concepts of reasonable limits, balance or flexibility' into Art 6(2) in the absence of any reference to them there might be seen as undermining or marginalising the presumption of innocence embodied in the provision.

17   [1993] 3 All ER 939, PC.

18   [1999] 4 All ER at 848–849.

19   [1988] CLJ 261, 265.

20   [1991] 3 NZLR 175.

21   [1999] 4 All ER 801 at 837. See also Lord Steyn at 835.

22   Ibid at 859.

Trial and punishment

4.39 For the purposes of the rule against duplicity, s 4A creates one offence.[1] An offence under s 4A of the 1986 Act is triable summarily only.[2] The maximum punishment is six months' imprisonment or a fine not exceeding level 5 on the standard scale, or both.[2] This, the same as for an offence under s 4 of the 1986 Act, can be contrasted with the maximum of a level 3 fine for the non-imprisonable offence under s 5 of the 1986 Act. It would seem to be inadequate for the worst cases of harassment in particular.

1   1986 Act, s 7(2). See paras **3.69–3.70** in respect of duplicity.

2   Ibid, s 4A(5).

Arrest

4.40 A constable may arrest without warrant anyone whom he reasonably suspects[1] is committing an offence under s4A.[2] This power is identical to the power in respect of a s 4 offence, save that s 17 of PACE does not apply. Otherwise the comments in paras **4.18–4.19** apply equally here. The present power of arrest is arguably more important than the offence itself since there is the potential for vociferous demonstrators and demonstrators who display 'shock pictures' (eg of aborted foetuses) to provide a constable with reasonable suspicion that they intended to cause distress. An arrest would be just as much an interference with freedom of expression as any subsequent conviction.

1   See para **3.68** fn 1.

2   1986 Act, s 4A(4).

CONDUCT LIKELY TO CAUSE HARASSMENT, ALARM OR DISTRESS

4.41 Section 5(1) of the 1986 Act provides that:

'A person is guilty of an offence if he –

(a) uses threatening, abusive or insulting words or behaviour, or disorderly behaviour, or

(b) displays any writing, sign or other visible representation which is threatening, abusive or insulting,

within the hearing or sight of a person likely to be caused harassment, alarm or distress thereby.'

4.42 Section 5 does not require that a person's threatening, abusive, insulting or disorderly conduct actually causes harassment, alarm or distress.[1] Where someone's conduct has such an effect, and was intended to, there is an overlap between s 4A and s 5. The higher maximum penalty for an offence under s 4A means that, in such a case, that offence is likely to be charged and that a charge for a s 5 offence alone will be limited to cases where the special requirements of s 4A are not satisfied or are unlikely to be provable.

---

1   See para **4.13** fn 5.

Prohibited conduct

4.43 This offence is similar to that under s 4A, in that:

(a) there must be threatening, abusive, insulting or disorderly words or behaviour, or the display of any writing, sign or other visible representation which is threatening, abusive or insulting;

(b) the words or behaviour need not be used towards another (unlike an offence under s 4);

(c) in relation to a writing, sign or other visible representation, the offence is limited to displaying and cannot be committed simply by distribution (unlike an offence under s 4).

What was said in paras **4.23–4.26** is equally applicable in the above respects in s 5, unless otherwise indicated. Two unreported cases show the application of that approach in the context of s 5. In *Herrington v DPP*,[1] the Divisional Court agreed with a magistrates' court that a man 'who had gone down the garden, turned and stared for a period of time at [a] lady's kitchen window when standing nude and facing his genitals towards her' was engaging in threatening behaviour for the purposes of s 5. Likewise, in *Lewis v DPP*,[2] the Divisional Court agreed that holding aloft outside an abortion clinic a placard showing a baby lying in a pool of blood and entitled '21 weeks abortion' was abusive and insulting.

---

1   (1992) unreported, DC.
2   (1995) unreported, DC.

4.44 A situation which seems to fall outside s 5 relates to someone who writes and/or delivers a threatening, abusive or insulting letter which is opened by its addressee. In *Chappell v DPP*,[1] Potter J, as he then was, with whom the other member of the Divisional Court agreed, said that he failed to see 'how a person writing and/or delivering a letter to another, who opens it in the absence of the sender, can, on any reasonable reading of s 5, be said to be a person who "uses words or behaviour ... within the hearing or sight of a person" who receives it'.

---

1   (1989) 89 Cr App R 82 at 89. Nor does he 'display' it: ibid, at 88; see para **4.25**. Also see para **4.32**.

4.45 Behaviour is not limited to overt behaviour. It would be open to a magistrates' court to find that the conduct of a 'Peeping Tom' constitutes insulting behaviour. Indeed, in *Vigon v DPP*,[1] where the accused chose to peep on women by setting up a partially concealed video camera in a women's changing room, the Divisional Court, dismissing an appeal against conviction under s 5, held that it was open to the magistrates to find that setting up the camera, switching it on and letting it run amounted to insulting behaviour. It is difficult to think of cases where non-overt insulting etc behaviour could satisfy all the requirements of an offence under s 4 or s 4A of the 1986 Act, so that in practice this decision is only of importance in relation to s 5. The decision extends s 5 well beyond the types of rowdy behaviour at which it was aimed. Indeed, there will not be many cases where non-overt behaviour will suffice for s 5 because, unless (as in *Vigon v DPP*) it is actually heard or seen by someone likely to be caused harassment, alarm or distress by it, it will not have been done in the hearing or sight of someone likely to be caused harassment, alarm or distress thereby.

---

1   (1998) 162 JP 115, DC.

Harassment, alarm or distress likely

4.46 'Harassment, alarm or distress' (see paras **4.28–4.30**) are not required actually to be caused to anyone. Instead, harassment, alarm or distress must be *likely* to be caused to a person in whose hearing or sight the accused's conduct occurs, not merely 'annoyance' or 'disturbance'. As in s 4, 'likely' imparts an objective requirement, and means 'probable' as opposed to 'possible'. No awareness of the risk need be proved by the prosecution. Unlike the situation in s 4A the accused must take his 'victim' as he finds him; it is no excuse that the victim is of a particularly sensitive disposition, or particularly vulnerable, for reasons unknown to him.[1] If, however, the conduct would have been unlikely to harass, alarm or distress a person without the special sensitivity or vulnerability, it will normally be necessary to produce the 'victim' as a witness to testify as to that sensitivity or vulnerability.

As said above, 'harassment, alarm or distress' are not defined by the Act and are somewhat vague terms. It would not, for example, be surprising to find magistrates convicting a person who in an abusive way has misused the Union Flag as some public protest, on the basis that this was likely to distress a person in whose sight it occurred.[2] The likely harassment etc need not be substantial in nature.

---

1   He may, however, have a defence under s 5(3)(a); see para **4.55**.
2   ATH Smith 'Public order law: the Government proposals' [1985] PL 533 at 537.

4.47 While the accused's conduct need not be directed towards another[1] (and written material need not be displayed by him to another), there must be a victim in the sense that what the accused does must be within the hearing or sight of a person likely to be caused harassment, alarm or distress thereby, although no likelihood of violence being provoked or feared is required. Where threatening etc conduct is directed at a person, such as a constable, who is not likely to be caused harassment, alarm or distress, the offence is nevertheless capable of commission if the conduct is in the hearing or sight of someone else who is likely to be caused harassment, alarm or distress thereby. In addition, it is not necessary, in a case where it is alleged that a person was likely to be caused alarm, that it was likely that that person would be caused alarm as to harm to himself. It is enough that he would be likely to be alarmed for the safety of an unconnected third party.[2]

1   This distinction between the words of s 5 and s 4 was acknowledged in *R v Ball* (1990) 90 Cr App R 378 at 380.
2   *Lodge v DPP* (1988) *The Times*, 26 October, DC.

4.48 It will be noted that the accused's conduct must be proved to have been in the hearing or sight of a person likely to be caused harassment, alarm or distress. This 'hearing or sight' test as opposed to one of 'presence' avoids any arguments about what would amount to 'presence'.[1] Conduct can be in someone's hearing (in particular) where he is some way away, as where abuse or insults are shouted through loudspeakers or where a group of youths run amok on a deserted housing estate tipping over dustbins, and the only person on the estate is an octogenarian cowering in an inside room at the sound of their disturbance. It may be that some types of conduct can be regarded as continuing, and that (for example) someone who paints graffiti on a wall while no one is around continues to display it as long as it remains visible and can commit the present offence once someone has sight of the graffiti.

Conversely, conduct clearly in the presence of someone who would be likely to be harassed, alarmed or distressed cannot be an offence under s 5 if it consists solely of spoken words of which he is unaware because he is deaf, or solely of written words of which he is unaware because he is blind or his view is obstructed. 'Hearing or sight' refers to the hearing or sight of a person likely to be caused harassment etc, whether or not he actually detected it. In the absence of evidence from an alleged 'victim', whether or not the accused's conduct was within an alleged victim's hearing or sight will be a matter of inference from all the circumstances.

1   What is meant by 'presence' can give rise to a degree of uncertainty: see para **3.57**.

4.49 It was held by the Divisional Court in *DPP v Orum*[1] that it is a question of fact in each case whether or not a person in whose hearing or sight the conduct occurred was likely to be caused harassment, alarm or distress. In answering it, the Court held, the magistrates must have regard to all the circumstances, including the time, the place, the nature of the conduct and the nature of the person(s) in whose hearing or sight it occurred. It is not enough (unlike the approach in riot, violent disorder and affray) that a hypothetical person in whose hearing or sight it occurs might have been harassed etc.

DPP v Orum was not cited in *R v Ball*,[2] where the Court of Appeal contemplated the possibility that the test 'under s 5' is 'objective throughout', ie objective likelihood is judged against the reaction of a reasonable person in hearing or sight of the behaviour, rather than an actual person who was in that situation. This conflicts with the decision in *DPP v Orum* and cannot be right on that ground or on the ground of the clear wording of s 5(1). Fortunately, the Court of Appeal in *Ball* did not find it necessary to decide the point, or to go into it in any great detail.

It might have been thought that s 5 would not cover behaviour that is only likely to cause harassment, alarm or distress *if* it is discovered, but it was held in *Vigon v DPP*, whose facts are set out in para **4.45**, that it was open to the magistrates to convict if they found 'that the [accused] was aware that, if the customer noticed the camera, it was likely to be distressed by it'. The reference to awareness by the court seems to suggest some confusion between the mens rea required as to the behaviour being insulting and the present requirement.

---

1   [1988] 3 All ER 449, DC; see para **4.51**.
2   (1990) 90 Cr App R 378, CA.

4.50 Although it must be proved that the accused's conduct occurred in the hearing or sight of a person likely to be caused harassment etc, that person does not have to give evidence, nor need he be identified by name. It can be sufficient for a constable or another person to give evidence that there was someone in hearing or sight of the accused's conduct and that in all the circumstances that person was likely to be caused harassment, alarm or distress. The absence of a requirement to produce a witness to testify as to the likelihood that he or she heard or saw the accused's conduct and was likely to be harassed, alarmed or distressed means that there can be a conviction in a case where the victim is fearful of reprisals and therefore unwilling to give evidence, but it weakens the protection against the inappropriate application of s 5. However, if the requirements of the offence are properly applied, that danger will be eliminated because the officer's evidence of who was present will have to be sufficiently detailed in order that the magistrates can decide whether that person (or persons) was likely to be alarmed etc and that likelihood will have to be proved. Of course, the prosecution's task will be easier if they have a witness to testify about the effect of the accused's conduct.

4.51 A consequence of the present requirement is that an offence under s 5 is unlikely to be committed where threatening, abusive etc conduct is used only in the hearing or sight of a constable, unless the constable is likely to be alarmed for the safety of an unconnected third party. In *DPP v Orum*,[1] two constables found D having a row with his girlfriend in the street in the early morning. They told him to quieten down and move on. He replied obscenely. An argument ensued and he was arrested and charged under s 5(1). On an appeal against dismissal of the information, the main issue was whether D's conduct fell within s 5(1), the magistrates having found that neither the girlfriend or any of the occupants of houses in the street had been, or were likely to be, harassed, alarmed or distressed by D's behaviour. Was it the law that a constable must be presumed not to be likely to suffer harassment etc? The Divisional Court answered 'no'. Glidewell LJ (with whose judgment the other judge, McCullough J , agreed) held as follows:

'I find nothing in the context of the 1986 Act to persuade me that a police officer may not be a person who is caused harassment, alarm or distress by the various kinds of words and conduct to which s 5(1) applies. I would therefore answer the question in the affirmative, that a police officer can be a person who is likely to be caused harassment and so on. However, that is not to say that the opposite is necessarily the case, namely it is not to say that every police officer in this situation is to be assumed to be a person who is caused harassment. Very frequently words and behaviour with which police officers will be wearily familiar will have little emotional impact on them save that of boredom. It may well be that, in appropriate circumstances, magistrates will decide (indeed, they might decide in the present case) as a question of fact that the words and behaviour were not likely to cause harassment, alarm or distress to either of the police officers. That is a question of fact for the magistrates to decide having regard to all the circumstances: the time, the place, the nature of the words used, who the police officers are and so on.'

The Court did not, however, send the case back to the magistrates to find, as a matter of fact, whether the constables had been likely to be harassed because the prosecution were more interested in having the point of law answered than in getting a conviction after the lapse of time involved.

In a case where there is a true likelihood of harassment, alarm or distress to a constable, it may well be that the accused's conduct is sufficiently grave for an offence under s 4, or, even, an affray, to have been committed. The danger, of course, is that magistrates may be too susceptible to finding that harassment etc of a constable was likely.

---

1   [1988] 3 All ER 449, DC. Also see *R v Ball* (1990) 90 Cr App R 378, CA; ATH Smith 'Assaulting and abusing the police' [1988] Crim LR 600 at 603.

4.52 We have seen[1] that, because s 4 requires that the violence intended or likely to be feared or provoked must be *immediate* violence, threats issued against persons or property some distance away fall outside the offence (save where they are likely to provoke immediate violence on the part of those to whom the threats, abuse or insults are directed or others then present). On the other hand, s 5 does not require a likely alarm to relate to something immediate. Consequently, if a gang in one part of a town were to utter in the presence of an innocent bystander threats directed at members of an ethnic group resident in another part, and those threats were likely to alarm him, an offence under s 5 would be committed.

---

1   See para **4.13**.

Public or private places

4.53 The position corresponds to that under s 4 or s 4A. An offence under s 5 may be committed in a public or a private place, except that no offence is committed where the words or behaviour are used, or the writing, sign or other visible representation is displayed, by a person inside a dwelling and the other person, within whose sight or hearing it occurs and who is likely to be harassed, alarmed or distressed thereby, is also inside that or another building.[1]

---

1   1986 Act, s 5(2). What is said in paras **4.10**, **4.32** and **4.33** applies equally here.

Mental element

4.54 The accused must either intend his words or behaviour, or the writing etc, to be threatening, abusive or insulting or be aware that it may be threatening, abusive or insulting, or (as the case may be) intend his conduct to be disorderly or be aware that it may be.[1] Consequently, a person who gives no thought to the nature of his conduct, or who honestly believes that there is no risk of it being threatening etc, does not commit this offence. The provisions in s 6(5) concerning intoxication, referred to in para **3.30**, apply equally to an offence under s 5.

Although the accused's conduct must be in the hearing or sight of a person likely to be caused harassment, alarm or distress thereby, it does not have to be proved that the accused intended this or was aware that it might occur. However, ignorance of the presence of such a person may give rise to the defence under s 5(3)(a) below and, in any event, may be relevant in relation to proof of the requirement that the accused must intend that his conduct be threatening, abusive, insulting or disorderly or be aware that it may be.

If the accused was aware that his conduct might cause harassment, alarm or distress, it by no means follows that he intended it to be threatening, abusive or insulting, or was aware that it might be.[2]

These requirements offer some protection to freedom of speech. The demonstrator who unwittingly uses language which is threatening, abusive, insulting or disorderly in expressing his opinions cannot be convicted under s 5, despite their likelihood of causing distress.

---

1   1986 Act, s 6(4). See para **4.34**. Section 6(4) is identical to s 6(3), set out in para **4.11** fn 2,
     except that it adds a reference to intention or awareness as to conduct being disorderly. The
     comments in para **4.11** fn 2 are equally applicable to s 5.
2   *DPP v Clarke* (1992) 94 Cr App R 359 at 366.

Defences

4.55 Section 5(3)(a) of the 1986 Act provides that it is a defence for the accused to prove that he had no reason to believe that there was any person within hearing or sight who was likely to be caused harassment, alarm or distress. As in the case of the defence under s 5(3)(b), the test of 'reason to believe' is an objective one. If a man shouts foul-mouthed abuse to the world at large when walking along an apparently deserted country lane, he would normally be able to prove that he had no reason to believe that there was someone resting behind a hedge (if, in fact, there had been). He would find it more difficult to prove the defence if he had shouted the abuse as he passed a cottage further down the lane.

The defence is not limited to those who have reason to believe that there is no one in earshot or sight of his conduct. It also applies to those who prove that, although they knew someone was in earshot or sight of their conduct, they had no reason to believe that that person or persons would be likely to be caused harassment, alarm or distress, for example because there was no reason to know of a particular sensitivity or vulnerability on the part of that person or persons.

Section 5(3)(b) provides a further related defence for an accused who alleges that he was inside a dwelling at the material time. It states that it is a defence for him to prove that he was inside a dwelling and had no reason to believe that the words or behaviour used, or the writing, sign or other visible representation displayed, would be heard or seen by a person outside that or any other dwelling.

Section 5(3)(c) provides that it is a defence for an accused to prove that his conduct was reasonable. In one case, anti-abortionists were charged with an offence under s 5 because of their abusive and insulting conduct in displaying pictures of a newly aborted foetus to persons entering an abortion clinic. It was held that their conduct, viewed objectively, was not reasonable.[1]

The defences in s 5(3)(b) and (c) correspond to those in s 4A(3). The comments about s 4A(3) in paras **4.36–4.38** apply equally to s 5(3).

---

1   *Morrow v DPP* [1994] Crim LR 58, DC.

Trial and punishment

4.56 For the purposes of the rule against duplicity, s 5 creates one offence.[1] An offence under s 5 is triable summarily only.[2] The maximum punishment is a fine not exceeding level 3 on the standard scale;[2] unlike an offence under s 4 or s 4A, punishment with imprisonment is not possible. Where the conviction concerns a 'football-related offence', a domestic and/or international football banning order may be made in the circumstances outlined in paras **8.35** and **8.45**.

---

1 1986 Act, s 7(2). See paras **3.69–3.70** in respect of duplicity.
2 Ibid, s 5(6).

Arrest

4.57 Section 5(4) of the 1986 Act provides a power of arrest after warning:

'A constable may arrest a person without warrant if –

(a) he engages in offensive conduct which [a] constable *warns* him to stop, and
(b) he engages in further offensive conduct immediately or shortly after the warning.'[1]

The constable need not be in uniform. As enacted, the power of arrest was limited to the officer who has personally administered the warning, but this limitation was removed by the Public Order (Amendment) Act 1996. Thus, where two constables are present, trying to restore order at a fracas, and one warns D to stop, the other officer may effect an arrest if D engages in offensive conduct immediately or shortly after the warning.

The reference in (a) to 'he engages in offensive conduct which a constable warns him . . .' seems literally to mean that the person must actually be engaged in the conduct when he is warned. If this is the correct interpretation, the power of arrest under s 5(4) will be severely limited, limited to the case where the constable observes the actual conduct and gives his warning while it is continuing. In any other case, an arrest would only be possible under s 25 of PACE, and then only if one of the general arrest conditions was satisfied. An alternative interpretation, viz that 'engages' means 'is or has been engaged' can only be made by perverting the apparent sense of 'engages' in (a) which would almost certainly impinge on the meaning of 'engages' in (b).

Offensive conduct means conduct which the constable reasonably suspects[2] to constitute an offence under s 5.[3] The conduct mentioned in (a) and the further conduct need not be of the same nature.[3] If a constable warns someone to stop using abusive language in a queue outside a chip shop and shortly afterwards that constable (or another) finds that person rampaging round a nearby housing complex, knocking dustbins over, an arrest can be made under s 5(4).

The requirement in (b) that the further offensive conduct occurs 'immediately or shortly after the warning' provides some limit on the power of arrest, but given the inherent elasticity of 'shortly after'[4] the limit cannot be regarded as a particularly strict one. Whether or not the limit applies will be a question of fact in each case. Further offensive conduct one or two minutes after the warning would seem to be 'shortly after' it, even if not 'immediately' after it, and so it might be held to be if it took place 20 minutes later but not, it is submitted, if it took place an hour later.

It would seem that the purpose of the warning is to give the accused a chance, by discontinuing his conduct, to escape arrest and, in all probability, prosecution.[5] However, the safeguard provided by the warning may often be of little value because there is no requirement that the warning should give time to comply and because the further conduct may be different as to which no warning was given.

1　　Italics added.
2　　See para **3.68** fn 1.
3　　1986 Act, s 5(5).
4　　'Immediately' seems to be redundant, since 'shortly after' seems to refer to a wider period of time.
5　　See Birch commentary [1991] Crim LR 715.

4.58 In terms of the definition of 'offensive conduct', it will be noted that the fact that no one within whose hearing or sight the behaviour in question occurred was harassed, alarmed or distressed is irrelevant if the constable reasonably suspects that someone in earshot or within sight of the behaviour is likely to be harassed etc by it. This can present problems for a constable where he is the only other person in whose hearing or sight the threatening etc words or behaviour occurs. We have seen[1] that in *DPP v Orum*[2] it was judicially recognised that a constable is less likely to be harassed, alarmed or distressed by threatening etc words or behaviour. Suppose that a constable in such a case knows for a fact that he is not harassed etc by the behaviour in question (although he knows most members of the public would have been). Does he have a power of arrest under s 5(4)? In *DPP v Orum*,[2] the Divisional Court answered the question in the negative. Glidewell LJ, with whose judgment McCullough J agreed, said:

> 'Counsel for the prosecution poses for our consideration a second question: if in fact a police officer is not likely to be caused harassment etc does he then have any power to arrest under s 5(4)? Theoretically, the answer to that question may be Yes, but in practice, in my view, it must almost invariably be No. The reason is this. If an officer is not caused harassment, alarm or distress, it is difficult to see how he can reasonably suspect, if he is the only person present, that an offence against s 5(1) has been committed since such causation is a necessary element in the offence. If he does not reasonably suspect that such an offence has been committed, then he has no power of arrest under s 5(4).'

1　　See para **4.51**.
2　　[1988] 3 All ER 449, DC.

4.59 Whether or not a person has been 'warned to stop' for the purposes of s 5(4)(a) depends on whether or not it has been conveyed to him that should he engage in further offensive conduct he would be breaking the law, a test which seems to go further than the words of s 5(4)(a), which seem to refer simply to a warning to stop present conduct as opposed to continuing or repeating it in the future. The above test was put forward in the decision of the Divisional Court in *Groom v DPP*.[1] D swore at H, made racial remarks and behaved in a threatening manner. A police officer observed this and asked D to apologise to H. D replied 'or else you will nick me?' The officer replied 'yes', whereupon D told her to 'get stuffed' and threatened her before she arrested him under s 5(4). D then assaulted her. At his trial for assault on the officer in the execution of her duty, D submitted that he had not been 'warned to stop' his offensive conduct and therefore the constable had not been acting in the execution of her duty in arresting him. Dismissing D's appeal against conviction, the Divisional Court held that, in ordinary English, to tell someone to stop something was not necessarily to warn him. A warning related to something in the future; to give a person cautionary notice or advice with regard to actions or conduct. Section 5(4), it held, did not specify the consequences of which a person should be warned; it did not say that he should be told that if he continued he would be liable to arrest; the warning did not have to be in any particular words. It must, however, have been contemplated that the instruction to stop would, of necessity, convey that should the conduct be repeated or continued the offender would be breaking the law.

The court emphasised that the concept of a warning was perfectly ordinary and required no exegesis. The tribunal of fact had to consider all relevant circumstances and reach a common sense conclusion as to whether or not a warning had been given. It held that it was impossible to say that the magistrates had been wrong to conclude that the conversation, taken as a whole, sufficiently conveyed to D that if he were to do the same sort of thing again he might be arrested, and that he would be breaking the law.

Bingham LJ, as he then was, added that, in analysing the effect of what people said and did in confused and violent, or potentially violent, situations, tribunals of fact should concentrate in a common sense way on the substance of what was said and done. The effect of the officer's communication was a question of fact for the magistrates which should not be interfered with unless they misdirected themselves in law or reached a plainly untenable conclusion, neither of which had happened.

The judgment in *Groom v DPP* also provides implicit authority for the point that, as in relation to a 'warning' about the risk of prosecution for certain motoring offences that is required by s 179 of the Road Traffic Act 1988 before a prosecution can be brought, unless certain other procedures have been adopted, a warning must be heard and understood by its addressee in order to be effective.[2]

---

1   [1991] Crim LR 713, DC.
2   The authority in respect of s 179 is *Gibson v Dalton* [1980] RTR 410, DC.

4.60 For such a minor offence, one wonders whether this specific power of arrest is necessary. It is certainly unusual for an offence that does not carry imprisonment. The police already have available their common law power to arrest for a breach of the peace (if there has been one) and their conditional power of arrest under s 25 of PACE. On the other hand, it can be argued that these powers are insufficient to give the police a power to stop hooligans from disturbing members of the public and to take prompt action to prevent a situation deteriorating. The effect of the necessary warning may be enough to stop the behaviour, so that an arrest is never necessary.

Conclusions

4.61 Situations in which s 5 tends to be charged are mainly abusive, insulting or threatening words or behaviour (one-half of cases), minor violent behaviour (one-eighth; the charge is useful where the victim is unwilling to press charges) and disorderly behaviour, a notable example being public house and food outlet disorder (one-fifth). Other situations are minor indecency, domestic disputes outside the home and minor football hooliganism.[1] Section 5 has undoubted utility; for example, as a curb on harassment or to protect other vulnerable sectors of the public against serious hooliganism. Nevertheless, s 5 is open to criticism in terms of its width and of its vagueness (of 'harassment, alarm or distress', in particular), which allows its boundaries to be settled in particular cases by the police and the magistrates.[2] It has been used not only against hooligans but also against those exercising moral or political opinions. As seen, protesters outside abortion clinics have been convicted under s 5.[3] Pickets or demonstrators shouting threats, abuse or insults at those acting contrary to their views will usually satisfy the requirements of s 5. Section 5 is therefore liable to criminalise conduct not deserving to be criminal and not intended by Parliament to be caught by it. According to one writer, by 1990, s 5:

> 'had been used quite indiscriminately, for example against juveniles for throwing fake snowballs, against a man who had a birthday party for his son in his back garden (he was charged even though he agreed to turn the music down), against two 19 year old males for kissing in the street, against a nudist on a beach and against another nudist in his own house [in fact, he was in his garden], and, most sinisterly, in the so-called Madame M case (successfully taken up by the National Council for Civil Liberties (NCCL)) against four students who were in the process of putting up a satirical poster during the last general election. It depicted the Prime Minister as a sadistic dominatrix.'[4]

As these examples suggest, the introduction of s 5 gave the police a useful resource which they were swift to utilise. A survey[5] of 470 public order cases from the 1988 records at five police stations in two police areas showed that 56% of the sample led to charges under s 5. The research supported the view that low-level nuisances of varying kinds which would not previously have been the subject of formal action were leading to arrest and charge under s 5, and that s 5 was proving useful where evidence might not support a more serious charge.

Concern about the use of s 5 was heightened:

– by national statistics which showed that 41,468 people were prosecuted or cautioned in 1990 for the still new offence; and

– by a study[6] into the use of s 5 charges in six police forces during 1990 that showed that in one-half of the s 5 cases involving threatening, abusive or insulting words or behaviour (25% of the total s 5 cases), the conduct was directed solely at the police. A common sequence was swearing at the officer, warning by officer, further swearing, arrest and charge. In such cases, s 5 was being used as a means to preserve respect for police authority (which was certainly not its intended purpose). Although the study showed that one-fifth of all s 5 cases ended in a binding over, the usual outcome where the police were the victim was a conviction followed by a fine. The study also indicated a disproportionate use of s 5 against Afro-Caribbeans. The repercussions of the Stephen Lawrence case may well be reflected in an improvement in this respect.

More recent data[7] show a fall in the total of cautions and prosecutions since 1990 (although there was a reversal of the continual decline in the last year's figures):

Number of offenders cautioned and defendants prosecuted and found guilty for an offence under s 5 of the Public Order Act 1986, 1987–1996

Outcome	1987	1988	1989	1990	1991	1992	1993	1994	1995	1996
Cautions	–	–	3,958	4,836	5,353	7,869	9,001	9,270	9,349	10,611
Prosecutions	12,660	32,493	37,358	36,632	30,247	27,796	22,456	22,425	21,798	23,887
Total Cautions and Prosecutions	–	–	41,316	41,468	35,600	35,665	31,457	31,695	31,147	34,498
Convictions	9,490	24,079	26,828	25,193	19,478	16,541	13,526	13,704	13,505	14,944

A study published in 1996[8] updated the 1990 findings,[6] and indicated that the police were still not limiting the operation of s 5 to the situations for which it was intended but were 'employing it too often in minor disorders where the police are verbally abused', although there was a significant improvement. Of the total number of s 5 cases, the police were the sole victims in 11% and both police and public were victims in a further 17% of cases.

While there has no doubt been a change for the better by police management in structuring discretion, there is still some way to go if s 5 is to be wholly true to its intended purpose. As Professor Ashworth has noted, 'Section 5 is an example of what can result from broadly defined offences with undemanding requirements of proof'.[9]

---

1   See the study cited below at fn 8.

2   See Bonner and Stone 'The Public Order Act 1986: steps in the wrong direction?' [1987] PL 202.

3   *DPP v Fidler* [1992] Crim LR 62, DC; *DPP v Clarke* [1994] Crim LR 58, DC.

4   Thornton *Decade of Decline: Civil Liberties in the Thatcher Years* (NCCL, 1990) 37. It is not clear how many of these prosecutions ended in convictions. The last one certainly did not.

5   Newburn et al 'Policing the streets' (1990) *Home Office Research Bulletin* 10; 'Increasing public order' (1991) 7 *Policing* 22.

6   Brown and Ellis *Policing Low-level Disorder: Police Use of the Public Order Act 1986* (1994) Home Office Research Study No 135.

7   This data is derived from Reid 'Public Order (Amendment) Act 1996' [1998] Crim LR 864 at 868.

8   Brown and Ellis 'Policing low-level disorder: police use of the Public Order Act 1986' (1996) *Home Office Research Bulletin* 38.

9   'Criminalising disrespect' [1995] Crim LR 98 at 100.

4.62 Section 5 would not seem to be contrary to Art 9 of the ECHR (freedom of thought) because it does not punish the accused for what he thought but for what he has done in execution of his thoughts. On the other hand, it may be contrary to Arts 10 (freedom of expression) or 11 (freedom of peaceful assembly and of association) of the ECHR. There are dicta of the European Court of Human Rights in *Müller v Switzerland*[1] to the effect that the protection of free speech under Art 10 extends equally to expressing ideas which 'offend, shock or disturb'.

It is arguable that reference to Arts 10 and 11 of the Convention could lead to conduct with a genuine political aim being regarded as reasonable on the basis that to criminalise it would be a drastic curb on the freedom to protest, which might be in breach of one, or both, of those articles, at least in respect of Art 11 if the assembly was peaceful.

However, both Art 10 and Art 11 allow such restrictions prescribed by law as are necessary in a democratic society for the prevention of disorder or the protection of the rights of others and it is submitted that, despite the width of s 5 (and in particular the vagueness of 'harassment, alarm or distress'),[2] s 5 would not be held to contravene the ECHR, although particular applications might be.

1   (1991) Ser A, no 133; 13 EHRR 212, ECtHR.
2   See paras **4.28–4.30**.

RACIALLY-AGGRAVATED PUBLIC ORDER OFFENCES[1]

4.63 Incidents of racial violence and harassment have increased substantially in recent years.[2] The impact of repeated acts of victimisation and violence on individuals is a matter of serious concern, as is the build-up of anger, fear and resentment among ethnic minority communities.

Racial incidents in England and Wales have been separately recorded by the police since 1988.[3] These have included incidents of verbal abuse and threatening behaviour, violence to the person and property damage. Figures have risen in almost every year since then. The number of racial incidents reported to the police (all forces in England and Wales) in 1988 were 4,383; in the year April 1995 to March 1996 they were 12,222.[4]

Data from the 1996 British Crime Survey suggest[4] that the above figures grossly understate the extent of the problem. The Survey estimated that the number of racially motivated offences against ethnic minorities in 1995 (as judged by the victims) was 143,000 – 15% of all offences against them, as opposed to 1% of all offences against white people in that year. In addition, a considerably higher percentage of members of ethnic minorities were found by the survey to have suffered racial harassment in 1995 than white people. Ethnic minorities also scored higher than white people on all the Survey's measures of fear of crime. In 1997, the New York-based group, Human Rights Watch, published a report showing that this country had one of the highest rates of racially motivated crime in Western Europe.[5]

1   Malik 'Racist crime: racially aggravated offences in the Crime and Disorder Act 1998 Part II' (1999) 62 MLR 409.
2   See *Racially Motivated Crime: A British Survey* (1994) Home Office Research and Planning Unit Paper 82. The police record as 'racial incidents' all incidents reported to them where any party suspects or alleges racial motivation, in accordance with the definition of a racial incident adopted in 1985 by the Association of Chief Police Officers, viz 'Any incident in which it appears to the reporting or investigating officer that the complaint involves an element of racial motivation; or any incident which includes any allegation of racial motivation made by any person': *Racial Violence and Harassment: A Consultation Paper* (Home Office, 1997) para 2.2.
3   *Racial Violence and Harassment: A Consultation Paper*, above, para 2.2.
4   *Ethnicity and Victimisation: Findings from the 1996 British Crime Survey* (1998) Home Office Statistical Bulletin Issue 6/98.
5   HL Deb, vol 584, col 577 (1997).

4.64 The criminal law is not lacking in offences which can successfully be charged in cases of racist violence or harassment or other conduct with a racial element. Part III of the Public Order Act 1986, dealt with in Chapter 5, contains a number of offences concerned with inciting racial hatred. In addition, the whole armoury of offences against the person, offences against public order, and so on, is available.

Racially aggravated conduct can also often be dealt with by the anti-social behaviour order, introduced by s 1 of the Crime and Disorder Act 1998, which is dealt with in Chapter 2.

In 1986, the Home Affairs Select Committee of the House of Commons described racial attacks and harassment as 'the most shameful and dispiriting aspect of race relations in Britain'.[1] In the year that followed, the Conservative government came under pressure to strengthen the law to deal with racially motivated violence and racial harassment. Concern about such conduct as a major problem was increased by notorious incidents such as the fatal stabbing in 1993 of Stephen Lawrence, as a result of what the coroner's jury found to be a racist attack. In the 1993–94 session of Parliament, the Home Affairs Select Committee of the House of Commons called for specific offences to deal with such conduct, and so did the Commission for Racial Equality in 1992.[2] The Government responded to that pressure to a limited extent by inserting, via the Criminal Justice and Public Order Act 1994, s 4A into the Public Order Act 1986.

The Labour Party manifesto in 1997 promised to create a new offence of racially motivated violence and a new offence of racial harassment. The Crime and Disorder Act 1998 achieved something different for two reasons. First, it provides a wider range of offences, not all requiring violence or harassment, which are simply aggravated versions of existing offences.[3] Second, it is not limited to 'racially motivated' conduct in the strict sense of that term – as will be seen later.

---

1   *Racial Attacks and Harassment* Home Affairs Select Committee, Third Report (1985/86; HC 409).

2   See *Racial Attacks and Harassment* Home Affairs Select Committee, Third Report (1993/94; HC 71); *Second Review of the Race Relations Act 1976* Commission for Racial Equality (1992).

3   It proved very difficult to define a single offence covering racial violence against the person, because the maximum punishment would have had to be set at a level inappropriate for some behaviour covered: *Racial Violence and Harassment: A Consultation Paper* (Home Office, 1997) para 5.4.

4.65 Part II of the 1998 Act introduced racially-aggravated offences parallel to certain 'basic' offences under the Offences Against the Person Act 1861, Criminal Damage Act 1971, Public Order Act 1986 and the Protection from Harassment Act 1997. For each new offence, if the racial aggravation element is proved, significantly greater maximum penalties will be available than for their basic offence counterpart. The reason is that the racial hostility involved in them causes a harm (to the victim, to his community and to good race relations) that is qualitatively different in type from that caused by the basic offence. The racially-aggravated offences are intended to 'send a strong message to society at large that such crime is unacceptable and that it will be dealt with very seriously by the police and the courts'.[1]

In addition, s 82 of the Crime and Disorder Act 1998 gave statutory effect to the sentencing principle in respect of other offences, that racial aggravation is an aggravating factor meriting a stiffer sentence.

With a few modifications, the above provisions enact proposals set out in a Home Office consultation paper published in 1997.[2] They are not without precedent in other jurisdictions. Many American States have enacted hate-crime legislation: either by introducing a specific offence to deal with violence or harassment motivated by, inter alia, race or by providing for a greater penalty for racially motivated unlawful conduct.[3] France has introduced offences relating to racial hatred and violence.[4] In 1994, Germany introduced legislation to extend criminal liability for neo-Nazi, racist and xenophobic attacks.[5] Aggravated offences are not wholly without precedent in other contexts in English criminal law. Examples of other aggravated offences are aggravated burglary and aggravated vehicle-taking.[6]

Clearly, the racially aggravated offences are a powerful symbol against racism and in favour of a tolerant society. Their effectiveness will depend on the commitment of the police and the CPS to enforce them. The *Stephen Lawrence Inquiry*[7] showed how under-performance and low priority can lead to the mishandling of cases, although there have been a number of new initiatives subsequently by the Home Secretary and the police aimed at improving police attitudes and ethos. It must be asked, however, whether such offences are the best way of achieving a tolerant society. It can be questioned whether highlighting the racial aspects of an offence does not magnify tensions and widen social divisions, making it more difficult to pursue more constructive preventive policies.[8]

---

1   *Racial Violence and Harassment: A Consultation Paper* (Home Office, 1997) para 2.4.
2   Ibid, para 3.
3   For examples, see Lawrence *Punishing Hate: Bias Crimes under American Law* (Harvard UP, 1999). Some of these statutes have been held to breach the First Amendment: see, for example, *Wisconsin v Mitchell* 124 L Ed 2d 436 (1993).
4   New Penal Code, Arts 624–3 to 624–6.
5   See Human Rights Watch/Helsinki *Germany for Germans: Xenophobia and Racist Violence in Germany* (Human Rights Watch, New York, 1995).
6   Theft Act 1968, ss 10 and 12A.
7   *The Stephen Lawrence Inquiry: Report of an Inquiry by Sir William Macpherson of Cluny* (Cm 4262, 1999).
8   For an assessment of arguments for and against 'hate crime' laws, see Hare 'Legislating against hate – The legal response to bias crimes' (1997) 17 OJLS 415. Also see Jacobs and Potter *Hate Crimes, Criminal Law and Identity Politics* (OUP, 1998) and Lawrence op cit (para **4.65** fn 3) chap 7, and, specifically, in relation to the present provisions, Brennan 'Racially motivated crime: the response of the criminal justice system' [1999] Crim LR 17.

4.66 In relation to the racially-aggravated public order offences, which are governed by s 31 of the 1998 Act, the basic offences are those under:

–   the Public Order Act 1986, s 4;
–   the Public Order Act 1986, s 4A;
–   the Public Order Act 1986, s 5.

The racially-aggravated public order offences are offences in their own right;[1] s 31 does not simply introduce new maximum sentences for the basic offences.

---

1   This is clear from the wording of the relevant sections. Any possible doubts would be resolved by reference to the principle established by the House of Lords in *R v Courtie* [1984] 1 All ER 740, viz where a greater maximum punishment can be imposed if a particular factual ingredient is established than if it is not, two or more distinct offences exist.

When is an offence racially aggravated?

4.67 The answer is provided by s 28(1) of the Crime and Disorder Act 1998 which states that an offence is racially aggravated for the purposes of the various racially-aggravated offences if:

(a) at the time of committing the offence, or immediately before or after doing so, the offender demonstrates towards the victim of the offence hostility based on the victim's membership of, or presumed membership of, a racial group; or

(b) the offence is motivated (wholly or partly) by hostility towards members of a racial group based on their membership of that group.

Definition of racial group

4.68 Section 28(4) of the Crime and Disorder Act 1998 provides that racial group means a group of persons defined by reference to race, colour, nationality (including citizenship) or ethnic or national origins. The result of the wording of the definition is that there is a substantial overlap between parts of it.

The definition of 'racial group' is clearly framed in somewhat flexible and elusive language so as to prevent argument over the precise meaning of 'race' and to leave no loopholes. Suppose, for example, that an immigrant from India attacks a Pakistani because of his hatred of Pakistanis. He could hardly be said to be motivated by, or to demonstrate, hostility towards that person on the basis of his colour, and it could be argued that Pakistanis do not constitute a single 'race'. On the other hand, as will be seen below, it could hardly be argued that Pakistanis do not all have the same national origin.[1]

Nevertheless, while there are understandable reasons behind the width and flexibility of the definition of 'racial group', its definition means that the provisions relating to racial aggravation go well beyond racist conduct as normally understood.

---

1   See the opinion of Lord Cross of Chelsea in *London Borough of Ealing v Race Relations Board* [1972] 1 All ER 105 at 118.

4.69 It will be noted from s 28(4) that to be a member of a racial group the person must be a member of a group of persons defined by reference to colour, race, nationality or ethnic or national origins. Sikhs, for example, are not a group defined by reference to colour, race or nationality, but (as we shall see) they are a group defined by reference to their ethnic origins.

The courts do not appear to have enlarged on the meaning of 'colour' or 'race' in the present context. 'Colour' clearly refers to skin colour, and not the colour of hair or eyes, but one cannot be more specific and one can only speculate about whether there are a limited number of colours in a spectrum or whether light brown is a different colour from medium brown and so on. It is doubtful whether the courts will ever need to consider the meaning of these terms, the issues which would arise would almost inevitably be dealt with by another part of the definition.

With respect to 'nationality (including citizenship)', the bracketed words indicate that 'nationality' here is being used to indicate the fact of being a citizen of a certain State, 'citizenship' being added to cover the case where nationality is described by that term by the law of the State in question, as under the British Nationality Act 1981. It is not easy to envisage situations where an offence would be motivated by, or demonstrate, hostility based purely on nationality in the above sense, as opposed to colour, race, national or ethnic origins. An example, however, would be where a person who had a hatred for a particular State and its citizens attacked a British-born person who was a naturalised citizen of that State after he had seen him presenting that State's passport.

The other two terms in the definition, 'national origins' and 'ethnic origins', call for more explanation.

4.70 'National origins' means something different from mere nationality in the sense of citizenship of a certain state.[1] 'Origins' is a reference to a connection with a nation by birth or descent.[2] 'National' refers to:

> '…"nationality" as meaning membership of a certain nation in the sense of race. Thus, according to international law, Englishmen and Scotsmen are, despite their different nationality as regards race, all of British nationality as regards citizenship … "[N]ational origins" means national in the sense of race and not citizenship. One result is that if a naturalised British citizen is attacked because he was born a German and the attacker has a grudge against Germans the attack will be motivated by his membership of a group defined by reference to national origins.'[3]

Further elucidation of 'national origins' can be derived from the speech of Lord Simon of Glaisdale in *London Borough of Ealing v Race Relations Board*, which was concerned with that term in s 1 of the Race Relations Act 1968 (the forerunner of the Race Relations Act 1976) in the context of racial discrimination:

> '"Nation" and "national", in their popular in contrast to their legal sense, are also vague terms. They do not necessarily imply statehood. For example, there were many submerged nations in the former Hapsburg empire. Scotland is not a nation in the eye of international law; but Scotsmen constitute a nation by reason of those most powerful elements in the creation of national spirit – tradition, folk memory, a sentiment of community. The Scots are a nation because of Bannockburn and Flodden, Culloden and the pipes at Lucknow, because of Jenny Geddes and Flora Macdonald, because of frugal living and respect for learning, because of Robert Burns and Walter Scott. So, too, the English are a nation – because Norman, Angevin and Tudor monarchs forged them together, because their land is mostly sea-girt, because of the common law and of gifts for poetry and parliamentary government, because (despite the Wars of the Roses and Old Trafford and Headingley) Yorkshiremen and Lancastrian feel more in common than in difference and are even prepared at a pinch to extend their sense of community to southern folk. By the Act of Union English and Scots lost their separate nationalities, but they retained their separate nationhoods; and their descendants have thereby retained their separate national origins. So, again, the Welsh are a nation – in the popular, though not in the legal, sense – by reason of Offa's Dyke, by recollection of battles long ago and pride in the present valour of their regiments, because of musical gifts and religious dissent, because of fortitude in the face of economic adversity, because of the satisfaction of all Wales that Lloyd George became an architect of the welfare state and prime minister of victory. To discriminate against Englishmen, Scots or Welsh, as such, would, in my opinion, be to discriminate against them on the ground of their "national origins".'[4]

---

1   *London Borough of Ealing v Race Relations Board* [1972] 1 All ER 105 at 112, per Viscount Dilhorne.
2   *London Borough of Ealing v Race Relations Board* [1972] 1 All ER 105, HL.
3   Ibid, at 108, per Lord Donovan.

4   Ibid, at 116.

4.71 In respect of 'ethnic origins', 'origins' has the same meaning as in 'national origins', ie connection by birth or descent. The term 'ethnic' is construed relatively widely and, although a cultural or religious group is not per se defined by reference to its ethnic origins, 'ethnic' is used in a sense wider than the strictly racial or biological. This was held by the House of Lords in *Mandla v Dowell Lee*,[1] where Lord Fraser of Tullybelton, with whose speech the other Law Lords agreed, said:

> 'For a group to constitute an ethnic group in the sense of the Race Relations Act 1976, it must, in my opinion, regard itself, and be regarded by others, as a distinct community by virtue of certain characteristics. Some of these characteristics are essential; others are not essential but one or more of them will commonly be found and will help to distinguish the group from the surrounding community. The conditions which appear to me to be essential are these: (1) a long, shared history, of which the group is conscious as distinguishing it from other groups, and the memory of which it keeps alive; (2) a cultural tradition of its own, including family and social customs and manners, often but not necessarily associated with religious observance. In addition, to these two essential characteristics the following characteristics are, in my opinion, relevant: (3) either a common geographical origin, or descent from a small number of common ancestors; (4) a common language, not necessarily peculiar to the group; (5) a common literature peculiar to the group; (6) a common religion different from that of neighbouring groups or from the general community surrounding it; (7) being a minority or being an oppressed or a dominant group within a larger community, for example a conquered people... and their conquerors might both be ethnic groups.'[2]

Pursuant to the above dictum, it is clear that Jews[3] are a group defined by reference to their ethnic origins, and so are Sikhs (as the House held in *Mandla*),[4] Romany gypsies,[5] the Scots and the English.[6] On the other hand, members of the 70-year old Rastafarian sect are not,[7] nor are Muslims,[8] and neither are tinkers or travellers.[9]

1   [1983] 1 All ER 1062, HL.
2   Ibid, at 1066–1067.
3   Also see *Seide v Gillette Industries Ltd* [1980] IRLR 427 at 430; and *Ansell v Police* [1979] 2 NZLR 53, NZCA (approved by Lord Fraser in *Mandla v Dowell Lee*).
4   The Sikhs were originally a religious community, although this is no longer purely so, founded at about the end of the fifteenth century, which is now a distinctive and self-conscious community, with its own written language (which a small proportion of Sikhs can read): *Mandla v Dowell Lee* [1983] 1 All ER 1062 at 1069, per Lord Fraser.
5   *Commission for Racial Equality v Dutton* [1989] 1 All ER 306, CA.
6   *Northern Joint Police Board v Power* [1997] IRLR 610, EAT.
7   *Dawkins v Crown Suppliers (PSB) Ltd* [1993] ICR 517, CA. See Parpworth 'Defining ethnic origins' (1993) 143 NLJ 610.
8   *Malik v Bartram Personnel Group* (1990), an Employment Tribunal decision, no 4343/90. On two occasions the Divisional Court has declined to make a declaration on the point on the ground that it was an academic or hypothetical one on the facts: *DPP v London Borough of Merton* (1998) unreported, DC; ibid (1999) unreported, DC.
9   *Commission for Racial Equality v Dutton*, above.

4.72 As can be seen, a group of persons defined by reference to religion is not a racial group and therefore falls outside the scope of Part II of the Crime and Disorder Act 1998. The result is that, while the commission of an offence specified in Part II that demonstrates hostility based solely on the victim's membership of a religion, for example the Jewish, Muslim, Rastafarian or Roman Catholic religion, or is motivated solely by hostility towards members of his religion, is not covered, the commission of one of these offences which demonstrates hostility based on the fact that the victim is black-skinned, or Irish, or Pakistani, or a Jew, or a Sikh is, because the 'attack' relates to his membership of a racial group. The essential difference between membership of a racial group and membership of a religious group is that the former is inherited whereas the latter involves personal choice. Of course, threatening, abusive or insulting behaviour towards a member of a group identified by reference to a religion may be open to the interpretation that it is an attack on him as a member of a racial group identified with it, for example as Jews (or Sikhs) are associated with the Jewish (or Sikh) religion.[1] In addition, it is open to question how many attacks etc are triggered solely by hostility towards a person's religion. It is likely that the vast majority of attacks on members of ethnic minority groups associated with a particular religion, for example the Muslim religion, are triggered by racial hostility, and not solely by religious hostility.

Abusive behaviour towards Muslims has been on the increase in recent years,[2] but the Government has resisted pressure to extend racially-aggravated offences so as to include religious aggravation, on the ground that it is more difficult to define whether someone is a member of a religious group, which involves a subjective as well as an objective element.[3] It has, however, established research on the nature and scale of religious discrimination in order to establish the size of the problem, including research into religious attacks. The question of religious aggravation is dealt with further in para **4.80**.

---

1   *Brownlie's Law of Public Order and National Security* (1981) p 17. Also see DGT Williams 'Racial incitement and public order' [1966] Crim LR 320 at 324; Hepple 'Race Relations Act 1965' (1966) 29 MLR 306 at 308.
2   See, for example, the report in *The Times* of 28 October 1998.
3   HC Deb, vol 314, col 895 (1998).

4.73 The definition of 'racial group' does not include a group or person identified by reference to their language.[1] Suppose a Welsh language protester causes distress to an English-speaking person who has a holiday home in Wales by using insulting or abusive words. It would be difficult to prove that he has committed a racially-aggravated public order offence on this ground. The reason is that it would be difficult to prove that he was demonstrating hostility to the person based on that person's membership of a racial group in terms of national or ethnic origins etc, or that he was motivated by hostility towards members of a racial group in such terms based on their membership of that group. His objection is to that person's language and it would seem to be a matter of indifference what that person's national or ethnic origins are. Nevertheless, a jury might be invited to consider whether any hostility demonstrated by, or motivating, the protester was based on his English national origins or the fact that he was English-speaking.

It may be noted, also, that 'racial group' does not include a group of persons defined by politics or culture; members of the National Front are not protected from vilification or abuse by the special protection of the new offences, nor are 'New Age Travellers'. Likewise, the new offences do not protect a person who is a victim because of his place of origin or residence. The fact that a person is a 'Brummie' or a 'Geordie' does not make him a member of a racial group defined in terms of residents of Birmingham or Newcastle.

---

1   See *Gwynedd County Council v Jones* [1986] ICR 833, EAT.

Racial aggravation

4.74 By s 28(1) of the Crime and Disorder Act 1998, any of the specified offences is racially aggravated if:

> '(a) at the time of committing the offence, or immediately before or after doing so, the offender demonstrates towards the victim of the offence hostility based on the victim's membership (or presumed membership) of a racial group, or
>
> (b) the offence is motivated (wholly or partly) by hostility towards members of a racial group based on their membership of that group.'

Thus, there are two types of racial aggravation, the first based on the *demonstration towards the victim* of *racial hostility* and the second based on *racially hostile motivation* towards members of a racial group. It is important to note that the demonstration of racial hostility is a separate, independent type of racial aggravation not requiring proof of a racially hostile nature, and not simply a means of proving or inferring racially hostile motivation, and that 'hostility' and 'hostile' are quite strong terms. The inclusion of the demonstration of racial hostility as a species of racial aggravation is intended to avoid the problems which can be encountered in proving a racially hostile motivation by placing the emphasis on the external manifestations of the conduct involved.

4.75 The concept of membership of racial group is not always an easy one to apply. There is clearly no problem where the group in question is defined by reference to colour, race or nationality: a person either is or is not a member of a group identified by reference to a particular colour, race or nationality. The difficulty relates to membership of a racial group identified by reference to its ethnic or national origins.

In *Mandla v Dowell Lee*,[1] Lord Fraser of Tullybelton said, obiter, that an ethnic group would be capable of including converts, for example, persons who marry into the group, and of excluding apostates. He added, 'Provided a person who joins the group feels him or herself to be a member of it, and is accepted by other members, he is ... a member'. It would seem that a convert can be a member of a group identified by reference to its ethnic origins – the question is not his origins but that of the group – and that a person may cease to be a member of such a group by abandoning its traditions and his identity with it. Lord Fraser thought that the same would be true of other types of racial group. It is inconceivable that this could occur in practice in terms of colour or race. On the other hand, it seems possible that one can convert in and out of a group defined by reference to its national origins. [2]

---

1   [1983] 1 All ER 1062 at 1067.
2   Also see *Gwynedd County Council v Jones* [1986] ICR 833 at 836.

4.76 The importance of the precise meaning of 'membership' in s 28(1)(a) is lessened by s 28(2), which provides that in s 28(1)(a) 'membership' in relation to a racial group includes association with members of that group. Thus, even if a convert does not become a 'member' in the strict sense of the term he is clearly in association with the group. So is a person who has not converted but is the spouse or adopted child of a member and thereby in association with that member and members of his family etc who are members of the group. Thus, if a white woman who is married to a Pakistani is attacked or abused because of her association with Pakistanis the offence will be racially aggravated.

There is no need for a provision about 'association' in s 28(1)(b) because s 28(1)(b) merely requires motivation by hostility 'towards members of a racial group', as opposed to an individual victim. It follows that s 28(1)(b) can be satisfied if the actual victim is not a member of the racial group towards whom hostility is proved to have been the motivation for the offence. If an attack on a white girl is shown to be motivated by her friendship with a black youth or youths, the hostility towards members of a racial group (black people) is made out without any need to prove that she, the actual victim of the offence, is technically a member of the racial group by association.[1]

---

1   Leng, Taylor and Wasik *Blackstone's Guide to the Crime and Disorder Act 1998* (Blackstone, 1998) p 46.

Demonstration of hostility based on victim's membership etc of a racial group

4.77 Section 28(1)(a) requires that 'at the time of committing the offence, or immediately before or after doing so, the offender demonstrates towards the victim hostility based on the victim's membership or presumed membership of a racial group'.

Although it was intended to make 'racial aggravation' easier to prove than if that term was limited to racially hostile motivation, it would be over-optimistic to assume that 'the demonstration of racial hostility' will always be easy to prove. The requirement that racial hostility must be demonstrated at the time of committing the offence, or immediately before or after doing so means that there must be some evidence of an overt demonstration of what could be found to be racial hostility during that period. A finding of racial aggravation under s 28(1)(a) could not be based *solely* on a person's previous statements indicating hostility to a racial group. Indeed, the evidence will have to be confined to the time of the alleged incident, unless the accused conducts his case in such a way as to let the prosecution adduce evidence of, or ask questions about, his character or previous convictions, or the facts are such that similar factual evidence is admissible (which will be rare).

The reference to 'hostility' seems to indicate that enmity or antagonism must be displayed on the stated ground. It might have been better if, as in a corresponding provision in Scots law,[1] reference had been made to the demonstration of malice and ill-will towards the victim. It is not obvious how hostility is going to be demonstrated other than by words, spoken or written.

Section 28(1)(a) does not require the hostility demonstrated to be based only on the victim's membership of a racial group, or even principally on it; this is confirmed by s 28(3)(b) referred to in para **4.80**. However, the more incidental the words or other conduct with a racial content, the more difficult it will be to prove that the accused has demonstrated racial hostility. In this context it must be emphasised that it is not enough simply to refer, for example, to the victim's race, the accused must be proved to have demonstrated 'hostility'. If the accused goes up to an Afro-Caribbean and, without any provocation, hurls racist abuse at him, there will clearly be no problem in proving that he has demonstrated hostility based on his victim's membership of a racial group. It will be difficult to do so where the accused is enraged when a careless driver drives into the back of his car at some traffic lights and, incensed, goes to the careless driver's car to 'have it out' with him. The careless driver tells the irate driver to 'F... off' in tones which clearly indicate that he is Irish, to which the still irate driver calls him a 'stupid Irish bastard who shouldn't be allowed on the road'. Arguably, here he is demonstrating hostility based on the careless driver's carelessness and rudeness but not on his Irishness. It would be different if the irate driver had said, 'All you bloody Irish are the same. Complete boneheads. I can't stand any of you'. The test would seem to be whether the hostility demonstrated is based *solely* on some other factor or factors, such as the victim's intransigence or carelessness or past conduct; if so the hostility will not have been demonstrated based on the victim's membership of a racial group. It would be different if it was proved that, although the hostility demonstrated was based primarily on some other factor it was also based on the victim's racial origins, as explained above. Such proof will normally be by way of the magistrates or jury drawing inferences from the evidence, but it must not be forgotten that the case must be proved beyond reasonable doubt; inferences should not be drawn too readily.

In relation to the requirement that the hostility must be demonstrated at the time of committing the offence, or immediately before or after doing so, reference can be made to case law on the offence of robbery. The definition of that offence refers to the use of threats of force 'immediately before or at the time of the stealing'. It has been held for the purposes of the offence that 'the time' of the stealing is not limited to the period (possibly a split second of time) during which the material act with mens rea of theft occurs, and that 'the time' of the stealing lasts as long as the theft can be said to be still in progress in common sense terms, ie so long as the accused is 'on the job'.[2] The addition by s 28(1)(a) of 'immediately after' is effective to extend that period. It means, for example, that what starts off as a 'simple' public order offence under s 4 of the 1986 Act and finished with racist abuse which would not satisfy s 4 (or even s 4A or s 5) is elevated to the aggravated category.

---

1   Crime and Disorder Act 1998, s 33.
2   *R v Hale* (1978) 68 Cr App R 415, CA; *R v Atakpu* [1993] 4 All ER 215 at 224; *R v Lockley* [1995] Crim LR 656, CA.

4.78 Sometimes hostility may be demonstrated towards someone in the mistaken belief that he is a member of a racial group, as where a Bangladeshi is the victim of hostility intended to be directed at a Pakistani. In such a case the offence will be racially aggravated because s 28(2) provides that the reference to 'presumed membership' in s 28(1)(a) means presumed by the offender. Likewise, if a white woman who has become a Muslim, and who is wearing a chador, a religious face covering, is the subject of a racial attack or racial abuse in the mistaken belief that she is a Pakistani, the offence will be racially aggravated. Similarly, if a racist threatens a white woman whom he mistakenly believes is associated with a Pakistani and his family, and the hostility he demonstrates is based on that association, his offence is racially aggravated because of the definition of 'membership' and 'presumed membership'.

Motivation by hostility towards members of a racial group based on their membership of that group

4.79 In terms of the second alternative meaning of 'racially aggravated' contained in s 28(1)(b), this has the effect in relation to the specified offences of making motive relevant to criminal liability, something which is exceptional,[1] but which has a modern precursor in the offence of reprisals against witnesses, jurors and others, contrary to s 51(2) of the Criminal Justice and Public Order Act 1994. It is likely only to be relied on where hostility to a particular victim based on race is not demonstrated, as, for example, where racist graffiti is painted on the wall of a block of council flats.

Proof of motivation by racial hostility could consist solely of evidence of statements made before or after the event or of evidence of membership of a racist group. Unlike s 28(1)(a), proof of racial aggravation under s 28(1)(b) does not depend on any statements or other evidence indicating racial hostility contemporaneous with the offence.[2]

It should be noted that the offence need not be motivated wholly by hostility towards members of a racial group based on their membership of that group, nor need it be principally so motivated. It may, for example, be motivated by religious, as well as racial, hostility. However, where it is partly so motivated, particularly where the racial motivation is subordinate to other motives, it will be particularly difficult to prove the necessary motivation.

Section 28(1)(b) does not require the accused to be motivated by racial hostility towards the victim of the offence but 'merely' by hostility 'towards members of a racial group'. Normally the victim will be a member of that group (and thus included within the ambit of that hostility) or at least be associated with it, but this is not a requirement of s 28(1)(b). A person who, motivated by hostility towards members of the Jewish community, shouts abuse at a bricklayer whom he knew was not Jewish who was working on the building of a synagogue would fall foul of s 28(1)(b), for example. It is for this reason that it was not necessary to extend to s 28(1)(b) the provision that membership of a racial group includes association with it.

---

1   Motive, good or bad, is normally irrelevant to criminal liability: *R v Sharpe* (1857) Dears&B 160; *Hills v Ellis* [1983] 1 All ER 667, DC; see para **9.67**, although it may affect the punishment imposed (as is confirmed in the case of a racist motive by the 1998 Act, s 82; see para **4.65**).

2   See *R v Ball* [1911] AC 47, HL; *R v Williams* (1987) 84 Cr App R 299, CA. Such evidence of non-contemporaneous matters would be excluded if in all the circumstances its admission would have such an adverse effect on the fairness of the proceedings that it ought not to be admitted; PACE, s 78. Evidence of the accused's membership of a racist group may be open to objection in terms of the ECHR, Art 11 (freedom of association): Hare 'Legislating against hate – the legal response to bias crimes' (1977) 17 OJLS 415 at 431.

4.80 The point just made is reinforced by s 28(3), which also makes a similar provision in respect of racial aggravation within s 28(1)(a). Section 28(3) provides that it is immaterial for the purposes of s 28(1)(a) or (b) whether or not the offender's hostility is also based, to any extent, on:

(a) the fact or presumption that any person or group of persons belongs to any religious group; or

(b) any other factor not mentioned in that paragraph.

This provision is particularly intended to allay the concerns of the Muslim community that the new offences would not do enough to protect them. The effect of the provision is to make clear that, even if religious hostility is the principal or main trigger for what is done, racial aggravation will be established if an element of racial hostility is proved. In reality, the provision does not add anything to s 28. It does not catch the case where people are attacked, threatened or harassed solely because of their religion. If D, an anti-Muslim fanatic, threatens a woman whom he knows is white, and whom he knows is not associated with members of an ethnic minority group, because she is wearing a chador or hajab as a badge of her religion the threat is not racially aggravated.

The result of the present law is that, if a Sikh and a Muslim, triggered by the hostility each feels for the other, utter threats to each other, the Sikh's demonstration of, or motivation by, hostility towards the Muslim religion will not make his threat racially aggravated. On the other hand, the Muslim's threat to the Sikh will be racially aggravated if, in part, it is triggered by hostility to Sikhs as an ethnic group, even if the principal trigger was hostility to the Sikh religion.

This problem is increased by the fact that religious hostility, unlike racial hostility,[1] has not yet been expressly identified as an aggravating factor when it comes to sentencing.

---

1   See para **4.65**.

The offences

4.81 Section 31(1) of the 1998 Act provides that:

'A person is guilty of an offence under this section if he commits –

(a) an offence under section 4 of the Public Order Act 1986 (fear or provocation of violence);

(b) an offence under section 4A of that Act (intentional harassment, alarm or distress); or

(c) an offence under section 5 of that Act (harassment, alarm or distress),

which is racially aggravated for the purposes of this section.'

Section 31(1) does not create one offence which can be committed in various ways; it creates three separate offences.[1]

---

1   Sections 4, 4A and 5 of the Public Order Act 1986 each create one offence: 1986 Act, s 7(2).

4.82 On a charge of an offence under s 31 the prosecution must prove that the accused has committed the relevant specified basic offence described above and that it was racially aggravated.

For the purposes of the aggravated offence under s 31(1)(c) the definition of racial aggravation in s 28(1) has effect in the way specified by s 31(7), the effect of s 31(7) being italicised, as follows:

(a) at the time of committing the offence, or immediately before or after doing so, the offender demonstrates towards *the person likely to be caused harassment, alarm or distress* hostility based on that person's actual or presumed membership of, or association with members of, a racial group; or

(b) the offence is motivated (wholly or partly) by hostility towards members of a racial group based on their membership of that group.

Trial and punishment

4.83 Unlike the basic offences under ss 4 and 4A of the Public Order Act 1986, the racially-aggravated versions of these two offences are triable either way.[1]

Section 31(4) of the Crime and Disorder Act 1998 provides the following maxima in respect of the aggravated versions of these offences:

(a) on summary conviction, imprisonment for a term not exceeding six months or a fine not exceeding the statutory maximum, or both;

(b) on conviction on indictment, imprisonment for a term not exceeding two years or a fine, or both.

Like the basic offence under s 5 of the Crime and Disorder Act 1998, the aggravated version of the s 5 offence is triable only summarily[2] and is not imprisonable. The maximum fine is one not exceeding level 4 on the standard scale.[2]

---

1   1998 Act, s 31(4).
2   Ibid, s 31(5).

Alternative verdicts

4.84 By section 31(6) of the Crime and Disorder Act 1998, where a person is charged with an aggravated s 4 offence or an aggravated s 4A offence, and the jury find him not guilty of it, they may return a guilty verdict in respect of the corresponding non-aggravated offence, notwithstanding that both basic offences are triable summarily only.

An alternative verdict of the second aggravated public order offence at a trial on indictment for the first of the three aggravated offences (ie guilty of an aggravated s 4A offence on a charge of an aggravated s 4 offence) is not provided for by the Crime and Disorder Act 1998. This is not surprising because an allegation of the first offence does not expressly or impliedly amount to or include all the elements of the second. It is for this reason that the alternative verdict provisions of the Criminal Law Act 1967 s 6(3)[1] are also inapplicable.

Where any of the three aggravated public order offences is tried summarily there cannot be an alternative conviction for the corresponding non-aggravated offence or, indeed, any offence.[2]

---

1   See para **3.73**.
2   See para **4.3**.

4.85 Although there can be an alternative conviction for the basic s 4 offence if the accused is acquitted in the Crown Court on a charge of violent disorder or affray,[1] there is no corresponding provision enabling an alternative verdict of the aggravated s 4 offence to be returned at a trial for violent disorder or affray. This is because offences of racially-aggravated violent disorder or affray have not been created. This is liable to lead to complications for the prosecution in a racially aggravated case where the prosecution wishes to charge violent disorder or affray. The points were well put by Viscount Colville of Culross at the Committee stage in the House of Lords:

> 'I respectfully suggest that what will happen in these circumstances is this. If the prosecution wish to prosecute someone for a racially aggravated public order offence, they will have to decide whether they are going to go for ordinary violent disorder,

ordinary affray – noble and learned Lords were right in saying that it will not be necessary for them in those circumstances to prove anything by way of racial aggravation – or they are going to go for racially aggravated threatening words and behaviour under ... [s 31]. There is no alternative. The two things are not an alternative. They cannot be, because of the way the legislation is drafted. If they wish to proceed, for instance, on affray, it will not be necessary for them to prove any racial aggravation. They will just prove an affray in the ordinary fashion. There will be no alternative of racially aggravated threatening words and behaviour under section 4, because it cannot be an alternative. They will therefore have to put two counts. They will have to have ordinary affray, which by definition will not have to be racially aggravated, and they will have to have a second count of racially aggravated threatening words and behaviour. What the jury will make of that, I really do not know.

There is an added complication. Having been confronted with non-racially aggravated affray and the alternative of a racially-aggravated offence, the jury will also have a third alternative under [s 31(6)] whereby they can find a non-racially oriented offence under section 4. If the noble and learned Lord really wants judges in the Crown Court to sum up, and the prosecution to proceed, upon that basis, we will do it. There is no problem. What will happen, I shudder to think; but that is what we will do because we are bound, as a matter of law, to do it ...'[2]

---

1 Public Order Act 1986, s 7.
2 HL Deb, vol 585, cols 1301–1302 (1998).

Arrest

4.86 None of the aggravated offences is an arrestable offence. Section 31 does, however, provide police officers with the same powers of arrest without warrant as are available for the corresponding basic offences.[1]

---

1 See paras **4.18–4.19** (but note that PACE, s 17, does not apply to the corresponding racially-aggravated offence), **4.40** and **4.57–4.60**.

Why not offences of racially-aggravated riot, violent disorder or affray?

4.87 It seems odd that the offences of riot, violent disorder and affray were not given an aggravated version. As already indicated, this is a potential source of difficulty in respect of alternative verdicts in the case of violent disorder and affray. These offences are the violent offences under the 1986 Act; those under ss 4, 4A and 5 can be described as non-violent ones. It is surprising that, for example, a race riot is not regarded as an aggravated offence and that the court's sentencing powers, after allowing for the element of racial aggravation under s 82 of the 1998 Act, are subject to the normal maximum for the offence. The Government gave two reasons. The first was that these offences 'are not directed against specific persons; they are mêlée or public order offences'.[1] This reason is not consistent with s 30, which provides the offence of racially-aggravated criminal damage. Criminal damage offences, including those involving racism, are frequently not directed against a specific individual or victim. As things now stand those who are guilty of taking part in a race riot are subject to a lower maximum penalty, 10 years' imprisonment, than those guilty of racially-aggravated criminal damage (14 years' maximum). The Government's second reason is equally unconvincing. It was that the aggravated offences were intended to be aimed at the 'main' violence and harassment offences directed against the person, and that riot, violent disorder and affray fell outside the area of such offences.[2]

1   HL Committee, vol 585, col 1281 (1998).
2   HC Committee B, col 329 (1998).

4.88 In the light of sentencing principle in s 82 of the Crime and Disorder Act 1998, one may question the need for the racially-aggravated public order offences and the other racially-aggravated offences. The sentencing principle enshrined in s 82 ensures that the element of racial aggravation can be reflected in sentence, and the requirement in s 82 to state in open court that racial aggravation has aggravated the sentence would satisfy the need for clear denunciation of a racially-aggravated offence.

The need to prove the element of racial aggravation in order to obtain a conviction may be a disincentive to a prosecution being instituted or continued for a racially-aggravated public order offence, particularly in cases described above where an alternative verdict is not (or may not be) available. Prosecutors may decide in such cases not to opt for alternative charges for the sake of simplicity, but simply to charge the basic offence and leave the element of racial aggravation to be taken into account under s 82.

PROTECTION FROM HARASSMENT ACT 1997

4.89 The 1997 Act was prompted by public concern about 'stalking', ie the persistent harassment of one person by another, normally of the opposite sex, by persistently following them or bombarding them with telephone calls or letters or similar obsessive conduct. As will be seen, however, the prohibition of harassment also applies to a much wider range of activities, some of them impinging on public order. Conduct involved in disputes between neighbours or in industrial disputes, racial harassment, protesters of various kinds, and the activities of the 'paparazzi' are all liable to be covered by it.

The law's response to harassment may take the form of civil proceedings initiated by the victim or of criminal proceedings. The 1997 Act improved the law in both respects. Before it, there was no tort of harassment and the basis on which an injunction could be granted was not entirely free from doubt, unless the parties were in a matrimonial or similar relationship; in addition, the normal remedy, civil contempt proceedings, was liable to be insufficient to deal with stalkers who broke an injunction against them. Likewise, until the 1997 Act, the remedy for harassment in criminal law was to secure a conviction for a non-fatal offence, such as assault occasioning actual bodily harm, or for some other offence, such as one under s 4 to s 5 of the Public Order Act 1986. The problem here was that some types of harassment might fall outside the terms of a particular offence and that the criminal law failed to deal with the obsessive person who tries to carry on harassment from his prison cell or after release from prison.

The 1997 Act provides civil and criminal remedies which both centre on breach of a prohibition of harassment contained in s 1 of the Act.[1]

1   The Act does not apply to any conduct certified by the Secretary of State to have been done on behalf of the Crown in relation to national security, the economic well-being of the UK or the prevention or detection of serious crime: 1997 Act, s 12.

Prohibition of harassment

4.90 The prohibition is framed as follows by s 1(1) of the 1997 Act:

'A person must not pursue a course of conduct –

(a) which amounts to harassment of another, and
(b) which he knows or ought to know amounts to harassment of the other.'

For there to be a 'course of conduct' there must be 'conduct'[1] on at least two occasions.[2] The conduct need not involve threatening, abusive or insulting words or behaviour. Any conduct will do if it amounts to harassment and is part of a course of conduct on at least two occasions. Two different types of conduct by an individual *can* amount to a course of conduct if they result in harassment. But whether pieces of conduct are a 'course of conduct' will depend on the length of the alleged course, the frequency of the conduct and the degree of similarity of the conduct. One piece of conduct in mid-May and a second similar piece in December of the same year could hardly be described as a 'course of conduct', whereas there would seem to be such a course if the second piece of similar conduct was in early June of the same year. Four pieces of similar conduct in mid-May, July, October and December of the same year would seem to be a course of conduct, although if the conduct was respectively a noisy argument with a third party, stealing a milk bottle from the doorstep, shouting abuse at the victim and blocking the victim's drive by parking across it it would probably not. At the other extreme, there is no reason why one piece of conduct quickly followed by another should not be a course of conduct; it would be different if the only conduct alleged cannot be divided into two pieces because it forms a continuum or if the two pieces were so close together that they could not be said to occur 'on two occasions'.

The reference to harassment of another here, and elsewhere in the Act, includes alarming that person or causing that person distress.[3] The meaning of 'harassment', 'alarm' and 'distress' would seem to be a question of fact, to be decided according to their ordinary, natural meaning.[4] What is said about these terms in paras **4.28–4.30** applies equally here. It need not be proved that any individual piece of conduct amounted to harassment etc, but it must be proved that the course of conduct did.

The objective nature of 'ought to know' in (b) is given a subjective aspect by s 1(2) of the 1997 Act, which provides that the person whose course of conduct is in question ought to know that it amounts to harassment of another if a reasonable person in possession of the same information would think the course of conduct amounted to harassment of the other.

---

1   A term which includes 'speech': 1997 Act, s 7(4).
2   Ibid, s 7(3).
3   Ibid, s 7(2).
4   See para **4.28**.

4.91 By s 1(3) of the 1997 Act, the prohibition of harassment in s 1(l) does not apply to a course of conduct

'if the person who pursued it proves[1] that:

(a) it was pursued for the purpose of preventing or detecting crime,

(b) it was pursued under any enactment or rule of law or to comply with any condition or requirement imposed by any person under any enactment, or

(c) in the particular circumstances the pursuit of the course of conduct was reasonable.'

The first defence clearly covers police officers or public officials acting in the course of their duty to prevent or detect crime. However, the wording is wide enough also to cover private individuals who claim that they are trying to stop or detect criminal activities. An example would be anti-vivisectionists trying to see if animal-cruelty offences were being committed in a laboratory. Such persons might find it difficult to prove that this was their purpose if there is no evidence to suggest that such offences had been committed on the premises or could reasonably be suspected to have been, or to be being, committed on the premises.[2]

The third defence is an important, albeit vague, curb on the width of the prohibition of harassment. It is of particular importance in terms of public protest and public order. Eady J stated in *Huntingdon Life Sciences Ltd v Curtin*[3] that the 1997 Act was not intended by Parliament to be used to clamp down on the discussion of matters of public interest or upon the rights of public protest and public demonstration which was so much part of our democratic tradition, and that he had little doubt that the courts would resist any wide interpretation of the Act. This does not, of course, mean that all public protest and public demonstrations will be reasonable conduct. In *Huntingdon Life Sciences* itself, Eady J continued an anti-harassment injunction against certain anti-vivisection protesters who had subjected a licensed animal-experimentation laboratory and its employees to a sustained campaign of harassment.

In *DPP v Moseley*,[4] Collins J stated that in determining whether conduct was reasonable a court had to balance the interests of the victim against the purpose and nature of the course of conduct pursued, including the right to peaceful protest. However, the Divisional Court agreed in that case that, if the course of conduct in question involved breach of an injunction, it could not be reasonable conduct, at least unless the circumstances were very special.[5]

The imposition of liability for breach of the prohibition of harassment raises the question of the compatibility of the 1997 Act with Arts 10 (freedom of expression) and 11 (freedom of peaceful assembly and association) of the ECHR. What was said earlier in this chapter about the compatibility of ss 4 to 5 of the Public Order Act 1986 with these Articles is equally applicable here.

---

1   On the balance of probabilities: see para **4.38** (in relation to criminal cases) and *Miller v Minister of Pensions* [1947] 2 All ER 372 (civil cases).

2   See Addison and Lawson-Cruttenden *Harassment Law and Practice* (Blackstone Press, 1998) p 39.

3   (1997) *The Times*, 11 December.

4   (1999) *The Times*, 23 June, DC.

5   See para **4.36** in relation to a similar defence to that under s 1(3)(c).

Civil remedy

4.92 Section 3(1) of the 1997 Act provides that an actual or apprehended breach of the prohibition of harassment may be the subject of a claim in civil proceedings by the person who is or may be the victim of the course of conduct in question. Proceedings may be brought in the High Court or a county court.

On such a claim:

(a) damages may be awarded for (among other things) any anxiety caused by the harassment and any financial loss resulting from the harassment;[1] and

(b) more importantly, an injunction may be granted for the purpose of restraining the defendant from pursuing any conduct which amounts to harassment (hereafter an 'anti-harassment injunction'). An application for an injunction appears to be a more common way of dealing with harassment than a prosecution for the offence under s 2 of the 1997 Act described below.

Because a breach of an injunction can result in criminal liability (see below), there are strong arguments that a higher standard of proof than the normal civil standard of 'on the balance of probabilities' is required of an applicant for an anti-harassment injunction. A similar argument can be made in respect of a claimant for damages under s 3, given that proof of a breach of the prohibition of harassment is proof of an offence contrary to s 2 of the 1997 Act (below). A similar issue was discussed in para **2.80** in relation to applications for an anti-social behaviour order. What was said there is equally applicable here.

In respect of a claim for damages, the special time-limit under s 11 of the Limitation Act 1986 of three years for (inter alia) breach of statutory duty, running from the date on which the cause of action accrued, or the date of the claimant's knowledge (if later), does not apply to a claim under s 3.[2] Instead, the normal tortious limitation period under s 2 of the 1986 Act seems to apply.

---

1   1997 Act, s 3(2).
2   Ibid, s 6.

Breach of injunction

4.93 Like a breach of any other injunction, breach of an anti-harassment injunction may result in civil contempt of court proceedings instituted by the victim. Such proceedings are, however, slow and in situations covered by the prohibition of harassment defendants are particularly liable to evade service of court documents. For such reasons, the 1997 Act makes special provision for breach of an anti-harassment injunction.

Where the High Court or a county court grants an anti-harassment injunction, and the claimant considers that the defendant has done anything that he is prohibited from doing by the injunction, the claimant may apply for the issue of a warrant for the arrest of the defendant.[1] Application must be made to a judge of the High Court or to a judge or district judge of a county court, depending on which type of court granted the injunction.[2] The judge or district judge to whom such an application is made may only issue a warrant if:

(a) the application is substantiated on oath, and

(b) the judge or district judge has reasonable grounds for believing that the defendant has done anything which he is prohibited from doing by the injunction.[3]

Where, without reasonable excuse,[4] a person subject to an anti-harassment injunction does anything prohibited by the injunction, he is guilty of an either-way offence.[5] The offence is punishable:

(a) on conviction on indictment, to imprisonment for a term not exceeding five years, a fine, or both; or

(b) on summary conviction, to imprisonment for a term not exceeding six months, a fine not exceeding the statutory maximum, or both.[6]

Like criminal liability for breach of an anti-social behaviour order, this is a rare example of a criminal sanction being applied to a breach of a civil order.

Special provision is made in respect of the interrelation of this offence and the law of contempt by s 3(7) and (8), as follows. Where a person is convicted of an offence under s 3(6) in respect of any conduct, that conduct is not punishable as a contempt of court. On the other hand, a person cannot be convicted of an offence under s 3(6) in respect of any conduct which has been punished as a contempt of court.

1   1997 Act, s 3(3).
2   Ibid, s 3(4).
3   Ibid, s 3(5).
4   The comments made about proof in relation to this defence in para **2.89** are equally applicable here. Also see para **2.90**.
5   1997 Act, s 3(6).
6   Ibid, s 3(9). By virtue of it maximum punishment, the offence is an arrestable offence: PACE, s 24(1).

Offences

Offence of harassment

4.94 Section 2(1) of the 1997 Act makes it an offence to pursue a course of conduct in breach of the prohibition on harassment in s 1. The offence is summary only, and punishable with six months' imprisonment or a fine not exceeding level 5 on the standard scale, or both.[1] The offence is an arrestable one,[2] something which the offences of common assault or battery or under ss 4–5 of the Public Order Act 1986 are not.

It would seem that an offence under s 2(1) is a continuing offence and that, provided the last piece of conduct relied on occurred within six months of the laying of the information, a magistrates' court may try that information, even though other pieces of conduct in that continuum that are relied on occurred before that period.[3]

1   1997 Act, s 2(2).
2   Section 2(3) added it to the list of arrestable offences in PACE, s 24(2).
3   Magistrates' Courts Act 1980, s 127(1).

Putting people in fear of violence

4.95 Section 4(1) of the 1997 Act provides a more serious offence, which does not centre on a course of conduct in breach of the prohibition on harassment, but on a course of conduct putting people in fear of violence. It provides that a person whose course of conduct causes another to fear, on at least two occasions, that violence will be used against him is guilty of an offence if he knows or ought to know that his course of conduct will cause the other so to fear on each of those occasions. This offence is of less relevance to public order.

The provisions relating to the s 4 offence are markedly similar to the provisions relating to the prohibition of harassment, in that:

(a) there must be a 'course of conduct', and 'conduct' includes 'speech'[1] and 'course of conduct' means conduct on at least two occasions;[2]

(b) the objective nature of 'ought to know' is given a subjective aspect by s 4(2), which provides that the person whose course of conduct is in question ought to know that it will cause another to fear that violence will be used against him on any occasion if a reasonable person in possession of the same information would think the course of conduct would cause the other so to fear on that occasion; and

(c) that it is a defence for the accused to prove[3] that –

   (i) his course of conduct was pursued for the purpose of preventing or detecting crime;

   (ii) his course of conduct was pursued under any enactment or rule of law or to comply with any condition or requirement imposed by any person under any enactment; or

   (iii) the pursuit of his course of conduct was reasonable for the *protection of himself or another or for the protection of his or another's property.*[4]

The distinguishing feature between an offence under s 2 and one under s 4 is, of course, that under s 4 the course of conduct must cause another to fear that *violence* will be used *against him.* It would seem that fear of violence against property is not enough. The prosecution does not have to prove under s 4(1) that violence feared was unlawful violence, but under the third defence in s 4(3) it will be a defence, in effect, for the accused to prove that the violence feared was not unlawful violence.

The offence under s 4 is an either-way offence. A person guilty of it is liable:

(a) on conviction on indictment, to imprisonment for a term not exceeding five years or a fine, or both; or

(b) on summary conviction, to imprisonment for a term not exceeding six months or a fine not exceeding the statutory maximum, or both.[5]

If on the trial on indictment of a person charged with an offence under this section the jury find him not guilty of the offence charged, they may find him guilty of an offence under s 2.[6]

By virtue of its maximum punishment an offence under s 4 is an arrestable offence.[7]

---

1   1997 Act, s 7(4).
2   Ibid, s 7(3).
3   See para **4.38**.
4   1997 Act, s 4(3).
5   Ibid, s 4(4).
6   Ibid, s 4(5).
7   PACE, s 24(1).

Restraining orders

4.96 Section 5 of the 1997 Act provides a back-up to conviction and sentence in respect of an offence under s 2 or s 4, to restrain further conduct by the offender of the type in question. This is an important provision because some types of people who engage in harassment, especially stalkers, get fixated and tend not to be easily deterred.

A court sentencing or otherwise dealing with a person convicted of an offence under ss 2 or 4 may (as well as sentencing him or dealing with him in any other way) make a restraining order.[1]

The order may, for the purpose of protecting the victim of the offence, or any other person mentioned in the order, from further conduct which (a) amounts to harassment, or (b) will cause a fear of violence, prohibit the convicted person from doing anything described in the order.[2] The order may have effect for a specified period or until further order.[3] It may be varied or discharged by the court which made it on application by the prosecutor, the convicted person or any other person mentioned in it.[4]

Breach of a restraining order constitutes an offence under s 5(5), which provides that, if without reasonable excuse[5] the defendant does anything which he is prohibited from doing by an order under this section, he is guilty of an offence. The offence is an either-way one. The maximum punishment is:

(a) on conviction on indictment, imprisonment for a term not exceeding five years or a fine, or both, or
(b) on summary conviction, imprisonment for a term not exceeding six months or a fine not exceeding the statutory maximum, or both.[6]

By virtue of its maximum punishment, an offence under s 5(5) is an arrestable offence.[7]

---

1   1997 Act, s 5(1).
2   Ibid, s 5(2),
3   Ibid, s 5(3).
4   Ibid, s 5(4).
5   The comments in paras **2.89–2.90** are equally applicable here.
6   1997 Act, s 5(6).
7   PACE, s 24(1).

Racially-aggravated harassment

4.97 Section 32(1) of the Crime and Disorder Act 1998 provides that:

'A person is guilty of an offence under this section if he commits –

(a) an offence under section 2 of the Protection from Harassment Act 1997 (offence of harassment); or
(b) an offence under section 4 of that Act (putting people in fear of violence),

which is racially aggravated for the purposes of this section.'

Section 32(1) does not create one offence which can be committed in more than one way; it creates two separate racially-aggravated offences which are offences in their own right.

On a charge of either of these aggravated offences the prosecution must prove that the accused has committed the relevant specified basic offence (set out above) and that it was racially aggravated (as defined in para **4.67**).

Trial, punishment and arrest

4.98 By s 32(3) of the 1998 Act, an aggravated offence within s 32(1)(a) is triable either way and on conviction on indictment is punishable more severely than an offence under s 2. The maximum punishment for an offence within s 32(1)(a) is:

(a) on summary conviction, imprisonment for a term not exceeding six months or a fine not exceeding the statutory maximum, or both;

(b) on conviction on indictment, imprisonment for a term not exceeding two years or a fine, or both.[1]

The maximum punishment on conviction on indictment for the aggravated offence within s 32(1)(b) is:

(a) on summary conviction, imprisonment for a term not exceeding six months or a fine not exceeding the statutory maximum, or both;

(b) on conviction on indictment, imprisonment for a term not exceeding seven years or a fine, or both.

Offences under s 32(1)(b) of the 1998 Act are arrestable offences by virtue of their maximum punishment.[2] Like an offence under s 2 of the 1997 Act, an offence falling within s 32(1)(a) has been added to the list of arrestable offences.[3]

---

1   1998 Act, s 32(3).
2   PACE, s 24(1).
3   1998 Act, s 32(2), amended the list in PACE, s 24(2), to this effect.

4.99 Section 32(7) of the 1998 Act provides that a restraining order under s 5 of the 1997 Act can be made in relation to a person convicted of an aggravated offence under s 32. The provisions of s 5 about duration, discharge or variation or breach of a restraining order are equally applicable when the order is made on a conviction under s 32.

Alternative verdicts

Trials on indictment
4.100 Section 32(5) and (6) of the 1998 Act provide for alternative verdicts at a trial on indictment of a person charged with an offence within s 32(1)(a) or s 32(1)(b).

If the jury find an accused not guilty of an offence under s 32(1)(b), they may find him guilty of the basic offence under s 4 of the 1997 Act under the general alternative verdict provisions relating to trials on indictment contained in s 6(3) of the Criminal Law Act 1967. On the other hand, s 6(3) would not entitle a jury to return an alternative verdict for the basic offence under s 2 of the 1997 Act if they find an accused not guilty of an offence under s 32(1)(a), because that basic offence is a summary one. Section 32(5) provides that in such a case the jury may find the accused guilty of the offence under s 2 of the 1997 Act.

In addition, if at trial on indictment for an offence under s 32(1)(b), the jury find the accused not guilty, they are permitted by s 32(6) to find him guilty of an offence under s 32(1)(a). In such a case the alternative verdict could not otherwise have been possible because the terms of s 6(3) of the Criminal Law Act 1967 could not be satisfied.

Summary trials
4.101 The inability of a magistrates' court to convict of an alternative offence has already been noted in para **4.3**.

PROVOCATION TO BREACH OF THE PEACE BY A PUBLIC PLAY

4.102 Section 6(1) of the Theatres Act 1968 provides that, with certain exceptions, if a public performance of a play (including an opera or ballet, but not a strip-session or sex show)[1] involves the use of threatening, abusive or insulting words or behaviour,[2] any person who (whether for gain or not) presented[3] that performance is guilty of a summary offence if he did so with intent to provoke a breach of the peace,[4] or if the performance as a whole was likely to occasion such a breach. The comments in para **4.5** about 'threatening, abusive or insulting words or behaviour' are equally applicable to this offence. The presenter must take his audience as he finds it. If insulting words are used, he is guilty if they are likely to occasion a breach of the peace by the particular audience, even though he does not intend to provoke a breach of the peace and even though his words might not have caused a hypothetical reasonable man to break the peace.[5] It is unsettled whether a presenter can be liable on the basis of unrehearsed additions not authorised by him.[6]

Although a performer who uses threatening etc words or behaviour cannot be convicted under s 6, unless he is also a presenter of the play, he will almost inevitably have committed an offence under ss 4, 4A or 5 of the Public Order Act 1986, in which case, unless what he did was unscripted, a presenter could in any event be convicted as an accomplice to that offence.

Section 7(2) of the 1968 Act sets out exceptions to the offence under s 6. It provides that s 6 does not apply to a performance given solely or primarily for one or more of the following purposes:

(a) rehearsal; or
(b) making a recording of the performance; or
(c) enabling the performance to be included in a broadcasting service.

However, if it is proved that the performance was attended by persons other than those directly connected with the giving of the performance or the doing in relation to it of any of the things mentioned in (b) or (c), the performance must be taken not to have been given solely or primarily for one or more of the stated purposes, and the above exceptions will not apply, unless the contrary is shown.

A prosecution requires the consent of the Attorney-General.[7] The offence is rarely, if ever, prosecuted. The maximum punishment is six months' imprisonment or a fine not exceeding level 5 on the standard scale, or both.[8]

---

1   According to s 18(1) of the Theatres Act 1968:

'"play" means –
(a) any dramatic piece, whether involving improvisation or not, which is given wholly or in part by one or more persons actually present and performing and in which the whole or a major proportion of what is done by the person or persons performing, whether by way of speech, singing or acting, involves the playing of a role; and
(b) any ballet given wholly or in part by one or more persons actually present and performing, whether or not it falls within paragraph (a) of this definition.'

'Public performance' includes any performance in a public place within the meaning of the Public Order Act 1936 (ie any highway and any other premises or place to which at the material time the public have or are permitted to have access, whether on payment or otherwise), and any performance which the public or any section of the public are permitted to attend, whether on payment or otherwise: ibid, s 18. Performances to members of theatre clubs fall within this definition. On the other hand, performances given on domestic occasions in a private dwelling do not.

2   Where a performance of a play was based on a script, then, in any proceedings for an offence under s 6 alleged to have been committed in respect of that performance:

(a)   an actual script on which that performance was based is admissible evidence of what was performed and of the manner in which the performance of any part of it was given; and

(b)   if such a script is given in evidence on behalf of any party to the proceedings then except in so far as the contrary is shown, whether by evidence given on behalf of the same or any other party, the performance is to be taken to have been given in accordance with that script: Theatres Act 1968, s 9(1).

In this context, 'script' is defined as meaning the text of the play (including musical or other notation) together with any stage or other directions for its performance, whether contained in a single document or not: ibid, s 9(2).

3   A person is not treated as presenting a performance by reason only of taking part in it as a performer: Theatres Act 1968, s 18(2)(c). Unlike the similar offence under the Public Order Act 1986, s 20 (para **5.40**), the present offence does not specifically catch those who 'direct' the play. Arguably, they also 'present' it but if so why does the 1986 Act refer to 'presents or directs'?

Where any offence under s 6 committed by a body corporate (see para **5.49**) is proved to have been committed with the consent or connivance of, or to be attributable to any neglect on the part of, any director, manager, secretary or other similar officer of the body corporate, or any person purporting to act in any such capacity, he as well as the body corporate is guilty of that offence and is liable to be proceeded against and punished accordingly: 1968 Act, s 16. With respect to this provision, see para **5.50**. An offence is only attributable to any neglect on the part of a director of a corporation if he was in breach of a duty to check the conduct (which resulted in the offence) of the person who committed the offence; normally there is no duty to check the conduct of an experienced member of staff whom one can expect to act in accordance with one's instructions unless there is something to prompt one into checking: *Lewin v Bland* [1985] RTR 171, DC.

4   See para **2.4**.

5   *Jordan v Burgoyne* [1963] 2 All ER 225, DC.

6   Compare s 20(2) of the 1986 Act; see para **5.43**.

7   Theatres Act 1968, s 8.

8   Ibid, s 6(2).

4.103 Section 10 of the Theatres Act 1968 provides that, if a constable of or above the rank of superintendent has reasonable grounds for suspecting:[1]

(a)   that an offence under s 6 has been committed in respect of a performance of a play; or

(b)   that a performance of a play is to be given and that such an offence is likely to be committed in respect of that performance,

he may make a signed written order under which any constable:

(a)   may require the person named in the order (ie the person suspected of having committed (or being likely to commit) the offence in question) to produce the actual script on which the performance was (or will be) based; and

(b)   if such a script is produced, may require the person so named to let him have it copied.

Failure without reasonable excuse to comply with one of these requirements is a summary offence.

1   See para **3.68** fn 1.

4.104 Section 15 of the 1968 Act provides that, if a justice of the peace is satisfied by information on oath that there are reasonable grounds for suspecting, as regards any premises specified in the information, that a performance of a play is to be given on those premises, and that an offence under s 6 is likely to be committed in respect of that performance, he may issue a warrant empowering any constable to enter the premises and to attend any performance of a play given there.

RELATED OFFENCES

4.105 The following offences involving threatening, abusive, insulting or disorderly behaviour are dealt with in Chapter 9:

–   being drunk and disorderly in a public place, contrary to s 91 of the Criminal Justice Act 1967;
–   use of profane or obscene language etc in a public place, contrary to s 28 of the Town Police Clauses Act 1847 or s 54 of the Metropolitan Police Act 1839;
–   riotous, violent or indecent behaviour in churches etc, contrary to s 2 of the Ecclesiastical Courts Jurisdiction Act 1860;
–   use of violence or intimidation or similar conduct, contrary to s 241 of the Trade Union and Labour Relations (Consolidation) Act 1992;
–   offences against local by-laws.

Offences relating to disorderly behaviour at public meetings, contrary to the Public Meeting Act 1908 and the Representation of the People Act 1983, are dealt with at the end of Chapter 6.

Chapter 5

INCITING RACIAL HATRED

INTRODUCTION

5.1   Before the Race Relations Act 1965, there was no offence specifically concerned with the incitement of racial hatred, although it was possible to use other offences against such incitement in certain circumstances. Provided that a racial propagandist published words, whether written or oral, which had a tendency to promote hostility between different classes of the population, with intent to cause such violence or disorder, he could be convicted of the common law offence of seditious libel (written words) or of seditious words (spoken words).[1] However, as the case of *R v Caunt*[2] (which was itself concerned with racial abuse) shows, the requirements of these offences are such that a prosecution is unlikely to succeed (it failed in *Caunt*), save in extreme cases. Alternatively, a prosecution could be brought under s 5 of the Public Order Act 1936 for words or behaviour conducive to a breach of the peace. Drawbacks were the need to prove the likelihood of a breach of the peace and the need for the accused's conduct to occur in a public place.

The increasingly multiracial nature of our society after 1945 led to the law being viewed as inadequate in dealing with abuse or insults which were directed at racial groups and 'poisoned' the social atmosphere, but which did not lead directly to a breach of the peace and were not likely to do so. Incidents at Fascist meetings increased the pressure for change. The result was the offence of incitement to racial hatred, which was introduced by s 6 of the Race Relations Act 1965.[3] After a number of statutory developments, the law on incitement to racial hatred is now governed by Part III (ss 17–29) of the Public Order Act 1986.

---

1   *R v Collins* (1839) 9 C&P 456 at 461; *R v Burns* (1886) 16 Cox CC 355 at 367; *R v Caunt* (1947) unreported; noted in 64 LQR 203. *R v Chief Metropolitan Stipendiary Magistrate, ex parte Choudhury* [1990] 1 WLR 986, DC.
2   (1947) unreported. The jury were directed that an article aimed at Jews could be seditious.
3   For a review of the law before Part III of the 1986 Act, see DGT Williams 'Racial incitement and public order law' [1996] Crim LR 320; Lester and Bindman *Race and Law* (Penguin, 1972) pp 360–365, 367–374 and 393; Leopold 'Incitement to hatred' [1977] PL 389; Gordon *Incitement to Racial Hatred* (Runnymede Trust, 1982); and Cotterell 'Prosecuting incitement to racial hatred' [1982] PL 378.

5.2   Part III provides six offences, all of which have to do with words, behaviour, material or visual images or sounds which are threatening, abusive or insulting and which are intended or likely to stir up racial hatred:

- using such words or behaviour or displaying such material;
- publishing or distributing such material;
- distributing, showing or playing a recording of such visual images or sounds;
- possessing such material or recording with a view to its being displayed, published, distributed or included in a programme service;
- presenting or directing a public play which involves such words or behaviour;

– including in a programme service a programme which involves such visual images or sounds.

The third and fourth offences were new; the others replaced earlier offences in an amended form to deal with defects in them. Part III also provided for the first time special powers ancillary to racial hatred offences.[1] As with the previous law on incitement to racial hatred, the sections seek to hold the balance between the stirring up of racial hatred and freedom of expression. They do not confer any power to ban processions or meetings by racist organisations because Governments have thought that this would excessively curtail freedom of speech, although such processions or such meetings (if trespassory) may be banned under ss 13 or 14A of the 1986 Act (Chapter 6) if their requirements are satisfied.

---

1   For a valuable discussion of theoretical and practical matters concerning Part III, see Wolffe 'Values in conflict: incitement to racial hatred and the Public Order Act 1986' [1987] PL 85.

5.3   The provisions in Part III of the 1986 Act have the potential to deal with many cases of incitement to racial hatred, although (as will be seen) the need to prove threatening, abusive or insulting conduct on the part of the accused means that the more insidious type of incitement not involving such conduct but 'dressed up' as apparently rational argument is not caught by them.

The effectiveness of the offences depends, of course, on the police giving priority to investigating such cases,[1] on a readiness to prosecute them[2] and on the attitude of judges, juries and magistrates. The track record is not an impressive one. Between 1987 and 1993 inclusive, the number of times the Attorney-General consented to a prosecution for an offence under Part III never exceeded three per year. In that period, there were seven convictions for such an offence.[3]

---

1   The police have been criticised for an apparent lack of commitment to the law on racial hatred. See, for example, *Police against Black People* (Institute of Race Relations, 1979), especially ch 18. This was confirmed by the *The Stephen Lawrence Enquiry: Report of an Enquiry by Sir William Macpherson of Cluny* (Cm 4262, 1999).
2   See paras **5.53–5.55**.
3   HC Deb, vol 239, Written answer, cols 485–486 (1994).

RACIAL HATRED

5.4   The offences in Part III of the 1986 Act have a number of common features. One is that they each require an intent that 'racial hatred' be stirred up or that 'racial hatred' be likely to be stirred up. Section 17 provides that racial hatred means hatred against a group of persons in Great Britain defined by reference to colour, race, nationality (including citizenship) or ethnic or national origins. Hereafter, such a group is described for convenience as a 'racial group'. The definition of racial group in s 17 is identical to that which applies in respect of racially-aggravated offences under Part II of the Crime and Disorder Act 1998, save that here 'colour' comes before 'race' (as to which there appears to be no significance) and that the hatred likely to be stirred up must be against a group of persons in Great Britain. The meaning of the key terms of the definition in s 17 was discussed in paras **4.68–4.73**. What is said there is equally applicable here.

5.5 As we have seen in para **4.72**, a group of persons defined by reference to religion is not a racial group and therefore falls outside the protection of Part III of the 1986 Act. The result is that, while behaviour encompassed by Part III which is likely to stir up hatred against a *religion*, for example the Jewish, Muslim, Rastafarian or Catholic religion, is not covered, behaviour which is likely to stir up hatred against Jews or Arabs or Pakistanis or the Irish or Romany gypsies[1] is, since they constitute racial groups. Of course, an attack on a religion may be open to the interpretation that it is likely also to stir up hatred against a racial group identified with it, for example as Jews are associated with the Jewish religion. Otherwise, in an extreme case, it may be that a prosecution for sedition based on conduct tending to cause hatred against a religious group would succeed.

Written or spoken words likely to stir up hatred against the Christian doctrine, or against God or Christ, can sometimes be dealt with by a prosecution for blasphemous libel or blasphemy respectively, and so can an attack on the formularies of the Church of England (but not an attack on other Christian denominations or other religions).[2]

As the Commission for Racial Equality said as long ago as 1976 '... it cannot be any more acceptable to stir up hatred against people because they are seen to be Muslims than to do so because they are Pakistanis'.[3] It has been pointed out that:

> 'This situation is made all the more nonsensical when you consider the possibility of a "religious conflict" between Sikhs and Muslims within Britain, resulting in a Muslim distributing a leaflet saying: "Stab a Sikh". These words would provide grounds for a prosecution in relation to the stirring up of "racial hatred" since Sikhs are considered to be an ethnic group. However, an almost identical leaflet, produced by a Sikh that said, "Stab a Muslim" would not.'[4]

There is evidence that militant racists are getting around Part III of the 1986 Act by referring to groups of people, eg Pakistanis, as Muslims with the intent thereby to stir up racial hatred towards those people because of their colour.[5]

---

1   *Commission for Racial Equality v Dutton* [1989] 1 All ER 306, CA.
2   *R v Lemon* [1979] 1 All ER 898, HL. In *Choudhury v UK* (1991) 12 HRLJ 172 the European Commission on Human Rights rejected a complaint under Art 9 of the ECHR (freedom of thought, conscience and religion) about the lack of an offence akin to blasphemy in respect of attacks on non-Christian religions.
3   *Second Review of the Race Relations Act* (CRE, 1976).
4   Jepson 'Tackling religious terminology that stirs up racial hatred' (1999) 149 NLJ 554.
5   Ibid. For a discussion of the need to reform the law so as to cover incitement to racial or religious hatred, and of the problems in doing so, see Poulter 'Towards legislative reform of the blasphemy and racial hatred laws' [1991] PL 371.

5.6 It was also pointed out in para **4.73** that 'racial group' does not include a group of persons defined by politics, language, culture or place of origin or residence.

5.7 In other jurisdictions, there are 'incitement to hatred offences' which are not limited to 'racial hatred'. In Canada, for example, there are offences of public incitement of hatred likely to lead to a breach of the peace, and of wilful promotion of hatred.[1] Nearer to home, the Northern Irish counterpart to Part III of the 1986 Act, contained in the Public Order (Northern Ireland) Order 1987,[2] covers incitement to hatred against any section of the public in Northern Ireland on grounds of religious belief, colour, race, nationality or ethnic or national origins. There is obviously much to be said for achieving legislative consistency with Northern Ireland.

---

1   Section 281.2 of the Canadian Criminal Code.
2   SI 1987/463 (NI 7). The provisions also prohibit conduct intended or likely to arouse fear of any section of the public in Northern Ireland on such grounds.

Racial hatred intended or likely

5.8 None of the offences under Part III of the 1986 Act requires an intent to provoke a breach of the peace, or the likelihood of such a breach (let alone that public disorder resulted), nor that it be proved that racial hatred was actually stirred up. Instead, it is 'merely' required that the accused should intend to stir up racial hatred by his conduct, or that such hatred is likely, having regard to all the circumstances, to be stirred up thereby (whether or not the accused realised this would be likely).[1] The rationale for the inclusion of the offences in a Public *Order* Act has been said to be that there is a threat to public order inherent in the conduct proscribed,[2] although this is hardly applicable to the offence of possessing racially inflammatory material.

'Stirring up hatred' is a much stronger thing than simply 'bringing into ridicule or contempt' or 'causing ill-will' or 'bringing into distaste';[3] at a minimum 'hatred' connotes intense dislike, enmity or animosity. It is for this reason that the common practice of chanting racialist abuse at football matches will not normally be caught by Part III, although it may be an offence under s 4, s 4A or s 5 of the 1986 Act or s 2 of the Football (Offences) Act 1991,[4] depending on the circumstances. The offences would have been easier to prove if only hostility or ill-will had to be intended or likely.

---

1   For minor qualifications to this statement see ss 20(2) and 22(4) and (5).
2   *Racial Discrimination* (Cmnd 6234, 1975), 30.
3   This is a gap. The mischief at which the offences are aimed can be achieved without the causing of hatred. In New South Wales the corresponding legislation refers to 'vilification': Anti-Discrimination (Racial Vilification) Act 1989.
4   See para **8.27**.

5.9 It is not enough simply that racial hatred in the abstract is intended or likely; it must be against a racial group. Moreover, the hatred against a racial group which is intended, or likely, to be stirred up must be in relation to a group in Great Britain, which is not surprising in an Act dealing with public order. Nevertheless, the 'Great Britain requirement' does not impose a major limitation because, given the multiracial nature of our society, it is hard to envisage a racist attack on a racial group abroad (including Northern Ireland) that would not be likely to stir up hatred against the same racial group in Great Britain.[1] Nevertheless, examples can be dragged from the recesses of the author's imagination. As far as he knows, there is no group of Eskimoes in Great Britain. If so, racist abuse of Eskimoes living in Northern Canada would not be caught by Part III of the 1986 Act, since it would not be likely to stir up hatred against a racial group in Great Britain. It was on the present ground that the Attorney-General is reported to have expressed the view that a prosecution was unlikely to succeed against those who publicly campaigned against the admission of Vietnamese boat people to Great Britain.[2]

1   It will be noted that *Great Britain*, not the *United Kingdom*, is the term used.
2   Bindman 'Incitement to racial hatred' (1982) 132 NLJ 299.

5.10 The truth of the contents of any written material or words is not a defence.[1]

1   *R v Birdwood* [1995] 6 Archbold News 2, CA (a decision in respect of offences under the 1986 Act, ss 19 and 23).

5.11 A defect with the law of incitement to racial hatred before the 1986 Act was that liability was limited to cases where racial hatred was likely to be stirred up. This meant that proof of an offence was difficult (if not impossible) in some types of case:

–   where the content of the words spoken or published was so contrary to the standards of decent humanity as to be likely to provoke sympathy for the racial group concerned rather than hatred of it;
–   where material was circulated only to a group or groups of people, such as clergymen or Members of Parliament, who might be unlikely to be incited to racial hatred. In the *Review of Public Order Law*,[1] the White Paper preceding the 1986 Act, it was said:

'At present, the more level-headed the recipients of racially inflammatory material, the more difficult it is to show that racial hatred is likely to be stirred up, even when the material itself is so threatening, insulting or abusive that this was clearly the intention of the distributor. The public order consideration is relevant here since the material may well find its way to other, less equable, audiences, although not directly distributed to them, and its effect may be to stir up racial hatred.'

As a result, the formula was recast to penalise conduct which either is intended to stir up racial hatred or is likely, having regard to all the circumstances, to stir up racial hatred. The necessary intent here would seem to be limited to a purposive one.[2] That purpose may be indicated by the content and manner of the accused's conduct. Where words are intended to stir up racial hatred but are unlikely to do so, the public order justification for the offences under Part III of the 1986 Act is less strong.

The test of likelihood is an objective one, and the accused is not required to know of the circumstances with regard to which it is applied. In relation to the likelihood of racial hatred being stirred up (assuming it is not intended), the prosecution has to prove that there were people (or, at least, a person) among the readership or audience who were likely to be stirred to racial hatred. This must be answered having regard to all the circumstances including (in the case, for example, of a publication) the type of person likely to buy it and the type of person whom it is likely to reach.[3] However, if it is not proved that any of the likely audience or readership was open to persuasion to feel racial hatred (as where the whole of the audience or readership are committed anti-racists), the prosecution must fail unless it is proved that the accused intended to stir up racial hatred.

As elsewhere in the 1986 Act, 'likely' means 'probable' and not just 'liable'.[4]

1   Cmnd 9510 (1985) para 6.6.
2   See para **4.35** fn 2.
3   *R v Owens* (1986) unreported, CA.
4   See para **4.15**.

5.12 By analogy with s 2 of the Obscene Publications Act 1959, which applies even though the article in question was directed only to those who are already depraved, since it is sufficient that it increases or maintains a state of corruption,[1] it would seem that those who already have racist opinions may be incited to further racial hatred.[2]

---

1   *DPP v Whyte* [1972] 3 All ER 12, HL.
2   *Review of Public Order Law* (Cmnd 9510, 1985) para 6.7.

Racial harassment not enough

5.13 The offences are not committed 'merely' by addressing threatening, abusive or insulting words or material *only* to members of a racial group whom they are designed to threaten, abuse or insult because the addresser cannot credibly be said to intend to stir up racial hatred among the addressees against themselves and such hatred is unlikely to be stirred up. Harassment per se of members of a racial group is not an offence under Part III. It may, however, give rise to liability for an offence under s 4, s 4A or s 5 of the 1986 Act, under s 31 of the Crime and Disorder Act 1998 (racially-aggravated Public Order Act offences), under the Protection from Harassment Act 1997 or under s 32 of the Crime and Disorder Act 1998 (offences of racially-aggravated harassment).

The criminal law does not deal with the expression of objectionable racially orientated views, such as the public advocacy, orally or in writing, of a discriminatory policy or course of action against an ethnic or racial group, where it cannot be proved that the stirring up of racial hatred was intended or likely. The major justification for making such expression criminal is that these views are so objectionable that their public utterance ought in itself to be an offence. It would, however, be open to a number of objections,[1] a particularly important one being that it would be totally inconsistent with the freedom of expression in a democratic society guaranteed by Art 10 of the ECHR, under which, provided the manner and the circumstances of the expression do not provoke unacceptable consequences, political proposals can be freely advocated, however odious.[2]

---

1   See *Review of Public Order Law* (Cmnd 9510, 1985) para 6.5.
2   *Handyside v UK* (1976) Ser A, no 24; 1 EHRR 737, ECtHR.

Threatening, abusive or insulting

5.14 All offences under Part III of the 1986 Act require that the material, words or behaviour in question are 'threatening, abusive or insulting'. These words do not bear an unusual legal meaning. Instead, as with offences under ss 4, 4A and 5, the magistrates or jury must decide as a question of fact whether the material etc was threatening, abusive or insulting in the ordinary meaning of those terms, and this is to be judged according to the impact which it would have on a reasonable member of the public.[1] If the material etc is threatening, abusive or insulting, it does not matter whether or not anyone who read, heard or witnessed it felt himself to be threatened, abused or insulted.[2]

The present requirement is a major limit on the offences, designed to avoid encroaching on freedom of speech, however unacceptable the content, simply because it is unacceptable, since if views are expressed in an apparently moderate or reasoned manner (ie without overt threats etc), they cannot result in a conviction, however upsetting they may be to a racial group, and even though they were intended or likely to stir up racial hatred. It may be that the main effect of the criminal law here is not to reduce the amount of incitement to racial hatred but simply 'to change the style of racialist propaganda, make it less blatantly bigoted, and therefore more respectable'.[3] It is arguable that it is over-restrictive to limit the offence to threatening, abusive or insulting words etc since the gist of the offence is incitement to racial hatred and if words etc are intended or likely to have that effect it should not matter how they were expressed. Moreover, it has been said that racist propaganda is probably most effective when expressed in apparently moderate terms rather than in abusive or insulting ones.[4]

1   *Brutus v Cozens* [1972] 2 All ER 1297, HL. See further, para **4.5**.
2   *Parkin v Norman* [1982] 2 All ER 583, DC.
3   Macdonald *Race Relations Act 1976* (Butterworths, 1977) p 139.
4   Peter Archer, QC, MP, HC Deb, vol 2, col 684 (1981).

THE OFFENCES

Use of words or behaviour or display of written material

5.15 Section 18(1) of the 1986 Act provides that a person who uses threatening, abusive or insulting words or behaviour, or displays any written material which is threatening, abusive or insulting, is guilty of an offence if:

(a) he intends thereby to stir up racial hatred; or
(b) having regard to all the circumstances, racial hatred is likely to be stirred up thereby.

Section 18 does not apply to words or behaviour used, or written material displayed, *solely* for the purpose of being included in a programme in a programme service.[1] In such a case, as we shall see, an offence *may* be committed under s 22 when the programme is transmitted. However, this does not mean that words or behaviour uttered, or written material displayed, in the studio are always exempt from s 18. They are caught by it if there is a studio audience because they will not be used or displayed *solely* for the purpose of being transmitted.

A particularly important application of s 18 is in relation to processions and meetings.

1   1986 Act, s 18(6). By the 1986 Act s 29, 'programme service' has the same meaning as in the Broadcasting Act 1990; see the 1990 Act, ss 201(1) and (2). Essentially, it refers to a television or radio broadcasting service or a cable programme service.

Prohibited conduct

In a public or private place

5.16 As in the case of an offence under ss 4, 4A or 5 of the Act, this offence may be committed in a public place or a private place.[1] It follows that racial abuse shouted at a private meeting in a hall or displayed on a poster in a students' union is covered by the offence, as is racial abuse spoken by one person to another in an office or garden. This was a change from the offence replaced by s 18, which could be committed only in a public place or at a public meeting. It reinforces the capacity of the offence to cover cases where no offence is caused to anyone and where there is no risk of imminent disorder.

There is one limit in relation to private places, which provides some recognition of the right to privacy (private life) guaranteed by Art 8 of the ECHR and the right of freedom of expression (including the freedom to receive and impart information without interference by the State) guaranteed by Art 10 of the ECHR. As in the case of an offence under ss 4, 4A or 5, an offence is not committed by the use of words or behaviour, or the display of written material, by a person inside a dwelling which are not heard or seen except by other persons in that or another dwelling.[2] Thus, racist taunts shouted from a house to people in the street or displayed on a poster on a window visible in the street are caught, but not racist abuse shouted inside a house or flat (and only audible within it or another house or flat) or a racist poster displayed in an inner room of a house. However, as worded, it also excludes the expression of racist abuse at a public meeting in a house or flat (although there is no reason why that abuse should have less adverse effects than if expressed at a meeting in an assembly hall) or such abuse by someone who has gained entry to a house or dwelling, although it does not exclude certain cases on a par with those in a dwelling (such as the private expression of views in a garden, office, pub or motor car).

It is a defence for the accused to prove[3] that he was inside a dwelling and had no reason to believe that his words or behaviour, or the written material displayed, would be heard or seen by a person outside that or any other dwelling.[4]

---

1   1986 Act, s 18(2).
2   Ibid. See para **4.10**. Save for the absence of 'as' before 'other living accommodation' the definition of 'dwelling' is identical to that given in s 8 of the 1986 Act in relation to offences in Part I of that Act.
3   See para **4.38**.
4   1986 Act, s 18(4).

Words, behaviour or display

5.17 Clearly, this offence deals with speakers, whether in the open air or an enclosed shopping centre or at a public meeting who utter threatening, abusive or insulting words. However, it also covers behaviour and the display of written material, quite apart from bringing racist gestures (such as a Nazi-style salute) within the Act, provided that the other requirements of s 18 are proved. Gestures are unlikely to satisfy these other requirements unless their context is clear. 'Behaviour' also covers racist mime shows, while the reference to 'display' catches exhibiting, showing or spreading out to view[1] 'written material'. Unlike the provisions in other offences in Part III relating to publication or distribution, the 'display' need not be to the public or a section of the public.

'Written material' includes any 'sign' or 'other visible representation',[2] terms which have been discussed in para **4.7**, with the result that displaying a racially inflammatory picture or holding up a racist placard or banner or wearing a swastika badge or a racist badge is caught if it is displayed in the prescribed way. The display of a book, pamphlet or leaflet is also covered, even though the offending material is contained within its covers.

'Other visible representation' does not include videos and films. It follows that the display of them cannot be an offence under s 18. Quite apart from the fact that a video, at least, cannot be said to be a visual representation, there is a special offence in s 21 dealing, inter alia, with corresponding conduct covered by s 18, in relation to videos and films. This offence also covers sound recordings; a person who plays a sound recording cannot be said to *use* words for the purposes of s 18.

---

1   See para **4.7** for further discussion of display.
2   1986 Act, s 29.

Mental element

5.18 We have already seen (paras **5.8–5.12**) that the prosecution must prove that the accused intended to stir up racial hatred by his words, behaviour or display or that such hatred was likely to be stirred up thereby. Where a person is proved to have intended to stir up racial hatred by his words etc, it is irrelevant that he was unaware and did not even have reason to suspect that they were threatening, abusive or insulting; he is responsible for them. On the other hand, s 18(5) provides that a person who is not shown to have intended to stir up racial hatred is not guilty of an offence under s 18 if he did not intend his words or behaviour or the written material to be, and was not aware[1] that it might be, threatening, abusive or insulting. Unlike comparable provisions in other offences in Part III, the accused does not have the burden of proving this lack of intent or awareness, although, no doubt, evidence must be adduced of such lack before the prosecution has to disprove it.[2] Of course, where a person intends to stir up racial hatred, he will almost inevitably intend his words or gestures to be threatening, abusive or insulting or be aware of the risk of this.

---

1   'Awareness' elsewhere in the 1986 Act has been construed in a subjective sense: *DPP v Clarke* (1992) 94 Cr App R 359, DC; para **4.11** fn 1.
2   Contrast the situation in offences under ss 4, 4A or 5, and their racially-aggravated versions, where the prosecution must prove the accused intended his conduct to be threatening etc, or be aware that it may be (see paras **4.11**, **4.34**, **4.54** and **4.82**).

Prosecution, trial, punishment and arrest

5.19 Prosecution, trial and punishment are dealt with in paras **5.53–5.59**.

Section 18(3) provides that a constable may arrest without warrant anyone whom he reasonably suspects is committing an offence under s 18.[1] The constable need not be in uniform. This power to arrest a person reasonably suspected to be committing a s 18 offence corresponds with the power of arrest under ss 3, 4 and 4A of Part I of the 1986 Act, ss 12, 13, 14 and 14A of Part II and s 31 of the Crime and Disorder Act 1998. It can be commended on grounds of consistency and the need on occasion for immediate action by the police to stop the offence continuing. Nevertheless, it is not easy to envisage cases where there would not be a power of arrest, whether at common law for actual or apprehended breach of the peace or under s 25 of PACE. The other offences under Part III do not give rise to the same need for immediate action; it is not surprising that no power of arrest in relation to them is conferred by the Act.

---

1   See, in relation to the terms of this power of arrest, the discussion of the corresponding power in ss 3, 4 and 4A in paras **3.68**, **4.18** and **4.40**.

Publishing or distributing

5.20 Section 19(1) of the 1986 Act provides that a person who publishes or distributes written material which is threatening, abusive or insulting is guilty of an offence if:

(a) he intends thereby to stir up racial hatred; or
(b) having regard to all the circumstances, racial hatred is likely to be stirred up thereby.

This is one of the few offences against public order which is in common sense terms liable to be committed by a company (or other corporation) through the acts and state of mind of one of its controlling officers.[1]

---

1   'Person' in s 19(1) includes a body corporate. 'Person' includes a body corporate unless a
     contrary intention appears: Interpretation Act 1978, s 5 and Sch 1. Since this offence is
     punishable by a fine as an alternative to imprisonment, it is clear that a body corporate may
     commit this offence and this is assumed by s 28 (para **5.50**). As to corporate liability, and the
     liability of directors etc, see para **5.49**.

Prohibited conduct

Publication or distribution

5.21 The accused must publish or distribute the written material to the public or a section of the public.[1] Writing the material is not, in itself, an offence under the 1986 Act or any other provision, unless it amounts to a 'display' of the material. The Act does not explain what constitutes 'publishing or distributing'. 'Distribute' does not seem to raise any problem, referring simply to some type of dealing out among a number of recipients.[2]

Elsewhere in the criminal law, 'publish' has been held to mean making known to someone else;[3] here the making known must mean making available to be known by the public or a section of the public. By analogy with the approach taken by the Court of Appeal in *R v Fellows*[4] in the context of obscene material, putting racist written material on the Internet and providing access to it by giving others a password or the like constitutes a publication of it. If so, the present offence can be committed provided that access is given to a section of the public at least.

---

1   1986 Act, s 19(3).
2   See, further, para **4.7**.
3   *Dew v DPP* (1920) LJKB 1166, DC; *Ransom v Burgess* (1927) 137 LT 530, DC.
4   [1997] 2 All ER 548, CA.

5.22 There is an obvious danger of an overlap between the 'display' of written material in s 18 and its 'publication' in s 19 since, while 'publishing' does not necessarily involve 'displaying', technically 'displaying' (ie exhibiting) written material necessarily involves 'publishing' it. 'Publishing' may be limited by 'displaying' so that the two sections are mutually exclusive, ie a person does not 'publish' under s 19 if he 'displays' written material under s 18. Certainly, the wise course where there is a 'display' is to charge an offence under s 18 lest the court is receptive to the type of argument just advanced.

To the public or a section of it

5.23 This requirement means that publication to an individual or group of people, or distribution to a group, does not constitute an offence under s 19, and provides recognition of the right to privacy and the right to receive and impart information without interference by the State. Under the offence replaced by s 19, the corresponding phrase to 'to the public' was 'to the public at large' (which clearly could not have meant the whole community), but nothing seems to turn on the omission of the last two words. 'The public' and 'section of the public' are not defined by the Act. In the only reported case which referred to the point under the previous legislation, *R v Britton*,[1] the Court of Appeal held that a distribution of racist pamphlets to members of a family living together in one house was not a distribution to 'the public at large'. There appears to be no minimum number of persons to whom publication or distribution must be made in order for it to be to 'the public' but to publish or distribute to one person alone, nor (it is submitted) to two or three, cannot be to do so to 'the public'. Ultimately, the question must be solved by common sense, the question being whether the publication or distribution has been on a scale and on a basis such as to be describable as being to 'the public'. It would seem that the basis must be random or indiscriminate publication or distribution.

---

1   [1967] 1 All ER 486, CA.

5.24 A publication or distribution only to members of a club or association is not a distribution to 'the public' but to a 'section of the public', as will be seen.

R v Britton is the only reported case to have dealt with the phrase 'section of the public'. The Court of Appeal held that the family was not a 'section of the public'. The Court's interpretation has been criticised on the ground that, in the light of the object of the offence, viz to punish those who attempt to stir up racial hatred, it is arguable that the section of the public to whom publication is in fact made is not a matter of concern. Nevertheless, it is submitted that the decision was sensible; a family group would not normally be described as a section of the public (and doubtless the same is true of other small, domestic groups). In *Britton*, Lord Parker CJ said, obiter, that 'section of the public' refers to some identifiable group, 'in other words members of a club or association'. It is submitted that the term is not limited to this but covers any identifiable group of people whose connection is not a private relationship (ie a personal, familial or domestic one), provided that the group is identifiable by some common interest or characteristic. If this is so, the employees of X Ltd are a section of the public, as are the inhabitants of houses in Y street, teachers, a football crowd and persons of West Indian descent.

Despite Lord Parker's dictum, it could be that members of a club or association will not form a section of the public if the club or association is essentially a private one, in that there is a procedure for election for membership which involves a genuine process of personal selection, so that entry into membership is not a formality with which any member of the public (or qualified member of the public, eg graduates or women) can comply[1] and thereby obtain membership. Such a view was taken in respect of 'section of the public' by the majority (4–1) of the House of Lords in *Charter v Race Relations Board*.[2] The case might, however, be distinguishable on the ground that it was concerned with the provision of facilities and services to a section of the public for the purposes of s 12 of the Race Relations Act 1968, an anti-discrimination provision.

---

1   Unless there is some 'obvious disqualification [sic] as might cause the manager of say a good
     restaurant to exclude' the applicant: *Charter v Race Relations Board* [1973] 1 All ER 512 at 516,
     per Lord Reid.
2   [1973] 1 All ER 512, HL.

Written material

5.25 For the offence to be committed, the publication or distribution must be of 'written material'. Such material includes any sign or other visible representation;[1] a racist cartoon or photograph in a magazine would therefore be covered. A fly-poster pasted on a wall or graffiti spray-painted on a bridge or road sign is certainly written material; subject to what was said in para **5.22**, it would seem to be published for the purposes of s 19 by the writer who also displays it for the purposes of s 18.

---

1   1986 Act, s 29.

Mental element

5.26 Although the prosecution must prove that the accused intended to stir up racial hatred by the publication or distribution or that such hatred was likely to be stirred up thereby (paras **5.8–5.12**), it does not have to prove any mens rea on the part of the accused in relation to the content of the written matter that he has published or distributed, although he will almost inevitably have had such mens rea if he is proved to have intended to stir up racial hatred. This makes a charge under s 19 more attractive than one under s 18 if it has the choice of alleging a publication or a display. However, under s 19(2), it is a defence for an accused who is not proved to have intended to stir up racial hatred to prove[1] that he was not aware[2] of the content of the matter and neither suspected nor had reason to suspect it of being threatening, abusive or insulting. The defence under s 19(2) is of obvious importance to innocent publishers or distributors, like newsagents. The test of no reason to suspect is a wholly objective test, ie the accused must prove that no reasonable person in his situation would have suspected that the content of the material was threatening, abusive or intimidating.[3]

---

1   See para **4.38**.
2   See para **5.18** fn 1.
3   See para **3.68** fn 1.

Prosecution, trial, punishment and arrest

5.27 Prosecution, trial and punishment are dealt with in paras **5.53–5.59**.

An offence under s 19 of the 1986 Act has been added to the list of arrestable offences in s 24(2) of PACE. As a result, provided the requirements of s 17 of PACE are satisfied, a constable has power to enter and search premises for the purpose of arresting someone for an offence under s 19.

Recordings

5.28 A videotape is not 'written material' within the Act's definition (referred to in para **5.25**), nor is a gramophone record or sound tape. Thus, a person who shows, sells or hires out a racist video, record or tape is not caught by the offence under s 19 (publishing or distributing written material). However, he is caught by s 21, which extends the law on racial hatred to such recordings.

5.29 Section 21(1) provides that a person[1] who distributes,[2] or shows or plays, to the public or a section of the public[3] a recording[4] of visual images or sounds which are threatening, abusive or insulting is guilty of an offence if:

(a) he intends thereby to stir up racial hatred; or

(b) having regard to all the circumstances, racial hatred is likely to be stirred up thereby.

The offence is not restricted to particular places; it can be committed, for example, at private meetings on private premises. By analogy with *R v Fellows*, referred to in para **5.21**, someone who puts racist visual images or sounds on the Internet and provides access to them thereby 'shows' them.

---

1 See paras **5.20** fn 1 and **5.49**.
2 See para **5.21**.
3 1986 Act, s 21(2).
4 'Recording' means any record from which visual images or sounds may, by any means, be reproduced, and references to the distribution, showing or playing of a recording are to its distribution, showing or playing to the public or a section of the public: 1986 Act, s 21(2).

5.30 Because the distribution, showing or playing must be to the public or a section of the public, a person who lends a friend a racist record or who shows a racist videotape on a domestic occasion in his own home does not commit an offence under s 21. Nor does someone commit that offence by playing a tape recorded racist message over the telephone to someone (or when someone receives such a message on an answerphone). In addition, by s 21(4), an offence is not committed where the showing or playing of a recording is done *solely* to enable it to be included in a programme service.[1] The purpose of this provision is to prevent overlap with s 22 (which is concerned with broadcasting and the transmission of programme services). However, if the showing or playing of the recording is not solely for the purpose of enabling the recording to be broadcast or transmitted by a programme service, as where there is a studio audience, s 21(4) does not apply and an offence can be committed under both ss 21 and 22. The mere fact that the recording is seen by the employees of a company as it is transmitted would not prevent the showing being solely for the purpose of transmission.

---

1 For the meaning of 'programme service', see para **5.15** fn 1.

Mental element

5.31 As with s 19, the prosecution does not have to prove any mens rea on the part of the accused in relation to the content of the recording. Likewise, it need not necessarily be proved that he intended racial hatred to be stirred up by the distribution, showing or playing, since it is enough that such hatred is likely in all the circumstances to be stirred up. However, under s 21(3), it is a defence for an accused who is not proved to have intended to stir up racial hatred to prove[1] that he was not aware of the content of the recording and did not suspect, and had no reason to suspect,[2] that it was threatening, abusive or insulting.

1   See para **4.38**.
2   See paras **3.68** fn 1 and **5.18** fn 1.

Prosecution, trial and punishment

5.32 See paras **5.53–5.59**.

Possession of racially inflammatory material

5.33 Section 23(1) of the 1986 Act provides that a person[1] who has in his possession written material[2] which is threatening, abusive or insulting, with a view to its being displayed, published, distributed[3] or included in a programme service[4] (whether or not by himself) is guilty of an offence if:

(a) he intends racial hatred to be stirred up thereby, or
(b) having regard to all the circumstances, racial hatred is likely to be stirred up thereby.

In the case of an intended publication or distribution, it must be to the public or a section of the public.[5] By analogy with the approach taken in relation to the law of obscenity,[6] racist written material held in electronic form in someone's personal computer would constitute the possession of written material and an offence under s 23(1) would be committed in relation to it if the other elements of the offence were proved.

Section 23(1) also provides that a person who has in his possession a recording of visual images or sounds (eg a film or sound or videotape) which are threatening, abusive or insulting, with a view to its being distributed, shown, played or included in a programme service (whether by himself or another) is guilty of an offence if:

(a) he intends racial hatred to be stirred up thereby; or
(b) having regard to all the circumstances, racial hatred is likely to be stirred up thereby.

In the case of an intended distribution, showing or playing it must be to the public or a section of the public.[5] Section 23(2) adds that 'for this purpose' (presumably whether the requisite intent or likelihood in the two offences is proved) regard must be had to such display, publication, distribution, showing, playing or inclusion in a programme service as the accused has, or it may reasonably be inferred that he has, in view.

1   See paras **5.20** fn 1 and **5.49**.
2   See para **5.25**.
3   See para **5.21**.
4   As to 'programme service', see para **5.15** fn 1.
5   1986 Act, s 29.
6   See *R v Fellows* [1997] 2 All ER 548, CA.

5.34 The Act does not define what is required for 'possession' in this context, but reference to other areas of the law suggests that actual custody is not necessary provided that there is control over the written material or recording. The fact that the accused must be in possession with a view to publication or distribution of the written material or recording in question means that it is unnecessary to go into some of the more abstruse points concerning that concept. A person can be in possession of written material or a recording if it is in his actual custody or within his control (as where it is in the custody of an employee of his on his behalf or where it is on premises occupied by him although he is elsewhere at the time).[1] The intended publication or distribution need not be by the person in possession. If racially inflammatory pamphlets printed by X are deposited with Y for safekeeping in his warehouse until X wishes to collect and distribute them, the present offence can be committed by X and by Y (as long as the pamphlets are in the warehouse) because, since Y (as well as X) is in control of the pamphlets, Y and X are in possession of them.

---

1   *Lockyer v Gibb* [1966] 2 All ER 653, DC.

5.35 Although the offence under s 23 was aimed at those who manufacture or supply racist material against whom it can be difficult to prove a specific instance of distribution, the offence is certainly not limited to them. Nevertheless, the requirement that an intended publication or distribution must be to the public (or a section of the public), a concept also inherent in the concept of broadcasting, means that many 'innocent' possessors of racist material will fall outside the offence. However, the offence would not be committed by a person who had been handed a racially inflammatory leaflet in the street if he then decided to give it to a friend because he would not have a view to publishing or distributing it to the public or a section of the public, as is required. Nor, for the same reason, would people, such as investigative journalists (or members of an anti-racist group), who collected racist material in order to use it as background material or to hand it to the police; but they would be caught if they intended to expose its harmful nature by publishing it in a booklet. A library unwittingly in possession of racially inflammatory material might seem to be likely to be convicted under s 23, if it was prosecuted (which is unlikely),[1] but it is submitted that a bona fide library would not find it difficult in most cases to prove the defence under s 23(3) mentioned in the next paragraph.

---

1   See para **5.53**.

Mental element

5.36 As with s 19, the prosecution does not have to prove any mens rea on the part of a person charged with possession contrary to s 23 in relation to the content of the written material or recording possessed by him. Likewise, it need not necessarily be proved that the accused intended racial hatred to be stirred up by the publication or distribution, since it is enough that, if the material or recording was published or distributed etc, racial hatred would be likely (having regard to all the circumstances) to be stirred up as a result of the publication or distribution. However, under s 23(3), it is a defence for an accused who is not proved to have intended to stir up racial hatred to prove[1] that he was not aware of the content of the written material or recording, and neither suspected nor had reason to suspect[2] it of being threatening, abusive or insulting. This is of obvious importance to 'innocent' possessors of racialist material, such as warehousemen.

---

1   See para **4.38**.
2   See para **3.68** fn 1.

5.37 Whether the person in possession of the written material or recording was in possession with a view to its publication or distribution may be disputed in a particular case, in which case the magistrates or jury would have to draw such inferences as seem reasonable from the quantity and nature of the material possessed.

Prosecution, trial and punishment
5.38 See paras **5.53–5.59**.

Entry and search
5.39 Section 24(1) of the 1986 Act provides that, if a justice of the peace is satisfied by information on oath laid by a constable that there are reasonable grounds for suspecting[1] that a person has possession of written material or a recording in contravention of s 23, the justice may issue a warrant authorising any constable to enter and search the premises where it is suspected that the material or recording is situated.[2] An application for a warrant may only be made by a constable, and only a constable may act under a warrant.

A constable entering or searching premises[3] in pursuance of a warrant issued under s 24 may use reasonable force if necessary.[4]

---

1   See para **3.68** fn 1.
2   The application for a search warrant, and its execution, must comply with ss 15 and 16 of PACE and the Code of Practice for the Searching of Premises (Code B).
3   'Premises' means any place, including, in particular: (a) any vehicle, vessel, aircraft or hovercraft; (b) any offshore installation; and (c) any tent or movable structure: 1986 Act, s 24(4).
4   1986 Act, s 24(3).

Public plays

5.40 Section 20(1) of the 1986 Act provides that, if there is given a public performance[1] of a play[1] involving the use of threatening, abusive or insulting words or behaviour, any person[2] who presents or directs that performance is guilty of an offence if:

(a) he intends thereby to stir up hatred; or
(b) having regard to all the circumstances (and, in particular, taking the performance as a whole) racial hatred is likely to be stirred up thereby.

---

1   See Theatres Act 1968, s 18 (see para **4.102** fn 1), applied by s 20(5) of the 1986 Act.
2   Including a body corporate; see paras **5.20** fn 1 and **5.49**.

5.41 For the purposes of s 20, a person does not present a play by reason only of taking part in it as a performer[1] (although he may be guilty under s 18 on the ground of using threatening etc words or behaviour), but if he takes part as a performer in a performance directed by another he is treated as a person who directed the performance if without reasonable excuse he performs otherwise than in accordance with that person's direction.[1]

A person is treated as having directed a performance of a play given under his direction, even though he was absent during the performance.[1] A performer is not to be treated as an accomplice to an offence under s 20 by reason only of taking part in the performance.

Unless a performer's offence under s 18 involves an unscripted addition to the performance, a producer or director would be guilty of a s 18 offence as an accomplice. Consequently, the rationale of the present offence is not obvious.

---

1   1986 Act, s 20(4).

5.42 The provisions of ss 9, 10 and 15 of the Theatres Act 1968 relating to production of a script (or a copy) and its use as evidence and to entry and attendance at a play, referred to in paras **4.102–4.104**, are applied to an offence under s 20 of the 1986 Act by s 20(6). Section 20(3) provides an identical set of exceptions in relation to a rehearsal, recording or broadcast as those laid down by s 7(2) of the 1968 Act.[1]

---

1   See para **4.102**.

Mental element

5.43 The prosecution must prove that the accused intended the performance to stir up racial hatred or that racial hatred is likely to be stirred up thereby. It is important to note that, in deciding (in a case where racial hatred was not intended to be stirred up by the play) whether racial hatred is likely to be stirred up by the performance, regard must be had to all the circumstances (such as the nature of the audience, the place where the play is performed and, in particular, taking the performance as a whole). It is for this reason that a performance of 'Othello' or 'The Merchant of Venice' is not caught by the present offence (at least, if the script is not substantially corrupted).

The prosecution does not have to prove any mens rea on the part of the accused presenter or director in relation to the content of the play. However, if he is not proved to have intended to stir up racial hatred, he has a defence if he proves[1] that he did not know and had no reason to suspect:[2]

(a) that the performance would involve the use of the offending words or behaviour; or

(b) that the offending words or behaviour were threatening, abusive or insulting; or

(c) that the circumstances in which the performance would be given would be such that racial hatred would be likely to be stirred up.[3]

These defences are of particular importance where the presenter or director is not present at a particular performance. Paragraph (a) provides a defence where the actor unauthorisedly departs from the script in a way which could not have been anticipated by the presenter or director. Paragraph (b) covers the case, for example, where words are insulting to a particular group in an audience, but the presenter or director had no reason to suspect this since the words would normally be unexceptionable and he had no reason to suspect the susceptibility of the particular group. Paragraph (c) deals with the case where, because of circumstances of which the presenter or director could not reasonably have been aware, an ostensibly 'innocent' play has become one which is likely to stir up racial hatred. It is difficult to envisage that the defences in (b) and (c) are likely to be available other than in rare cases.

---

1   See para **4.38**.
2   See para **3.68** fn 1.
3   1986 Act, s 20(2).

Prosecution, trial and punishment
5.44 See paras **5.53–5.59**.

Inclusion in programme service

5.45 Section 22(1) of the 1986 Act provides that, if a programme[1] involving the use of threatening, abusive or insulting visual images or sounds is included in a programme service,[1] each of the persons[2] mentioned in the next paragraph is guilty of an offence if:

(a) he intends thereby to stir up racial hatred; or
(b) having regard to all the circumstances, racial hatred is likely to be stirred up thereby.

---

1   A 'programme' includes any advertisement and any other item included in the 'programme service': 1986 Act, s 29, applying the Broadcasting Act 1990, s 202(1). As to 'programme service', see para **5.15** fn 1.
2   See paras **5.20** fn 1 and **5.49**.

5.46 Liability is extended not only to the person using the offending words or behaviour in question, but also to producers and directors of the programme, and to the person providing the programme service.[1]

However, if the latter, or a producer or director, is not proved to have intended to stir up racial hatred, he has a defence if he proves[2] that he did not know and had no reasonable cause to suspect[3] that the programme would involve the use of the offending material, *and* that it was not reasonably practicable for him to remove it.[4]

In addition, a person who is not proved to have intended to stir up racial hatred is not guilty of an offence if he did not know, and had no reason to suspect, that the offending material was threatening, abusive or insulting.[5] It will be noted that the accused does not have to prove this exclusion from liability.

---

1   1986 Act, s 22(2).
2   See para **4.38**.
3   See para **3.68** fn 1.
4   1986 Act, s 22(3).
5   Ibid, s 22(6).

5.47 Two further defences are also provided by s 22.

It is a defence for a person by whom the programme was produced or directed who is not shown to have intended to stir up racial hatred to prove[1] that he did not know and had no reason to suspect:

(a) that the programme would be included in a programme service; or
(b) that the circumstances in which the programme would be so included would be such that racial hatred would be likely to be stirred up.[2]

It is also a defence for a person by whom offending words or behaviour were used and who is not shown to have intended to stir up racial hatred to prove[1] that he did not know and had no reason to suspect:

(a) that a programme involving the use of the offending material would be included in a programme service; or

(b) that the circumstances in which a programme involving the use of the offending material would be so included, or in which a programme so included would involve the use of the offending material, would be such that racial hatred would be likely to be stirred up.[3]

---

1   See para **4.38**.
2   1986 Act, s 22(4).
3   Ibid, s 22(5).

Prosecution, trial and punishment
5.48 See paras **5.53–5.59**.

GENERAL POINTS ABOUT THE OFFENCES

Offences by corporations

5.49 It may well be that a corporation, particularly a limited company, may be involved in the publication, distribution, broadcasting or possession etc of racially inflammatory material. In such a case, it can be criminally liable for an offence under Part III of the 1986 Act, like other offences, provided that the conduct and state of mind of a 'controlling officer' who can be identified with the corporation falls within the requirements of the section in question.[1]

---

1   Officers who can be identified with the corporation are those who constitute the 'directing mind and will' of the corporation, such as directors and others who manage the affairs of the corporation and, in addition, any person to whom those responsible for the general management of the corporation have delegated some part of their functions of management, giving him full discretion to act independently of instructions from them; within the scope of his delegation, the delegate acts as the corporation: *Tesco Supermarkets Ltd v Nattrass* [1971] 2 All ER 127, HL. See further, Card, Cross and Jones *Criminal Law* (1998) paras 21.50–21.59.

   The above statement of the law has been concerned with the personal liability of corporations. The wording of the offences under Part III makes it impossible that a corporation can be held vicariously liable for any of them through the acts of an inferior employee.

5.50 The fact that a corporation is criminally liable does not prevent the conviction, as well, of the individual who physically committed the offence nor the conviction of any other person who aided or abetted its commission. In addition, s 28(1) of the 1986 Act casts the net wider so as to catch directors and the like whose guilt as an accomplice might be hard to prove, as well as those who are undoubtedly guilty under ordinary principles. The subsection provides that, where a corporation is guilty of an offence under Part III and the offence is proved to have been committed with the consent or connivance of any director, manager,[1] secretary or other similar officer of the corporation, or a person who was purporting to act as such, he, as well as the corporation, is guilty of that offence. Unlike s 16 of the Theatres Act 1968, referred to in para **4.102** fn 3, s 28(1) does not extend to imposing liability on any director etc to whose neglect an offence is proved to have been attributable, which widens liability beyond that covered by the law of complicity.

An individual who is liable under this provision is by its express terms guilty of the same offence as that committed by the corporation; he does not commit, nor is he guilty of, some separate offence created by the provision. An obiter dictum by the Court of Appeal in *R v Wilson*[2] that such a provision creates an offence ancillary to that committed by the corporation, and when it applies the individual is guilty of 'that offence', cannot be correct, given the unequivocal wording of the provision.

A person 'consents' to the commission of an offence by a corporation if he is aware of what is going on and agrees to it.[3] 'Connivance' is generally regarded as involving wilful blindness as to the commission of the offence,[4] which must no doubt be coupled in this context with acquiescence in it. A person who consents to, or connives at, an offence committed by a corporation (through another person's conduct) may be guilty of that offence as an accomplice; and this is so even in the case where he does nothing positive, if he had a right of control over that other person. The importance of this part of the provision is that it makes the task of the prosecution less difficult, since it is enough for them to prove consent or connivance by a person of the specified type and they do not have to prove that it amounted to aiding, abetting, counselling or procuring.

Section 28(2) deals with the case where, as in the case of some clubs or associations which are corporate bodies, the affairs of the corporation are managed by its members. It provides that, in such a case, s 28(1) applies in relation to the acts or defaults of a member in connection with his functions of management as it applies to a director.

---

1   Ie someone managing in a governing role the affairs of the corporation, as opposed to someone with a day-to-day management function: *R v Boal* [1992] 3 All ER 177, CA.
2   [1997] 1 All ER 119 at 121.
3   *Huckerby v Elliott* [1970] 1 All ER 189, DC.
4   *Somerset v Hart* (1884) 12 QBD 360.

5.51 It must be emphasised that the above has been concerned with corporate bodies. Unless it is an incorporated body, an association (including a political party) cannot, save in a few exceptional offences, itself be rendered criminally liable for the acts of its committee or senior members, let alone its ordinary members, nor can the provisions of s 28 apply. On the other hand, a member of the committee, or indeed any member, can be convicted of an offence under Part III perpetrated by someone else (eg another member of the committee) if he can be proved to be an accomplice to it under general principles (ie to have aided, abetted, counselled or procured it). However, since minutes may not be kept of (say) a decision by an association to publish or produce a racially inflammatory publication, it may be difficult to identify the individuals (perpetrators and accomplices) involved in it. A fortiori, there may be a problem with fly-posting in the name of an association.

Parliamentary and court reports

5.52 None of the above offences applies to a fair and accurate report of:

(a) proceedings in Parliament;[1] or

(b) proceedings publicly heard before a court or tribunal exercising judicial authority.[2]

However, in the case of a report of the proceedings of a court or tribunal, the exemption applies *only* if the report is published contemporaneously with those proceedings or, if it is not reasonably practicable or would be unlawful to publish a report of them contemporaneously (eg because of the law of contempt of court), it is published as soon as publication is reasonably practicable[3] and lawful.[4] This limitation is designed to prevent racists from avoiding criminal liability by subsequently simply publishing, distributing or the like, a verbatim report (including the offending material) of a criminal trial for an offence under Part III that had been proved to have been committed. If racial hatred is intended or likely to be stirred up, thereby an offence is committed.

In the case of reports of proceedings in Parliament and of reports of proceedings before a court or tribunal, the exemption from liability only applies to a fair and accurate report. No doubt the case law on 'fair and accurate' in the similarly worded provision in s 3 of the Law of Libel Amendment Act 1888 is equally applicable to the present defence. To be 'fair and accurate', the report must be fair and impartial, although it need not be verbatim.[5] In addition, it should convey to its readers the substance of what has taken place in court as if they had been present.[6]

No defence is provided in relation to bona fide newspaper reports of speeches whose makers are later convicted under s 18 of the 1986 Act. Editors must therefore be careful. The resulting restriction on the publication of the details of speeches on racial matters raises once again the balance between freedom of expression (by the press, here) and the rights of racial groups.

---

1   1986 Act, s 26(1).
2   Ibid, s 26(2).
3   See para **6.9** fn 2.
4   1986 Act, s 26(2).
5   *Lewis v Levy* (1858) EB&E 537; *Andrews v Chapman* (1853) 3 Car & Kir 286; *Turner v Sullivan* (1862) 6 LT 130.
6   *Furniss v Cambridge Daily News Ltd* (1907) 23 TLR 705 at 706 per Cozens-Hardy, MR; *Burnett and Hallamshire Fuel Ltd v Sheffield Telegraph and Star Ltd* [1960] 2 All ER 157.

Prosecutions

5.53 No prosecution for an offence under Part III of the 1986 Act may be instituted, except by or with the consent of the Attorney-General.[1] The same applies to conspiracy or attempt to commit such an offence or aiding, abetting, counselling or procuring its commission.[2] The requirement of the Attorney-General's consent is intended to ensure that the legitimate exercise of freedom of expression is not inhibited by the fear of frivolous prosecutions and to ensure that prosecutions are only brought against the ringleaders and organisers of incitement to racial hatred.[3] This justification does, however, raise the question of the desirability of drafting the legislation in potentially wide terms, but leaving it to the Attorney-General to prosecute only when he thought it appropriate, in an effort to allay concerns about the extent of the intervention of the law. The appropriateness of leaving the boundaries of freedom of expression in the hands of a member of the government, albeit a distinguished lawyer, may be open to doubt. Many racial hatred offences have political overtones; should it be in the hands of a politician to decide whether to prosecute? Where, as here, the interests of the State are not directly affected, there seems to be no reason why a prosecution should depend on the Attorney-General's wishes.

It is alleged that the requirement of the Attorney-General's consent in effect precludes prosecutions other than in the most blatant cases because Attornies-General have shown excessive caution in bringing prosecutions, on the ground that an unsuccessful prosecution does more harm than good to racial equality.[4] It may also be that the inclusion of the offences in a Public Order Act means that, unless public order is clearly threatened, there is a reluctance to prosecute. If this is so, it is a misplaced view. The gravamen, and origins, of the offences lie in the view that racial hatred poses a diffused threat to public order and has a corrosive effect per se on society.

The charge of excessive caution appears to be borne out by the statistics given in para **5.3**.

---

1   1986 Act, s 27(1). The function of the Attorney-General under s 27 may be exercised by the
     Solicitor-General: Law Officers Act 1997, s 1. As to the terms in which consent may be given,
     see *R v Cain* [1975] 2 All ER 900, CA; see para **3.34**.
2   See, respectively, the Criminal Law Act 1977, s 4(3); Criminal Attempts Act 1981, s 2(2);
     Accessories and Abettors Act 1861, s 8. The requirement for the Attorney-General to institute,
     or consent to, a prosecution for an offence under Part III does not prevent an arrest without
     warrant, or the issue or execution of a warrant for the arrest of a person for such an offence,
     or the remand in custody or on bail of a person charged with such an offence: Prosecution of
     Offences Act 1985, s 25.
3   HL Deb, vol 268, col 1012 (1965).
4   Bindman 'Incitement to racial hatred' (1982) 132 NLJ 299; Cotterell 'Prosecuting incitement
     to racial hatred' [1982] PL 378.

5.54 A consent to a prosecution of a person for an offence or offences under ss 18–23 does not extend to the prosecution of that person for conspiracy to contravene any of these sections,[1] nor (it is submitted) to the prosecution of that person for an attempt to contravene any of them. Such a charge must be the subject of a fresh consent.

---

1   *R v Pearce* (1980) 72 Cr App R 295, CA.

5.55 If a private individual or anyone else is aggrieved by the Attorney-General's failure to prosecute, he has no choice but to grin and bear it. Not only can he not bring a prosecution, but also he cannot bring a civil action on the basis of an alleged offence under one of these sections. This was held in *Thorne v British Broadcasting Corporation*,[1] where Thorne, a person of German origin resident in Britain, alleged that the BBC had conducted sustained propaganda of racial hatred against the Germans. He sought to bring a civil action for an injunction to restrain the BBC from disseminating racialist abuse in breach of s 6 of the Race Relations Act 1965 (incitement to racial hatred). His claim was struck out by the Court of Appeal on the ground that s 6 only created a criminal offence, and that any remedy for its breach was under the Attorney-General's exclusive control. The only exception would seem to be that, in the event of repeated offences, an individual could bring a relator action for an injunction in the name of the Attorney-General and with his consent, but the courts will not interfere if the Attorney-General refuses in the exercise of his discretion to consent.[2]

A decision by the Attorney-General not to prosecute is not judicially reviewable.[3]

1   [1967] 2 All ER 1225, CA.
2   *Gouriet v Union of Post Office Workers* [1977] 3 All ER 70, HL.
3   *R v Solicitor-General, ex parte Taylor* [1996] 1 FLR 206, DC.

Duplicity

5.56 We have already seen (in paras **3.69**, **4.17**, **4.39** and **4.56**) that, for the purposes of the rules against duplicity, each of ss 1–5 of the 1986 Act creates one offence. Likewise, s 27(2) of that Act provides that, for the purposes of the rules against charging more than one offence in the same count or information, each of the offence-creating sections in Part III creates one offence. Consequently, for example, a count in an indictment (or an information) charging an accused under s 19 with publishing or distributing written material which is threatening, abusive or insulting with intent to stir up racial hatred thereby or in circumstances where racial hatred is likely to be stirred up thereby is not bad for duplicity.

Trial and punishment

5.57 The offences under Part III of the 1986 Act are triable either way. The maximum punishment is:

(a) two years' imprisonment or a fine, or both, on conviction on indictment; and
(b) six months' imprisonment or a fine not exceeding the statutory maximum, or both, on summary conviction.[1]

These amounts may be compared with the much lower maxima for the summary offences involving threatening, abusive or insulting words or behaviour under ss 4, 4A and 5 of the Act, which have elements in common with offences under Part III. This provides a clear indication of the gravity attached to offences of racial hatred by Parliament. Depending on the circumstances, an offence under Part III (in reality an offence under ss 18, 19 or 23 is the obvious candidate) connected to a designated football match can result in the making of a domestic football banning order under Part IV of the 1986 Act and/or an international football banning order under Part II of the Football Spectators Act 1989 as explained in paras **8.30–8.58**.

1   1986 Act, s 27(3).

Forfeiture

5.58 Section 25 of the 1986 Act provides for the forfeiture of racially inflammatory material following a conviction:

(a) under s 18 in relation to the display of written material; or
(b) under s 19 (publication or distribution), or s 21 (distribution etc of a recording), or s 23 (possession).

There is no power of forfeiture in other cases. It follows, for example, that the court cannot order forfeiture of the script following a conviction under s 20.

Section 25(1) obliges a magistrates' court by which, or the Crown Court before which, a person is convicted of such an offence to order to be forfeited any written material or recording produced to the court and shown to its satisfaction to be the written material or recording to which the offence relates. Forfeiture is not limited to things found in the convicted person's possession.

Since a forfeiture order is mandatory once the court is satisfied of the specified condition, it is not surprising that there is no procedure for giving notice to a person not already before the court (eg an owner of material possessed by the accused at the material time) that an order under s 25(1) may be made.

Section 25(1) may be contrasted with the similarly worded forfeiture provision under s 66 of the Criminal Justice and Public Order Act 1994, referred to in para **7.90**, which gives the court a discretion as to ordering forfeiture.

Although a forfeiture order made under the present section is undoubtedly a sentence within the meaning of s 50(1) of the Criminal Appeal Act 1968, there is no right of appeal from the Crown Court to the Court of Appeal against it, because it is a sentence fixed by law.[1] For the same reason, a person convicted by a magistrates' court cannot appeal against sentence to the Crown Court against the imposition of a forfeiture order under the present section.[2] However, an accused, or someone else with a sufficient interest, can obtain judicial review of a forfeiture order made by a magistrates' court in an appropriate case. Judicial review of a forfeiture order under s 25 may also be available to someone convicted in the Crown Court.[3]

Of course, if an appeal against conviction is successful the court will quash a forfeiture order imposed under s 25(1).

---

1   Criminal Appeal Act 1968, s 9(1).
2   Magistrates' Courts Act 1980, s 108(3).
3   This depends on whether the order is a 'matter relating to trial on indictment'. If it is, judicial review is not available: Supreme Court Act 1981, s 28(3). In *R v Maidstone Crown Court, ex parte Gill* [1986] Crim LR 737, DC, a forfeiture order imposed on a third party under drugs legislation by the Crown Court as a trial court was judicially reviewed.

5.59 It is submitted that an order under s 25 amounts to an additional penalty and cannot be combined with an absolute discharge or a conditional discharge.[1] On this basis, if there is material to forfeit under s 25(1), an absolute or conditional discharge cannot be ordered.

A forfeiture order under s 25 does not take effect until the expiry of the ordinary time within which an appeal (whether against conviction or against sentence) may be instituted or, where an appeal is instituted, until it is finally decided or abandoned.[2] The effect of this provision is simply to suspend the operation of the forfeiture order. However, until the determination of an appeal (or the expiry of time for an appeal) the written material or recording will remain with the court authorities or the police or (sometimes) Customs and Excise. If there is no appeal or an appeal fails, the order will come into effect; if an appeal succeeds, the written material or recording must be returned.

Strangely, no provision is expressly made for the disposal or destruction of written matter which has been forfeited, but it is implicit that this can be done once the order is in effect.

1   *R v Hunt* [1978] Crim LR 697, CA; *R v Savage* (1985) 5 Cr App R (S) 216, CA. Note the decisions in these cases would now be different because the forfeiture orders there were made under the Powers of Criminal Courts Act 1973, s 43, s 12(4) of which (as amended by the Criminal Justice Act 1988) now expressly permits such a combination. The reasoning, however, in these cases remains applicable to forfeiture orders under other statutes.

2   1986 Act, s 25(2).

European Convention on Human Rights

5.60 A prosecution under Part III of the 1986 Act clearly constitutes an interference by the state with Art 10 (freedom of expression) of the ECHR, although in extreme cases it may be that Art 17 of the ECHR (nothing in the ECHR to be construed as implying a right for any state, group or person to engage in conduct aimed at (inter alia) the destruction of any right or freedom in the Convention) could be relied on to limit the ambit of Art 10. Indeed, Art 17 was relied on in the context of extreme racist material in *Glimmerveen v Netherlands*[1] by the European Commission of Human Rights. The Commission held that the dissemination of extreme opinions maintaining racial supremacy and spreading racial hatred was outside the protection of Art 10 because of its potential to undermine public order and the rights of the targeted minority. However, in *Handyside v UK*,[2] the European Court explained that Art 10 applies 'not only to information or ideas that are favourably received, or are regarded as inoffensive or as a matter of indifference, but also to those that offend, shock or disturb the State or any sector of the population'.

It is submitted that the interference with freedom of expression under Art 10 in the present context is in principle necessary in a democratic society for the protection of the rights and freedoms of others, and may in a particular case also be so necessary to prevent disorder or crime. The concept of proportionality inherent in 'necessary in a democratic society' would seem to be satisfied in respect of the actual application of Part III by its provisions referred to earlier which protect the right to privacy and the freedom to receive and impart information. There may, however, be some applications of Part III (eg private discussions between a group of acquaintances) where this would not be the case.[3] An example is provided by *Jersild v Denmark*.[4] J, a journalist, had arranged for three youths, members of a racist group, to appear on a serious television programme where he conducted an interview with the three youths who expressed extreme racist views. The interview was broadcast without any disclaimer. It was not intended by J to promote racist views but to express them. The youths were convicted of making racist statements, and J of aiding and abetting them. The majority of the European Court of Human Rights (12–4) held that the conviction of J for aiding and abetting the youths was disproportionate to the protection of the rights of the targeted minorities and that the interference with his freedom of expression under Art 10 could not be justified under Art 10(2). The key factors were that J did not himself express the racist views, that the interview was part of a serious programme aimed at an informed audience and that its presentation showed clearly that its aim was not racism, but to expose and analyse the causes of racism.

---

1   (1978) 18 D&R 187, 4 EHRR 260, Eur Comm HR. In *Jersild v Denmark*, discussed in the text, the European Court, without referring to Art 17, pointed out that the racist remarks of the three youths referred to did not have the protection of Art 10.
2   (1976) Ser A, no 24; 1 EHRR 737, at para 49.
3   The present prosecution policy in respect of Part III offences means that a prosecution would be inconceivable in such instances.
4   (1994) Ser A, no 298; 19 EHRR 1, ECtHR. For a discussion of this case, see Wintermute (1995–96) 6 King's College LJ 143.

Other racist offences

5.61 The offence of racist chanting at a designated football match is dealt with in para **8.27**.

The Crime and Disorder Act 1998 introduced various offences of racially-aggravated assault, racially-aggravated criminal damage, racially-aggravated public order offences and racially-aggravated harassment. The racially-aggravated public order offences and racially-aggravated harassment are dealt with in paras **4.81–4.87** and **4.97–4.99**. The other offences are outside the scope of this book.

Chapter 6

PROCESSIONS AND ASSEMBLIES

INTRODUCTION

6.1 Processions and assemblies are an important manifestation of the freedoms of expression and of assembly and association. The vast majority of public processions and assemblies pass off peacefully, but policing them takes a great deal of police time and money, and even a peaceful march or demonstration can have a serious impact on the life of a locality in a non-violent way. Sometimes a procession or assembly develops into public disorder. This chapter deals with provisions specifically aimed at the regulation of processions and assemblies. It must not be forgotten, however, that there are other constraints on public processions and assemblies. For example, their mere occurrence may constitute the tort of trespass, or result in criminal liability for wilful obstruction of the highway (contrary to s 137 of the Highways Act 1980) or the common law offence of public nuisance (both of which are dealt with in Chapter 9) or for breach of regulations or a by-law. In addition, the general preventive powers of a police officer to prevent a breach of the peace (described in Chapter 2) are applicable to a procession or assembly. Quite apart from this, a wide range of offences may be committed by those involved. Such constraints are not circumscribed by the special provisions set out below. This is also true of remedies in civil law. The fact that the necessary advance notice of a public procession has been given, or that conditions have been imposed on a public procession or assembly, for example, does not preclude an interested party obtaining an injunction in respect of it.

The powers described in this chapter, like the common law breach of the peace powers, impact on the freedom of speech and peaceful assembly in a way which a prosecution for an offence committed during a procession or assembly does not. The powers to impose conditions and to ban mentioned below can reduce or neutralise the impact of a procession or assembly or, of course, prevent it taking place and having any effect. Punishing those who 'misbehave' at a procession or assembly does not have this consequence; indeed, the consequent publicity tends to increase the effect.

6.2 Statutory powers to control the routes of processions have existed since the Metropolitan Police Act 1839 and the Town Police Clauses Act 1847. However, it was not until 1936 that s 3 of the Public Order Act 1936 provided a general statutory power to impose conditions on, or to ban, public processions. That section, prompted by the violence induced by processions organised by the British Union of Fascists and opposed by Communists in the East End of London, was repealed and replaced by the 1986 Act.

Section 3(1) of the 1936 Act empowered a chief constable (or the Commissioner of the Metropolitan Police or of the City of London Police) to impose conditions on the conduct of an actual or proposed public procession, if he had reasonable grounds for apprehending that the procession might occasion serious public disorder.

Section 3(2) of the 1936 Act provided that, if a chief constable was of the opinion that his powers under s 3(1) would not be sufficient to prevent serious public disorder being occasioned by a public procession in a particular local authority district, he had to apply to the district council for an order prohibiting for up to three months all public processions or any class thereof. An order required the Home Secretary's consent. Section 3(3) contained a similar provision with respect to the City of London and Metropolitan Police areas; however, in those two, orders prohibiting processions were made by the respective Commissioner, with the Home Secretary's consent.

A person who knowingly failed to comply with any conditions imposed under s 3(1), or who organised or assisted in organising any public procession held or intended to be held in contravention of an order under s 3(2) or (3) (or who incited another to take part in such a procession), committed a summary offence.

6.3 The 1936 Act did not deal with assemblies, although there was (and remains) a power for public bodies or officials to forbid or control meetings on land whose management is vested in the Crown (eg Trafalgar Square and Hyde Park)[1] or in a local authority or other statutory body.[2]

---

1   See the Trafalgar Square Regulations 1952, SI 1952/776, made under the Trafalgar Square Act 1844 and the Royal and Other Parks and Gardens Regulations 1977, SI 1977/217, made under the Parks Regulations Act 1872.
2   See the by-laws referred to in paras **9.97–9.102**, especially para **9.98**.

6.4 Concern over public disorder and various events in the 1970s and early 1980s, particularly the Brixton Riots in 1981 and disorder associated with the 1984–85 miners' strike, coupled with the cost of policing them, led to the strengthening by Part II (ss 11–16) of the Public Order Act 1986 of the controls over the holding and conduct of public processions and assemblies. These provisions, like the ones they replace, are preventive in nature. The principal changes made were:

–   the introduction of advance notice requirements for public processions;
–   the extension of the grounds on which conditions may be imposed on public processions; and
–   the introduction of a power to impose conditions on public assemblies (but not to prohibit them).

A power to prohibit 'trespassory assemblies' was added in 1994.

These provisions raise in a crucial way the balance between the right to the freedom of expression and of association (which includes rights to march and to protest) under the ECHR and the right to peace on the streets and elsewhere.

THE LAW ON PUBLIC PROCESSIONS

'Public procession'

6.5 For the purposes of the 1986 Act, a 'public procession' is defined by s 16 of the 1986 Act as a procession in a public place. 'Public place' is in turn defined by s 16 as:

'(a) any highway ... and
(b) any place to which at the material time the public or any section of the public has access, on payment or otherwise, as of right or by virtue of express or implied permission.'

Although a procession will normally occur in a place open to the air, this is not a requirement of the definition of a public procession.

'Any highway' in (a) refers to roads and streets (and the verges and pavements alongside them), footpaths or bridleways, and cycle tracks, provided in each case that there is a public right of passage over them.[1]

The definition in (b) embraces not only places of common resort, but also private property to which the public have access otherwise than as trespassers. Whether a place is a 'public place' is a question of degree and fact.[2] If the public or any section of it have access to a place by express or implied permission, eg to enter a shopping precinct, it is irrelevant that the occupier of the place has the right to refuse entry or to restrict who may enter.[3] It is nevertheless a 'public place' under the present definition. So, for example, are the grounds of a cathedral or church; an Easter procession in a cathedral close, for example, is a public procession.[4]

Since the public must have access, by right or permission, at the material time, a place which is open at certain times but closed at others is a public place when it is open but not when it is closed; a pub car park bearing a notice that it was for use only by customers was held to be no longer a public place an hour after closing time.[5] A place to which people have, or are permitted to have, access is only a public place if the class of such persons is wide enough for them to be described as 'the public' or a 'section of the public', a term discussed in another context in para **5.24**. The grounds of a National Trust property or of a football club will, for example, be a public place at a time when they are only open to members of the Trust or supporters' association because a section of the public will have access to them.

A place can be a 'public place' even though access is dependent on payment. Stadia, public parks, and the like are public places on occasions when access is permitted to any member of the public or section of the public on payment for a ticket. It is not necessary, of course, that all who gain access should have paid for a ticket.

Whether or not a procession is 'public' seems to depend only on its locus. As already indicated, a procession restricted to members of a club, trade union, political party and so on on a road or public place is, therefore, a public procession.

---

1   See para **9.74**.
2   *R v Waters* (1963) 47 Cr App R 149, CCA.
3   *Lawrenson v Oxford* [1982] Crim LR 185, DC.
4   Such a procession would, however, be exempt from the advance notice requirement in the Public Order Act 1986, s 11: para **6.10**.
5   *Sandy v Martin* [1974] Crim LR 258, DC.

6.6   The definition in s 16 of the 1986 Act leaves unanswered the question 'What is a procession?' Lord Denning adopted the *Oxford English Dictionary* definition in the following observation in *Kent v Metropolitan Police Commissioner*:[1]

'A public procession is the act of a body of persons marching along in orderly succession – see the *Oxford English Dictionary*. All kinds of processions take place every day up and down the country – carnivals, weddings, funerals, processions to the Houses of Parliament, marches to Trafalgar Square and so forth.'

This definition comes close to that given to 'procession' by Lord Goddard CJ in *Flockhart v Robinson*,[2] viz 'A procession is not a mere body of persons; it is a body of persons moving along a route'. Although Lord Goddard's definition did not expressly require the body of persons to move in orderly succession, it is clear from the Divisional Court's decision that there is such a requirement. In that case, after a lawful procession had broken up to disperse, a group moved into an area where processions were prohibited. Initially, the group was in loose formation and not in ranks, and in the form of a rabble, but in due course it spontaneously adopted an orderly formation. The Divisional Court held that at that point it became a procession.

Presumably, the body of persons must be moving along for a common purpose, a requirement made in an Australian case.[3]

A number of points can be added. First, as was indicated in *Flockhart v Robinson*, no prior arrangement is required for a 'procession'; it can arise spontaneously. Second, although there cannot be a procession consisting only of one person walking a given route (even if for some ceremonial purpose), the statements about the meaning of 'procession' do not indicate the minimum number required for a procession, except to make it clear that a body of persons must be involved, which leaves uncertainty about how many people constitute a body; certainly more than two. Moreover, unlike the definition of a public assembly,[4] the definition of a *public* procession does not prescribe a minimum number. Consequently, it is impossible to say in advance when a lone charity walk becomes a procession when joined by others. Third, there is nothing in the above statements, except Lord Denning's, to require the body of persons to be on foot. Consequently, it is submitted, a convoy of vehicles (such as a carnival parade) is a procession if it moves in orderly succession. Indeed, this is assumed to be so by the law relating to the wearing of seat belts![5]

---

1   (1981) *The Times*, 15 May, DC.
2   [1950] 2 KB 498 at 502.
3   See DGT Williams *Keeping the Peace* (Hutchinson, 1967) p 62.
4   See para **6.57**.
5   The Motor Vehicles (Wearing of Seat Belts) Regulations 1993, SI 1993/176: with respect to the requirement that adult passengers in the front seat of a motor vehicle wear a seat belt, there is an exemption in respect of a person who is riding in a vehicle which is taking part in a procession that is held to mark or commemorate an event if either the procession is one commonly or customarily held in a police area or areas, or notice in respect of the procession has been given in accordance with the Public Order Act 1986, s 11.

Advance notice

6.7   Section 11 of the 1986 Act provides a national requirement for advance written[1] notice of certain types of public procession. There is no corresponding general statutory provision requiring notice of an assembly. Until the 1986 Act, there was no general statutory provision in England and Wales requiring advance notice to be given of a procession; in comparison there was (and is) such a general requirement in Scotland, Northern Ireland and many West European countries.[2] However, in some 92 local authority areas[3] in England and Wales, local Acts required advance notice of processions. None of these local provisions survived the 1986 Act.[4]

It must be emphasised that the requirement of advance notice is not the same as introducing a requirement of a police permit for a procession. Subject to the powers to impose conditions or to ban processions, discussed below, everyone remains free to march, whether or not they have complied with the requirement of advance notice. The function of s 11 is to alert the police so that they can make the necessary policing arrangements and to serve as the formal trigger for discussion between police and organisers designed to agree the ground rules for a march, and thereby obviate the need for formal conditions or bans.[5]

---

1   See para **4.7** fn 2.
2   *Review of the Public Order Act 1936 and Related Legislation* Cmnd 7891 (Home Office, 1980), para 66.
3   *Review of Public Order Law* (Cmnd 9510, 1985), para 4.3.
4   Many of these provisions were repealed successively as a result of the Local Government Act 1972, s 262, in the years up to 1986. The rest were repealed by the 1986 Act, s 40(3) and Sch 3.
5   House of Commons Home Affairs Select Committee Fifth Report, HC 756 (1980), para 35.

6.8   Clearly, where a demonstration is likely to be large, or likely to provoke a significant counter-demonstration, the police will need time to have discussions with the organisers and to keep order and to preserve the ordinary activities of everyday life. Such arrangements may involve them in calling in members of other forces under mutual aid arrangements, and the more time they have the better will be the arrangements. They will also need time to enable them to take steps to prevent serious disruption of public and private transport and other consequences of a public procession, and to give them time to consider the need for any banning order.

Notification of processions had generally been given to the police before the 1986 Act.[1] However, the processions which were most likely to lead to violence and serious disorder tended to be those which were not notified. For example, in March 1985, the Metropolitan Police learnt about a proposed National Front march in Greenwich only as a result of leaflets left at a London railway station; eventually the march was banned under s 3(3) of the Act of 1936.[2] In 1985, in Staffordshire, no notice was given of the March for Jobs, with the result that large numbers of police officers had to be deployed to keep open a number of alternative routes.[3] Following a number of events, concern was expressed at the absence of a national requirement for advance notice, and such a requirement was recommended by the Home Affairs Select Committee and by Lord Scarman in his report on the Brixton riots of 1981.[4]

---

1   In his *Report on the Disorders at Red Lion Square* Cmnd 5919 (1975), paras 128 and 129, Lord Scarman stated that the police were notified in at least 80% of cases and that generally no difficulty was experienced in finding out about unnotified processions.
2   HC Deb, vol 89, col 798 (1986).
3   HL Deb, vol 479, col 477 (1986).
4   Cmnd 8427 (1981), para 7.45.

When must notice be given?
6.9   Section 11(1) of the 1986 Act requires written notice of a proposal to hold a public procession only where the procession is intended:

(a) to demonstrate support for or opposition to the views or actions of any
     person[1] or body of persons;
(b) to publicise a cause or campaign; or
(c) to mark or commemorate an event.

These three categories cover most types of procession, including (for example)
any procession expressing opposition to, or support for, a political issue, any
procession by a political organisation or pressure group, any procession,
including a sponsored walk, in support of a campaign or cause, and any procession
to commemorate the winning of a sporting event or the death of a person (with
the general exception of a funeral procession, see below).

    On the other hand, it follows from the wording of s 11(1) that organisers of
processions that are of no interest to the police, such as crocodiles of school
children, tourists following a guide, or a party of ramblers, are not required to give
advance notice.

    In addition, s 11(1) provides that the obligation to give advance notice does
not apply where 'it is not reasonably practicable[2] to give *any*[3] advance notice' of the
procession. This is intended to exempt spontaneous processions, such as one
arising out of a sense of grief or loss arising from an accident or other tragedy, or
out of some political or military action. It would also cover a spontaneous
procession which breaks away from a procession in respect of which notice has
been given. The test of practicability is vague, to be judged by the police in the first
instance and ultimately by a court if the exemption is raised by way of defence on a
prosecution for non-compliance with s 11.

    It will be noted that the exemption provision in s 11(1) refers simply to
'advance notice', and not advance *written* notice. Interpreted literally, this is odd
because it suggests that advance oral notice can be sufficient to satisfy the advance
notice requirement. In addition, a literal interpretation would seem to limit the
exemption to such an extent as to deprive it of effect; there will be very few
processions, indeed, where it would not be reasonably practicable to give oral
notice, by telephone at least, of a spontaneous procession which is about to set off,
although the very spontaneity of the procession might mean that the organisers (if
there can be said to be organisers of such a procession) may not think about the
need to inform the police.

    Although the present type of advance notice provision will not generally
constitute an interference with Art 11 of the ECHR (freedom of peaceful
assembly),[4] a Convention right under the Human Rights Act 1998, it is arguable
that to criminalise someone who organises a spontaneous peaceful procession
would be an interference. Moreover, it is submitted that the reference to 'advance
notice' must refer to advance written notice, if the exemption is to have any real
meaning, and that this can be supported by reference to s 11(1) as a whole, the
material parts of which are: 'Written notice shall be given in accordance with this
section of a proposal to hold a public procession intended (a) to demonstrate
support ... unless it is not reasonably practicable to give any advance notice of the
procession.' The second reference to advance notice, being contained in an
'unless clause', must be construed by reference to the main provision expressed in
terms of advance written notice. Unless s 11(1) is interpreted in this way, it would
breach Art 11 since it would not seem to be a justifiable restriction on that freedom
under Art 11(2). Even construed as referring to advance written notice not being
reasonably practicable, the exemption is of limited effect. Cases will be rare where

a delay to deliver a written notice, however brief the period of advance warning, will render a procession meaningless or deprive it substantially of effect. As said above, the problem with spontaneous processions is that the organisers may simply not think about the need to give advance notice of any kind.

---

1 In this context, 'person' includes a corporate body: Interpretation Act 1978, s 5 and Sch 1.
2 'Practicable' is defined by the *Shorter Oxford English Dictionary* as 'capable of being carried out in action' or 'feasible' (adopted by Lord Goddard LCJ in *Lee v Nursery Furnishings Ltd* [1945] 1 All ER 387 at 389), and by *Webster's Dictionary* as 'possible to be accomplished with known means or resources' (adopted by Parker J in *Adsett v K & L Steelfounders and Engineers Ltd* [1953] 1 All ER 97 at 98). 'Reasonably practicable' imposes a less strict standard than 'practicable': ibid.
3 Italics added.
4 *Rassemblement Jurassien, Unité Jurassienne v Switzerland* (1979) 17 D&R 93, ECommHR.

Exempt processions

6.10 Quite apart from the limited exception just described, some types of procession are exempted from the requirement of advance written notice. Written notice does not have to be given of a funeral procession *organised by a funeral director in the normal course of his business.*[1] The words italicised would seem to forestall a highly charged political procession associated with a funeral (such as those which have been organised at the funerals of some IRA members) from claiming exemption.

Nor does written notice have to be given of a procession which is *commonly or customarily* held in the police area (or areas) in which it is intended to be held.[1] The apparent reason for this exemption is that the police will already know about the procession, its route, its time and so on. However, there is no guarantee that these matters will remain unchanged from year to year.

The meaning of this exemption is somewhat obscure since it does not indicate in further detail what is meant by 'commonly or customarily'. In *Review of Public Order Law,*[2] the White Paper preceding the 1986 Act, the Government proposed 'a general exemption for processions of a religious, educational or ceremonial character customarily held in an area'. Although the exemption does not use this terminology, it is clear that such processions (eg the annual Royal British Legion marches on Remembrance Sunday, the Lord Mayor's Show, annual carnival processions, and graduation processions in Oxford) would fall within it. However, it appears that any procession, not only Lord Mayors' processions or trade union marches on May Day, but also a procession by a political organisation or trade union movement will not require advance notice if it is commonly or customarily held in the police area (or areas) in question, even though it is not religious, educational or ceremonial in nature. Does this mean that, by commonly holding marches, even violent ones, in a police area, an organisation can win its spurs, so to speak, and thereby acquire an exemption from the advance notice requirement? Could it have been said that the CND's Aldermaston marches at Easter in the late 50s and early 60s had become customarily held so that, had s 11 existed then, advance notice would not have been required? In short, what does 'commonly or customarily' require? What frequency is required for 'commonly'? What period of time for 'customarily'? It is submitted that a precise definition of either adverb is not possible in the present context, although it may well be that, as a question of fact, it will be obvious whether a procession is commonly or customarily held in a police area.

There is no express requirement that a 'commonly or customarily held procession' must be commonly or customarily held along the same route in the police area(s) in question, although there is if they are so held in a different area (or areas) each year. Nevertheless, it can be argued that the present exemption is not applicable where the commonly or customarily held procession follows a different route each year. This would certainly be the view if a purposive construction is made of the present exemption.

It is unfortunate that this exemption is not clearer, since if it does not apply but the organiser, believing that his procession is commonly or customarily held, does not give notice, criminal liability is incurred. In cases of doubt, the advice must be to give advance notice.

---

1   1986 Act, s 11(2).
2   Cmnd 9510 (1985), para 4.5.

Who must give notice and to whom?

6.11 Section 11(1) does not say who must give the written[1] notice, but in practice it will be one or more of the organisers.[2] The notice need not be formal. For example, sending a handbill advertising a march can constitute a written notice, although like any other such notice it must satisfy the requirements of the present section in order to be effective. The notice must be given to the police. Notice to the local authority or any other body is not required, although in practice one can expect the police to relay the information in the notice to other services, for example bus companies, likely to be affected by the procession.

---

1   See para **4.7** fn 2.
2   See para **6.38**, in respect of this term.

Delivery

6.12 By s 11(4)(a), notice must be delivered to a police station in the police area[1] in which it is proposed the procession will start.[2] The notice need not be delivered at a police station in the district (or in the police division) in which the procession is intended to start. If another Jarrow march is held, notice need only be given at a police station somewhere in the Durham police area; the expectation, of course, is that the police force in that area would pass the information on to other forces along the route.

The Act does not define 'police station'; presumably it includes a sub-station which is open only for certain hours a day.

It is noteworthy that the police are not obliged by the section (or anything else) to acknowledge receipt of a notice.

---

1   By the Police Act 1996, s 1(2), there are 43 police areas: (a) the 41 listed in Sch 1 to the
     Police Act 1996; (b) the Metropolitan Police district; and (c) the City of London police area.
2   If it is proposed to start the procession in Scotland and cross into England, notice must be
     delivered to a police station in the first police area in England on the proposed route:
     s 11(4)(b).

6.13 A notice may be delivered by post, but only if the recorded delivery service is used;[1] otherwise it must be delivered by hand[2] and it would seem that this requires that (as in the case of recorded delivery) the notice should actually be handed over and not just put through a letter box. As can be seen, delivery by fax or e-mail is not permitted.

A posted notice must be actually delivered[3] at least six clear days before the date when the procession is intended to be held.[1] So must a notice delivered by hand, except that, if that is not reasonably practicable, a notice delivered *by hand* will be validly delivered if delivered as soon as delivery is reasonably practicable.[2] This means that, normally, if it is proposed to hold a march at 3 pm on 8 August, notice must be delivered before midnight on 1 August. Six clear days seem an unnecessarily long period for the police to have sufficient time to conduct discussions with the organisers, and to make their own preparations, although it may be noted that 28 days' notice must be given in the special context of Northern Ireland (where conditions on processions are imposed by the independent Parades Commission).[4] In contrast, only a handful of the notice provisions in local Acts required six clear days or even three; the overwhelming majority required 36 hours or less. The system apparently worked with these shorter periods.

Neither the police nor anyone else have any power to dispense with the various requirements as to notice, so as to allow, for example, notice to be given by telephone, fax or e-mail.

---

1   1986 Act, s 11(5).
2   Ibid, s 11(6).
3   The Interpretation Act 1978, s 7 (under which a document sent by post is deemed to have been served when posted and to have been delivered in the ordinary course of post) does not apply. The effect of this exclusion is that a notice sent by post must actually be delivered at a relevant police station at least six clear days before the date when the procession is *intended* to be held.
4   Public Processions (Northern Ireland) Act 1998, ss 6 and 8.

6.14 The six clear days requirement is not invariable since it does not apply in the case of delivery of the notice by hand if it is not reasonably practicable[1] to deliver the notice in compliance with it.[2] This exception is intended for marches, arranged at short notice in response to some unexpected event, where it is reasonably practicable to give *some* written[3] notice, but it would not be reasonably practicable to give the normal period of notice. Examples of such a case would be a march to the Embassy of a State which has announced the execution of a political prisoner within 24 hours or a march to protest at government policies when the Prime Minister makes a totally unexpected visit the next day.

---

1   See para **6.9** fn 2.
2   1986 Act, s 11(6).
3   See para **4.7** fn 2.

6.15 The exception is unlikely to apply in many cases since it will usually be practicable to give six clear days' notice and to wait for it to expire, even though this may not be particularly expedient because by the time the notice has expired the media will have lost interest in the issue in question and the feelings of those involved may have moderated.

It must not be forgotten that the fact that it is not reasonably practicable to give six clear days' notice does not mean that no notice need be given. Written notice must still be given as soon as reasonably practicable, unless as we saw in para **6.9**, it is not reasonably practicable to give any written notice.

One situation where the exception may prove to be particularly important is where an extremist group gives the minimum period of advance notice. In such a case, the exception could permit a counter-march by opponents to take place at the same time, which might be less likely to lead to disorder than if the opponents were limited to lining the route of the former march to protest.

Where less than six clear days' notice is given, organisers will proceed with the march within the six clear days at their own risk.

6.16 Compliance with the requirements of s 11 of the 1986 Act does not provide any form of immunity in respect of the subsequent procession. In some other jurisdictions, there is such an immunity: in New South Wales, for example, those who give notice to which the police do not object and who process peacefully are protected from prosecution for obstruction of the highway or other public nuisance.[1]

The advance notice requirement may discourage people from exercising their right of freedom of expression. Clearly, it prevents spontaneous processions arising out of 'lawful' meetings, unless it can be said that no notice need be given as it would be impracticable to give any written notice.

If the police agree to accept less than six clear days' notice or to accept notice by telephone etc, there is nothing in the Act to stop them changing their mind and later alleging a breach of the requirement. However, it is submitted that it would be an abuse of process for them to institute a prosecution for the offence of non-compliance with the notice requirement, referred to below.[2]

---

1   Summary Offences Act 1988 (New South Wales), Part 4.
2   See *R v Croydon JJ, ex parte Dean* (1994) 98 Cr App R 76, DC; *Postermobile Plc v Brent LBC* (1997) *The Times*, 8 December, DC.

Contents of the notice

6.17 A notice required under s 11(1) must specify the date of the proposed procession, its proposed starting time and route, and the name and address of the person (or one of the persons) proposing to organise[1] it.[2] It is not required to specify the nature of the procession, its proposed finishing time, the estimated number of participants, or the arrangements for its control being made by the organiser(s). This is surprising; these matters would seem to be part of the minimum that the police must know in order to consider whether to exercise their powers under ss 12 or 13, below.

It is the practice for police forces to make available forms of notice incorporating provision for more information than is required to be specified by s 11(1). This is to facilitate the planning of the policing of the procession and traffic management and the determination of whether or not to impose conditions on the procession or to seek a prohibition of it (see paras **6.25–6.34** and **6.43–6.51**). Failure to supply such additional information is not, of course, a contravention of the advance notice requirement.

---

1   See para **6.38**.
2   1986 Act, s 11(3).

Offences

6.18 Although failure to comply with the requirements of s 11 does not render the procession unlawful, offences may be committed by the organisers.

Section 11(7) provides:

'Where a public procession is held, each of the persons organising it is guilty of an offence if –

(a) the requirements of this section as to notice have not been satisfied, or
(b) the date when it is held, the time when it starts, or its route, differs from the date, time or route specified in the notice.'

Both offences are similar in that there is no exemption for someone who became an organiser after notice should have been given, in that the use of the present tense in respect of 'persons organising it' indicates that somebody who has ceased to be a person organising the procession when it takes place is not guilty (this, however, would seem to require some positive act of quitting involvement in the procession or its planning), and in that no offence is committed if the procession is never held. In the case of a spontaneous procession where some written notice was reasonably practicable it may not be easy to prove who are the persons organising it. Indeed, the absence of any definition of 'organise' is liable to cause difficulties, in this and the other offences in Part II.[1]

In respect of an offence under s 11(7)(b), the deviation is not required to be substantial. No doubt the de minimis principle applies, but otherwise organisers who start the procession 30 minutes after the notified time or who deviate from the notified route so that the procession can shelter during a torrential downpour in a hall (at the invitation of an authorised person) commit an offence, unless they can rely on one of the defences outlined shortly.

Both of these offences are summary offences. The maximum punishment is a fine not exceeding level 3 on the standard scale;[2] it is not punishable with imprisonment.

There is no record of any prosecution for breach of s 11. No doubt this is mainly because advance notice is given in respect of the vast majority of processions.[3]

It must be emphasised that liability for either offence is limited to the organisers of the procession; it is not an offence simply to participate knowingly in a procession for which advance notice has not been given etc.

---

1   See para **6.38**.
2   1986 Act, s 11(10).
3   Of 75 protest marches observed in London in a research study in 1990–91, only three failed to give notice at all; three gave less than the minimum period and five complied only minimally. The rest exceeded the minimum requirement, the mean length of notice being 55.5 days: Waddington *Liberty and Order* (UCL Press, 1994) p 70.

6.19 These offences are unusual in their nature, since the prohibited conduct can be characterised as involving the state of affairs of being an organiser in the circumstances that the requirements as to notice have not been satisfied or (as the case may be) that one or more of the specified details of the procession differs from that stated in the notice. No act or omission at the material time on the part of the organiser need be proved. It is not necessarily going to be a defence to delegate responsibility to one of the other organisers (subject to the possible availability of a defence under s 11(8) below). Unless one of the two defences described below can be successfully claimed, an organiser can be convicted simply on the basis of an administrative error.

6.20 If the prosecution proves the prohibited conduct in one or other of the two above ways the accused must be convicted, since no mental element need be proved by the prosecution, unless the accused can prove[1] one of the two defences set out below. It is by no means obvious why a mental element does not have to be proved by the prosecution, particularly since such a requirement is made in relation to similar offences under ss 12–14.

---

1   See para **4.38**.

Defences

6.21 Section 11(8) of the 1986 Act provides that it is a defence for the accused to prove:

(a) that he did not know of the failure to satisfy the requirements of this section or (as the case may be) the difference of date, time or route;
(b) that he did not suspect the failure or (as the case may be) the difference; and
(c) that he had no reason to suspect the failure or (as the case may be) the difference.

Provided these requirements are satisfied an organiser can escape liability, for example, on the ground of delays in the post or of changes in the notice made without consultation or agreement by a co-organiser. It is clear that (a) and (b) are subjective matters, ie the magistrates must try to ascertain the actual state of mind of the accused at the time of the offence. On the other hand, (c) is a wholly objective matter, additional to the above subjective tests, ie that the accused must prove that the reasonable man in his situation would not have suspected the failure to satisfy the requirements of s 11 or (as the case may be) the difference of date, time or route.[1]

---

1   See para **3.68** fn 1.

6.22 The defence under s 11(9) is limited to the second variant of the offence. The subsection provides that, to the extent that an alleged offence turns on a difference of date, time or route, it is a defence for the accused to prove that the difference arose from something beyond his control (eg because a road on the notified route had been closed to repair a burst water main or because a hooligan element had seized control of the march) or from something done with the agreement of a police officer (of whatever rank) or by his direction, for example a condition imposed under s 12. Where the difference resulted from something done with the agreement of a police officer or by his direction, it seems particularly unfair to place the burden of proof on the accused. It is doubtful whether a failure to start on time because the band which is to lead the procession has been delayed is a circumstance beyond the organisers' control if they have decided to postpone the procession until the band arrives, but it might be different if it was the sole organiser of the procession who was unavoidably late in arriving.

6.23 Section 11(8) and (9) is open to objection on the ground that it is dangerous to allow people to be convicted of an offence unless they prove something; the burden of disproving a defence ought to be on the prosecution (once there is evidence of the defence). What is said in para **4.38** about cases where the burden of proof is placed on the accused is equally applicable here.

Arrest

6.24 There is no specific power of arrest for an offence under s 11. However, a police officer who reasonably suspects[1] that an offence under s 11 has been, or is being, committed may arrest without warrant any person whom he reasonably suspects[1] of having committed, or being in the course of committing, that offence if it appears to him that the service of a summons is impracticable or inappropriate because one of the five general arrest conditions under s 25 of PACE is satisfied.

---

1   See para **3.68** fn 1.

Imposing conditions on public processions

6.25 Conditions may be imposed under s 12 of the 1986 Act on any public procession (including one exempt from the need for advance notice) not only beforehand but also when the procession is assembling or even during it. Conditions are not, however, frequently imposed. For example, between February 1990 and New Year's Eve 1992 conditions were imposed on only four processions in the Metropolitan Police district.[1] Instead, processions will generally be subject to informal arrangements negotiated between the police and the organisers. The greatest practical importance of the power to impose conditions is that, like the power to ban under s 13, it provides a legal framework for such negotiations and gives the police bargaining power in them.[2] Conditions are likely to be imposed only where there have not been negotiations or where the police suspect that an informal arrangement will not be kept.

---

1   Waddington 'Dying in a ditch: use of police powers in public order' (1993) 21 *Int J Sociology of Law* 335 at 338.

2   As to the process of such negotiation, see Waddington *Liberty and Order* (UCL Press, 1994) ch 4.

Who can impose conditions?

6.26 The power to impose conditions on public processions is conferred on a person called 'the senior police officer'. By s 12(2) of the 1986 Act, this term means:

> '(a) in relation to a procession being held, or to a procession intended to be held in a case where persons are assembling with a view to taking part in it, the most senior in rank of the police officers present at the scene, and
>
> (b) in relation to a procession intended to be held in a case where paragraph (a) does not apply, the [...] [chief constable (or, in the case of the City of London or Metropolitan Police, the respective Commissioner of Police),[1] or the delegate of such person].'[2]

The power to impose conditions under (a) means that, if circumstances require, the 'senior police officer' can convert previously negotiated arrangements (whose breach is no offence) into formal conditions (whose breach is). Moreover, even if conditions have been imposed under (a) or (b) there is nothing to stop the senior police officer present at the scene from imposing additional conditions to those imposed by his chief constable or, indeed, to prevent any constable from overriding any conditions, by whomsoever imposed, by virtue of his common law powers relating to a breach of the peace.

Decisions about the imposition of conditions, particularly when made in advance, can involve political judgments as well as operational ones. Indeed, where the ground relied on is the risk of serious disruption to the life of the community, the element of political judgment predominates. Operational judgments have traditionally, and rightly, been entrusted to the police, but involving the police in political judgments is liable to impugn the public perception of their neutrality. It is interesting to note that the corresponding provision to s 12 in Northern Irish law has been replaced by a provision whereby the advance imposition of conditions on public processions has been entrusted instead to an independent Parades Commission by s 8 of the Public Processions (Northern Ireland) Act 1998, subject to review on application by the chief constable by the Secretary of State. It is worth noting that the political judgment aspect is recognised by ss 13 and 14A of the 1986 Act in respect of bans on public processions and trespassory assemblies, which must be made and/or approved by elected politicians.

---

1   Section 12(2)(b) uses the term 'chief officer of police'. This term is defined by s 101 of the Police Act 1996 and applied by s 5 of and Sch 1 to the Interpretation Act 1978, as meaning:
     (a)   in relation to a police force maintained for each police area (see below) outside London by a police authority, the Chief Constable;
     (b)   in relation to the Metropolitan Police force and the City of London police force, the respective Commissioner of Police.
     This definition has the effect of excluding the chief constables of entities such as the Transport Police or Ministry of Defence Police from the term 'chief officer of police' for the purposes of the 1986 Act, ss 12–15.
2   See para **6.93**.

6.27 At any time before people are 'assembling' with a view to participating in a procession only the chief constable or respective Commissioner can impose conditions (unless he has delegated his functions under s 15).[1] The Act does not say whether 'assembling' means assembling at the scene of the start point of a procession or assembling in a wider sense, such as where a group reaches the vicinity of the start or boards a train to travel to it.

Where a march is actually under way (or the intending participants are assembling), the senior police officer will be the most senior officer (by rank) present at the scene. It is submitted that where there is more than one officer present of the most senior rank, the most senior of them will be the one with the longer or longest period of service in that rank.[2] 'Present at the scene' seems to require actual physical presence there, as opposed to some kind of constructive presence away from the 'scene' (eg by radio). It is a moot point whether an officer hovering over the scene in a helicopter is 'present' at it. The senior police officer may theoretically only be of a junior rank, he may even be a probationary constable or special constable, since the power to impose conditions is conferred on '*the* senior police officer' (whose definition in (a) above is not limited by rank), and not on a senior police officer. The result is that the responsibility for imposing conditions on the spot may be in the hands of a young and inexperienced police constable. While this is unlikely in relation to large processions as a whole, it could be so in the case of a small procession. Where the procession is a large one, it is arguable that there may be more than one 'scene', in which case the 'senior police officer' present at an individual scene could impose conditions. This interpretation would be liable to produce conflicting conditions and is unnecessary when the police have instant modes of communication. In any event, the reference to the most senior officer 'present at *the* scene' in s 12(2) seems to indicate a contrary interpretation. On this interpretation, the 'scene' may be an extensive one if the procession is large; physical presence proximate to some part of it would seem to be presence at the scene.

---

1   See para **6.93**.
2   See para **7.5** fn 1.

The grounds

6.28 The senior police officer only has power to impose conditions if, having regard to the time or place at which and the circumstances in which any public procession is being held or is intended to be held[1] and to its route or proposed route, he *reasonably believes* that:

(a) it may result in serious public disorder, serious damage to property or serious disruption to the life of the community; or

(b) the purpose, whether express or not, of the persons organising it is the intimidation of others with a view to compelling them not to do an act they have a right to do, or to do an act they have a right not to do.[2]

These grounds are clearly more extensive than those which would permit the senior police officer to impose conditions under his breach of the peace powers.

For the purpose of the requirement that the senior police officer must 'reasonably believe' one of the specified matters, 'belief' is something more than 'suspicion', a term defined in para **3.68** fn 1.[3] 'Reasonably believes' means that the grounds on which the person concerned formed the belief must be sufficient to induce in a reasonable person the required belief.[4] However, it is not enough that the person concerned has reasonable grounds to believe that the specified facts exist, he must also actually believe that they do.[5]

The existence of the reasonable grounds, and of the belief founded on them, is ultimately a matter to be decided in the light of the circumstances disclosed by the evidence.

---

1   The comments in para **6.61** about the corresponding terms in s 14 are equally applicable to s 12.
2   1986 Act, s 12(1).
3   *R v Forsyth* [1997] 2 Cr App R 199, CA.
4   *McArdle v Egan* (1933) 150 LT 412, CA; *Nakkuda Ali v Jayaratne* [1951] AC 66, PC; *R v IRC, ex parte Rossminster Ltd* [1980] 1 All ER 80 at 84, 92, 103 and 104, HL.
5   See *R v Banks* [1916] 2 KB 621, CCA; *R v Harrison* [1938] 3 All ER 134, CCA, which were concerned with 'reasonable grounds for suspecting'.

Serious public disorder/serious damage

6.29 Conditions cannot be imposed simply because the senior police officer reasonably believes that there will be public disorder or damage falling short of serious disorder or damage. In such a case, conditions imposed would be invalid. A prosecution for breach of a condition would fail, and the decision to impose the condition could be challenged by judicial review (see paras **6.95–6.99** below).

'*Serious* public disorder' and '*serious* damage[1] to property' would seem to refer to the level or geographic extent of the disorder or damage. The serious disorder or damage apprehended need not be on the part of those in the procession; it suffices that it is reasonably believed that the procession will result in others causing such disorder or damage. Consequently, the opponents of a procession can, by threatening violence or damage, cause conditions to be imposed on it.

---

1   'Damage' presumably includes 'destroy'. See, further, para **6.77** fn 2.

Serious disruption

6.30 This ground is open to criticism on the bases that it is too vague (the Act provides no definition of 'serious disruption' and it is more likely than the two grounds above to engender genuine differences of opinion) and too widely drawn (arguably it renders redundant the first two grounds).[1] It certainly extends the basis for imposing a condition beyond the demands of 'public order' as that term is normally understood (and to a greater extent than any other ground); it seems to be based on the preservation of an orderly society, which is a different thing.

Of course, any public procession is liable to cause inconvenience or disruption to community life, but it will only suffice to impose conditions if the risk is of *serious* disruption to the life of the community (and whether or not there is such a risk depends partly on the place in question, eg whether it is a village or an inner city district). It will be noted that, although 'disruption' means more than inconvenience, the dividing line is vague (as is that between 'mere' disruption and serious disruption). There is a danger that this ground tilts the scales too far against those who wish to march; too far against the right to demonstrate in favour of the right to go shopping or to drive one's car.[1] 'Community' is also vague. It would seem to bear its ordinary relevant meaning, viz a group of people living, working or trading in the same locality, but this begs the question of what that locality is. In London, for example, is the locality/community in respect of a march in Oxford Street, Oxford Street, Inner London, the whole Metropolitan area, or what?[2] The narrower the answer is the more easily the test of serious disruption can be satisfied. Controlling any temptation for the senior police officer to impose conditions and thereby make policing easier on the grounds of serious disruption to the life of the community is not helped by the vagueness of those terms.

In forming a view as to the present ground, 'it is appropriate for the senior officer to take account not only of physical matters such as the disruption of traffic and the blocking of streets, but also of the annoyance and upset which may be caused to a community by a procession passing through it, if it is shown that as a consequence there is disruption to life in that community'.[3] Disruption does not have to be long-lasting in order to be serious; serious disruption can occur temporarily.[4]

Under the present heading, the police can impose conditions as to route or time in order to limit serious traffic congestion (eg in the rush hour), or to prevent a bridge being blocked, or to limit serious disruption to the owners and customers of shops adjoining the route of the procession.

It should also be noted that the reasonable belief must relate to the risk that the procession itself may result in serious disruption; it is not enough that the senior police officer reasonably believes that persons en route to, or leaving, the procession may seriously disrupt the life of the community.

The serious disruption anticipated need not be serious disruption by individual members of the procession. Consequently, it suffices if it is reasonably believed that the holding of a procession in itself is liable to lead to serious disruption of the life of the community by the opponents of it.

The Act does not provide any criteria to enable the balance to be held between the assemblers and the general public. The test is simply whether or not there is a reasonable belief that something serious may result from the assembly which would seriously disrupt the life of the community, serious disruption to community life being judged according to a reasonable person's perception of the life of the community.

---

1 See Bonner and Stone 'The Public Order Act 1986: steps in the wrong direction?' [1987] PL 202.

2 Ewing and Gearty *Freedom under Thatcher* (Clarendon Press, 1990) p 121.

3 *Re Murphy* [1991] 5 NIJB 88 at 113, per Hutton LCJ (with reference to the Northern Irish provision identical to the grounds under s 12(1), which was repealed by the Parades (Northern Ireland) Act 1998).

4 *Re Armstrong* (1992) unreported, NIQBD, cited by Hadfield 'Public order police powers and judicial review' [1993] Crim LR 915 at 922.

Intimidation

6.31 This ground empowers the police to impose conditions on the organisers of processions if they reasonably believe that the *purpose* of the organisers is the *intimidation* of others *with a view to compelling them to refrain from doing something they have a right to do* (eg to work) *or to do something they have a right not to do* (eg to refuse to join a strike). Marches by animal rights protesters on a vivisection laboratory, for example, may be made subject to conditions under the present ground if the organisers' purpose is intimidation with a view to compelling the laboratory to abandon vivisection. The words italicised constitute a limit on this ground that is more apparent than real because intimidation rarely occurs with some other end solely in view. However, it is doubtful whether an intimidatory racist march through an area inhabited by ethnic groups would fall within the present ground, unless the organisers had a view to compelling members of the groups to refrain from living there or to refrain from doing something else they had a right to do, like trading or being on the streets during the march. Of course, such a march might give rise to a risk of serious public disorder (or perhaps of serious disruption to the life of the community), in which case it could be made the subject of conditions on that ground.

The fact that there must be a reasonable belief that the *purpose* of the organisers is 'intimidation of others with a view to compelling ...' does provide some limit on the present ground. It is not enough in itself that it is reasonably believed that such intimidation will occur as a result of conduct intended to compel others to do or refrain from something. Nor is it enough if the organisers' purpose is intimidation with a view to persuading (as opposed to compelling, ie coercing); there is, however, a fine dividing line between these two concepts which is open to exploitation by the senior police officer if that officer is inclined to impose conditions.

6.32 One point which remains to be resolved is whether conditions may be imposed where the purpose of the organisers of a procession is the intimidation of *one* person. The provision speaks of the 'intimidation of others' but it would be consistent with its spirit that it should apply in such a case. There seems to be nothing in s 12 to exclude the normal rule[1] of the statutory interpretation that words in the plural include the singular.

Another point which remains to be resolved is the meaning of 'intimidation' itself. The Act does not define the term. In relation to the offence under s 241(1)(a) of the Trade Union and Labour Relations (Consolidation) Act 1992 (intimidation with a view to compelling another to abstain from doing any act which he has a legal right to do etc), 'intimidates' includes putting a person in fear by an exhibition of force or violence or the threat of force or violence, whether to persons or property.[2] If, as it is submitted would be so, a threat to cause economic loss, eg to disrupt a business, would not constitute 'intimidation', a condition could not be made in respect of a march by striking workers on their place of work, which was intended by them to disrupt business at the work place.

In any event, 'intimidate' is a strong word and would probably not extend to conduct merely inducing feelings of discomfort, as opposed to putting in fear. If it did,[3] there would be a significant extension of the law, particularly since the essence of the ground is whether a police officer reasonably believes that the organisers' purpose is intimidation.

---

1   Interpretation Act 1978, s 6.
2   Para **9.39**.
3   A Metropolitan stipendiary magistrate took the view that it did not in *Police v Reid* [1987] Crim LR 702. For a discussion of intimidation in another context, see para **9.39**.

The conditions

6.33 Section 12(1) provides that, in a case falling within the above provisions, the senior police officer may give directions imposing on the persons organising or taking part in the procession any conditions which appear to him necessary to prevent 'such' serious disorder, damage or disruption or intimidation (ie the serious disorder or the like which he reasonably believes may result from the procession), including conditions prescribing the route of the procession or prohibiting it from entering any public place specified in the direction.

Section 12 does not limit the types of condition which may be imposed. Other examples are the number of those in the procession and the number in line abreast on the route, the starting point and time and duration of the procession, the prohibition of the wearing of uniforms or masks or of the carrying of flags or banners, the use of loudhailers, the number and disposition of stewards, the provision of first aid facilities and the use of vehicles.

6.34 It will have been noted that the senior police officer may impose such conditions as 'appear to him to be necessary to prevent' (a subjective assessment) serious public disorder, serious damage, serious disruption, or the intimidation of others. Although the conditions are not required 'reasonably' to appear necessary to the senior police officer, there must be some relationship between the apprehended serious disorder or the like and a condition imposed. If there is not, the condition may be challenged in legal proceedings, as explained in paras **6.94–6.99**. This is important. Otherwise, it could be possible for a disguised, but virtually unchallengeable, ban on a particular march to be made (or for a march to be neutralised) by imposing such stringent conditions that it could not be held (or could not be held with any effect). This is particularly significant in the light of the fact that the power to ban processions under s 13 does not extend to banning a particular procession.

Procedural matters

6.35 Where a direction is given by a chief police officer by virtue of s 12(2)(b) (ie in advance of the procession or its assembly), it must be given in writing.[1] On the other hand, a direction given under s 12(2)(a) (ie during the procession or when it is assembling) need not be given in writing; clearly written notice will normally be impracticable in such a case. There are no requirements as to when the conditions (even when written) must be communicated,[2] nor as to the particular form of a direction, nor need a direction given in advance be given by a particular time before the procession (ie there is nothing corresponding to s 11). But, of course, it is in the interests of the police that the organisers (and participants) have adequate knowledge of any conditions imposed. One reason is that proof of an offence involving a breach of condition requires knowledge on the part of the accused.

---

1   1986 Act, s 12(3). As to 'writing', see para **4.7** fn 2.
2   Contrast the Metropolitan Police Act 1839, s 54, para 9 (offence of wilful disregard of, or non-compliance with, regulations or directions made by the Commissioner as to the route to be taken to prevent obstruction at times of public processions); this offence can only be committed by a person who has been acquainted with the regulations or directions. See para **6.100**.

6.36 The senior police officer present at the scene is not required to be in uniform, nor to identify himself as the senior police officer to the organisers of the procession or to participants. The absence of such requirements could theoretically be the cause of misunderstanding or confusion when he gives a direction, particularly in a situation of urgency: 'Who is he to give us orders?' could be the response. In practice, it is likely in many cases that the negotiations which will already have taken place will remove any doubts in the minds of the organisers as to who is the senior police officer, and it is unlikely that he will not be in uniform.

Offences

6.37 A person who 'organises a public procession and knowingly fails to comply with a condition' imposed under s 12 commits a summary offence, whose maximum punishment is three months' imprisonment or a fine not exceeding level 4 on the standard scale, or both.[1] As in the case of an offence under s 11, the accused must still be an organiser at the time of non-compliance. An organiser 'knowingly' fails to comply with a condition not only when he actually knows of this, but also when he is wilfully blind as to the non-compliance.[2] It must be emphasised that an organiser is not guilty of the present offence merely because the procession does not comply with a condition; he himself must have failed to comply. Thus, an organiser does not commit the offence if the breach of condition is caused by undisciplined members of the procession, although they may be guilty of the offences referred to in the next paragraph. An organiser who fails to comply has a defence if he proves[3] that the failure arose from circumstances beyond his control.[4] It would seem that one type of such circumstance would be where the conditions have been overriden by a constable under his breach of the peace powers.[5]

---

1   1986 Act, s 12(4) and (8).

2   'Knowingly' does not limit the mens rea to actual knowledge since it also includes wilful
     blindness: *Roper v Taylor's Central Garages (Exeter) Ltd* [1951] 2 TLR 284, DC; *Ross v Moss*
     [1965] 3 All ER 145, DC; *Westminster City Council v Croyalgrange Ltd* [1986] 2 All ER 353, HL.
3   See para **4.38**.
4   1986 Act, s 12(4).
5   Williams 'Processions, assemblies and the freedom of the individual' [1987] Crim LR 167 at
     172.

6.38 It remains to be decided exactly what constitutes 'organising' a procession. Clearly, someone who plans the procession in advance, in terms of date, time, route etc is an organiser (along with others who share such functions). If this was not the case, the obligation imposed by s 11 to give advance notice would be nonsensical. In *Flockhart v Robinson*,[1] Finnemore J, dissenting, stated:

> 'The mere fact that a person takes part in a procession would not of itself be enough. I do not think that the fact the defendant was the leading person in the procession would by itself be enough, although it might be some evidence to be considered ... I think organising a procession means something in the nature of arranging or getting up or planning a procession ...'

However, 'organising' is not *limited* to involvement in pre-planning. The Divisional Court in *DPP v Baillie*[2] concluded in a case where the dissemination of information about a free festival was of crucial importance (since such information was unlikely to be given publicly) that this provided sufficient evidence of organising an assembly. Subject to the obiter dictum of Lord Goddard below, this would seem to be equally applicable to a procession. The Court clearly thought this was a borderline case but considered that, in the light of the absence of a public announcement (and thus the elevation of the accused's role as a disseminator of information), there was just enough evidence to support the magistrates' decision that he was 'organising' the assembly. It did not attempt a definition of 'organising'.

Finnemore J's view that 'organising' is *limited* to arranging or planning is not correct for another reason: the majority in *Flockhart v Robinson* held that things done during a procession by someone not involved in its planning can constitute organising it. In that case D, who had earlier in the day organised a lawful procession in the City of London, was seen walking in the West End at the head of a loose formation of supporters. After a traffic check, the supporters became a compact body marching in close formation behind him, at which point, it was found as a fact, they had spontaneously and without prior arrangement become a public procession. Thereafter, D gave the members of the procession words or signs of command at traffic crossings and as to route. The majority of the Divisional Court held that he had organised the procession thereby. Lord Goddard CJ said:[3]

> ' "Organised" is not a term of art. When a person organises a procession, what does he do? A procession is not a mere body of persons: it is a body of persons moving along a route. Therefore the person who organises the route is the person who organises the procession ... By indicating or planning the route a person is in my opinion organising a procession.'

Lord Goddard added that: 'There is no other way of organising a procession.' This obiter dictum is most doubtful, there is no reason for excluding those who make other plans or arrangements from 'organising' a procession.

According to the statement which formed part of Lord Goddard's ratio decidendi, marshals and stewards are among those who 'organise' a procession. Unless 'organising' in s 11 and s 12 have different meanings, the scope of the offences under s 11 is liable to be wider than one might have expected, since s 11 seems to refer naturally to those who plan a procession in advance.

---

1   [1950] 2 KB 498 at 504–505.
2   [1995] Crim LR 426, DC.
3   [1950] 2 KB at 502–503.

6.39 By s 12(5) of the 1986 Act, a person who takes part in a public procession and knowingly[1] fails to comply with a condition imposed under s 12 is guilty of a summary offence punishable with a fine not exceeding level 3 on the standard scale, except that it is a defence under s 12(9) to prove[2] that the failure arose from circumstances beyond his control. For a conviction under s 12(5), it must be proved not only that the condition applied to the accused, and that *he* failed to comply with it (since it is irrelevant that others did not), but also that he knew that it did;[3] clearly the police must take care in the way that they publicise conditions imposed.

It is questionable whether the defence under s 12(9) will be proved if it is merely proved that there has been a breakdown of organisation or communication. On the other hand, the defence would be proved if a marcher proved that he was being inescapably borne along by the pressure of other marchers when the condition was broken. In this type of case, however, an accused would seem to have the common law defence of impossibility,[4] in respect of which he would not have more than an evidential burden.[5]

---

1   See para **6.37** fn 2.
2   See para **4.38**.
3   For a view to this effect see *Brickley v Police* (1988) *Legal Action* July 21, Crown Court on appeal (charge of corresponding offence in respect of a condition under 1986 Act, s 14).
4   The courts have sometimes construed an offence as one in which such a defence cannot operate, see, for example, *Davey v Towle* [1973] RTR 328, DC; *Sparks v Worthington* [1986] RTR 64, DC. It might be held that the effect of the defence in s 12(9) is to exclude the common law defence.
5   See, for example, *Hill v Baxter* [1958] 1 All ER 193 at 196, per Devlin J.

6.40 The offence committed by participants can be illustrated as follows. Suppose that the police have imposed the condition that a march shall not proceed down the High Street. On reaching the High Street, the first part of the march obeys the condition, but part of the march proceeds down the High Street. None of the first part of the procession commits an offence. Of those who proceed down the High Street, anyone who knows of the condition (but not any others) commits an offence unless he or she proves that the failure to comply arose from circumstances beyond his or her control.

Although no offence is committed under s 12 by those who are mere spectators at a procession or by others (such as journalists) who do not actually participate in the procession, they could be made subject to a direction under the police's breach of the peace powers, and be liable for wilfully obstructing a constable in the execution of his duty if they do not comply with such a direction.[1]

---

1   See paras **2.16** and **9.65–9.67**.

6.41 A person who incites another to commit the 'participants' offence' mentioned in para **6.39** is also guilty of a summary offence,[1] but is liable to a greater penalty (viz three months' imprisonment or a fine not exceeding level 4 on the standard scale, or both).[2] Thus, if A, a member of a procession subject to a condition, incites B to break that condition and B does so, knowing of it, A commits a more serious offence than B, whether or not he (A) also breaks the conditions. Strictly speaking, the present offence is not necessary because incitement to commit a summary offence is punishable as the common law offence of incitement; the importance of the present offence is that it provides a higher maximum punishment than is possible for the common law offence of incitement in relation to a summary offence (where the maximum is the same as for the offence incited).[3]

Incitement requires an element of persuasion or encouragement[4] or of threats or other pressure,[5] which may be implied as well as expressed. The mere expression of a hope that someone should fail to comply with a condition would not suffice. The solicitation must come to the notice of a person intended to act on it, although it need not be effective in any way.[6] If the solicitation does not reach the mind of another, because (for example) a shout soliciting the commission of the 'participants' offence' cannot be heard above the crowd or a letter is lost in the post, the person making it is not only not guilty of the present offence of incitement, but also not guilty of an attempt to commit the present offence since it is a summary offence.[7] The solicitation need not be directed to a particular person.[8]

It appears that the accused must have an intention that the person incited should take part in a public procession, knowing of the failure to comply with a condition imposed under this section.

The disparity in maximum sentence between those who organise marches or incite marchers to disregard police conditions and the rank and file reflects a perceived distinction in the gravity of the conduct in question. It is unlikely that sentences of imprisonment would be imposed on organisers or inciters, except in cases where their flagrant disregard of a condition imposed has had severe consequences or where they have persistently failed to comply with conditions.

---

1   1986 Act, s 12(9).
2   Ibid, s 12(6).
3   Magistrates' Courts Act 1980, s 45(3).
4   *R v Hendrickson* [1977] Crim LR 356, CA.
5   *Race Relations Board v Applin* [1973] 2 All ER 1190, CA; *Invicta Plastics Ltd v Clare* [1976] RTR 251, DC.
6   *R v Krause* (1902) 18 TLR 238 at 243.
7   See Criminal Attempts Act 1981, s 1, especially s 1(4).
8   *R v Most* (1881) 7 QBD 244, CCR.

European Convention on Human Rights

6.42 The imposition of conditions on a procession is an interference with the freedom of peaceful assembly guaranteed by Art 11 of the ECHR, a Convention right under the Human Rights Act 1998.[1] Whether they can be justified under Art 11(2) on the ground that they are prescribed by law and are necessary in a democratic society in the interests of public safety, for the prevention of disorder or crime or for the protection of the rights of others will depend on the facts. So will any justification under Art 10(2) in relation to any interference with the freedom of expression guaranteed by Art 10.

---

1   It has, indeed, been held that ECHR, Art 11, protects the right to organise and participate in a peaceful public demonstration: *Rassemblents Jurassien, Unité Jurassienne v Switzerland* (1979) 17 D&R 93, ECommHR.

Prohibition of processions

6.43 The prohibition of a public procession should be a measure of last resort. The ground for making an order prohibiting public processions remains the same as under the 1936 Act, viz the apprehension of serious public disorder (coupled with the insufficiency with the powers of the police to impose conditions to prevent it); the extension of the grounds for the imposition of conditions was not applied to banning orders. The power under s 13 of the 1986 Act to prohibit a procession is limited to future processions. It is inapplicable to a procession which has commenced. However, in such a case, or indeed in advance of a procession, a constable may in appropriate circumstances prohibit a procession if he reasonably believes that this is necessary to prevent a breach of the peace.[1] Wilful failure to comply with such a prohibition will amount to an offence of wilfully obstructing a constable in the execution of his duty.[2] The duration of such a prohibition would necessarily be very limited.

---

1   See para **2.16**.
2   See paras **9.65–9.67**.

6.44 So far, the use of the power originating in s 3 of the Public Order Act 1936 has been cyclical. It was used frequently up to 1951. From then until 1981 it was rarely used. Between 1982 and 1987 banning orders became far more common (on average 16 a year).[1] Between 1987 and 1993, there were no bans on processions in London,[2] and only a few in the rest of the country. Police caution in this respect may be due to a police view that it is better to control a procession than to prompt an ill-organised and hostile march or assembly in response to a ban on a procession.

---

1   *Review of Public Order Law* (Cmnd 9510, 1985) para 4.7.
2   Waddington *Liberty and Order* (UCL Press, 1994) pp 58–61.

The procedure

6.45 As with its predecessor, s 13 of the 1986 Act provides separate procedures for the provinces and for the City of London police area and Metropolitan Police district. However, both procedures depend on the relevant chief officer of police[1] reasonably believing[2] that, because of the particular circumstances existing in any district[3] or part of it (in the provinces) or in his police area or part of it (in London), the power under s 12 to impose conditions will be insufficient to prevent the holding of public processions[4] in that district/area or part from resulting in serious public disorder.[5]

Examples of cases where there may be the necessary reasonable belief would be where there have been recent public disturbances in the district (or part) or tension is running high there or where a number of processions are being planned by rival groups for the same date or period.

---

1   See para **6.26** fn 1.
2   See para **6.28**.
3   'District' in this context means a local government district (including a unitary authority area) in England or the area of a county council or county borough council (both of which types of council are unitary authorities) in Wales: Local Government Act 1972, ss 1(1), (3) and (4), 20(1) and (3), Sch 1, Pt I, and Sch 4, Pts I and II.
4   For definition, see paras **6.5–6.6**.
5   1986 Act, s 13(1) and (4).

6.46 Section 13(1) of the 1986 Act provides that, where a *chief constable* has such a reasonable belief,[1] he 'shall' (ie is required to do so)[2] apply for an order prohibiting holding of all public processions (or of any class of them) in the district or part concerned. The chief constable is not required to give the grounds for his belief. His application must specify the period (up to three months)[3] for which a ban is sought and, if a prohibition limited to a class of processions is sought, it must specify that class.

The application for an order must be made to the council of the district. On receiving such an application, a council may with the consent of the Home Secretary make an order either in the terms of the application or with such modifications as may be approved by the Home Secretary.[4] The council can refuse a request for an order. It cannot be forced to make an order by the Home Secretary. On the other hand, it cannot make one with modifications imposed by it.

An order cannot be made by a council of its own volition, however desperate the situation; an application by the chief constable is an essential prerequisite.

An order under s 13 need not be in writing,[5] but if it is not it must be recorded in writing as soon as practicable[6] after being made,[7] a tougher requirement than 'as soon as reasonably practicable', which appears in s 11 in relation to the advance notice requirement thereunder.

---

1   See para **6.28**.
2   It has been claimed that the chief constable has a discretion (Wallington 'Some implications for the policing of industrial disputes' [1987] Crim LR 180), but this is hard to reconcile with the natural meaning of 'shall' in its context. Cf the use of 'may' in the corresponding provision in the 1986 Act, s 14A, para **6.78**.
3   Ie three calendar months: Interpretation Act 1978, s 5 and Sch 1.
4   1986 Act, s 13(2).
5   See para **4.7** fn 2.
6   See para **6.9** fn 2.
7   1986 Act, s 13(6).

6.47 Under s 13(4), essentially the same provisions apply where the Commissioner of the City of London Police or the Commissioner of the Metropolitan Police has the reasonable belief referred to above. There are two important differences. One is that, if a Commissioner has the requisite reasonable belief, he '*may*' (ie is not required to do so) act under s 13(4). The second important difference is that a Commissioner himself makes a banning order (subject to the consent of the Home Secretary); he does not have to apply to a council for it to make an order. At the time of writing, the Home Secretary is the police authority for the two London forces. The provisions of s 13(4) will not be affected when the

Metropolitan Police Authority created by the Greater London Authority Act 1999, begins operations. The reason seems to be that in the heart of London (Trafalgar Square, Westminster and Whitehall) at least, many processions are of a national nature, be they State Processions or protest marches, and that as national considerations are at issue it would be inappropriate for a local authority's consent to be required.

6.48 The involvement of local councils is said to add the necessary elements of local knowledge and political accountability, and the involvement of the Home Secretary to add political accountability and consistency, in the making of orders.[1] By way of comparison, in Scotland, the Civic Government (Scotland) Act 1982 empowers a local authority to ban an individual procession, after consulting the chief constable; ministerial consent is not required. This can, however, be contrasted with Northern Ireland where bans on public processions can only be imposed by the Secretary of State for Northern Ireland after consultation where practicable with the independent Parades Commission and the Chief Constable of the RUC.[2]

The involvement of the local council can have disadvantages. One is that it may impart an undesirable degree of party political controversy into the decision to ban a march.[3] Another is that the involvement of the local council and the Home Secretary is unnecessarily cumbersome; speed of response is often of the essence. Another disadvantage is that a procession in one district may have serious repercussions elsewhere, and therefore its prohibition is not an appropriate matter for a local authority, and that the exclusion of the local council from the process would avoid the need for a chief constable to have to seek prohibition order after prohibition order from different councils in his area if a march is to go through different districts or if the organisers keep switching it from district to district. Imagine the complications which could ensue if some district councils were agreeable to a ban and others refused to order it.

---

1   *Review of Public Order Law* (Cmnd 9510, 1985) para 4.15.
2   Public Processions (Northern Ireland) Act 1998, s 11.
3   *Review of the Public Order Act 1936 and Related Legislation* (Cmnd 7891, 1980), para 50.

Notice of bans

6.49 There is no requirement for the giving of notice of a banning order, although no doubt the local authority or Home Secretary will take steps to do so, partly because otherwise the procession will take place and partly because criminal liability for breach of an order depends on knowledge of its existence. Nevertheless, it is unfortunate that certain minimal requirements, in terms of the nature of the advance publicity and the time at which notice must be given, have not been imposed.

Terms of a ban

6.50 Like an order under s 3 of the 1936 Act, an order under s 13 may only prohibit all public processions or any class of public procession specified in it in the district/area or part concerned. 'Class of public procession' is a somewhat vague term but it does not seem to have caused difficulties in practice and the term does provide flexibility to deal with the wide range of situations in which it may be necessary to make a prohibition order. 'Class of procession' can be defined by inclusion (eg 'processions of a political character') or by exclusion. In *Kent v*

Metropolitan Police Commissioner,[1] a 28-day ban on all processions held in the Metropolitan Police district 'except those traditionally held on May 1 to celebrate May Day and those of a religious character customarily held' was upheld on an application for its judicial review. The most common type of ban is a class ban prohibiting 'all public processions except those of a religious, educational, festive or ceremonial character commonly held'.

The absence of a power under s 13 to ban a single procession results in some unfairness because 'the innocent [ie those who were not the cause of a ban] suffer with the guilty'.[2] A proposal[2] for such a power was not enacted because of a fear that a specific-ban power would leave the police open to allegations of political bias.[3] It would, however, have helped to prevent the manipulation of the present system whereby one group can effectively stop another from marching, even though the latter's march might well have been peaceful, by the expedient of indicating an intention to march itself at the same time, anticipating correctly that this will lead to a ban on marches. It would seem that if it was known that only one march was intended on a particular day a ban of that single march could be achieved by the simple expedient of a blanket or class ban. This would not be an abuse of power. In addition, there is no reason why a ban on a single march should not be imposed under the power to prevent a breach of the peace.

An order can be revoked or varied by a subsequent order made in the same way, ie in accordance with the procedures set out in paras **6.46** and **6.47**.[4] It is uncertain whether an order can be relaxed for a particular procession in this way, but it is submitted that to permit this would be inconsistent with s 13(1) or (4), as the case may be.

There is nothing to prevent a fresh order being made in the same or different terms on the expiry of an earlier order.

---

1   (1981) *The Times*, 15 May, CA.
2   *Review of Public Order Law* (Cmnd 9510, 1985) para 4.14.
3   In *Christians against Racism and Fascism v UK* (1980) 21 D&R 138, the wish to avoid
     discrimination was accepted by the European Commission on Human Rights as a justification
     for blanket bans.
4   1986 Act, s 13(5).

6.51 Banning orders in wide terms can seriously limit the right to demonstrate and to protest of groups who are not responsible for the disturbances etc which have resulted in the order. For example, in the early 1980s, after race riots in Brixton and other disturbances, a series of orders in similar terms to those in the order in *Kent v Metropolitan Police Commissioner*[1] were made by the Metropolitan Police Commissioner (with the Home Secretary's consent). The Metropolitan Police district covers a densely populated area of 786 square miles. The effect of the series of bans was that, during their period of operation, seven CND marches, a student march to the House of Commons, a procession by a fair and a carnival procession in Fulham and other processions were all banned, even though the bans had been caused by other people's disturbances.

Although an order under s 13 can prohibit public processions for up to three months, orders will not normally have this duration, but a much shorter one. They may be as short as 24 hours (and could theoretically be even shorter), although a weekend is the most common duration.[2] Bans for longer than 30 days have been exceptional.[3]

1   (1981) *The Times*, 15 May, CA.
2   HC Standing Committee G: Report cols 630, 664 and 665 (1986).
3   Marston and Tain *Public Order Offences* (1995) p 123.

Offences

6.52 A person who 'organises[1] a public procession the holding of which he knows[2] is prohibited by virtue of an order' under s 13, is guilty of a summary offence, for which the maximum penalty is three months' imprisonment or a fine not exceeding level 4 on the standard scale, or both.[3] It would seem that this offence can be committed by organising a banned march before it takes place, and even if it does not occur.

A person who takes part in a public procession, knowing[2] that its holding is prohibited by virtue of an order under s 13, is also guilty of a summary offence,[4] as is someone who incites[5] another to commit this offence.[6] A person who commits the former offence is liable to a fine not exceeding level 3 on the standard scale.[7] A person convicted of incitement under s 13(9) is punishable in the same way as an organiser.[8]

Unlike the corresponding offences under s 12, the offences relating to organisers and participants are not provided with any special defence.

1   See the comments about organising in paras **6.37–6.38**. The wording of the present offence is more amenable to the possibility of convicting an organiser of it of committing the offence before any procession occurs in the circumstances referred to there.
2   'Knowledge' has the same meaning as in s 12, see para **6.37** fn 2.
3   1986 Act, s 13(7) and (11).
4   Ibid, s 13(8).
5   See para **6.41**.
6   1986 Act, s 13(9).
7   Ibid, s 13(12).
8   Ibid, s 13(13).

European Convention on Human Rights

6.53 The banning power under s 13 might appear to be in breach of Arts 10 and 11 of the ECHR on the ground that banning a march anticipated as peaceful could not be justified under Arts 10(2) or 11(2) as being necessary in a democratic society to prevent disorder or crime or to protect the rights and freedoms of others. However, in *Christians against Racism and Fascism v UK*,[1] the European Commission on Human Rights held that a two-month ban on processions in London, which was intended to prevent marches by the National Front, was justified in the interests of public safety where the risk of disruption or violence (not necessarily on the part of the marchers) outweighed the restriction on the freedom of peaceful assembly. It therefore rejected as manifestly ill-founded an argument that a ban under the predecessor to s 13 contravened Art 11, since there was a real danger of disorder which, it concluded, could not be prevented by a less stringent measure. In *Platform 'Ärtze für das Leben' v Austria*,[2] it was held by the European Court of Human Rights that there is a positive obligation on the police to take 'reasonable and appropriate measures' to provide protection for a peaceful demonstration against violent disturbance by counter-demonstrators, so that a threat of violent disruption could not of itself justify banning a peaceful demonstration if disorder could be prevented by less far-reaching methods.

1   (1980) 21 D&R 138, ECommHR.
2   (1988) Ser A, no 139; 13 EHRR 20, ECtHR.

THE LAW ON PUBLIC ASSEMBLIES

6.54 Public assemblies are more common than public processions, and their possible range is wide. Examples are demonstrations outside embassies, pickets and demonstrations in support of pickets, street carnivals (such as that held in Notting Hill), rallies of scooterists at seaside resorts, pop festivals, and football matches and other sporting events (whether there are spectators or not). Sometimes, of course, a public assembly becomes a public procession (just as a public procession can become a public assembly when it stops at its destination); when those assembled become an assembly on the move to a destination, the provisions on public processions mentioned above become applicable.

6.55 Until the 1986 Act, there were no general statutory powers specifically designed to control public assemblies, although in appropriate circumstances they could be, and can still be, banned or subjected to conditions by the police under their common law powers associated with their duty to deal with or prevent a breach of the peace, which were explained in Chapter 2.[1] In addition, the statutory provisions described in paras **6.100–6.103** can apply to many demonstrations (eg a sit-down in a road or street). Moreover, many local authorities have passed by-laws dealing with public meetings in their area.[2]

1   Nothing in the 1986 Act affected the common law powers to deal with or prevent a breach of
      the peace: 1986 Act, s 40(4).
2   See paras **9.97–9.99**.

6.56 In the light of major disorder associated with static demonstrations in the 1970s and early 1980s, the then Government decided[1] that it was no longer acceptable that they should be completely exempt from control, and that the police should have statutory preventive powers to minimise the risk of disorder or disruption at public assemblies by imposing conditions. On the other hand, the Government rejected a requirement of advance notice[2] on the ground that, in the light of the large number of public assemblies, the administrative burden would far outweigh the information gain.[3] The provisions enabling conditions to be imposed on those organising or taking part in public assemblies are contained in s 14 of the 1986 Act. Unlike the common law power referred to above, conditions can be imposed well in advance of the public assembly, ie at a time when a breach of the peace is not imminent. The comments in para **6.42** about the relationship of s 12 of the 1986 Act to Arts 10 and 11 of the ECHR are equally applicable to s 14.

1   *Review of Public Order Law* (Cmnd 9510, 1985) para 5.2.
2   The Home Affairs Select Committee had recommended an advance notice period of 72
      hours.
3   *Review of Public Order Law* (Cmnd 9510, 1985) para 5.4.

Imposing conditions on public assemblies

What is a 'public assembly' under s 14?

6.57 Section 14 of the 1986 Act is limited to 'public assemblies', which are defined by s 16 as assemblies of 20 or more people in a 'public place' which is wholly or partly open to the air. It is noteworthy that no minimum number is prescribed for a public procession.

'Assembly' is not defined by the 1986 Act, nor is there a common law definition. The *Shorter Oxford English Dictionary* defines an 'assembly' as 'gathering ... together, the state of being collected or gathered. The coming together of persons or things, gathering of persons, a number of people together.' In the context of a non-public order offence, the Divisional Court has held that an 'assembly' means no more than a gathering of persons, and one which could be stationary or in motion.[1] It has been suggested that the concept of an 'assembly' is probably wider than the term 'meeting' and includes any coming together of persons, including processions, political vigils, pickets, prayer meetings, demonstrations, a group at a cenotaph ceremony, families watching the changing of the guard, flag sellers acting in concert, sandwich men walking in a line abreast and a cycling club en route.[2] Where there is a gathering moving along a route in an orderly fashion, it is a procession[3] as well as an assembly, and is therefore better dealt with under the wider statutory powers in respect of public processions. On the other hand, a group of 20 or more demonstrators walking round in circles outside a foreign embassy, or 20 or more solstice celebrants walking round Stonehenge in circles, would constitute an assembly only. It would seem irrelevant whether those gathered are standing, sitting, crawling and so on. There is no need for the members of the gathering to share a common purpose, although often they will.

---

1   *DPP v Roffey* [1959] Crim LR 283, DC.
2   *Brownlie's Law of Public Order and National Security* (1981) p 31.
3   See para **6.6**.

6.58 To be a public assembly, the assembly of 20 or more must be held in a public place. Assemblies held in a private place are not covered by s 14. The definition of 'public place' in s 16 of the 1986 Act was set out in para **6.5**.

The assembly must also be held in a place wholly or partly open to the air. Assemblies in a wholly enclosed public place are not covered by s 14 because it was thought that to apply the condition-making power to them would tilt the balance too far against the freedoms of expression and of assembly and because serious public disorder was less common at indoor meetings.[1] The reference to a place partly open to the air gets round the problems which might arise if, for example, the assembly consisted of people sitting in the grandstands of a football ground. For a further discussion of what is meant by a place partly in the open air in another context, see para **7.72**.

Assemblies in a private place or wholly indoors can, of course, be regulated under the powers of the police to prevent a breach of the peace.

---

1   *Review of Public Order Law* (Cmnd 9510, 1985) para 8.17.

6.59 Provided that they satisfy the definition of 'public assembly', there are no limits on the types of assembly which may be subjected to conditions. In particular, there is no exemption for assemblies of pickets who, in contemplation or furtherance of a trade dispute, are acting in accordance with s 220 of the Trade Union and Labour Relations (Consolidation) Act 1992 for the purpose only of peacefully communicating information, or peacefully persuading others to abstain from working. Given the seriousness of the grounds for the imposition of a condition (para **6.60**), there is no good reason why any public assembly should be exempt. Properly conducted assemblies, *including picketing in accordance with s 220 of the Act of 1992*, are unlikely to satisfy one of the grounds for the imposition of a condition (although this may not be so if the assembly is threatened or opposed by opposition groups).

Who can impose conditions, and when, and on whom?

6.60 Conditions may only be imposed if the 'senior police officer', having regard to the time or place at which and the circumstances in which a public assembly is being held or is intended to be held, reasonably believes[1] that one of the specified grounds are satisfied.[2] These grounds, which are the same as apply to the imposition of conditions on a public procession, are that:

(a) the assembly may result in serious public disorder, serious damage to property or serious disruption to the life of the community; or

(b) the purpose of the persons organising it is the intimidation of others with a view to compelling them not to do an act they have a right to do, or to do an act they have a right not to do. The obvious example of a situation where this ground might be satisfied is non-peaceful picketing.

'Senior police officer' bears a similar meaning as in the case of the imposition of conditions on public processions.[3] Where an assembly is being held, the term means the most senior in rank of the police officers present at the scene; where an assembly is intended to be held it means chief officer of police, ic the chief constable or (in London) the relevant Commissioner. Unlike the corresponding provision in s 12, the definition in s 14(2) does not specifically deal with where the participants are assembling; its wording suggests that conditions may be imposed only by the chief constable or Commissioner since the assembly is still at the 'intended' as opposed to 'being held' stage. This would seem to be highly impractical.

Conditions may be imposed by the senior police officer on the persons organising or taking part in the assembly. They may be imposed either in writing or orally, unless they are imposed in relation to an assembly intended to be held (in which case the chief constable or Commissioner must give them in writing[4]).[5]

---

1   See para **6.28**.
2   1986 Act, s 14(1).
3   See paras **6.26–6.27**.
4   See para **4.7** fn 2.
5   1986 Act, s 14(3).

6.61 The opening words of s 14(1) of the 1986 Act are: 'If the senior police officer, having regard to the time or place at which and the circumstances in which any public assembly is being held or is intended to be held, reasonably believes...'

This means that the valid exercise of the power to make conditions depends on a public assembly as defined by s 16 being *in fact* held or intended. It is not enough that the senior police officer reasonably believes that such an assembly is being held or is intended. In addition, despite the reference to the need for the senior police officer to have regard to the 'time *or* place' at which any public assembly is being held or is intended to be held appearing to be disjunctive, both time and place must be known before the power to impose conditions can be exercised.[1] In respect of the place, this is self-evident because, unless one knows where an intended assembly is going to be held, one cannot be certain whether or not it is going to be held in a public place which is wholly or partly in the open air (ie whether it will be a public assembly). While the time of the assembly must be known, it is submitted that, while it need not be known precisely, it must be possible to pin it down to a particular period. These points gain support from the rather patchy judgment in this respect of McCowan LJ, with whom Buxton J agreed, in *DPP v Baillie*,[2] where a direction containing conditions had been made in respect of a proposed assembly, whose precise location was never disclosed (all that was known was that one should go to Andover or to Crawley Down, north of Andover) at a particular weekend (or possibly a series of weekends). In these circumstances it was held that the direction did not come within s 14(1).

---

1   This is implicit in *DPP v Baillie* [1995] Crim LR 426, DC.
2   Above. This is a brief report. The transcript is available on LEXIS.

Conditions that may be imposed

6.62 Section 14(1) of the 1986 Act provides that the senior police officer may give directions imposing on those organising or taking part in the assembly such conditions as appear to him necessary[1] to prevent disorder, damage, disruption or intimidation of the type described above. This corresponds to s 12(1). However, 'in order to prevent the imposition of conditions whose effect would be tantamount to a ban',[2] the provision is more restrictive since, unlike s 12, it limits conditions to those which prescribe the place at which the assembly may be (or continue to be) held, its maximum duration, or the maximum number of persons who may constitute it.[3] Thus, demonstrators and the like can be told where to assemble or stand, for how long they can do so and how many may do so, but not (for example) when the assembly must commence or whether loudhailers may be used or about what may be worn or displayed.[4] Presumably, conditions about where an assembly may be held include negative ones (ie as to where it may not be held).

---

1   See para **6.34**.
2   *Review of Public Order Law* (Cmnd 9510, 1985) para 5.6.
3   1986 Act, s 14(1).
4   Other matters of this type may be dealt with by other parts of the law, eg those relating to uniforms, offensive weapons and threatening, abusive or insulting behaviour.

6.63 It has been argued that a condition cannot be imposed reducing the numbers at an assembly below 20 'because the group is no longer an assembly'.[1] While the point about the numerical condition which may be imposed is correct, as explained below, the reason would seem not to be. The reason why the point is correct lies in the wording of s 14(1) of the 1986 Act, the relevant parts of which are:

> 'If the senior police officer, having regard to the time or place at which and the circumstances in which *any public assembly* is being held or is intended to be held, reasonably believes ... he may give directions imposing on the persons organising or taking part in *the assembly* such conditions as to the place at which the assembly may be (or continue to be) held, *its* maximum duration, or the maximum number of persons who may constitute *it* ...'.[2]

From this, it can be seen that 'it' at the end of this quotation refers to the anticipated (or existing) *public assembly*. An assembly will cease to be a 'public assembly' if its numbers fall below 20 with the result that a condition that an assembly must constitute a number below that will not be a condition on the number of persons who can constitute a public assembly. Provided, however, that its requirements are satisfied, the common law power to prevent a breach of the peace might be utilised by the police to reduce the number at an assembly below 20.

---

1   Thornton *Public Order Law* (1987) p 154.
2   Italics added.

6.64 The limitation on the type of conditions which may be imposed is intended to prevent the imposition of conditions whose effect would be equivalent to the prohibition of the assembly. Nevertheless, there is the potential here for conditions to be imposed which require a public assembly in the open air to be re-sited so far away as to render it impossible to hold it or which render it less effective or completely ineffectual for some other reason. A vigil limited to five people across the road from the place in question is going to be far less effective than one of 100 people at the doors of the place itself. It all depends on what the 'senior police officer' believes to be necessary. As with the imposition of conditions on processions, there is a danger of conditions being imposed which are tantamount to disguised bans or which, at least, deprive a demonstration of any effect on its intended target. The power is controversial. It involves the police in making what will inevitably be regarded as a political decision, and it requires sensitivity in its exercise if freedom of assembly and confidence in the police are not to be undermined.

6.65 The width of the present power is shown by the fact that if they reasonably apprehend (say) serious public disorder the police could even impose conditions limiting the number of spectators at a football match. Conditions could also be imposed (on the ground of serious disruption to the life of the community) on static demonstrations outside embassies or which block a road; conditions here might relate to the number of demonstrators or the duration or position of the demonstration. On the other hand, it is not easy to see how conditions could validly be imposed on a peaceful group of parents protesting outside the council offices about the lack of zebra crossings in their area, or on a small peaceful picket outside a furriers' to persuade customers not to buy furs, since one of the above conditions (eg reasonable belief in serious public disorder) is very unlikely to be satisfied, although another offence may be committed, for example obstruction of the highway.

6.66 An example of a direction under s 14 is provided by that in *DPP v Baillie*,[1] which was held invalid for the reason explained in para **6.61**.

'Re: PROPOSED FESTIVAL ON 12th JUNE ET SEQUENTES AT NW HAMPSHIRE

Within the meaning of Section 14, Public Order Act 1986 this event or any similar event of the type proposed is a public assembly which may result in serious public disorder, serious damage or serious disruption to the life of the community.

You are hereby directed to satisfy the following conditions: –

1. Any event must be licenced in accordance with the Local Government (Miscellaneous Provisions) Act 1982 in respect of Public Entertainment and Environmental Health.
2. The place will be subject to advance agreement with the Police to ensure the life of the community is not disrupted by noise nuisance from whatever source associated with the event.
3. The Maximum Duration will be subject to advance agreement with the Police to ensure there is no public disorder or disruption to the life of the community caused by noise at unsociable hours.
4. The maximum number of persons who constitute the assembly will be subject to advance agreement with the Police to ensure:
   (i) There is no public disorder caused by overcrowding and/or inadequate lighting.
   (ii) There is no damage caused to roadside verges and neighbouring property resulting from inadequate arrangements for off street parking.
   (iii) There is no damage or disruption to the life of the community resulting from inadequate sanitary arrangements.
   (iv) There is no disruption to the life of the community resulting from too great a volume of traffic for the access and egress routes to and from the assembly.

You are advised that a person who organises or takes part in an assembly and fails to comply with a condition under this section is guilty of an offence and liable to arrest.

(Signed)

Assistant Chief Constable'

The Divisional Court in *DPP v Baillie* did not comment on the validity of the conditions as such, but it is arguable that condition 1 was invalid because it does not as such refer to the place, duration or numbers of the assembly, as opposed to the legally necessary attribute (a licence) of the use (a festival) to which the proposed place (wherever that was) was to be put. On the other hand, the condition could be construed as a condition as to the place at which the assembly had to be held, ie a place licensed under the Local Government (Miscellaneous Provisions) Act 1982.

The other three conditions are questionable on the ground of vagueness because they depend for their resolution on the matters in question being agreed in advance.

---

1   See para **6.61** fns 1 and 2.

6.67 The formal imposition of conditions under s 14 is uncommon. As with s 12, the greater significance of s 14 is that organisers of public assemblies will informally agree (and be more prepared to agree) to certain matters, knowing that, if they do not, conditions relating to those matters can be imposed.

Offences

6.68 Section 14(4)–(6) provides summary offences dealing with those who organise or participate in a public assembly and knowingly[1] fail to comply with a condition imposed under s 14, or who incite[2] another so to participate, which correspond to those relating to public processions, and the same comments apply as in relation to them. Likewise, a person charged with the offence of organising or participating has a defence if he proves[3] that the non-compliance was due to circumstances beyond his control.

The nature of an assembly means that what is said about 'organising' in respect of a procession[4] is not wholly applicable. It appears from the decision in *DPP v Baillie*[5] that a purveyor of information as to the time and place of an assembly can be an 'organiser' if this role is of crucial importance. This suggests that 'organiser' is to be interpreted liberally. In this case, D published his telephone number as a declared source of information about the time and location of free festivals. He directed some callers (who were under-cover police officers) on a Friday to Andover, and then to Crawley Down, with instructions to ring back, indicating that there would be a festival that weekend. The police imposed various conditions, set out in para **6.66**, on the assembly. D continued to give the directions. The Divisional Court upheld the Crown Court's decision to allow D's appeal against conviction for knowingly failing to comply, as an organiser of an assembly, with a condition imposed under s 14. The Divisional Court held that there was just sufficient evidence for a prima facie case that D was an organiser as his role as the purveyor of information as to the time and place of the festival was of crucial importance. It held, however, that there was insufficient evidence to show that the police were 'having regard to the time or place at which and the circumstances in which any public assembly is being held or intended to be held … [W]e do not even know that the intended assembly was going to be held in a public place as defined in s 16 of the Act'. The Divisional Court left open the question whether the 'organiser' offence could be committed before the public assembly to which the direction containing conditions referred was held. While this point may seem to be of obvious importance where the assembly in question is never held or when there is still time for compliance before the assembly is held, it is impossible to understand how any of the conditions could be broken by an 'organiser' before the assembly was held.

Since there will no longer be a public assembly if numbers fall below 20, and since the conditions imposed only apply to such an assembly, none of these offences can be committed at a time when the assembly has fallen below that level, although one of them could be committed at a later stage if the numbers assembled have then reached 20 or more.

By s 14(8)–(10), the maximum punishment is the same as for the corresponding offences relating to processions.[6]

---

1   See para **6.37** fn 2.
2   See para **6.41**.
3   See para **4.38**.
4   See para **6.38**.
5   [1995] Crim LR 426, DC.
6   See paras **6.37**, **6.39** and **6.41**.

Prohibition of trespassory assemblies

6.69 Sections 70 and 71 of the Criminal Justice and Public Order Act 1994 inserted into the 1986 Act ss 14A, 14B and 14C, which respectively provide a general statutory power for the first time to prohibit an assembly in the open air, if it is trespassory, provide various offences in relation to the contravention of a prohibition, and provide a power to stop people proceeding to a banned assembly.

When the Public Order Act 1986 was drafted, the Government decided against a power to ban static demonstrations on the ground that this would be a substantial limitation on the freedoms of expression and of assembly which would go further than strictly necessary, particularly as assemblies were a more important means of exercising freedom of speech than marches.[1] Sections 14A–14C mark a limited, compromise position based on a perceived need to protect communities from the risk of serious disruption caused by trespassory assemblies and to protect ancient monuments from damage caused by assemblies, such as 'free festivals' attracting 'New Age Travellers' and assemblies at Stonehenge at the summer solstice.

Previously, the only preventive power, a limited one, available was the common law power to prevent a reasonably apprehended imminent breach of the peace. This power extends to prohibiting a meeting in appropriate circumstances,[2] but it does not cover many of the anticipated situations covered by s 14A of the 1986 Act.

1   *Review of Public Order Law* (Cmnd 9510, 1985) para 5.3.
2   See para **2.16**.

6.70 The power under s 14A of the 1986 Act to prohibit a trespassory assembly is limited to future assemblies. It is inapplicable if an assembly has commenced; in such a case, however, a constable may be able to prohibit the continuance of the assembly, if he reasonably believes that this is necessary to prevent an imminent breach of the peace.[1] Failure to comply with such a prohibition amounts to the offence of wilfully obstructing a constable in the execution of his duty.[2] In addition, in the circumstances covered by ss 61 or 69 of the Criminal Justice and Public Order Act 1994, a police officer may direct trespassers to leave land in the open air. Nevertheless, not all assemblies caught by the preventive power under s 14A will, when they occur, be susceptible to the exercise of the above powers.

1   See para **2.16**.
2   See paras **9.65–9.67**.

The grounds for prohibition

6.71 As in the case of the powers under s 13 of the Public Order Act 1986 to ban processions, s 14A of the 1986 Act provides separate procedures for the provinces and for the City of London police area and the Metropolitan Police district. Both procedures depend on the relevant chief officer of police[1] reasonably believing[2] that an assembly is intended to be held in his police area at a place on land in the open air to which the public has no right of access or only a limited right of access and that the assembly:

(a) is likely to be held without the permission of the occupier of the land or to conduct itself in such a way as to exceed the limits of any permission of his or the public's right of access; and

(b) may result –
    (i) in serious disruption to the life of the community; or
    (ii) where the land, or a building or monument on it, is of historical, architectural, archaeological or scientific importance, in significant damage to the land, building or monument.[3]

The power to prohibit can operate only where the police have advance notice of the assembly. Clearly, problems can arise in the case of ad hoc assemblies, especially if organisers use covert means to organise them. Unlike public processions, there is no requirement for advance notice.

---

1   See para **6.26** fn 1.
2   See para **6.28**.
3   1986 Act, s 14A(1) and (4).

Type of assembly

6.72 The chief officer of police must reasonably believe[1] that an 'assembly' is intended to be held at a place on land in the open air to which the public has no right of access or only a limited right of access.

For the purposes of s 14A of the 1986 Act, an 'assembly' has the same meaning as in s 14 viz an assembly of 20 or more people.[2] The Act does not further define an 'assembly'. What is said in para **6.57** about this term is equally applicable here. It is irrelevant whether or not the assembly is a public one. An open-air sit-in by students or workers on private premises, for example, is an assembly for the purposes of s 14A.

There is no exemption for assemblies of pickets who, in contemplation or furtherance of a trade dispute, are acting in accordance with s 220 of the Trade Union and Labour Relations (Consolidation) Act 1992 for the purpose only of peacefully communicating information, or peacefully persuading others to abstain from working.

---

1   See para **6.28**.
2   1986 Act, s 14A(9).

6.73 It is irrelevant whether the anticipated assembly is open to the public or is private, but it must be held on land in the open air.[1] This can be contrasted with the power to impose conditions on a public assembly under s 14 of the Public Order Act 1986; there the assembly may be held wholly or partly in the open air. The land on which it is reasonably believed that the assembly is intended to be held must be land to which the public has no legal right of access or only a limited right of access. 'Land' here includes land forming part of any highway. 'Public' includes a section of the public, a term discussed in another context in para **5.27**. In relation to a 'limited right of access by the public to land', this means that their use of it is restricted to use for a particular purpose (as in the case of a highway) or is subject to other restrictions.[1] Parks, public squares in towns and places like Stonehenge are all land to which the public have a limited right of access.

---

1   1986 Act, s 14A(9).

Lack of permission or excess of permission or right

6.74 The anticipated assembly must reasonably be believed to be trespassory in nature. The chief officer of police must reasonably believe[1] that the intended assembly *is likely* to be held without the permission of the occupier of the land or to conduct itself in such a way as to exceed the limits of any permission of his or the limits of the public's right of access.[2] For this purpose, the occupier is the person entitled to possession of the land by virtue of an estate or interest held by him in the land.[3]

This is a major limitation on s 14A of the 1986 Act. Cases where there is a reasonable belief that serious disruption will be caused by mass meetings held in public squares in towns, or in parks, with the permission of the occupier are not caught, unless it is reasonably believed that the meetings are likely to conduct themselves in such a way as to exceed the terms of the permission. Nor, likewise, are they caught in relation to agricultural shows or fetes held with such permission.

Because 'land' in s 14A includes land forming part of the highway, it follows, for example, that an intended assembly of 20 or more on the highway (which may be trespassory, depending on the circumstances)[4] can be the trigger for an order under s 14A.

---

1   See para **6.28**.
2   1986 Act, s 14A(1)(a).
3   Ibid, s 14A(9).
4   See para **6.86**.

Serious disruption or significant damage

6.75 The chief officer must reasonably believe that the intended assembly may result in:

(a) serious disruption to the life of the community; or
(b) where the land, or a building or monument on it is of historical, architectural, archaeological or scientific importance, in significant damage to the land, building or monument.

It will be noted that the reasonable belief need merely be that one of these two things *may* occur, which is a lower standard than that of likelihood in relation to the trespass element.

6.76 The first of these alternative grounds is the same as one which applies to the imposition of conditions on a public procession or assembly; what is said in para **6.30** is equally applicable here mutatis mutandis.[1]

It could be said that 'serious disruption to the life of the community' covers serious public disorder, but the fact that ss 12 and 14 distinguish serious public disorder, serious damage and serious disruption to the life of the community suggests that in s 14A 'serious disruption to the life of the community' does not include serious disorder or damage. The fact that the alternative ground specifically deals with damage to real property in the case of historic sites etc seems to confirm this view. Thus, it would seem that a reasonable belief that an assembly is likely to lead to theft, or pollution (damage) through lack of toilet facilities, or damage to woodland when it is vandalised for firewood cannot provide a ground for an order. On the other hand, 'serious disruption to the life of the community' certainly is capable of covering the obstruction of the highway or the generation of noise, if sufficiently serious.

The Act does not provide any criteria to enable the balance to be held between the assemblers and the general public. The test is simply whether or not there is a reasonable belief that something may result from the assembly that would seriously disrupt the life of the community, serious disruption to community life being judged according to a reasonable person's perception of the life of the community.

---

1   Also see Fitzpatrick and Taylor 'Trespassers *might* be prosecuted' [1998] EHRLR 292 at 298.

6.77 The second alternative ground, a reasonable belief, where the land, or a building or monument on it, is of historical, architectural, archaeological or scientific importance, that the trespassory assembly may result in significant damage to the land, building or monument,[1] is aimed at incursions such as those by mass trespassers at Stonehenge at summer solstice time.

Neither s 14A nor any other provision defines what makes land, or a building or monument on it, of historical, architectural, archaeological or scientific importance, which is a matter of objective fact (as opposed to reasonable belief on the part of the chief officer). It would seem indisputable that this terminology includes scheduled monuments and designated areas of archaeological import-ance within the meaning of the Ancient Monuments and Archaeological Areas Act 1979, such as Stonehenge, ancient monuments and historic buildings managed by the Historic Buildings and Monuments Commission under the National Heritage Act 1983, and sites of special scientific interest listed under the Wildlife and Countryside Act 1981. However, there is no reason why other land, buildings or monuments, for example those vested in the National Trust, should not be covered if they are of importance in one of the specified ways. Once one gets outside premises covered by the three Acts, s 14A becomes uncertain in its application, since the question is raised about the requisite importance of them. It would have been better if the present ground had been limited to land, monuments and buildings specified by the three statutes. It would have covered the types of case at which the ground is aimed. Yet again, the vagueness of a public order law provision can be criticised. It is arguable that the reference to 'historical importance' is insufficiently precise to satisfy the requirement of 'prescribed by law' made by Art 11(2) of the ECHR.

In relation to the requirement that it must be reasonably believed that the assembly may result in significant damage, 'significant damage' would seem to mean more than minimal damage but not to require the damage to be serious. If it meant 'serious damage', that term would have been used as in ss 13 and 14 of the 1986 Act. Unlike 'damage' in s 61 of the Criminal Justice and Public Order Act 1994, 'damage' in s 14A is not expressly stated to include the deposit of any polluting matter, although such deposit may well constitute damage in the ordinary legal sense of that term.[2] The deposit of polluting matter is liable to have particularly serious consequences in some areas of special scientific interest.

1   As opposed to property in or on them.
2   'Damage' would seem to bear the same meaning as under the Criminal Damage Act 1971,
     save that it must include 'destruction'. Property is damaged if it suffers permanent or
     temporary physical harm or permanent or temporary impairment of its use or value: *Morphitis
     v Salmon* [1990] Crim LR 48, DC; *R v Whiteley* [1991] Crim LR 436, CA. Grass can be
     damaged by being trampled on: *Gayford v Chouler* [1898] 1 QB 316, and land can be damaged
     by having rubbish dumped on it: *R v Henderson* (1984) unreported, CA; such conduct impairs
     the utility or value of the grass or land.

The procedure

6.78 Where a chief constable has a reasonable belief in one of the grounds set out above, he may[1] apply for an order prohibiting for a period specified in the order the holding of all trespassory assemblies in the district or a part of it.[2]

As in the case of a banning order under s 13, the application must be made to the council of the district[3] in which the trespassory assembly is believed to be intended to take place. On receiving such an application, the council of the district may, with the consent of the Home Secretary, make an order either in the terms of the application or with such modifications as may be approved by the Home Secretary.[4]

It will be noted that the chief constable's application must be for an order banning all trespassory assemblies in the district in question or part of it. It is not permissible for the council, by way of modification, to limit its order to a particular trespassory assembly or class of trespassory assembly.

It is noteworthy that in Scotland ministerial approval is not required.[5]

1   Note 'may' is used in s 14A, rather than 'shall' (ie must) as in the 1986 Act, s 13.
2   1986 Act, s 14A(1).
3   As defined in para **6.45** fn 3.
4   1986 Act, s 14A(2)(a).
5   Ibid, s 14A(2)(b).

6.79 If the Metropolitan Police Commissioner or the City of London Police Commissioner has a reasonable belief in the conditions set out above, the Commissioner himself may, with the consent of the Home Secretary, make an order prohibiting for a period specified in the order the holding of all trespassory assemblies in his police area or part of it, as specified in the order.[1]

1   1986 Act, s 14A(4).

6.80 The comments made in paras **6.45–6.48** about the corresponding procedures under s 13 of the 1986 Act apply equally well here.

6.81 An order under s 14A of the 1986 Act need not be made in writing but, if it is not, it must be recorded in writing as soon as practicable[1] after being made.[2] It is unfortunate that certain minimal requirements, in terms of notice, the nature of the notice and the time at which it must be given, have not been imposed, albeit there would have had to have been allowances for emergencies.

An order can be revoked or varied by a subsequent order made in the same way as the order.[3]

---

1   See para **6.9** fn 2.
2   1986 Act, s 14A(8).
3   Ibid, s 14A(7).

Terms of a ban

6.82 The prohibition order will apply either to the district (provinces) or area (metropolis) in which it is reasonably believed that the assembly is intended to be held, or a part of it, as specified in the order. An order under s 14A operates to prohibit *any* assembly which:

(a)   is held on land in the open air to which the public has no right of access or only a limited right of access; and
(b)   takes place in the prohibited circumstances, ie without the permission of the occupier of the land or so as to exceed the limits of any permission of his or the limits of the public's right of access.[1]

This indicates that a 'trespassory assembly' must be 'trespassory' in the sense that it must involve the commission of the tort of trespass by those taking part, either by entering land to which they have no right of access, or by exceeding a limited right of access to land. As can be seen, an assembly that has triggered a prohibition order is not completely banned; it can go ahead, for instance in a non-trespassory way, in the district or area covered by the order.

---

1   1986 Act, s 14A(5).

6.83 The duration and area of an order prohibiting a trespassory assembly are not left at large. Section 14A(6) of the 1986 Act provides significant limitations. It states that no order under s 14A shall prohibit the holding of (trespassory) assemblies for a period exceeding four days or in an area represented by a circle with a radius of five miles[1] from a specified centre, which need not (it appears) be the centre of, or even on, the land where it is believed that the assembly is intended to be held. This could be of importance, for example, where that land is adjacent to an estuary; the land coverage could be increased by choosing a centre further inland. A five-mile radius is a large area to put into quarantine. There is nothing in the 1986 Act to prevent a number of concurrent or consecutive orders being made in appropriate cases in relation to different areas so that the district is covered by a number of intersecting circles of prohibition or so that the prohibition is extended over a longer period than the critical four days.

As already stated, a prohibition order must prohibit *all* trespassory assemblies in the area in question; it cannot discriminate between such assemblies by banning a particular class of them or a specified one.

---

1   Ie five miles in a straight line on a horizontal plane: Interpretation Act 1978, s 8.

Offences

6.84 Section 14B creates three offences.

A person who organises an assembly, knowing that it is prohibited by an order under s 14A, commits a summary offence, whose maximum punishment is three months' imprisonment or a fine not exceeding level 4 on the standard scale, or both.[1] A person who takes part in an assembly, knowing that it is prohibited by an order under s 14A, is also guilty of a summary offence, punishable with a fine not exceeding level 3 on the standard scale.[2] A person who incites another to commit an offence of knowingly taking part in a prohibited assembly also commits a summary offence that is punishable with three months' imprisonment or a fine not exceeding level 4 on the standard scale, or both.[3]

The comments made in para **6.52** about the corresponding offences under s 13 are equally applicable here.

---

1   1986 Act, s 14B(1) and (5).
2   Ibid, s 14B(2) and (6).
3   Ibid, s 14B(3) and (7).

6.85 Central to all three offences is that the assembly must be prohibited under s 14A, and an assembly is prohibited only if, within the area and duration of the prohibition order, it:

(a) is held on land in the open air to which the public has no right of access or only a limited right of access; and
(b) takes place in the prohibited circumstances, ie without the permission of the occupier of the land or so as to exceed the limits of any permission of his or the limits of the public's right of access.[1]

Normally, there is no problem in determining whether these conditions are satisfied. Their application, however, in the case of assemblies on the highway has been the subject of a difference of judicial opinion as to whether the public's right of access to the highway is still limited to the right to pass or re-pass and activities incidental to passage, as traditionally understood,[2] or could also include the right to hold a public assembly in certain circumstances. The majority decision of the House of Lords in 1999 in *DPP v Jones*[3] established that the latter is the case.

---

1   See para **6.82**.
2   See, in particular, *Ex parte Lewis* (1888) 21 QBD 191, DC; *Harrison v Duke of Rutland* [1893] 1 QB 142, CA; *Hickman v Maisey* [1900] 1 QB 752, CA.
3   [1999] 2 All ER 257, HL.

6.86 The background to *DPP v Jones* was an attempt by a group of people to enter the site of Stonehenge in 1985. They had clashed with the police and since then the site had been fenced and the public denied access. In 1995, the local chief constable, fearing protests to mark the tenth anniversary of the clash, applied for and was granted an order under s 14A banning trespassory assemblies within four miles of Stonehenge for four days. During that period, a police inspector counted 21 people on the grass verge of the A344 adjacent to the fence surrounding Stonehenge.[1] Some were bearing banners with legends such as 'Free Stonehenge'. None of them was behaving in a destructive or violent manner, or causing any obstruction to other users of the highway. The police inspector asked the 21 to leave. Three of them, including Dr Jones and Mr Lloyd, did not. They were arrested and convicted by a magistrates' court for taking part in a trespassory assembly.

Dr Jones and Mr Lloyd appealed successfully to the Crown Court but the Divisional Court allowed an appeal by the Director of Public Prosecutions. From that decision Dr Jones and Mr Lloyd appealed to the House of Lords. By a majority of 3 to 2, the House allowed those appeals because the assembly had not been shown to have exceeded the public's right of access to the highway.

Because each of the three Law Lords in the majority adopted slightly different reasoning, it is difficult to determine the ratio of the case. The least that it decides, however, is that it is not necessarily in excess of the public's right of access to the highway to assemble on the highway, and that an assembly which (as in that case) is peaceful and non-obstructive of the rights of passage of other users of the highway is not in excess of the public's right of access if it is a reasonable use of the highway.

Lord Irvine LC thought that, provided an assembly 'does not amount to a public or private nuisance and does not obstruct the highway by unreasonably impeding the primary right of the public to pass and re-pass ... there is a right of peaceful assembly on the highway'.[2]

Lord Hutton acknowledged that the public's right of access to the highway should include the right of assembly in some cases. He said:

> 'If, as in my opinion it does, the common law recognises the right of public assembly, I consider that the common law should also recognise that in some circumstances this right can be exercised on the highway, provided that it does not obstruct the passage of other citizens, because otherwise the value of the right is greatly diminished.'[3]

Lord Hutton emphasised, however, that his opinion that the appeal be allowed was based on the fact that the assembly in question had been found by the Crown Court to be a reasonable use of the highway, adding: 'I would not hold that a peaceful and non-obstructive public assembly on a highway is always a reasonable user and is therefore not a trespass.'[4] Lord Clyde, the third member of the majority, took a similar view, although he expressed it differently, by saying that he was 'prepared to hold that a peaceful assembly which does not obstruct the highway does not necessarily constitute a trespassory assembly' (and that the assembly in question was not trespassory).

---

1   Presumptively, such a verge is part of the highway: see para **7.97**.
2   [1999] 2 All ER 257 at 265.
3   Ibid, at 293.
4   Ibid, at 297.

6.87 The decision in *DPP v Jones* clearly narrows the scope of s 14A insofar as it relates to assemblies on highways.

Whether a peaceful, non-obstructive assembly exceeds the public's limited right to be on the highway because it is unreasonable is a matter of fact and degree. This was acknowledged by all three members of the majority who recognised that this permits the court to take into account the size and duration of the obstruction and its obstructiveness.[1]

What was said in *Jones v DPP* applies equally to all kinds of highway, including public footpaths and bridleways across private land, although the determination of what is reasonable may be affected according to whether the assembly is on a road or on, say, a public footpath across private land.[2]

---

1   [1999] 2 All ER 257 at 265, 287 and 297–298.
2   Ibid, at 265 and 297–298, per Lord Irvine LC and Lord Hutton.

6.88 Lords Irvine and Hutton emphasised that it would be unsatisfactory if a peaceful assembly on the highway which was a reasonable use of it constituted a trespassory assembly in circumstances where it would not constitute the offence under s 137 of the Highways Act 1980 of wilful obstruction of the highway without lawful excuse (because the reasonable use would be a lawful excuse).[1] Lord Irvine found it 'satisfactory that there is a symmetry in the law between the activities on the public highway which may be trespassory and those which may amount to unlawful obstruction of the highway'.[2] This satisfaction is not, however, completely well-founded because the decision of the majority as a whole does not go this far: it is limited to *non-obstructive* peaceful assemblies (ie, it seems, ones which are not actually obstructions, but only potentially so), whereas there can be a lawful excuse under s 137 of the 1980 Act in the case of actual as well as potential obstructions.

---

1   [1999] 2 All ER 257 at 266 and 295 per Lords Irvine LC and Hutton.
2   Ibid, at 266.

European Convention on Human Rights

6.89 A ban under s 14A inevitably restricts the freedom of peaceful assembly guaranteed by Art 11 of the ECHR. In addition, it may be noted that Art 11 covers 'meetings in public thoroughfares',[1] so that, even after *DPP v Jones*, the application of s 14A to an obstructive peaceful assembly on the highway or to a non-obstructive one which is an unreasonable use of the highway will be a restriction for the purposes of Art 11.

The principal problem, in justifying a s 14A ban under Art 11(2), is that there is no need under s 14A to prove that an assembly threatened public safety, public order or the rights of others. In *Pendragon v UK*,[2] the European Commission of Human Rights held on the facts that a ban under s 14A was not in breach of Art 11. The order in question had been made in respect of all trespassory assemblies within a four-mile radius of Stonehenge for a four-day period over the summer solstice. Like previous orders, it had been prompted by serious disorder at Stonehenge during summer solstices in the early 1980s. P conducted a Druid service attended by more than 20 people arrested within the four-mile exclusion zone during the period of the order; he was arrested when he refused to leave. The Commission held, by a majority, that the ban had not been in breach of Art 11 because the restriction on P's freedom of peaceful assembly was prescribed by law, Stonehenge needed protection, the past disorder there at the summer solstice justified steps being taken to prevent disorder (a legitimate aim under Art 11(2)), and the steps taken by the order were proportionate to that aim and therefore 'necessary in a democratic society'. The Commission noted that the ban did not affect groups of less than 20 and that it was open to P to practise his religion in a smaller group, even within the four-mile exclusion zone. In this case, need to prevent a recurrence of the past disorder at the summer solstice was instrumental to the Commission's decision. A ban might well be held to be an unjustifiable restriction on the freedom of assembly under s 14A if there was no evidence that any likely assembly in the area would endanger public safety or order (as opposed, simply, to being disruptive), or if public safety or order could effectively be ensured by less extreme methods.

The same arguments apply to a justification under Art 10(2) in respect of any interference with freedom of expression under Art 10 resulting from a ban.

---

1   *Rassemblement Jurassien, Unité Jurassienne v Switzerland* (1979) 17 D&R 93, ECommHR; *G v FRG* (1989) 60 D&R 256, ECommHR.

2   (1998) Application no 31416/96, ECommHR. The Commission also rejected a complaint
      under the ECHR, Art 14, on the ground that there was no evidence that Druids were treated
      differently from other groups in terms of entry to the Stonehenge area at the summer
      solstice. Also see *Chappell v UK* (1987) 53 D&R 241; 10 EHRR 510, ECommHR. Also see *Friedl
      v Austria* (1995) 21 EHRR 83, ECommHR.

Power to stop people proceeding to banned assembly

6.90 If a constable in uniform[1] reasonably believes[2] that a person is en route to an
assembly in an area to which a s 14A order applies and that the assembly is likely to
be one prohibited by that order, he may:

(a) stop that person; and
(b) direct him not to proceed in the direction of the assembly.[3]

   This power is a considerable one to control developing situations before
people reach the site of an assembly. It is a controversial one because it impinges
on the rights to freedom of expression and to freedom of assembly and association
as a means of protecting the life of the local community and ancient monuments
and historic buildings. It is subject to the proviso that it may only be exercised in
the area to which the order applies.[4] A person who fails to comply with a direction
of the present type that he knows has been given commits a summary offence,[5]
punishable with a fine not exceeding level 3 on the standard scale.[6] A constable in
uniform may arrest without warrant anyone whom he reasonably suspects[7] to be
committing this offence.[8]

   Although the UK has not ratified the Fourth Protocol to the Convention (Art
2 of which guarantees freedom of movement), it is arguable that stopping people
under s 14C may breach Art 11 (or Art 10) of the ECHR in any event, depending
on the circumstances

1   See para **6.92**.
2   See para **6.28**.
3   1986 Act, s 14C(1).
4   Ibid, s 14C(2).
5   Ibid, s 14C(3).
6   Ibid, s 14C(5).
7   See para **3.68** fn 1.
8   1986 Act, s 14C(4).

GENERAL

Arrest without warrant

6.91 None of the offences under ss 11–14A of the 1986 Act are arrestable
offences. Arrest without warrant is as follows.

6.92 A constable in uniform may arrest without warrant anyone whom he
reasonably suspects[1] is committing an offence under ss 12, 13, 14 or 14A.[2]

   Generally, the powers accorded to a constable are not dependent on him
being 'in uniform' although, for example, the powers under s 14C of the 1986 Act
and various police powers under Part V of the Criminal Justice and Public Order
Act 1994 and Part II of the Criminal Law Act 1977 depend on the constable being
in uniform. Case law indicates that a constable who is in uniform except for his

helmet is 'in uniform', since he is easily identifiable as a constable.[3] In *Taylor v Baldwin*,[4] a 'breathalyser case', it was left open whether a constable who was hatless and wearing a raincoat over (and concealing) his uniform was 'in uniform'. However, the Divisional Court did state that the whole purpose of the statutory requirement of 'a constable in uniform' was to ensure that persons required to undergo a breath test knew that the person asking for the breath specimen was a constable in uniform. It has been held that, in the absence of evidence to the contrary, a court is entitled to presume that a police officer on duty in public was in uniform.[5]

The necessity for this specific power of arrest is open to question. Quite apart from the common law power to arrest for an actual or apprehended breach of the peace, in many instances where a police officer reasonably suspects that one of these offences is being committed, it will appear that the service of a summons is impracticable because one of the general arrest conditions in s 25 of PACE will be satisfied. The power of arrest under s 25 of PACE may be exercised by a police officer who is not in uniform.

Where none of the general arrest conditions under s 25 of PACE is satisfied it is questionable why there should be a power of arrest for these summary offences. A particular reason for saying this is that an arrest in such a case is more likely to do more harm (in terms of inflaming the situation) than good (in terms of keeping the law and the peace). It is certainly odd that when PACE was passed a specific power of arrest was given in relation to offences under other sections of the 1936 Act, but not in relation to offences under s 3 of it (which contained the powers to impose conditions on or to ban processions), and that two years later such a power was thought necessary in relation to ss 12–14. By way of contrast, there is no specific power of arrest under the Act for offences under s 11 relating to the requirement of advance notice. Clearly, there was no need.

1　See para **3.68** fn 1.
2　1986 Act, ss 12(7), 13(10), 14(7) and 14B(4).
3　*Wallwork v Giles* [1970] RTR 117, DC.
4　[1976] RTR 265, DC.
5　*Richards v West* [1980] RTR 215, DC; *Gage v Jones* [1983] RTR 508, DC.

Delegation of chief officer's powers

6.93　The size and complexity of modern police forces, particularly the Metropolitan Police Force, means that it will not always be possible or practicable for a chief officer of police to exercise his exclusive functions in relation to the imposition of conditions in advance and the prohibition of public processions and trespassory assemblies. This is recognised by s 15 of the Act, which provides that:

(a)　a chief constable may delegate any of his functions under ss 12 to 14A to an assistant chief constable; and

(b)　in the City of London and the Metropolitan Police district, the respective Commissioners may delegate any of the functions to an Assistant Commissioner of Police.

It is up to the chief officer to decide whether or not he wishes to delegate any of the above functions (although in practice he will doubtless decide to do so); he does not require the consent of his police authority, any local authority or the Home

Secretary. Likewise, it is up to the chief officer to decide the extent of any delegation, and any conditions to which it is subject.

Challenging a condition or ban

No appeal against merits

6.94 Those aggrieved by the imposition of a condition on a procession or assembly or by a ban on a procession or trespassory assembly do not have a right of appeal against its merits, for example to the local magistrates' court or to a Crown Court judge.[1] Such a procedure would be quicker, cheaper and more convenient than an application for judicial review, and it could involve an inquiry by persons with knowledge of local conditions into the merits of a banning order or of conditions imposed in advance, although it could not have dealt with on-the-spot conditions. On the other hand, affording a right of appeal against police operational decisions would have been novel and open to the objections that the courts are not in the position to make decisions about public order matters (eg whether a procession is likely to cause serious public disorder) and that they should not be involved in making decisions about operational matters (as opposed to questions of law) for which they are not well equipped.

1   For proposals for a right of appeal, see, eg, *Brownlie's Law of Public Order and National Security* (1981) p 58; Thornton *We Protest* (NCCL, 1985).

Judicial review[1]

6.95 The imposition of a condition or of a ban is open to challenge directly by an application to the High Court for judicial review, or collaterally, in certain cases,[2] as a defence to a prosecution under ss 12–14A of the 1986 Act.

1   See Hadfield 'Public order police powers and judicial review' [1993] Crim LR 915.
2   Those of substantive or procedural ultra vires, just as a by-law may be impugned by way of defence in these cases: *Boddington v British Transport Police* [1998] 2 All ER 203, HL.

6.96 Judicial review does not permit a court to hold a decision invalid simply because the court disagrees with its merits; it merely permits it to do so if it is proved that the decision has not been reached in the proper way. This covers cases which are substantively or procedurally ultra vires, including ones made on the basis of an abuse of discretion. In this context, the courts can examine the exercise of a discretionary power and hold it invalid on the ground that it has been exercised in bad faith, ie intentionally abused for extraneous purposes. The courts can also so act where powers have been misused in good faith, as where they have been used for an unauthorised purpose or without regard to legally relevant considerations or on the basis of legally irrelevant considerations.[1] An order which banned an individual procession could, for example, be impugned, since it would be substantively ultra vires.

1   *Westminster Corpn v London and North Western Rly Co* [1905] AC 426, HL; *Padfield v Minister of Agriculture, Fisheries and Food* [1968] 1 All ER 694, HL; *Congreve v Home Office* [1976] 1 All ER 697, CA; *Secretary of State for Education and Science v Tameside Metropolitan Borough Council* [1976] 3 All ER 665, HL.

6.97 Quite apart from abuse or misuse of power, the imposition of conditions (or their nature) under s 12 or s 14, or of a ban (or its nature) under s 13 or s 14A, can be examined by the court on an application for judicial review in the light of the *Wednesbury*[1] principle, whereby an executive decision can be impugned if it is such that no reasonable authority could have made it. This is a restricted ground of review. The courts have shown a reluctance to disagree with the operational decisions of a police officer, particularly a *chief* officer of police.[2] More specifically the decision in *Kent v Metropolitan Police Commissioner*,[3] indicated that the courts would be reluctant to interfere with orders made under ss 12–14A of the 1986 Act. There, the general secretary of the CND, on behalf of its members, challenged as being too wide a 28-day ban on all processions in the Metropolitan Police district from April 25, 1981 'except those traditionally held on May 1 to celebrate May Day and those of a religious character customarily held'. The ban had been imposed in the light of disorder and was unrelated to the activities of the CND. It was alleged that the Commissioner had not directed his mind sufficiently to the matters to be considered and, especially, that the ban would affect a large number of processions over a large area. The Court of Appeal accepted that CND marches were commonly and peacefully held and that it was dealing with a fundamental freedom – the right to demonstrate and to protest on matters of public concern. Despite this, and despite the fact that the evidence of the Commissioner was described by Sir Denis Buckley as meagre, the Court of Appeal unanimously held that the ban was valid; it was for the applicant to prove that there were no grounds or no reasonable grounds for the prohibition, and unless this was proved the courts would not interfere. It appears from this decision that, in the absence of evidence of bad faith, the courts would be extremely slow to intervene,[4] and that the courts would be particularly reluctant to interfere with a 'banning order' because of the involvement of a number of bodies in its making, as opposed to a police officer alone,[5] however senior, in the case of the imposition of a condition. In *Kent v Metropolitan Police Commissioner*, when saying that the court could not say that the Commissioner had been wrong to conclude that the ban was necessary, the Divisional Court indicated that this was so especially when the Home Secretary had agreed with it.[6] The test of proportionality applied to interferences with a Convention right under the Human Rights Act 1998 holds out the prospect of a greater degree of judicial intervention.[7]

---

1   *Associated Provincial Picture Houses Ltd v Wednesbury Corpn* [1947] 2 All ER 680, CA.
2   *R v Metropolitan Police Comr, ex parte Blackburn (No 1)* [1968] 1 All ER 763, CA; ibid *(No 3)* [1973] 1 All ER 324, CA; *Mohammed-Holgate v Duke* [1984] 1 All ER 1054, HL; *R v Chief Constable of Sussex, ex parte International Trader's Ferry Ltd* [1999] 1 All ER 129, HL.
3   (1981) *The Times*, 15 May, CA.
4   Marston and Tain *Public Order Offences* (1995) p 123.
5   That officer may, of course, have consulted others, including (in the case of an advance condition) the local authority, but the decision will be his.
6   The Court of Appeal stated that the applicant had a remedy because he could apply to have the order varied (see para **6.50**).
7   See para **1.24**.

6.98 A problem with judicial review in the present context is the element of time. Except where it is sought by a person who has been prosecuted for an offence under ss 12–14A, there is little point in obtaining a judicial review after the procession or assembly has taken place or should have taken place. Unless the police have advance notice well in advance of a procession or assembly (and only six clear days' notice is required for some processions, and none for others or for assemblies) and announce well in advance any conditions imposed, there will be little time in which to make an order under s 12 or s 14, let alone for that order to be challenged by seeking judicial review before the procession or assembly commences. A similar point can be made about a prohibition on processions or trespassory assemblies made shortly before the planned date of a procession. A fortiori, there will normally be no chance of seeking judicial review before it takes effect if a condition is imposed while a procession or assembly is in progress. It has, however, been claimed that judicial review 'after the event can be significant as a guide to future conduct'.[1]

If it is possible to apply in time for leave to commence judicial review proceedings (the first step in obtaining judicial review) and leave is granted, interim relief can be granted pending the full hearing. Where the relief sought includes certiorari or prohibition, the grant of leave will, if the court so directs, operate as a stay of the order impugned until the determination of the application or until the court otherwise directs. When any other type of relief is requested, the court may grant an interim injunction that will have the same practical effect.[2] The granting of leave in the present context necessitates an expedited hearing of the substantive application for judicial review.

---

1   DGT Williams 'Processions, assemblies and the freedom of the individual' [1987] Crim LR 167 at 179.
2   Civil Procedure Rules 1998, Sch 1, RSC Ord 53, r 3(10); *R v Secretary of State for Education and Science, ex parte Avon County Council (No 2)* [1991] 1 All ER 282, CA.

6.99 Of course, it is not only those in favour of a procession or assembly who may want to challenge the police or local authority or Home Secretary. What if the chief constable refuses to impose a condition on a march despite the overwhelming views of local inhabitants or that the local authority refuses an application by the chief constable for the ban of another march?

Certainly, neither the local police authority nor the Home Secretary is entitled to require a chief constable to exercise any of his powers, and the same is true of the Home Secretary in relation to the two London forces.[1] Moreover, although a chief constable or Commissioner's refusal to impose a condition or ban can be questioned in the courts in judicial review proceedings, an application will succeed only in extreme cases.

This is shown by the following statement by Slynn J (as he then was) in *R v Metropolitan Police Comr, ex parte Lewisham BC*,[2] where the council unsuccessfully tried to obtain an order of mandamus against the Commissioner to ban a National Front march. Slynn J said:

'No doubt I have power to grant mandamus. Circumstances could arise in which I could make an order. For example if the Commissioner failed to take into account all relevant matters or if the Commissioner was of the opinion that his powers to prevent serious public disorder under subsection (1) [of the Public Order Act 1936, s 3, imposition of conditions], ... and other powers, were not sufficient to prevent public disorder, but nevertheless failed to take action. Or if the Commissioner took a view of the circumstances which was wholly untenable, I consider that the court could intervene.'[2]

The position would be the same if judicial review was sought of a local authority's (or a London Commissioner's) refusal to ban a procession.

As above, time may be a major constraint on the practical possibility of seeking judicial review and if it is sought the role of the court is limited.

1   *R v Metropolitan Police Comr, ex parte Blackburn (No 1)* [1968] 1 All ER 763, CA.
2   (1977) unreported. The case is referred to as a news report in *The Times* of 12 August 1977. The statement quoted in the text is quoted in *Brownlie's Law of Public Order and National Security* (1981) p 52.

REGULATION OF ROUTES ETC

6.100 Under s 52 of the Metropolitan Police Act 1839 and s 22 of the City of London Police Act 1839, the relevant Commissioner of Police may make regulations and give directions to prevent the obstruction of streets in the Metropolitan Police district and the City of London, respectively. Such regulations and directions are a means of prior control over processions and assemblies additional to those under Part II of the Public Order Act 1986.

Section 52 of the Metropolitan Police Act empowers the Metropolitan Police Commissioner:

(a) to make regulations –

   (i)   for the route to be observed by all carts, carriages, horses and persons, and
   (ii) for preventing obstruction of the streets and thoroughfares in all times of public processions, public rejoicings or illuminations; and

(b) to give directions to the constables for keeping order and to constables and traffic wardens for preventing any obstruction to the thoroughfares in the immediate neighbourhood of Her Majesty's palaces and public offices, Parliament, law courts, theatres and other places of public resort, and in any case when the streets or thoroughfares may be thronged or may be liable to be obstructed.

By s 54, para 9, of the 1839 Act , 'every person' commits a summary offence 'who, after being made acquainted with the regulations or directions' made under s 52 'shall wilfully disregard or not conform himself thereunto'. The maximum punishment is a fine not exceeding level 2 on the standard scale. The Divisional Court has held that to give someone a summary of a direction (as opposed simply to state its existence) is sufficient to acquaint him with it.[1]

The width of the power to give directions under s 52 of the 1839 Act is shown by its use to create roadblocks in the Wapping area during the long-running News International dispute in the mid-1980s, which had a significant effect on residents.[2]

1   *Needham v DPP* (1994) unreported, DC.
2   *No Way in Wapping* (NCCL, 1986).

6.101 In addition to the legislative provisions mentioned above, the sessional orders made on the first day of each session by both Houses of Parliament require the Metropolitan Police Commissioner to take care that the streets leading to Parliament are kept open and that no obstruction is permitted to hinder the passage of Lords and Members of Parliament to and from Parliament. The power to make sessional orders is part of the power of Parliament in relation to Parliamentary proceedings which exists under Parliamentary privilege.[1]

The present type of sessional order is enforced by directions given to all constables each year by the Metropolitan Police Commissioner under s 52 of the Metropolitan Police Act 1839, directing them that all assemblies or processions of persons shall be dispersed and shall not be in or proceed along any street or open place within a specified area on any day on which Parliament is sitting, and directing them to prevent or remove any cause of obstruction within that area. The directions do not apply to a peaceful assembly or procession which is not capable of causing an actual obstruction.[2] The Metropolitan Police show a greater preparedness to enforce sessional orders than they do to exercise their powers under ss 12–14 of the 1986 Act. Their practice is to stop a procession to which the directions apply at the boundary of the area referred to in the directions and to allow those in the procession to proceed independently to the Houses of Parliament to lobby.[3]

A breach of the directions is, of course, an offence under s 54, para 9, of the 1839 Act. On the other hand, unless the conduct takes place within the precincts of the Houses of Parliament, contravention of a requirement made by a police officer acting under a sessional order per se would seem not to be an offence, such as obstructing a constable acting in the execution of his duty, because of the opinion of the Divisional Court in *Papworth v Coventry*[4] that a sessional order itself can have no effect outside the walls and precincts of the Houses of Parliament.

---

1   *Erskine May's Parliamentary Practice* 22nd edn (ed Limon and Mackay) (Butterworths, 1997) pp 6, 65 and 180.
2   See *Papworth v Coventry* [1967] 2 All ER 41, DC.
3   Waddington *Liberty and Order* (UCL Press, 1994) pp 66–68.
4   [1967] 2 All ER 41, DC. In *Despard v Wilcox* (1910) 102 LT 103, DC, the court had left open how far beyond the precincts of the Houses of Parliament a sessional order could extend. Also see *Pankhurst v Jarvis* (1910) 101 LT 946, DC, where Lord Alverstone CJ was of the view that the power to make a sessional order extended to include control of the access and passages of the House. In this case, a conviction for obstructing a constable by pushing against a police cordon in front of St Stephen's entrance to the House of Commons in breach of a sessional order in order to present a petition was upheld.

6.102 In the provinces, there is a similar power of prior control under s 21 of the Town Police Clauses Act 1847,[1] although it is vested in the local authority and not in the chief constable. Section 21 provides that the local authority:

'... may from time to time make orders for the route to be observed by all carts, carriages, horses, and persons, and for preventing obstruction of the streets, within the limits of the Special Act, in all times of public processions, rejoicings, or illuminations, and in any case[2] when the streets are thronged or liable to be obstructed, and may also give directions to the constables for keeping order and preventing any obstruction of the streets in the neighbourhood of theatres and other places of public resort; and every wilful breach of any such order shall be deemed a

separate offence against this Act, and every person committing any such offence shall
be liable to a penalty not exceeding [level 3 on the standard scale].'

---

1   This provision applies, like the 1847 Act s 28, referred to in para **9.18**, throughout England
    and Wales outside Greater London: ibid.
2   'In any case' is construed ejusdem generis with 'public procession' etc: *Brownsea Haven
    Properties Ltd v Poole Corpn* [1958] 1 All ER 205, CA, so that a more general order (in that case
    creating, in effect, a one-way street for the holiday season) is invalid: ibid.

6.103 Regulations, orders or directions under the above powers may be challenged by way of judicial review, or by way of defence to a charge of breaking them,
according to the principles set out in paras **6.96** et seq.[1]

---

1   See, for example, *Papworth v Coventry* [1967] 2 All ER 41, DC.

DISORDERLY CONDUCT AT MEETINGS

6.104 Disorderly conduct at a meeting, public or private, may result in criminal
liability. For particularly grave cases of disorder, there are the serious offences
against public order, such as riot; in less grave cases charges of other offences, such
as the offences under ss 4, 4A or 5 of the Public Order Act 1986 or the offence of
wilfully obstructing a constable in the execution of his duty, would suffice. The
powers to deal with a breach of peace described in Chapter 2 are also available to
prevent or deal with disorder, eg the power to enter premises to prevent disorder.

6.105 In addition, special provision is made for disorderly behaviour at *public*
meetings by the Public Meeting Act 1908, which was passed in an attempt to
prevent the deliberate disruption of public meetings by the suffragettes. Section
1(1) of that Act provides that any person who at a lawful public meeting acts in a
disorderly[1] manner for the purpose of preventing the transaction of the business
for which the meeting was called together is guilty of a summary[2] offence. Merely
asking questions or simple disapproval or making points which the chairman of
the meeting does not like is not enough. On the other hand, violence or a threat of
violence is not required, so that boisterous heckling will suffice if done for the
purpose of preventing the transaction of business (which includes the expression
of points of view). The maximum punishment is six months' imprisonment or a
fine not exceeding level 5 on the standard scale, or both. It is also an offence under
s 1(2) of the Act to incite others to act in the way described.

---

1   'Disorderly' is not defined by s 1, nor is it defined in other criminal statutes where it appears:
    see Criminal Justice Act 1967, s 91 – disorderly behaviour while drunk in a public place;
    Public Order Act 1986, ss 4A and 5 – disorderly words or behaviour etc. As to the approach to
    disorderly, see para **4.24**.
2   Criminal Law Act 1977, Sch 1.

6.106 The term 'public meeting' is not defined but appears to be used in the sense
that the meeting is open to the public or a section of the public.[1] Meetings which
are open to the public held on private premises are therefore public meetings.[2]
The Act only applies to lawful meetings, whether indoors or outdoors. The fact
that a meeting is held on a highway does not render it unlawful merely because it is

so held.[3] However, the circumstances in which the meeting is held may make participants liable for the offence of obstructing the highway, in which case the meeting will be unlawful. A meeting does not cease to be lawful simply because there is disorderly opposition from others.[4]

---

1   As to this phrase in another context, see para **5.24**. Note 'public meeting' is defined for the purposes of the offence under the Public Order Act 1936, s 1: ibid, s 9.

2   'A public meeting should be one which is genuinely open to the public, and usually on a first-come, first-served basis, although many public meetings keep sections of the meeting place reserved for interested parties, such as the organisers of the meeting or the officers of the club holding the meeting. It is irrelevant whether payment is required before entry or not. If the meeting is a ticket-holders-only meeting, the sale or provision of tickets must be made to the public or a section of it, although there is no need for extensive publicity, before a meeting becomes public': Thornton *Public Order Law* (1987) p 158.

3   *Burden v Rigler* [1911] 1 KB 337, DC.

4   *Beatty v Gillbanks* (1882) 9 QBD 308. This point does not seem to have been doubted by the Divisional Court in *Duncan v Jones* [1936] 1 KB 218

6.107 Section 1(3) of the 1908 Act empowers a constable who reasonably suspects a person of committing an offence under s 1(1) or (2) to require that person to declare to him immediately his name and address. However, the constable may do so only if requested by the chairman of the meeting. If the person requested refuses or fails to declare his name *and* address or gives a false name *and* address, he commits a summary offence, punishable with a fine not exceeding level 1 on the standard scale; this offence is not imprisonable.

The requirements of s 1(3) are liable to cause problems for the constable, since there may be a fine dividing line between forcibly making points or asking questions that the chairman does not like, and acting in a disorderly manner for the purpose of preventing the transaction of business.

There is no specific power of arrest in relation to any of the above offences. If the general arrest conditions under s 25 of PACE are satisfied, however, a constable can arrest for an offence under s 1(1), (2) or (3) of the 1908 Act.

6.108 The 1908 Act has been little used but has not been repealed. It appears that the police have not been keen to enforce it, partly because s 1 contains no power of arrest and partly because they have taken the view that they ought not to interfere except to prevent a breach of the peace (as opposed to securing a hearing for a lawful speaker).[1]

---

1   *Brownlie's Law of Public Order and National Security* (1981) p 21.

Disorderly conduct at an election meeting

6.109 Section 1 of the 1908 Act does not apply to election meetings to which s 97 of the Representation of the People Act 1983 applies. Section 97 of the 1983 Act provides a similar summary offence (prosecuted as the offence of illegal electoral practice) to that under s 1 of the 1908 Act in relation to disturbances at election meetings.

Section 97(1) of the 1983 Act makes it an offence for a person at a lawful public meeting to act, or to incite others to act, in a disorderly manner for the purpose of preventing the transaction of the business for which the meeting was called together. For the purpose of this offence, 'lawful public meeting' refers to three types of meeting. First, it means a political meeting held in any constituency between the date of the issue of the writ for the return of a Member of Parliament for the constituency and the date at which a return to the writ is made. Secondly, it refers to a meeting held with reference to a local government election in the electoral area for the election in the period beginning with the last date on which notice of the election may be published in accordance with the local government election rules and ending with the day of the election.[1] Thirdly, it means a political meeting in connection with a European Parliamentary election between the last date on which notice of the election may be published and the date of the poll.[2]

An offence contrary to s 97 of the 1983 Act is not punishable with imprisonment, but only with a fine not exceeding level 5 on the standard scale.[3]

---

1   1983 Act, s 97(2).
2   The European Parliamentary Elections Regulations 1999, SI 1999/1214, Art 3(1) and Sch 1, apply s 97 to these elections.
3   1983 Act, s 169.

6.110 A constable has an identical power to require a person's name and address to that set out in s 1(3) of the Public Meeting Act 1908 where the officer reasonably suspects a person of committing an offence contrary to s 97(1); a refusal to supply a name and address, or a failure to do so, is a summary offence punishable in the same way as an offence under s 1(3) of the 1908 Act.[1]

There is no specific power of arrest in respect of an offence under s 97 of the 1983 Act, but the power of arrest under s 25 of the 1984 Act is available in the same way as in respect of an offence under s 1 of the Public Meeting Act 1908.

---

1   1983 Act, s 97(3).

Chapter 7

COLLECTIVE TRESPASS OR NUISANCE ON LAND

INTRODUCTION

7.1   A number of high-profile cases of public disorder in the 1980s and early 1990s involving 'New Age Travellers', anti-hunt saboteurs, those attending 'raves', and squatters led to Part V of the Criminal Justice and Public Order Act 1994, which provides a range of law enforcement powers and offences to deal with collective trespass and nuisances engendered by such groups of people and others. Promoted by the Government as essential for the maintenance of public order and private rights, the provisions were opposed by many on the grounds that they were unfair, excessive and contrary to principle.

The use of the first three sets of provisions dealt with in this chapter (failure to leave or re-entry on land after direction to leave, aggravated trespass and powers relating to raves), each of which involves in whole or part the giving by the police of a direction to leave land, has been examined in a Home Office Research Study,[1] which is referred to at appropriate points. The Study focused first on the extent to which the new provisions have been used and the degree to which their use has resulted in cautions and prosecutions, and secondly on the ways in which police officers have applied the provisions, the impact of their use and the issues that have emerged. The Study drew on interviews in 14 police forces with a total of 64 officers who have policed the kinds of disorder addressed by the provisions. Although there have been relatively few prosecutions for offences under these provisions, they have been effective in enabling the police to prevent the activities in question or to disperse those participating in them.

---

1   *Trespass and Protest* (1998). This study covered the first 18 months of the existence of these provisions.

FAILURE TO LEAVE OR RE-ENTRY TO LAND AFTER POLICE DIRECTION TO LEAVE

7.2   Section 39 of the Public Order Act 1986, enacted as a direct result of mass trespasses in the early 1980s by groups of hippies, Hells Angels and others, causing damage to property and/or threatening local inhabitants, enabled a senior police officer to give a direction to leave land. A direction could be given only if the senior police officer present at the scene reasonably believed that two or more had entered as trespassers and were present with the common purpose of residing on the land, that reasonable steps had been taken to ask them to leave, and that any of them had caused damage to property on the land or threatened, abused or insulted the occupier or a member of his family or an employee or agent of his, or that the trespassers had brought more than 12 vehicles on to the land. It was an offence for a person to fail to leave land, or to return to it, knowing that a direction had been given which applied to him.

7.3   Section 39 did not prevent mass trespasses by New Age Travellers and others in various locations. The then Government's view was that s 39 was not strong enough. As a result, the Criminal Justice and Public Order Act 1994 repealed s 39 of the Public Order Act 1986 and replaced it with stronger provisions set out in s 61 of the 1994 Act.[1]

---

1   Section 62 introduced a power to seize vehicles.

7.4   While s 61 clearly applies in the types of mass trespass described in the last paragraph, it can also apply in the case of smaller, less publicised trespasses. For example, it has been applied in the case of trespasses by gypsies and travellers, although police willingness to use s 61 against gypsies varies from force to force.[1] Section 61 is, in fact, applicable even though the number of trespassers may only number two.

Powers to direct 'unauthorised vehicular campers' to leave land are also possessed by local authorities under s 77 of the 1994 Act (see paras **7.97–7.111**).

---

1   *Trespass and Protest* (1998) p 7. See, further, para **7.21**.

Direction to leave etc

7.5   The starting point for the provisions under s 61 of the 1994 Act is a direction to leave under s 61(1), which can be given only by 'the senior police officer present at the scene'. The 1986 Act defined 'the senior police officer' as 'the most senior in rank of the police officers present at the scene', but this definition does not appear in the 1994 Act. Presumably, the courts will interpret seniority for the purposes of s 61(1) by reference to rank, and not by reference to age or (subject to the next sentence) by length of service. It is submitted that where there is more than one officer present of the most senior rank, the most senior of them will be the one with the longer or longest period of service in that rank.[1]

---

1   Support for this can be found in an unreported magistrates' court decision in respect of the same phrase in the 1994 Act, s 69, referred to in *Trespass and Protest* (1998) p 45.

7.6   The reference in s 61 to 'the senior police officer' can be contrasted with s 63, which provides a power, exercisable only by a police superintendent or above, to direct ravers to leave land. The senior police officer present at the scene may only be of a junior rank. Thus, responsibility for imposing conditions on the spot may be in the hands of a junior police officer, although this is unlikely to occur in the case of large-scale trespasses (where directions are normally given by an inspector or chief inspector).

'Senior police officer *present at the scene*' prevents a direction being given by, say, a superintendent who is in charge of the operation, but is not so present; the direction will have to be given by the senior subordinate officer who is present at the scene.[1] 'Present at the scene' would seem to require actual physical presence at the scene, as opposed to some kind of constructive presence (eg by radio). 'Scene' is a vague term. It is submitted that 'present at the scene' does not necessarily require presence on the land being trespassed on. A police officer would be present at the scene if, for example, he was on the other side of a hedge dividing that land from land under a separate occupier. It is a moot point whether it would cover a police officer hovering over the scene in a helicopter.

---

1   An unreported decision by a magistrates' court (*Trespass and Protest* (1998) pp 44–45) which appears to be to the contrary in respect of the same phrase in the 1994 Act, s 69, is simply wrong.

7.7   Section 61(1) provides that, in order to give a direction to leave, the senior officer present at the scene must reasonably believe[1] that four conditions are satisfied, viz:

(a)   that two or more persons are trespassing on land;

(b)   that they are present there with the common purpose of residing there for any period;

(c)   that reasonable steps have been taken by or on behalf of the occupier to ask them to leave; and

(d)   (i)   that any of those persons has caused damage to the land or to property on the land or used threatening, abusive or insulting words or behaviour towards the occupier, a member of his family or an employee or agent of his; or

(ii)   that those persons have between them six or more vehicles on the land.

These circumstances need not, of course, actually exist. It is the reasonable belief that they do which triggers the power to make a direction.

---

1   See para **6.28**.

Two or more trespassers

7.8   The senior police officer must reasonably believe that two or more people are trespassing, as against the occupier of land,[1] on it. If the people concerned are known to be on the land with the occupier's consent, s 61 is inapplicable, no matter how much disturbance is caused to the locality. It appears that the reasonable belief must relate to the two or more being trespassers in civil law (ie being on land in the possession of another without a right by law or licence to be there), regardless of whether the trespassers know this.[2] This may be a source of difficulty for the senior police officer since, quite apart from any dispute as to the basis on which the people concerned are on the land, police officers are not normally trained in the civil law relating to trespass.

---

1   1994 Act, s 61(9).

2   Trespass is a legal concept, the definition of which is founded in the law of tort. According to that law, any intentional or negligent entry onto land is a trespass if the land is in the possession of another who does not expressly or impliedly permit the entry and entry is without a right in law to do so.

A permission or legal right to enter may be limited to a particular area of land or the purpose of entry. If an entrant with a limited permission or right enters part of the land that he is not entitled to enter or enters land for some purpose other than a permitted one, his entry to the part or the land (as the case may be) will be as a trespasser: *Westwood v Post Office* [1973] 1 All ER 283, CA, reversed on other grounds [1973] 3 All ER 54, HL. This rule is especially important in relation to public access to a highway that extends only to a right of passage and certain other activities: see para **6.85**.

If a person is deliberately on land, it is no defence that he did not mean to trespass because he thought he was legally entitled to be there: *Beseley v Clarkson* (1861) 3 Lev 37.

7.9 Under s 39 of the 1986 Act, it was the initial entry which had to be trespassory, but this is not required by s 61 of the 1994 Act. Thus, the present condition will be satisfied if the senior police officer reasonably believes that two or more have entered the land in question as trespassers or that, although they entered with a licence (permission, express or implied) from the occupier, they have become trespassers because the licence has been effectively revoked or has expired.[1] It follows that, if the senior police officer reasonably believes that travellers who have camped on a farmer's field with his permission have been notified that the permission is revoked or that the period of permission for a caravan rally in a field has expired, the present condition will be satisfied because he will have a reasonable belief that those concerned are trespassing as against the occupier of the land.

Tenants who fail to quit land when their lease expires do not become trespassers in civil law (because they remain in law in possession of the land),[2] although it is doubtful whether the senior police officer can reasonably be expected to know this. If he is aware of the relevant law, he would certainly not have a reasonable belief that the tenants were trespassers and could not make a direction to leave.

---

1   *Wood v Leadbetter* (1845) 13 M&W 838; *Hillen & Pettigrew v ICI (Alkali) Ltd* [1936] AC 65, HL.
     A licensee who holds over after the termination of the licence becomes a trespasser after the
     lapse of a reasonable time to leave and remove his property: *Minister of Health v Bellotti* [1944]
     1 All ER 238.
2   *Hey v Moorhouse* (1839) 6 Bing NC 52.

7.10 The reasonably believed trespass must have begun; there is no power to make a direction on the basis that two or more people are about to enter land as trespassers. On the other hand, the reasonably believed trespass need not have begun at the same time on the part of each person. It is clear from s 61(1) that the trespass (or trespasses) must be in relation to land that has the same occupier, but it is not necessary that the trespass should relate to the same part of that piece of land. For example, it will be enough if the reasonable belief relates to X having entered and remained on North Field as a trespasser and Y on South Field as a trespasser, provided both fields are part of a contiguous set of plots of land whose occupier is the same.

7.11 At least two people reasonably believed to be trespassers must be present on the land for a requirement to leave to be made. If it is known that all but one have left the land to go shopping, a direction to leave cannot be made at that time. While the shoppers could be said to be still residing on the land, it cannot be said that they are present on it at the time. A fortiori, a direction cannot be made against a single trespasser-camper.

7.12 Section 61 applies to common land (as that term is defined in s 22 of the Commons Registration Act 1965)[1] as well as other types of 'land'.[2] Because of its nature, common land is vulnerable to mass incursions. Entry onto common land for a purpose outside a right in common is a trespass, and so is such an entry by a person who does not have a right in common. Section 61(7) deals with the problem that it may be impossible to establish who is the occupier of common land, and therefore to establish a trespass. It provides that in its application to common land s 61 has effect as if:

'(a) references in it to trespassing or trespassers were references to acts and persons doing acts which constitute either a trespass as against the occupier or an infringement of the commoners' rights; and

(b) references in it to "the occupier" included the commoners or any of them or, in the case of common land to which the public has access, the local authority[3] as well as any commoner.'

All or any of the commoners, or a local authority referred to in (b), can make the request to leave by s 61(1).[3] However, if one commoner or such a local authority permits persons to be on the land they will not be trespassers as against other commoners or the local authority.[4]

---

1 'Common land as defined in s 22 of the Commons Registration Act 1965' means:
   (a) land subject to rights of common (as defined by the Act, see below) whether those rights are exercisable at all times or only during limited periods;
   (b) waste land of a manor not subject to rights of common;
   but does not include a town or village green or any land which forms part of a highway.
      'Rights of common' as defined in s 22 of the Commons Registration Act 1965 include rights of beastgate or cattlegate and rights of sole or several vesture or herbage or of sole or several pasture, but do not include a right held for a term of years or from year to year.
2 Directions have been made under s 61 in relation to a wide range of sites, including car parks, playing fields, farmland, industrial estates, vacant or derelict land, business parks, grass verges and building sites: *Trespass and Protest* (1998) p 8.
3 Ie a county council, London borough council, district council or parish council in whose area the land or part of the land is situated: Commons Registration Act 1965, s 22(1), applied by the 1994 Act, s 61(9).
4 1994 Act, s 61(8)(b).

7.13 'Land' in s 61 does not include buildings, other than 'agricultural buildings'[1] and 'scheduled ancient monuments'[2] (such as Stonehenge and the ruined Kenilworth Castle).[3] Consequently, s 61 does not apply where the reasonable belief is merely that persons are trespassing in someone's house or factory. The reason is that the mischief at which s 61 is aimed is the invasion of open spaces. The exclusion of buildings which are not agricultural or scheduled monuments is not as serious as it may seem, because s 6 of the Criminal Law Act 1977 prohibits the use of force in gaining entry to any premises, and s 7 provides redress against those who refuse to leave residential premises, including land attached to a house, at the request of a displaced residential occupier or a protected intending occupier.[4] If all buildings had been included in s 61, there would have been obvious implications for factory or student sit-ins and for organisations who temporarily 'occupy' buildings.

---

1 Ie agricultural buildings within the meaning of paras 3–8 of Sch 5 to the Local Government Finance Act 1988, eg barns, cowsheds or deep-litter units at a farm and greenhouses at a market garden.
2 Ie scheduled monuments within the meaning of the Ancient Monuments and Archaeological Areas Act 1979.
3 1994 Act, s 61(9).
4 See paras **7.128–7.139**.

7.14 In addition, 'land' does not include land forming part of a 'highway'[1] (which term includes lay-bys or 'oxbows' left by road straightening or, rebuttably,[2] the verges of a highway), unless it falls within the classification in s 54 of the Wildlife and Countryside Act 1981 (footpath, bridleway or byway open to all traffic or road used as a public path) or is a cycle track under the Highways Act 1980 or the Cycle Tracks Act 1984.[3] Encampments blocking footpaths and bridleways are not unknown.

Assemblies on the highway may be subject to an order under s 14A of the Public Order Act 1986, described in Chapter 6, and unauthorised vehicular campers are subject to controls under ss 77 and 78 of the 1994 Act, discussed below.[4] Those who obstruct free passage along the highway may be convicted of obstructing the highway, contrary to s 137 of the Highways Act 1980, or of the common law offence of public nuisance.[5] A local authority has powers under s 143 of the 1980 Act to require someone who has put his tent, caravan or other structure on the highway to remove it, but it must give him one month in which to do so. Injury to a person or property can be dealt with by charging an appropriate offence.

---

1   See para **9.74**.
2   See para **7.97**.
3   1994 Act, s 61(9). Section 54 of the Wildlife and Countryside Act 1981 distinguishes between three types of 'road used as a public path' which must be shown on every definitive map and statement which county and London borough councils are required by s 53 of that Act to keep for their area:
  (a)   a byway open to all traffic, ie a highway over which the public have a right of way for vehicular and all other kinds of traffic, but which is used by the public mainly for the purpose for which footpaths and bridleways are so used;
  (b)   a bridleway, ie a highway over which the public have the following, but no other, rights of way, ie a right of way on foot and a right of way on horseback or leading a horse, with or without a right to drive animals of any description along the highway;
  (c)   a footpath, ie a highway over which the public have a right of way on foot only, other than such a highway at the side of a public road.
  By s 329(1) of the Highways Act 1980, 'cycle track' means a way constituting or comprised in a highway, being a way over which the public have the following, but no other, rights of way, ie a right of way on pedal cycles (other than pedal cycles which are motor vehicles under the Road Traffic Act 1988) with or without a right of way on foot.
4   See paras **7.96–7.109**.
5   See paras **9.72–9.96**.

Present with the common purpose of residing

7.15 The senior police officer must reasonably believe that two or more trespassers are present on the land with the common purpose of residing there for any period. The section does not require this to be the only purpose; the trespassers may have others (eg to repair one of their vehicles on the land). There is no requirement for a prior common agreement to reside. It is enough that it is reasonably believed that the two or more trespassers have the common purpose to reside even though it is clear that each has formed it independently and is not acting in concert with the other(s).

The 1994 Act does not define what is meant by 'residing', except that s 61(9) states that a person may be regarded as having the purpose of residing in a place notwithstanding that he has a home elsewhere. As implied by s 61(9), 'residing' at a place can be described as 'living there' or 'having a home there', however temporarily. Clearly, this condition excludes those trespassers who are simply ramblers, birdwatchers, sit-down demonstrators, hare-coursers and most other trespassers, unless (as is unlikely) the senior officer makes a reasonable mistake about their intentions and reasonably believes that they are there for the purpose of residing there. It is submitted that, where trespassers are on land with their mobile homes, the main target of the offence, the senior police officer will have reasonable grounds to believe that they are present with the common purpose of residing there, unless it is apparent that they are there for a wholly temporary purpose, such as shopping. An area of potential difficulty is where travellers trespass in a roadside field and claim that they are there because they need to repair one of their vehicles or to have a 'brew-up'. If this is reasonably believed to be the only purpose of the trespass, a direction cannot be given. On the other hand, if it is reasonably believed that this is not the only genuine common purpose and that residence on the land is the common purpose (or one of them) a direction can be given.

Request to leave

7.16 The senior police officer must reasonably believe that reasonable steps have been taken by or on behalf of the occupier[1] to ask the trespassers to leave. There is no limit on who may act on behalf of the occupier; it could be anyone with the occupier's authority. Where there is a dispute between two people as to who is the occupier of the land, the senior police officer will have a reasonable belief in the present respect (and as to the fact that they are trespassers) if both of the claimants have directed the persons on the land to leave.[2]

Reasonable steps mean steps which, viewed objectively and in the light of all the circumstances, are reasonable. A request made by shouting from a house, by loudhailer or by notices, may suffice, depending on the circumstances, including the number of trespassers, the distance between them and a person making an oral request, and so on.

If the occupier cannot be traced and there is no one to act on his behalf, or if for some reason a request to leave cannot be made, the police must fall back on other powers, eg their breach of peace powers, if they wish to intervene in disorder or nuisance on the land.

---

1 Ie the person entitled to possession of the land by virtue of an estate or interest held by him: s 61(9); but not a bare or contractual licensee. In relation to common land, see s 61(7)(b), referred to in para **7.12**. It is enough in the case of common land that it is reasonably believed that one of the commoners or the appropriate local authority has taken such steps: s 61(8); see para **7.12**.
2 *Neizer v Rhodes* (1995) SCCR 799, High Ct of Justiciary.

Damage, threats etc or possession of vehicles

7.17 The senior police officer must reasonably believe that one of the following conditions is satisfied:

(a) that any of the trespassers has caused damage to the land or to property[1] on the land or used threatening, abusive or insulting words or behaviour towards the occupier[2] of the land, a member of his family or an employee or agent of his; or

(b) that the trespassers have between them six or more vehicles on the land.

It follows from this requirement that overnight campers, for example, are outside the scope of s 61, provided that they have not caused damage to property on the land or used threatening etc words or behaviour or have six or more vehicles with them.

1   The 1994 Act, s 61(9) provides that 'property' in this context means property within the
     meaning of the Criminal Damage Act 1971, s 10(1), viz:
        '... property of a tangible nature, whether real or personal, including money and –
        (a)   including wild creatures which have been tamed or are ordinarily kept in captivity,
              and any other wild creatures or their carcasses if, but only if, they have been reduced
              into possession which has not been lost or abandoned or are in the course of being
              reduced into possession; but
        (b)   not including mushrooms growing wild on any land or flowers, fruit or foliage of a
              plant growing wild on any land.'
     'Mushroom' includes any fungus and 'plant' includes any shrub or tree: Criminal Damage
     Act 1971, s 10(2).
2   See para **7.16** fn 1.

7.18 In relation to (a), above, it appears that it is irrelevant that the reasonably
believed damage was trivial. It is also irrelevant that the damage was accidental and
not even recklessly caused, or was to the trespasser's own property. The damage
need only be caused by one trespasser; likewise, threatening words or behaviour
need only be used by one trespasser. If 20 people are peacefully camped on the
land, and are causing no trouble at all except by the fact of their alleged trespass
but the 21st person cuts down a tree, the police may act.

'Damage' seems to bear the same meaning as under the Criminal Damage
Act 1971,[1] save that it must include 'destruction' and that, by s 61(9), it includes
for the purpose of s 61 'the deposit of any substance capable of polluting the land'
(such as diesel oil or excrement). Such deposit is a major problem in the type of
case at which s 61 is aimed and the provision in s 61(9) puts it beyond doubt that it
constitutes 'damage' for present purposes, although it was hardly necessary to do
so because it had already been held that dumping rubbish on land can constitute
'damage' to it.[2] It is submitted that those who allow their animals to excrete on
land can be said thereby to damage it (since the pollution results from their failure
to exercise their right of control over their animals). The fact that the power to
make a direction extends to the case where the reasonable belief relates to
damage to something forming part of the land (as well as to damage to the land
itself) is important. Conduct such as tearing branches from saplings or trampling
grass are common examples of damage in the type of case at which s 61 is aimed.

Since wild mushrooms and the flowers, fruit or foliage of a wild plant are not
property for present purposes,[3] a direction cannot be given if the senior police
officer simply reasonably believes that such things, as opposed to a wild plant itself,
have been damaged.

1   Property is damaged if it suffers permanent or temporary physical harm or permanent or
     temporary impairment of its use or value. See, further, para **6.77** fn 2.
2   In *R v Henderson* (1984) unreported, CA.
3   See para **7.17** fn 1.

7.19 In relation to a reasonable belief that threatening, abusive or insulting words
or behaviour have been used, there can be no doubt that 'threatening, abusive or
insulting' do not bear a special technical meaning but must be understood in their
ordinary sense.[1] Such words or behaviour must be reasonably believed to have
been used 'towards' the occupier,[2] a member of his family or an employee or agent
of his, ie in the physical presence of, and in the direction of, that person directly.[3]

However, they need not be reasonably believed to have been used with intent to cause fear of violence or to provoke violence or to have been likely to cause such fear or provocation.

---

1   See para **4.5**.
2   As defined by s 61 (9); see para **7.16** fn 1.
3   *Atkin v DPP* (1989) 89 Cr App Rep 199, DC; see para **4.8** (threatening words or behaviour towards another, contrary to the Public Order Act 1986, s 4).

7.20 In relation to (b), in para **7.17**, 'vehicle' expressly includes any vehicle, or any caravan as defined in s 29(1) of the Caravan Sites and Control of Development Act 1960,[1] a term which covers a motor-camper, a bus or motor coach adapted for human habitation, and similar vehicles.[2] There is no reason why 'vehicle' should not also include bicycles, tricycles, carts and perambulators. If so, six cyclists who have trespassed with their tents in a field for an overnight stay can be caught by s 61. This is liable to render the application of the section absurd.

The reference to six or more vehicles is surprising given that the minimum number of persons who need be reasonably believed to be involved is two, but it may result from a desire to exclude gypsy camps generally from s 61, although the number postulated is too low to have this effect in many cases, since it would only need three caravans and three cars or lorries to exceed it. The number has been reduced from 12 to six by s 61 so as to catch trespassing encampments falling below the previous threshold, which are nevertheless large enough to cause significant disturbance to the occupier of the land, his family etc. Whatever the reason, any choice of number would have been open to accusations of arbitrariness. For example, the presence of five buses, each full of 50 people is a more substantial intrusion than the presence of two trespassers with a tent who collect on the land six motor cycles as scrap. Provided that they are peaceful and damage nothing, determined mass trespassers can evade the provisions of s 61 by bringing no more than five vehicles, however large, on to the land, or by bringing that number on to A's field and the same number on to B's adjacent field.

The senior police officer's belief must relate to the two or more trespassers 'having between them' six or more vehicles on the land at that time. This simply requires the trespassers to be in possession or control of the vehicles. It is irrelevant whether those trespassers brought them on to the land. Indeed, there is no reason why the vehicles should not belong to the occupier of the land if they have been commandeered by the two or more trespassers.

It is irrelevant that a vehicle is not in a fit state for use on roads.[3] Moreover 'vehicle' includes 'any chassis or body, with or without wheels, appearing to have formed part of such a vehicle, and any load carried by, and anything attached to, such a vehicle (sic)'.[3] This raises the interesting question of whether, where the body and chassis of a vehicle have been separated, there are one or two vehicles. It is submitted that such double-counting is not permissible. The importance of these provisions is, of course, that s 61 catches a couple of scrap merchants who break up vehicles on land on which they have trespassed with their caravan, including those who have taken over the business from other trespassers who brought the vehicles on to the land.

---

1   1994 Act, s 61(9). The *Shorter Oxford English Dictionary* defines vehicle as 'a means of conveyance provided with wheels or runners for the carriage of persons or goods'. The statutory meaning of 'vehicle', where no express definition is provided, must be established in

the light of the construction and nature of the contrivance and the circumstances of its use: *Boxer v Snelling* [1972] RTR 472, DC.

2   The 1960 Act, s 29(1) defines a 'caravan' as:

'... any structure designed or adapted for human habitation which is capable of being moved from one place to another (whether by being towed, or by being transported on a motor vehicle or trailer) and any motor vehicle so designed or adapted, but does not include –

(a)   any railway rolling stock which is for the time being on rails forming part of a railway system, or

(b)   any tent.'

A 'caravan' does not include a construction without wheels, made of four prefabricated panels, bolted together and dragged onto a concrete base, since it does not possess the quality of mobility, and cannot be towed away by a trailer or single vehicle: *Carter v Secretary of State for the Environment* [1994] 1 WLR 1212, CA.

A vehicle is not 'adapted' so as to constitute a 'caravan' unless it has been physically altered for human habitation: *Backer v Secretary of State for the Environment* [1983] 2 All ER 1021. Accordingly, a vehicle is not 'adapted' for human habitation merely because by some means short of physical alteration, such as putting furniture in it, it is made suitable for human habitation: ibid.

3   1994 Act, s 61(9).

The making of the direction

7.21 If, but only if, the senior police officer reasonably believes that the four conditions set out in para **7.7** are satisfied, he may direct any or all of those persons whom he reasonably believes to be trespassing on the land and to be present there with the common purpose of residing there to leave the land. The Association of Chief Police Officers' guidance document on Part V of the 1994 Act[1] reminds officers that s 61 confers a power not a duty to evict, and advises a multi-agency approach. The discovery of a trespassory New Age Traveller or gypsy site usually leads to discussions between the police, the local authority and the landowner about who should take responsibility. Where there has been a regular problem with unauthorised vehicular camping it is likely that it will be addressed in the local community safety plan drawn up under the Crime and Disorder Act 1998 and a multi-agency approach agreed under it. Particularly in a simple case, a landowner may apply for a possession order or an injunction, or the local authority may use its powers in relation to unauthorised vehicular campers dealt with in paras **7.96–7.109**; alternatively, especially if there has been crime or disorder, the police may act under s 61.[2] There is no clear dividing line between the use of one of three options. A factor influencing police involvement is the ownership of the land. Where there is evidence of damage (as opposed to personal threats) the police are less likely to act under s 61 if the land is owned by a public organisation (eg the Forestry Commission), a large company or a major landowner. In such a case, they tend to look initially to the owner to use the civil law to remove the trespassers, and to use s 61 only if the landowner has tried and failed so to remove them. They are much more likely to act when the landowner is an individual or small organisation.[3] Linked to the issue of the exercise of discretion is the use of resources involved in applying s 61. At least one police force has adopted a policy of not using s 61 at all,[3] a judicially reviewable abdication of discretion.

Although it has been stated that the senior police officer has 'an entirely unfettered discretion to act on the information which is available',[4] his exercise of discretion to make a direction can be challenged on an application for judicial review on the same grounds as a challenge to the imposition of a condition or a ban on a public procession or assembly.[5]

Home Office Circular 45/94 states:

> 'The decision whether or not to issue a direction to leave is an operational one for the police alone to take in the light of all the circumstances of a particular case. But in making this decision the senior police officer at the scene *may* wish to take account of the personal circumstances of the trespassers, for example the presence of elderly persons, invalids, pregnant women, children and other persons whose well-being may be jeopardised by a precipitate move.'[6]

This is a weaker statement than that which applies to the exercise of local authorities in respect of their powers to direct the removal of unauthorised vehicular campers.[7] In *R v West London Magistrates' Court, ex parte Small*,[8] which concerned an application for leave to apply for judicial review of a direction under s 61, Collins J was satisfied that it was arguable that considerations of 'common humanity' should be taken into account by the senior police officer, although he did not need to decide the point. Unless he is required to do so, a local authority wishing to make a removal direction against unauthorised vehicular campers under s 77 could avoid its duty to have regard to such considerations[7] by encouraging the police to make a direction under s 61. The Divisional Court's approach to a corresponding Circular in respect of unauthorised vehicular campers[7] suggests that, when the matter has to be decided, it will be held that there is a duty to have regard to considerations when making a decision under s 61.

A direction cannot apply to persons not present at the time the reasonable belief is formed; this is the effect of the structure of s 61(1). Where the people in question are reasonably believed by the senior police officer to be persons who were not originally trespassers but have become trespassers on the land, because, for example, an express permission to be on the land has been withdrawn, he must reasonably believe that the second, third and fourth conditions listed in para **7.7** are satisfied in relation to the time after those persons became trespassers before he can make a direction under s 61(1).[9]

---

1   Issued in Spring 1999 by the ACPO Public Order Sub-Committee.
2   Similar guidance in relation to unauthorised vehicular campers is given by *Managing Unauthorised Camping: A Good Practice Guide* (DETR/Home Office, 1998).
3   *Trespass and Protest* (1998) pp 8–10.
4   *R v Wiltshire Constabulary, ex parte Taylor* (1992) unreported, DC.
5   See paras **6.96–6.98**. A problem with judicial review is that the time taken to obtain it may exceed that for which the direction is effective, although interim relief may be ordered when the application for leave to apply for judicial review is made, as explained in para **6.98**.
6   Italics added.
7   See para **7.101**.
8   (1998) unreported.
9   1994 Act, s 61(2).

7.22 Section 61 does not empower a police officer to stop people proceeding to a gathering in respect of which a direction has been made under s 61. However, sometimes the senior police officer (or any police officer or, indeed, anyone else) may be able to prevent entry by relying on the common law powers to take steps to prevent or deal with an imminent breach of the peace.[1]

---

1   See paras **2.7–2.18**.

7.23 A direction under s 61(1) need not be communicated to its addressees by the senior police officer giving it since, if it is not so communicated, it may be communicated to them by any police officer at the scene;[1] at large gatherings, communication may have to be made by a number of police officers. The requirement of communication does not mean that every addressee of the communication must be addressed personally. Communication may be oral (eg by the use of a loudhailer) or in writing (eg by notices or leaflets). In some cases leaflets have only been given to owners of vehicles, and if the owners were not with their vehicles, the leaflets were pasted to windscreens or put inside the vehicle. Strangely, there is no provision corresponding to s 63 (the 'raves provision') whereby persons are treated as having had a direction communicated to them if reasonable steps have been taken to bring it to their attention. There is no obligation to record in writing the issue of an oral direction and its detail and grounds, let alone any right for a person directed to obtain a copy of such a record. If such safeguards were regarded as necessary after a stop and search under PACE, why did Parliament not consider them necessary here? That said, a written record or some other record will be the norm. In some forces, the communication of a direction is video-recorded to assist in proof of communication to an individual.[2] If no sort of record of the issue of a direction, of the addressees of the direction, and of its terms and grounds, has been taken, it may be difficult for the police to prove that an accused was subject to a direction or had the necessary mental element on a charge of one of the offences involving breach of a direction.

By analogy with case law on a direction under s 69 of the 1994 Act,[3] there will be a direction to leave under s 61 if what is stated, albeit vague and uncertain, conveys to an addressee that he must leave the land; no other detail is required. The ACPO guidance document for Part V of the 1994 Act provides a model written direction that is of commendable clarity. It contains warnings about the criminal consequences and the associated powers to arrest and to seize vehicles, if the direction is not complied with. These warnings are not required by the legislation.

A police officer communicating a direction under s 61 need not be in uniform. This is unfortunate because it is desirable that public order policing is carried out by uniformed officers so that there can be no mistaking the authority with which their instructions are given. It is noteworthy that the power of arrest conferred by s 61(5) can be exercised only by a police officer in uniform (see para **7.32**).

---

1   1994 Act, s 61(3).
2   *Trespass and Protest* (1998) p 10.
3   See para **7.61**.

7.24 The senior police officer's power to issue a direction under s 61(1) is not limited to directing the trespassers to leave the land. He can also direct them to remove any vehicles or other property they have with them on the land.[1] The senior police officer should take care to ensure that removal of any vehicles or other property is included in the direction and that the communication of it makes this clear; otherwise it may be difficult to prove the necessary mental element against someone who leaves without removing such things.

It is interesting to note that, on its literal construction, a direction to remove applies to any vehicle or other property that the trespassers have with them, regardless of whether they brought it on to the land or not and regardless of whether or not they own it or have any other lawful right to it. It is submitted that it would be absurd if a direction to remove property extended to property to which the trespassers had no lawful right, and that under the 'golden rule' of construction[2] the power to direct removal should not be construed so as to have this effect.

In the cases surveyed in the Home Office study, directions always led to the land being cleared of persons and vehicles. However, it was often necessary to back up directions before they were effective, for example by the attendance of a large number of officers, with the associated threat of arrest or vehicle-seizure; token arrests; and towing away some of the vehicles on to the highway.[3]

---

1   1994 Act, s 61(1).
2   For the classical exposition of the golden rule, see *Grey v Pearson* (1857) 6 HL Cas 61 at 106, per Lord Wensleydale.
3   *Trespass and Protest* (1998) p 11.

Offences

7.25 If a trespasser directed to leave complies with a direction under s 61(1), he commits no offence. On the other hand, he commits an offence under s 61(4) if, knowing that a direction under s 61(1) has been given which applies to him:

(a) he fails to leave the land as soon as reasonably practicable; or
(b) having left, he again enters the land as a trespasser within the period of three months beginning with the day on which the direction was given.

The wording of para (a) of s 61(4) is so different from that of para (b) that the two paragraphs must create separate offences. Consequently, a charge of contravention of both paragraphs must be charged in two informations,[1] otherwise it will be bad for duplicity, although both informations may be contained in the same document.[2]

A direction comes into effect as soon as it is made. Technically, there is no 'period of grace' in which a person subject to it can make arrangements in respect of a place to go etc. In practice, however, officers give a deadline for vacating the land when communicating the direction.

If it is subsequently found that the senior police officer did not have a requisite reasonable belief, or that the direction was not made by the senior police officer, an offence contrary to s 61(4) will not have been committed, since there will not have been a direction under s 61(1).[3]

---

1   Magistrates' Courts Rules 1981, r 12.
2   Ibid. See *Shah v Swallow* [1984] 2 All ER 528, HL. If, however, an information charges both offences, the prosecution may, even at the trial stage, elect on which offence it wishes to proceed. Failing a decision, the information will be dismissed: Magistrates' Courts Rules 1981, r 12.
3   Even if this was not so, the accused might be able to rely on the defence of reasonable excuse referred to in para **7.30**.

Prohibited conduct

7.26 In the offence under s 61(4)(a), this consists of failing to leave the land as soon as reasonably practicable after a direction under s 61(1) has been given which applies to the person so failing. Surprisingly, no offence expressly appears to be committed by a person who leaves the land in compliance with a direction but who does not remove a vehicle or property which he has been required to move by the direction. However, if the interpretation given to the identical words in s 39 of the 1986 Act is adopted (and there can be no real doubt that it will be, despite the fact that a corresponding offence in s 77(3) of the 1994 Act expressly refers to a failure to remove a vehicle or property), failing to leave includes failing to remove a vehicle or other property which one has been directed to remove.[1]

Because the offence is committed only by failing to leave the land 'as soon as reasonably practicable',[2] which refers to the practicability of moving out (and not the practicality of going to reside somewhere else legally), a person does not commit an offence if it is not reasonably practicable to leave when the direction is given. Even though it may be practicable for D personally to leave, he will not commit an offence if it is not reasonably practicable for him to take his vehicle with him (eg where his motor caravan has broken down, is not towable and is awaiting a low-loader or, even, where he cannot afford to pay the cost of a tow).

---

1   *Krumpa v DPP* [1989] Crim LR 295, DC.
2   See para **6.9** fn 2. It was held in *Krumpa v DPP* that 'as soon as reasonably practicable' in the corresponding offence under s 39 of the Public Order Act 1986 meant that the trespassers should leave as soon as they objectively reasonably could in the circumstances, not when a reasonable police officer believed was practicable.

7.27 Section 61(4)(b) deals with the case where a person, having left the land after a direction had been given, enters the land again as a trespasser within a three-month period[1] beginning with the day on which the direction is given. For example, if that day is 1 August, the three-month period will end on 31 October, so that an entry on 1 November will not be an offence under s 61(4)(b), unless a subsequent direction to leave has been given which applies to him. The purpose for which the entry is made is irrelevant; s 61(4)(b) is not limited to entry with intent to reside on the land.

Like an offence under s 61(4)(a), the present offence can be committed by one person alone, even though the direction to leave which preceded it and on which it depends can only be given if there is a reasonable belief that two or more persons are trespassing on the land.

The most important application of s 61(4)(b) is likely to be in relation to a person who has complied as soon as reasonably practicable with a direction to leave (so that he is not guilty of an offence under s 61(4)(a)). If he enters the land again as a trespasser within the three-month period, he will commit an offence under s 61(4)(b). However, difficulties in recording the identity of the trespassers have meant that the police have rarely had sufficient evidence to prove that someone had returned to the land after being directed away. As a result of this evidential problem, if a group of trespassers returned to a site within three months officers tend simply to give another direction rather than seeking to deal with the matter as an offence under s 61(4)(b).[2]

---

1   Ie a three-calendar-month period: Interpretation Act 1978, s 5 and Sch 1.
2   *Trespass and Protest* (1998) pp 11–12. Video-recording has been used as a method of recording the identity of trespassers: ibid. See para **7.23**.

7.28 Both offences refer to failing to leave, or re-entering, *the land*. 'The land' (as opposed to a term such as 'the site [of the trespass]') is susceptible to an interpretation which extends the area in question beyond the particular place or part in which the trespass has occurred.

Of course, if the direction specifies the boundaries of the land which must be left, as where the direction is along the lines of 'You are trespassing on this farm. You must all leave it and this means that you must leave the following area ...', there will be no problem in determining the land to which the direction applies. However, if the area specified is not in accordance with the principles set out below it will be ineffective to the extent of the excess.

It is submitted that, if the direction does not specify the extent of 'the land' that must be left, 'the land' should be interpreted as extending to contiguous areas of land which have the same occupier. If this is correct, the following examples illustrate the position where trespassers in Green Field, which is occupied by Farmer Giles, are directed under s 61(1) to leave 'the land'.

(a) The trespassers simply leave Green Field and enter Brown Field, an adjoining field on Farmer Giles' farm which is also occupied by him, by passing through a connecting gateway between the two fields, and set up camp there. It is submitted that the trespassers fail to leave 'the land'.

(b) The trespassers leave Green Field, enter Brown Field and proceed across it to a gateway connecting Yellow Field to Brown Field. They pass through into Yellow Field and set up camp there. Yellow Field is also on Farmer Giles' farm and is occupied by him. It is submitted that the trespassers fail to leave 'the land'.

(c) The trespassers leave Green Field and enter Red Field which is immediately opposite across a stream (or a road) by crossing a connecting bridge (or by crossing the road). They set up camp on Red Field. Red Field is also part of Farmer Giles' farm and is occupied by him. In law, the bed of the river and the road (or, if it has been adopted by the highway authority, the subsoil of the road)[1] will be vested in Farmer Giles. It is submitted that the two fields can therefore be regarded as contiguous and that Red Field is part of the land to which the direction applies and that the trespassers have failed to leave it.

Assuming that the above is accepted, the trespassers in (a), (b) and (c) can be dealt with for an offence under s 61(4)(a). It is not a question of a new direction to leave having to be made in relation to the new field in which they set up camp, which would be possible anyway only if the various conditions for a direction were satisfied in relation to the new field. A contrary interpretation of 'the land' would deprive s 61 of much of its force in the above type of case.

The above situations may be contrasted with the following. The trespassers leave Green Field and move out onto the road referred to above. They travel along the road, past farmland occupied by Farmer Jenks and Farmer Archer on either side of the road. A mile later they pull off the road onto Black Field, which is occupied by Farmer Giles. This field is a separate holding, ie it is not contiguous to Green, Brown, Yellow and Red Fields referred to above, despite having the same occupier. This time the trespassers have not failed to leave 'the land' nor, having left 'the land', have they re-entered it within three months. Therefore, in relation to their trespass in Black Field, they must be dealt with by a fresh direction if the conditions for a direction are satisfied in relation to Black Field.

If the submission as to the meaning of 'the land' made above is correct, an extensive area of land will be protected by a direction to leave, and the supporting offence of failing to leave, in the case of a large estate of contiguous parcels of land which have the same occupier throughout, but not if the estate is let to tenant farmers (because each holding will have a separate occupier).

---

1   There may be exceptions to this normal rule.

Mental element

7.29 When he fails to leave (or enters again), an accused must know that a direction to leave has been given which applies to him, which he will if he actually knows of this or is wilfully blind[1] as to whether such a direction has been given. This would seem to require that the direction should make clear the obligation being imposed. Although it appears that vague and uncertain words can suffice for a direction,[2] one would have thought that in such a case there would be problems in proving the requisite knowledge on the accused's part. However, in *Capon v DPP*[3] the Divisional Court stated, in relation to a corresponding offence under s 69, that: 'If A says something to B which B hears, the court is entitled to conclude that B knows and understands what A has said in the absence of some contrary indication'.[4] This is questionable: a person can understand the ordinary meaning of language without understanding its impact and effect on him.[5]

The structure of the offences under s 61(4) suggests that it would be irrelevant to an accused's liability that he was mistaken as to the land to which the direction applied and thought he was leaving it by moving to a contiguous field occupied by the same person.

It is unclear whether a mental element attaches to the trespass for the purpose of the offence under s 61(4)(b). In civil law, it is not required for trespass that a person who enters as a trespasser should know or be aware of the risk of being a trespasser. On the other hand, where an offence involving trespass is concerned, it is arguable that the normal requirement of mens rea as to that element applies. It applies in respect of burglary,[6] and it is submitted that it should apply here and that knowledge or wilful blindness as to entry as a trespasser must be proved. If this is correct, a person who re-enters as a trespasser, having been misled into believing that he now has the occupier's permission, would not be guilty of an offence under s 61(4)(b).

---

1   See para **6.37** fn 2.
2   *Capon v DPP* (1998) *The Independent*, 23 March, DC; a full report is available on LEXIS.
3   See para **7.61**, where the facts of this case are set out.
4   The court stated that there was evidence to support a finding that the accused knew a
     direction had been given, as there was no contrary indication that any of them did not
     understand what was said (which was odd because there was evidence that one of them had
     said: 'I don't understand'; see para **7.61**).
5   Mead, cited in para **7.61** fn 2, at 873.
6   *R v Collins* [1973] 2 All ER 1105, CA.

Defences

7.30 It is a defence for the accused to prove:[1]

'(a)   that he was not trespassing on the land, or
 (b)   that he had a reasonable excuse for failing to leave the land as soon as reasonably
        practicable or, as the case may be, for again entering the land as a trespasser.'[2]

It is submitted that the defence of 'not trespassing' in (a) must refer to not trespassing at the time that the senior police officer forms his reasonable belief (after all, he may be wrong), and not the time of the prohibited conduct. Otherwise, the defence will be inoperable in relation to the 're-entering' offence, because the fact that the prosecution has to prove the element of trespass as part of its proof of the prohibited conduct would mean that there would be no need for a defence of 'no-trespass' to be proved by the accused, and a defence which is clearly intended to apply to both offences would be inapplicable to one of them.

It is not obvious what could be a reasonable excuse for failing to leave land, which would not also prevent it being established that the accused failed to leave as soon as reasonably practicable. 'Reasonable excuse' is likely to have more significance in relation to the offence of re-entry. It might, for example, be a reasonable excuse to re-enter to collect something which had been left behind. In other contexts, it has been held that whether there is a reasonable excuse depends on whether a reasonable man would think the excuse reasonable in the circumstances,[3] but that as a matter of law there are limitations as to what a reasonable man thinks.[4] This is likely to be the approach taken by the courts in relation to the present provision. Analogy with 'reasonable excuse' in the context of failing to provide a specimen under drink-drive law suggests that it is not a reasonable excuse in relation to an offence under s 61 (4) (a) that the accused did not think he was a trespasser.[5] It has been held in relation to a similarly worded offence under s 69 of the 1994 Act that it is not a reasonable excuse that the accused mistakenly believed that the person giving the direction was not entitled to do so or had remained to establish what offence was in issue.[6] It can be seen from all this that a claim of reasonable excuse will rarely succeed.

---

1   See para **4.38**.
2   1994 Act, s 61 (6).
3   *Bryan v Mott* (1975) 62 Cr App R 71, DC.
4   Ibid; *Evans v Hughes* [1972] 3 All ER 412, DC.
5   *R v Downey* [1970] RTR 257, CA; *R v Reid* [1973] 3 All ER 1020, CA.
6   *Capon v DPP* (1998) *The Independent*, 23 March, DC. A full report is available on LEXIS. See para **7.61**.

Trial and punishment

7.31 An offence under s 61 (4) is summary only.[1] The maximum punishment is three months' imprisonment or a fine not exceeding level 4 on the standard scale[1] or both.

---

1   1994 Act, s 61 (4).

Arrest

7.32 The purpose of s 61 of the 1994 Act is to give the occupier of the land a swifter remedy for recovering possession of it than the available (and possibly costly) civil remedy. Consequently, s 61(5) is of crucial importance since it provides that a constable in uniform[1] who reasonably suspects[2] that a person is committing one of the above offences may arrest him without a warrant. However, where a substantial number are so suspected, the police may be inhibited from making arrests; each arrest reduces the number of officers available to deal with the rest by one or (normally) two.

Where there is only a reasonable suspicion that the accused has committed the offence, or if the officer who reasonably suspects that the accused is committing the offence is not in uniform, he can only arrest the accused if the requirements of s 25 of PACE are satisfied.

---

1   See para **6.92**.
2   See para **3.68** fn 1.

Seizure

7.33 Section 62 of the 1994 Act provides powers of seizure which are supplementary to the police powers provided by s 61. It provides that, if a direction has been given under s 61 and a constable reasonably suspects[1] that any person to whom the direction applies has, without reasonable excuse:

(a) failed to remove any vehicle[2] on the land which appears to the constable to belong to him or to be in his possession or under his control; or

(b) entered the land as a trespasser with a vehicle within a three-month period beginning with the day on which the direction was given;

the constable (who is not required to be in uniform) may seize and remove that vehicle. It is no bar to seizure of a vehicle that it is someone's home.

Paragraph (a) above, covers not only the case where the trespassers have quit, leaving their vehicles behind, but also the case where they fail to leave, unreasonably claiming that they cannot remove their vehicles.

It will be noted that this power does not extend to property other than vehicles, such as scrap metal and animals, about which a direction under s 61(1) may be made. The vehicles are the 'key'; if they go, the trespasser will almost inevitably follow. It will also be noted that the constable need not have reasonable grounds for the view that he takes as to whether or not the vehicle belongs etc to that person in (a), although he must have such grounds in relation to his suspicion that the person has failed to remove the vehicle.[3]

The police have been wary about using their new powers to seize and retain vehicles, not because of the ECHR, but because of the high level of organisation and expertise involved and the possibility of disorder. Their view has been that the exercise of those powers would require a very serious situation where all else had failed.[4]

---

1   See para **3.68** fn 1.
2   'Vehicle' bears the same meaning as in s 61 (para **7.20**): 1994 Act, s 62.
3   A seizure of a caravan or the like might give rise to a breach of the ECHR, Art 8, and the seizure of any possessions might constitute a breach of the ECHR First Protocol, Art 1; see paras **7.110** and **7.111**.
4   *Trespass and Protest* (1998) pp 12–13.

Retention and disposal

7.34 Any vehicle seized and removed under the above power may be retained in accordance with regulations made by the Home Secretary,[1] currently the Police (Retention and Disposal of Vehicles) Regulations 1995.[2] Regulation 3(1) provides that, after a vehicle has been seized, it must be passed into and remain in the custody of a constable or other person authorised under reg 3 by the chief officer of police for the area in which the vehicle was seized ('the authority') until:

(a) the authority permits it to be removed from its custody by a person appearing to it to be the person from whom the vehicle was seized or the owner of the vehicle; or

(b) it has been disposed of or destroyed under the Regulations.

By reg 4(1) the authority must, as soon as it is able after the vehicle has been taken into its custody, take such steps as are practicable[3] to serve a 'removal notice' on the person from whom the vehicle was seized, except where the vehicle has been removed from its custody under reg 5, below. A removal notice must contain the following 'specified information' to the extent that it is ascertainable: (a) the vehicle's registration mark; and (b) the make of the vehicle.[4]

The notice must state:

(a) where the vehicle was seized;

(b) where it is now being kept;

(c) that the addressee must claim the vehicle on or before the date specified in the notice, being a date not less than 21 days from the day when the notice is served on him;

(d) that unless the vehicle is claimed on or before that date the authority intends to destroy or dispose of it;

(e) that charges are payable by the person from whom the vehicle was seized in respect of its removal and retention, and that it may be retained until they are paid.[5]

The notice must be served by delivering it to the person to whom it is directed by leaving it at, or by sending it by registered post or recorded delivery to, his usual or last known place of abode.[6]

By s 67(4) of the 1994 Act, any authority is entitled to recover from someone from whom a vehicle has been seized the prescribed charges[7] in respect of the removal, retention, disposal and destruction of the vehicle by the authority. Any such charges are recoverable as a simple contract debt, so that a court order is not required.[8] Any authority having custody of the vehicles under the regulations is entitled to retain custody until any such charges are paid.[9]

Regulation 5(1) provides that, subject to s 67(4) and to reg 6 (below), if a person satisfies the authority that he is the person from whom the vehicle was seized the authority must permit him to remove the vehicle from its custody. However, the authority is not obliged to do so if it reasonably believes that that person is not the owner of the vehicle or authorised by the owner to remove it; in such a case it is not prevented from returning the vehicle to its owner.[10]

Although the power under s 67 is not strictly a power of forfeiture, it is so in effect because reg 6(1) provides that, where the authority has been unable to serve a removal notice on the person on whom the vehicle was seized or, following the service of such a notice, the vehicle has not been removed from its custody under the Regulations, the authority may dispose of or destroy the vehicle in accordance with the following rules. If the authority is satisfied that the person on whom it has served or attempted to serve a removal notice is the owner of the vehicle, it may dispose of or destroy the vehicle at any time,[11] except that it may not do so:

(a) during the period of three months starting with the date on which the vehicle was seized;

(b) if the period in (a) above has expired, until after the removal date specified in the removal notice; or

(c) if not otherwise covered by (a) or (b) above, during the period of seven days starting with the date on which the vehicle is claimed under reg 5 above.[12]

On the other hand, where the authority is not satisfied that the person on whom it has served or attempted to serve a removal notice is the owner of the vehicle, it may only dispose of or destroy the vehicle if, after checking the vehicle registration records and taking any other steps to find the vehicle's owner as appear to it to be practicable:

(a) it fails to find such a person, allowing a reasonable time for any person or body from whom it has requested information to respond to the request; or

(b) it finds such a person but he fails to comply with a removal notice served on him, or he is a person on whom it has already served or attempted to serve a removal notice.[13]

Thereafter, it may dispose of or destroy the vehicle at any time, subject to the three periods referred to at note 12 above.

An authority which disposes of or destroys a vehicle under the Regulations must, where it is possible to do so, give prescribed information relating to the disposal or destruction of the vehicle to the person from whom it was seized, to any person who appears to the authority to have been its owner immediately before its disposal and to the Secretary of State (if the vehicle has a GB registration mark, or to another specified person or persons if it has some other sort of mark).[14]

In addition, when the authority disposes of the vehicle it must pay the net proceeds of sale to any person who within a one-year period beginning with the sale date satisfies it that at the time of the sale he was the vehicle's owner.[15]

It is no bar to the exercise of the power of destruction or disposal that, as may well be the case, the vehicle is the home of the person from whom it was seized.

Particularly in the light of the fact that the above provisions, which can culminate in effect in a forfeiture, do not depend on a conviction, their application may contravene Art 1 of the First Protocol of the ECHR (no person to be deprived of possessions except in the public interest) and, since the seizure is an executive action carried out without a court order, Art 6 of the ECHR (right to fair and public hearing).[16] If the vehicle seized is someone's home, there would seem to be a breach of Art 8 of the ECHR (right to respect for home) since it is difficult to see how such a seizure could be 'necessary in a democratic society in the interests of public safety, for the prevention of disorder or crime, or for the protection of the rights and freedoms of others'.

---

1   1994 Act, s 67(1).
2   SI 1995/723. The power to make regulations is exercisable by statutory instrument which is subject to annulment in pursuance of a resolution of either House of Parliament: s 67(8).
3   See para **6.9** fn 2.
4   Regs 2(2) and 4(3).
5   Reg 4(3).
6   Reg 4(4).
7   The prescribed sums for the purpose of s 67(4) of the 1994 Act are: (a) in respect of removal, £105; (b) in respect of retention, £12 for each 24-hour period during which the vehicle is in the authority's custody: reg 9(1). For the purposes of (b) above, each 24-hour period is reckoned from noon on the first day after removal during which the place at which the vehicle is stored is open for claiming vehicles before noon: reg 9(2).
8   1994 Act, s 67(6).
9   Ibid, s 67(7).
10   Reg 5(2).

11 Reg 6(2).
12 Reg 6(5).
13 Reg 6(3) and (4).
14 Reg 7(1). As to the prescribed specification, see reg 7(2).
15 Reg 8(1). If it appears to the authority that more than one person is the owner of a particular vehicle, such one of them as the authority thinks fit shall be treated as its owner for the purposes of reg 8(1): reg 8(2). In reg 8(1), 'the net proceeds of sale' means any sum by which the proceeds of sale exceed the aggregate of such sums as may be payable under the Regulations in respect of the removal and retention of the vehicle: reg 8(3).
16 *Mats Jacobsson v Sweden* (1990) Ser A, no 180; 13 EHRR 79, ECtHR.

Need

7.35 Trespasses on land in the open air of the type covered by s 61 can, of course, be dealt with otherwise than by using the criminal process. Quite apart from the occupier's right to use reasonable force to prevent trespassers entering land or to eject them, the civil law offers protection. The occupier may obtain a possession order (which can be granted whether or not the identity of the trespasser is known). The trouble with this remedy is that it is not a speedy one and the costs of obtaining it will be borne by the 'victim' unless a defendant is named and a costs order is made against him. Moreover, the order may not be effective.

Conduct of the type in question is attended by the clear risk of a breach of the peace, since the landowner and/or others may well reasonably be prompted to take action. The result is that the police can prevent the trespass taking place or continuing by exercising their common law power to prevent a breach of the peace by stopping the would-be trespassers entering the area of the land in question or (as the case may be) requiring them to leave.[1] If those concerned disobey, they will commit the offence of wilfully obstructing a constable in the execution of his duty. If they use or threaten force or behave in an abusive or insulting way or in some other threatening way, this can be dealt with by a prosecution for an appropriate offence against the person or an offence against public order, such as riot, violent disorder or affray or an offence under ss 4, 4A or 5 of the Public Order Act 1986. With the exception of common assault or battery, such offences are either arrestable or carry with them a specific power of arrest, quite apart from the possibility of arrest for breach of the peace or under s 25 of PACE. If damage is caused, liability for criminal damage (an arrestable offence) is possible. Where vehicles are used to enter land, the non-arrestable offence of driving without lawful authority on land which does not form part of a road, contrary to s 34 of the Road Traffic Act 1988, is committed.

With the exception of an offence under s 5 of the Public Order Act 1986 and of the last offence, all these offences are more serious than an offence under s 61.

The availability of the power to bind over to keep the peace should also be borne in mind.

In common with the above procedures and powers, s 61 is unlikely to do more than solve the 'local problem'. The end result of a direction under s 61 is liable simply to be to move the trespassers on to cause trouble elsewhere.

Police figures for 1995 show that officers across 15 forces gave a direction to leave land 67 times under s 61 and that there were no cases in which the police seized vehicles under s 62. The use of s 61 varied widely from force to force: one force used it 16 times, while the majority used it either once or twice. The number of people being directed from land in each of the instances also varied widely, ranging from 3 to 46. The number of motorised vehicles and caravans evicted ranged from 6 to 52, with the average number evicted being around a dozen. Perhaps reflecting the police's success in enforcing s 61, the statistics below[2] show that prosecutions for an offence under s 61 are rare.

	Cautions	Prosecutions	Convictions
1995	5	4	3
1996	13	4	0

1   *Moss v McLachlan* [1985] IRLR 76, DC.
2   *Trespass and Protest* (1998) pp 16–17.

7.36 Section 61 criminalises trespassers who refuse to leave and extends the law into areas previously dealt with by civil law and county court eviction procedures. It also interferes with the freedom of assembly under Art 11 of the ECHR and with the right to respect for private and family life under Art 8. Both Articles only permit such interference with these rights as is in accordance with the law and is necessary in a democratic society for, inter alia, the prevention of disorder or crime, for the protection of health or morals, or for the protection of the rights and freedoms of others. Insofar as a direction may be made against a trespasser who is reasonably believed to have damaged the land or property on it, or to have threatened, etc, the occupier, etc, or to have been an accomplice to such conduct, the interference with the freedoms of assembly and of private and family life involved in a direction under s 61 may well be justified under Arts 11 and 8 as being necessary in a democratic society to prevent disorder or crime, where the conduct is liable to lead to a breach of the peace, or in any event to protect the rights and freedoms of others (the occupier, his family, etc) from such conduct, although the range of other offences and powers applicable in such a situation would seem to make special provision unnecessary. However, except (arguably) where a breach of the peace is liable to result from the conduct of others, such justification would not apply in relation to a trespasser who was not reasonably believed to be associated, as perpetrator or accomplice, with that conduct, or where the trigger for a direction is simply a reasonable belief that the trespassers have six or more vehicles with them on the land. In such a case, the use of a civil remedy against such a person would seem to be as far as is necessary in a democratic society to protect the rights and freedoms of the occupier, etc. In any event, the absolute ban on re-entry as a trespasser (for whatever purpose) seems to be disproportionate and open to challenge.

AGGRAVATED TRESPASS

7.37 Sections 68 and 69 of the Criminal Justice and Public Order Act 1994 deal with trespassers who seek to intimidate, to obstruct or to disrupt people engaged in a lawful activity on the land. Section 68 makes such conduct an offence, while s 69 provides the police with a power corresponding to that under s 61 to direct people to leave the land. These provisions were aimed particularly at the activities of anti-hunt saboteurs who go beyond peaceful protest. However, they also cover, for example, animal rights supporters who seek to disrupt shooting at game, to intimidate those working in laboratories involving procedures on animals or to obstruct a horserace, and environmental protesters. Their application with regard to protesters demonstrating to prevent contractors building a new road, such as the Newbury by-pass, has been one of the most important areas in which they have been applied.

The offence

7.38 By section 68(1) of the 1994 Act:

> 'A person commits the offence of aggravated trespass if he trespasses on land in the open air and, in relation to any lawful activity which persons are engaging in or are about to engage in on that or adjoining land in the open air, does there anything which is intended by him to have the effect –
>
> (a) of intimidating those persons or any of them so as to deter them or any of them from engaging in that activity,
> (b) of obstructing that activity, or
> (c) of disrupting that activity.'

For the purposes of the rule against duplicity, s 68(1) creates one offence consisting of one piece of prohibited conduct which can be committed with one or more of three intents.[1] Thus, where more than one intent is alleged in respect of the same conduct there is no need for more than one charge.

---

1   *Nelder v DPP* (1998) *The Times*, 8 June, DC. The report is very brief. The full text is on LEXIS.

7.39 There is some overlap between this offence and an offence under s 5 of the Public Order Act 1986 where trespassers engage in conduct with intent to intimidate people engaged in a lawful activity or to obstruct or disrupt that activity. A significant distinction, however, is that no defence of reasonable conduct is available under s 68, unlike s 5 of the 1986 Act.

Prohibited conduct

7.40 The prohibited conduct consists of trespassing on land in the open air and, in relation to any lawful activity that people are engaging in or about to engage in on that or adjoining land in the open air, doing something. Nothing is required to result from that 'something'.

7.41 In relation to the first element, a trespass[1] on land in the open air, there is no need for an entry on to that land to be as a trespasser; the offence can be committed by someone who goes onto the land lawfully but then becomes a trespasser by remaining after the expiry of his licence. Likewise, a person lawfully on land may become a trespasser by entering part of it from which he is excluded. Thus, university students who are lawfully on the campus by virtue of their licence to be there become trespassers, and can be convicted of the present offence, if they hold a noisy sit-in in the cordoned-off square outside the administration block to disrupt a royal walkabout. Unlike the offence under s 61, there is no prescribed minimum number of trespassers – one is enough, although instances of the offence being committed by one person in isolation are unlikely (and a prosecution of that person even less likely).

---

1   See para **7.8** fn 2.

7.42 The requirement that the trespass must be on land in the open air gives the offence under s 68 a narrower locational ambit than the offence under s 61. Animal rights extremists who invade a dutch barn in which a livestock auction is being held, in order to obstruct it, cannot commit the present offence.[1] Nor, a fortiori, can protesters who trespass in a broiler house to prevent egg collection or who invade a circus ring during a performance. On the other hand, hunt saboteurs who trespass in a field clearly trespass on land in the open air, and so do members of the crowd who stage a disruptive protest by trespassing on the pitch at Old Trafford. In the case of a designated association football match, pitch invaders may be convicted for the less serious offence[2] of football pitch invasion under s 4 of the Football (Offences) Act 1991 and are more likely to be charged with it since no intent to intimidate, obstruct or disrupt need be proved.

---

1   Unless their conduct en route to the barn satisfies the terms of s 68.
2   See paras **8.25**, **8.28** and **8.29**.

7.43 Like 'land' in s 61 of the 1994 Act, 'land' in s 68 does not include land forming part of a highway (unless that highway is a footpath or bridleway or one of the other categories excluded by s 61(9), described in para **7.14**).[1] Thus, although a human chain blocking a village street to prevent the passing of a hunt is a trespass, it cannot constitute aggravated trespass, but a similar blockage of a footpath or bridleway will. Both pieces of conduct can, of course, constitute the less serious offence of obstructing the highway, contrary to s 137 of the Highways Act 1980, or the more serious one of public nuisance. However, if protesters on any highway only obstruct it partially, neither offence will be committed if their use of the highway is reasonable.[2] Indeed, a non-obstructive demonstration on any highway does not constitute a trespass if it involves such a use.[3]

  Where a demonstration takes place in proximity to a road, it may not be easy for the prosecution to prove that protesters were not on the highway if they allege they were. Clearly fine questions of demarcation can arise.

---

1   1994 Act, s 68(5).
2   See paras **9.72–9.96**.
3   See para **6.86**.

7.44 The second piece of conduct required by s 68(1) is that the accused trespasser must do something (with the requisite intent to intimidate etc) in relation to any lawful activity which persons are engaging in or are about to engage in on that land in the open air or adjoining land in the open air. It will be noted that s 68(1) requires the accused to do something. That 'something' must be a distinct and overt act other than the act of trespassing.[1] That act must be specified in the information.[1]

  A failure to do something, with the requisite intent, is not enough. Hunt saboteurs who have assembled in a field by a footbridge over a river for a briefing and who refuse to move when the hunt suddenly comes on the scene and wishes to cross the river, cannot be convicted of an offence under s 68, whereas they could if with intent to obstruct the hunt they had formed themselves into a human chain or given drugged meat to the hounds or stood on an earth to prevent a fox being dug out. Likewise, a person can be convicted of the offence if, during a game shoot, he shouts abuse at the participants or lets off maroons to scare away the birds, or if, during a Test match, he runs on to the pitch to disrupt play.

---

1   *DPP v Barnard* (1999) 96(42) LSG 40.

7.45 The requirement that the act must be done in relation to any lawful activity which persons are engaging in or about to engage in raises a number of points.

First, although as a matter of interpretation the plural includes the singular, this rule gives way to a contrary express or implied intention.[1] It is submitted that the use of 'person' in relation to who can commit the offence and then the use of 'persons' in the present context provides that contrary intention, so that a trespasser cannot commit aggravated trespass if he acts only in relation to one person engaged in a lawful activity.

Secondly, the actual or imminent lawful activity must be on the land trespassed on or adjoining land in the open air. Thus, animal rights protesters who trespass in the open air to interfere with operations in an adjacent intensive rearing shed do not commit the present offence. What constitutes adjoining land is open to speculation. There is no problem where the lawful activity is on a contiguous plot of land, which has the same occupier, to that trespassed on, since that plot (eg a field) will be part of the land trespassed on. But what if two plots have separate occupiers? Clearly, a field on Green Farm occupied by Farmer Giles which abuts a field on Bridge Farm occupied by Farmer Archer is 'adjoining land', but what if the field on Green Farm is separated from Bridge Farm by a field on a third farm, Home Farm, or if the two fields are separated by a road or a stream? The *Shorter Oxford English Dictionary* defines adjoining as 'lying close, being contiguous, to or with'. It would be surprising if 'adjoining land' was held not to include land separated by a road or a stream but, beyond that, it is not obvious that other land in separate occupation not immediately contiguous could be held to be 'adjoining'. It is noteworthy that the Government resisted the use of 'neighbouring' in substitution for 'adjoining' on the ground that it was too imprecise and liable to cover too large an area.[2] This is yet another example of uncertainty in the provisions described in this chapter.

Thirdly, it remains to be seen how 'about to' will be interpreted. It is submitted that while 'about to' must not be interpreted as 'immediate', ie taking place or accomplished without delay, it must mean 'imminent', ie 'liable to happen soon'. Any wider interpretation would make the offence far too extensive.

---

1   Interpretation Act 1978, s 6.
2   HL Deb, vol 556, col 1497–1498 (1994).

7.46 'Lawful activity' is defined by s 68(2). It provides that activity on any occasion on the part of a person or persons on land is 'lawful' for the purposes of s 68 if he or they may engage in the activity on the land on that occasion without committing an offence or trespassing on the land. Thus, the activity of a shooting party on land which they have a licence to be on or of ramblers walking along a footpath is a lawful activity, and so is the activity of felling a tree or constructing a road if the necessary permissions have been given. On the other hand, the activity of people, even the occupiers of the land, digging for badgers is not a lawful activity because it is an offence under s 2 of the Protection of Badgers Act 1992. Acts by trespassers in relation to such an activity are not caught by s 68, nor are such acts in relation to a hunt which is itself trespassing.

Provided that an activity is intrinsically lawful, as where a highway authority is clearing the route of a new road with lawful authority, a collateral illegality, such as a breach of the health and safety regulations by those clearing the route, will not prevent there being a lawful activity.[1]

---

1   *Hibberd v DPP* [1997] CLYB 1251, DC.

7.47 In addition, the mere fact that at some point during the accused's prohibited conduct the activity of his opponents was incidentally unlawful does not prevent an offence being committed if that prohibited conduct with the prescribed intent occurred to an appreciable extent when that activity was lawful. This was held by the Divisional Court in *Nelder v DPP*.[1] While hunt saboteurs were trespassing, the hunt servants took the hounds on to a railway line. In doing so, they (unlike the rest of the hunt who remained on land where they were permitted) were trespassers. The saboteurs followed the huntsman and hounds and began a noisy disruptive protest. The hounds ran off the line through fields in which the hunt was permitted to be, pursued by the hunt servants. The saboteurs ran along with the hounds continuing their noisy disruption. Indeed, the magistrate found the whole activity of the hunt was disrupted.

The Divisional Court dismissed appeals against convictions for aggravated trespass by a number of the saboteurs. It agreed with the magistrate that as a matter of fact and degree, at any rate by the time that the trespass by the hunt servants and hounds had ended, the hunt's activity had become lawful so that by thereafter maintaining their protest for an appreciable time over an appreciable distance, the saboteurs had committed the prohibited conduct with intent to obstruct or disrupt that lawful activity. Simon Brown LJ, with whom Hooper J agreed, said:

> 'Clearly, if the hunt's central objective had been, for example, to hunt land over which they had no permission to go or upon which hunting was banned, then the mere fact that they proposed also to engage in some lawful hunting in the vicinity would not make their activity, as a whole, lawful. That, however, was not this case. Equally, had the protesters confined their protest to the period whilst a significant part of the hunt was trespassing, then too no offence here could properly be found established. That, too, however, was not the case.'

---

1   See para **7.38** fn 1. This part of the case is not in *The Times* report.

7.48 The accused's conduct must be done '*in relation to* any lawful activity'. What is required for this 'relational' element remains to be judicially determined but presumably it requires the accused's act to be directed at the lawful activity.

7.49 The meaning of the reference to 'activity which persons are *engaging* in or about to *engage* in' in s 68(1) is not clear. Does 'engaging/engage' require that something is actively being done or about to be done actively by the persons concerned? If it does not, the aggravated trespass provisions are particularly wide in their scope. Hooligans who trespass in a field and scatter in all directions the sheep grazing there may be said to do an act in relation to the sheep and in relation to the farmer and his shepherd, and do so with intent to disrupt the operation of the farm, but it is submitted that they do not do so in relation to an activity in which the farmer and the shepherd are engaging or about to engage in.[1] It would be different if the farmer and shepherd were engaged in driving the sheep into a pen at the time.

---

1 A similar point may be made about environmental protesters who trample on a genetically modified crop in a field in which they are protesting, although they may be guilty of criminal damage.

Mental element

7.50 The accused is required by s 68(1) to do his act 'in relation to any lawful activity which persons are engaging in or are about to engage in' with the intention[1] that it should have one of the following effects:

(a) of intimidating[2] those persons or any of them so as to deter them or any of them from engaging in the lawful activity;
(b) of obstructing[3] that activity; or
(c) of disrupting[4] that activity.

The requirement of 'intent' must be stressed. Proof that conduct had one of these three effects is not required. On the other hand, it is not sufficient that the accused was merely reckless as to the risk of one of the three effects occurring.

By way of example of the present requirement, a trespassing animal rights protester commits aggravated trespass if he shouts threats of violence at those engaged in a pheasant shoot on the land, or if he fires maroons to scare away the pheasants, or if he seeks to divert the attention of the shoot, because he will have, respectively, an intention to intimidate the shooters, an intention to obstruct their lawful activity and an intention to disrupt it. Anti-motorway campaigners will commit aggravated trespass if they sit down in front of excavating machines with the intention of obstructing the excavation work, and so will someone who runs onto a Test match pitch to make a political protest by disrupting play. Indeed, a group who hold a peaceful picket on the steps of the town hall as a protest against a cut in funds for voluntary advice services, intending thereby to disrupt or obstruct council workers in carrying out their jobs, commit the present offence, however well-intentioned they may be. Likewise, trespassing pickets in the open air who try to prevent 'scabs' entering the workplace commit aggravated trespass if they shout threats of violence at them with intent that their words should have the effect of intimidating them so as to deter them from engaging in work. However, a charge of the slightly more serious offence of intimidation under s 241 of the Trade Union and Labour Relations (Consolidation) Act 1992[5] is more likely. Nevertheless, the fact that such conduct is aggravated trespass is important since it can serve as a trigger for a direction to leave under s 69.

In contrast, trespassing pickets who merely sought peacefully to persuade 'scabs' would not be caught, because of lack of a requisite intent. A fortiori, trespassing ramblers do not commit the offence if their conduct does not go beyond trespassing.

There is an element of overlap between the three intended effects, particularly those of obstruction and disruption.[6]

1   Although the accused must have the necessary intent when he does the act in question, he
     need not have that intent when his trespass begins: *Lucy v DPP* (1997) 73 P&CR D25, DC.
2   It is submitted that 'intimidating' will be construed in the same way as in relation to the
     offence under s 241(1)(a) of the Trade Union and Labour Relations (Consolidation) Act
     1992; see para **9.39**.
3   By analogy with the offence of obstructing a constable in the execution of his duty,
     'obstructing' does not require an assault. In general, any conduct which makes it more
     difficult for a person to do what he is legally entitled to do amounts to 'obstructing' him: see
     para **9.66**.
4   The intended disruption is not required to be serious; cf the use of 'serious disruption' in the
     1986 Act, ss 12 and 14.
5   See para **9.48**.
6   *Nelder v DPP* (1998) *The Times*, 8 June, DC; see para **7.38** fn 1.

7.51 It is submitted that the wording of s 68(1), which requires the accused to do
something 'intended by him to have the effect of' intimidating etc, indicates that
'intention' here is limited to intention in its purposive sense[1] and that if such an
intent is not proved but it is proved that one of the required effects was virtually
certain to result from D's conduct, and that D foresaw this result as virtually
certain, it will not be possible (as it otherwise would be)[2] for the magistrates to find
that D intended that effect. If the necessary intent is limited to a purposive one,
huntsmen who know that their conduct, or the conduct of their pack, will terrify a
frail couple in the garden in which they trespass, but who do not aim that conduct
to have this effect, cannot be guilty under s 68, even if it could be said that they had
acted in relation to a lawful activity in which the couple were engaging.

1   As to intention, see para **4.35** fn 2. It is submitted that the context in which 'intention'
     appears in s 68(1) limits that term to its purposive meaning. A finding of intention from
     foresight of virtual certainty is not possible in all offences of 'intention'; the nature of the
     offence or context in which the word 'intention' appears in a definition of the offence may
     preclude the possibility of a finding of intention from foresight and limit 'intention' in that
     offence to a purposive intention: see, for example, *R v Ahlers* [1915] 1 KB 616. It is submitted
     that there is such a preclusion in respect of the present offence.
2   *R v Woollin* [1998] 4 All ER 103, HL.

7.52 The requirement that the accused should do something which is intended
by him to have the effect of intimidating, obstructing or disrupting is clearly
satisfied where what is done is in itself intended to have the effect of intimidating,
obstructing or disrupting the lawful activity in question. Thus, if trespassing
anti-hunt protesters blow horns, or spray a scent-confusing spray in front of the
hounds, with the intent of disrupting the hunt by their conduct, the requirement
of mens rea is clearly satisfied.

What, however, if an accused's act was merely done with intent to do a further
act, which is not committed, and thereby to intimidate, obstruct or disrupt a lawful
activity? Suppose that a trespassing anti-hunt protester is arrested as he runs
towards a hunt with the intention that when he is within distance he will do
something whose effect will be to intimidate, obstruct or disrupt the hunt. The
words of s 68(1) would seem to indicate that this will not satisfy the requirement of
mens rea. However, in *Winder v DPP*,[1] the Divisional Court held that, if the act
done by the trespasser (eg running in the above example) was done towards an
intended intimidation, obstruction or disruption, the requirement of mens rea

would be satisfied. This interpretation would seem to stretch the clear words of s 68(1) beyond any permissible bounds.

The Divisional Court recognised that there could be problems of remoteness with its interpretation of the offence. However, in terms of the facts of the case, it thought that remoteness was not a stumbling block. Schiemann LJ giving the Court's judgment said:

> 'The running after the hunt was sufficiently closely connected to the intended disruption as to be, in the words of the Criminal Attempts Act 1981, "more than merely preparatory". It was intended to get the appellants sufficiently close to the hunt in a sufficiently short time to enable them there to disrupt it ... That conclusion sufficed to justify the conviction.'[2]

The view that D's act of running was 'more than merely preparatory' to the intended disruptive conduct is a more generous view than has been taken in respect of this phrase under the Criminal Attempts Act 1981.[3] Surely the running was merely preparatory to the intended disruptive conduct. In any event, it is hard to accept that 'more than merely preparatory' was meant by the court to be the test of remoteness because it could not conceivably have been satisfied in the two examples of the offence given by the Divisional Court, which illustrate that the offence is wider than even the facts of *Winder* indicate:

> 'Suppose a trespasser on open land says to a third party "go over the brow of that hill and there throw some stink bombs" so as to disrupt the lawful activity – be it a hunt, be it a concert, be it a birthday celebration for the farmer's daughter – which is going on there. Is the trespasser guilty of the s 68 offence, whether or no the third party throws the stink bombs and whether or no the members of the hunt know of the trespasser's existence? Clearly the act of giving the instruction does not in itself disrupt but it is intended in due course to result in acts which have that effect. We think that such a trespasser is guilty.
>
> The same goes for a trespasser who, wishing to disrupt a lawful activity, but out of sight, picks up a stone with a view to throwing it in the midst of those carrying out the lawful activity. We do not consider that the drafting of the section would require a court to hold that since picking up a stone in itself harmed no-one no offence [under s 68] was committed.'[2]

These examples are tantamount to allowing the police power of arrest associated with s 68 to be used not for the acts themselves but to prevent a remote possibility of a further substantive offence in the future.[4]

---

1   (1996) 160 JP 713, DC.
2   Ibid, at 719.
3   See, for example, *R v Gullefer* [1990] 3 All ER 882, CA; *R v Geddes* (1996) 160 JP 697, CA.
4   See Mead 'Human Rights Act – a panacea for public protest?' (1999) 4 J Civ Lib 7.

7.53 No requirement of mens rea is expressly made as to the fact that the accused is trespassing. By analogy with the offence of burglary,[1] it would seem that there is a mental element required in this respect that it would consist of actual knowledge or wilful blindness.

---

1   *R v Collins* [1972] 2 All ER 1105, CA.

Prevention of evil – a defence?

7.54 A claim that a trespasser was acting to prevent some evil occurring will not succeed if the above requirements are satisfied. Necessity is a very narrow defence[1] whose terms are not going to be satisfied where the victims of the trespassory conduct are engaged in a lawful activity.

---

1   Card, Cross and Jones *Criminal Law* (1998) paras 20.41–20.42.

Trial, punishment and arrest

7.55 By s 68(3) of the 1994 Act, aggravated trespass is a summary offence; the maximum punishment is the same as for offences under s 61, viz three months' imprisonment or a fine not exceeding level 4 on the standard scale, or both.

A constable in uniform[1] who reasonably suspects[2] that a person is committing the offence of aggravated trespass may arrest him without warrant.[3] As with an offence under s 61, the police may be inhibited from making arrests where a substantial number are so suspected, because of the effect of making each arrest on the available police manpower.

---

1   See para **6.92**.
2   See para **3.68** fn 1.
3   1994 Act, s 68(4). For a power of arrest in other circumstances, see PACE, s 25. Compare the offence under the Football (Offences) Act 1991, described in para **8.28**, which is an arrestable offence under PACE, s 24(2).

Direction to leave land

The power

7.56 Section 69(1) of the 1994 Act provides:

'If the senior police officer present at the scene reasonably believes –[1]

(a)   that a person is committing, has committed or intends to commit the offence of aggravated trespass on land in the open air; or

(b)   that two or more persons are trespassing on land in the open air and are present there with the common purpose of intimidating[2] persons so as to deter them from engaging in a lawful activity or of obstructing[3] or disrupting a lawful activity,

he may direct that person or (as the case may be) those persons (or any of them) to leave the land.'

As can be seen from this provision, it is not necessary for an offence of aggravated trespass to have been committed before a direction can be made under s 69.[4] Section 69 is especially useful in two situations: to get rid of trespassers before there is a major confrontation; and, if the confrontation does occur, to limit it and prevent it getting out of hand.

---

1   See para **6.28**.
2   See para **7.50** fn 2.
3   See para **7.50** fn 3.
4   *Capon v DPP* (1998) *The Independent*, 23 March, DC. A full report is available on LEXIS.

7.57 'Lawful activity' and 'land' bear the same meaning as in s 68.[1] 'The senior police officer' who alone has power to make a direction has been discussed in paras **7.5** and **7.6**.

---

1   1994 Act, s 69(6).

7.58 In relation to the alternative conditions which must be reasonably believed, that in (a) calls for no comment additional to that made above, save to say that 'commit' here presumably means commit by perpetration, rather than aiding or abetting.

7.59 The second alternative condition, (b), deals with the case where there is no reasonable belief that a particular individual trespasser on land in the open air is committing, has committed or is about to commit aggravated trespass, but there is a reasonable belief that two or more trespassers on land in the open air were present there with the common purpose of intimidating people so as to deter them from engaging in a lawful activity or of obstructing or disrupting a lawful activity but not necessarily with the intention of doing anything personally to that effect. It seems odd that the common purpose of intimidating etc is not expressly limited to a lawful activity on the land or adjoining land in the open air (as in the case of aggravated trespass). On a literal interpretation of s 69(1), it appears that, if the senior police officer reasonably believes that two or more trespassers on land in the open air are present there with the common purpose of intimidating the medical staff of an adjacent abortion clinic from performing lawful abortions, which they are about to engage in, he may direct them to leave. This is so different from the other types of situation covered by ss 68 and 69 that this literal interpretation should be resisted and the land on which the activity occurs be regarded as impliedly required to be land in the open air.

Although it must reasonably be believed that the two or more are present with the requisite common purpose, they need not be believed to be present as a group, or pursuant to an agreement. Nor need that purpose be their only purpose.

The direction

7.60 If the senior police officer present at the scene[1] reasonably believes[2] that one or other of the two conditions is satisfied, he may direct the person (or persons)[3] whom he reasonably believes is committing, has committed or intends to commit the offence or (as the case may be) those persons (or any of them) present with the common purpose to leave the land.[4] If it is not communicated to the person (or persons) concerned by the police officer giving it, the direction may be communicated to them by any police officer present at the scene.[5] A police officer communicating a direction need not be in uniform.[6] There is no power to direct a person to remove any vehicle or other property which he has with him on the land, but such a power may be implied, as it was in the case of the similar power in s 39 of the Public Order Act 1986.[7] However, the fact that the corresponding police powers to make a direction under s 61 (para **7.24**) and s 63 (para **7.82**) expressly include the power to direct the removal of any vehicles or other property (and are accompanied by ancillary provisions about police seizure, removal and detention of vehicles which have not been removed) is a strong argument against such an implication.

The direction is not required to be in writing. Although there are obvious advantages in putting it in writing, this will often be impracticable. The officer who gives an oral direction is not obliged to record it, although it will be sensible to do so; see para **7.23**.

---

1   See paras **7.5** and **7.6**.
2   See para **6.28**.
3   Interpretation Act 1978, s 6.
4   As to challenging a direction by an application for judicial review, see paras **6.96–6.98**.
5   1994 Act, s 69(2).
6   For criticism, see para **7.23**.
7   *Krumpa v DPP* [1989] Crim LR 295, DC.

7.61 As in the other provisions in this chapter centring on a direction to leave, s 69 does not specify a precise formula of words and information. Analogy with the case law on a 'warning to stop' under s 5(4) of the Public Order Act 1986[1] suggests that the issue is the substance, and not the form, of what was stated and whether it conveys sufficiently to the addressee that he must leave. Moreover, an approach along such lines was taken by the Divisional Court in *Capon v DPP*,[2] although the court's perception of what was required in the latter respect was a surprisingly low one. One might have expected a direction, in order to be valid,

–   to state the power which is being exercised and the grounds for the direction (just as the grounds for an arrest must be given);
–   to identify sufficiently the land to be left; and
–   to indicate generally or specifically who is subject to it.

It is clear from *Capon v DPP* that what is required is much less.

D, E and F were anti-hunt protesters. They had trespassed on farmland, aiming to observe (and video) the digging out of a fox to see if any offences were committed by the hunt. A conversation took place between D, E and F and Sergeant C, the senior police officer at the scene:

D (to C):	'We are going to video from here because this is where they are going to be digging …'
C (to D):	'… that … is interfering with the hunt. You either leave the land or you're arrested. It's as simple as that.'
D:	'I'm not prepared to leave the land because I don't believe I'm committing any offence.'
C:	'I believe you are.'
D:	'I have no intention of disrupting it …'
C:	'In that case, I'm arresting you for aggravated trespass.'
(to E)	'Are you leaving the land? …'
E:	'No.'
F:	'How are we disrupting it?'
C:	'Your presence is disrupting it.'
(to E)	'In that case you're arrested for aggravated trespass.'
(to F)	'Are you leaving the land?'
F:	'Aggravated trespass?'
D:	'We are here quite peacefully, we are simply videoing what is going on.'
C:	'Are you leaving the land?'
F:	'I don't understand …'
C:	'In that case you're arrested as well for aggravated trespass. …'

D, E and F were subsequently convicted of failing to leave land after a police direction to do so. They appealed unsuccessfully to the Crown Court which found that there was sufficient evidence for C to have a reasonable belief that the three were committing an offence under s 68, and that his words constituted a direction within s 69(1). D, E and F appealed to the Divisional Court. Dismissing their appeals, that court held that C's words to each of them were sufficient to amount to a direction within s 69(1). The words to D, within the hearing of the other two – 'You either leave the land or you're arrested' – were plainly imperative. With respect to the words spoken to E and F, Lord Bingham CJ, with whom Dyson J agreed, said:

> 'It is a question of fact whether the statements ... were pure questions inviting the answer "yes" or "no" in a neutral manner, or whether in the context they were imperatives masquerading as questions ... An imperative may masquerade as a question without ceasing to be an imperative. [That] depends on the context, the relationship between the parties and the tone of voice. The court resolved these issues against the appellants and I can find ... no reason to criticise that decision, which indeed seems ... plainly right.'

Even allowing for the matters referred to in the last sentence, it is difficult to see how vague questions to D and E could have amounted to a direction to them within s 69(1), but the decision seems so to regard them.

Capon v DPP shows that, depending on the facts, there can be a direction under s 69 despite the absence of an express reference to the power being used or to the land which must be left.

Lord Bingham stated that it was irrelevant in the context that C had not made it clear, by reference to the statute or section relied on or otherwise, that the direction was being made under s 69. The appellants were far from ill-informed about the effect of the Act and C had made repeated reference to 'aggravated trespass'; it was abundantly clear that C considered the appellants to have committed aggravated trespass and was telling them to leave.

In terms of the non-identification of the land, Lord Bingham stated:

> 'An unqualified direction to leave would ordinarily in my judgment be understood as being a requirement to leave the land on which those persons were trespassing ... It is possible to imagine cases in which there could be doubt about the land which a person was being directed to leave, and questions of possible difficulty could arise if persons left one area of land and were prosecuted for failing to leave another part of the land in question or for being present in another area of the same land. None of those questions however arises in this case.'

The warning required in s 5(4) of the 1986 Act has been judicially construed as requiring that what is required as a response is conveyed. As will be apparent, no such requirement was made in *Capon v DPP*.

Capon v DPP is a worrying decision whose standing in terms of the ECHR and the Human Rights Act 1998 has been questioned in the following terms:

> 'A direction in such terms as permitted here could fall foul of the *Sunday Times*[3] test at Strasbourg level, and therefore under the HRA. The European Court in that case considered whether or not an injunction under the then common law of contempt was a permissible restriction, within Art 10(2), upon the right of free expression contained in Art 10. For a restriction to be justified under Art 10(2) it needs to have been "prescribed by law" and, for the Court in the *Sunday Times* case, the question was

whether or not the law had been sufficiently precisely defined so as to enable the citizen to regulate his or her conduct. It could be said that the direction given here would not have been "prescribed by law" under Art 11(2), in that sense, and could therefore constitute an unjustifiable interference with the rights of peaceful protest. Possibly, arrests under s 69 would also fail to accord sufficient protection to liberty under ECHR Art 5 since that article guarantees that no one shall be deprived of their liberty "save . . . in accordance with a procedure prescribed by law". It will be the duty of higher courts under the HRA to interpret primary legislation so as to be Convention compliant so far as is possible and so a future Divisional Court may be required to limit or read words into ss 68 and 69 by redefining a "direction" as being one which includes a further warning that failure to leave will itself be an offence, rendering the trespasser liable to arrest.'[4]

---

1   See paras **4.57–4.60**.
2   (1998) *The Independent*, 23 March, DC; a full report is available on LEXIS. For extensive
     criticism of this decision, see Mead 'Will peaceful protesters be foxed by the Divisional Court
     decision in *Capon v DPP?*' [1998] Crim LR 870.
3   (1979) Ser A, no 30; 2 EHRR 245, ECtHR.
4   Mead above at 873.

Offences

7.62 A person directed to leave under s 69(1) of the 1994 Act commits an offence under s 69(3) if, knowing[1] that such a direction has been given which applies to him:

(a) he fails to leave the land as soon as practicable;[2] or
(b) having left, he again enters the land as a trespasser within a three-month period beginning with the day on which the direction was given.

As in the case of an offence under s 61(4), these two[3] offences depend on a direction to leave having been validly given. If a power to direct removal of vehicles or other property is implied into s 69, it is submitted that 'failing to leave' would include failing to remove a vehicle or property that one has been directed to remove.[4]

The three-month period referred to in the second offence is significant because it extends the protection of a direction under s 69 to events, such as sporting events, which take place over a period of time. Its compatibility with Art 10 of the ECHR (freedom of expression) is doubtful. Is a three-month period 'necessary in a democratic society' for any of the legitimate aims under Art 10(2), ie is it proportionate to any pressing social need? It seems unlikely that it is.

It is a defence to a charge of either of the above offences for the accused to prove[5] that he was not trespassing on the land, or that he had a reasonable excuse for failing to leave the land as soon as practicable or, as the case may be, for again entering the land as a trespasser.[6]

The two offences essentially correspond with those under s 61, and what is said in paras **7.26–7.30** is equally applicable here.[7] There is one apparent difference; the failure to leave offence under s 61(4) is only committed by a failure to leave as soon as reasonably practicable, whereas the present corresponding offence appears to be stricter because it is committed by a failure to leave as soon as it is practicable to do so, presumably whether reasonably practicable or not. Whether this difference was unintentional is not known.

1   See paras **7.29** and **6.37** fn 2.
2   See para **6.9** fn 2.
3   See para **7.25**.
4   See first paragraph of para **7.26**.
5   See para **4.38**.
6   1994 Act, s 69(4). See para **7.30**.
7   Note, in addition, that it was held in *Capon v DPP*, para **7.61** fn 2, that it is not a reasonable excuse that the accused has not committed an offence under s 68.

Trial and punishment

7.63 An offence under s 69(3) of the 1994 Act is a purely summary one. The maximum punishment is the same as for an offence under s 61 or s 68, three months' imprisonment or a fine not exceeding level 4 on the standard scale, or both.[1]

1   1994 Act, s 69(3).

Police powers

7.64 A constable in uniform[1] who reasonably suspects[2] that a person is committing the above offence may arrest him without a warrant.[3] There is no power to enter the land to make the arrest, but it would be unusual if the occupier did not consent.

Some groups of anti-hunt protesters and animal rights activists have worn balaclavas and masks to conceal their identity while trespassing. If an authorisation to stop and search for offensive weapons or dangerous instruments has been given under s 60 of the 1994 Act, a constable in uniform[1] is empowered also to require a person to remove any item which he reasonably believes that person is wearing wholly or mainly for the purpose of concealing his identity, and to seize any item which he reasonably believes any person intends to wear wholly or mainly for that purpose.[4]

Failure to stop or to remove an item when required is a summary offence, punishable with a maximum of one month's imprisonment or a fine not exceeding level 3 on the standard scale, or both.[5] Failure to remove an item is yet another offence which has been added to the list of arrestable offences in s 24(2) of PACE.[6]

An authorisation under s 60 can be given where a police officer of the rank of inspector (or above) reasonably believes[7] that:

(a) incidents involving serious violence may take place in any area in his locality, and that it is expedient to give an authorisation under the section to prevent their occurrence; or

(b) that persons are carrying dangerous instruments or offensive weapons in any locality in his police area without good reason.

In such a case, that officer may give an authorisation that the powers conferred by the section are to be exercisable at any place within that locality for a specified period not exceeding 24 hours.

Where an inspector gives such an authorisation he must, as soon as it is reasonably practicable[8] to do so, cause an officer of or above the rank of superintendent to be informed.

The authorisation may be extended once only for a further 24 hours on the authority of an officer of or above the rank of superintendent, where expedient, having regard to offences committed, or reasonably suspected to have been committed, in connection with the activity. Thereafter further use of the powers requires a new authorisation.

Such authorisations must be in writing and must specify the grounds on which it is given and the locality and the duration of their validity. If it is not practicable to do this at the time it must be done as soon as possible. It is for the authorising officer to determine the period of time in which he proposes to exercise these powers. It should be the minimum period he considers necessary to deal with the risk of violence.

1   See para **6.92**.
2   See para **3.68** fn 1.
3   1994 Act, s 69(5). For a power of arrest without warrant in other cases, see PACE, s 25.
4   1994 Act, s 60(4A). See Code of Practice for the Exercise by Police Officers of Statutory Powers of Stop and Search (Code A), para 1.8 and Notes for Guidance 1A and 1AA. Any item seized under s 60(4A) must be retained by the police for two months. During that period the person from whom the item was seized may apply for its return. After the two-month period, or the determination of an unsuccessful application, whichever is later, the item must be destroyed or otherwise disposed of, unless its retention is required for the purpose of criminal proceedings: Police (Retention and Disposal of Items Seized under s 60 of the Criminal Justice and Public Order Act 1994) Regulations 1999, SI 1999/269, reg 3. This regulation does not apply if the item is one to which the Police (Property) Regulations 1997, SI 1997/1908 apply: ibid, ie property in the possession of the police to which the Police (Property) Act 1897 applies (property in their possession in connection with the investigation of a suspected offence) and property forfeited by a court under the Powers of Criminal Courts Act 1973, s 43.
5   Ibid, s 60(8).
6   Crime and Disorder Act 1998, s 27.
7   See para **6.28**.
8   See para **6.9** fn 2.

Concluding points

7.65 One may doubt the need for ss 68 and 69. The range of offences described in para **7.35**, almost all of them more serious, is available to deal with the conduct covered by s 68. However, some cases of acts done with intent to obstruct or disrupt will only be caught by s 68. In addition, s 69 gives the police a new power to deal with a public order situation. Without ss 68 and 69 the police might only have had available in many cases their common law breach of the peace powers which are not wholly appropriate for the kinds of behaviour involved and are restrictive in terms of subsequent process since usually the only possible process is binding over. The police welcomed ss 68 and 69, as can be seen from the following statistics for cautions, prosecutions and convictions.[1]

		Cautions	*Prosecutions*	*Convictions*
Aggravated trespass (s 68)	1995	7	111	64
	1996	14	359	211
Failure to leave land (s 69)	1995	11	15	12
	1996	0	27	4

1   *Trespass and Protest* (1998) pp 53–54. In 1995 there were 122 arrests for aggravated trespass and directions were given under s 69 on 17 occasions: ibid. In the first three months of the conflict over the Newbury bypass, there were 356 arrests for aggravated trespass and this resulted in the increase in prosecutions under s 68 in 1996: ibid pp 49 and 58.

7.66 The provisions in ss 68 and 69 determine the line between two freedoms – to pursue a lawful activity and to express an opinion. Common examples of activities in respect of which ss 68 and 69 have been applied have been the activities of hunt saboteurs and anti-road building protesters.[1] A direction, arrest or conviction under s 68 or s 69 in these and other cases could raise issues of a breach of Art 11 of the ECHR, which provides for a right to freedom of peaceful assembly, subject to limitations prescribed by law and which are necessary in a democratic society for the prevention of disorder or crime, or, inter alia, for the protection of the rights and freedoms of others. Article 11 has been held by the European Court of Human Rights to protect the right to hold public demonstrations so long as they are peaceful.[2]

In addition, the use of banners, placards, shouting or horns to intimidate or disrupt a lawful activity on the land which led to a direction, arrest or conviction under s 68 or s 69 could raise issues of a breach of Art 10, which provides a right to freedom of expression. This right (which includes the right to hold opinions, and receive and impart ideas without interference from public authority) is subject to such limitations as may be prescribed by law and are necessary in a democratic society for the prevention of disorder or crime, or inter alia, for the protection of the rights of others.

Could the interference with the exercise of the freedom of expression by the application of s 68 or s 69 be justified under Art 10, as being necessary for the prevention of crime or disorder, for example by those carrying out the lawful activity if they were provoked into a violent reaction, or for the protection of the rights of others, viz those carrying out the lawful activity? The question, it must be remembered, is whether the interference is 'necessary in a democratic society' for one of these purposes, and in determining this regard must be had to the 'duties and responsibilities' that the exercise of the freedom of expression carries with it in such a society.

It is possible to think of situations within the terms of the ECHR where criminal liability is justified as necessary in a democratic society to prevent disorder and/or protect others' rights, as where the accused intentionally causes the person carrying out a lawful activity to be intimidated. However, the problem is that, as already seen, there are other situations covered by s 68 where criminal liability is doubtfully necessary in a democratic society, because it is disproportionate to the harm suffered. It is unarguable that in such a society mere trespass should be an offence. In addition, is it necessary in a democratic society to impose criminal liability on a person whose conduct has not caused intimidation, disruption or obstruction of a person carrying out a lawful activity,[3] and was not even likely to do so, simply because he did an act in relation to it that was intended to have that effect? The decision in *Winder v DPP* and the two examples given in it[4] are powerful examples of a disproportionate application of the law. The rights of the victims must also be recognised here, but they can be protected by the existing civil law. It is submitted that the terms of s 68 cannot be justified under Art 10(2) in respect of many of its applications. Nor can they be so justified, for similar reasons, under Art 11(2) in relation to their interference with the freedom of assembly.

The power under s 69 to direct a trespasser to leave land is, arguably, the part of the aggravated trespass provisions most open to challenge under the ECHR on the basis of its disproportionality. Additional to the arguments concerning s 68, the following reasons can be adduced. First, there is no discretion in respect of the ban on re-entry within a three-month period. A prohibition against re-entry for three months irrespective of any consideration as to the nature and seriousness of the conduct giving rise to the making of the direction would seem open to successful challenge under Art 11 of the ECHR. Secondly, given the potential extent of the 'land' to which the ban may extend, the restriction may also be disproportionate in area, as well as time, and therefore clearly not be necessary for this reason as well in a democratic society for the protection of any relevant interest.

---

1   See *Daily Telegraph* (1991) November 7; *The Guardian,* (1994) November 21; *The Times* (1995) June 17, and the cases referred to above.
2   *Ezelin v France* (1991) Ser A, no 202; 14 EHRR 362, ECtHR. Also see *G v FRG* (1989) 60 D&R 256, ECommHR.
3   Purposeful disruption prevents an assembly being lawful and therefore takes it outside Art 11: *Christians against Racism and Fascism v UK* (1980) 21 D&R 138, ECommHR.
4   See para **7.52**.

POWERS IN RELATION TO RAVES

7.67 Sections 63–65 of the Criminal Justice and Public Order Act 1994 deal with 'raves'. Raves are loud and usually take place at night. The music is commonly of low frequency, can easily penetrate buildings and can be heard over long distances. The number of people making their way to a rave can cause severe congestion (and even blocking, by parked cars) on approach roads for several miles around. Public hygiene problems can be caused if there is inadequate provision for sanitation and rubbish. (There is also the problem of drug abuse at raves but this is not the mischief at which ss 63–65 are aimed.) Prior to the Act, the only available means under the general law to deal with an unlicensed rave which had the permission of the landowner were the common law power of the police to deal with an actual or apprehended imminent breach of the peace, which could extend to forbidding the rave or turning would-be attenders back in the event of a breach of the peace being apprehended, the law of public nuisance,[1] a prosecution in respect of the provision of an unlicensed public entertainment under the provisions referred to in para **7.69**, and the powers of a local authority under the Environmental Protection Act 1990[2] to deal with a statutory noise nuisance. However, local authorities can have problems in responding rapidly and effectively to raves, particularly because raves tend to be 'one-offs' in a particular location and the venue is often kept secret until the last minute.[3]

It is for these reasons that the 1994 Act gave the police powers to prevent unlicensed raves from being set up and to stop them if they have started (s 63), to seize sound equipment if necessary (s 64) and to redirect people who are on their way to a rave (s 65).

1   See paras **9.92–9.96**. See *R v Shorrock* [1993] 3 All ER 917, CA.
2   For a brief description, see para **7.73**.
3   See Scarmer 'The party's over' (1990) 10 (Winter/Spring) *Socialist Lawyer* 4.

What is a 'rave' for the purposes of the Act?

7.68 Parliament did not insert 'rave' in the actual body of the Act; the term appears only in the heading to ss 63–66 and in the marginal notes to ss 63 and 65. Rather more prosaically, we are told by s 63(1) to what that section applies and therefore what is a 'rave' to which the heading and marginal note refer. Section 63(1) provides that s 63:

> 'applies to a gathering on land in the open air of 100 or more persons (whether or not trespassers) at which amplified music is played during the night (with or without intermissions) and is such as, by reason of its loudness and duration and the time at which it is played, is likely to cause serious distress to the inhabitants of the locality.'

7.69 There is one exception. Section 63 does not apply to a gathering licensed by a local authority entertainment licence,[1] of which there are two types: public and private.

In London or (where the licensing system has been adopted) in other areas, no place may be used for, inter alia, any public dancing or music except under, and in accordance with the terms and conditions of, a public entertainment licence.[2] The terms and conditions imposed can include conditions to prevent unreasonable disturbance to the neighbourhood by noise. In the determination of whether or not to grant a licence, and (if it is granted) on what terms, the balance is intended to be struck between the interests of the inhabitants and the interests of those who want to hold or to attend an entertainment that might cause distress. The provision of a public entertainment (ie public dancing or music) without a public entertainment licence, or the breach of a term or condition of such a licence, results in criminal liability on the part of an organiser or manager of the entertainment (if there is no licence), or of the licensee (if there is a breach of a licence), and (in either event) of any other person who allowed the premises or place to be used for the entertainment.

Private entertainment licences are governed by the Private Places of Entertainment (Licensing) Act 1967, which contains essentially similar provisions and offences in relation to the use of a place for private dancing or music promoted for gain, whether in London or (where the system has been adopted) the provinces.

This brief account shows that the sensible way for the intending holder of a rave to proceed is to seek a public or private entertainment licence, if it is to be held in an area where the licensing system applies. Of course, the nature of a rave means that his application way well fail. If it does, or if he does not apply for a licence, he will commit an offence under the above legislation if the rave goes ahead, and he, his assistants and those attending, can also be dealt with under the powers in ss 63–65 of the 1994 Act.

1   Section 63(9). In any proceedings under the present provisions it would be for the accused to prove that there was a licence in respect of the gathering: Magistrates' Courts Act 1980, s 101.
2   London Government Act 1963, Sch 12; Local Government (Miscellaneous Provisions) Act 1982, Sch 1.

100 or more

7.70 The requirement that, for s 63 to apply, there must be 100 or more people involved seems somewhat arbitrary. Gatherings of less than 100 involving the playing of loud amplified music for a long time can cause serious distress to the locality. If the loud music is the essential mischief behind s 63, why should there be any minimum number required to be in attendance? The danger with fixing any number is that the devious can always get round it, for example by issuing only 90 tickets to a ticket-only event with only nine organisers etc in attendance. A figure as high as 100 will exclude most private parties in people's gardens at which loud music is played. Those who have suffered during summer nights might think that such events should have been dealt with by s 63; it appears that a distinction is to be perceived between raves, which are attended by youngsters, and garden parties, which are more likely to be attended by those of an older generation, a distinction not necessarily based on the volume of noise generated.

Trespass unnecessary

7.71 There are two features of the definition of a 'rave' which distinguish the present provisions from those described previously in this chapter. The first is that they are not limited to trespassory conduct or gatherings.

The place

7.72 The second distinction is that, unlike the provisions relating to aggravated trespass, the present provisions are not limited to activities completely in the open air because s 63(10) states that 'land in the open air' in the definition of a 'rave' 'includes a place partly open to the air', a phrase also used in the context of s 14 of the Public Order Act 1986 (imposition of conditions on public assembly). There must be limits to what 'partly open to the air' means, especially as the term is related to land in the open air. Is a warehouse with one window open 'partly open to the air'? Surely not. Otherwise many indoor raves would be covered, which would be hard to accept when the definition of a rave specifies land in the open air and simply qualifies it by saying that that can cover a place partly open to the air. Mr David Maclean, the then Minister of State at the Home Office, stated at the Committee stage in the House of Commons that a dutch barn was a place partly open to the air and that so was an aircraft hangar without doors.[1] These examples are acceptable, although the latter only just. The Minister of State also stated that a marquee would be regarded as partly open to the air.[2] If he meant a marquee open at one side, this is acceptable, but not if he meant an almost wholly enclosed marquee (eg one whose flaps are down, with only a normal door-size opening left open). Canvas offers little, or no, insulation against noise. It is unfortunate that raves in enclosed marquees should be exempt from the present provisions.

Definitional difficulties such as the present one have inhibited the use by the police of their rave powers; on occasions where they did not use those powers because of definitional problems they have relied on other public order powers or negotiated a nuisance-reducing solution with the rave organisers.[3]

Although 'rave' and 'acid house party' are sometimes used interchangeably, the latter is the more appropriate for an event inside a building, which in itself can only be controlled through the provisions referred to in paras **7.69** and **7.73**.

1   Col 592 of the report of the Committee (1994).
2   Ibid, col 593.
3   *Trespass and Protest* (1998) p 25.

7.73 It is typical of the piecemeal nature of the 1994 Act that it confines itself to raves on land in the open air or a place partly open to the air, and does not deal with noisy unlicensed musical parties, organised on a commercial basis in warehouses and other empty buildings. These parties are common in some parts of London and some large cities. They can be just as disturbing as a 'rave'. However, they can only be dealt with by a prosecution for not having an entertainment licence or by the cumbersome statutory nuisance procedure under ss 79–82 of the Environmental Protection Act 1990.

Under ss 80 and 81 of the 1990 Act, a local authority that (through its environmental health officers) is satisfied that a statutory nuisance exists or is likely to occur can serve an abatement notice, failure to comply with which is an offence. Alternatively, by s 82 of the 1990 Act, a person aggrieved by an actual statutory nuisance may bring proceedings in a magistrates' court, which can order abatement and fine the defendant. The fly-by-night nature of the organisers of commercial parties of the present type means that these provisions are of little use.

The statutory nuisance procedure applies to all types of premises, but where the premises from which noise is emitted are a dwelling in an area in which the Noise Act 1996 has been adopted by the local authority that Act provides a more adequate system of control.

Spontaneous gatherings

7.74 Although the present provisions appear to be aimed at organised gatherings, there is no requirement to this effect. A spontaneous gathering of 100 or more trespassers can be a 'rave', if the other conditions are satisfied, just like a party attended by 100 or more which is organised and advertised by the landowner and to which admission is by ticket only.

Amplified music

7.75 A crucial part of the statutory definition of a 'rave' is that there must be amplified music played during the night. For the avoidance of doubt, 'music' is defined as including sounds wholly or predominantly characterised by the emission of a succession of repetitive beats.[1] Presumably, the amplified sound need not have been generated at the time or (in the case of a disco) originally by the playing of a traditional musical instrument, but may be noise electronically generated by a computer.

1   1994 Act, s 63(1)(b).

During the night

7.76 The amplified music must be played 'during the night', although it need not be played continuously. If it is only played at some other time, the gathering is not a 'rave' even though the gathering continues through the night. (Provided the amplified music is played during the night, it is irrelevant that it is also played during the day.) 'Night' is not defined for present purposes. Is it sundown to sunrise or some other variable period related to the sun? If it is, the protection against raves will be more limited in the summer than in the winter, which would be odd since raves are more common in the summer. This is another example of the vagueness of the present provisions, which will have to be sorted out eventually by the courts and which does not assist the police,[1] nor organisers of gatherings who are trying to keep within the law. The problem is, of course, at the edges. All would agree that midnight or 2 am is 'at night' but there would be disagreement in relation to 9 pm and even more controversy about 8 pm or 6 am. This uncertainty can be contrasted with other statutory provisions. For example, under the Night Poaching Act 1828,[2] 'night' is defined as being from one hour after sunset to one hour before sunrise.

The playing of loud music during the day can also cause considerable upset. However, there is a difference between the degree of distress caused by loud noise in the day and loud noise at night. Moreover, to extend the definition of a 'rave' to include all-day gatherings would have caught all-day charity discos and carnivals which are generally thought deserving.

---

1   Although it had not caused problems in the first five years of s 63's operation, according to the ACPO Guidance Document.
2   Night Poaching Act 1828, s 12.

Serious distress

7.77 By reason of its loudness and duration, and the time at which it is played, the amplified music played must be such as is likely to cause serious distress to the inhabitants of the locality. Whether or not those participating in the gathering realise this is irrelevant. The drafting of s 63(1) of the 1994 Act leaves much to be desired, but it seems that the music which is likely to cause serious distress need not be that played during the night. If music played during the day is likely to cause serious distress, it is irrelevant that its volume is turned down at night and is not likely to cause that degree of distress.

'Serious distress' is not defined by the Act. It is another vague term. Clearly, it means more than simple nuisance or annoyance. For example, being kept awake at night is distressing, but is it seriously distressing?

7.78 It will be noted that the question of serious distress is judged in relation to the loudness and duration of the music and the time at which it is played. Because the question is one of likely serious distress to the inhabitants of the locality, the loudness and time of the music which would suffice in a built-up area might well not suffice in a country area where the nearest inhabitants were some distance away. However, if there is only one inhabitant in the locality and he is likely to be caused serious distress, the present condition would be satisfied since (as there is no express or implied contrary intent in the provision) the plural includes the singular.[1]

---

1   Interpretation Act 1978, s 6.

Duration of a rave

7.79 Section 63(1)(a) of the 1994 Act provides that a 'rave' continues during intermissions in the music. It also provides that, where the gathering extends over several days, the 'rave' continues throughout the period during which amplified music is played at night (with or without intermissions). In such a case, then, a gathering of 100 or more on land in the open air which lasts from 2 pm on

Thursday to 6 pm on the following Monday is certainly a 'rave' throughout the period from the beginning of 'night' on the Thursday to the end of 'night' on the Monday, if amplified music etc is played on each of the four nights and is likely to cause serious distress. It is a moot point whether the period of the rave commences at 2 pm on the Thursday and/or ends at 6 pm on the Monday, since it is not clear that those two times can be said to fall within 'the period during which amplified music is played at night'. Of course, as soon as the number gathered together falls below 100, a gathering which was a 'rave' will cease to be so.

Direction to leave

Who can direct?

7.80 Section 63(2) of the 1994 Act provides a police power in this respect. Unlike the powers to direct trespassers to leave under ss 61 and 69, the power is not exercisable by the 'senior police officer present at the scene', but only by an officer of at least the rank of superintendent. The superintendent need not personally communicate the direction and there is no requirement that he should be present when forming the necessary judgement and/or when making the direction. He could make the direction at his headquarters, for example, and communicate it to an officer at the scene.

The grounds

7.81 A superintendent does not have to wait for numbers to build up to rave dimensions, since he can give a direction under s 63(2) if he reasonably believes[1] that, as respects land in the open air (including land partly open to the air):

(a) two or more people are making preparations for the holding there of a 'rave';
(b) 10 or more people are waiting for a 'rave' to begin there; or
(c) 10 or more people are attending a 'rave' that is in progress.

'Exempt persons' (see para **7.82**) can be counted in for the above purpose. There may be difficulty in relation to ground (a) or (b) since the superintendent's reasonable belief must relate, inter alia, to all the factors required to constitute a 'rave'. Suppose, for example, that a superintendent reasonably believes that four people are on land in the open air preparing for a nocturnal loud-music gathering, or that 12 are waiting for such a gathering to start there. He cannot give a direction under s 63 unless he can be said reasonably to believe that 100 or more will attend the gathering (and therefore that it would be a rave). It is unusual to require a reasonable belief as to a minimum number as large as 100 as a precondition of the exercise of a power.

Ground (c) seems odd since, if a superintendent reasonably believes that 10 or more are attending a rave, he must ipso facto also reasonably believe that 100 or more are doing so (otherwise he cannot reasonably believe that the thing attended is a 'rave').

---

1   See para **6.28**.

The direction

7.82 A direction under s 63(2) is a direction that those persons referred to in the last paragraph and any others who come to prepare or wait for or to attend the rave are to leave the land and to remove any vehicles or other property which they have with them.[1] The direction is a direction to leave etc the land on which the site of the rave is situated, and not just part of the land or the place partly open to the air in which the gathering is to take place or is taking place. If Parliament had intended so to limit the area to which a direction applies, it would have used a term such as 'the site', which is used in relation to the associated power to stop and re-direct in s 65 (see para **7.86**). It would seriously impair the effectiveness of s 63 if a direction to leave could be satisfied simply by moving from one part of the land to another. As to what constitutes 'the land' to which a direction applies, reference should be made to para **7.28**. What is said there is equally applicable here. Although s 63(2) speaks in terms of a 'direction that . . .', and does not specifically require the direction to be communicated to its addressees, s 63(3) indicates that it must be so communicated, either by the superintendent giving it or by any police officer at the scene. The communicating officer is not required to be in uniform. An officer can be at the scene without being on the land in question; communication over a wall or hedge would do.[2]

By analogy with case law on a direction under s 69 of the 1994 Act, there will be a direction under s 63 if what is stated conveys to an addressee that he must leave the land (and this is a requirement which can be satisfied by vague and uncertain language) and no other detail is required. The ACPO Guidance Document contains a suggested format for a direction under s 63. It contains warnings about the criminal consequences of a breach of the order and the related power of arrest and about the power to seize property which is not removed. These warnings are not required by the legislation.

One of the troubles with making a direction during a rave can be actually communicating it to each individual. For this reason, s 63(4) provides that people are to be treated as having had a direction communicated to them if reasonable steps have been taken to bring it to their attention. Thus, the mere fact that a person did not hear (or see) a direction because of the noise (or strobe lights) at the rave will not prevent an effective communication to him if reasonable steps have been taken to bring the direction to his attention, although it may make it difficult to prove one of the offences referred to in para **7.83**. Nevertheless, because such steps must be taken, the police will have to be careful that they take them in relation to latecomers to a rave if the direction is to apply to latecomers.

As explained in para **7.23**, it is advisable for the officer making the direction to record it in writing.

A direction to leave does not apply to the occupier of the land in question, any member of his family, any employee or agent of his, or any person whose home is situated on the land.[3] Unscrupulous occupiers who organised raves might try to exploit this exemption by appointing the ravers as their agents, but they would not succeed because the ravers would not be appointed to conduct any transaction of a type undertaken by an agent. Most raves occur, are organised by, or take place with the permission of the occupier of the land. In such cases, an injunction against the occupier and/or a statutory nuisance-abatement notice served on him under s 80 of the Environmental Protection Act 1990 can be powerful means of preventing the rave taking place, provided there is time for them to be made.

---

1   For the power to enter land to communicate a direction, see para **7.87**. As to challenging a
     direction by an application for judicial review, see paras **7.21** and **6.96–6.98**.
2   As to 'present at the scene', see para **7.6**.
3   1994 Act, s 63(5) and (10). 'Occupier' has the same meaning as in s 61: s 63(10); see para
     7.16 fn 1.

Offences

7.83 The holding of a 'rave' is not, in itself, an offence. However, s 63(6) of the 1994 Act provides that if a person knowing[1] that a direction has been given which applies to him:

(a) fails to leave the land as soon as reasonably practicable;[2] or
(b) having left, again enters the land within a period of seven days beginning with the day on which the direction was given;

he commits an offence and is liable on summary conviction to imprisonment for a term not exceeding three months' imprisonment or a fine not exceeding level 4 on the standard scale, or both. Save that the re-entry period is seven days, and not three months, that the re-entry need not be as a trespasser, and that 'land' includes a place partly open to the air, the above two offences are identical to those in s 61(4) in relation to a direction under s 61, and the reader is referred to paras **7.25–7.29**.

Because it can be impossible to record in writing each attendee being told to leave, some forces have video-taped an officer giving a direction through a set of loud-hailers to provide some evidence that those addressed 'knew of the direction'.[3] For the same reasons as in relation to an offence under s 61(3) (b), arrest or prosecution for the offence under s 63(6)(b) rarely, if ever, occurs. Instead, suspected re-entrants are directed away again.[3]

It is a defence for the accused to prove[4] that he had a reasonable excuse[5] for failing to leave the land as soon as reasonably practicable[2] or, as the case may be, for again entering the land.[6] On the other hand, where the direction has been made in advance of an event, which the accused knows is a ticket-only event limited to below 100, this does not prevent a conviction under s 63(6), unless the direction itself is invalid on the ground that its maker did not have the specified reasonable belief.[7]

Most of those who have been directed to leave have done so. In 1995, for example, directions to leave under s 63 were made on nine occasions (the numbers directed ranging from 12 to 50) and no formal action was brought in respect of either of the above two offences; in 1996 one person was cautioned and seven were prosecuted, four being convicted.[3]

---

1   See paras **7.29** and **6.37** fn 2.
2   See para **6.9** fn 2.
3   *Trespass and Protest* (1998) pp 29–30.
4   See para **4.38**.
5   See para **7.30**.
6   1994 Act, s 63(7).
7   Allen and Cooper 'Howard's way – a farewell to freedom?' (1995) 58 MLR 364 at 381.

Arrest

7.84 By s 63(8) of the 1994 Act, a constable in uniform[1] who reasonably suspects[2] that a person is committing one of the above offences may arrest him without a warrant.[3] Entry to effect an arrest may be authorised by a superintendent; see para **7.87**.

---

1   See para **6.92**.
2   See para **3.68** fn 1.
3   For a power of arrest without warrant in other cases, see PACE, s 25.

Human rights

7.85 A direction under s 63 or an arrest or conviction for breach of it will involve a restriction or penalty on the exercise of the right to freedom of peaceful assembly guaranteed by Art 11 of the ECHR. In the light of the terms of s 63, it is far from clear that such a restriction or penalty could be justified under Art 11(2) as one 'prescribed by law and . . . necessary in a democratic society . . . for the prevention of disorder or crime, . . . or for the protection of the . . . rights of others . . .', which would seem to be the only possible relevant justifications.

Power to stop persons proceeding

7.86 Section 65 of the 1994 Act provides the police with a significant (and controversial) power to stop people proceeding to a rave (whether by road or otherwise). By s 65(1), a constable in uniform,[1] who reasonably believes[2] that a person is on his way to 'a gathering to which s 63 applies' in relation to which a direction under s 63 is in force, may:

(a) stop that person; and
(b) direct him not to proceed in the direction of the rave.

This power may only be exercised within five miles[3] of the boundary of *the site* of the 'rave'[4] (as opposed to the land on which the site is situated, which may be a larger area). It is not limited to those on their way by road, nor to those on their way to attend the rave. A direction not to proceed may be given to anyone en route, eg someone delivering sound equipment, except the occupier of the land where the 'rave' is taking place, or a member of his family, or any employee or agent of his, or anyone whose home is situated on that land.[5]

The reference in s 65(1), to 'a gathering to which s 63 applies' indicates that the requirements of s 63(1) (ie the definition of a 'rave') must be satisfied. It is not enough simply that a direction has been made on the basis that the decision-maker reasonably believed that they were satisfied. It is doubtful, however, whether this distinction will impact on police practice. Once a direction has been made, the power under s 65 is likely to be exercised. It would, however, be important if the offence below is charged. The prosecution might find it difficult in some cases to show a valid exercise of the power if the accused alleges that the gathering was not one to which s 63 applied.

It is a summary offence for a person, knowing that a direction under s 65(1) has been given to him, to fail to comply with it; the maximum punishment is a fine not exceeding level 3 on the standard scale.[6] A constable in uniform[1] who reasonably suspects[7] that a person is committing this offence may arrest him without a warrant.[8]

The power to turn away under s 65 is used more frequently than the power to make a direction under s 63. For example, on 32 occasions in 1995 instructions were given to officers to turn people away; the numbers involved ranged from 45 to 500.

There are obvious similarities between this power and that in s 14C of the Public Order Act 1986 in relation to trespassory assemblies.[9] For the reasons stated in relation to that power, it is arguable that the exercise of the present power involves a breach of Art 11 of the ECHR. Indeed, the uncertainties surrounding the definition of a 'gathering to which s 63 applies' provide an additional argument, to the effect that the power is insufficiently precisely formulated to enable an individual to foresee to a reasonable degree the legal consequences of his conduct, and therefore the interference is not prescribed by law.

1 See para **6.92**.
2 See para **6.28**.
3 'Five miles' means five miles in a straight line on a horizontal plane: Interpretation Act 1978, s 8.
4 1994 Act, s 65(2).
5 Ibid, s 65(3) and (6).
6 Ibid, s 65(4).
7 See para **3.68** fn 1.
8 1994 Act, s 65(5).
9 See para **6.90**.

Entry and seizure

Entry
7.87 A police superintendent (or above) who reasonably believes[1] that circumstances exist that would justify the giving of a direction under s 63 of the 1994 Act may authorise any constable to enter the land in question without a warrant for any of the following purposes:

(a) to ascertain whether such circumstances exist;
(b) to communicate a direction to leave under s 63(2);
(c) to make an arrest without warrant under s 63(8); or
(d) to exercise the power of seizure and removal under s 64(4), described in the next paragraph.[2]

1 See para **6.28**.
2 1994 Act, s 64(1), (2) and (3).

Seizure
7.88 Section 64(4) of the 1994 Act provides that, if a police officer reasonably suspects[1] that a person to whom a direction under s 63 applies has without reasonable excuse:

(a) failed to remove any vehicle or sound equipment on the land which appears to the officer to belong to him or to be in his possession or under his control; or
(b) entered the land as a trespasser with a vehicle or sound equipment within a seven-day period beginning with the day on which the direction was given;

the constable, who need not be in uniform, may seize and remove that vehicle or sound equipment. It will be noted that there is no power under s 64 to seize 'other property' which the person concerned may have been directed to remove under s 63, eg lighting equipment and tents.

'Vehicle' has the same meaning as in s 61.[2] 'Sound equipment' is defined by s 64(6) as meaning equipment designed or adapted for amplifying music and any equipment suitable for use in connection with such equipment; 'music' bears the meaning given in para **7.75**.

As in the case of s 62, (a) covers property of those who have quit the land and left the property behind and those who have not yet left.

It will be noted that, if a person subject to a direction enters the land with the permission of the occupier within seven days with a vehicle or sound equipment, a police officer authorised under s 64 does not have a power to seize and remove it because the power of seizure on entry is limited to cases where entry is as a trespasser.

Section 64(4) does not authorise seizure of any vehicle or sound equipment belonging to the occupier of the land, to any member of his family, to any employee or agent of his, or to anyone whose home is situated on the land,[3] even if such a person is the organiser of the rave or concerned in its management. Clearly, in some cases, police officers will have to be careful lest liability for wrongful interference with the goods of such people is incurred.

---

1   See para **3.68** fn 1.
2   1994 Act, s 64(6); see para **7.20**.
3   Ibid, s 64(5).

7.89 As in the case of a vehicle seized and removed under s 62(1) of the 1994 Act, any vehicle seized and removed under the above power may be retained in accordance with regulations made by the Home Secretary.[1] In the light of the fact that these provisions can be applied even though a rave may never have been held, or even planned, there is perhaps an even stronger case for saying that application of them in the present context may contravene Art 1 of the First Protocol of the ECHR (no person to be deprived of possessions except in the public interest) and, since the seizure is an executive action, Art 6 of the ECHR (right to fair and public hearing) or, if the vehicle seized is someone's home, Art 8 of the ECHR (right to respect for home).[2]

Any sound equipment seized and removed under s 64(4) may be retained until the conclusion of proceedings[3] against the person from whom it was seized for an offence under s 63.[4] Unlike the position in respect of vehicles, there is no power to retain sound equipment thereafter (so that it must be returned, unless a forfeiture order, see below, is made), nor to recover from its owner any costs in respect of storage etc of sound equipment.

Once a rave has begun, the police have been reluctant to attempt seizure during its continuance because of the risk of disorder.[5]

---

1   1994 Act, s 67(1). The regulations referred to in para **7.34** also apply to a vehicle seized and removed under s 62(1). So do the comments made about them.
2   See para **7.34**.
3   By the 1994 Act, s 67(9), 'conclusion of proceedings' against a person means: (a) his being sentenced or otherwise dealt with for the offence or his acquittal; (b) the discontinuance of the proceedings; or (c) the decision not to prosecute him, whichever is the earlier.
4   1994 Act, s 67(2).
5   *Trespass and Protest* (1998) pp 26–27.

Forfeiture of sound equipment on conviction

7.90 Section 66(1) of the 1994 Act empowers (but does not oblige) a magistrates' court in which a person is convicted of an offence under s 63 in relation to a gathering to which s 63 applies[1] to order the forfeiture of any sound equipment seized from him under s 64(4) (see para **7.88**) or in his possession or under his control at the time of his arrest for an offence under s 63 or of the issue of a summons in respect of such an offence,[2] if the court is satisfied that it has been used at the 'rave'. The court may make a forfeiture order under s 66(1) whether or not it also deals with the offender in respect of the offence in any other way,[3] except that it cannot combine such an order with one of absolute or conditional discharge because it amounts to an additional penalty.[4]

As in the case of forfeiture orders under other provisions, in considering whether to make an order under s 66(1), a court must have regard to:

(a) the value of the property; and
(b) the likely financial and other effects on the offender of the making of the order (taken together with any other order contemplated by the court).[5]

This repeats the wording of s 43(1A) of the Powers of Criminal Courts Act 1973. In *R v Highbury Corner Stipendiary Magistrates' Court, ex parte Di Matteo*,[6] where that provision was in issue, it was held that if the defendant is being sentenced for more than one offence the court must consider the total effect of the sentence.[7]

An order under s 66(1) operates to deprive the offender of his rights, if any, to the property forfeited, and the property must (if not already in their possession) be taken into the possession of the police.[8] The order does not affect the rights of anyone else.

---

1   See para **4.68**.
2   1994 Act, s 66(13).
3   Ibid, s 66(2).
4   See para **5.59** fn 1.
5   1994 Act, s 66(3).
6   (1991) 92 Cr App R 263, DC.
7   In *R v Buddo* (1983) 4 Cr App R (S) 268, DC, it was held that if a forfeiture order is combined with a prison sentence or a substantial fine there is a risk of 'overdoing the punishment'.
8   1994 Act, s 66(4).

Determining claims

7.91 Where sound equipment has been forfeited under s 66(1), a magistrates' court may, on application by a claimant, other than the offender from whom the property was forfeited, make an order for delivery of it to the applicant if it appears to the court that he is the owner of the property.[1] This would seem to require the claimant to produce some evidence of ownership. Such an application must be made within six calendar months of the forfeiture order being made.[2] An application cannot succeed unless the claimant satisfies the court that he had not consented to the offender having possession of the property or that he did not know, and had no reason to suspect, that the property was likely to be used at a 'rave'.[3] An order for delivery does not affect the right of any person besides the offender to take, within the period of six calendar months from the date of that order, proceedings for the recovery of the sound equipment from the person in possession of it in pursuance of the order.[4] However, on the expiration of the six-month period that right ceases.[4]

1   1994 Act, s 66(5).
2   Ibid, s 66(7).
3   Ibid, s 66(8).
4   Ibid, s 66(4).

Other points

7.92 The Home Secretary has power to make regulations[1] for the disposal of forfeited sound equipment, and for the application of the proceeds of any sale of it, where there has not been a successful application by a claimant.[2] The Police (Disposal of Sound Equipment) Regulations 1995[3] apply where not less than six months have expired from the date on which the forfeiture order under s 66(1) was made and either no application by a claimant of the property has been made under s 66(5), or no such application has succeeded.[4] Where an application has been made within the six-month period, or within that period the person on whose conviction the court ordered the forfeiture of the property has appealed against conviction or sentence, the application of the regulations is suspended until the application or appeal has been determined.[5]

Regulation 3 provides that property to which the regulations apply must be disposed of by sale or, if a police superintendent (or above) is satisfied that the nature of the property is such that it is not in the public interest to sell it, by other means in accordance with his directions. The proceeds of any sale must be paid to the police authority and applied in accordance with reg 4.

A forfeiture order under s 66(1) is a 'sentence' within the meaning of s 108(3) of the Magistrates' Courts Act 1980 and therefore an appeal may be made against it to the Crown Court. Alternatively, an appeal against it may be made by case stated to the High Court on the ground that it is wrong in law or in excess of jurisdiction.

1   The power to make regulations is exercisable by statutory instrument which is subject to
     annulment in pursuance of a resolution of either House of Parliament.
2   1994 Act, s 66(10).
3   SI 1995/722.
4   Reg 2(1).
5   Reg 2(2).

UNAUTHORISED VEHICULAR CAMPERS[1]

Abolition of local authority duty to provide sites for gypsies

7.93 Part II (ss 6–12) of the Caravan Sites Act 1968 sought to tackle a perceived widespread problem of unauthorised gypsy encampments by increasing the number of public sites for gypsies and providing powers to deal with gypsies who did not use such a site when it was available. Section 6 of the 1968 Act obliged local authorities to provide sites for 'gypsies', defined by s 16 of the Act as 'persons of nomadic habit of life, whatever their race or origin, but [not including] members of an organised group of travelling showmen, or persons engaged in travelling circuses, travelling together as such'. In *R v South Hams District Council, ex parte Gibb*,[2] the Court of Appeal held that this definition imported the requirement that there should be some recognisable connection between the wandering or travelling of those concerned and the means whereby they made or sought their livelihood. Consequently, persons, such as New Age Travellers, who moved from place to place merely as the fancy might take them and without any connections between the movement and their means of livelihood fell outside the definition.

By the time the 1994 Act was enacted, more than 300 sites had been provided by local authorities in England and Wales and 46% of gypsy caravans were accommodated on them.[3] Compliance with the duty under s 6 of the 1968 Act was facilitated by s 70 of the Local Government, Planning and Land Act 1980, which gave the Government the power to pay a capital grant of 100% to local authorities in respect of capital expenditure in establishing gypsy caravan sites.

In August 1992, the Government issued a consultation paper[4] proposing the abolition of the duty of local authorities to provide sites for gypsies.

---

1 Harrison 'Travellers' tales' (1994) Sol Jo 368; Sandland 'Travelling back to the future?' (1994) 144 NLJ 750.
2 [1994] 4 All ER 1012.
3 HL Deb, vol 555, col 1122 (1994). A further 24% were on authorised private sites and 10 per cent on land owned by the gypsies themselves (albeit many were without planning permission).
4 *Reform of the Caravan Sites Act 1968* (Department of the Environment/Welsh Office).

7.94 The proposal was implemented by s 80(1) of the 1994 Act, which also repealed s 70 of the 1980 Act.

A local authority may still establish further caravan sites under s 24 of the Caravan Sites and Control of Development Act 1960 if it wishes, but it is no longer legally required to do so and central Government funds are not available.

The repeals were prompted by the Government's view in 1994 that the 1968 Act had failed in its purpose (since the number of gypsies camping unauthorisedly, a consistent average of about 3,000 caravans each year, had not fallen since 1981 because of an increase in the number of gypsy caravans), by its wish to stop its commitment to open-ended funding of sites, by its view that to continue to impose a duty on local authorities without grant support was not appropriate, and by its desire to encourage gypsies to establish their own sites through the normal planning system. The Government considered that many gypsies would wish to buy sites for which they would apply for planning permission. However, it is not easy for gypsies to obtain such permission,[1] and the Government made it more difficult for gypsies to obtain planning permission in the green belt because the Department of the Environment Circular 1/94 (Welsh Office Circular 2/94) withdrew guidance that it was appropriate to permit caravan sites there on a 'special case' basis. Now it is the policy that as a rule it will not be appropriate to make provision for gypsy sites in such areas. The repeal of the duty to provide sites not only left the problem of unauthorised gypsy encampments unresolved, but inevitably led to an increase in such encampments.[2]

---

1 Research published in 1991 by the Department of the Environment stated that the planning permission refusal rate for gypsies who have applied for permission is extremely high, perhaps 90%, compared with a success rate of 80% for all applicants: HL Deb, vol 555, cols 1132 and 1198 (1994).
2 For a discussion of the need for reform of the law relating to gypsies and travellers, and proposals for reform, see Morris and Clements (eds) *Gaining Ground: Law Reform for Gypsies and Travellers* (University of Hertfordshire Press, 1999).

Other changes

7.95 Under s 12 of the 1968 Act, the Secretary of State for the Environment had power to designate a local authority if he was satisfied that the needs of gypsies in its area were met. By the time the 1994 Act was passed, only 38% of local authorities had been designated. The effect of designation was two-fold. First, s 10 of the 1968 Act made unauthorised camping in a caravan in a designated area by a gypsy an offence. Secondly, designation gave a local authority powers to act rapidly against unauthorised camping by gypsies because s 11 empowered a magistrates' court in any designated area on complaint by the local authority to order a caravan on land in the authority's area in contravention of s 10 to be removed together with anyone residing in it. The order could authorise the local authority to take reasonable steps to ensure that the order was complied with. If a local authority was not designated, the only remedy available to deal with unauthorised gypsy encampments (as with any other unauthorised campers) was for the occupier of the land to obtain a civil possession order.

In its Consultation Paper of August 1992, referred to in para **7.93**, new powers for local authorities to move from land all unauthorised vehicular campers were proposed. These proposals were implemented by ss 77–79 of the Criminal Justice and Public Order Act 1994, which replaced ss 10–12 of the 1968 Act. Sections 77–79 apply to all unauthorised vehicular campers, whatever type of vehicles are involved, and to local authorities in general. Like the other provisions referred to in this chapter, the police will be involved in their operation. The propriety of involving the police in what are essentially social and environmental issues and the enforcement of private rights is questionable.

Sections 77–79 are unnecessary in many cases where the activities of unauthorised vehicular campers threaten public order; s 61 of the 1994 Act is often available in such a case.

Directing unauthorised vehicular campers to leave[1]

7.96 Powers to direct unauthorised vehicular campers to leave are given by s 77 of the 1994 Act to a county council, district council (including a unitary authority) or London borough council (in England) or a county council or county borough council (in Wales),[2] hereafter 'the local authority'.

---

1   Campbell 'Gypsies: the criminalisation of a way of life' [1995] Crim LR 28; Morris and
    Clements (eds) *Gaining Ground: Law Reform for Gypsies and Travellers* (University of
    Hertfordshire Press, 1999), especially ch 4.
2   1994 Act, s 77(6) and (7). These powers are also given to the Common Council of the City of
    London and the Council of the Isles of Scilly: s 77(6).

Unauthorised vehicular campers

7.97 For the purposes of s 77, unauthorised vehicular campers are people residing in a vehicle or vehicles (of whatever type):

(a) on any land in the open air forming part of a highway;
(b) on any other unoccupied land in the open air;
(c) on any occupied land in the open air without the consent of the occupier.[1]

It is irrelevant that no harm or nuisance is being caused by the campers.

'Occupier' means the person (or persons) entitled to possession of the land by virtue of an estate or interest held by him (or them).[2] The 'highway' here means any type of highway,[3] including footpaths and bridleways. If fences or hedges have been put up to separate the adjoining land from the highway, there is a rebuttable presumption of law that the highway extends to the whole space between the fences or hedges and is not confined to such part of the highway as may have been made up.[4] The present provisions can be contrasted with those in ss 61 and 68, from which many highways are excluded.[5]

Although (a) and (b) above do not refer to absence of consent or authority, it is submitted that s 77(1) is concerned only with unauthorised vehicular campers. In *R v Beaconsfield Justices, ex parte Stubbings*,[6] Sir John Donaldson MR interpreted the identical list ((a)–(c)) in s 10 of the Caravan Sites Act 1968 as referring only to unauthorised vehicular campers. That this is also the case in respect of s 77(1) is supported by the fact that 'unauthorised campers' appears in the heading to the group of sections starting with s 77 and in the marginal note to s 77.[7] 'Unauthorised vehicular campers' is used here as a convenient label for those listed above.

In *Beaconsfield Justices, ex parte Stubbings*, which was concerned with campers on occupied land, Sir John Donaldson MR held that the authority contemplated is the consent of the occupier of the land. As Sir John Donaldson stated, obiter, in the case of (b) (unoccupied land), there is no occupier to give consent. In relation to the highway in (a), Sir John said that likewise there is no occupier to give consent 'or no occupier could conceivably give consent'. In the case of the highway, however, it is submitted that the highway authority can give consent, and that the grant of such consent will prevent vehicular camping being unauthorised. This is important because oxbows and other redundant parts of the highway are sometimes places to which local authorities direct unauthorised campers. If, as will often be the case, the local authority concerned is the highway authority, its consent will mean that the camping is not unauthorised in such a case. Thus, it could not make a direction to leave against such campers without first revoking its consent.

---

1   1994 Act, s 77(1) and (6).
2   Ibid, s 77(6).
3   See para **9.74**.
4   See *A-G v Beynon* [1969] 2 All ER 263, and authorities cited therein.
5   See paras **7.14** and **7.43**.
6   (1987) 85 LGR 821 at 831.
7   Marginal notes and headings are not debated by Parliament and are therefore not part of the Act. The result is that they may only be looked at to determine the purpose, as opposed to the scope, of the section (*DPP v Schildkamp* [1969] 3 All ER 1640, HL; *R v Kelt* [1977] 3 All ER 1099, CA), although it may be that headings have a wider use: *DPP v Schildkamp* above, at 1656. Even in their limited sphere of operation, marginal notes in particular carry little weight and cannot oust a meaning indicated by some part of the Act itself.

7.98 No minimum number of persons is specified. However, s 77(1) speaks of 'persons . . . residing in a vehicle or vehicles . . . on . . . land' and it would seem that there must be at least two people residing in a vehicle or vehicles on the land. Admittedly, words in the plural in a statutory provision include the singular (unless the contrary intention appears from the Act),[1] but it seems that a contrary intention does appear because elsewhere in s 77(1) the subsection refers to a 'vehicle or vehicles' and this must imply that if Parliament had meant 'persons' to mean 'person or persons' it would have said so. There is no reason, in principle, assuming the present provisions are necessary, why a single camper should be excluded from them; the mischief is the same, albeit on a smaller scale. It is interesting to note that s 77(2) contemplates that a direction can be given to one person. 'Residing . . . on . . . land' is not without its difficulties. At first glance, there appears to be nothing to stop the local authority directing one unauthorised vehicular camper whose vehicle is a mile apart from another individual camper's on the highway or other unoccupied land in the local authority's area to leave. However, the direction is to leave '*the* land' which suggests the idea that the two or more vehicular campers must be camping on a discrete area or parcel of land, as does common sense.

---

1   Interpretation Act 1978, s 6.

7.99 The Act does not define 'residing', except that s 77(6) says that a person may be regarded as residing on any land notwithstanding that he has a home elsewhere. As implied by s 77(6), 'residing' at a place can be described as 'living there' or 'having a home there', however temporarily. It has been held that a 'residence' 'denotes the place where an individual eats, drinks and sleeps'.[1] 'Residence' continues in a place, of course, during temporary absences, such as absence for shopping or on business, as long as the vehicle remains there as the person's habitation.

The requirement of residence in a vehicle or vehicles excludes those who are unauthorisedly on land, for example, a lay-by, to effect repairs to their caravan or to have a picnic. Of course, if a vehicle-repairer decides to set up home there, and does so, while the repair is effected, he will be residing there. The requirement also excludes those who, although they have vehicles with them, are residing in tents.

The vehicular camping must be in the open air.[2] Those who park a vehicle in a barn and live in it, for example, are not caught by s 77. Section 4 of the Vagrancy Act 1824 may be relevant in these cases. That section provides that a person wandering abroad and lodging in any barn or outhouse, or in any deserted or unoccupied building, or in the open air, or under a tent, or in any cart or wagon, and not giving a good account of himself commits a summary offence punishable with up to three months' imprisonment or a fine not exceeding level 3 on the standard scale. In addition, the provisions of s 61 of the 1994 Act or of s 6 of the Criminal Law Act (below) may be relevant.

---

1   *North Curry (Inhabitants)* (1825) 4 B&C 953 at 959.
2   1994 Act, s 77(6).

7.100 In s 77, 'vehicle' includes a caravan[1] or any other vehicle whether mechanically propelled or horse-drawn, such as a minibus, bus, saloon car or van, and whether or not it is in a fit state for use on roads.[2] For obvious reasons, 'vehicle' also includes any body, with or without wheels, appearing to have formed part of such a vehicle.[2] Thus, campers cannot get round the provisions relating to unauthorised campers by removing the wheels from their caravan and supporting it up on bricks.

---

1   As defined by the Caravan Sites and Control of Development Act 1960, s 29(1): 1994 Act, s 77(6); see para **7.20**.

2   1994 Act, s 77(6).

The direction

7.101 A local authority may direct persons who appear to the authority to be unauthorised campers in the authority's area, 'and any others with them', to leave the land and remove the vehicle or vehicles and any other property (such as scrap metal or animals) they have with them on the land.[1] The power of a local authority itself to make a direction instead of having to apply in the first instance to a magistrates' court for an order requiring unauthorised campers to leave provides a fast-track procedure; the quicker the action, the less the nuisance and the mess which may well have to be cleared up.

A direction may be made simply because it 'appears' to the local authority that there are unauthorised campers on the land in the authority's area; it does not have to have reasonable grounds for the view which it forms, nor need a site be available in the authority's area on which the campers may lawfully reside in their vehicle. Non-statutory guidance has been issued to local authorities in *Gypsy Sites Policy and Unauthorised Camping*,[2] a Departmental Circular issued in 1994, and *Managing Unauthorised Camping: A Good Practice Guide*,[3] published in 1998. This guidance notes that eviction is only one of the available options, and that unauthorised vehicular camping cannot be dealt with in isolation (because otherwise the most that can be achieved is shifting people from site to site). The Circular sets out guidance as to how local authorities should approach their powers under the 1994 Act in the context of their other statutory duties relating to children, education and housing. It advises local authorities to take into account the effect of an eviction on the education of any children and on the provision of any health or welfare services to those occupying the site. The *Good Practice Guide* is stronger. It states that inquiries must be carried out and local authorities must consider welfare issues when deciding whether to proceed with eviction. This guidance is legally obligatory. The Divisional Court held in 1995 that, when deciding whether to make a direction, and if so to whom, the local authority must consider the relationship of its proposed action to the various statutory provisions and humanitarian considerations that would arise, such as those outlined in the Circular, and to make its decision accordingly.[4] Failure to do so can result in a local authority's removal direction and the subsequent magistrates' court removal order being quashed on an application for judicial review.[4]

The considerations in the guidance should be kept under review so far as there are any changes after a direction has been made, when the local authority decides whether to apply for a removal order under s 78 of the 1994 Act.[4]

Any inquiries as to the personal circumstances of a vehicular camper by a local authority must be conducted before, and not after, a direction to leave has been made, otherwise unsatisfactory delay can occur.[5] Failure to make proper inquiries before making a direction cannot be cured by consideration at a later stage (eg before applying for a removal order under s 78).[4] Where any inquiries are only made after the direction, the direction can be quashed by an order of certiorari on an application for judicial review.[6]

Both the Circular and the *Good Practice Guide* emphasise the need for toleration. The Guide states: 'Encampments must be "tolerated" where enquiries have revealed specific welfare needs ... "[T]oleration" can be defined as a willingness to delay initiating eviction proceedings and/or to give generous periods for compliance once proceedings have been started'.[7] Sites can be tolerated 'for a matter of days, weeks, months or years, depending on the circumstances'.[8]

---

1   1994 Act, s 77(1). As to challenging a direction by an application for judicial review, see paras **7.21** and **6.96–6.98**.
2   DOE 18/94; Welsh Office 76/94.
3   DETR/Home Office.
4   *R v Lincolnshire CC, ex parte Atkinson; sub nom Wealden DC, ex parte Wales; Wealden DC, ex parte Stratford* (1995) 8 Admin LR 529, DC.
5   *R v Wolverhampton MBC, ex parte Dunne* [1997] 29 HLR 745, DC.
6   Ibid. A removal order (see para **7.107**) made by a magistrates' court when a direction made in such circumstances is not complied with will likewise be quashed: ibid.
7   *Good Practice Guide*, para 5.2.
8   Ibid, para 5.5.

7.102 Insofar as a direction relates to the removal of a vehicle or vehicles which the unauthorised campers or others with them have with them on the land, the definition given in para **7.100** of a 'vehicle' should be borne in mind; it includes a vehicle not in a fit state to be used on a road. It must be added that the term 'vehicle' includes any load carried by, and anything attached to, a vehicle.[1] Consequently, for example, the local authority may direct the removal of a bus whose wheels have been removed, or an unroadworthy coach, or scrap metal which is loaded on a lorry. It is not obvious why a 'load' was specified as being a vehicle because it would have been 'other property' even if not so specified.

A direction operates to require persons who re-enter the land within the period of its operation with vehicles or other property to leave and remove the vehicles or other property in the same way as it operates when initially given.[2] It is submitted that in this context 'persons' and 'vehicles' include the singular. The present provision does not apply if the re-entry is not 'with vehicles or other property', but read literally it would seem that, unless the re-entry is in the nude, a person who re-enters would necessarily do so 'with other property' (his clothes and shoes). This cannot have been intended, but it is not clear what the limit is on 'other property'.

---

1   1994 Act, s 77(6).
2   Ibid, s 77(4).

Notice

7.103 Notice of a direction must be served on the persons to whom the direction applies; it is sufficient for this purpose for the direction to specify the land and (except where the direction applies to one person only) to be addressed to all occupants of the vehicles on the land, without naming them.[1] There appears to be a lacuna here because the direction can extend to 'any others with [the unauthorised vehicular campers]' who would seem not necessarily to be occupants of a vehicle. A direction does not apply to a locality, but only to people on the land when the direction was made, and can only be contravened by such persons;[2] clearly it is important to have an accurate record of those people.

Where it is impracticable to serve notice of a direction under s 77 on a person named in it, the direction is treated as duly served on him if a copy of it is fixed in a prominent place to the vehicle concerned.[3] Where a direction is directed to the unnamed occupants of vehicles, it is treated as duly served on them if a copy is fixed in a prominent place to every vehicle on the land at the time when service is thus effected.[3] In addition, in either case, the local authority must take such steps as may be reasonably practicable[4] to secure that a copy of a notice is displayed on the land (otherwise than by being fixed to a vehicle) in a manner designed to ensure that it is likely to be seen by anyone camping on the land.[5]

Notice of a direction must be given by the local authority to the owner of the land in question and to any occupier of it unless, after reasonable inquiries, the local authority is unable to ascertain the name and address of the owner or occupier.[6] The owner or occupier is entitled to be heard in any proceedings following from a breach of a direction.[6]

---

1   1994 Act, s 77(2).
2   *R v Lincolnshire CC, ex parte Atkinson; sub nom Wealden DC, ex parte Wales; Wealden DC, ex parte Stratford* (1995) 8 Admin LR 529, DC.
3   1994 Act, s 79(2).
4   See paras **6.9** fn 2 and **7.26** fn 2.
5   1994 Act, s 79(3).
6   Ibid, s 79(4).

Offences

7.104 By s 77(3) of the 1994 Act, it is an offence if a person, knowing that a direction under s 77(1) has been given which applies to him:

(a) fails, as soon as practicable, to leave the land or remove from the land any vehicle or other property which is the subject of the direction; or

(b) having removed any such vehicle or property again enters the land with a vehicle within the period of three months beginning with the day when the direction was given.

The re-entry is not required to be for the purpose of residing on the land.

Save that the offence in (a) refers to failing as soon as practicable, rather than failing as soon as reasonably practicable, that the offence in (a) expressly refers to a failure to remove a vehicle or other property that is the subject of a direction which applies to the accused, and that the offence in (b) does not require the re-entry to be as a trespasser, the above two offences are similar to those in s 61(4), and the reader is referred to paras **7.25–7.29**.

Where a person to whom a direction to remove a vehicle or other property fails to do so in circumstances where the thing does not belong to him and is not in his possession or control, interesting issues are raised. Presumably, he would have the defence of lawful authority (or belief in lawful authority) to a charge of taking a conveyance, contrary to s 12 of the Theft Act 1968, if he removed a vehicle, but it seems odd to involve a person in criminal liability for failing to remove something that is not even under his physical control.

It would seem that, if A and B are directed to remove a vehicle on the land, and A does so, B cannot be convicted of the first of the two offences above if he leaves the land after A has removed the vehicle, because it has become impossible for him to remove it.

The second of the two offences does not seem to be strictly necessary in the light of the provision in s 77(4) that a direction under s 77(1) operates to require those who re-enter land within three months of the direction with vehicles or other property to leave and remove the vehicles or other property as it operates in relation to persons and vehicles and other property on the land when the direction was given.

Defences

7.105 It is a defence for the accused to prove[1] that his failure to leave or to remove the vehicle or other property as soon as practicable, or his re-entry with a vehicle, was due to illness, mechanical breakdown or other immediate emergency.[2] Unlike s 61, s 77 does not provide a wider defence of reasonable excuse. The fact that there is no lawful alternative site available in the locality is irrelevant to liability.

---

1   See para **4.38**.
2   1994 Act, s 77(5).

Trial and punishment

7.106 An offence under s 77(3) is triable only summarily.[1] The maximum punishment is a fine not exceeding level 3 on the standard scale. Imprisonment cannot be imposed.[2] There is no specific power of arrest for an offence under s 77(3). The only statutory power of arrest in relation to it would be that of a constable under s 25 of PACE if one of the general arrest conditions is satisfied, but this is unlikely to be utilised against a person residing in a vehicle on the land because of the provisions in s 78 of the 1994 Act for an order for removal.

---

1   1994 Act, s 77(3).
2   Compare the offence under the Vagrancy Act 1824 referred to in para **7.99**.

Order for removal

7.107 An order of removal may be made under s 78 of the 1994 Act. It may only be made on the complaint of a local authority.[1] If it is satisfied that 'persons and vehicles[2] in which they are residing are present on land' in the complainant authority's area in contravention of a direction under s 77, a magistrates' court may make an order (hereafter an 'order for removal') requiring the removal of any vehicle or other property that is present on any land and any person residing in it.[3] A magistrates' court cannot refuse to make an order under s 78 on the grounds of the merits of the local authority's decision to make a direction under s 77[4] (although that decision can be challenged in judicial review proceedings), nor on the ground that there is nowhere else in the locality for the camper(s) to go (either permanently or temporarily). Although the word 'may' in s 78(1) gives the magistrates a discretion, it is a strictly limited discretion to decline to make an order in certain special circumstances, eg where the requisite formalities have not been carried out[5] or where an occupier had undertaken to leave by a particular date, thus rendering an order unnecessary.[6]

Where a complaint is made under s 78, a summons requiring the person or persons to whom it is directed to appear before the magistrates' court may be directed to:

(a) the occupant of a particular vehicle on the land; or
(b) all occupants of vehicles on the land, without naming him or them.[7]

The provisions described in para **7.103** relating to the service etc of a direction under s 77 are equally applicable to the service of a summons mutatis mutandis.

If the defendant is absent and the court does not proceed in his absence but adjourns the hearing, it may not (contrary to the normal rule) issue a warrant for his arrest.[8]

---

1   1994 Act, s 78(1).
2   Or a person and a vehicle: Interpretation Act 1978, s 6.
3   1994 Act, s 78(1). The legality of any direction may only be challenged before the magistrates on the ground of substantive or procedural ultra vires; otherwise it must be challenged by way of judicial review of the local authority's decision: see *Shropshire CC v Wynne* (1997) 96 LGR 689, DC.
4   *R v Wolverhampton MBC, ex parte Dunne* (1997) 29 HLR 745, DC; *Shropshire CC v Wynne*, above.
5   *R v Wolverhampton MBC, ex parte Dunne*, above, at 754.
6   *Shropshire CC v Wynne*, above. The Divisional Court's statement that the issue of reasonableness was one for the local authority to determine when it made the direction under s 77 does not mean that its decision on this matter cannot be challenged in judicial review proceedings under the *Wednesbury* principle.
7   1994 Act, s 78(5).
8   Ibid, s 78(6).

7.108 An order for removal may authorise the local authority to take such steps as are reasonably necessary to ensure that the order is complied with and, in particular, may authorise the authority, by its officers and employees:

(a) to enter upon the land specified in the order; and
(b) to take, in relation to any vehicle or property to be removed in pursuance of the order, such steps for securing entry and rendering it suitable for removal as may be specified.[1]

However, the local authority must not enter on any occupied land unless it has given the owner and 'occupier' (as defined in para **7.97**, which term does not include an unauthorised camper) at least 24 hours' notice of its intention to do so, or unless after reasonable inquiries it is unable to ascertain their names and addresses.[2]

---

1   1994 Act, s 78(2).
2   Ibid, s 78(3).

7.109 By s 78(4), a person who wilfully obstructs a person in the exercise of any power conferred on him by a removal order commits an offence. The offence is triable only summarily and is punishable with a fine not exceeding level 3 on the standard scale. Imprisonment cannot be imposed. It is submitted that 'wilfully obstructs' bears the same meaning as in the offence of wilful obstruction of a constable in the execution of his duty, dealt with in paras **9.65–9.67**. Examples in the present context include forcible resistance or digging a trench, whether this makes it impossible or simply difficult for the persons exercising the power to do so.

Human rights

7.110 Sections 77–79 of the 1994 Act interfere with the right to respect for a person's private and family life and for his home (which is guaranteed by Art 8 of the ECHR).

The European Commission on Human Rights held in *G & E v Norway*[1] that a minority group is in principle entitled to claim the right to respect for its particular lifestyle as being 'private life', 'family' or 'home'[2] within Art 8, although on the facts of that case there had not been a sufficient interference with it (the Lapps' deprivation of 2.8 square km in Northern Norway) to constitute a breach of Art 8. Although ss 77 and 78 are not limited to them, they interfere far more substantially with gypsies and travellers who seek to follow a traditional nomadic existence. In the case of gypsies, at least, ss 77 and 78 also contravene Art 14 (enjoyment of ECHR rights to be secured without discrimination on any ground such as, eg, social origin or other status).

In relation to Art 8, the question would be whether, in the light of the abolition of the duty to provide accommodation for gypsies and the powers under s 61, interference by a local authority or a court removal order under ss 77 or 78 in a particular case, was justified under Art 8(2) as necessary in a democratic society for one of the purposes stated there, the possible candidates being the interests of public (highway) safety, the protection of health or the protection of the rights and freedom of others in terms of the environment. In *Buckley v UK*,[3] the first case referred to the European Court of Human Rights concerning the rights of a gypsy community, which related to a refusal of planning permission in respect of three caravans occupied by a gypsy and her family, the Court refused to consider whether the above sections were contrary to Arts 8 or 8 and 14 together. It dismissed the application by a majority on the basis that a broad margin of appreciation applied in planning cases in balancing the public interest and the right of the individual to respect for his home. It is not easy to see how the application of the two sections in such circumstances can always be said to be necessary in a democratic society for one of the stated purposes. It is noteworthy that the European Commission on Human Rights has declared admissible a number of applications relating to the operation of ss 77 and 78 on the ground that there were serious issues of fact and law arising from the application to those sections of Arts 8 and 14.

The application of ss 77 and 78 may also contravene Art 11 of the ECHR (freedom of assembly).

---

1   Applications no 9278/81 and 9415/81; 35 D&R 30, ECommHR.
2   An illegally stationed caravan is a 'home' for the purposes of Art 8: *Buckley v UK* RJD 1996-IV 1271; (1997) 23 EHRR 101, ECtHR.
3   RJD (1996) 1996-IV 1271; 23 EHRR 101, ECtHR.
4   See, for example, *Beard v UK* (1998) 25 EHRR CD 28, ECommHR.

SQUATTERS

7.111 In terms of the criminal law, squatters do not commit an offence simply by squatting but they may incur liability for the offence of using violence to secure entry or (in the case of residential premises only) the offence of adverse occupation, contrary to ss 6 and 7 of the Criminal Law Act 1977 respectively.

Towards the end of 1993 it was estimated that 90% of squatters were in council houses (3,000 council houses), 9% in shops or offices and 1% in privately owned residential property.[1] While reports of the genuinely homeless who moved into empty council houses might have evoked some public sympathy, there was none in relation to the growing trend towards squatting in commercial premises by 'pirate traders' who engaged in unfair competition with other retailers. An example was provided by a news report in June 1994 concerning an organisation which set up at least 70 'squat shops' around Britain. It operated by sending locksmiths to empty shops at night, who would replace the locks and hand the new keys to a squatting manager. By the next morning the shops would be stocked. The shop managers slept on the premises, making it impossible for landlords to take repossession without a possession order, with the attendant delays which go with such an order. By the time the possession order could be enforced, the squatters would have moved, taking the remaining stock back to the organisation.[2]

With the exception of special provisions under ss 6 and 7 of the Criminal Law Act 1977 (referred to in paras **7.134** and **7.136**), which only apply to a displaced residential occupier or a protected intending (residential) occupier, those entitled to possession who cannot regain it peacefully can only lawfully regain possession by invoking the civil law and obtaining a possession order; displaced residential occupiers and protected intending occupiers may, of course, prefer this course of action to that of acting under the special provisions. During the time taken for the possession order to be obtained and enforced by eviction, squatters can cause damage to the premises.

---

1   (1993) *The Times*, 5 November.
2   (1994) *The Times*, 16 June.

7.112 To strengthen the law against squatters, a fast-track interim possession order for the recovery of premises was introduced in 1995, non-compliance with which attracts criminal sanctions under the Criminal Justice and Public Order Act 1994. In addition, that Act extended the provisions under ss 6 and 7 of the Criminal Law Act 1977 in favour of displaced residential occupiers and protected intending (residential) occupiers. In view of the alternative offered by the provisions of the Criminal Law Act 1977 in many cases of squatting in residential premises, the procedure for an interim possession order is of particular importance in relation to squatting in commercial premises.

Interim possession order

7.113 The procedure for such an order is provided by Part II of Ord 24 of the County Court Rules 1981 set out in Sch 2 to the Civil Procedure Rules 1998. As its name implies the order provides an interim stage before a (final) possession order is obtained under Part I of Ord 24. In a case where the interim order procedure is potentially available, an applicant for a full possession order is not constrained to use the interim procedure.

7.114 By Ord 24, r 8, the interim possession order procedure only applies to premises within the meaning of s 12 of the Criminal Law Act 1977, viz a building, or part of a building under separate occupation (such as a flat), any land ancillary to a building, and the site comprising any building or buildings together with any land ancillary thereto.[1] 'Building' in the context of s 12 includes any immovable structure, and any movable structure, vehicle or vessel designed or adapted for residential purposes.[2] A caravan or houseboat is an obvious example of the latter. As the definition shows, land may only be 'premises' under s 12 if it is 'ancillary to a building', which it is if it is adjacent to it and used (or intended for use) in connection with the occupation of that building or any part of it.[2] It follows from this definition that an interim possession order cannot be made against trespassers, such as 'New Age Travellers', on open land (ie land not ancillary to a building).

An application for an interim possession order is made to the county court for the district in which the premises are situated.

Order 24, r 9, sets out the conditions for an interim possession order application. It provides that, in proceedings for a possession order under Part I of Ord 24, an application may be made for an interim possession order where:

'(a) the only claim made in the proceedings is for the recovery of premises;

(b) the claim is made by a person who –

   (i)   has an immediate right to possession of the premises; and
   (ii) has had such a right throughout the period of unlawful occupation complained of;

(c) the claim is made against a person (not being a tenant holding over after the termination of the tenancy) who entered the premises without the applicant's consent and has not subsequently been granted such consent, but no application for an interim possession order may be made against a person who entered the premises with the consent of the person who, at the time of entry, had an immediate right to possession of the premises; and

(d) the claim is made within 28 days of the date on which the applicant first knew, or ought reasonably to have known, that the respondent, or any of the respondents, was in occupation.'

Order 24, r 10, governs the issue of the application for an interim possession order. The applicant must file:

(a) a claim form;
(b) a witness statement or affidavit in support; and
(c) an application notice;

each of which must be in the prescribed form, together with sufficient copies for service on the respondent.

On the filing of these documents, the court must:

(a) issue the claim forms and the application for an interim possession order;
(b) fix an appointment for the application to be considered; and
(c) insert the time of that appointment in the application notice referred to above and in the copy served on the respondent.

The time fixed for consideration of the application for an interim possession order must be as soon as possible after the documents have been filed, but not less than *three days*[3] after the date on which the application for an interim possession order is issued.

Order 24, r 11(1) provides that within 24 hours[4] of the issue of the application for an interim possession order, the applicant must serve the following documents on the respondent:

(a) the application notice; and
(b) the prescribed form of respondent's witness statement or affidavit, which must be attached to the application notice.

Because the application applies to all occupiers, whether or not their names are known to the applicant, r 11(2) requires that these documents be served by the applicant fixing a copy of them to the main door or other conspicuous part of the premises and, if practicable, inserting through the letter-box at the premises a copy of the documents in a sealed, transparent envelope addressed to 'the occupiers'. Additionally, but not alternatively, r 11(3) provides that the applicant may place stakes in the ground at conspicuous parts of the premises to each of which shall be fixed a sealed transparent envelope addressed to 'the occupiers' and containing a copy of the documents.

At or before the time fixed for consideration of the application for an interim order, the applicant must file a witness statement or affidavit of service in the prescribed form in relation to the documents mentioned in Ord 24, r 11(1). In addition, at any time before the time fixed for consideration of the application, the respondent may file a witness statement or affidavit in the prescribed form in response to the application.

Order 24, r 12, deals with the consideration of the application. If the respondent has filed a witness statement or affidavit in accordance with the above rule, he *may* attend before the court when the application for an interim possession order is considered *to answer such questions on his or the applicant's witness statement or affidavit* as the *court* may put to him. The parties' affidavits are read in evidence; no oral evidence can be adduced except in response to questions put by the court. If the court so directs, an application may be dealt with in private and in the absence of one or both of the parties.

Order 24, r 12 also provides that, in deciding whether to grant an interim possession order, the court must have regard to whether the applicant has given or is prepared to give undertakings in support of his application:

(a) to reinstate the respondent if, after an interim order has been made, the court holds that the applicant was not entitled to the order;

(b) to pay damages in such a case;

(c) not to damage the premises pending the final determination of the possession proceedings;

(d) not to grant a right of occupation to any other person pending such a determination;

(e) not to damage or dispose of any of the respondent's possessions pending such determination.

By Ord 24, r 12(5), the court must make an interim possession order if:

(a) the applicant has filed an affidavit of service of the notice of application; and

(b) the court is satisfied[5] that the conditions specified in Ord 24, r 9, are met and that any undertakings given by the applicant as a condition of making the order are adequate.

An interim possession order must be in a prescribed form and must be to the effect that the respondent vacate the premises specified in the claim form within 24 hours[4] of *service* of the interim possession order.

If the court makes an interim possession order, it must fix a return date for the hearing of the claim which must be not less than seven days[3] after the making of the order, when confirmation of the order by the grant of a final possession order will be considered in open court. Where an interim order is made, the court officer must submit a draft of it as soon as possible to the judge or district judge by whom it was made for approval, and when the draft order has been approved the court must insert in the order the time limit for service under r 13 below.

By Ord 24, r 13, an interim possession order must be served within 48 hours[4] of the judge or district judge's approving the draft order. The applicant must serve copies of the claim form, the applicant's witness statement or affidavit and the interim possession order in accordance with r 11(2) or (3) or in such other manner as the court may direct. If the interim order is not served within the time limit specified by r 13 or by any order extending or abridging time, the applicant may apply to the court for directions for the application for possession to continue *under Part I of Ord 24* as if it had not included a claim for an interim possession order.

Order 24, r 14(2) provides that the interim possession order *expires on the return date.* On the return date, the court may make such order as appears appropriate, including making a final order for possession or dismissing the claim.[6] An order may be made on the return date in the absence of one or both parties.[7]

By Ord 24, r 15, a respondent who has vacated the premises pursuant to an interim possession order may apply for that order to be set aside before the return date in urgent cases.

---

1   Criminal Law Act 1977, s 12(1)(a).
2   Ibid, s 12(2).
3   Not including a day on which the court office is closed: Ord 1, r 9(4). Compare the corresponding time period for a full possession order.
4   Any time during which the court office is closed is *not* to be disregarded in calculating this period: Ord 24, r 8(2).
5   On the balance of probabilities: see, eg *Miller v Minister of Pensions* [1947] 2 All ER 372.
6   Ord 24, r 14(3).
7   Ibid, r 14(4).

7.115 The procedures relating to an interim possession order can be contrasted with the existing summary procedure for 'full' possession orders against squatters in the High Court (Ord 113 of the Rules of the Supreme Court 1965 contained in Sch 1 to the Civil Procedure Rules 1998) and county courts (Ord 24, Pt 1, of the County Court Rules 1981 contained in Sch 2 to the Civil Procedure Rules 1998). An interim possession order can be made earlier than can a possession order after service of the claim form.[1] Another contrast relates to enforcement of the order.

Enforcement of a 'full' possession order is done by county court bailiffs or, in the case of a High Court order, the Sheriff; when it occurs depends on their waiting lists. Delays of six weeks or so in the enforcement of an order are not uncommon. Most orders are county court orders and the bailiffs, unlike the Sheriff, have no right to enlist police help to carry out the eviction (although bailiffs are normally accompanied by the police when enforcing a possession order). In comparison, an interim possession order cannot be enforced by the execution of a warrant of possession by a county court bailiff.[2] Instead, it is enforced through the medium of the criminal law. Those who are present on the premises as trespassers during the currency of an interim possession order commit an offence and can be arrested by the police, who (as with the other provisions in this chapter) have had yet another burden heaped on them. The ever-increasing involvement of the police as, in effect, bailiffs in social issues such as squatting[3] poses problems for the police in terms of their function and relationships in society. This was the first time that breach of a possession order had been made a criminal offence. Indeed, the idea of a criminal offence for breach of a civil order seemed to be novel, although it has subsequently been adopted in respect of a breach of a civil order under s 3 of the Protection from Harassment Act 1997 or breach of an anti-social behaviour order under s 1 of the Crime and Disorder Act 1998.

1   A possession order cannot be made not less than five days (residential premises) or two days (other premises) after service of the claim form, unless the court abridges these times in a case of urgency: RSC Ord 113, r 6; CCR, Ord 24, r 4.
2   CCR, Ord 24, r 13(3).
3   The police already had such a function in respect of squatters in the strictly limited circumstances set out in the Criminal Law Act 1977, s 7: see para **7.136**.

Trespassing during currency of interim possession order or re-entering as trespasser thereafter

7.116 Section 76(2) of the 1994 Act provides that a person who is present on the premises as a trespasser at any time during the currency of an interim possession order served in accordance with the County Court Rules 1981[1] commits an offence, subject to the terms of s 76(3). Section 76(3) provides that no offence is committed by a person if:

(a) he leaves the premises within 24 hours of the time of the service of the order and does not return; or
(b) a copy of the order was not fixed to the premises in accordance with rules of court (ie Ord 24, r 11 of the County Court Rules 1981).[2]

The offence under s 76(2) is a wide one. Indeed, it is wider than might appear at first glance for two reasons. First, by s 76(6), those in occupation of premises when an interim possession order is served are deemed to be present as trespassers for the purposes of s 76, so that they must leave within 24 hours or be guilty of an offence under s 76(2). If they claim to be lawfully entitled to be on the premises, they will have to take this up at a full hearing after they have left.

Secondly, as careful reading of s 76(2) indicates, this offence can be committed not only by those in respect of whom the interim possession order was made but by others, for example a second group of squatters to whom the original squatters (who have left in obedience to an order) have passed on the keys, provided a copy of the order was fixed to the premises in the correct way. Thus, there is no need in such a case for the lawful owner or occupier during the currency of an interim possession order to start proceedings all over again against a new group of squatters, although proof of the offence depends on proof of a trespass.

1   This requirement is made by the 1994 Act, s 76(1).
2   See para **7.14**.

7.117 By s 76(4) of the 1994 Act, a person who was in occupation of the premises when the order was served but who leaves them commits an offence if he re-enters the premises as a trespasser or attempts to do so after the expiry of the order but within the period of one year beginning with the day of the service of the order.[1] (If the re-entry is during the currency of the order, an offence is, of course, committed under s 76(2)). Whether s 76(4) itself creates two offences is an open question. This is a point which has important implications in respect of the law which applies. Section 3 of the Criminal Attempts Act 1981 applies to specific statutory offences of attempt which are *expressed as an offence of attempting to commit* another offence, rules which correspond to those in s 1 of that Act for the general statutory offence of attempt. Thus, s 3(3) of the 1981 Act provides that a person is guilty of an attempt under a special statutory provision if, with intent to commit the relevant full offence, he does an act which is more than merely preparatory to the commission of that offence. In addition, s 3(4) and (5) of the 1981 Act provides the same rules as in s 1 of that Act in relation to 'impossible attempts'. The precise meaning of the words italicised remains to be determined.

A specific statutory offence of attempt created by a separate section or subsection from the full offence is 'expressed as an offence of attempting to commit another offence', but it is by no means obvious that the same is true where (as in s 76) the full offence and the attempt are expressed in the same provision. (If 'entering' and 'attempting to enter' are separate offences, an information charging both would be bad for duplicity.) The structure of the provision is of obvious importance, and it should be noted that the words used in s 76(4) are '... enters the premises or attempts to do so after the expiry of the order ...' It is submitted that this is more easily interpreted as a reference to two offences than if the words had been 'enters or attempts to enter the premises after the expiry of the order ...', but it cannot be claimed with complete confidence that the present provision creates two offences. If it is held that 'attempts to enter' in s 76 is not within the scope of s 3 of the 1981 Act, it could be that that Act would nevertheless be applied by analogy. Alternatively, it might be that the rules relating to the common law offence of attempt, which was abolished by the 1981 Act, would apply.

As an offence under s 76 is only triable summarily, it would not have been an offence to attempt to enter but for its express inclusion in s 76(4).[2]

---

1   It would seem that it will always have to be proved that re-entry (actual or attempted) was as a
     trespasser. The deeming provision in s 76(6), referred to in para **7.116**, relates to deemed
     presence as a trespasser.
2   Criminal Attempts Act 1981, s 1(4).

Mental element

7.118 No mental element is expressly required to be proved by s 76 in relation to an offence thereunder. The fact that the offences of failing to leave and of re-entering under ss 61, 63, 69 and 77 of the 1994 Act all expressly require proof that the accused knew that a direction to leave had been made which applies to him strongly, but not conclusively,[1] suggests that the presumption of statutory interpretation[2] that mens rea is required to be proved is rebutted where the allegation is one of failing to leave, contrary to s 76(2), or re-entering as a trespasser, contrary to s 76(4). However, it is submitted that, even if these offences do not require proof of mens rea, a full mental element for attempt must be proved where an attempt to re-enter, contrary to s 76(4), is in issue. It is of the essence of an attempt that the accused should be proved to have intended to commit the full offence alleged to have been attempted.[3]

---

1   *Cundy v Le Cocq* (1884) 13 QBD 207, DC; *Neville v Mavroghenis* [1984] Crim LR 42, DC;
     Pharmaceutical Society of Great Britain v Storkwain Ltd [1986] 2 All ER 635, HL; cf *Sherras v de
     Rutzen* [1895] 1 QB 918, DC.

2   *Sweet v Parsley* [1969] 1 All ER 347, HL; *Gammon (Hong Kong) v A-G of Hong Kong* [1984] 2 All
     ER 503, PC.
3   Such an intent is required to be proved under the Criminal Attempts Act 1981 and was so
     required in respect of the common law offence of attempt.

Trial, punishment and arrest

7.119 As already indicated, an offence under s 76(2) or s 76(4) is only triable
summarily. The maximum punishment is six months' imprisonment or a fine not
exceeding level 5 on the standard scale, or both.[1] This can be contrasted with the
lower maxima for the similar offences already referred to in this chapter, where
the maximum is normally three months or level 4, or both. The reason why it
should be higher for the present offences is not readily apparent.

1   1994 Act, s 76(5).

7.120 A constable in uniform[1] may arrest without warrant anyone who is, or whom
he reasonably suspects[2] to be, guilty of an offence contrary to s 76.[3] The power of a
constable under s 17 of PACE to enter (by force, if need be) and search any
premises for the purpose of arresting a person whom he has reasonable grounds
for believing is on the premises extends to an offence contrary to s 76.[4] However,
unlike all but one of the other powers of entry under s 17 of PACE,[5] the power of
entry and search to arrest a person for an offence contrary to s 76 may be exercised
only by uniformed police officers.

1   See para **6.92**.
2   See para **3.68** fn 1.
3   1994 Act, s 76(7). For a power of arrest without warrant in other cases, see PACE, s 25.
4   1994 Act, Sch 10, para 53. What is said about this power in para **4.18** applies equally here.
5   Entry and search to arrest for an offence under the Criminal Law Act 1977, ss 6, 7, 8 and 10.

Interim possession order: false or misleading statements

False or misleading statements to obtain an order

7.121 The procedure for the grant of an interim possession order is open to attack
on the ground that it gives rise to the risk of abuse by unscrupulous landlords.
Section 75(1) of the 1994 Act provides that a person commits an offence if, for the
purpose of obtaining an interim possession order, he:

(a) makes a statement which he knows to be false or misleading in a material
     particular; or
(b) recklessly makes a statement which is false or misleading in a material
     particular.

Section 75(1) may create two separate offences, each with its own state of mind as
to the falsity etc. Provisions of this type are common but, with rare exceptions,
such as s 3 of, and Sch to, the Property Misdescriptions Act 1991, they are not
structured in the (a) and (b) form used here. Instead, they are expressed in terms
of making any statement 'which he knows to be false in a material particular or
recklessly makes any statement which is false in a material particular'. It is
submitted that, despite its structure, there is only one offence under s 75(1), since
the conduct is identical in each case, for which one of two states of mind as to the
falsity etc is required.

Prohibited conduct

7.122 What is required is the making of a statement which is false, or (although literally true) misleading, in a material particular. For this purpose, a statement means any statement, in writing or oral and whether as to fact or belief, made in or for the purpose of the proceedings.[1] Statutory offences of making false statements are quite common; offences of making false or misleading statements less so. Since it has been held in the context of similar offences that a statement may be false not only on account of what it expressly states, but also on account of what it omits, conceals or implies, even though it is literally true, on the ground that there is such a partial statement of the facts that what is withheld makes what is stated false,[2] it is not easy to see the function of 'misleading' unless it is simply to make it clear that a statement of the latter type falls within s 75. It could be that a statement not caught by the above is 'misleading' if it is nevertheless liable to deceive. Such a statement will be rare. An offence of the present type, unlike perjury, is not committed where a person makes a statement which is in fact true which he does not believe to be true.

---

1   1994 Act, s 75(4).
2   *R v Lord Kylsant* [1932] 1 KB 442; *R v Bishirgian* [1936] 1 All ER 586.

7.123 The statement made must be false or misleading in a material particular. A statement is false or misleading in a material particular if it is likely to affect the recipient of the information in taking or refraining from taking a course of action.[1]

---

1   *R v Mallett* [1978] 3 All ER 10, CA (concerned with 'material particular' in Theft Act 1968, s 17).

Mental element

7.124 The accused must not only make his statement for the purpose of obtaining an interim possession order, but he must also know (ie actually know)[1] or be reckless that his statement is false or misleading in a material particular. The structure of the words used here indicates that it is not enough that the accused knows or is reckless that the fact is false or misleading. He must also know that it is false or misleading in a material particular.

It is a moot point whether recklessness is limited to subjective recklessness, which is not very different from 'without belief in its truth' in perjury, or whether it means *Caldwell* recklessness, a considerably wider concept. There are arguments both ways.

A person would act with subjective recklessness as to a statement being false or misleading in a material particular if, when he made the statement false or misleading in a material particular, he actually realised that the statement might be so false or misleading, provided it was unjustifiable for him to take the risk that it was.[2] On the other hand, an accused would be *Caldwell* reckless (under the test laid down by Lord Diplock in the House of Lords and adopted by the majority in *Caldwell*)[3] if the risk that the statement was false or misleading in a material particular would have been obvious to a reasonable person as more than negligible and either the accused has not given any thought to the possibility of there being some kind of risk or he has recognised that there is some risk involved and he has nevertheless persisted in his conduct.

In *Caldwell,* Lord Diplock's remarks about *Caldwell* recklessness were directed towards statutory offences in whose definition the word 'reckless' or 'recklessly' appears, as in s 75. Any doubts about whether he intended his remarks to have a wider application appear to be resolved by his statement in *R v Lawrence* that 'The conclusion of the majority [in *Caldwell*] was that the adjective "reckless" when used in a criminal statute, ie the Criminal Damage Act 1971' meant *Caldwell*-type recklessness and that 'the same must be true of the adverbial derivative "recklessly"'.[4]

However, even where 'reckless' or 'recklessly' appears in the statutory definition of a statutory offence, it is not an invariable rule that *Caldwell* recklessness suffices, since the courts have recognised that there can be exceptions to it.[5] In *Large v Mainprize,*[6] the Divisional Court applied the subjective test of recklessness, without reference to *Caldwell,* to the statutory offence of recklessly furnishing false information as to a fishing catch. This decision provides particularly persuasive authority in relation to the meaning of recklessness in the present offence.

---

1   The use of 'recklessness' as an alternative to knowledge, precludes knowledge including 'wilful blindness', a species of subjective recklessness, as it otherwise would: *Roper v Taylor's Central Garages (Exeter) Ltd* [1951] 2 TLR 284, DC.
2   *R v Briggs* [1977] 1 All ER 475, CA; *R v Stephenson* [1979] 2 All ER 1198, CA.
3   *Commissioner of Police of the Metropolis v Caldwell* [1981] 1 All ER 961.
4   [1981] 1 All ER 974 at 981.
5   See *R v Satnam* (1984) 78 Cr App R 149, CA; *R v Breckenridge* (1984) 79 Cr App R 244, CA.
6   [1989] Crim LR 213, DC

False or misleading statements to resist an order

7.125 Since it will be possible for an alleged squatter on residential premises to make a response to the application for an interim possession order, it was thought that parity of treatment should be extended to those who make statements which are false or misleading in a material particular (as the accused knows or as to which he is reckless) for the purpose of resisting the making of an interim possession order. This is done by s 75(2) of the 1994 Act. The comments made above about the offence under s 75(1) are equally applicable mutatis mutandis to this offence.

Trial, punishment and arrest

7.126 An offence under s 75(1) or (2) is triable either way. The maximum punishment:

(a) on conviction on indictment, is imprisonment for a term not exceeding two years or a fine, or both;
(b) on summary conviction, is imprisonment for a term not exceeding six months or a fine not exceeding the statutory maximum, or both.[1]

These provisions correspond to those in most other statutory offences of making materially false statements.

Unlike the other offences contained in the preceding sections in this chapter, no power to arrest without warrant a person suspected of committing an offence under s 75 is expressly provided, nor is the offence an arrestable offence under s 24 of PACE. The absence of a specific power of arrest is not surprising since the conduct is not such as to necessitate an arrest as a matter of urgency.

---

1   1994 Act, s 75(3).

ENTERING AND REMAINING ON PROPERTY

7.127 Part II of the Criminal Law Act 1977 contains a number of offences relating to entering and remaining on property. Although these offences are often associated with 'squatters', the relevant provisions extend to situations other than squatting.

The two major offences in Part II of the 1977 Act are using or threatening violence for securing entry to premises, and adverse occupation of residential premises. Both offences are triable only summarily and are punishable with a maximum of six months' imprisonment or a fine not exceeding level 5 on the standard scale, or both.[1] They were amended by ss 72–74 of the Criminal Justice and Public Order Act 1994.

The definitions of the various offences in Part II refer to 'premises', as defined by s 12 (see para **7.114**). The two major offences also refer to 'access' to premises, and this means any part of any site or building within which those premises are situated which constitutes an ordinary means of access to those premises (whether or not that is its sole or primary use),[2] such as a communal hallway or staircase in a block of flats.

---

1   1977 Act, ss 6(5) and 7(5). 'No rule of law ousting the jurisdiction of magistrates' courts to try
     offences where a dispute of title to property is involved shall preclude magistrates' courts
     from trying offences under [Part II of the 1977 Act]': ibid, s 12(8).
2   Ibid, s 12(1)(b).

Violence for securing entry

7.128 Section 6(1) of the 1977 Act provides that any person who, without lawful authority, uses or threatens violence for the purposes of securing entry into any premises for himself or any other person, is guilty of an offence, provided that:

(a) there is someone present on those premises at the time who is opposed to the entry which the violence is intended to secure; and

(b) the person using or threatening the violence knows that that is the case.

Prohibited conduct

7.129 The crux of this offence is the use or threat of violence for the purpose of securing entry into premises on which a person opposed to the entry is present: actual entry is not required. It is immaterial whether the entry which the violence is intended to secure is for the purpose of acquiring possession of the premises or for some other purpose.[1] Thus, while the use or threat of violence in order to conduct a 'sit-in' in premises is an obvious example of the present offence, so is the use or threat of violence in an unsuccessful attempt to gate-crash a party. The violence used or threatened may be directed against a person or property,[1] and the offence can be committed even though the violence is not directed towards a person or thing on the premises but towards someone or something outside them, provided always that it is done for the purpose of securing entry to them.

'Violence' is a word with an everyday meaning. Consequently, whether or not violence occurs is a question of fact and the term should not be subjected to legal definition by the courts.[2] While magistrates are likely to find that the use of force on a person or smashing a door or window constitutes violence, they are unlikely to find that forcing a window catch or Yale lock with a piece of wire does.

---

1   1977 Act, s 6(4).
2   See *Brutus v Cozens* [1972] 2 All ER 1297, HL; and *Dino Services Ltd v Prudential Assurance Co Ltd* [1989] 1 All ER 422, CA, discussed in para **3.15**.

7.130 The requirement that someone must be present on the premises at the time of the use or threat of violence who is opposed to the entry that the violence is intended to secure means that if D breaks into P's house, in order to squat in it, while P and his family are on holiday, D does not commit the present offence, although he may well be guilty of criminal damage and will commit an offence under s 7 of the 1977 Act if he fails to leave when P requests him to on his return. Even if a person is present on the premises at the time, no offence is committed unless he (or at least one of a number of persons on the premises) is opposed to the intended entry. In order for a person to be opposed to the intended entry, it must be against his will, but he need not offer opposition to it. It is uncertain whether he must know of it in order that the offence be committed by the accused, or whether it is enough that there is present on the premises someone who, to the knowledge of the entrant, would wish to oppose his entry, or who has a duty to oppose it. This is a matter of obvious importance where the only person present on the premises is asleep at the time or, as in the case of a large factory, the premises are large and the night watchman is unaware of the intended entry. The latter interpretation would seem preferable. Otherwise there would be a significant lacuna in the offence.

The fact that s 6 does not apply to the use of violence to gain entry to unoccupied premises is consistent with the mischief of the offence – the prevention of disorder, since there will not normally be a risk of disorder in such a case.

Mental element

7.131 It is implicit that the accused must intentionally or recklessly (in the subjective sense of that term) use or threaten violence. In addition, s 6(1) requires that this be done for the purpose of securing entry into any premises for the accused or any other person. Section 6(1) also requires that the accused should know[1] that there is a person on the premises at the time of the use or threat of violence and that that person is opposed to the entry which the violence is intended to secure.

---

1   'Knowledge' includes wilful blindness, see para **6.37** fn 2.

Without lawful authority

7.132 No offence is committed if the accused has 'lawful authority' to use or threaten violence for securing entry into the premises. A number of statutes give constables power to enter premises by violence, if need be, to arrest someone and/or search them. The threat or use of violence pursuant to such powers would clearly be with lawful authority. The same would be true in relation to any other person, such as a court officer enforcing a possession order, who has power to use force to enter premises for a particular purpose, provided he was acting pursuant to that power.

On the other hand, s 6(2) provides that the fact that a person has any interest in or right to possession or occupation of any premises does not constitute lawful authority for the use or threat of violence by him or anyone else for the purpose of securing entry into them. It follows that, if the landlord of rented premises or the occupier of a lock-up shop uses violence to re-enter his premises and evict squatters, he will have no lawful authority for his action. This means that, unless it is possible to effect a peaceful re-entry, landlords and other non-residential occupiers must seek to recover possession in the civil courts

Displaced residential occupier and protected intending occupier

7.133 Special provision is made for persons falling within the definition of a 'displaced residential occupier' or 'protected intending occupier' of premises or any access to them.

Any person who was occupying the premises in question as a residence immediately before being excluded from occupation by anyone who entered those premises, or any access to those premises, as a trespasser is a 'displaced residential occupier' of them or any access to them,[1] except that the term does not cover a person who was himself occupying the premises as a trespasser before being excluded from occupation.[2] Obviously, a householder who discovers squatters in his house when he returns from work or from holiday is a displaced residential occupier. Since the definition does not talk in terms of 'principal' residence, a person displaced from his weekend cottage in the country while he is living in his flat in town would also seem to be a displaced residential occupier.

Only an individual, ie not a company or other legal person, can be a 'protected intending occupier' (PIO). Examples are the purchaser of a freehold, or someone awarded a council house tenancy, who has not yet taken up occupation. There are three types of 'protected intending occupier' under the involved definition of that term in s 12A of the 1977 Act.

The first type is an individual who, at the time of the request to leave:

(a) has in the premises in question a freehold interest or leasehold interest with not less than two years still to run; and
(b) requires the premises for his own occupation as a residence; and
(c) is excluded from occupation of them by a person who entered them, or any access to them, as a trespasser; and
(d) holds, or a person acting on his behalf holds, a written statement,[3] signed by him and witnessed by a magistrate or commissioner for oaths, which –

   (i) specifies his interest in the premises; and
   (ii) states that he requires the premises for occupation as a residence for himself.[4]

The purpose of the statement is to enable the police to identify the PIO and thereby prevent abuse of these provisions.

The second type of PIO is an individual who, at the time of the request to leave:

(a) has a tenancy of the premises (other than a tenancy falling within the other two definitions) or a licence to occupy them granted by a person with a freehold interest or a leasehold interest with not less than two years still to run in the premises;

(b) requires the premises for his own occupation as a residence;

(c) is excluded from occupation of the premises by a person who entered them, or any access to them, as a trespasser; and

(d) holds, or a person acting on his behalf holds, a written statement[3]

    (i) which states that he has been granted a tenancy of those premises or a licence to occupy them;

    (ii) which specifies the interest in the premises of the person who granted that tenancy or licence to occupy ('the landlord');

    (iii) which states that he requires the premises for occupation as a residence for himself; and

    (iv) which is signed by the landlord and by the tenant or licensee and witnessed by a magistrate or commissioner for oaths.[5]

The third type of PIO is an individual who, at the time of the request to leave:

(a) has a tenancy of the premises in question (other than a tenancy falling within the other two definitions) or a licence to occupy them granted by a local authority, the Housing Corporation, the Welsh Assembly, or a registered social landlord within the meaning of the Housing Act 1985;

(b) requires the premises for his own occupation as a residence;

(c) is excluded from occupation of them by a person who entered them, or any access to them, as a trespasser; and

(d) has been issued by or on behalf of the authority referred to in (a) with a certificate stating that the authority etc is one to which these provisions apply and that he has been granted a licence or tenancy by it to occupy the premises as a residence.[6]

---

1   1977 Act, s 12(3) and (5).

2   Ibid, s 12(4). Section 12(6) provides that anyone who enters or is on or in occupation of any premises by virtue of (a) any title derived from a trespasser, or (b) any licence or consent given by a trespasser or by a person deriving title from a trespasser, is himself to be treated as a trespasser for the purposes of Part II of the 1977 Act, and phrases involving a reference to a trespasser are to be construed accordingly. In addition, s 12(7) provides that anyone who is on any premises as a trespasser does not cease to be a trespasser by virtue of being allowed time to leave the premises, nor does anyone cease to be a displaced residential occupier of any premises by virtue of any such allowance of time to a trespasser.

3   If a person makes a statement for the purposes of this provision that he knows to be false in a material particular, or if he recklessly makes such a statement that is false in a material particular, he commits an offence (s 12A(8)) and is liable on summary conviction to imprisonment for a term not exceeding six months or a fine not exceeding level 5 on the standard scale, or both: s 12A(10). What was said about a similar offence in paras **7.121–7.124** is equally applicable here.

4   1977 Act, s 12A(2) and (3).

5   Ibid, s 12A(4) and (5).

6   Ibid, s 12A(6) and (7).

7.134 Even a displaced residential occupier or PIO does not have lawful authority to use or threaten violence to secure entry to his home. However, s 6(1A) of the 1977 Act provides that the offence under s 6(1) does not apply to a person who is a displaced residential occupier or a PIO of the premises in question or who is acting on behalf of such an occupier. This exemption does not have to be proved by the accused. Instead, if he adduces sufficient evidence (ie evidence which raises a reasonable doubt) that he was, or was acting on behalf of, such an occupier he is presumed to be, or to be acting on behalf of, such an occupier unless the contrary is proved by the prosecution. This exemption applies only to a charge under s 6. However, if such an occupier is charged with assault or some other offence he may have the general defence[1] of using reasonable force to terminate a trespass or (if he has unsuccessfully asked the trespasser to leave) in the prevention of crime.[2]

---

1   Criminal Law Act 1967, s 3.
2   The trespasser's failure to leave on request will be an offence under s 7, below.

Power of arrest

7.135 Section 6(6) of the Criminal Law Act 1977, empowers a constable in uniform[1] to arrest without a warrant anyone who is, or whom he with reasonable cause suspects[2] to be, guilty of an offence under s 6.[3] The constable may enter (by force if need be) and search any premises where he has reasonable grounds for believing that the person to be arrested is, for the purpose of arresting him.[4]

---

1   See para **6.92**.
2   See para **3.68** fn 1.
3   Powers of arrest under Part II of the 1977 Act were preserved by PACE, s 26(2) and Sch 2.
4   PACE, s 17. What is said about this power in para **4.18** applies equally here.

Adverse occupation of residential premises

7.136 The relevant provision is s 7 of the 1977 Act. Section 7(1) of the 1977 Act provides that any person who is on any premises (including any access to them)[1] as a trespasser after having entered as such[2] is guilty of an offence if he fails to leave those premises on being required to do so by or on behalf of:

(a) a 'displaced residential occupier' of them; or
(b) an individual who is a 'protected intending occupier' of them.[3]

The main purpose of this offence is to give a residential occupier or a PIO of premises who has been excluded from them by trespassers, such as squatters, a swifter remedy for recovering possession of them than the available civil remedy. He can request them to leave, and, if they do not, may call on a constable in uniform,[4] who may arrest without warrant those who are, or whom he, with reasonable cause, suspects[5] are guilty of the offence.[6] The constable has the power of entry and search for this purpose referred to at the end of para **7.135**.[7]

---

1   1977 Act, s 7(4).
2   What is said in para **7.133** fn 2 about entry as a trespasser seems to be equally applicable here.
3   Where the offence relates to a PIO, a document purporting to be a *certificate* under the 1977 Act, s 12A(6)(d) is to be received in evidence and, unless the contrary is proved, is deemed to have been issued by or on behalf of the authority stated in the certificate: s 12A(9)(b).
4   See para **6.92**.
5   See para **3.68** fn 1.
6   1977 Act, s 7(6).
7   PACE, s 17(1).

Prohibited conduct

7.137 What is required is a failure to leave premises (or access to them) by a person who is on those premises (or access) as a trespasser, having entered as such, and who has been required to leave by or on behalf of a person of the specified type. It seems that someone who fails to leave immediately is caught. This can be contrasted with the offences of failing to leave after a direction to do so under ss 61, 63, 68 and 76 of the Criminal Justice and Public Order Act 1994, discussed above, which are committed by a failure to leave as soon as practicable or reasonably practicable. The requirement that the accused must have entered the premises as a trespasser means that a person who remains on premises after the termination of a tenancy or licence does not commit the present offence, since his original entry on them (to which s 7 must refer)[1] was not as a trespasser.

The offence does not simply consist of failure by a trespasser to leave premises, since such failure only constitutes the offence if a request to leave has been made by, or on behalf of, a 'displaced residential occupier' or a 'protected intending occupier' of the premises. Failure to leave premises despite a request by the landlord of them or any other type of occupier is not an offence.

---

1 See Professor Griew's annotations to the 1977 Act, s 7, in [1997] *Current Law Statutes.*

Mental element

7.138 Presumably, at the time of committing the offence, ie when he fails to leave on being required to do so, the accused must know that he is a trespasser and entered as such, or be wilfully blind as to this. Whether he knew that he was a trespasser when he entered would seem to be irrelevant. An unwitting entry without a lawful right or the occupier's permission constitutes an entry as a trespasser for the purposes of the law of trespass.[1]

---

1 See para **7.8**.

Defences

7.139 Three defences are provided by the Act, the burden of proof in each case being on the accused.[1]

(a) Where the request to leave was made by, or on behalf of, a person claiming to be a PIO, the accused has a defence if the person requesting him to leave failed at that time to produce a written statement, or certificate, complying with the Act, despite being asked to do so by the accused.[2]

(b) It is a defence that the accused believed that the person requiring him to leave was not a displaced residential occupier or a PIO of the premises, or someone acting on his behalf.[3]

(c) It is a defence that the premises in question are or form part of premises used mainly for non-residential purposes, and that the accused was not on any part of the premises used wholly or mainly for residential purposes.[4] This means, for instance, that people involved in a factory sit-in do not commit the present offence if they fail to leave when required by a resident caretaker, so long as they are not in his flat or in part of the premises used wholly or mainly for access to, or in connection with, the flat.

---

1 See para **4.38**.
2 1977 Act, s 12A(9). See para **7.134** as to such a statement or certificate. The statement or certificate need not be shown to the trespasser in its entirety. Provided that the matters requiring to be certified are displayed it is not necessary that any other part (eg the PIO's address) is: *R v Forest JJ, ex parte Hartman* [1991] Crim LR 641, DC.

3   Ibid, s 7(2).
4   Ibid, s 7(3).

Other offences

7.140 In order to fulfil this country's international obligations to protect the inviolability of diplomatic and similar premises, s 9(1) of the 1977 Act makes it an offence simply to enter as a trespasser premises that are or form part of an embassy, consulate, the private residence of a foreign diplomatic agent, or other similar premises. Alternatively, it is an offence under s 9(1) to be on such premises as a trespasser even though the initial entry was lawful. It is a defence in either case for the accused to prove[1] that he believed that the premises in question were not premises to which s 9 applies.[2] An offence under s 9(1) is only triable summarily; the maximum punishment is six months' imprisonment or a fine not exceeding level 5 on the standard scale, or both.[3] A constable in uniform[4] may arrest without warrant anyone who is, or whom he, with reasonable cause, suspects to be, in the act of committing an offence under s 9.[5] A prosecution under s 9 requires the Attorney-General's consent.[6]

1   See para **4.38**.
2   1977 Act, s 9(3).
3   Ibid, s 9(5).
4   See para **6.92**.
5   1977 Act, s 9(7).
6   Ibid, s 9(6). As to this requirement, see paras **5.53–5.55**.

Chapter 8

FOOTBALL HOOLIGANISM

INTRODUCTION

8.1   Association football hooliganism is not a new phenomenon.[1] However, in the last three or four decades, football hooliganism, particularly where it involves gangs or groups who associate themselves with particular teams, has been a cause of particular concern. Football hooliganism is mainly associated with matches involving national, Football Association Premier League or Football League teams. For some time steps have been taken to minimise hooliganism, such as segregation of rival supporters; detailed planning with the police, opposition and rail and coach operators; ensuring that terraces are free from objects that can be used as missiles; and the use of closed-circuit television systems in grounds.

The police have undertaken extensive covert operations against hooligan ringleaders and the Football Section of the National Criminal Intelligence Service collates intelligence on serious and persistent hooligans.

A number of statutory provisions have been enacted specifically designed to deal with football hooliganism. Most of these are based on proposals made in the mid 1980s by the White Paper, *Review of Public Order Law*,[2] and the Popplewell Reports on crowd safety and control at sports grounds,[3] and in 1990 in the Taylor Report on the Hillsborough Stadium disaster in 1989.[4]

---

1   For a brief history of hooliganism connected with sport, see paras 5.3–5.19 of the Final Popplewell Report (*Report of Committee of Inquiry into Crowd Safety and Control at Sports Grounds*) (Cmnd 9710, 1986). For a useful background to this chapter, see Greenfield and Osborn 'After the Act: the (re)construction and regulation of football fandom' [1996] 1 J Civ Lib 7.
2   Cmnd 9510 (1985).
3   Cmnd 9585 (Interim) and Cmnd 9710 (Final) (1986).
4   *The Hillsborough Stadium Disaster: Report of Inquiry* (Cm 962, 1990).

8.2   Intoxication among supporters can be a major cause of hooliganism. The Sporting Events (Control of Alcohol etc) Act 1985 provides for various restrictions, centring on the possession or supply of alcohol and drunkenness which, with one exception mentioned in para **8.9**, are wholly concerned with one type of sporting event, viz an association football match. The licensing provisions in the 1985 Act, which have undoubtedly contributed to the control or prevention of disorder, are outside the ambit of this book and are not dealt with here.

Subsequently, other pieces of legislation have been enacted to deal with the problem of football hooliganism:

–   the Football (Offences) Act 1991, which created three offences governing the throwing of missiles, indecent or racist chanting and pitch invasion;
–   Part IV of the Public Order Act 1986, which provides for orders excluding football hooligans from prescribed football matches;
–   the Football Spectators Act 1989, which controls the admission of spectators to designated football matches and also provides for international football banning orders being made against football hooligans;

– s 166 of the Criminal Justice and Public Order Act 1994, which introduced an offence in respect of football-ticket touting; and

– the Football (Offences and Disorder) Act 1999, which toughened-up the above provisions in a variety of ways along lines proposed in a Home Office consultation paper.[1]

---

1   *Review of Football Related Legislation* (1998).

8.3   Legislation primarily addressed at crowd safety has also had a dampening effect on crowd disorder. The Safety of Sports Grounds Act 1975, amended in the light of the Final Popplewell Report, gives the Secretary of State power to designate as a sports ground requiring a local authority certificate under the Act any ground which in his opinion has a capacity for more than 5,000 spectators (in the case of a ground of a Football Association Premier League clubs or Football League club) or for more than 10,000 (in the case of any other club).[1] Numerous designation orders have been made under the Act; quite a number of them relate to rugby union, rugby league and cricket grounds. An either-way offence is committed if spectators are admitted to a designated ground in respect of which an application for a safety certificate has not been made or in breach of such a certificate.[2] The Fire Safety and Safety of Places of Sport Act 1987 provides a similar system of certification in respect of stands at undesignated grounds where there is covered accommodation for 500 or more spectators.

Sections 8–13 of the Football Spectators Act 1989 (1989 Act) are designed to control the admission of spectators to football matches designated for the purposes of Part I of that Act, which are described in para **8.35**. They do so by establishing a Football Licensing Authority whose function is to grant licences, in appropriate cases, to admit spectators to a ground to watch a designated football match there. The licence may contain conditions. In particular, the Secretary of State can require the authority to include in any licence requirements as to the seating of spectators. The Secretary of State has done so in the Football Spectators (Seating) Orders 1994, 1995, 1996, 1997 and 1999.[3] All-seat accommodation has undoubtedly contributed to the reduction of crowd disorder, as well as to crowd safety. It is an either-way offence to admit persons to unlicensed premises, or to permit them to remain there, during a period relevant to a designated football match.[4] It is a summary offence to contravene any terms or condition in a licence.[5] Both offences can be committed only by someone who is a 'responsible person'; such a person has a defence if he proves that the contravention took place without his consent and that he took all reasonable precautions and exercised all due diligence to avoid the commission of such an offence.

Sections 2–7 of the Football Spectators Act 1989 provide for a national membership scheme that would be administered and enforced by a Football Membership Authority, under which (generally) only members of the scheme would be authorised spectators at a designated football match. Attendance at such a match by someone who was not an authorised person would be an offence. These sections have not yet been implemented. In the light of the Taylor Report, it is considered unlikely that they will ever be implemented. For this reason, they are not discussed further in this book.

---

1   1975 Act, s 1(1).
2   Safety at Sports Grounds Act 1975, s 12.

3   SI 1994/1666, SI 1995/1706, SI 1996/1706, SI 1997/1677, SI 1999/1926.
4   Football Spectators Act 1989, s 9.
5   Ibid, s 10.

8.4   These statutory changes, along with improved police strategies and better management by clubs referred to above, seemed significantly to reduce the level of disorder at football grounds and among those travelling to or from them. Figures for the 1998/99 season, however, revealed an increase on the previous season after six years of falling arrest rates. Overall, arrests for football-related violence and hooliganism rose slightly from 3,307 to 3,341, but there were larger increases in arrests for violent disorder (up from 52 to 100) and for assault (up from 110 to 133).[1]

The problem is that it appears that there is a hard core of 100–200 offenders who are responsible for most of the disorder. Using the Internet (sometimes 'closed' websites) and other modern technology, they plan and coordinate it.[2] They have not been deterred so far and are unlikely to be deterred by the changes made by the Football (Offences and Disorder) Act 1999. The problem, as with so much of recent criminal law, is that the volume of offences and police powers aimed at a minority is likely to create tension and ill-feeling and confrontation between the ordinary fan and the police.

1   Information supplied by the National Criminal Intelligence Service. The NCIS website is http://www.ncis.co.uk.
2   See report in (1999) *The Guardian* 9 September.

SPORTING EVENTS (CONTROL OF ALCOHOL ETC) ACT 1985

Alcohol on coaches, trains etc

8.5   Sections 1 and 1A of the Sporting Events (Control of Alcohol etc) Act 1985 (1985 Act) provide a number of summary offences whose aim is to prevent drunken behaviour by football fans en route to or from matches, and to prevent them arriving at grounds drunk. These offences are offences of:

– causing or permitting the carriage of alcohol on a specified vehicle;
– being in possession of alcohol on such a vehicle; and
– being drunk on a specified vehicle.

Vehicles specified

8.6   Section 1 of the 1985 Act provides these offences in relation to public service vehicles (ie coaches, buses and the like)[1] and railway passenger vehicles. It does not apply to all such vehicles, but only to those which are being used for the principal purpose of carrying passengers for the whole or part of a journey[2] to or from a 'designated sporting event'.[3] Thus, s 1 does not apply to a bus or train on a normal scheduled service because it is not being used for the principal purpose of carrying passengers to or from a designated sporting event, even if the majority of the passengers are travelling to or from a match, since the words 'used' and 'principal purpose' must refer to use by, and the principal purpose of, the bus or railway company.[4] However, s 1 does apply to a 'football special' or to a coach or train chartered by the supporters' club, provided that it is travelling to or from a designated sporting event.

The limitation of s 1 to public service vehicles and passenger trains means that s 1 can easily be avoided by the use of other forms of transport. The gap has been partially plugged by s 1A of the 1985 Act, which was added by Sch 1 to the Public Order Act 1986. This provides substantially identical offences to those in s 1 which it applies to Transit or minibus-type vehicles, which are quite often observed full of football supporters on match days.

Section 1A applies to a motor vehicle[5] which:

(a) is not a public service vehicle but is adapted to carry more than eight passengers, and
(b) is being used for the principal purpose of carrying two or more passengers for the whole or part of a journey[2] to or from a designated sporting event.[6]

It will be noted that the definition is not limited to minibuses. It therefore includes the few types of private car which are adapted to carry more than eight passengers. The requirement in (b) that the vehicle must be carrying two or more passengers (including the driver) is designed to ensure that those who travel alone, or with one passenger, to a match, having bought alcohol while doing the family shopping at the supermarket, are not caught. It was thought it would neither be fair nor sensible to catch such persons. If so, why stop at two?

If supporters wish to avoid the provisions of ss 1 or 1A, they need merely travel by a scheduled bus or train service or by private car, or by some other means of transport. However, under British Railways by-laws the carriage of alcohol on trains, including normal scheduled train services, going to or from a place where there is a football match can be banned, breach of a ban being an offence.[7]

It is not obvious why ss 1 and 1A should between them be limited to, basically, buses, coaches, minibuses and trains being used for the principal purpose of transporting football supporters. There is no evidence that the use of these types of transport is likely to aggravate the risk of drunken behaviour by football fans en route to or from matches or the risk of them arriving at grounds drunk; so why should the type of transport matter?

---

1   For the purposes of ss 1 and 1A, 'public service vehicle' has the same meaning as in the
     Public Passenger Vehicles Act 1981: 1985 Act, ss 1(5) and 1A(5). Section 1(1) of the 1981 Act
     defines a public service vehicle as a motor vehicle (other than a tramcar) which:
     (a)   if adapted to carry more than eight passengers, is used for carrying passengers for hire
            or reward; or
     (b)   if not so adapted, is used for carrying passengers for hire or reward at separate fares in
            the course of a business of carrying passengers.
     For a discussion of this definition, see English and Card *Butterworths Police Law* 6th edn
     (Butterworths, 1999) pp 316–321.
2   As to what is meant by a 'journey to or from a match' see para **8.35**.
3   1985 Act, s 1(1).
4   Compare Birch 'Bottles, booze and bobbies' (1985) 149 JPN 596.
5   'Motor vehicle' means a mechanically propelled vehicle intended or adapted for use on
     roads: 1985 Act, s 1A(5).
6   1985 Act, s 1A(1).
7   British Railways Board By-laws, Art 3(A). These by-laws continue to have effect in relation to
     any independent railway company which is the subject of a transfer scheme, as well as in
     relation to the track, infrastructure and stations transferred to Railtrack. There is a
     corresponding provision in relation to the London underground: London Transport
     Executive Railways By-laws.

Designated sporting event

8.7   'Designated sporting event' is defined by s 9(3) of the 1985 Act. It 'means a sporting event or proposed sporting event for the time being designated, or of a class designated, by order made by the Secretary of State'.[1] It also 'includes a designated sporting event within the meaning of Part V of the Criminal Justice (Scotland) Act 1980'.[2] A designation order made by the Secretary of State may apply to events or proposed events outside Great Britain as well as those in England and Wales.

---

1   An order under s 9(3) must be made by statutory instrument and is subject to annulment in pursuance of a resolution of either House of Parliament: 1985 Act, s 9(8).The Act does not apply to sporting events where all competitors take part otherwise than for reward and to which all spectators are admitted free of charge: s 9(6).

2   Part V of the 1980 Act has been re-enacted as Part II of the Criminal Law (Consolidation) (Scotland) Act 1995, but a consequential amendment to this effect to the 1985 Act, s 9(3), has not been made.

Sporting event ... designated ... by the Secretary of State

8.8   The Sports Grounds and Sporting Events (Designation) Order 1985[1] made by the Secretary of State, specifies the following classes of sporting events:

(a) (i)   association football matches in which one or both teams represent a Football League club or a Football Association Premier League club;

  (ii)   international association football matches (including semi-professional and schoolboy ones);

  (iii) association football matches (other than those already specified) in the European Champion Clubs Cup, European Cup Winners' Cup or UEFA Cup,

  provided in each case that the match takes place at the ground of an association football club which is a member of the Football Association or the Football Association of Wales or at Wembley Stadium;

(b) association football matches within the jurisdiction of the Scottish Football Association;

(c) association football matches at a ground outside Great Britain:

  (i)   in which one or both teams represent the Football Association or Football Association of Wales or a Football Association Premier League or Football League club; or

  (ii)   in competition for the European Champion Clubs Cup, European Cup Winners' Cup or UEFA Cup and one or both teams represent a club which is a member of the Football Association or the Football Association of Wales.

Matches involving club teams belonging to other leagues in England and Wales are not designated, nor is a match between a club in one of the two leagues and a club that is not if it is played at the latter's ground. Consequently, for example, an FA Cup match between Yeovil Town and Manchester United which is to be played at Yeovil's ground is not a designated sporting event.

---

1   SI 1985/1151.

Designated sporting event ... Part V of the Criminal Justice (Scotland) Act 1980[1]

8.9 All matches in the Scottish Football League or in the Highland Football League, all Scottish Football League and Scottish Football Association cup matches, all football matches in the three European cups, and soccer internationals, provided in each case that they take place at a designated ground, have been designated by the Sports Grounds and Sporting Events (Designation) (Scotland) Order 1980.[2] The grounds designated by the Order are Hampden Park and the grounds of members of the Scottish Football League or of the Highland Football League. In addition, the Order designates rugby internationals at Murrayfield as a designated sporting event.

---

1   See para **8.7** fn 2.
2   SI 1980/2030.

Causing or permitting carriage of alcohol on a vehicle

8.10 Section 1(2) provides that a person who knowingly causes or permits intoxicating liquor[1] to be carried on a vehicle to which s 1 applies is guilty of an offence:

(a) if the vehicle is a public service vehicle and he is the operator[2] of the vehicle or the employee or agent of the operator; or

(b) if the vehicle is a hired vehicle (eg a chartered train or a football special) and he is the person to whom it is hired or the employee or agent of that person. Thus, an organiser of the supporters' club (or his agent) can be convicted if he permits intoxicating liquor to be carried on a chartered train, but a train guard employed by the operator who fails to prevent this cannot.

Section 1A(2) provides that a person who knowingly causes or permits intoxicating liquor to be carried on a motor vehicle to which s 1A applies is guilty of an offence:

(a) if he is its driver; or

(b) if he is not its driver but is its keeper,[3] the employee or agent of its keeper, a person to whom it is made available (by hire, loan or otherwise) by its keeper or the keeper's employee or agent, or the employee or agent of a person to whom it is so made available.

---

1   By virtue of the 1985 Act, s 9(7), this has the same meaning as in the Licensing Act 1964, s 201, viz spirits, wine, beer, cider, and any other fermented, distilled or spiritous liquor, except:

    (a)   any liquor of an original gravity not exceeding 1016° and of a strength not exceeding 1.2%;

    (b)   perfumes;

    (c)   flavouring essences recognised by the Customs and Excise Commissioners as not being intended for consumption as or with dutiable alcoholic liquor;

    (d)   spirits, wine or made-wine so medicated as to be, in the opinion of the Commissioners, intended for use as a medicine and not as a beverage.

2   Per the 1985 Act, s 1(1), 'operator' has the same meaning as in the Public Passenger Vehicles Act 1981. That meaning is given by the 1981 Act, s 81, viz the operator of a vehicle is the driver, if he owns the vehicle; and in any other case, the person for whom the driver works (whether under a contract of employment or any other description of contract personally to

do work). Special provision is made for the case where the vehicle is hired by one holder of a PSV operator's licence to another holder.

3   The statement in the 1985 Act, s 1A(5), that 'keeper' means the person having the duty to take out a licence for the vehicle under the Vehicles Excise and Registration Act 1994 is not very helpful, since he is described by that provision as the person 'keeping the vehicle'.

8.11 The causing or permitting of the carrying of liquor on the vehicle must be done 'knowingly'.[1] There seems no doubt that 'knowingly' applies to 'permit' as well as to 'cause', but it would probably not matter if it did not since 'permit' has generally been construed by the courts as importing the same or similar requirement of mens rea as 'knowingly', and many of these cases have concerned public service vehicles.[2] A person 'causes' someone else to do something if it is done on his actual authority, express or implied, or in consequence of his exercise of some influence on the acts of the other person.[3] 'Permit' is capable of at least three different meanings depending on its context. It can mean 'authorising', or 'assenting to or agreeing to' or 'not taking reasonable steps to prevent something within one's power'. It is submitted that in the present context, particularly the alternative mode of commission of 'causing', 'permitting' here bears the third, widest meaning.[4]

The maximum punishment for an offence under s 1(2) or s 1A(2) is a fine not exceeding level 4 on the standard scale.[5] A person convicted of an offence under s 1(2) may be made subject to a domestic and/or an international footballing order, as explained in paras **8.34** and **8.45**.

---

1   'Knowingly' includes 'wilful blindness': see para **6.37**.
2   *Goldsmith v Deakin* (1933) 150 LT 157, DC; *Newell v Cross, Newell v Cook* [1936] 2 All ER 203, DC; *Evans v Dell* [1937] 1 All ER 349, DC; *McLeod (or Houston) v Buchanan* [1940] 2 All ER 179, HL; *Reynolds v GH Austin & Sons Ltd* [1951] 1 All ER 606, DC; *Roper v Taylor's Central Garages (Exeter) Ltd* [1951] 2 TLR 284, DC; *Vehicle Inspectorate v Nuttall* [1999] 3 All ER 833, HL.
3   *A-G of Hong Kong v Tse Hung-lit* [1986] 3 All ER 173, PC.
4   As it did in *Vehicle Inspectorate v Nuttall* above (offence of causing or permitting a breach of the tachograph regulations).
5   1985 Act, s 8(a).

Possession of alcohol on a vehicle

8.12 Section 1(3) makes it an offence for a person to have intoxicating liquor in his possession while on a vehicle to which s 1 applies. There is a corresponding offence under s 1A(3) in relation to motor vehicles to which s 1A applies. The maximum punishment for either offence is three months' imprisonment or a fine not exceeding level 3 on the standard scale, or both.[1] In the case of a conviction under s 1(3), the court can make a domestic football banning order and/or an international football banning order in the circumstances outlined in paras **8.34** and **8.45**.

'Possession' is a notoriously elusive concept. Chameleon-like it can change its definition depending on its context. Thus, case law about 'possession' in other offences must be handled with care. Although physical custody is not necessary for possession in some other offences, since physical control is enough for their purposes,[2] it is submitted that the mischief and wording of the present offences require a narrower definition. The offences are concerned with having intoxicating liquor in one's possession while on a motor vehicle of a specified type. Although a test of physical control can be satisfied, and one can be in possession, in relation to one's personal effects that are at home or in one's car while one is travelling on a bus, it is submitted that one does not have them in one's possession while travelling on the bus. It would seem that 'has in his possession while on a motor vehicle' is akin to the phrase 'has with him' in offences relating to offensive weapons and firearms; there is a similarity of phraseology and also of mischief (the prevention of people having weapons or liquor available to them which if used may cause a public order situation). 'Has with him' in relation to weapon offences requires either that the person is carrying the weapon or that it is near to him and readily accessible to him.[3] On this basis, a person would have liquor in his possession while on a coach if he had a can of beer in his jacket pocket, whether he was wearing the jacket or the jacket was in the luggage rack above his seat, but not (it would seem) if the can was in the locked luggage locker underneath the passenger compartment to which he did not have ready access nor (certainly) if the jacket containing the can had been left at home. It would obviously be absurd if the present offence could be committed in the last situation.

To be in possession, knowledge of the thing's quality is not required, so that a person can be in possession of a bottle of beer which he has found and put in his pocket even though he believed it only contained ginger beer.[4] However, possession cannot begin until the person concerned is aware that the thing is in his 'control'.[5] Thus, if a hip-flask is slipped into someone's pocket or bag and he does not have the vaguest idea that it is there, he does not have possession of it.

In the case of liquor in a parcel, packet or other container in a person's physical control, he is in possession of that liquor if he knows that he is in control of that container and that it contains something, even though he thinks that the thing is something different in kind from liquor and even though he has no right to open the container to check its contents.[6]

Possession once begun continues as long as the thing is in the person's control, even though he has forgotten about it or mistakenly believes it has been destroyed or disposed of.[7]

This is what is required for possession. What about mens rea as to the nature of the thing possessed, ie that it is intoxicating liquor? In the absence of any words importing such a requirement as to the nature of the thing possessed (ie that it is intoxicating liquor), it is submitted that it is likely that this offence will be construed as not requiring proof of such mens rea (and as not even permitting a reasonably mistaken belief that the thing is not intoxicating liquor to excuse the accused), just as the House of Lords did in *Warner v Metropolitan Police Comr*[8] in relation to the offence of unauthorised possession of an illicit drug, and just as the Court of Appeal has in respect of offences of having with one a firearm or offensive weapon.[9]

---

1   1985 Act, s 8(b).
2   *Lockyer v Gibb* [1966] 2 All ER 653, DC; *R v Boyesen* [1982] 2 All ER 161 at 163, per Lord Scarman.
3   *R v Pawlicki* [1992] 3 All ER 902, CA.
4   *Warner v Metropolitan Police Comr* [1968] 2 All ER 356; *Searle v Randolph* [1972] Crim LR 779, DC; *R v McNamara* (1988) 87 Cr App R 246, CA.
5   See, for instance, *Lockyer v Gibb* above; *R v Ashton-Rickhardt* [1978] 1 All ER 173, CA; *R v Boyesen* above at 163, per Lord Scarman; *R v Conway* [1994] Crim LR 826, CA (cases of offence of possession of drugs); *R v Cugullere* [1961] 2 All ER 343, CCA (having with one offensive weapon). Cf *R v Lewis* (1988) 87 Cr App R 270, CA (offence of possession of drugs), where the court stated that it was not necessary that D should have had actual knowledge that

the thing was under his control, since it was enough that he ought to have imputed to him knowledge that it was.

6   *R v McNamara* (1988) 87 Cr App R 246; *R v Waller* [1991] Crim LR 381, CA; *R v Steele* [1980] Crim LR 689, CA.

7   *R v Buswell* [1972] 1 All ER 75, CA; *R v Martindale* [1986] 3 All ER 25, CA (cases on possession of drugs); *R v McCalla* (1988) 87 Cr App R 372, CA (having with one offensive weapon); cf *R v Russell* (1984) 81 Cr App R 315, CA.

8   [1968] 2 All ER 356, HL.

9   *R v McCalla* above; *R v Vann* [1996] Crim LR 52, CA; *R v Hussain* [1981] 2 All ER 287, CA (possession of firearm without certificate); *R v Bradish* [1990] 1 All ER 460, CA (possession of prohibited weapon). Compare *R v Russell*, above.

Being drunk on a vehicle

8.13 Section 1(4) provides that a person who is drunk on a vehicle to which s 1 applies is guilty of an offence. There is a corresponding offence under s 1A(4) in relation to motor vehicles to which s 1A applies. The maximum punishment for these offences is a fine not exceeding level 2 on the standard scale.[1] In the case of a conviction under s 1(4), the court can make a domestic football banning order and/or an international football banning order in the circumstances explained below.[2] It is clear from the long title of the 1985 Act and its provisions that (as in the case of the offence of being drunk and disorderly)[3] the intoxication must be due to the consumption of intoxicating liquor (as opposed to drugs or some other substance). It is submitted that, as elsewhere in the criminal law, 'drunk' refers to a person who, by taking intoxicating liquor, has lost the power of steady self-control.[3]

1   1985 Act, s 8(c).
2   See paras **8.34** and **8.45**.
3   See para **9.17**.

A gap

8.14 The 1985 Act does not grapple with one of the major problems relating to football hooliganism, namely heavy drinking by many fans in pubs outside the ground before the match, often coupled with their late arrival at the ground and the consequent frustration suffered by them, with inevitable consequences in terms of public disorder.[1] These cases fall to be dealt with, if at all, under the general law of offences against the person, against property or against public order.

1   A consultation paper preceding the Football (Offences and Disorder) Act 1999 (*Review of Football Related Legislation* (Home Office, 1998)) proposed that, for potentially volatile matches, courts should be able to impose bans on alcohol sales at pubs and off-licences around football grounds, which would extend to the carrying and consumption of alcohol in the area. This proposal has not been implemented.

Police powers

8.15 Section 7(3) of the 1985 Act provides that a constable may stop a public service vehicle to which s 1 applies or a motor vehicle to which s 1A applies (but not, for obvious reasons, a railway passenger vehicle) and may search such a vehicle or a railway passenger vehicle if he has reasonable grounds to suspect that an offence under s 1 or s 1A is being or has been committed in respect of that vehicle. The provisions of s 2 of PACE and the Stop and Search Code (Code A) apply to such a search.

The power to search under s 7(3) is to search the vehicle, and not a person on board it. There is, however, a general power under s 7(2) for a constable to search a person whom he reasonably suspects is committing or has committed an offence under the Act. This is discussed in para **8.24**.

Alcohol, containers, fireworks etc at designated sports grounds

8.16 Sections 2 and 2A of the 1985 Act provide two offences relating to the possession of alcohol, containers, fireworks and the like at a designated sports ground, and one relating to being drunk at such a ground.

Designated sports ground
8.17 A 'designated sports ground' is defined by s 9(2) of the 1985 Act as any place:

(a) used (wholly or partly) for sporting events where accommodation is provided for spectators; and
(b) for the time being designated, or of a class designated, by order[1] made by the Secretary of State.

In the Sports Grounds and Sporting Events (Designation) Order 1985[2] made by the Secretary of State, the following grounds, all of them (with one exception) association football grounds, have been designated: the home grounds of all football clubs that are members of the Football Association or the Football Association of Wales; any other ground in England and Wales used occasionally or temporarily by such a club, or used for international matches; Wembley Stadium (which is not simply a football ground), and the ground of Berwick Rangers.

---

1   The order must be made by statutory instrument and is subject to annulment in pursuance of a resolution of either House of Parliament: 1985 Act, s 9(8).
2   SI 1985/1151.

Period of designated sporting event
8.18 Offences under ss 2 and 2A of the 1985 Act can only be committed during 'the period of a designated sporting event'.[1] Normally, this is the period beginning two hours before the start of the event or (if earlier, as where the start is delayed) two hours before the time at which it is advertised to start and ending one hour after the end of the event. There are special provisions where the event is postponed to a later day or simply does not take place. The provisions about 'the period of a designated sporting event' are set out in s 9(4) of the 1985 Act as follows:

> 'The period of a designated sporting event is the period beginning two hours before the start of the event or (if earlier) two hours before the time at which it is advertised to start and ending one hour after the end of the event, but –
>
> (a) where an event advertised to start at a particular time on a particular day is postponed to a later day, the period includes the period in the day on which it is advertised to take place beginning two hours before and ending one hour after that time, and
> (b) where an event advertised to start at a particular time on a particular day does not take place, the period is the period referred to in paragraph (a) above.'

The effect of this provision can be illustrated by the following examples concerning a designated sporting event advertised as starting at 3 pm on Saturday 1 November.

Example 1

Assuming that the match starts at 3 pm on 1 November, the period under the definition is from 1 pm until one hour after the end of the match. Since a football match normally lasts one hour forty minutes, including half-time, but excluding any stoppages for injury etc, the period will end at 5.40 pm; unless the match is abandoned at 4.15 pm or, being a cup-tie, goes into extra time and ends at 5.20 pm. In these special cases the period will end at 5.15 pm or 6.20 pm, respectively.

Example 2

If the start of the match is postponed or delayed until later on 1 November and starts at 4 pm, the period under the definition is still from 1 pm (two hours before the advertised start-time) and ends one hour after the end of the match (approximately 6.40 pm).

Examples 1 and 2 are derived from an application of the opening words of s 9(4).

Example 3

If the match is postponed to 7.30 pm on Wednesday 5 November (at which time it then takes place), s 9(4)(a) governs the 'relevant period' on *1 November.* Under this, the period on *1 November* is from 1 pm (ie two hours before the advertised start time) until 4 pm (ie one hour after that time). In addition, as explained in example 1, on *5 November* the period will be from 5.30 pm until approximately 10.10 pm.

Example 4

If the event simply does not take place, ie it is abandoned before the start and not postponed until a later date, the relevant provision is s 9(4)(b). Under this the period on *1 November* will be the same as that referred to in the first part of example 3, ie 1 pm until 4 pm.

One situation does not seem to be adequately covered by the definition. This is where an event is postponed until later in the same day but then does not take place. For example, suppose the start of the event on 1 November is postponed from 3 to 5 pm because of inclement weather and then abandoned at 5 pm. The period, having started from 1 pm (see Example 2) will end at 4 pm (see Example 4), although the crowd will still be there anticipating the 5 pm start. Consequently, an occurrence between 4 pm and 5 pm while the crowd are still at the ground or are dispersing cannot constitute an offence under s 2.

---

1   For the definition of a 'designated sporting event', see para **8.7**.

Possession of alcohol etc at designated ground

8.19 Section 2(1) of the 1985 Act provides that a person who has intoxicating liquor[1] or an article to which s 2 applies in his possession:[2]

(a) at any time during the period of a designated sporting event when he is in any area of a designated sports ground *from which the event may be directly viewed;* or

(b) while entering or trying to enter a designated sports ground at any time
   during the period of a designated sporting event at the ground;

is guilty of an offence, whose maximum punishment is three months' imprisonment or a fine not exceeding level 3 on the standard scale, or both.[3] This offence is
a relevant offence for the purposes of a domestic and/or an international football
banning order, as explained later.

By way of derogation from the general definition of the period of a
designated sporting event, a different period, laid down by s 5A of the 1985 Act,
applies for the purposes of the present offence in respect of a *room* in a designated
sports ground from which the designated sporting event may be directly viewed to
which the public are not admitted (eg the directors' room). This is a 'restricted
period' beginning 15 minutes before the start of the event (or advertised start if
earlier) and ending 15 minutes after the end of the event or 15 minutes after the
advertised start (if the event is postponed to a later day or cancelled).

---

1   See para **8.10** fn 1.
2   What is said about 'having in his possession' in para **8.12** is equally applicable here.
3   1985 Act, s 8(b).

8.20 The reference to an article to which s 2 applies is to various types of drinks
containers, for example bottles or a crushed-up can, which can be used as missiles
or weapons. Because these are not offensive weapons per se (except in the case of a
deliberately broken bottle or the like), a conviction for possessing an offensive
weapon is most unlikely if a container is not actually used to cause injury, because
the necessary intent to use it to cause injury would be impossible to prove.
Consequently, but for s 2 it would not normally be possible for the police to take
preventive action before a container was used offensively. Section 2 is, however,
open to the objection that it lowers too far the threshold of criminal liability, and
places at risk of arrest, prosecution and conviction persons whose possession of an
article is wholly innocent.

To turn to detail, s 2(3) states that an article to which s 2 applies is any article
capable of causing injury to a person struck by it, being:

(a) a bottle, can or other portable container (including such an article when
   crushed or broken) which is for holding any drink and is of a kind which,
   when empty, is normally discarded or returned to, or left to be recovered by,
   the supplier; or
(b) part of an article falling within (a).

However, the definition expressly does not apply to anything that is for holding
any medicinal product. The wording of this exception does not require the
medicinal product to be possessed for a medicinal purpose of the possessor or
another.

Arguably, the definition covers a coconut but it is submitted that it does not in
fact do so, since a coconut is not an article 'which is for holding any drink', words
which suggest the creation of the thing *before* any drink is inserted.

The container need not be made specifically to hold alcohol, and it is
irrelevant that it has never contained alcohol or that it is broken. An empty
lemonade bottle is caught, as is a coke tin. On the other hand, a re-usable plastic
drinks container, a mug, a thermos flask or a hip flask is not (although the latter is
likely to excite suspicion of possession of alcohol), since it is not the kind of

container which is normally discarded or returned to, or left to be recovered by, the supplier. Nor, it is submitted, is a plastic 'pop' bottle or a carton of orange caught since in itself (ie when empty) it is not an article capable of causing injury. This is an additional reason for excluding the re-usable plastic container. This is to presuppose that the tendency to cause injury must be assessed in relation to an empty container; any drinks container, however soft, is likely to cause injury if it is full when it is used as a missile.

Possession of fireworks etc

8.21 Section 2A(1) of the 1985 Act, which is essentially aimed at reducing the risk of fire, was added by Sch 1 to the Public Order Act 1986. It makes identical provision to s 2(1) in relation to the possession of a firework or of distress flares, fog signals, canisters of smoke or visible gas and similar articles. Matches and cigarette lighters are expressly excluded.[1]

An offence under s 2A(1) is punishable in the same way as one under s 2(1),[2] except that a domestic or international football banning order may not be made.

For the same reasons as are given at the end of para **8.12**, the offences under s 2(1) and s 2A(1) of the 1985 Act are likely to be construed as ones of strict liability in relation to the nature of the item possessed.

It is a defence for a person charged with an offence under s 2A(1) to prove[3] that he had possession with lawful authority;[4] it is not surprising that no such defence is provided for a s 2(1) offence. As with an offence under s 2(1), no defence of 'lawful excuse' or 'reasonable excuse' is provided.

In the absence of an authoritative definition of 'lawful authority' it is suggested that 'lawful' requires the authority be 'supported by law', as stated by Napier J in the South Australian case of *Crafter v Kelly*,[5] and that 'authority' must refer to a legal power or authorisation from a public source such as a public official. This appears to have been the view taken by Grantham J, obiter, in the Divisional Court in *Dickins v Gill*,[6] who treated 'without due authority' in the offence of possessing a die for a postage stamp, contrary to s 6 of the Post Office (Protection) Act 1884, as referring to the authority of the Crown. A similar view was taken in *Grieve v Macleod*[7] by the accused's counsel and the sheriff-substitute who tried the case. They both stated that they thought that 'lawful authority' in s 1(1) of the Prevention of Crime Act 1953 implied 'some kind of official licence or permission'; this point was not dealt with by the High Court of Justiciary on appeal.

Unfortunately, all this does not advance our understanding in concrete terms since the question remains 'when can there be an authority supported by law to be in possession of one of the specified things in the specified circumstances?' Presumably, the intention of the draftsman was to ensure that the present offence did not apply where a squad of police officers were sent to a football ground, at which a serious disturbance was taking place, armed with CS gas canisters or the like. Whether they had lawful authority to possess them would doubtless have to be answered ultimately by falling back on s 3 of the Criminal Law Act 1967 (use of reasonable force in preventing crime or arresting offenders) or on the common law rule authorising reasonable force to be used to stop or prevent a breach of the peace.

---

1   The full list of articles to which s 2A(1) applies is set out in s 2A(3), viz 'any article or
    substance whose main purpose is the emission of a flare for purposes of illuminating or
    signalling (as opposed to lighting or heating) or the emission of smoke or a visible gas; and

in particular applies to distress flares, fog signals, and pellets and capsules intended to be used as fumigators or for testing pipes, but not to matches, cigarette lighters or heaters.'

2   See para **8.19**.
3   See para **4.38**.
4   1986 Act, s 2A(2).
5   [1941] SASR 237 at 244.
6   [1896] 2 QB 310, DC.
7   1967 SLT 70, High Ct of Justiciary.

8.22 The offence under s 2A(1) is necessary only for the least serious cases, since possession of the articles in question will be an offence under s 5 of the Firearms Act 1968 (possession of prohibited weapon) if a canister etc contains a noxious gas or liquid, or under s 1 of the Prevention of Crime Act 1953 (having offensive weapon) or s 3 of the Criminal Damage Act 1971 (possession of thing with intent to use it to destroy or damage) if the thing is intended to be used to cause personal injury or damage to property, respectively.

Being drunk at designated ground

8.23 Section 2(2) of the 1985 Act provides that a person who is drunk[1] in a designated sports ground[2] at any time during the period of a designated sporting event[3] at that ground, or who is drunk while entering or trying to enter such a ground at any time during the period of a designated sporting event at that ground, is guilty of an offence. The maximum punishment is a fine not exceeding level 2 on the standard scale.[4] A domestic and/or international banning order may be made. Since the offence can be committed only during the period of a designated sporting event at the designated sports ground, a drunk who climbs into Manchester United's football ground at 3 am as a prank does not commit the present offence, nor any other offence under the 1985 Act.

The necessity for this offence is open to doubt, given that it is already an offence to be found drunk in a public place and an offence to be drunk and disorderly in a public place.[5]

Because of the existence of these two offences, the need for the offence of being drunk on a vehicle[1] is also open to doubt.

1   See para **8.13**.
2   See para **8.17**.
3   See para **8.18**.
4   1985 Act, s 8(c).
5   See Licensing Act 1872, s 12, and Criminal Justice Act 1967, s 91 (para **9.17**).

General police powers under the 1985 Act

8.24 A constable may, at any time during the period of a designated sporting event[1] at any designated sports ground,[2] enter any part of the ground for the purpose of enforcing the 1985 Act.[3] It will be noted that the constable's power of entry is not limited to the 'public' parts of the ground; if necessary for the purposes of enforcing the 1985 Act, he can enter the directors' suite or the manager's office.

In addition, a constable may search a person whom he has reasonable grounds to suspect is committing or has committed an offence under the 1985 Act, and may arrest such a person.[4] The reasonable suspicion must relate to the particular person searched. Whether 'reasonable grounds to suspect' exist is an objective question, depending on a consideration of all the evidence.[5] Guidance as to when reasonable suspicion can exist in respect of 'stop and search' is provided by the Stop and Search Code (Code A).[6] Searches of supporters entering grounds cannot be carried out under a general belief that such persons are likely to commit these offences and this is specifically stated in the Code. If a person is seen to be carrying a supermarket bag with the distinctive bulge of a 'four-pack', or the outline of bottles etc can be seen inside coat pockets, then a reasonable suspicion exists. Because the reasonable suspicion must relate to the individual searched, wholesale searches of supporters are most unlikely to be permissible under this power.

Note 1D to Code A provides that nothing in the Code affects the routine searching of persons entering sports grounds or other premises, *with their consent or as a condition of entry*. The searches which take place outside soccer grounds do not generally take place with consent (although they may be accepted under the belief that the police have a right to do so) and a search as a condition of entry to a sports ground is not a search that should be conducted by a police officer, even if he is paid by the proprietor of the ground to do duty there. If a proprietor makes such a condition, it should be enforced by his own stewards as it is no part of a police officer's duty to enforce the private rights of such proprietors.

In relation to the use of force, in respect of the above powers, what was said in para **8.15** is equally applicable.

---

1   Para **8.18**.
2   Para **8.17**.
3   1985 Act, s 7(1).
4   Ibid, s 7(2).
5   See para **3.68**.
6   See para A1.6.

FOOTBALL (OFFENCES) ACT 1991

8.25 Football hooliganism can take a variety of forms. Normally, it involves acts of personal violence or vandalism that are equally common in other places on other occasions and that are adequately dealt with by the general offences against public order described in Chapters 3 and 4 or by the various offences against the person. There are, however, certain types of behaviour at sporting events which, while not limited to football matches, most commonly or seriously occur there. They are the chanting of racist or indecent abuse, pitch-invasion and missile-throwing. These manifestations of football hooliganism could have been dealt with by an offence of disorderly conduct at a football ground, consideration of which was recommended by the Final Popplewell Report,[1] but such an offence was not enacted in the Public Order Act 1986. Three offences recommended in the Taylor Report[1] to deal with such conduct were, however, introduced by the Football (Offences) Act 1991:

–   throwing objects;
–   indecent or racist chanting;
–   pitch invasion.

These offences can only be committed at an association football match designated, or of a type designated, for the purposes of the 1991 Act by the Secretary of State.[2] The Football (Offences) (Designation of Football Matches) Order 1999[3] designates any association football match:

(a) in which one or both of the participating teams represents a club which is for the time being a member (whether a full or associate member) of the Football League or the Football Association Premier League, or represents a club, country or territory outside England and Wales; and
(b) which is played at a sports ground which is designated by order under s 1(1) of the Safety of Sport Grounds Act 1975 (para **8.3**), or registered with the Football League or the Football Association Premier League as the home ground of a club that is a member of the Football League or the Football Association Premier League at the time is played.

References in the Act to things done at a designated football match include anything done there in the period beginning two hours before the start of the match or (if earlier) two hours before the advertised start time and ending one hour after the end of the match. If the match does not take place on the advertised day, the period is two hours before the advertised start time until one hour after that time.[4] This terminology is similar to that used in other offences in this chapter.[5]

---

1   See para **8.1**.
2   Football (Offences) Act 1991, s 1(1). Technical rules relating to the making of the order are set out in ibid, s 1(1).
3   SI 1999/2462.
4   Football (Offences) Act 1991, s 1(2).
5   For a further discussion, see para **8.18**.

Throwing objects

8.26 If a missile is proved to have hit someone, its thrower (if identified, and identification is a major problem in the case of missile-throwing) can be convicted of a battery (common assault) or a more serious offence against the person, and if no one is hit but it is proved that someone was put in fear of being hit by the missile, its thrower can be convicted of an assault (common assault).

In addition, whether or not it can be proved that anyone was hit by the missile, a number of other offences can be charged against a missile thrower.

A general missile offence has not been created but, as was pointed out in para **3.14**, missile-throwing is expressly stated by s 8 to constitute 'violence' for the purposes of Part I of the Public Order Act 1986. It follows that those who throw or threaten to throw a missile may be guilty of violent disorder or affray if the terms of one of those offences are satisfied. In addition, missile-throwing may well also constitute an offence contrary to ss 4, 4A or 5 of the Act and the missile-thrower will also be guilty (if he intended to use it to cause injury) of having with him an offensive weapon in a public place, contrary to s 1 of the Prevention of Crime Act 1953, in relation to his possession of the missile before throwing it.

There can be occasions when none of the above offences can be proved against an individual. In such cases, s 2 of the 1991 Act is important. It makes it an offence to throw anything at or towards:

(a) the playing area or any area adjacent to the playing area to which spectators are not generally admitted; or

(b) any area in which spectators or other persons are or may be present;

without lawful authority[1] or excuse (which it is for the accused to prove).[2]

Thus, those who throw objects onto the pitch, into the players' tunnel etc, or into spectator areas will commit offences. Those who may prove a 'lawful excuse' would presumably include vendors who throw packets of crisps etc into the crowd, or spectators who throw money to such persons, and people who throw the ball back onto the pitch.

---

1   See para **8.21**.
2   See para **4.38**.

Chanting

8.27 Section 3(1) of the 1991 Act makes it an offence to *engage or* take part in 'chanting' of an indecent or racist nature. 'Chanting' means the repeated uttering of words or sounds (*whether alone or* in concert with one or more others),[1] and 'racist nature' means consisting of or including matter which is threatening, abusive or insulting to a person by reason of his colour, race, nationality (including citizenship) or ethnic or national origin.[2] As enacted, an offence could be committed only by 'taking part' in such chanting. Solo performers were not caught. This was changed by the Football (Offences and Disorder) Act 1999 which added to s 3 the words italicised above. Unlike the more serious offences[3] under ss 4–5 of the Public Order Act 1986 or s 18 of that Act,[4] or under s 31 of the Crime and Disorder Act 1998, s 3 renders indecent or racist chanting an offence per se.

---

1   1991 Act, s 3(2)(a).
2   Ibid, s 3(2)(b). As to these terms, see paras **4.68–4.76**.
3   Except for that under s 5, which carries the same maximum fine.
4   See paras **4.2**, **4.21**, **4.41**, **4.81** and **5.15**.

Pitch invasion

8.28 By s 4 of the 1991 Act, it is an offence for a person to go onto the playing area, or any area adjacent to the playing area to which spectators are not generally admitted, without lawful authority[1] or lawful excuse (which it is for the accused to prove).[2]

Those who would have a lawful excuse for going onto the pitch include trainers and official first aiders. People who run onto the pitch to escape a fire in the stand or to avoid being crushed clearly also have a lawful excuse. It is not easy to obtain a conviction where spectators surge forward onto the pitch as it is possible to contend that they were carried forward unwillingly by the momentum of the crowd. If this cannot be disproved, a conviction for an offence under s 4 will not be possible, since a person cannot generally be convicted if his conduct was beyond his control.[3]

In relation to pitch invasions, these are normally simply boisterous expressions of feelings by spectators. As such, although annoying and disruptive to the game, they do not merit a greater sanction than expulsion from the ground by the club's agents. If there is violence (actual or threatened) to persons or property, this can be dealt with by charging an appropriate offence against the person or property or one of the offences in Part I of the Public Order Act 1986. The need for this offence is questionable.

---

1   See para **8.21**.
2   See para **4.38**.
3   See Card, Cross and Jones *Criminal Law* (1998) para 19.43.

Arrest, trial and punishment

8.29 All three offences have been added to the list of arrestable offences in s 24(2) of PACE. They are triable summarily only[1] and punishable with a fine not exceeding level 3 on the standard scale;[1] they are not punishable with imprisonment. They are relevant offences for the purpose of a domestic and/or an international football banning order.[2]

---

1   1991 Act, s 5(2).
2   See paras **8.35** and **8.45**.

DOMESTIC FOOTBALL BANNING ORDERS (DFBOs)

8.30 Part IV of the Public Order Act 1986 deals with these. It implements proposals made in the Final Popplewell Report.[1] Section 31 of the 1986 Act empowers a magistrates' court or the Crown Court on conviction of a person of certain offences to make a DFBO prohibiting him from entering any premises in England and Wales for the purpose of attending any prescribed football match there. Originally Part IV referred to an 'exclusion order',[2] but that order was re-named as a domestic football banning order, and the provisions relating to it strengthened, by the Football (Offences and Disorder) Act 1999, which in particular substituted a new s 30 and a new s 31.

The power to make DFBOs is intended to further the preventive aims of the Sporting Events (Control of Alcohol) Act 1985, but, unlike most of the provisions in that Act, DFBOs are not directly concerned with alcohol. Their purpose is to enable a court to ban convicted football hooligans from football matches; such orders are particularly useful (and particularly likely to be made) against the ringleaders of the hooliganism.

Despite the clear mischief of the provisions about DFBOs, such orders are not limited to offenders who were spectators. The provisions *could* be applied to anyone, such as a player or club manager, who satisfies the relevant criteria.

---

1   See para **8.1**.
2   In April 1999, 450 exclusion orders were in force: HC Deb, vol 329, col 511.

8.31 At present, DFBOs can only be made in relation to attendance at *any* association football match prescribed by the Secretary of State by an order made, and subject to annulment, in the same way as a designation order referred to in para **8.7**.[1] The Secretary of State has potentially very wide powers to extend the relevant provisions to other types of sporting event including modifying them.[2] No extension has yet been made.

By the Public Order (Domestic Football Banning) Order 1999,[3] an association football match is a prescribed match if it is one:

(a) in which one or both of the participating teams represents a club which is for the time being a member (whether a full or associate member) of the Football League or the Football Association Premier League, or represents a club, country or territory outside England and Wales, and

(b) which is played at a sports ground which is designated by order under s 1(1) of the Safety of Sports Grounds Act 1975,[4] or registered with the Football League or the Football Association Premier League as the home ground of a club which is a member of the Football League or the Football Association Premier League at the time the match is played.

---

1   1986 Act, s 36.
2   Ibid, s 37(1) and (2). The affirmative procedure would apply to the making of an extension order, see ibid, s 37(3). This would provide a measure of Parliamentary scrutiny.
3   SI 1999/2460.
4   See para **8.3**.

8.32 Section 30(1) of the 1986 Act provides that a court by or before which a person is convicted of an offence to which s 31 applies, or the Crown Court when dealing with someone committed for sentence for such an offence, has power to make a DFBO 'prohibiting him from entering any premises for the purpose of *attending* any prescribed football match *there*'; it does not extend to prohibiting a person entering a pub to watch a match on a wide screen. As is indicated by the italicised words, a DFBO can relate only to football grounds.

'Premises' in s 30(1) clearly bears its normal legal meaning of buildings, land with a building (eg a football stand) on it and land which is not built upon provided that it has a defined boundary.[1] However, the limits of 'premises' may be vague. For example, is the club car park on the edge of the ground and outside the curtilage of the stands and pitch part of the premises? The answer to this question could be important in relation to an alleged breach of a DFBO by a supporter en route to the stands. It is submitted that the answer is 'yes' provided that the area in question is obviously part of the parcel of land.

A DFBO will apply to any prescribed match, *whatever the venue and whatever the club*. This is sensible. Clearly, a DFBO would not be very effective if it barred a person only from the ground at which the offence was committed. There is no power simply to ban from matches at a particular ground or from particular types of game (eg international matches), nor to ban a person from entering a ground on a match day otherwise than to attend a match (eg to go to the souvenir shop).

---

1   *Andrews v Andrews* [1908] 2 KB 567 at 570, per Buckley LJ; *Whitley v Stumbles* [1930] AC 544, HL; *Bracey v Read* [1962] 3 All ER 472.

8.33 Section 30(4) of the 1986 Act provides that a DFBO cannot be made on its own but only *in addition* to a sentence or an absolute or conditional discharge. Thus, it cannot be made in relation to a person who has not been convicted but who has been bound over.

8.34 Subject to s 30(4) of the 1986 Act, where a court has power to make a DFBO in relation to the accused, it is obliged by s 30(2) of the 1986 Act to make a DFBO 'if it is satisfied that there are reasonable grounds to believe that making the order would help to prevent violence or disorder at or in connection with prescribed football matches'. If it is not so satisfied, it must state this in open court,[1] and give its reasons for not being satisfied.[2] This marks a radical change of emphasis from the original s 30, under which a court could not make an order unless it was so satisfied. Now a court must justify a failure to make an order. The use of 'if it is satisfied that' rather than the more usual provision in a sentencing provision such as 'if it appears to the court that' or 'if in its opinion' raises the question of the degree of satisfaction which the court must have. Since the satisfaction does not relate to a matter which the prosecution must prove, the rule in *Woolmington v DPP* is not strictly applicable. The wording of s 30(2) is suggestive that the standard of satisfaction is simply 'on the balance of probabilities'.

---

1   In *R v Denbigh Justices, ex parte Williams* [1974] 2 All ER 1052, DC, Lord Widgery CJ stated as
     follows, in the context of a submission that a hearing had not been in open court:
         'The trial should be "public" in the ordinary common-sense acceptation of that term. The
         doors of the courtroom are expected to be kept open, the public are entitled to be
         admitted, and the trial is to be public in all respects ... with due regard to the size of the
         courtroom, the conveniences of the court, the right to exclude objectionable characters
         and youth of tender years, and to do other things which may facilitate the proper conduct
         of the trial.'
2   1986 Act, s 30(3).

Offences to which s 31 applies

8.35   For a DFBO to be made, the offence of which a person is convicted must be 'an offence to which s 31 applies'. The list of offences to which s 31 applies is the same as the list of 'relevant offences' provided by Sch 1 to the Football Spectators Act 1989 for the purposes of an international football banning order; Sch 1 to the 1986 Act is applied to the present provisions by s 31(1) of the 1986 Act, as substituted by the Football (Offences and Disorder) Act 1999. It is as follows:

'(a)   an offence under section 2(1) or 5(7) [of the Football Spectators Act 1989];[1]

(b)   any offence under s 2 of the Sporting Events (Control of Alcohol etc) Act 1985 (alcohol containers at sports grounds) committed by the accused at any designated football match or while entering or trying to enter the ground;[2]

(c)   any offence under section 5 of the Public Order Act 1986 (harassment, alarm or distress) or any provision of Part III of that Act (racial hatred)[3] committed during a period relevant to a designated football match at any premises while the accused was at, or was entering or leaving or trying to enter or leave, the premises;

(d)   any offence involving the use or threat of violence by the accused towards another person committed during a period relevant to a designated football match at any premises while the accused was at, or was entering or leaving or trying to enter or leave, the premises;

(e)   any offence involving the use or threat of violence towards property committed during a period relevant to a designated football match at any premises while the accused was at, or was entering or leaving or trying to enter or leave, the premises;

(f)   any offence under section 12 of the Licensing Act 1872 (persons found drunk in public places, etc) of being found drunk in a highway or other public place committed while the accused was on a journey to or from a designated football match being an offence as respects which the court makes a declaration that the offence related to football matches;

(g) any offence under section 91(1) of the Criminal Justice Act 1967 (disorderly behaviour while drunk in a public place) committed in a highway or other public place while the accused was on a journey to or from a designated football match being an offence as respects which the court makes a declaration that the offence related to football matches;[4]

(h) any offence under section 1 of the Sporting Events (Control of Alcohol etc) Act 1985 (alcohol on coaches or trains to or from sporting events) committed while the accused was on a journey to or from a designated football match as respects which the court makes a declaration that the offence related to football matches;[5]

(i) any offence under section 5 of the Public Order Act 1986 (harassment, alarm or distress)[3] or any provision of Part III of that Act (racial hatred)[3] committed while the accused was on a journey to or from a designated football match being an offence as respects which the court makes a declaration that the offence related to football matches;

(j) any offence under section 4 or 5 of the Road Traffic Act 1988 (driving etc when under the influence of drink or drugs or with an alcohol concentration above the prescribed limit) committed while the accused was on a journey to or from a designated football match being an offence as respects which the court makes a declaration that the offence related to football matches;

(k) any offence involving the use or threat of violence by the accused towards another person committed while one or each of them was on a journey to or from a designated football match being an offence as respects which the court makes a declaration that the offence related to football matches;

(l) any offence involving the use or threat of violence towards property committed while the accused was on a journey to or from a designated football match being an offence as respects which the court makes a declaration that the offence related to football matches;

(m) any offence under the Football (Offences) Act 1991;[6]

(n) any offence under section 5 of the Public Order Act 1986 (harassment, alarm or distress) or any provision of Part III of that Act (racial hatred)[3] –

    (i) which does not fall within paragraph (c) or (i) above,

    (ii) which was committed during a period relevant to a designated football match, and

    (iii) as respects which the court makes a declaration that the offence related to that match or to that match and any other football match which took place during that period;

(o) any offence involving the use or threat of violence by the accused towards another person –

    (i) which does not fall within paragraph (d) or (k) above,

    (ii) which was committed during a period relevant to a designated football match, and

    (iii) as respects which the court makes a declaration that the offence related to that match or to that match and any other football match which took place during that period;

(p) any offence involving the use or threat of violence towards property –

    (i) which does not fall within paragraph (e) or (l) above,

    (ii) which was committed during a period relevant to a designated football match, and

    (iii) as respects which the court makes a declaration that the offence related to that match or to that match and any other football match which took place during that period;

(q) any offence under section 166 of the Criminal Justice and Public Order Act 1994
     (sale of tickets by unauthorised persons) which relates to tickets for a football
     match.'[7]

Schedule 1 to the Football Spectators Act 1989 provides that any reference to an
offence in the above list includes:

(a) a reference to any attempt, conspiracy or incitement to commit that offence;
     and
(b) a reference to aiding and abetting, counselling or procuring the commission
     of that offence.

Schedule 1 to the 1989 Act also provides that, for the purposes of paras (f)–(l)
above:

(a) a person may be regarded as having been on a journey to or from a designated
     football match whether or not he attended or intended to attend the match
     (as where someone goes to an all-ticket match without a ticket, intending to
     cause trouble outside the ground); and
(b) a person's journey includes breaks (including overnight breaks).

This leaves open the question of when a journey to or from a match begins and
ends. Is someone, who leaves home en route to a match via a pub where he has
arranged to meet up with friends, on a journey to the match as soon as he leaves
home or only when he leaves the pub to go to the ground? This is of obvious
importance if he commits an offence under paras (f)–(l) before he gets to the pub
(or while he is in it). It is submitted that a person is on a journey *to* a match as soon
as he departs from somewhere with the principal purpose of going to a match and
that he is on a journey *from* a match when he departs from the ground until he
reaches his home, place of work or some other place where his presence is not
referable to being en route from the match.

A declaration of the types referred to in paras (f)–(l) and (n)–(q) above is
referred to elsewhere in the 1989 Act as a 'declaration of relevance'.[8] Unless the
offender waives the requirement or the court is satisfied that the interests of justice
do not require more notice to be given, a court may not make a declaration of
relevance as respects any offence unless it is satisfied that the prosecutor gave
notice to the offender, at least five days before the first day of the trial,[9] that it was
proposed to show that the offence related to football matches, to a particular
football match or to particular football matches (as the case may be).[10] A person
convicted of an offence in respect of which a declaration of relevance is made can
appeal against its making as if it was a sentence passed for the offence.[11] A DFBO
made on conviction of a relevant offence must be quashed if the making of the
declaration of relevance is quashed on appeal.[12]

The references in Sch 1 to the 1989 Act to designated football matches are
references to designated football matches for the purposes of Part I of the Football
Spectators Act 1989.[13] These are exactly the same as prescribed matches for the
purposes of a DFBO, viz: any association football match played in England or
Wales:

(a) in which one or both of the participating teams represents a club which is for
     the time being a member (whether a full or associate member) of the
     Football League or the Football Association Premier League, or represents a
     club, country or territory outside England and Wales; and

(b) which is played at a sports ground which is designated by order under s 1(1) of the Safety of Sports Grounds Act 1975 (see para **8.3**), or registered with the Football League or the Football Association Premier League as the home ground of a club which is a member of the Football League or the Football Association Premier League at the time the match is played.[14]

However, in paras (h), (i), (k), (l), (n), (o) and (p) references to designated football matches also include references to football matches played abroad designated for the purposes of Part II of the Football Spectators Act 1989,[15] as to which see para **8.44**.

The references in paras (c)–(e) to a 'period relevant to a designated match' mean one of the following periods:

'(a) the period beginning –

  (i) two hours before the start of the match, or
  (ii) two hours before the time at which it is advertised to start, or
  (iii) with the time at which spectators are first admitted to the premises,

whichever is the earliest, and ending one hour after the end of the match;

(b) where a match advertised to start at a particular time on a particular day is postponed to a later day, or does not take place, the period in the advertised day beginning two hours before and ending two hours after that time.'[16]

The references in paras (n)–(p) to the 'period relevant to a designated match' bear the same meaning, except that the reference to a designated football match includes one to a match designated under Part II of the 1989 Act, 24 hours is substituted for the periods of two hours and one hour, and para (a)(iii) does not apply.[17]

---

1 Offences of unauthorised attendance at designated football match and offence of making a false statement to join national football membership scheme. These offences have not been brought into force; see para **8.3**.

2 See paras **8.19** and **8.23**.

3 See paras **4.41** and **5.2**. It is odd that a conviction for the racially-aggravated version of the s 5 offence under the Crime and Disorder Act 1998, s 31 (para **4.81**) has not been added to this list. Whilst the relevant offence under the *1998* Act, s 31 clearly requires proof of the elements of s 5, it is a separate offence from that under the 1986 Act, s 5, and is therefore not an offence to which the *1986* Act, *s 31* applies.

4 See para **9.17**.

5 See paras **8.10**, **8.12** and **8.13**.

6 See para **8.25**.

7 See para **8.59**.

8 1989 Act, s 14(9), applied by the 1986 Act, s 31(2).

9 The legislation does not indicate what is the first day of the trial in an either-way case where the accused indicates an intent to plead guilty in 'plea before venue' proceedings and is committed for sentence.

10 1989 Act, s 23(1) and (2), applied by the 1986 Act, s 31(2).

11 Ibid, s 23(3), applied by the 1986 Act, s 31(2). Also see the Criminal Appeal Act 1968, ss 10 and 50, and the Magistrates' Courts Act 1980, s 108.

12 1989 Act, s 23(4), applied by the 1986 Act, s 31(3).

13 Ibid, s 14(6), applied by the 1986 Act, s 31(2).

14 Football Spectators (Designation of Football Matches in England and Wales) Order 1999, SI 1999/2461, art 3 and Sch.

15 1989 Act, s 14(6), applied by the 1986 Act, s 31(2).

16 1989 Act, s 14(6) applying s 1(8) thereof, applied by the 1986 Act, s 31(2).

17 1989 Act, s 14(6), applying s 1(8A) thereof, applied by the 1986 Act, s 31(2).

Giving notice of order etc

8.36 Where a court makes a DFBO, its clerk[1] (in the case of a magistrates' court) or the appropriate officer (in the case of the Crown Court) is required by s 34(1) of the 1986 Act to:

(a) give a copy of it to the person to whom it relates; and
(b) (as soon as reasonably practicable)[2] send a copy of it to –

  (i)   the chief officer of police for the police area in which the offence leading to the order was committed; and
  (ii) any person prescribed by order by the Secretary of State.

In relation to 'any prescribed person', the Chief Executive of the Football Association and the Football Banning Orders Authority[3] have been prescribed.[4] This ensures that the relevant details are circulated to clubs and other football organisations, although it is not expected that all clubs will be notified about each DFBO.

The Act does not say when the order comes into effect. It would seem that it comes into effect on its pronouncement in court (and not only on service on the offender, if later).[5] If this is correct, the operation of the order will not be affected by a failure to deliver it to the offender.

---

1   The Magistrates' Courts Act 1980, s 141, as applied by the 1986 Act, s 35(3), provides that this reference to a clerk of a magistrates' court is a reference to the clerk to the justices for the petty sessions area for which the court is acting; and that, where there is more than one clerk to the justices, anything that that Act requires or authorises to be done by or to the clerk to the justices shall or may be done by or to any of the clerks or by or to such of the clerks as the magistrates' courts committee having power over the appointment of clerks to justices for that area generally or in any particular case may direct.
2   See para **6.9** fn 2.
3   See para **8.48**.
4   Public Order (Domestic Football Banning) Order 1999, SI 1999/2460.
5   This point is made by Marston and Tain *Public Order Offences* (1995) p 195. They rely on the reasoning in *Walsh v Barlow* [1985] 1 WLR 90, DC (community service order operative even though not served on the offender).

Photographs

8.37 For a DFBO to be effective a photograph of the person subject to it needs to be available to the police. Section 35 of the 1986 Act makes provision for a photograph to be taken of such a person.

At the instance of the prosecutor of the offence for which a DFBO is made, a court which makes a DFBO may make an order requiring a constable to photograph the person concerned or to cause such a photograph to be taken.[1] The Act assumes that this order will normally be made at the time of the DFBO, but there is nothing in the Act to prevent that order being made subsequently (although the offender should be given the chance to appear). The order also requires the person concerned to attend at a specified police station within seven clear days of the order at a time specified in the order in order to have his photograph taken.[2] A person who fails to comply with the order may be arrested without warrant by a constable in order that his photograph may be taken.[3] He does not, however, commit an offence under the Act, although (depending on the circumstances) he may be guilty of obstructing a constable in the execution of his duty. That offence will also be committed if the person deliberately makes it more difficult for the photograph to be taken.[4] There is no express provision to use force to take the photograph. It is likely that the court would imply a power to use reasonable force, otherwise the order and the power of arrest would be deprived of much of their effect.

An arrest under s 35 is akin to an arrest under s 27 of PACE for non-compliance with a fingerprinting requirement. It is not an arrest for an offence and therefore s 30 of PACE (arrestee to be taken to a police station as soon as practicable) and Part IV of PACE (detention of subject) do not apply. Nevertheless, at common law the arrestee should be dealt with reasonably by taking him to a police station without delay for the photograph to be taken. The following provisions of PACE do apply to someone arrested under s 35: s 28 (information to be given on arrest); s 32(1) and (2)(a) (search on arrest); s 54 (search at police station); ss 56 and 58 (right to have someone informed of arrest and access to legal advice). In addition, the Code of Practice on Detention (Code C) applies.

Since photographs taken under s 35 will remain the property of the police, the police will determine what use will be made of them, including circulating them through the National Criminal Intelligence Service. However, they are not obliged to do so, nor to send a copy of the photograph to any prescribed person to whom a copy of the DFBO must be sent under s 34.

---

1   1986 Act, s 35(1)–(3).
2   Ibid, s 35(1).
3   Ibid, s 35(4). For the taking of photographs, see also the Code of Practice for the Identification of Persons by Police Officers (Code D).
4   Obstructing a constable is dealt with in paras **9.65–9.67**.

8.38 Since the effectiveness of a DFBO may depend on a photograph of the offender being available to the police, it may appear odd that the court has a discretion as to whether to order a photograph to be taken. It can be anticipated that normally such an order will be made, but no obligation is placed on the court to make it since it would be otiose if the offender had recently been made subject to another DFBO (and an order for a photograph) or if, for some other reason, eg that the offender was photographed at the police station at the time of charge, the police had a photograph. The sentence of an offender to immediate imprisonment would seem to preclude the making of a photograph order, but the offender may already have been photographed on charge and he will be photographed for the purposes of imprisonment.[1]

---

1   This point is made by Marston 'Exclusion orders under the Public Order Act 1986' (1987) 84 LSG 2426.

Duration of order

8.39 A DFBO has effect for such period as specified in it,[1] which must be not less than one year and not more than three.[2]

1   1986 Act, s 32(1).
2   Ibid, s 32(2).

Appeal against order

8.40 Where it has been made by a magistrates' court, an offender can appeal to the Crown Court against the making of a DFBO or its length, just as he can appeal against any other sentence.[1] An appeal to the Crown Court is by way of re-hearing.[2] The Crown Court can revoke the DFBO or reduce or increase its length.[3] An appeal against the making of an order by a magistrates' court, or the length thereof, or against the determination of an appeal from a magistrates' court to the Crown Court, can be made to the High Court by case stated, but only on the ground that it is wrong in law or in excess of jurisdiction.[4]

Where the Crown Court has made a DFBO, either after a conviction in that Court or on a committal for sentence, the offender can appeal with the leave of the Court of Appeal[5] to the Court of Appeal (Criminal Division) against the order or against its length.[6] As in the case of any other appeal against sentence, the Court of Appeal may quash the order or reduce its length but may not increase its length.[7]

1   Magistrates' Courts Act 1980, s 108.
2   Supreme Court Act 1981, s 79.
3   Ibid, s 48.
4   Magistrates' Courts Act 1980, s 111; Supreme Court Act 1981, s 28.
5   Criminal Appeal Act 1968, s 11(1). Alternatively, an appeal can be made if the sentencing
        judge grants a certificate that the case is fit for appeal against sentence: ibid, s 11(1A).
6   Ibid, ss 9 and 10.
7   Ibid, s 11(3).

Application for termination of order[1]

8.41 A person made subject to a DFBO may apply for its termination. The application must be made to the court by which it was made, and can be made at any time after the order has been in effect for one year.[2] It follows that an order of less than one year's duration is not terminable.

In determining the application, the court will have regard to the person's character, his subsequent conduct, the nature of the offence which led to the order and any other circumstances of the case.[3] If the court refuses the application, a further one *must not* be entertained within six months.[4] This limit, and the one-year qualifying period just mentioned, are clearly intended to control the number of applications for termination. Both periods are mandatory. The court may order the applicant to pay all or part of the costs of an application for termination.[5] The potentiality of this is a further disincentive to an application for termination.

If an order terminating a DFBO is made, it will have to specify the date from which the order ceases to have effect.[3] For obvious reasons, a copy of the order must be sent to the same people, subject to the same conditions, as a copy of the DFBO;[6] see para **8.36.**

The power to rescind or suspend orders under s 63(2) of the Magistrates' Courts Act 1980 does not apply to a DFBO.[7]

1   See Broadbent 'Terminating exclusion orders' (1989) 133 Sol Jo 11.
2   Public Order Act 1986, s 33(1). In the case of a DFBO made by a magistrates' court, an application for termination may be made to any magistrates' court acting for the same petty sessions area: ibid, s 33(5). In the case of an order made by the Crown Court, the application must be made to the same Crown Court.
3   Ibid, s 33(2).
4   Ibid, s 33(3). Six months means six calendar months: Interpretation Act 1978, s 5 and Sch 1.
5   1986 Act, s 33(4).
6   Ibid, s 34(2).
7   Ibid, s 33(6).

Breach of order

8.42 By s 32(3) of the 1986 Act, a person who enters premises in breach of a DFBO is guilty of a summary offence punishable with a maximum of six months' imprisonment or a fine not exceeding level 5 on the standard scale, or both. The offence is an arrestable offence under s 24(2) of PACE. As noted in para **8.32**, a person is not in breach of a DFBO if he enters a football ground solely for a purpose other than attending a prescribed football match. It is not a breach of a DFBO simply to commit a football-related offence other than one involving entry to premises to attend a prescribed match.

On conviction for the above offence, there is no power to extend the order broken nor to make a further DFBO in relation to that offence.

It is not a separate offence for a person, for example a turnstile operator, to admit a person in breach of a DFBO, but such a person may be convicted of the offence under s 32(3) of the 1986 Act as an accomplice if the relevant mens rea required of an accomplice can be proved.

8.43 The DFBO provisions of the 1986 Act will be repealed if a day is ever appointed under s 27(2) of the Football Spectators Act 1989 for the commencement of s 2 of that Act (national membership scheme provision), except for the purposes of the making under s 33 of the 1986 Act of applications after that date to terminate DFBOs and the communication of termination orders under s 34(2) thereof.[1] In the light of the Taylor Report,[2] it is most unlikely that s 2 of the 1989 Act will ever be brought into force.

1   Football Spectators Act 1989, s 27(5).
2   See para **8.1**.

INTERNATIONAL FOOTBALL BANNING ORDERS (IFBOs)

8.44 DFBOs simply require their subjects to stay away from prescribed matches in England and Wales. They do not go further and require their subjects to report to the police when matches are taking place, but international football banning orders – which are designed to prevent their subjects travelling abroad to watch designated matches – do.

Part II of the Football Spectators Act 1989 deals with IFBOs. They were originally called restriction orders,[1] but they were re-named, and the relevant law strengthened, by the Football (Offences and Disorder) Act 1999. Part II applies in relation to football matches played in any country (or territory),[2] including Scotland, outside England and Wales that are designated football matches.[3]

In this context 'designated football match' is defined by s 14(2) of the 1989 Act as meaning any match of a type designated by order for the purposes of Part II of the Act by the Secretary of State or a particular match so designated.[4] So far, only types of match (as opposed to particular matches) have been designated. The list of types of match designated by the Secretary of State for the purpose of Part II is contained in the Football Spectators (Designation of Football Matches outside England and Wales) Order 1990.[5] By that Order, the following association football matches outside England and Wales involving:

(a) a national team appointed by the Football Association to represent England or the Football Association of Wales to represent Wales; or
(b) a team representing a club which is, at the time the match is played, a member (full or associate) of the Football League or the Football Association Premier League; or
(c) a team from a club in England or Wales playing in a competition organised by or on behalf of UEFA

are designated football matches for the purposes of Part II of the Act.

In relation to such matches, it is provided that reporting is obligatory only for such persons subject to an IFBO as are required to report under s 19(3) of the 1989 Act, referred to in para **8.50**.

---

1   In April 1999, 113 restriction orders were in force: HC Deb, vol 329, col 510.
2   1989 Act, s 14(9).
3   Ibid, s 14(1).
4   Ibid, s 14(2). The order must be made by statutory instrument and is subject to annulment in pursuance of a resolution of either House of Parliament: ibid, s 14(3). An order under s 14(2) may, in relation to any description of football matches specified therein, direct that reporting is obligatory for all persons subject to IFBOs or that reporting is obligatory only for such persons subject to IFBOs as are required to report under s 19(3)(b) (see para **8.50**): ibid, s 19(8).
5   SI 1990/732.

When can an international football banning order be made?

8.45 An IFBO can be made under s 15 or s 22 of the 1989 Act.

Section 15(1) of the 1989 Act empowers a court by or before which a person is convicted of a relevant offence, or the Crown Court when dealing with someone committed for sentence, to make an IFBO against him. Section 15(3) provides that, like a DFBO,[1] an IFBO made under s 15 may be made only in addition to a sentence or an absolute or conditional discharge.

Offences which are relevant offences for the purposes are listed in Sch 1 to the 1989 Act. They are set out in para **8.35**, as are related provisions made by Sch 1 to and ss 14 and 23 of the 1989 Act. A proposal made in a consultation paper[2] before the enactment of the Football (Offences and Disorder) Act 1999 that the courts should have power to impose an IFBO on known but unconvicted football hooligans on the basis of information presented to a court by the police has not been enacted. Not surprisingly, the idea of making such an order against someone on the basis of 'we can't prove it, but we know he's guilty' rang alarm bells.

As in the case of a DFBO, where a court has power to make an IFBO in relation to an accused, it is obliged, subject to s 15(3), to make an IFBO if satisfied that there are reasonable grounds that making the order would help to prevent violence or disorder at or in connection with 'designated football matches' as defined in para **8.44**.[3] If it is not so satisfied, it must state this in open court and give its reasons for not being satisfied.[4] As with the corresponding provision for DFBOs this provision contains a change of emphasis from that originally enacted.

---

1   See para **8.33**.
2   *Review of Football Related Legislation* (Home Office, 1998).
3   1989 Act, s 15(2).
4   1989 Act, s 15(2A). The comment in para **8.34** is equally applicable here.

8.46 Section 22 of the 1989 Act governs the making of an IFBO as a result of a conviction for a 'corresponding offence' committed outside England and Wales. A 'corresponding offence' is not simply a foreign offence corresponding to one under English law. Instead, it is an offence under the law of a country outside England and Wales specified in an Order in Council; a foreign offence can only be specified if it appears to Her Majesty to correspond to an offence listed in Sch 1 to the 1989 Act.[1] For this purpose, an offence specified in an Order in Council under that subsection is regarded as corresponding to an offence specified in Sch 1 notwithstanding that any period specified in the Order is longer than any corresponding period specified in that Schedule.[2] At the time of writing, orders have been made in respect of Italy, Scotland, Sweden, Norway, Republic of Ireland and France.[3]

The procedure under s 22 is initiated by laying an information before a justice of the peace for any area in which someone resides, or is believed to reside, to the effect that he has been convicted of a corresponding offence in a country outside England and Wales.[4] The justice may then:

(a)   issue a summons directed to that person requiring him to appear before a magistrates' court for that area to answer to the information; or

(b)   issue a warrant[5] to arrest that person and bring him before a magistrates' court for that area.[6]

Where the person concerned comes before the magistrates' court, the court, if satisfied that:

(a)   he is ordinarily resident in England and Wales; and

(b)   has been convicted in the country outside England and Wales of the corresponding offence;

may, unless it appears that the conviction is the subject of proceedings in a court of law in that country questioning the conviction, make an IFBO in relation to him.[7] However, as in the case of an order under s 15, a magistrates' court which has power to make an IFBO under s 22 is under a duty to do so if it is satisfied that there are reasonable grounds to believe that making the order would help to prevent violence or disorder at or in connection with designated football matches.[8] Likewise, where a magistrates' court decides not to make an IFBO, it must state in open court that it is not so satisfied and give its reasons.[9]

The Orders in Council made so far specify the authority in the foreign country which is to certify the conviction of the person of a corresponding offence, the nature and circumstances of the offence and whether or not the conviction is the subject of proceedings in that country questioning it.[10] A document in the form specified in the Order in Council is admissible in any proceedings relating to an IFBO as evidence of the facts stated in the certificate.[11] The facts stated in the document are taken to be proved in proceedings under s 22 unless the contrary is proved, provided that there is proof that the person subject to the proceedings is the person whose conviction is set out in the document.[12]

---

1   1989 Act, s 22(1).
2   Ibid, s 22(1A).
3   All the orders are entitled the Football Spectators (Corresponding Offences in [name of country]) Order. Their citations are respectively SI 1990/992, SI 1990/993, SI 1992/708 (these three were amended by SI 1992/1724), SI 1996/1634, SI 1996/1635 and SI 1998/1266.
4   1989 Act, s 22(2).
5   No warrant may be issued unless the information is written and substantiated on oath: ibid, s 22(3).
6   Ibid, s 22(2).
7   Ibid, s 22(4). In such proceedings, the court has the same powers (except that it cannot remand the person in custody), and the proceedings must be conducted as near as possible in the like manner, as if the proceedings were the trial of an information for a summary offence: ibid, s 22(6).
8   Ibid, s 22(5).
9   Ibid, s 22(5A).
10   Provision is made for this by the 1989 Act, s 22(9).
11   Ibid, s 22(10). A document in the specified form is taken to be such a document unless the contrary is proved: ibid.
12   Ibid, s 22(11).

Effect of an IFBO

8.47 An IFBO means an order of the court under ss 15 or 22 of the 1989 Act requiring the person to whom the order applies to report to a police station on the occasion of designated football matches.[1]

Section 15(5) of the 1989 Act requires the order to specify the police station[2] in England or Wales at which the person subject to the order must report initially. By s 15(5A), the court may, if it thinks fit, impose conditions in the order with which the person subject to it must comply. Those conditions may include conditions about the surrender of his passport not more than five days before the date of each designated football match in respect of which he is required to report.[3] This new power is obviously a powerful reinforcement to an order.[4] The imposition of a passport-surrender condition would not seem to be a breach of Art 12(1) of the International Covenant on Civil and Political Rights, which provides that everyone shall have the right to leave any country, including his own, because Art 12(2) permits this right to be restricted by law where necessary to protect public order (*ordre public*) or the rights and freedoms of others. The UK is not a party to Protocol 4 of the ECHR, Art 2 of which guarantees freedom of movement and the freedom to leave any country, including one's own, although restrictions may be placed by law on such freedoms if necessary in a democratic society for the maintenance of *ordre public*, for the prevention of crime or for the protection of the rights and freedoms of others. Whether the imposition of such a condition would infringe EU Council Directive 73/148, which confers on nationals of Member States wishing to go to another Member State as recipients of services[5] a right of free movement, is rather more problematical, since it has not yet been established in what circumstances a Member State may prevent an individual leaving its jurisdiction in order to receive a service in another Member State.[6]

The duty to report is a duty:

(a) to report initially to the police station specified in the order within five days beginning with the date of the making of the order; and

(b) subject to any exemption,[7] to report on the occasion of designated football matches when required to do so under s 19(3) of the 1989 Act to the police station in England and Wales specified in the notice by which the requirement is imposed at the time or between the times specified in the order.[8] The provisions of s 19(3) are set out in para **8.50**.

Where the subject of the IFBO is sentenced to, or is already serving, a term of imprisonment, the duty to report is suspended until his discharge from prison. In such a case, the order has effect, if he is discharged more than five days before the expiry of the period for which the order has effect and he was precluded by his imprisonment from reporting initially, as if it required him to report initially to the police station named in the order within the five-day period beginning with the date of his discharge.[9] It would seem that if the discharge is less than five days before the expiry of the order, the order is a dead letter because the initial obligation under it is one which must be fulfilled within five days.

The duty to comply with conditions imposed by an IFBO is a duty, subject to any exemption, to comply with those conditions when required to do so under s 19(3).[10]

---

1   1989 Act, s 14(4).

2   The Football Spectators Restriction Orders Authority (the predecessor to the Football Banning Orders Authority; see para **8.48**) circulated (letters of 20 April 1990 and 8 June 1990) to clerks to the justices a directory of police stations nominated by chief officers of police as suitable for the purpose of initial reporting.

3   1989 Act, s 15(5B). A surrendered passport must be returned as soon as reasonably practicable (see para **6.9** fn 2) after the match has taken place: ibid, s 15 (5C).

4   The above provisions of s 15 also apply to an order under s 22, as do ss 16–21 referred to below: 1989 Act, s 22(8).

5   In *Luisi v Ministero del Tesero* Cases 286/82 and 26/83 [1984] ECR 377, the European Court of Justice held that 'tourists, persons receiving medical treatment and persons travelling for the purpose of education or business' are 'recipients of services' who enjoy the right of free movement under Community law. Football supporters in a foreign country would seem to be 'tourists'.

6   Weatherill and Beaumont *EC Law* 2nd edn (Penguin, 1995) p 603.

7   See para **8.51**.

8   1989 Act, s 16(2).

9   Ibid, s 16(3).

10 Ibid, s 16(3A).

Giving notice of order etc

8.48 Section 18 of the 1989 Act makes similar, but not identical, provision to that in respect of a DFBO.

Where a court makes an IFBO, the clerk[1] of the court (in the case of a magistrates' court) or the appropriate officer (in the case of the Crown Court):

(a) must give a copy of it to the person to whom it relates;

(b) must (as soon as reasonably practicable)[2] send a copy of it to the enforcing authority;

(c) must (as soon as reasonably practicable)[2] send a copy of it to the police station (addressed to the officer responsible for the police station) at which the person subject to the order is to report initially; and

(d) in a case where the person subject to the order is sentenced by the court to or is serving a term of imprisonment, must (as soon as reasonably practicable)[2] send a copy of it to the governor of the prison or other person to whose custody he will be committed or in whose custody he is, as the case may be.[3]

The 'enforcing authority' referred to in (b) means such organisation established by the Secretary of State under s 57 of the Police Act 1996 (common services organisations) as the Secretary of State designates for the purposes of Part II of the 1989 Act.[4] The Secretary of State has designated the Football Banning Orders Authority for this purpose.[5] Presumably, an order comes into effect on its pronouncement in court.[6]

Where a person subject to an IFBO is discharged from prison and, in the case of a person who has not reported initially to a police station, is discharged more than five days before the expiry of the IFBO, the prison governor or person in whose custody he is, as the case may be, must (as soon as reasonably practicable)[2] give notice of his discharge to the enforcing authority.[7]

---

1   1989 Act, s 18(4), applies the Magistrates' Courts Act 1980, s 141, to this term in s 18, in the same way as is done in respect of a DFBO, see para **8.36** fn 1.
2   See para **6.9** fn 2.
3   1989 Act, s 18(1). As to service of documents, see ibid, s 25(1). 'Imprisonment' includes any form of detention: ibid, s 14(9).
4   Ibid, s 14(7). The designation must be by order made by statutory instrument: ibid.
5   Football Spectators (Designation of Enforcing Authority) Order 1999, SI 1999/2459.
6   See para **8.36**.
7   1989 Act, s 18(3). As to service of documents, see ibid, s 25(1).

Duration of order

8.49 Unless previously terminated, an IFBO has effect in relation to a person convicted of a relevant offence for a period determined by the court making the order:

(a) which begins with the date of the making of the order;
(b) which is not longer than the maximum period; and
(c) which is not shorter than the minimum period.[1]

The maximum period:

(a) in a case where the person was sentenced in respect of that offence to a period of imprisonment[2] taking immediate effect, is 10 years; and
(b) in any other case, is five years.[3]

The minimum period:

(a) in a case where the person was sentenced in respect of that offence to a period of imprisonment[2] taking immediate effect, is six years, and
(b) in any other case, is three years.[4]

---

1   1989 Act, s 16(1).

2   'Imprisonment' includes any form of detention: 1989 Act, s 14(9).
3   Ibid, s 16(1A).
4   Ibid, s 16(1B).

Reporting procedure

8.50 Once an IFBO has been made, the system is as follows. Where a person subject to an order reports initially at the police station specified for that purpose by the order, the police officer responsible for that police station may make such requirements of that person as are determined by the enforcing authority[1] to be necessary or expedient to give effect to IFBOs.[2] A person who fails, without reasonable excuse, to comply with any such requirement commits a summary offence punishable with a fine not exceeding level 2 on the standard scale.[3]

Section 19(3) of the 1989 Act requires the enforcing authority[1] during the currency of an IFBO to perform the following functions,[4] on the occasion of any designated football match:

(a) Where the match is one for which reporting is obligatory for all persons subject to IFBOs, the authority must, by written notice to that person:

    (i)   require him to report to the police station specified in the notice at the time or between the times specified in the notice; and

    (ii) require him to comply with the conditions (if any) imposed by the order (s 19(3)(a)).

(b) Where the match is one for which reporting is obligatory for such persons only as are required to report under this paragraph, the authority must, if that person is one as respects whom s 19(4) below is satisfied, by written notice to that person:

    (i)   require him to report to the police station specified in the notice at the time or between the times specified in the notice; and

    (ii) require him to comply with the conditions (if any) imposed by the order (s 19(3)(b)).

Section 19(4) prohibits the imposition of requirements under (b) by the enforcing authority unless imposing them is, in their opinion, necessary or expedient in order to reduce the likelihood of violence or disorder at, or in connection with, the designated football match; and the authority may establish criteria for determining whether requirements under (b) ought to be imposed on any person or class of persons.

1   Ie the Football Banning Orders Authority; see para **8.48**.
2   1989 Act, s 19(2).
3   1989 Act, s 19(6) and (7). What is said about 'reasonable excuse' in paras **8.56–8.57** is equally applicable here.
4   In exercising their functions the authority must have regard to any guidance issued by the Secretary of State under the 1989 Act, s 21: ibid, s 19(5).

8.51 A person subject to an IFBO may apply for an exemption from all or any of the duties to report (after the initial report) or to comply with a condition:

(a) as respects a particular designated football match; or

(b) as respects designated football matches played during a period.[1]

The application must be made 'to the authority empowered to grant exemptions ... ("the exempting authority")',[1] ie to the enforcing authority[2] or, if the application is for an exemption as respects matches (or a particular match) to be played within a five-day period beginning with the date of the application, the officer responsible for a police station.[3] However, such an officer must not grant an exemption without referring the matter to the enforcing authority, unless he considers that it is not reasonably practicable to do so.[4]

The exempting authority must exempt the applicant from all or any of his duties if he shows to its satisfaction:

(a) that there are special circumstances which justify his being so exempted; and
(b) that, because of those circumstances, he would not attend the match or matches if he were so exempted.[5]

The effect of an exemption is that the duties of the enforcing authority under s 19(3) of the 1989 Act[6] and of the subject of the order to report and/or comply with a condition are suspended in respect of any match to which it applies.[7] The availability of an exemption is of obvious importance where the subject of an IFBO has to attend a funeral or take an examination elsewhere, at a time when he is due to report on the occasion of a match.

A person aggrieved by a refusal to grant an exemption may appeal to a magistrates' court acting for the petty sessions area in which he resides.[8] Before doing so, he must give the exempting authority notice in writing[9] of his intention to do so.[8] The magistrates' court may make such order as it thinks fit.[10]

---

1   1989 Act, s 20(1).
2   Ie the Football Banning Orders authority; see para **8.48**.
3   1989 Act, s 20(2).
4   Ibid, s 20(3). As to reasonably practicable, see para **6.9** fn 2.
5   Ibid, s 20(4). In reaching a decision, the exempting authority must have regard to any guidance issued by the Home Secretary under the 1989 Act, s 21: ibid, s 20(5).
6   See para **8.50**.
7   1989 Act, s 20(6).
8   Ibid, s 20(7).
9   See para **6.9**.
10   1989 Act, s 20(8). The court may order the appellant to pay all or part of the costs of an appeal: ibid, s 20(9).

8.52 By s 20(10) and (11) of the 1989 Act, a summary offence, punishable with a fine not exceeding level 3 on the standard scale, is committed by someone who, in connection with an application for exemption:

'(a)   makes a statement which he knows to be false or misleading in a material particular or recklessly makes a statement which is false or misleading in a material particular, or
(b)   produces, furnishes, signs or otherwise makes use of a document which he knows to be false or misleading in a material particular or recklessly produces, furnishes, signs or otherwise makes use of a document which is false or misleading in a material particular.'

What is said about the similar offence under s 75 of the Criminal Justice and Public Order Act 1994 in paras **7.121–7.124** is equally applicable here.

Appeal against order

8.53 What is said in para **8.40** about an appeal against a DFBO is equally applicable to an appeal against an IFBO made under s 15. Appeal lies to the Crown Court against the making of an IFBO under s 22 of the 1989 Act.[1]

---

1   1989 Act, s 22(7).

Application for termination of order

8.54 An IFBO may be terminated on the application of the person to whom it applies. The relevant provisions are contained in s 17 of the 1989 Act. They are identical to those which apply to the termination of a DFBO (see para **8.41**), except that an application for termination cannot be made unless two-thirds of the period of the IFBO has elapsed.[1]

Where an IFBO is terminated, the clerk[2] of the magistrates' court or the appropriate officer of the Crown Court, as the case may be:

(a) must give a copy of the terminating order to the person to whom the IFBO relates;

(b) must (as soon as reasonably practicable)[3] send a copy of it to the enforcing authority; and

(c) in a case where the person subject to the IFBO is serving a prison sentence, must (as soon as reasonably practicable)[3] send a copy of the terminating order to the prison governor or other person in whose custody he is.[4]

---

1   1989 Act, s 17(1).
2   See para **8.48** fn 3.
3   See para **6.9** fn 2.
4   1989 Act, s 18(2). As to service of documents, see ibid, s 25(1).

Breach of order

8.55 By s 16(4) of the 1989 Act, a person who, without reasonable excuse, fails to comply with the duty to report, or the duty to comply with conditions imposed by an IFBO, commits a summary[1] offence, which is punishable with imprisonment for a maximum of six months or a fine not exceeding level 5 on the standard scale, or both.[1]

---

1   1989 Act, s 16(5).

8.56 In the context of other offences, it has been held that whether there is a reasonable excuse depends on whether a reasonable person would think the excuse reasonable in the circumstances,[1] but as a matter of law there are limitations as to what a reasonable person might think.[2] This is likely to be the approach taken by the courts in relation to the present provision.

In terms of other offences of 'failing', the limits of what a reasonable person would think a reasonable excuse have been particularly well developed in respect of offences of failing to supply a specimen under the drink-drive legislation. It is submitted that the case law there can be applied by analogy to the present offence. According to that case law, a reasonable person would not think it a reasonable excuse that the accused mistakenly believed that the order to report was invalid.[3] On the other hand, the fact that the accused was physically or mentally incapable of complying (or there is a substantial risk to his health or safety if he complies) with the duty to report in the order is capable of amounting to a reasonable excuse.[4] This would, for example, cover cases where he is confined to bed by illness or injury. Likewise, if the offence is construed as one of strict liability, it would seem that the fact that the accused is mentally incapable of understanding what he is required to do (as where he is a recent immigrant with little understanding of English) can amount to a reasonable excuse.[5]

It remains to be seen whether there could be a reasonable excuse if the failure was due to difficulty in complying or the disruptive effect of complying, as when one of the accused's children or parents was ill or his employer would not give him time off to report.

1   *Bryan v Mott* (1975) 62 Cr App R 71, DC.
2   Ibid; *Evans v Hughes* [1972] 3 All ER 412, DC.
3   *R v Downey* [1970] RTR 257, CA; *R v Reid* [1973] 3 All ER 1020, CA.
4   *R v Lennard* [1973] 2 All ER 831, CA.
5   *Chief Constable of Avon and Somerset Constabulary v Singh* [1988] RTR 107, DC. An alleged
     linguistic difficulty must be scrutinised very carefully: *DPP v Whalley* [1991] Crim LR 211, DC.
     Compare *R v Densu* [1998] Crim LR 345, DC (strict liability offence of possessing offensive
     weapon in a public place without lawful authority or reasonable excuse; held ignorance that
     the thing is an offensive weapon cannot amount to a reasonable excuse).

8.57 Clearly, an evidential burden of establishing reasonable excuse is placed on the accused, but on whom is the legal burden? Unlike some statutory provisions,[1] no express burden of proving reasonable excuse is placed on the accused. The question therefore is whether without reasonable excuse is an essential (or integral) element of the offence or an 'exception, proviso, excuse or qualification'. If it is the latter, the onus of proof would be on the accused by virtue of s 101 of the Magistrates' Courts Act 1980. However, it would seem that the phrase is an essential element of the offence, and that there is therefore no more than an evidential burden on the accused in respect of reasonable excuse (if it is raised) and that, once that is satisfied, it is for the prosecution to disprove reasonable excuse beyond reasonable doubt. In *Polychronakis v Richards & Jerrom Ltd*,[2] it was stated that, where 'reasonable excuse' is a defence, it is not for the accused to prove it unless the specific statutory provisions so requires. This is in line with other authority,[3] although not all.[4] The fact that placing the onus of proof of 'reasonable excuse' on the accused might be incompatible with the presumption of innocence in Art 6(2) of the ECHR[5] is a strong argument for placing the burden of proof on the prosecution in relation to it.

1   See, for example, Prevention of Crime Act 1953, s 1.
2   [1998] Env LR 347 DC.
3   *R v O'Boyle* [1973] RTR 445, CA; *Mallows v Harris* [1979] RTR 404, DC (reasonable excuse);
     Jaggard v Dickinson [1980] 3 All ER 716, DC; *Nagy v Weston* [1965] 1 All ER 78, DC; *Hirst v
     Chief Constable of West Yorkshire* (1986) 85 Cr App R 143, DC (lawful excuse).
4   See *Gatland v Metropolitan Police Comr* [1968] 2 All ER 100, DC.
5   See para **4.38**.

Arrest

8.58 As enacted, the offence under s 16(4) of the 1989 Act was not an arrestable offence, nor was there a specific power of arrest. A problem revealed by events surrounding the World Cup in 1998 was that police officers were seeing individuals subject to IFBOs leaving the country, knowing full well that they would be failing to comply with their IFBOs, but unable to do anything about it in terms of making an arrest.

Section 84(2) of the Crime and Disorder Act 1998 sought to fill this gap by adding an offence under s 16(4) of the 1989 Act to the growing list of arrestable offences in s 24(2) of PACE. It is doubtful, however, whether this will enable the police to arrest in a case such as that just mentioned. The reason is that the power to arrest without warrant in advance given to the police by s 24(7) of PACE requires the police officer to have reasonable grounds for suspecting that the arrestee is *about to commit* an arrestable offence. By the very nature of things, a person at a port or airport or at a Eurostar station en route to a football match abroad can hardly be said to be 'about to commit' an offence that cannot be committed until the time specified in the notice requiring him to report at a police station, which will almost certainly be some time after embarkation.[1] The imposition in the order of a condition requiring the offender to surrender his passport before a relevant match will be far more effective.

---

1   Since the duty to report is 'on the occasion' of a designated match, it would be impermissible for the reporting time period to be significantly greater than the 'occasion' (ie the time of the occurrence of the match: *Shorter Oxford English Dictionary*).

FOOTBALL TICKET TOUTING

8.59 One of the recommendations of the Taylor Report[1] was a specific offence of touting tickets for, and on the day of, a football match. Lord Justice Taylor (as he then was) gave two reasons. First, sales by touts undermine the segregation of supporters, which is necessary to guard against disorder inside football grounds. Secondly, the presence of touts outside football grounds on the day of a match, especially an all-ticket match, acts as a focus for disorder as people strive to obtain tickets from them. Four years on from the report, s 166 of the Criminal Justice and Public Order Act 1994 implemented Lord Justice Taylor's recommendation.

The offence under s 166 does not currently apply to ticket touts at sporting events other than designated association football matches, nor does it apply to ticket touts outside theatres or other places of entertainment. Ticket touting is undoubtedly a problem at other sporting events, such as Wimbledon, and outside some West End theatres because of the obstruction caused by the touts, some of whom are over-enthusiastic in their sales technique, and many people object to the profits that touts make out of selling scarce tickets at inflated prices. In addition, touts may be selling tickets that have been stolen or which have been forged. The activities of such touts, however, do not give rise to the public order issues referred to in the previous paragraph, and it is the maintenance of public order to which s 166 is addressed. In addition, touts who engage in threatening or insulting behaviour, or who obstruct the highway, or who knowingly sell stolen, forged or invalid tickets, can be convicted of offences under the Public Order Act 1986, the Highways Act 1980, the Theft Act 1968 or the Forgery and Counterfeiting Act 1981.

Section 166(6) of the 1994 Act empowers the Secretary of State to make an order by statutory instrument[2] amending s 166 so that it applies 'to any *sporting* event, or category of sporting event, for which 6,000 or more tickets are issued for sale'.[3] It is unlikely that this power will be used unless, and until, public disorder at other sporting events necessitates action in the same way that public disorder necessitated action in relation to football matches.

Where a sporting event lasts for more than a day, an order under s 166(6) would only apply to it in respect of any day in respect of which 6,000 or more tickets had been issued for sale. Thus, a cricket match scheduled to extend over several days could only come within the scope of an order under s 166(6) where tickets issued for sale for a particular day (rather than all the days together) totalled 6,000 or more. This is the effect of s 166(8) which provides that, where an order has been made under s 166(6), s 166 applies, with any modifications made in the order, 'to any part of the sporting event specified or described in the order, provided that 6,000 or more tickets are issued for sale for the day on which that part of the event takes place'.

---

1   See para **8.1**.
2   No such order can be made unless a draft has been laid before, and approved by, a resolution of each House of Parliament: 1994 Act, s 172(5).
3   As to proof of the numbers of tickets issued for sale, see 1994 Act, s 166(7).

Prohibited conduct

8.60 Section 166(1) of the 1994 Act provides that it is an offence for an unauthorised person to sell, or offer or expose for sale, a ticket for a designated football match in any public place or place to which the public has access or, in the course of a trade or business, in any other place. The offence recommended in the Taylor Report was limited to the day of the match; this limit does not appear in the offence under s 166.

Sale etc of ticket by unauthorised person
8.61 A person is 'unauthorised' unless he is authorised in writing to sell tickets for the match by the home club or by the organisers of the match.[1] 'Authorised by the home club' presumably means authorised by or on behalf of its management. The offence is not limited to professional ticket touts; it can be committed, for example, by a person who sells a ticket at face value to a friend in a pub because he is no longer able to attend the match.

No sale need be proved. It is enough that the unauthorised person offered to sell a ticket or simply exposed it for sale. Consequently, merely standing passively outside a ground displaying a fistful of tickets can suffice, even though it would not amount to an offer to sell.[2] An advertisement of football tickets in a newspaper would not be caught by s 166 because it is not an offer to sell[3] and could hardly be described as an exposure for sale.

Section 166(1) speaks of the sale etc of a ticket. In fact, it also covers the sale etc of fake tickets as well as of bona fide ones, since a 'ticket' is defined as meaning anything which purports to be a ticket.[4] However, in the case of the sale or offer or exposure for sale of a fake ticket a charge of obtaining property (the purchase price) by deception or of attempting to do so would be more appropriate.

---

1   1994 Act, s 166(2)(a).
2   *Fisher v Bell* [1961] 1 QB 394, DC.
3   *Partridge v Crittenden* [1968] 2 All ER 421, DC.
4   1994 Act, s 166(2)(b).

For designated football match

8.62 The ticket must be for a 'designated football match'; originally this meant a football match, or a football match of a description, for the time being designated under s 1(1) of the Football (Offences) Act 1991, referred to in para **8.25**, but a new definition of the term in s 166 was substituted by the Football (Offences and Disorder) Act 1999, s 10. A 'designated football match' for the purposes of s 166 now means a football match of a description, or a particular football match, for the time being designated for the purposes of Part I or Part II of the Football Spectators Act 1989.[1] The two designation orders are described in paras **8.31** and **8.44**. These cover association football matches at Wembley Stadium or the National Stadium in Cardiff or at the home ground of a Football League or Football Association Premier League club, and also (and this extends s 166) matches abroad involving the English or Welsh team, matches abroad involving such a club or UEFA matches abroad involving any English or Welsh club.

---

1   1994 Act, s 166(2)(c).

Place of commission

8.63 The prohibited conduct may be committed by anyone in 'a public place or a place to which the public have access'.[1]

Whether a place is a 'public place' is a question of degree and fact.[2] There are similar definitions of 'public place' in other criminal statutes. With the caveat that the phrase must be read in its context, reference may be made to the discussion of the definition in the context of Part II of the Public Order Act 1986 in para **6.5**. A 'public place' in s 166 clearly refers to the 'highway' and to any other place, for example common ground, to which the public have access as of right. It probably also includes any place to which the public have access, on payment or otherwise, by virtue of express or implied permission, such as a pub, shop or the car park of a football ground, during times when it is open (but not when it is closed).[3]

The point is immaterial because such a place will be a 'place to which the public have access'. In other statutory offences, 'public place' is defined as including any place to which at the material time the public have or are permitted access, whether on payment or otherwise. The omission here of any reference to permission certainly does not narrow the phrase used. The question is one of whether the public qua public have access to the place in question. It is not enough that any member of the public can enter it. For example, any member of the public can enter someone's front garden to go to the front door, but this does not make the garden a place to which the public have access because, despite the implied licence to enter, it is not qua members of the public that such people enjoy access but qua lawful visitors.[4] A communal area in a block of flats where there is nothing to prevent access by the public is, on the other hand, a place to which the public have access.[5] There is no need to provide evidence of public use.[6] It can be inferred from the facts that a place, albeit enclosed, was publicly owned and was open for any member of the public to use it, that it is a public place.[6]

The proximity of the place to the football ground in question is immaterial, so that the offence is not limited to sales etc outside the ground or near it.

Where the sale is in the course of a trade or business, the prohibited conduct is not limited to places that are public or to which the public have access; it may be committed in any other place as well. Thus, the net is cast wider against professional ticket touts; for example, a professional ticket tout who, in a telephone call from his own home, offers to sell a ticket can be convicted.

1   1994 Act, s 166(1).
2   *R v Waters* (1963) 47 Cr App R 149, CA.
3   *Sandy v Martin* [1974] Crim LR 258, DC.
4   *R v Edwards (Llewellyn)* (1978) 67 Cr App R 228, CA; *DPP v Fellowes* (1993) 157 JP 936, DC.
5   *Knox v Anderton* (1983) 76 Cr App R 156, DC.
6   *Cummings v DPP* [1999] COD 288.

Mental element

8.64 No mental element is prescribed for this offence. If the presumption that mens rea is required to be proved[1] is held not to be rebutted when the section is construed on this point, the mental element required will be actual knowledge or wilful blindness[2] as to the elements of the prohibited conduct. However, the nature of the offence, its maximum penalty,[3] and the fact that other offences in the 1994 Act expressly require proof of mens rea is very likely to lead a court to hold that the presumption is rebutted. The issue of the mental element requirement is not especially important here because it is difficult to conceive of many cases where, the prohibited conduct under s 166 having been proved, the existence of the accused's knowledge or wilful blindness as to its component parts could be in doubt. The only realistic possibility would relate to the issue of lack of authorisation; cases could occur where an accused thought that he had been authorised to sell tickets when he had not been authorised in writing or when a purported written authorisation was invalid.

1   *Sweet v Parsley* [1969] 1 All ER 347, HL; *Gammon (Hong Kong) Ltd v A-G of Hong Kong* [1984] 2 All ER 503, PC.
2   See para **6.37**.
3   See para **8.65**.

Arrest, trial and punishment

8.65 An offence under s 166 of the 1994 Act has been added to the list of arrestable offences in s 24(2) of PACE.[1] The offence is triable summarily only.[2] It is not punishable with imprisonment. The maximum fine is a fine not exceeding level 5 on the standard scale.[2] A domestic and/or international football banning order may only be made against the convicted person.[3]

1   1994 Act, s 166(4).
2   Ibid, s 166(3).
3   See paras **8.35** and **8.45**.

8.66 Section 32 of PACE provides police officers with powers of search in certain circumstances where a person is arrested elsewhere than at a police station. Inter alia, a police officer may search the arrested person for anything that may be evidence relating to an offence, and may enter and search any premises (including any vehicle) in which he was when arrested or immediately before he was arrested for evidence relating to the offence for which he was arrested. By s 166(5) of the 1994 Act, this provision has effect, in relation to s 166, as if the police officer's power to enter and search any vehicle extended to any vehicle which he has reasonable grounds for believing[1] was being used for any purpose connected with the offence, for example because it contains some of the tout's stock of tickets. Consequently, if the vehicle is so connected, a police officer may enter and search it even though the tout is not in the vehicle when or immediately before he was arrested.

---

1   See para **6.28**.

Chapter 9

MISCELLANEOUS PUBLIC ORDER OFFENCES

PROHIBITION OF POLITICAL UNIFORMS AND QUASI-MILITARY ORGANISATIONS

9.1 The Public Order Act 1936 is the relevant statute. Prosecutions under the Act have not been common, but it continues to have a significant deterrent effect.

Prohibition of political uniforms

9.2 Section 1(1) of the 1936 Act provides:

'Subject as hereinafter provided, any person who in any public place, or at any public meeting wears uniform signifying his association with any political organisation or with the promotion of any political object shall be guilty of an offence:

Provided that, if the chief officer of police[1] is satisfied that the wearing of any such uniform as aforesaid on any ceremonial, anniversary, or other special occasion will not be likely to involve risk of public disorder, he may, with the consent of the Secretary of State, by order[2] permit the wearing of such uniform on that occasion either absolutely or subject to such conditions as may be specified in the order.'

Section 1 was enacted in response to the increasing use of uniforms by political groups, particularly the British Fascist Movement.

---

1   See para **6.26** fn 1.
2   This order must be in writing. It may be revoked or varied by a subsequent order in writing: 1936 Act, s 9(3).

9.3 An offence under s 1 of the 1936 Act can only be committed 'in any public place or at any public meeting'. 'Public place' in s 1 bears its common form definition referred to earlier in other offences, viz 'any highway and any other premises or place to which at the material time the public have or are permitted to have access, whether on payment or otherwise'.[1] In relation to 'public meeting', 'meeting' means a meeting held for the purpose of the discussion of matters of public interest or for the purpose of the expression of views on such matters, and 'public meeting' includes any 'meeting' in a public place and any meeting which the public or any section of the public[2] are invited to attend, whether on payment or otherwise.[3]

---

1   1936 Act, s 9(1); see para **6.5**, but note that the context of a provision can affect the meaning to be ascribed to it.
2   See para **5.24** on this phrase in another context.
3   1936 Act, s 9(1).

9.4 The 1936 Act does not provide any definitions in relation to the requirement that the accused must be proved to have been wearing a uniform signifying his association with any political organisation or with the promotion of any political object. It is not necessary that a complete outfit be worn. In *O'Moran v DPP*,[1] the

Divisional Court held that 'wearing' implies one or more items of 'wearing apparel', such as a beret,[2] dark glasses,[2] or a pullover,[2] trousers or a jacket. The reference to 'wearing apparel' excludes things like badges[2] or armbands or, a fortiori, banners, flags or emblems signifying association with a political organisation etc. There may be an argument about armbands. It is submitted that, unlike those things recognised as wearing apparel, which intrinsically have the function of protecting the wearer quite apart from the communication of any message, the sole function of an armband is the communication of a message or messages, and that armbands are not wearing apparel. Badges, armbands, banners and flags may, however, amount to a visible representation for the purposes of an offence under s 4, s 4A or s 5 of the Public Order Act 1986,[3] although the prosecution might have difficulty in proving the other requirements of one of these offences. Alternatively, or in addition, carrying, wearing or displaying such an item may be conduct likely to occasion violence (and therefore be a breach of the peace) and entitle a police officer to seize the item,[4] or may constitute the offence under s 3(1) of the Prevention of Terrorism (Temporary Provisions) Act 1989 described in para **9.10**.

1   [1975] 1 All ER 473 at 480, DC.
2   So held in *O'Moran v DPP* [1975] 1 All ER 473, DC.
3   Chapter 4.
4   See para **2.18**.

9.5   In deciding whether what was worn was 'uniform', different considerations arise according to whether the accused was alone or with others. If someone alone wears a soldier's clothes it is not necessary to prove that that was a uniform of any sort; it is clear and judicial notice can be taken of it.[1] On the other hand, if an isolated individual is wearing an article, for example a black beret, the article would not be regarded as a uniform unless there is proved that the beret has been recognised and is known as uniform. In contrast, if a number of people are together wearing the article in order to indicate that they are together and in association, the article can be regarded as a uniform without proof that it has previously been used as such.[1] In *O'Moran v DPP*,[2] where there was evidence that eight men had marched in military style, dressed in dark glasses, black berets and dark clothing, at the funeral of a fellow member of the IRA, the Divisional Court held that they were wearing uniform for the purposes of s 1 of the 1936 Act.

As this case indicates, and as was expressly recognised in it, subject to the de minimis rule, there is no need for the articles in question to cover all or major parts of the body; a uniform can consist of a single item of wearing apparel that is a distinguishing mark.

1   *O'Moran v DPP* [1975] 1 All ER 473 at 480.
2   [1975] 1 All ER 473, DC.

9.6   The wearing of the uniform must signify the accused's association with any political organisation or with the promotion of any political object. Those who wear British Legion or Scout uniforms in public in connection with the objects of the respective organisation do not, for example, commit an offence under s 1 of the 1936 Act.

'Association' in this context seems to refer to adherence to, although not necessarily membership of, an organisation.[1] The crucial thing is that the offence is committed by someone who wears wearing apparel constituting a uniform which signifies his association in the specified way. It is not expressly required that an accused should be aware of the significance of what he wears. It would be unfortunate if the offence was construed to catch someone who inadvertently wore clothing which signified his association in the specified way. It is submitted that the requirement that the reference in s 1(1) to wearing uniform 'signifying his association' refers to signifying his *actual* association. This must be correct. Otherwise, film actors or those dressed up for a fancy dress party, for example, would be caught by s 1.

It has not yet been determined what is meant by 'political' in this context. In the context of charitable trusts law and extradition law, 'political' has been interpreted as having a wider meaning than 'party political'. It has been held that a 'political object' means the object of overthrowing or changing the government or inducing it to change its policy (and a 'political association' would seem to be one whose objects are of this type).[2] Of course, charitable trusts and extradition are different contexts, and it may be that a court would decline to apply the meaning accorded to 'political' in relation to them to that term in s 1. In such a case, it might prefer to leave the meaning of the term, as an ordinary word, for the court to decide as a question of fact, as has been done in respect of other words in common usage.[3] If this approach is the correct one, a decision as to the meaning of the term would not be upset on appeal unless it was such that it was unreasonable in the sense that no court acquainted with the ordinary use of language could reasonably have reached it.[4]

---

1   The wording of the 1936 Act, s 2(1) (see para **9.11**) seems to confirm this.
2   For a review of the cases, see *R v Radio Authority, ex parte Bull* [1995] 4 All ER 481, DC; [1997] 2 All ER 561, CA.
3   See, for example, *Brutus v Cozens* [1972] 2 All ER 1297, HL.
4   Ibid, at 1299, per Lord Reid.

9.7   Lord Widgery CJ in *O'Moran v DPP*[1] took the view that the wearing of uniform signifying the accused's association with any political organisation may be proved in either of two ways:

> 'It is open to the prosecution ... to show that the particular article relied on as uniform has been used in the past as the uniform of a recognised association, and they can by that means, if the evidence is strong enough ... prove that the black beret, or whatever it may be, is associated with a particular organisation ... [I]t is not necessary for them to specify the particular organisation because in many instances the name of the organisation will be unknown or may have been recently changed. But if they can prove that the article in question has been associated with a political organisation capable of identification in some manner, then that would suffice ...
>
> Alternatively, ... the significance of the uniform and its power to show the association of the wearer with a political organisation can be judged from the events to be seen on the occasion when the alleged uniform was worn. In other words it can be judged and proved without necessarily referring to the past history at all because ... if a group of persons assemble together and wear a piece of uniform such as a black beret to indicate their association one with the other, and furthermore by their conduct indicate that that beret associates them with other activity of a political character, that is enough ...
>
> Applying that to the instant case, ... [i]f you look at the picture as presented outside the church ... you would find these men in uniform and in a uniform which associated them with the other activities then going on. If one examined what those activities

were, it would become abundantly clear that they were activities of a political character. Thus the chain of responsibility under the section would be complete.'

---

1   [1975] 1 All ER 473 at 481.

9.8   Where a person is charged before any court with an offence under s 1 of the 1936 Act, no further proceedings in respect of it may be taken against him without the consent of the Attorney-General.[1]

An offence contrary to s 1 is triable only summarily.[2] The maximum punishment is three months' imprisonment or a fine not exceeding level 4 on the standard scale, or both.[2]

---

1   1936 Act, s 1(2). Also see paras **5.53–5.55**.
2   1936 Act, s 7(2).

9.9   An offence contrary to s 1 of the 1936 Act is not an 'arrestable offence', but a constable may arrest without warrant anyone whom he reasonably suspects[1] to be committing it.[2] For this purpose, he may enter and search any premises on which he has reasonable grounds for believing that the suspect is.[3]

---

1   See para **3.68** fn 1.
2   1936 Act, s 7(3).
3   PACE, s 17. What is said in para **4.18** about this power applies equally here.

A related offence

9.10   Section 3(1) of the Prevention of Terrorism (Temporary Provisions) Act 1989 makes it a summary offence for a person in a public place:[1]

(a)   to wear *any item of dress*; or
(b)   to wear, carry or display *any article*,

in such a way or in such circumstances as to arouse reasonable apprehension that he is a member or supporter of a proscribed organisation.

The wording of this offence clearly covers things such as badges and armbands, and banners, flags and emblems, as well as wearing apparel. The following organisations are proscribed organisations for the purposes of s 3: the Irish Republican Army and the Irish National Liberation Army.[2]

The maximum punishment for an offence under s 3(1) is six months' imprisonment or a fine not exceeding level 5 on the standard scale, or both.[3] A prosecution may only be instituted by or with the consent of the Attorney-General.[4]

---

1   'Public place' is defined by the 1989 Act, s 3(3) in essentially the same terms as in the Public Order Act 1936, s 9(1); see para **9.3**.
2   Prevention of Terrorism (Miscellaneous Provisions) Act 1989, Sch 1.
3   Ibid, s 3(1).
4   Ibid, s 19(1). See paras **5.53–5.55**.

Prohibition of quasi-military organisations

9.11 Section 2(1) of the Public Order Act 1936 was enacted in response to the growth in the mid-1930s of private armies, especially Fascist ones. It provides:

'If the members or adherents of any association of persons, whether incorporated or not, are –

(a) organised or trained or equipped for the purpose of enabling them to be employed in usurping the functions of the police or of the armed forces of the Crown;[1] or

(b) organised and trained or organised and equipped either for the purpose of enabling them to be employed for the use or display of physical force in promoting any political[2] object, or in such manner as to arouse reasonable apprehension that they are organised and either trained or equipped for that purpose;[1]

then any person who takes part in the control or management of the association, or in so organising or training as aforesaid any members or adherents thereof, shall be guilty of an offence under this section.'

This prohibition does not prevent the employment of a reasonable number of persons as stewards to assist in the preservation of order at any public meeting held upon private premises, or the making of arrangements for that purpose or the instruction of persons to be so employed in their lawful duties as such stewards, or their being furnished with badges or other distinguishing signs.[3]

It will be noted that it is not an offence simply to be a member or adherent of an association of the type described in s 2(1).

---

1 Proof of things done or of words written, spoken or published (whether or not in the presence of any party to the proceedings) by any person taking part in the control or management of an association or in organising, training or equipping members or adherents of an association is admissible as evidence of the purposes for which, or the manner in which, members or adherents of the association (whether those persons or others) were organised or trained, or equipped: 1936 Act, s 2(4).

2 See para **9.6**.

3 1936 Act, s 3(6). It is, however, an either-way offence (maximum imprisonment 10 years) to belong to or profess to belong to a proscribed organisation: Prevention of Terrorism (Temporary Provisions) Act 1989, s 2.

9.12 Section 2 is not concerned with those who control or manage private security undertakings or security organisation within undertakings. These bodies are not concerned with usurping the functions of the police or armed forces nor (as far as the writer is aware) organised and trained/equipped for the use or display of force in promoting any political object.

On the other hand, it is arguable that those who control, manage or train local vigilante groups may contravene s 2(1)(a) because such groups do not necessarily act in support of the police but instead act independently of the police (and with the opposition of the police); in such a case the group would seem to be usurping the functions of the police. This doubt would not have arisen if, like s 1 and the other parts of s 2, the association was required to be 'political' or have a political object. Admittedly, the preamble[1] refers to the Act being 'An Act to prohibit ... the maintenance by private persons of associations of a military or similar character' and the marginal note[2] to s 2, the material part of which is set out at the heading to para **9.11**, refers to quasi-military organisations, but neither of these can affect what appears to be the clear wording of s 2(1)(a).

Section 2(1)(b) is clearly limited to those who participate in managing, controlling or training members or adherents of quasi-military associations by the references to organisation *and training* or organisation *and* equipment and to the promotion of any political object. There are two limbs to s 2(1)(b): the first is concerned with the management etc of an association whose members etc are organised etc for the use or display of force to attain a political object, and the second with the managers etc of an association whose members etc are organised etc in such a manner as to *arouse reasonable apprehension* that they are organised and either trained or equipped for the use or display of force for a political purpose. In relation to the latter limb, the Court of Criminal Appeal in *R v Jordan*[3] approved a direction by the trial judge along the following lines:

> 'Reasonable apprehension means an apprehension or fear which is based not upon undue timidity or excessive suspicion or still less prejudice but one which is founded on grounds which to you appear to be reasonable. Moreover the apprehension or fear must be reasonably held by a person who is aware of all the facts ... you must try to put yourselves in the position of a sensible man who knew the whole of the facts.'

The Court of Criminal Appeal held that the fact that there was no evidence of actual attacks or plans for attacks on opponents did not necessarily remove grounds for reasonable apprehension.

---

1   A preamble cannot affect the interpretation of a statute if the body of the Act is clear and
    unambiguous: *Powell v Kempton Park Racecourse* [1899] AC 143 at 157, per Earl of Halsbury LC.
    Also see *A-G v Ernest Augustus of Hanover* [1957] 1 All ER 49 at 58, per Lord Normand.
2   Marginal notes may only be looked at to determine the purpose, as opposed to the scope of,
    the section: *DPP v Schildkamp* [1969] 3 All ER 1640, HL; *Tudor Grange Holdings Ltd v Citibank
    NA* [1991] 4 All ER 1 at 13, per Browne-Wilkinson VC; *DPP v Johnson* [1995] 4 All ER 53, DC.
    They carry little weight and cannot oust a meaning given by the section itself.
3   [1963] Crim LR 124.

9.13 It is a defence for a person charged with the offence of taking part in the control or management of an association of a type described above to prove[1] that he neither consented[2] to nor connived[2] at the organisation, training or equipment of members or adherents of his association in contravention of s 2.[3]

---

1   See para **4.38**.
2   See para **5.50**.
3   1936 Act, s 2(1) proviso.

9.14 No prosecution under s 2(1) of the 1936 Act may be instituted without the consent of the Attorney-General,[1] which has been granted most sparingly.

An offence under s 2(1) is triable either way.[2] The maximum sentence on conviction on indictment is two years' imprisonment or an unlimited fine, or both; on summary conviction it is six months' or a fine not exceeding the statutory maximum, or both.[2]

By s 2(3), the High Court has power, on the application of the Attorney-General, to order the disposal of property belonging to any association whose

members or adherents are organised, trained or equipped in contravention of
s 2(1).

---

1   1936 Act, s 2(2). Also see para **5.53**.
2   1936 Act, s 7(1).

9.15 An offence contrary to s 2 of the 1936 Act is not an arrestable offence. Arrest
without warrant is only possible if it is by a constable and the terms of the
conditional power of arrest under s 25 of PACE are satisfied.

If a High Court judge is satisfied by information on oath that there is
reasonable ground for suspecting[1] that an offence under s 2 has been committed,
and that evidence of its commission is to be found at any premises or place
specified in the information, he may, on an application by a police officer of or
above the rank of inspector, grant a search warrant authorising any such officer
named in the warrant (and anyone else named in the warrant and any other police
officers) to enter the premises or place within one month,[2] from the date of the
warrant.[3] If necessary, the officer(s) may enter by force.[3] They may search the
premises or place and anyone found there, and seize anything found as a result
which the officer concerned has reasonable grounds for suspecting[1] to be
evidence of the commission of an offence under s 2.

---

1   See para **3.68** fn 1.
2   Ie one calendar month: Interpretation Act 1978, s 5 and Sch 1.
3   1936 Act, s 2(5).

Unlawful Drilling Act 1819

9.16 Under s 1 of this Act it is an offence:

(a) to attend a meeting for the purpose of training or drilling any other person or
     persons in the use of arms or military exercises without any lawful authority
     from Her Majesty or a Secretary of State, or any officer deputed by him for the
     purpose; or
(b) to attend a meeting where such training or drilling occurs for the purpose of
     being trained or drilled (or actually to be trained or drilled at such a
     meeting).

Both offences are triable only on indictment. They are Class 3 offences.[1]
Proceedings must be commenced within six calendar months of the offence.[2] The
maximum punishment for offence (a) is seven years' imprisonment; for offence
(b) it is two years.[3]

Any justice of the peace, constable, or other person acting in their aid or
assistance, may disperse any meeting where unlawful training or drilling occurs,
and may arrest anyone present at it or anyone aiding, assisting or abetting it.[4]

---

1   See para **1.9** fn 5.
2   Unlawful Drilling Act 1819, s 7.
3   Ibid, s 1.
4   Ibid, s 2.

DRUNK AND DISORDERLY

9.17 Section 91(1) of the Criminal Justice Act 1967 states that 'any person who in any public place is guilty, while drunk, of disorderly behaviour' commits a summary offence, punishable with a fine not exceeding level 3 on the standard scale; the offence is not imprisonable. The offence is a relevant offence for the purposes of a DFBO or an IFBO[1] in the circumstances set out in para **8.35**.

A person 'who in any public place is guilty (sic), while drunk, of disorderly behaviour' may be arrested without warrant by any person.[2] Despite the wording, it appears to be enough that the arrester believes (presumably on reasonable grounds) that the person arrested is 'guilty'.[3] Although some degree of immediacy is required, the disorderly conduct need not continue up to the very moment of arrest. Thus, if an offender flees and is pursued, the fact that he has ceased to be disorderly when the pursuer catches up with him does not prevent an arrest being made.[4] Moreover, it is not necessary that the person effecting the arrest should personally have witnessed the drunkenness and disorderly behaviour; he can act on the basis of what someone else tells him (as where a complaint is made to a constable by a private citizen who has just witnessed the behaviour).[5] Where a constable has power to arrest a person under s 91, the constable may take that person to a treatment centre for alcoholics.[6]

In s 91, 'public place' includes any highway and any other premises or place to which at the material time the public have or are permitted to have access, whether on payment or otherwise.[7] This is the same definition as in s 1 of the Public Order Act 1936, referred to in para **9.3**.

For the purposes of s 91, 'drunk' refers to a person who has taken intoxicating liquor to such extent that he has lost the power of steady self-control;[8] it does not refer to a person who has been affected as a result of glue-sniffing or taking drugs.[9] 'Disorderly' is an ordinary English word, and whether an accused was disorderly is a question of fact for the magistrates, just as it is on a charge of an offence contrary to s 4A or s 5 of the Public Order Act 1986; see para **4.24**.

---

1   Football Spectators Act 1989, Sch 1.
2   Criminal Justice Act 1967, s 91(1). PACE, s 26, did not repeal this power of arrest: *DPP v Kitching* (1990) 154 JP 293, DC.
3   In *Fay v DPP* [1998] COD 339, DC, the Court spoke in terms of the arrester's belief when dealing with an arrest under s 91. In *Wills v Bowley* [1982] 2 All ER 654, where a comparable power of arrest, since repealed, existed under the Town Police Clauses Act 1847, s 28, the House of Lords said that the power was not confined to cases where the offence had in fact been committed, but extended to cases where a constable honestly believed on reasonable grounds that it had been.
4   *Fay v DPP*, above.
5   *Fay v DPP*, above. Unlike the repealed power under the 1847 Act, s 28, the present power is not limited to cases where the offence is committed within the 'view' of the arresting constable.
6   Criminal Justice Act 1972, s 34.
7   Criminal Justice Act 1967, s 91(4). Communal areas in a block of flats have been held to be a 'public place' in circumstances where there is nothing to prevent access: *Knox v Anderton* (1983) 76 Cr App R, DC. In *Williams v DPP* (1992) 95 Cr App R 415, DC, the landing of a communal block of flats, to which access could be gained only by way of a key, security code, tenants' intercom or the caretaker was held not to be a 'public place', because only those admitted by or with the implied consent of the occupiers of the flats had access. People with access were, therefore, not present as members of the public.

8   *Shorter Oxford English Dictionary.*'Drunk' means what an ordinary person would consider to be
     such, and not merely, eg, unfit to drive: *R v Presdee* (1927) 20 Cr App R 95, CCA.
9   *Neale v E (A Minor)* (1983) 80 Cr App R 20, DC; *Lanham v Rickwood* (1984) 148 JP 737, DC;
     where the accused has taken a mixture of drink and drugs, the magistrates' court must be
     sure that his intake of intoxicating liquor alone is such as to make him drunk: *Lanham v
     Rickwood.*

TOWN POLICE CLAUSES ACT 1847, s 28

9.18 Although originally adoptive, this provision now applies throughout
England and Wales,[1] except in Greater London.[2] It contains a host of offences
dealing with obstruction, annoyance or danger in any street.

Most of these offences do not have the maintenance of public order as their
mischief but are concerned with public safety (eg the offences of making a slide on
ice in the street, of kite-flying in the street and of leaving open a cellar in the
street), with public health and the environment (eg the offences of hanging
clothes in the street, of beating carpets in the street, of throwing nightsoil, rubbish
etc onto the street and of keeping a pigsty in the street) and with the regulation of
traffic in the street (eg the offences of furiously riding or driving any horse or
carriage or furiously driving cattle in the street, and of not exercising proper
control over a wagon or cart).

1   Public Health Act 1875, s 171; Local Government Act 1972, Sch 14, para 23.
2   Local Government Act 1972, Sch 14, para 26.

9.19 The offences under s 28 of the 1847 Act which can be said to have the
maintenance of public order as their mischief are the offences of:

–   wantonly discharging any firearm, or throwing or discharging any stone or
     other missile, or making any bonfire, or throwing or setting fire to any
     firework;[1]
–   wilfully causing any obstruction in any public footpath or other public
     thoroughfare (see para **9.89**);
–   publicly offering for sale or distribution or exhibiting to public view any
     profane book, paper, print, drawing, painting or representation, or singing
     any profane or obscene song or ballad, or using any profane or obscene
     language.

'Obscene' in s 28 does not bear the specialised meaning given to that term
for the purposes of the Obscene Publications Act 1959 by s 1(1) of that Act.
Instead, it would seem to have the meaning given by the courts to 'obscene' in
the context of other offences where it is used in its ordinary dictionary sense
of shocking, lewd, indecent and so on.[2] It has been contrasted with 'indecent'
on the basis that, while both involve offending against the recognised
standards of propriety, 'indecent' is at the lower end of the scale and
'obscene' at the upper end.[3] Unlike 'obscenity' under the Obscene Publications Act, which can be satisfied by a tendency to deprave and corrupt in a
non-sexual way (eg by advocating drug-taking),[4] it is clear that obscenity
elsewhere in the law is limited to offending against standards of propriety or
decency.

'Profane' in its dictionary sense means blasphemous, taking God's name in vain, outraging sacred things.[5] It would be unfortunate in our multi-cultural society if it was limited to blasphemous conduct in its legal sense (ie limited to attacks on the Christian religion, God, Christ and other persons sacred to the Christian religion, calculated to outrage and insult a Christian's religious feelings).[6]

It could be that the Divisional Court would hold that the meaning of 'obscene' and 'profane' in the present context is simply one of fact for the magistrates (and not a question of law);[7] in which case it would not interfere with the magistrates' understanding of the term unless it was one which no reasonable bench could reach.[7]

In each offence, the conduct in question must occur in a 'street' (which, for the purpose of the above offences, includes any road, square, court, alley and thoroughfare, or public passage).[8] In addition, as with all offences under s 28, the prohibited conduct is required to be 'to the obstruction, annoyance or danger, of the residents or passengers'. 'Residents' refers to occupiers of residential premises in the street, and 'passengers' to passers-by.[9] In *Hoogstraten v Goward*,[10] it was held that 'passengers' means passers-by, that a police officer who was a passer-by was a 'passenger'[11] and that it was open to a court to find that he was annoyed at being abused by obscene language. There seems no reason why s 3 of the 1847 Act, which makes similar provision to s 6 of the Interpretation Act 1978, should not apply to 'passengers', so that the term includes a 'passenger'. On the other hand, the reference to 'the residents' may indicate a contrary intention to the application of the singular, although it can hardly mean all the residents. It would seem that prohibited conduct in the street can be to the annoyance of residents, although they may not be in the street at the time. It is not necessary to call any person who has been obstructed, annoyed or endangered as a witness,[9] but the requisite obstruction, annoyance or danger to residents or passengers must be proved by the prosecution.

---

1   By s 80 of the Explosives Act 1875, it is a summary offence to throw, cast or fire any firework in or onto any highway, street, thoroughfare or public place. The maximum punishment is a fine not exceeding level 5 on the standard scale. Cases covered by this offence include throwing in a street a firework that fails to explode, or the firing of a firework in any street or public place. There are no exceptions to this offence; even the celebration of 'Guy Faulkes' must be restricted to the use of fireworks otherwise than in streets or public places. The offence is more easily proved than the summary offence under the Town Police Clauses Act 1847, s 28, or the summary offence under s 161 of the Highways Act 1980 (maximum punishment a fine not exceeding level 1) of discharging any firework within 50 feet of the centre of a highway which consists of or comprises a carriageway in consequence of which a user of the highway is injured, interrupted or endangered.

2   *R v Anderson* [1971] 3 All ER 1152, CA (Post Office Act 1953, s 11, offence of posting indecent or obscene article).

3   *R v Stanley* [1965] 1 All ER 1035, CCA (Post Office Act 1953, s 11); *Galletly v Laird* 1953 SC (J) 16 (Burgh Police (Scotland) Act 1892).

4   *John Calder (Publications) Ltd v Powell* [1965] 1 All ER 159, DC.

5   It was accorded this meaning in *Armstrong v Moon* (1894) 13 NZLR 517, NZSC.

6   *R v Lemon* [1979] 1 All ER 898, HL.

7   See para **4.5**.

8   Town Police Clauses Act 1847, s 3. The 'street' includes the carriageway and footway at the sides. In addition, for the purposes of the third offence listed above, any place of public resort or recreation ground belonging to or under the control of the local authority, and any unfenced ground adjoining or abutting upon any street, is deemed to be a 'street', in

addition to the general definition of 'street' given in the text: Public Health Acts Amendment Act 1907, s 81; Local Government Act 1972, Sch 14, paras 23 and 26.

9   *Woolley v Corbishley* (1860) 24 JP 773, DC; *Read v Perrett* (1876) 1 Ex D 349, DC.

10   [1967] Crim LR 590, DC.

11   For the purposes of another offence (indecent exposure) under the 1847 Act, s 28, to which the deeming provision referred to in footnote 8 above applies, it has been held that police officers who witnessed the accused masturbating in a public lavatory were not 'passengers' because they were there for the special purpose of apprehending people committing acts which had given rise to complaints, as opposed to resorting to the lavatory (a place of public resort) for a purpose for which people normally resorted to it: *Cheesman v DPP* [1992] QB 83, DC.

9.20 An offence contrary to s 28 of the 1847 Act is triable summarily only. It is punishable with a maximum of 14 days' imprisonment *or* a fine not exceeding level 3 on the standard scale.

Since it is neither an arrestable offence nor subject to a special power of arrest, arrest for it is only possible under the conditional power of the police under s 25 of PACE or for breach of the peace.

METROPOLITAN POLICE ACT 1839, s 54

9.21 This provision is limited to the Metropolitan Police district.[1] It covers a similar agglomeration of offences to that covered by s 28 of the 1847 Act, spanning the same range of mischiefs. A major distinction is that there is no general requirement that an offence be committed 'to the obstruction, annoyance or danger of residents or passengers'. Save for this distinction, and that the conduct must occur 'in any thoroughfare or public place',[2] s 54 contains three public order offences that are similarly worded to those mentioned in para **9.19** under s 28 of the 1847 Act, viz:

–   Selling or distributing or offering for sale or distribution, or exhibiting to public view, any profane book, paper, print, drawing, painting or representation, or singing any profane, indecent, or obscene song or ballad, or using any profane, indecent or obscene language to the annoyance of the inhabitants or passengers;[3] The word 'indecent' does not appear in the corresponding offence under the 1847 Act. It would seem that this bears the type of meaning referred to in para **9.19**, as opposed to the meaning given to that term in the context of the offence under the Ecclesiastical Courts Jurisdiction Act 1860, s 2, referred to in para **9.31**. Where profane, indecent or obscene language, at least, is alleged, it suffices for the prosecution to prove that the language was calculated (ie likely) to annoy; proof of actual annoyance is not required.[3]

–   Wantonly discharging any firearm or throwing or discharging any stone or other missile, to the damage or danger of any person, or making any bonfire, or throwing or setting fire to any firework.

–   Wilfully causing any obstruction in any thoroughfare (see para **9.90**).

1   Ie Greater London (excluding the City of London, the Inner Temple and the Middle Temple): see London Government Act 1963, s 76.

2   'Public place' is not defined by the Act. No doubt the courts will apply a test similar to the common-form ones to be found in the various statutes referred to elsewhere in this book.

9.22 Strangely, an offence under s 54 of the 1839 Act is slightly less serious than one under s 28 of the 1847 Act. The offence is triable summarily only. It is not imprisonable; the maximum fine is one not exceeding level 2 on the standard scale. What was said in para **9.20** about arrest without warrant is equally applicable to the present offence.

9.23 Most of the conduct which constitutes an offence under s 28 of the 1847 Act and under s 54 of the 1839 Act is also an offence under other statutory provisions. Quite a few of the offences are concerned with conduct which is unlikely to occur in modern society. Both sections would benefit from rationalisation to avoid duplication and to make them appropriate to the third millenium. The effect of this might be their complete repeal.

BOMB HOAXES

9.24 Bomb hoaxes have the potential to cause panic and disorder. They are therefore properly the subject of this book. Bomb hoaxes can result in conviction for public nuisance provided that a 'class of the public' is affected by the hoax,[1] but since the enactment of s 51 of the Criminal Law Act 1977 the appropriate offence to charge, whatever the number of persons affected by a bomb hoax, is an offence under that section. There are three offences under s 51: placing an article, dispatching an article, and sending a false message, in each case with the appropriate intent.

1   *R v Madden* [1975] 3 All ER 155, CA. Public nuisance is dealt with in para **9.92**. Other offences which could be charged in respect of a bomb hoax are threatening to destroy or damage property, contrary to the Criminal Damage Act 1971, s 2, and wasting police time, contrary to the Criminal Law Act 1967, s 5(2).

Placing or dispatching an article

9.25 Section 51(1) of the 1977 Act provides:

'A person who –

(a)   places any article in any place whatever; or
(b)   dispatches any article by post, rail or any other means whatever of sending things from one place to another,

with the intention (in either case) of inducing in some other person a belief that it is likely to explode or ignite and thereby cause personal injury or damage to property is guilty of an offence.
   In this subsection, "article" includes a substance.'

Although the marginal note to s 51 is 'Bomb hoaxes', neither of the two offences under s 51 are limited to harmless articles; placing or dispatching a real bomb with the necessary intent constitutes an offence under s 51. However, a charge for causing (or attempting to cause) an explosion contrary to s 2 (or s 3) of the Explosive Substances Act 1883, would be more appropriate; these are indictable only offences punishable with a maximum of life imprisonment.

9.26 The offence of placing an article requires proof that the accused placed an article in any place whatsoever with the intention of inducing in some other person a belief that it was likely to explode or ignite and thereby cause personal injury or damage to property. As can be seen, the offence can be committed in a purely private place, although generally the conduct covered by the offence occurs in a place to which the public have access.

An example of the present offence would be where D places under a seat at a railway station a parcel to which wires are connected together with something which resembles a timing device, with the intention of inducing a railway passenger or railway worker to believe that the parcel is likely to explode and thereby cause personal injury or damage to property. Indeed, simply placing an unadorned parcel with the requisite intent can suffice. The placing must be done with the requisite intent. Someone who mislays something, and on realising what has happened fails to collect it intending to cause the specified belief in another, cannot be convicted of the present offence; he cannot be said to have 'placed' the thing with the requisite intent. It must be stressed that the belief of another referred to above that must be intended need not actually be caused. It is submitted that the intended belief must be to cause the specified belief by the placing of the article; it does not constitute the present offence (although it is an offence under s 51(2) of the 1977 Act) to place an article intending to cause the requisite belief by a subsequent phone-call to someone. The intent to cause the requisite belief can be (and will usually be) a generalised one. As already implied, and as stated by s 51(3), it is not necessary for an offence under s 51(1) for the accused to have any particular person in mind as the person in whom he intends to induce the specified belief.

9.27 The offence of dispatching requires proof that the accused dispatched any article by post, rail or any other means from one place to another with the intention of inducing in another person a belief that it is likely to explode or ignite and thereby cause personal injury or damage to property.

The present offence is not committed by someone who posts a real parcel bomb, disguised as an 'innocent parcel', which blows up immediately it is opened, as he intended it should, because it cannot be said that he intended to induce anyone to believe that the article is likely to explode etc; his intention was that it should explode before the recipient had time to realise what the contents of the parcel were and he certainly did not intend that anyone else should. The appropriate charge is one under s 2 of the Explosive Substances Act 1883.

A typical example of the present offence is where someone puts in the post a suspicious parcel of the size and weight to be a bomb with a ticking mechanism inside it, addressed to a prominent politician.

The comments made in para **9.26** above about the requisite intent are equally applicable to the present offence.

Of the three offences in s 51, this offence is the least appropriately described as a public order offence.

Messages known or believed to be false

9.28 Section 51(2) of the Criminal Law Act 1977 provides:

> 'A person who communicates any information which he knows or believes to be false to another person with the intention of inducing in him or any other person a false

belief that a bomb or other thing liable to explode or ignite is present in any place or location whatever is guilty of an offence.'

Despite the marginal note to s 51 referred to above, the prohibited conduct does not require the information to be false. The crux of the offence is that the accused must be proved:

(a) to have known the information was false (which is only possible if the information was false) or believed it was false (and one can believe a thing is false, even if it is not); and

(b) to have communicated the information with the requisite intent.

The requisite intent is what must be proved; it is irrelevant that no one had the specified belief as a result of the accused's conduct. It is not necessary that the accused had any particular person in mind in whom he intended to induce the specified belief.[1] Rather oddly, the offence requires that the intent be to induce a false belief that a bomb etc *is* present somewhere. Hoaxers who report a 'suspicious package' at a time of terrorist activity, intending to induce a belief that there *may be* a bomb there would seem to lack the necessary intent.

Although the offence is most commonly committed by means of a telephone call, it can be committed by any means of communication. The message need not be specific as to a location.[2] People who telephone the police, or anyone else, in the belief that that information is true, or may possibly be true, do not commit the present offence, even if they can be said to have the requisite intent, because they will not know or believe that the information communicated is false.

---

1   Criminal Law Act 1977, s 51(3).
2   *R v Webb* (1995) *The Times*, 19 June, CA (999 call, saying 'There is a bomb'; held sufficient for an offence under s 51(2)).

Trial, punishment and arrest

9.29 An offence under s 51 of the 1977 Act is triable either way.[1] The maximum punishment on conviction on indictment is seven years' imprisonment; on summary conviction it is six months' imprisonment or a fine not exceeding the prescribed sum (ie the statutory maximum), or both.[1] By virtue of their maximum sentence, offences under s 51 are arrestable offences under s 24(1) of PACE.

---

1   Criminal Law Act 1977, s 51(4).

DISTURBANCE IN CHURCH, CERTIFIED PLACE OF WORSHIP OR BURIAL-GROUND

9.30 Disturbances occasionally occur in churches and other religious places. Such conduct may well be caught by other offences mentioned elsewhere in this book, particularly those under ss 4 to 5 of the Public Order Act 1986.[1] However, s 2 of the Ecclesiastical Courts Jurisdiction Act 1860 provides an offence specifically concerned with such conduct.

Section 2 of the 1860 Act provides that any person[2] commits an offence if he is:

'... guilty of riotous, violent, or indecent behaviour in England[3] in any cathedral church, parish or district church, or chapel of the Church of England, or in any chapel of any religious denomination, or in England in any place of religious worship duly certified under the Places of Worship Registration Act 1855, whether during the celebration of divine service,[4] or at any other time, or in any churchyard, or burial-ground, or who shall molest, let, disturb, vex, or trouble, or by any other unlawful means disquiet or misuse any preacher duly authorised to preach therein, or any clergyman in Holy Orders ministering or celebrating any sacrament or any divine service,[4] rite, or office in any cathedral, church or chapel, churchyard, or burial-ground.'

It has not been determined how many offences are embraced by s 2 of the 1860 Act. Arguably, the early reference to riotous, violent or indecent behaviour in any cathedral etc is to three ways of committing one offence, and the later reference to molesting, letting, disturbing, troubling etc any preacher etc is a reference to various ways of committing one or two other offences. It would give rise to potential problems under the rule against duplicity[5] if each of the modes of conduct specified in the two parts constituted a separate offence. On the other hand, the two parts of s 2 are sufficiently distinct to make it difficult to accept that s 2 simply creates one offence capable of commission in any of the ways specified.

---

1   Chapter 4.
2   Including a clerk in holy orders: *Vallancey v Fletcher* [1897] 1 QB 265, DC.
3   At the time of enactment, 'England' was construed as including 'Wales' and must be so interpreted now.
4   'Divine service', in relation to the Church of England at least, covers all the services of that Church, including the celebration of the sacraments: *Matthews v King* [1934] 1 KB 505, DC. Assuming it is legally valid, the question whether the celebrant complied with the ceremonial law of the Church of England is irrelevant: ibid.
5   See paras **3.69–3.70**.

First part of s 2

9.31 In terms of an offence under the first part of s 2 of the 1860 Act, which requires riotous, violent or indecent behaviour, 'riotous' is construed in accordance with s 1 of the Public Order Act 1986.[1] This means that the term is redundant because proof of riot requires, inter alia, that one person uses unlawful violence and that a minimum of 11 others use or threaten unlawful violence. It would be surprising if a prosecutor focussed on an allegation of riotous behaviour when the alternative of violent or indecent behaviour by the accused alone suffices.

'Violent behaviour' in s 2 is not defined, unlike 'violence' in Part I of the Public Order Act 1986. The fact that 'riotous' and, as we shall see, 'indecent' bear legal meanings suggests that the meaning of 'violent' *here* is a question of law, although whether conduct satisfies that meaning is a question of fact. It is submitted that it refers to the use of force against person or property; that force must, of course, be unlawful (ie not legally justified) because the normal private and public defences of self-defence, prevention of crime and so on are applicable to any offence under s 2. On the other hand, like the other behaviour referred to in s 2, it cannot be justified by a claim of right.[2]

'Indecent behaviour' in s 2 does not refer to anything in the nature of tending to corrupt or deprave; it is used without any sexual connotation. This was stated by

Lord Parker CJ in *Abrahams v Cavey*,[3] with whose judgment Diplock LJ and Widgery J agreed. Lord Parker also stated that: 'it ["indecent"] is used in the context of riotous, violent or indecent behaviour, to put it quite generally, within the genus of creating a disturbance in a sacred place'.[3] As a result the Divisional Court upheld the conviction of a number of people who had interrupted a church service, attended by the then Prime Minister, during the Labour Party conference. One of them had shouted: 'Oh you hypocrites, how can you use the word God to justify your policies?' Later there were other interruptions by other accused, two of whom addressed the congregation from their pews and prevented the Prime Minister reading the second lesson. Whether or not conduct is indecent under the above test has to be judged in the context of where it occurred; something which might not constitute a disturbance if said or done in the street may be a disturbance if done during a church service, for example.[4]

---

1   See para **3.39**.
2   *Vallancey v Fletcher* [1897] 1 QB 265, DC.
3   [1967] 3 All ER 179 at 182.
4   *Worth v Terrington* (1845) M&W 781. Also see *R v Farrant* [1973] Crim LR 240, in which the Crown Court upheld a magistrates' court conviction for indecent behaviour in a churchyard where the accused and an assistant had engaged, fully dressed and with no sexual connotation, in a black magic ceremony in a churchyard.

9.32 The disturbance must occur in any church or chapel of the Church of England, or in any chapel of any religious denomination, or in any place of religious worship certified under the Places of Worship Registration Act 1855, or in any churchyard, or burial-ground. It is irrelevant when the disturbance occurs; it can occur whether or not a service is taking place. There is no reason why anyone else should be present besides the accused.

A place of worship certified under the 1855 Act may include a meeting place for Protestant Dissenters or other Protestants, a meeting place for persons of the Roman Catholic denomination or Jewish religion, and any place of meeting for religious worship of any other body or denomination, eg the Muslim and Sikh religions; such places must be certified under the 1855 Act.

The reference to a 'burial-ground' is not in terms restricted in any way; it would be open to a court to hold that the term extends to a municipal cemetery. 'Churchyard' reflects the essentially Christian society of the mid-nineteenth century. Presumably a yard attached to a Mosque or Hindu temple is a 'churchyard' for the purposes of s 2.

Second part of s 2

9.33 The second part of s 2 of the 1860 Act makes it an offence to molest, let, disturb, vex or trouble, or by any other unlawful means disquiet or misuse any preacher authorised to preach in a church, chapel or a certified place of religious worship, or any clergyman in Holy Orders ministering or celebrating any sacrament anywhere[1] or any divine service, rite or office in any cathedral, church or chapel, churchyard, or burial-ground.

The first half of these provisions is concerned with unlawfully molesting, disturbing or the like any preacher (presumably whether ordained or not) authorised to preach in one of the places to which an offence described in the previous paragraphs applies while he or she can be said to be a 'preacher'. This certainly seems to cover the time while he or she is actually preaching or is en route to or from the pulpit or the like. Whether the term extends over a longer period, for example during a service at which someone is going to or has preached is uncertain. The mischief of this provision seems to be interfering with preaching, in which case a narrow interpretation along the lines just indicated seems preferable. After all if violent or indecent behaviour occurs, there will be an offence under the first part of s 2; indeed, the definition of 'indecent behaviour' seems to render redundant the present provision.

The same is true of the latter half of the second part of s 2. This is limited to molesting, disturbing etc a clergyman in Holy Orders (ie an episcopally ordained priest)[2] ministering or celebrating a sacrament, service or rite or office.[3]

1   *Matthews v King* [1934] 1 KB 505, DC. Thus, whilst it is an offence unlawfully to molest etc any clergyman in holy orders performing a sacrament, eg of communion, in a playing field or at an open air camp, unlawfully molesting him while he is conducting a service, rite or office of some other kind is only an offence if it occurs in a church, chapel, churchyard or burial-ground.

2   *Glasgow College of Art v A-G* (1848) 1 HL Cas 800 at 823, per Lord Cottenham, LC; *Bishop of St Albans v Fillingham* [1906] P 163.

3   These words do not apply to a clergyman in Holy Orders who is taking the collection during a divine service: *Cope v Barber* (1872) LR 7 CP 393, DC.

Trial, punishment and arrest

9.34 An offence contrary to s 2 of the 1860 Act is triable only summarily.[1] The maximum punishment is two months' imprisonment *or* a fine not exceeding level 1 on the standard scale.[1] The only statutory power of arrest available to a police officer is the conditional power of arrest under s 25 of PACE. By s 3 of the 1860 Act, a churchwarden (presumably only in the Church of England)[2] may arrest a person who has committed an offence under s 2 'immediately and forthwith' afterwards. In addition to these statutory powers, the common law power to arrest for a breach of the peace may be available.[3]

1   Ecclesiastical Courts Jurisdiction Act 1860, s 2.

2   Churchwardens have special legal powers and duties under the Canon Law which applies to the established church, eg the duty to prevent behaviour of the type referred to in s 2 in a church during divine service: see Revised Canons Ecclesiastical G 13.

3   See paras **2.7–2.10**.

Related offences

9.35 The offence under s 2 of the 1860 Act overlaps with a number of other offences.

–   Section 36 of the Offences Against the Person Act 1861 makes it an either-way offence[1] to obstruct or prevent by threats or force a clergyman or other minister in or from celebrating divine service[2] or otherwise officiating in a place of divine worship, or in or from undertaking a burial service, or to assault a clergyman engaged in any of the above activities. The maximum term of imprisonment on conviction on indictment is two years.

–   Section 7 of the Burial Laws Amendment Act 1880 penalises as an indictable only offence, maximum imprisonment two years,[3] the same sort of behaviour as specified under s 2 of the 1860 Act at any burial under the Act (ie any burial without Church of England rites).

–   Section 59 of the Cemeteries Clauses Act 1847 makes it a summary offence for a person to play any game or sport, or discharge firearms (except at a military funeral) in a cemetery to which the Act applies (ie any cemetery authorised by an Act of Parliament incorporating the Cemeteries Clauses Act 1847), or who shall wilfully and unlawfully disturb any persons assembled in such a cemetery for the purpose of burying a body there, or who shall commit any nuisance in the cemetery. This offence is not an imprisonable one; the maximum fine is one not exceeding level 1 on the standard scale. The Cemeteries Clauses Act 1847 is now in operation only in relation to a few cemetery companies.

–   Articles 18 and 19 of the Local Authorities Cemeteries Order 1977[4] prohibit nuisances or wilful disturbances in a cemetery, or wilful interference with any burials there, or with any grave or other memorial and flowers thereon, and games and sports in a cemetery. Contravention of these provisions is a summary offence, punishable with a fine not exceeding level 1 on the standard scale.

---

1   Magistrates' Courts Act 1980, s 17(1) and Sch 1.
2   As to the meaning of divine service, see *Matthews v King* [1934] 1 KB 505, DC; para **9.30** fn 4.
3   See *Archbold* (2000), para 27.7.
4   SI 1977/204; made under the Local Government Act 1972, s 214. 'Cemetery' includes any burial-ground or other place set aside for the internment of the dead, including any part of such a place *set aside for the internment of ashes*. The general exclusion of crematoria from the provisions discussed in this part may be noted. The reason seems to be historic.

Reform

9.36   There are obvious overlaps between the various offences mentioned in this part, as well as with the offences under ss 4, 4A and 5 of the Public Order Act 1986. In 1985, the Law Commission concluded that the first part of s 2 of the 1860 Act should be retained in a modernised form, but that it was undesirable that the 'clutter' of other offences mentioned above should be retained 'particularly because they are never used'.[1] In 1998, a Home Office Consultation Paper, *Reforming the Offences Against the Person Act 1861*, endorsing another Law Commission report,[2] proposed the repeal of s 36 of the 1861 Act.

Despite its archaic language, s 2 can be supported as protecting the expression of religious belief and places of worship on the ground that they are attended by particular sensitivities, albeit that it provides special protection to the episcopally ordained clergymen of the Christian religion. On the other hand, in an increasingly secular society this argument is open to doubt when the offending conduct simply constitutes a disturbance. Moreover, where the offending conduct is a manifestation of the freedom of expression guaranteed by Art 8 of the ECHR, interference by the State with that freedom via arrest, prosecution and punishment for an offence under s 2 will have to be justified as necessary in a democratic society for the relevant legitimate aims, the prevention of disorder or the protection of the rights of others. Unless there was a clear risk of violence by the persons committing the offending conduct or that it would reasonably provoke the object of it, it might be difficult to establish that the interference was proportionate to the legitimate aim.

---

1   *Criminal Law: Offences Against Religion and Public Worship* Law Com no 145 (1985).
2   *Criminal Law: Offences Against the Person and General Defences* Law Com no 218 (1993).

LABOUR RELATIONS: INTIMIDATION

9.37 Section 241(1) of the Trade Union and Labour Relations (Consolidation) Act 1992 provides:

> 'A person commits [a summary] offence who, with a view to compelling another person to abstain from doing or to do any act which that person has a legal right to do or abstain from doing, wrongfully and without legal authority –
>
> (a)   uses violence to or intimidates that person or his wife or children, or injures his property,
> (b)   persistently follows that person about from place to place,
> (c)   hides any tools, clothes or other property owned or used by that person, or deprives him of or hinders him in the use thereof,
> (d)   watches or besets the house or other place where that person resides, works, carries on business or happens to be, or the approach to any such house or place, or
> (e)   follows that person with two or more other persons in a disorderly manner in or through any street or road.'

Section 241(1) is not directly concerned with picketing. Indeed, despite the title of the Act in which it appears, it is not confined to the context of trade disputes,[1] although that is its normal application. Section 241(1) deals with a range of acts which amount to attempts to prevent a person from exercising his own freedom of choice as to whether or not he does or does not do something he is entitled not to do or to do.

Section 241 of the 1992 Act re-enacted s 7 of the Conspiracy and Protection of Property Act 1875, whose provisions seemed to have fallen into disuse until the miners' strike of 1984–85 during which 643 charges were preferred under it, mostly for 'watching and besetting'.[2] It is unfortunate that the opportunity was not taken in 1992 to amend the archaic wording of the provision. There must be doubts about the need for s 241 in the light of the offences in ss 4, 4A and 5 of the Public Order Act 1986 in particular.

---

1   For examples of the application of s 241 in other contexts, see *DPP v Fidler* [1992] 1 WLR 91, DC (para **9.45**); *DPP v Todd* [1996] Crim LR 344, DC, where it was held that the offence could apply to an anti-motorway construction protester who took up a position in a dismantled crane preventing workmen from progressing with the construction.
2   Wallington 'Policing the miners' strike' (1985) 14 ILJ 145 at 150–151.

Prohibited conduct

9.38 An offence under s 241 of the 1992 Act may be committed by any of the following range of conduct done with a view to compelling another person (hereafter 'that person') to abstain from doing something which he is legally entitled to do, and vice versa. In the absence of a provision to the contrary, it is submitted that the wide disparity in the conduct specified means that, for the purposes of the rule against duplicity, s 241 sets out five separate offences, despite the fact that s 7 of the 1875 Act was held in Scotland and Ireland to create only one offence for this purpose.[1]

---

1   *Clarkson v Stewart* (1894) 32 SLR 4, Ct of Session; *Wilson v Renton* (1909) 47 SLR 209, High Ct of Justiciary; *Hardy v O'Flynn* [1948] IR 343.

Using violence to or intimidating the other person or his wife or children, or injuring his property

9.39 The social structure pre-supposed by the reference to 'that person, his wife or children' is an example of the archaic nature of the contents of s 241. The use of violence[1] to a person or injury to property will invariably involve the commission of another offence. In *R v Jones*,[2] the Court of Appeal, although not wishing to define 'intimidation' in the predecessor to s 241 exclusively, stated that it 'includes putting persons in fear by the exhibition of force or violence or the threat of force or violence; and there is no limitation restricting the meaning to cases of violence or threats of violence to the person'. Thus, a threat to injure property can suffice. On the other hand, it has been held that 'abuse, swearing and shouting' does not itself amount to a threat of violence for the purposes of the tort of intimidation,[3] which is not surprising. There is also authority of some ambiguity that it is not intimidation for present purposes to threaten to deprive a worker of his livelihood,[4] or to 'black' an employer's business.[5]

It is a moot point whether a threat to break a contract with the other person can amount to intimidation for the purpose of s 241. In *Rookes v Barnard*,[6] the House of Lords held that such a threat can suffice for the tort of intimidation. If it could suffice for 'intimidation' in s 241, the present type of offence would be considerably extended and it would put into doubt the cases referred to at the end of the previous paragraph. It is submitted that the application of the criminal law in such cases would be unjustified in the absence of a clear indication in s 241.

It is also a moot point whether the intimidation must succeed in putting a person in fear or whether it is enough that it is likely to do so.[7]

There can be no doubt that intimidation can be by a threat (of the appropriate type) implicit in conduct. For example, participation in a mass picket may amount to intimidation because of the 'terror that [the] very numbers convey'.[8]

So far it has been assumed that the meaning of 'intimidation' in s 241 is a question of law. It is arguable that, as an everyday word of the English language, it is a question of fact for the court whether the accused's conduct was 'intimidating' in the ordinary sense of that term. We have seen the adoption of this approach in respect of other terms, such as 'threatening, abusive or insulting', in public order offences.[9] There is support for such an approach in the present context. Speaking in relation to the predecessor to s 241, the Divisional Court stated in *Gibson v Lawson*,[10] 'Intimidate is not, as has often been said by judges of authority, a term of art – it is a word of common speech and everyday use; and it must receive, therefore, a reasonable and sensible interpretation according to the circumstances of the case as they arise from time to time'.

---

1   See para **3.15**.
2   (1974) 59 Cr App R 120 at 125.

3   *News Group Newspapers Ltd v Society of Graphical and Allied Trades '82 (No 2)* [1987] ICR 181 at 204.

4   *Gibson v Lawson* [1891] 2 QB 545, DC.

5   *Wood v Bowron* (1867) LR 2 QB 21; *Curran v Treleavan* [1891] 2 QB 560. Compare *Judge v Bennett* (1887) 52 JP 247 (employer informed in terms strong enough to make him fear his shop would be picketed: held intimidation).

6   [1964] 1 All ER 367, HL.

7   The only authority on the point is persuasive. In *R v McCarthy* [1903] 2 IR 146 it was held that there must be evidence that the victim was actually put in fear. On the other hand, in *Agnew v Munrow* (1891) 28 Sc LR 335 the suggested test was whether the accused's act would induce 'serious apprehension of violence in the mind of a man of ordinary courage'.

8   *R v Bonsall* [1985] Crim LR 550, Crown Ct. Also see *Thomas v National Union of Mineworkers (South Wales Area)* [1985] 2 All ER 1 at 30, per Scott J.

9   See para **4.5**.

10   [1891] 2 QB 545 at 559. Also see *R v Baker* (1911) 7 Cr App R 89, CCA.

Persistently following the other person from place to place

9.40 This type of offence does not require any violence or threat of violence, nor is disorderly conduct required.[1] The mere act of following is enough, provided it is persistent and from place to place. In *Smith v Thomasson*,[2] Hawkins J said that it was impossible to define generally what was meant by 'persistently follows'. In that case, the requirement was held to be satisfied where the accused followed a worker who had emerged from a factory being picketed by the accused through three streets; the accused had not tried to speak to the worker and had on one occasion overtaken him. Thus, doggedly following a worker's footsteps can amount to 'persistently following' him. The following need not be on foot; it can be by one car following another car, for example.

1   *Kennedy v Cowie* [1891] 1 QB 771, DC.

2   (1891) 16 Cox CC 740, DC. Also see the Irish case *R v Wall* (1907) 21 Cox CC 401.

Hiding any tools, clothes or other property owned or used by the other person or depriving him or hindering him in the use thereof

9.41 In *Fowler v Kibble*,[1] a civil case, the Court of Appeal held that, because the activity (like any other activity under what is now s 241) must be wrongful independently of s 241, there could be no breach of s 241 where a worker, acting on instructions of officials of a miners' union, did not let miners who were not members of the union have safety lamps, because such deprivation was not wrongful.

1   [1922] 1 Ch 487, CA.

Watching or besetting the house or other place where the other person resides, works or carries on business or happens to be, or the approach to any such house or place

9.42 There is persuasive authority that the meaning of 'watching' is a question of fact.[1] This can be supported by reference to *Brutus v Cozens*[2] on the ground that the word is an ordinary word of the English language and the context does not show that it is being used in an unusual sense. The same cannot, however, be said of 'besetting', an archaic term (and therefore not an ordinary word of the English language) defined by the *Shorter Oxford English Dictionary* as meaning 'surround with hostile intent, besiege, assail on all sides; occupy and make impassable (a gate, road, etc); close round, hem in'. While the present provision has traditionally been applied to those standing outside the place concerned, its application in *Galt (Procurator Fiscal) v Philp*[3] to strikers who barricaded and locked themselves inside their workplace, thereby preventing entry by would-be workers, is consistent with the dictionary definition of 'beset'.

It has been held that the watching or besetting need not be for more than a short time.[4] There is no warrant for a direction to a jury in an Irish case involving the predecessor to s 241 that 'Watching means persistent watching'.[5]

In practice, 'watching or besetting' is usually only charged in respect of watching or besetting private residences.[6]

---

1   *A-G v O'Brien* (1936) 70 *Irish Times Law Reports* 101.
2   [1972] 2 All ER 1297, HL. See para **4.5**.
3   [1984] IRLR 156, High Court of Justiciary.
4   *Charnock v Court* [1899] 2 Ch 35, High Ct.
5   *R v Wall* (1907) 21 Cox CC 401 at 403, per Palles CB.
6   Thornton *Public Order Law* (1987) p 56.

Following the other person with two or more persons in a disorderly manner through a street or road

9.43 This provision differs from that referred to in para **9.40** in that no persistence is required and that, on the other hand, the accused's following must be with two or more others, must be in a disorderly manner and must be in a street or road. Whether the following is in a disorderly manner is a question of fact, depending on the conduct of the accused and all the circumstances of the case.[1] In *Elsey v Smith (Procurator Fiscal)*,[2] the High Court of Justiciary held that there was enough evidence to entitle the sheriff-substitute to find that a following was disorderly where strikers had followed a fellow worker in a car in a way which appeared to have given rise to an altercation.

---

1   *R v McKenzie* [1892] 2 QB 519, DC.
2   [1983] IRLR 292, High Court of Justiciary.

General requirement: 'wrongfully'

9.44 Each of the types of conduct described above must be done wrongfully and without legal authority. The latter would seem to be a defence and is dealt with in para **9.46**.

The requirement that the accused's conduct must be wrongful has received little judicial attention. It is now clear that it means that it must be unlawful, ie tortious, independently of s 241 of the 1992 Act, and that it is not enough that the conduct has no legally accepted justification. This was the view of the Court of Appeal in *Ward Lock and Co Ltd v The Operative Printers' Society*,[1] which was followed by the Court of Appeal in *Fowler v Kibble*.[2] In a more recent decision, *Thomas v National Union of Mineworkers (South Wales Area)*,[3] Scott J decided that these authorities established that, to be an offence under s 241, conduct had to be tortious. Examples of torts which may be relevant in this area are those of public nuisance, intimidation, trespass to land, assault and battery. Scott J referred to *J Lyons & Co Ltd v Wilkins*,[4] decided before *Ward Lock*, where both at the interlocutory stage and at the trial stage the Court of Appeal had been of the view that it was enough that conduct of the type specified by s 241 had no legal justification. Scott J stated that he would had have considerable difficulty in understanding and applying the principles expressed in that case had it not been for the guidance provided by the two Court of Appeal cases referred to above, which represented the law. Clearly, he thought that *J Lyons & Co Ltd* was wrong on the present point.

It is unusual for criminal liability to depend on proof that the conduct in question is tortious.[5] Strangely, however, it seems that conduct in contemplation of or in furtherance of a trade dispute that would otherwise involve tortious liability but which is immune from liability by virtue of the statutory immunities in s 219 of the 1992 Act nevertheless remains wrongful for the purposes of s 241.[6]

---

1   (1906) 22 TLR 327, CA.
2   [1922] 1 Ch 487, CA.
3   [1985] 2 All ER 1.
4   [1896] 1 Ch 811, CA; [1899] 1 Ch 255, CA.
5   For a discussion of the point discussed above, see the contrasting views of Carty 'The legality of peaceful picketing on the highway' [1984] PL 600 and Bennion 'Mass picketing and the 1875 Act' [1985] Crim LR 64.
6   *Galt (Procurator Fiscal) v Philp* [1984] IRLR 156, High Court of Justiciary.

Mental element

9.45 Section 241(1) of the 1992 Act requires that the accused must have acted with a view to *compelling* someone to abstain from doing something which he had a right to do, or to do something which he has a right to abstain from doing. A person acts with a view to achieving something when it is his purpose or aim to achieve it.[1] Purpose must be distinguished from motive, ie the reason why someone acts.[2] If a person acts in one of the specified ways with the aim of compelling workers to abstain from working, for example, it is irrelevant that his motive is to secure the improvement of working conditions.[3]

It is insufficient to act simply with the purpose of persuading someone to abstain from doing something he has a right to do, and vice versa.[4] In *DPP v Fidler*,[5] two separate groups, one in favour of abortion and the other opposed to it, were stationed outside an abortion clinic. The accused were in the latter group. They confronted women using the clinic with verbal abuse and reproach and with photographs and models showing the physical consequences of abortion. The accused were charged with watching and besetting, contrary to what is now s 241. The Divisional Court held that on the above facts the accused were not guilty. Although their intention was to prevent abortions being carried out at the clinic, they had acted with a view to persuading women not to have abortions there rather than with the necessary view to compelling the relevant person to cease performing lawful abortions at the clinic. It held that in the absence of evidence 'that anyone was either prevented, or likely to be prevented, or intended to be prevented from undergoing an abortion in the strict sense of being unable to do so', the purpose of the accused did not amount to compulsion.[6]

For the avoidance of doubt, it should be noted that the intended compulsion need not succeed.[7]

---

1   *J Lyons & Co Ltd v Wilkins* [1899] 1 Ch 255 at 270, per Chitty LJ.

2   Ibid; *DPP v Fidler* [1992] 1 WLR 91, DC.
3   *Allied Amusements v Reaney* (1936) 3 WWR 129.
4   *DPP v Fidler*, above. See also *R v McKenzie* [1892] 2 QB 519, DC; *R v Bonsall* [1985] Crim LR
       150, Crown Ct.
5   [1992] 1 WLR 91, DC.
6   The Divisional Court, however, held that the accused had a case to answer in respect of
       charges of threatening, insulting or abusive words or behaviour, contrary to the Public Order
       Act 1986, s 5, and remitted the case to the justices in this respect.
7   *Agnew v Munro* (1891) 18 R (J) 22, High Ct of Justiciary.

Without legal authority

9.46 It is submitted that this is a defence so that it needs to be considered by the magistrates only if there is evidence which raises it as an issue, as is the case where the phrase appears in the definition of other offences.

The onus of proving the defence is not expressly placed on the accused. It is submitted that, notwithstanding s 101 of the Magistrates' Courts Act 1980, which places the burden on the accused at a summary trial to prove any 'exception, exemption, proviso, excuse or qualification', 'without legal authority' is an essential element in the definition of the various offences and the accused does not have the burden of proving legal authority. Instead, once the issue of legal authority has been raised the accused must be acquitted unless the prosecution disproves legal authority beyond reasonable doubt. This accords with the approach taken to similar phrases in other offences where the burden of proof has not been placed expressly on the accused.[1]

1   See, for example, para **9.79**. Such an approach would also be compatible with the
       presumption of innocence in the ECHR, Art 6(2); see para **4.38**.

9.47 'Legal authority' is not expressly defined by the statute. What is said in para **8.21** about '*lawful* authority' no doubt provides some general guidance about '*legal* authority'. More specifically and practically the phrase refers particularly (but not only) to s 220 of the 1992 Act. This provides:

'(1) It is lawful for a person in contemplation or furtherance of a trade dispute[1] to attend –

(a)   at or near his own place of work,[2] or
(b)   if he is an official of a trade union, at or near the place of work of a member of the union whom he is accompanying and whom he represents,

for the purpose only of peacefully obtaining or communicating information, or peacefully persuading any person to work or abstain from working.

(2) If a person works or normally works –

(a)   otherwise than at any one place, or
(b)   at a place the location of which is such that attendance there for a purpose mentioned in subsection (1) is impracticable,

his place of work for the purposes of that subsection shall be any premises of his employer from which he works or from which his work is administered.

(3) In the case of a worker not in employment where –

(a) his last employment was terminated in connection with a trade dispute, or

(b) the termination of his employment was one of the circumstances giving rise to a trade dispute,

in relation to that dispute his former place of work shall be treated for the purposes of subsection (1) as being his place of work.

(4) A person who is an official of a trade union by virtue only of having been elected or appointed to be a representative of some of the members of the union shall be regarded for the purposes of subsection (1) as representing only those members; but otherwise an official of a union shall be regarded for those purposes as representing all its members.'

The effect of s 220 is to confer an immunity from criminal liability in respect of offences under s 241 or from tortious liability in respect of a person's attendance in contemplation or furtherance of a trade dispute provided its terms are satisfied. The exemption does not apply to other offences. Thus, for example, it does not apply to the offence of obstructing the highway, contrary to s 137 of the Highways Act 1980, by pickets who seek peacefully to persuade.[3]

Section 220 has been described as providing 'a narrow but nevertheless real immunity'.[4] It is narrow because, in respect of criminal liability under s 241 or of tortious liability, it does not render lawful the activities in general of pickets, but only their attendance in the specified place for the specified purposes of peacefully obtaining or communicating information or peacefully persuading any person to work or abstain from working. It does not render lawful, for example, attendance outside a worker's home for such a purpose or congregating in such large numbers as to show (or to show in some other way) a purpose physically to prevent people getting into their workplace to work.[5] The immunity is also narrow by virtue of its limitation to trade disputes. It does not apply, for example, to animal rights protesters picketing a laboratory.

The Code of Practice on Picketing brought into effect under s 204 of the 1992 Act by the Employment Code of Practice (Picketing) Order 1992,[6] states, inter alia, that 'pickets and their organisers should ensure that in general the number of pickets does not exceed six at any entrance to or exit from a workplace; frequently a smaller number will be appropriate'. Failure to observe a provision of the Code does not give rise to legal liability.[7] On the other hand, the Code is admissible in court proceedings and can be taken into account by the court in determining a question to which it is relevant.[8]

---

1   'Trade dispute' is defined by the 1992 Act, s 244. The test as to whether there is a 'trade dispute' is an objective one: *British Broadcasting Corporation v Hearn* [1978] 1 All ER 111, CA; *NWL Ltd v Woods* [1979] 3 All ER 614, HL. In order for a person to act 'in contemplation or furtherance' of a trade dispute, that dispute must be imminent, so that the action is done in expectation of and with a view to it, or the dispute must be already existing, so that the act is done in support of one side to it: *Conway v Wade* [1909] AC 506 at 512, per Lord Loreburn LC; *Bent's Brewery Co v Hogan* [1945] 2 All ER 570; but cf *Health Computing v Meek* [1980] IRLR 437. If there is a trade dispute, the question of whether a person acts 'in contemplation or furtherance' of it is a subjective one, ie does the person have a genuine belief that his actions will further the interests of one party to the dispute? See *Express Newspapers Ltd v McShane* [1980] 1 All ER 65, HL; *Duport Steels v Sirs* [1980] 1 All ER 529, HL. The fact that a person's actions, considered objectively, are not reasonably capable of furthering the dispute is relevant only insofar as it casts doubt on the genuineness of that person's alleged subjective belief: ibid.

2   See 1992 Act, s 246; *Rayware Ltd v Transport and General Workers Union* [1989] 3 All ER 583, CA.

3   *Tynan v Balmer* [1966] 2 All ER 133, DC; *Broome v DPP* [1974] 1 All ER 314, HL.
4   *Broome v DPP* [1974] 1 All ER 314 at 325, per Lord Salmon.
5   *Young v Peck* (1912) 29 TLR 31; *R v Bonsall* [1985] Crim LR 150, Crown Ct.
6   SI 1992/476.
7   1992 Act, s 207(1).
8   Ibid, s 207(3).

Trial, punishment and arrest

9.48 An offence under s 241(1) of the 1992 Act is triable summarily only and punishable with imprisonment for a maximum of six months or a fine not exceeding level 5 on the standard scale, or both.[1]

1   1992 Act, s 241(2).

9.49 An offence under s 241(1) is not an arrestable offence, but a constable may arrest without warrant anyone whom he reasonably suspects to be committing such an offence.[1]

1   1992 Act, s 241(3). As to 'reasonably suspects', see para **3.68** fn 1.

ASSAULTING, WILFULLY OBSTRUCTING OR RESISTING A CONSTABLE IN THE EXECUTION OF HIS DUTY

9.50 Section 89 of the Police Act 1996, which re-enacted earlier identical offences, provides:

'(1) Any person who assaults a constable[1] in the execution of his duty, or a person assisting a constable in the execution of his duty, shall be guilty of an offence and liable on summary conviction to imprisonment for a term not exceeding six months or to a fine not exceeding level 5 on the standard scale, or to both.

(2) Any person who resists or wilfully obstructs a constable[1] in the execution of his duty, or a person assisting a constable in the execution of his duty, shall be guilty of an offence and liable on summary conviction to imprisonment for a term not exceeding one month or to a fine not exceeding level 3 on the standard scale, or to both.'[2]

In the absence of a provision to the contrary or any authority on the point, it is submitted that, for the purposes of the rule against duplicity,[3] there are two offences under s 89(2): one requiring resistance, and the other wilful obstruction.

Like the offences of obstructing the highway, public nuisance and some of the other offences in this chapter, offences under s 89 apply to a wide range of activities, many of which do not involve issues of public order. The explanation which follows concentrates on those aspects of the offences liable to be relevant in the context of public order.

1   The constable does not have to be in uniform. A constable is anyone holding the office of constable, whatever his rank in a particular police force: *Lewis v Cattle* [1938] 2 KB 454 at 457.

'Constable' includes special constables. Unlike other constables who are members of a police force established by a police authority (who can exercise their powers throughout England and Wales and the adjacent United Kingdom waters), a special constable can only exercise his powers in the police area for which he is appointed, and any adjacent United Kingdom waters, and any police area contiguous to his own: Police Act 1996, s 30(1)–(3).

'Constable' also includes those who hold office as police officers under police forces established for specific purposes. See, eg, British Transport police (British Transport Commission Act 1949, s 53; Railways Act 1993, s 132), Civil Aviation police (Civil Aviation Act 1982, s 57), and Ministry of Defence police (Ministry of Defence Police Act 1987, s 1).

2   By the Police Act 1996, s 89(3), s 89(1) and (2) are extended to a constable who is a member of the Royal Ulster Constabulary or a Scots police force when he is executing a warrant, or otherwise acting in England or Wales, under a statutory power to do so in England and Wales.

3   See paras **3.69–3.70**.

In the execution of his duty[1]

9.51   The key point about these offences is that the constable must be acting in the execution of his duty when the prohibited conduct occurs. A magistrates' court cannot convict an accused of one of these offences if it is not proved that the constable was acting in the execution of his duty at the material time.[2]

---

1   Lidstone 'A policeman's duty not to take liberties' [1976] Crim LR 617; Ross 'Two cases on obstructing a constable' [1977] Crim LR 187–192.
2   *Chapman v DPP* (1989) 89 Cr App R 190, DC; *Riley v DPP* (1989) 91 Cr App R 14, DC; *Kerr v DPP* [1995] Crim LR 394, DC.

9.52   Proof that the constable was on duty at the material time is not in itself sufficient to prove that he was acting in the execution of his duty.[1] On the other hand, to be acting in the execution of his duty, a constable need not be doing something which he is compelled by law to do (in the sense that he will commit an offence or a tort or a breach of a requirement of the police discipline regulations, eg disobedience to a lawful order, if he does not). This was held by the Divisional Court in *Coffin v Smith*,[2] where the court disapproved two cases, *R v Prebble*[3] and *R v Roxburgh*,[4] which suggested the contrary. In *Coffin v Smith*, constables who had been summoned to a boys' club whose leader was ejecting some troublemakers, in order to ensure that they left, were assaulted. It was held that the constables were at the club in the fulfilment of their duty to keep the peace and were clearly acting in the execution of their duty. *Prebble* would seem in any event to be distinguishable.[5] There, a constable, who at the landlord's request, had turned some people out of a public house, was held not to have been acting in the execution of his duty. The court found that there was no nuisance or danger of breach of the peace, and the constable was merely assisting the landlord in enforcing a private right, which does not appear to be part of a constable's general duties.

---

1   Indeed, it may not even be necessary because the duties imposed on a constable arise by virtue of his office and the powers of a constable are exercisable by virtue of his status as such. It is, therefore, arguable that an 'off-duty' constable can act in the execution of his duty if the requirements set out below are satisfied. See Freeland 'Can an off-duty constable be assaulted in the execution of his duty?' (1999) 163 JPN 170.
2   (1980) 71 Cr App R 221, DC.
3   (1858) 1 F&F 325.
4   (1871) 12 Cox CC 8.
5   For support for this distinction, see Smith and Hogan *Criminal Law* (1999) p 416.

9.53 To be acting in the execution of his duty a constable's conduct must fall within the general scope of a duty imposed on him by law by virtue of his office, and he must not be acting unlawfully at the time.

The following statement by the Court of Criminal Appeal in *R v Waterfield*,[1] which was applied in *Coffin v Smith*, is regarded as a classic one on the point:

> 'In most cases it is probably more convenient to consider what the police constable was actually doing and in particular whether such conduct was prima facie an unlawful interference with a person's liberty or property. If so, it is then relevant to consider whether (a) such conduct falls within the general scope of any duty imposed by statute or recognised at common law and (b) whether such conduct, albeit within the general scope of such a duty, involved an unjustifiable use of powers associated with that duty.'

---

1   [1963] 3 All ER 659 at 661.

9.54 The duties of a constable are derived from the common law and from statute. There is no exhaustive list of the common law duties of a constable, but they include duties to take all steps which appear to the constable necessary to protect life and limb and property, to keep the peace, to prevent crime, to detect crime and to bring an offender to justice.[1] As can be seen, these common law duties are widely drawn. A constable directing traffic on a road for reasons of safety (the normal reason for directing traffic) is acting within his general duty to protect persons and property.[2]

The fact that the judges have been reluctant to reduce within specific limits the general terms in which the common law duties of a constable have been expressed[3] does not aid the exposition or application of the law. It also makes it easier for the courts to extend police powers.

---

1   *R v Waterfield* [1963] 3 All ER 659, CCA; *Rice v Connolly* [1966] 2 All ER 649 at 651; *Ludlow v Burgess* [1971] Crim LR 238, DC; *Pedro v Diss* [1981] 2 All ER 59, DC; *Coffin v Smith* (1980) 71 Cr App R 221, CA.
2   *Johnson v Phillips* [1975] 3 All ER 682, DC. Compare *Hoffman v Thomas* [1974] 2 All ER 233, DC (constable directing driver to participate in traffic survey not acting in execution of common law duty, but see para **9.55**).
3   See, for example, the statement of the Court of Criminal Appeal in *Waterfield* above at 661.

9.55 It is possible for a statute to give constables powers whose exercise cannot be related to one of the general common law duties. It may be that a constable exercising such a power is acting in the execution of his duty, and an assault on, obstruction of or resistance to, him when so acting can be an offence under s 89. However, where, as is commonly the case, the statute provides a special offence of failing to comply with an exercise of the power (eg to request something) the present offences, and a fortiori that of wilful obstruction, may be impliedly excluded by the words of the statute. An example of the problems which can arise can be seen by reference to s 35 of the Road Traffic Act 1988, sub-s (1) of which makes it an offence, where a constable is engaged in the regulation of road traffic, for a driver to fail to comply with a direction given 'by the constable in the execution of his duty', while sub-s (2) provides that, where a traffic survey is being carried out, and a constable gives a direction to a driver for the purposes of the survey, the driver is guilty of a separate offence if he fails to comply with the direction. The separate provision in s 35(2) and the use of 'in the execution of his duty' in s 35(1) but not in s 35(2) strongly suggests that a constable acting under s 35(2) is not acting 'in the execution of his duty' for the purposes of offences under s 89 of the Police Act 1996.

9.56 The test as to whether a constable is acting lawfully is objective, with the result that the legality of his conduct is judged on the facts as they actually were and not on the facts as the constable mistakenly believed them to be.[1] Thus, a constable may be acting outside the execution of his duty even though he is acting in good faith. In *Kerr v DPP*,[2] for example, a constable who restrained the accused, mistakenly believing that the accused had been arrested by a colleague, was held not to have been acting in the execution of his duty (because he was exceeding his powers, although he would not have been if the facts had been as he believed them to be).

---

1   *Kerr v DPP* (1994) 158 JP 1048, DC.
2   (1994) 158 JP 1048, DC.

9.57 Usually, but not necessarily, whether or not a constable's conduct within one of his common law duties is lawful depends on whether or not he has a power to act as he does and whether or not he has made a justifiable use of that power. Most police powers are now statutory, but there do remain the common law powers concerning breaches of the peace, described in Chapter 2, which are frequently the basis on which a constable is acting in the execution of his duty in prosecutions under s 89, and the courts can also recognise other common law powers. An example is provided by *Johnson v Phillips*,[1] where the Divisional Court held that a constable has power (doubtless based on principles of necessity) to direct drivers to disobey traffic regulations if such a direction is reasonably necessary for the protection of life or property, although the power under what is now s 35(1) of the Road Traffic Act 1988 did not extend this far. As a result, a driver who refused a constable's direction to reverse up a one-way street to avoid blocking the passage of ambulances removing injured people was held rightly convicted of obstructing the constable in the execution of his duty. No doubt a court would take a similar view where, for example, a constable acting within his duty to protect life and limb ordered people to clear an area during a bomb scare, and hold that he had a power to give such a direction.

---

1   [1975] 3 All ER 682, DC.

9.58 The question of lawful action can give rise to fine distinctions. It has been held, for example, that a constable, like any other member of the public, has an implied licence to enter the front gate of private premises and knock on the door if on lawful business, and the same is true of the 'public' part of a shop or other business premises when it is open for business.[1] A constable entering premises in this way for the purpose of inquiring about an offence is acting in the execution of his duty until he has been told to leave by the occupier or someone acting with his authority and a reasonable time has been allowed for him to go:[2] if a constable remains on the premises after an implied licence has been revoked his presence is unlawful and he is not acting in the execution of his duty.

It frequently happens that a constable performing one of his duties does something to a person or his property, such as detaining him or entering his house without consent to search it, which would be unlawful unless authorised by a positive legal power. In such a case, the question arises whether he has such a power (either at common law or under a statute) and, if he has, whether he has exercised it correctly and without exceeding it; if his conduct does not fall within the proper execution of a power he is not acting in the execution of his duty.[3] For example, as a constable has no power physically to detain a person for questioning without making an arrest, he will be acting unlawfully and therefore not in the execution of his duty if he does so.[4] On the other hand, since physical contact that is generally acceptable in the ordinary conduct of everyday life is not unlawful,[5] taking hold of a person's arm or tapping him on the shoulder not in order to detain him, but to speak to him or draw something to his attention, does not take a constable outside the execution of his duty because his act is not unlawful.[6]

There is clearly a fine distinction between physical restraint by grasping someone's arm to detain him for questioning and tapping someone on the shoulder in order to attract his attention so that he can be questioned. Two cases which illustrate the fine distinction to be drawn are *Donnelly v Jackman*[7] and *Bentley v Brudzinski*.[8] In the former, a constable wished to question the accused about an offence which he had cause to believe that the accused had committed. After repeated unsuccessful requests to the accused to stop to speak to him, the constable tapped the accused on the shoulder. The accused made it plain that he had no intention of stopping to speak to the constable, who again tapped the accused on the shoulder, whereupon the accused hit him. The Divisional Court dismissed an appeal against a conviction for assaulting the constable in the execution of his duty on the ground that the magistrates were correct in regarding the tappings on the shoulder as a trivial interference with the accused's liberty that were insufficient to take him outside the execution of his duty. Commenting on this case, the Divisional Court in *Collins v Wilcock*,[9] stated:

> 'It appears that they [the Divisional Court] must have considered that the justices were entitled to conclude that the action of the officer, in persistently tapping the defendant on the shoulder, did not in the circumstances of the case exceed the bounds of acceptable conduct, despite the fact that the defendant had made it clear that he did not intend to respond to the officer's request to stop and speak to him; we cannot help feeling that this is an extreme case.'

In *Bentley v Brudzinski*, the constable having caught up with the accused, said, 'Just a minute'; then, to attract his attention, he placed his hand on the accused's shoulder. The accused then hit the constable. The Divisional Court dismissed the prosecutor's appeal against the dismissal of an information alleging an assault on the constable in the execution of his duty. It appears that the court thought that the magistrates were entitled to hold that the constable's act was done not merely to attract the accused's attention, but as part of an attempt unlawfully to detain him.

---

1   *Robson v Hallett* [1967] 2 All ER 407, DC; *McArdle v Wallace* [1967] Crim LR 467, DC.
2   *Davis v Lisle* [1936] 2 All ER 213, DC; *McArdle v Wallace*, above. Where the occupier or someone with his authority purports to revoke the licence, but refuses to cooperate with the constable so that his identity can be confirmed, the licence will not be revoked before the constable has had a reasonable time to satisfy himself as to that person's identity: *Ledger v DPP* [1991] Crim LR 439, DC. Also see *R v Thornley* (1981) 72 Cr App R 302, CA.
3   *R v Waterfield* [1963] 3 All ER 659, CCA.
4   *Kenlin v Gardiner* [1966] 3 All ER 931, DC; *Collins v Wilcock* [1984] 3 All ER 374, DC.
5   *Collins v Wilcock* above; see Card, Cross and Jones *Criminal Law* (1998) para 6.15.

6   *Donnelly v Jackman* [1970] 1 All ER 987, DC; *Collins v Wilcock*, above; *Mepstead v DPP* [1996] Crim LR 111, DC; cf *Bentley v Brudzinski* (1982) 75 Cr App R 217, DC.
7   [1970] 1 All ER 987, DC. See Evans 'Police power to stop without arrest' (1970) 33 MLR 438; Lanham 'Arrest, detention and compulsion' [1974] Crim LR 288.
8   (1982) 75 Cr App R 217, DC.
9   [1984] 3 All ER 374 at 379.

9.59 It is not enough that a constable has a relevant power in the circumstances and is exercising it; he will not act in the execution of his duty if he purports instead to exercise some other non-existent power or fails to exercise the power correctly. For example, if a constable arrests someone saying 'I am nicking you for common assault', a non-arrestable offence, when if he had thought about it he could have arrested for a breach of the peace or been satisfied that one of the general arrest conditions in PACE, s 25, was satisfied, the arrest is unlawful.[1] Likewise, an arrest without warrant in circumstances where the constable is entitled so to arrest is nevertheless unlawful if he uses unreasonable force[2] or if he fails to comply with the requirements in s 28 of PACE as to the information to be given on arrest. However, if an arrest is initially lawful but becomes unlawful because the constable does not give the arrestee his reasons as soon as is practicable, the constable will be acting in the execution of his duty up to the point of time at which the arrest becomes unlawful.[3]

1   *Edwards v DPP* (1993) 97 Cr App R 301, DC.
2   Criminal Law Act 1967, s 3(1).
3   *DPP v Hawkins* [1988] 3 All ER 537, DC.

9.60 Normally, proof of the legality of the conduct of the constable alleged to have been acting in the execution of his duty will be done by direct evidence, but inferences drawn from circumstantial evidence can suffice. This was held in *Plowden v DPP*.[1] During a large demonstration, constable X saw D holding on to the back of another, unidentified, uniformed constable's jacket, shouting abusively and apparently trying to prevent an arrest. D continued to be abusive when warned and was arrested by constable X. There was no direct evidence as to the purpose of the unidentified officer in acting as he did, but the magistrates found that a breach of the peace was in progress. They convicted the accused of obstructing the unidentified officer in the execution of his duty. On appeal to the Divisional Court, the question was whether they were correct on the evidence before them to find that that officer had been so acting. The Divisional Court held that the justices were entitled to infer from the facts found by them, including the breach of the peace, that the unidentified constable was acting in the execution of his duty in trying to prevent the breach of the peace when obstructed by D.

1   [1991] Crim LR 850, DC.

Assaulting a constable in the execution of his duty

9.61 As in the case of other offences of 'assault', 'assault' in s 89(1) of the Police Act 1996 is not limited to an assault in its strict sense but also includes a battery.[1] Because assault and battery are separate offences, the offence of assault on a constable in the execution of his duty involves two separate offences: assault in its strict sense on a constable in the execution of his duty and battery in such circumstances, and a conviction of assault and/or battery on a constable in the execution of his duty will be quashed under the rule against duplicity.[1]

A person is guilty of an assault if he intentionally or subjectively recklessly causes another person (the victim) to apprehend the application to his body of immediate, unlawful force. A person is guilty of battery if he intentionally or subjectively recklessly applies unlawful force to the body of another person (the victim).[2]

---

1   *Jones v Sherwood* [1942] 1 KB 127, DC; *DPP v Taylor; DPP v Little* [1992] 1 All ER 299, DC.
2   *Fagan v Metropolitan Police Comr* [1968] 3 All ER 442, DC; *R v Venna* [1975] 3 All ER 788, CA; *R v Kimber* [1983] 3 All ER 442, DC. For an explanation of the two offences, see Card, Cross and Jones *Criminal Law* (1998) paras 6.18–6.26.

Prohibited conduct

9.62 Proof of the actus reus of an offence under s 89(1) requires proof of the actus reus of assault or of battery, as appropriate, and that the victim was a constable acting in the execution of his duty (or someone assisting such a constable).

9.63 A person who is being lawfully arrested or detained is not entitled to use reasonable force in order to resist or escape.[1] On the other hand, a person who is being arrested or detained unlawfully is so entitled.[2] The same distinction applies where force is used to enable another person to resist or escape arrest or detention. Although a person who uses unreasonable force to resist a wrongful arrest or the like by a constable cannot be convicted of assaulting a constable in the execution of his duty, he can be convicted of common assault if it has also been charged.

---

1   *Kenlin v Gardiner* [1966] 3 All ER 931, DC.
2   *Pedro v Diss* [1981] 2 All ER 59 at 64.

Mental element

9.64 It must be proved that the accused had the mens rea for assault or battery, as the case may be.

It is unnecessary for the prosecution to prove that the accused knew that his victim was a constable acting in the execution of his duty.[1] The offence is one of strict liability in these respects, the rationale being the public policy of giving constables special protection when carrying out their duties.[2]

However, if the accused, not knowing that his victim is a constable, applies force to a constable, who is exercising one of his powers, and that force would be reasonable if the victim had not been a constable (because he would not have the power in question), the accused does not commit an offence under s 89(1). The reason is that, whether or not his mistake is reasonable, he lacks the mens rea required for the assault (ie battery) part of the offence, since he does not intend to apply *unlawful* force to his victim.[3] (This is important because in many cases where someone assaults a constable in the execution of his duty, not knowing that the victim is a constable, that person may think that he is being attacked.) On the other hand, if the accused knows that his victim is a constable, but mistakenly believes that the constable is acting in excess of his powers, he is not excused; his mistake, even if reasonable, is not one of fact but one of law relating to the powers of the constable.[4]

1   *R v Forbes* (1865) 10 Cox CC 362; *R v Maxwell* (1909) 2 Cr App R 26; *McBride v Turnock* [1964] Crim LR 456, DC; *Kenlin v Gardiner* [1966] 3 All ER 931, DC; *R v Brightling* [1991] Crim LR 364, CA; Howard 'Assaulting policemen in the execution of their duty' (1963) 79 LQR 247.
2   *Blackburn v Bowering* [1994] 3 All ER 380 at 384, per Leggett LJ.
3   *Blackburn v Bowering* [1994] 3 All ER 380, DC. See Fairweather and Levy 'Assaults on the police: a case of mistaken identity' [1994] Crim LR 817.
4   *R v Fennell* [1970] 3 All ER 215, CA.

Wilful obstruction

Obstruction[1]

9.65 The offence of obstructing a constable in the execution of his duty may be committed without anything in the nature of an assault.[2] It is commonly charged in public order situations: for example, against those who refuse to move on, against those who refuse to obey other instructions, and against those who interfere with the exercise of police powers of arrest or search. A police threat of arrest and/or prosecution for obstruction is extremely influential 'on the ground'.

1   Austin 'Obstruction – the policeman's best friend?' [1982] CLP 187; Gibbons 'The offence of obstruction' [1983] Crim LR 21; Lidstone 'The offence of obstruction' [1983] Crim LR 29.
2   Compare Scotland where a physical obstruction is required: *Curlett v M'Kechnie* 1938 JC 176.

9.66 In general, any conduct which actually prevents a constable from carrying out his duty or makes it more difficult for him to do so amounts to obstructing him.[1] Where a positive act has this effect it constitutes an obstruction, even though it is not unlawful independently of its operation as an obstruction[2] and even though the constable is unaware of it.[3] Examples of obstruction are hampering a constable in making an arrest, facilitating the escape of a suspected offender, non-compliance with a lawful request made by a constable in order to prevent a breach of the peace,[4] and refusing to open a door when lawfully requested to do so by a constable seeking to exercise a power of entry.[5]

It amounts to an obstruction to give a warning to someone who is already committing an offence in order that the commission of the offence may be suspended while there is a danger of detection,[6] and the same is the case where a warning is given to someone who is about to commit an offence in order that its commission may be postponed until after the danger of detention has passed.[7] On the other hand, it is not an obstruction where a warning is given to a person who has not committed an offence and in order to discourage him from ever doing so.[8]

1   *Hinchcliffe v Sheldon* [1955] 3 All ER 406, DC; *Rice v Connolly* [1966] 2 All ER 649, DC; *Lewis v Cox* [1984] 3 All ER 672, DC. An intent that one's conduct should have such an effect is insufficient in itself; there must be an actual obstruction, as defined above: *Bennett v Bale* [1986] Crim LR 404, DC.
2   *Dibble v Ingleton* [1972] 1 All ER 275, DC; *Neal v Evans* [1976] RTR 333, DC.
3   *Burton v DPP* (1998) unreported, DC; *DPP v Hamandishe* (1999) 5 Archbold News 3, DC.
4   See, for example, para **2.16**.
5   *Lunt v DPP* [1993] Crim LR 534, DC.
6   *Betts v Stevens* [1910] 1 KB 1, DC.
7   *Green v Moore* [1982] 1 All ER 428, DC.
8   *Bastable v Little* [1907] 1 KB 59, DC.

Wilful

9.67 The obstruction must be 'wilful', which in this context has the following meaning.

–   The accused's conduct which resulted in the obstruction must have been deliberate and intended by him to bring about a state of affairs which, regarded objectively, prevented or made it more difficult for the constable to carry out his duty, whether or not the accused appreciated that that state of affairs would have that effect or that it would in law amount to an obstruction.[1] Thus, to do something deliberately that in fact makes it more difficult for a constable to carry out his duties is not enough; there must be an intention that the deliberate conduct should result in that state of affairs. There is no need for any hostility towards the constable,[2] nor need the conduct be 'aimed at' him;[3] it is irrelevant that the obstructor's motive is public spirited or is neutral towards the constable, but based on what the obstructor considers to be a higher priority.

The above is well illustrated by *Hills v Ellis*[4] where D intervened in a lawful arrest by a constable in order to draw his attention to the fact that, as D believed, he was arresting the wrong man. The Divisional Court held that as D's deliberate conduct had resulted in a state of affairs that made it more difficult for the constable to carry out his duty, and as D had intended that state of affairs, D was guilty of wilful obstruction, despite the fact that he was actuated by good motives and not by hostility towards the constable.

It has not yet been decided whether the accused must have known that the person obstructed is a constable, but it has been held that there could not be a conviction for wilful obstruction in a case where the accused reasonably believed that that person was not a constable.[5]

–   In *Rice v Connolly*,[6] it was held that 'wilfully' meant not only 'intentionally', but also 'without lawful excuse'. This is rather surprising since 'wilfully' seems to refer to the accused's state of mind, whereas the question of 'lawful excuse' generally relates to factual matters surrounding conduct which excuse it.

The requirement that the obstruction must be without lawful excuse means that a failure or refusal to do something requested by a constable cannot amount to wilful obstruction unless the person requested is under a legal duty to do the thing requested. Therefore, unless a constable has a legal right to require a person to do something (and thereby to impose a legal duty on him to do it), a failure by that person to do the thing when requested by the constable cannot constitute a wilful obstruction because, although it makes it more difficult for the constable to carry out his duties, there will be a lawful excuse for that failure. This is of great importance; it prevents simple disobedience to a constable's instructions or lack of cooperation amounting to an offence in many cases. Thus, as there is no general *legal* duty to answer questions put by a constable, a mere refusal to answer such questions is not a wilful obstruction[7] (unless a special duty to answer exists in the circumstances). Nor, according to the Divisional Court in *Green v DPP*,[8] is it a wilful obstruction to advise someone else not to answer police questions, even if that advice is given in an abusive way. On the other hand, the court held, if a third party, by his abusive, persistent and unruly behaviour, went well beyond the exercise of his legal rights and prevented communication between the constable and the suspect or made it more difficult, he would be wilfully obstructing the constable. A case that seems very much on the borderline is *Ricketts v Cox*,[9] where it was held by the Divisional Court that a refusal to answer police questions which is accompanied by an abusive and hostile attitude, including threats, was a wilful obstruction. In the light of the decision in *Green v DPP*, it would seem that, but for the threats (to which, admittedly, the court did not give much attention in *Ricketts v Cox*), there would not have been an obstruction because, threats apart, the person would only be exercising his right not to answer police questions. In cases like *Green v DPP* and *Ricketts v Cox* a charge under s 4, s 4A or s 5 of the Public Order Act 1986 may often be the appropriate course. It is, of course, a wilful obstruction deliberately to give a constable false information if this makes it more difficult for him to carry out his duty.[10]

An example of a constable's power to require a person to do something is his power to order persons obstructing the highway to remove themselves;[11] consequently, failure to comply with such an order is a wilful obstruction. Likewise, a right possessed by a constable to enter premises for law enforcement purposes implies a duty on those inside the premises to let the constable in at his request; failure to comply is a wilful obstruction.[12] Another example is provided by *Johnson v Phillips*, referred to in para **9.57**. Lastly, under his powers to prevent a breach of the peace,[13] a constable can require various things to be done so as to prevent such a breach; a mere omission by a person required to do something under this power will amount to a wilful obstruction.

In these examples, the duty to act is imposed by the requirement made by the constable, but such a requirement is not essential; the duty may arise simply by operation of a statutory provision.

1   *Hills v Ellis* [1983] 1 All ER 667, DC; *Moore v Green* [1983] 1 All ER 663, DC.

2   *Moore v Green*, above (where the decision apparently to the contrary in *Willmott v Atack* [1976] 3 All ER 794, DC, was explained). Also see *Hills v Ellis*, above.

3   *Lewis v Cox* [1984] 3 All ER 672, DC (not following a statement to the contrary by Griffiths LJ in *Hills v Ellis* [1983] 1 All ER 667 at 670).

4   [1983] 1 All ER 667, DC. Also see *Lewis v Cox*, above.

5   *Ostler v Elliott* [1980] Crim LR 584, DC. The statement in ATH Smith *Offences against Public Order* (1987) p 192, referring to *Ostler v Elliott* as its authority, to the effect that the prosecutor must show that the defendant was aware that the person obstructed was a constable, is not borne out by the wording of the brief report of the decision in that case. The decision in *Ostler v Elliott*, as stated in the text, is along the same lines as in *R v Tolson* (1889) 23 QBD 168, CCR (a bigamy case) and represents a halfway-house between a requirement of full mens rea and strict liability. Despite the use of 'wilfully' in the definition of an offence, this halfway interpretation would be in line with the policy reasons behind the offence in s 89(1) of the 1996 Act being one of strict liability.

6   [1966] 2 All ER 649, DC.

7   *Rice v Connolly* [1966] 2 All ER 649, DC.

8   (1991) 155 JP 816, DC.

9   (1981) 74 Cr App R 298, DC; strongly criticised by Lidstone 'The offence of obstruction' [1983] Crim LR 29 at 33-35.

10   *Rice v Connolly*, above. An extreme case where there was held to be an obstruction by giving information is *Ledger v DPP* [1991] Crim LR 439, DC, where the obstruction consisted of the accused identifying himself to constables as 'Freddy and the Dreamers', which he did not intend to be believed and was not believed by them.

11   *Tynan v Balmer* [1966] 2 All ER 133, DC; *Kavanagh v Hiscock* [1974] 2 All ER 177, DC.

12   *Hinchcliffe v Sheldon* [1955] 3 All ER 406, DC; *Lunt v DPP* [1993] Crim LR 534, DC.
13   See Chapter 2.

Resistance

9.68 Like obstruction, the offence of resisting a constable in the execution of his duty does not require an assault. The fact that there has been an assault does not preclude a conviction on a charge of obstruction or resistance, but a charge of assault contrary to s 89(1) of the 1996 Act is normally more appropriate in such a case. On the other hand, unlike 'obstruction', resistance implies that some sort of physical conduct is required.

The wide meaning given to 'obstruction' probably renders 'resistance' otiose, since anyone who resists seems to obstruct (although the converse is not true). However, 'resisting' is a more appropriate word in certain cases, such as where a person arrested by a constable tears himself away.

The resistance is not required to be wilful. There can be no doubt that an intent to resist must be proved, but it remains to be seen what mens rea, if any, is required as to the fact that the person resisted is a constable. Analogy with the offence of assaulting a constable in the execution of his duty[1] suggests that it is irrelevant that the accused was ignorant (even though reasonably) that the person resisted was a constable. However, analogy with the offence of obstructing a constable suggests that a person cannot be convicted if he reasonably believed that the person resisted was not a constable.[2]

1   See para **9.64**.
2   See para **9.67**.

Arrest

9.69 An offence under s 89 of the 1996 Act is not an arrestable offence, nor is there a specific power of arrest for it.

The offence of assault contrary to s 89(1) will always involve a breach of the peace and accordingly the common law power to arrest for breach of the peace is available in relation to it. So is the general conditional power of arrest under s 25 of PACE.

The offences of obstruction and of resistance under s 89(2) will not necessarily involve an actual or imminent breach of the peace,[1] and only if it does can there be an arrest (under the common law power just referred to),[2] unless the general conditional power of arrest under s 25 of PACE is available.

Often an arrest for obstruction is preceded by a warning that a continuation of the conduct in question will lead to arrest. However, such a warning is not a pre-requisite of a valid arrest.

1   See paras **2.3–2.6**.
2   *Gelberg v Miller* [1961] 1 All ER 291, DC; *Wershof v Metropolitan Police Comr* [1978] 3 All ER 540, DC.

Related offences

9.70 To deal with particular mischiefs, a substantial number of statutes provide offences relating to obstructing public officials, other than constables, while they are executing particular functions.

An example of particular relevance to public order is provided by s 10(1) of the Criminal Law Act 1977, whereby:

> '... a person is guilty of an offence if he resists or intentionally obstructs any person who is in fact an officer of a court[1] engaged in executing any process issued by the High Court or by any county court for the purpose of enforcing any judgment or order for the recovery of any premises or for the delivery of possession of any premises.'

Section 10(2) limits the application of this offence to orders for possession made under RSC Ord 113 or CCR Ord 24. These Orders provide a summary procedure for obtaining orders for possession of premises or any other place against squatters, including any whom the plaintiff cannot identify. The s 10 offence can be useful in a public order context where a court officer is seeking to evict collective trespassers. For example, at the long-running Newbury bypass protest, obstruction of the under-sheriff seeking to enforce High Court possession orders and aggravated trespass were the most common charges. It is a defence for the accused to prove on the balance of probabilities[2] that he believed that the person he was resisting or obstructing was not an officer of the court.[3] Although, unlike many of the other related provisions, s 10(1) speaks of 'intentionally', as opposed to 'wilfully', obstructs, it is unlikely that a refusal to answer a question asked by an officer of the court for the execution of his order constitutes an offence, since there is no legal duty to answer and thus there seems to be no culpable omission.[4]

An offence under s 10(1) is triable only summarily. It is punishable with a maximum of six months' imprisonment or a fine not exceeding level 5 on the standard scale, or both.[5]

---

1   Ie any sheriff, under-sheriff, deputy sheriff, bailiff or officer of a sheriff (High Court process) or bailiff or other person who is an officer of a county court within the meaning of the County Courts Act 1959.
2   See para **4.38**.
3   Criminal Law Act 1977, s 10(3).
4   *Swallow v LCC* [1916] 1 KB 224, DC.
5   Criminal Law Act 1977, s 10(4). A magistrates' court is not precluded from trying an offence under s 10 by the rule of law ousting the jurisdiction of such a court to try offences where a dispute of title to property is involved: ibid, s 12(8).

9.71 Unlike the offence of obstructing a constable, there is a specific power of arrest for the present offence. A police officer in uniform[1] or any officer of a court may arrest without warrant anyone who is, or whom he, with reasonable cause, suspects[2] to be guilty of an offence under s 10.[3] A police officer in uniform may enter and search any premises for the purpose of arresting a person for an offence under s 10 if he has reasonable grounds for believing[4] that the person whom he is seeking is on the premises.[5]

---

1   See para **6.92**.
2   See para **3.68** fn 1.

3   Criminal Law Act 1977, s 10(5). This power of arrest is preserved by PACE, s 26(2) and Sch 2.
4   See para **6.28**.
5   PACE, s 17. What is said about this power in para **4.18** applies equally here.

OBSTRUCTION OF THE HIGHWAY

9.72 As a corollary to the common law right to pass and re-pass along the highway,[1] there are statutory offences of obstructing the highway. Such obstruction is punishable at common law.

1   *Harrison v Duke of Rutland* [1893] 1 QB 142; *Hickman v Maisey* [1900] 1 QB 753.

Highways Act 1980, s 137

9.73 Section 137(1) of the Highways Act 1980 provides 'If a person, without lawful authority or excuse, in any way wilfully obstructs the free passage along a highway, he is guilty of [a summary] offence. . .' This offence is commonly charged in instances of public disorder on the highway, including passive sit-down demonstrations, picketing and leafletting.

Prohibited conduct

9.74 The prohibited conduct is obstruction of free passage along a highway. Section 328(1) of the 1980 Act defines 'highway' for the purposes of that Act as meaning the whole or part of a highway other than a ferry or waterway. Where a highway passes over a bridge or through a tunnel, that bridge or tunnel is regarded for the purposes of the Act as part of the highway.[1]

To discern the meaning of 'highway' in the above definition, one has to turn to the general definition at common law in the absence of a general statutory definition. At common law, a highway is a way over which there exists a public right of passage, on foot, with vehicles, on horseback or accompanied by a beast of burden or cattle,[2] ie a right for all Her Majesty's subjects at all times to pass and re-pass without let or hindrance.[3] A highway will cease to be such on its final closure as such, for example by a court order, but not simply because it is temporarily closed to passage for some reason.

As can be seen, a 'highway' has a different meaning from a 'road' in road traffic legislation, which is defined as 'any highway and any other road to which the public has access'.[4]

1   Highways Act 1980, s 328(2).
2   Thus, bridleways and footpaths are 'highways', if there is a public right of passage along
     them. Pavements alongside a carriageway which is a highway are part of the highway and so,
     rebuttably (see para **7.97**), are the verges of the highway.
3   *Ex parte Lewis* (1888) 21 QBD 191 at 197.
4   Road Traffic Act 1988, s 192.

9.75 There can be an obstruction of free passage along a highway, even though there is not a complete blockage of it. It is enough that more than de minimis the space available to the public for passing or re-passing is diminished.[1]

It follows that there can be an obstruction if there is an occupation of part of a road, which results in other road-users being denied the use of the road as a whole.[2] There can likewise be an obstruction if a crowd gathers on the highway where it is addressed by someone, even though traffic still has room to pass by.[3] Indeed, even the conduct of a single protester standing on the highway can constitute an obstruction.[4] Someone juggling firesticks in a pedestrian precinct has been held guilty of obstructing the highway.[5]

There must, however, be some sort of physical interference on the highway with free passage along it. Simply to cause fear to users of the highway cannot amount to an obstruction. This was held by the Divisional Court in *Kent County Council v Holland*,[6] where the accused allowed his rotweiler dogs to act in a menacing way behind a fence separating his land from a path constituting a highway. Pedestrians on the path were put in fear, but, the Court said, the highway was not obstructed.

---

1   See *Seekings v Clarke* (1961) 59 LGR 268, DC; *Hirst v Chief Constable of West Yorkshire* (1987) 85 Cr App R 143 at 151, per Glidewell LJ. The *Shorter Oxford English Dictionary* defines 'obstruct' as 'place or be an obstacle in (a passageway . . .); make difficult or impossible to pass through. . .'.
2   *Hirst v Chief Constable of West Yorkshire* (1987) 85 Cr App R 143, DC.
3   *Homer v Cadman* (1886) 50 JP 454, DC; *Arrowsmith v Jenkins* [1963] 2 All ER 210, DC.
4   *Scarfe v Wood* [1969] Crim LR 265, DC.
5   *Waite v Taylor* (1985) 149 JP 551, DC.
6   (1997) 161 JP 558, DC.

9.76 An activity can constitute an obstruction on the highway whether or not the conduct in question occurs on the highway. What is required is conduct that results in the consequence that free passage along a highway is obstructed. Somebody standing off the highway who causes a crowd to gather on the highway can be convicted of obstructing it as a perpetrator, rather than simply as an accomplice to their obstruction.[1]

An obstruction can be caused by an omission to act, at least if the accused was under a legal duty to act, which results in an obstruction of the highway or its continuance.[2]

There can be an obstruction of the highway by picketing, even though the picketing is lawful under s 220(1) of the Trade Union and Labour Relations (Consolidation) Act 1992,[3] referred to in para **9.47**. Likewise, there can be an obstruction of the highway where someone stands on the highway handing out leaflets or people assemble there with banners.[4]

It is not necessary to prove an actual obstruction, ie that any particular person was obstructed.[5] Consequently, the fact that no one was inconvenienced in using the highway by the accused's conduct does not in itself mean that there has not been an obstruction,[6] although whether the obstruction was actual or potential is a relevant factor in determining whether or not the accused's conduct was an unreasonable use of the highway for the purposes of the defence of lawful excuse.[7]

---

1   *Fabbri v Morris* [1947] 1 All ER 315, DC; see para **9.82**.
2   In *Arrowmith v Jenkins* [1963] 2 All ER 210, DC, Lord Parker CJ spoke of obstruction by an act or omission.
3   *Broome v DPP* [1974] 1 All ER 314, HL.
4   *Hirst v Chief Constable of West Yorkshire* (1987) 85 Cr App R 143, DC.

5   *Wolverton UDC v Willis* [1962] 1 All ER 243, DC (obstruction offence under Town Police
     Clauses Act 1847, s 28); *Read v Perrett* (1876) 1 Ex D 249, DC (a similar obstruction offence
     under Metropolitan Police Act 1839, s 60).
6   *Nagy v Weston* [1965] 1 All ER 78, DC; *Cooper v Metropolitan Police Comr* (1985) 82 Cr App R
     238, DC.
7   *Nagy v Weston* above; *Cooper v Metropolitan Police Comr*, above; see para **9.82**.

9.77 Even if conduct can be said to be an obstruction, a court can dismiss a
prosecution on the ground that the obstruction was de minimis in terms of the
amount of space occupied by the obstruction compared with the total available
space or in terms of the duration of a complete obstruction.[1] If the amount of
space is negligible or the duration transient, a court may well apply the de minimis
rule. The de minimis exception is a narrow one: in *Torbay Borough Council v Cross*,[2]
the Divisional Court held that displays of goods outside a shop, which projected by
no more than 5% of the total width of the pavement, constituted an obstruction
which was more than de minimis.

On the other hand, in *Kent County Council v Holland*,[3] the Divisional Court
held that the occasional protusion of the jowls of rotweiler dogs through a mesh
fence which was the boundary to a footpath was so minimal in time and degree
that the magistrates were entitled to find that (and their Lordships agreed with
that finding) that it could not be said to amount to a physical obstruction of the
highway.

1   *Seekings v Clarke* (1961) 59 LGR 268, DC; *Wolverton UDC v Willis* [1962] 1 All ER 243, DC (see
     para **9.76** fn 5).
2   (1995) 159 JP 682, DC.
3   (1997) 161 JP 558, DC.

Mental element
9.78 The accused's obstruction of the highway must be 'wilful'. 'Wilful' is a term
whose requirements have been construed differently in different offences. There
are offences requiring 'wilfulness' which have been construed as ones of strict
liability,[1] but it is submitted that the present offence is one requiring full mens rea,
for the reasons set out below.

In modern times, the prevalent judicial approach has been to construe
'wilfully' so as to require proof of a subjective mental element as to the element(s)
of the prohibited conduct to which it relates.[2] Particularly important is that, in
relation to the (now repealed) similar offence under s 72 of the Highways Act 1835
of wilfully obstructing the free passage of any highway, it was held by the Divisional
Court in *Eaton v Cobb*[3] that a person had not wilfully obstructed free passage of the
highway where that obstruction was not intentional. Consequently, it held, that
offence had not been committed by the accused who, having checked in his
mirror and concluded that it was safe to do so, had flung open his car door in the
path of a cyclist.

This view is a more liberal one than that put forward in two other cases. In
Hirst v Chief Constable of West Yorkshire,[4] the Divisional Court referred to 'wilful' as
meaning 'deliberate', but this is an over-simplification and may mean the same as
was said by the Divisional Court in *Arrowsmith v Jenkin*,[5] viz someone wilfully
obstructs who 'intentionally, as opposed to accidentally, that is, by an exercise of
his or her free will, does or omits to do something which will cause an obstruction

or the continuance of an obstruction'. Awareness of the risk of the obstruction is not necessary under this approach.

It is submitted that, by analogy to the case of the offence of wilfully obstructing a constable in the execution of his duty,[6] it must be proved that the accused's conduct which resulted in the obstruction of the highway must have been deliberate and intended by him to bring about a state of affairs which in fact amounted to that obstruction, whether or not the accused appreciated that that state of affairs would have that effect or that in law it would amount to an obstruction. Arguably, as in some other contexts, subjective recklessness (ie awareness of an unjustified risk of causing an obstruction) should suffice in the alternative.[7]

---

1 For example *Cotterill v Penn* [1936] 1 KB 53, DC; *Maidstone BC v Mortimer* [1980] 3 All ER 552, DC.
2 See, for example, *Bullock v Turnbull* [1952] 2 Lloyd's Rep 303, DC; *R v Sheppard* [1980] 3 All ER 899, HL; *R v Gittins* [1982] RTR 363, DC. As to 'wilfully' in general, see Andrews 'Wilfulness: a lesson in ambiguity' (1981) 1 *Legal Studies* 303.
3 [1950] 1 All ER 1016, DC.
4 (1987) 85 Cr App R 143, DC.
5 [1963] 2 All ER 210, DC.
6 See para **9.67**.
7 Held in *R v Sheppard*, above, that awareness of risk suffices for statutory offence of wilful neglect of child.

Without lawful authority or excuse

9.79 Although s 101 of the Magistrates' Courts Act 1980 places the burden on the accused at a summary trial to prove any 'exception, exemption, proviso, excuse or qualification', it has been held that in s 137 the prosecution must prove that there was no lawful authority or excuse,[1] if evidence has been adduced in support of such a defence. No reference was made to the predecessor to s 101 but this approach is in line with that taken in other cases where phrases such as 'without lawful authority or excuse' or 'without reasonable excuse' are employed and the burden of proof has not expressly been placed on the accused.[2] Such an approach can also be supported on the ground that such phrases are an essential element of the definition of the offence in which they appear; to place the burden of proving them on the accused would be incompatible with the presumption of innocence in the ECHR, Art 6(2).

---

1 *Nagy v Weston* [1965] 1 All ER 78, DC; *Hirst v Chief Constable of West Yorkshire* (1987) 85 Cr App R 143, DC.
2 *Mallows v Harris* [1979] RTR 404, DC; *Jaggard v Dickinson* [1980] 3 All ER 716, DC. Contrast *Gatland v Metropolitan Police Comr* [1968] 2 All ER 100, DC.

9.80 It is a trite statement, but needs to be made, that an obstruction of the highway is not without lawful authority if it is authorised by law.[1] The following are examples of such authorisation. A police road block set up in accordance with the provisions of s 4 of PACE is clearly effected with lawful authority. A police officer who causes an obstruction by the exercise of his powers to direct traffic will do so with lawful authority and those who are stopped will also have such authority. Lawful authority also includes permits and licences granted under statutory provisions.[2] Street traders and charity-collectors who are licensed to operate on the highway and are acting within the terms of their licence obstruct the highway with lawful authority.

A mistaken belief that one has lawful authority is no defence,[3] however reasonable the belief, although, by analogy with a similarly worded defence under s 19 of the Firearms Act 1968, a genuine belief (reasonable or not) in facts which, if true, would constitute lawful authority can constitute a lawful excuse.[4]

The previous practice of the police or of a local authority in condoning the obstruction by failing to take proceedings in respect of the same obstruction for a substantial period, although it was known to them, does not constitute lawful authority.[5] It may, however, amount to a lawful excuse.

---

1   See para **8.21**.
2   *Hirst v Chief Constable of West Yorkshire* (1987) 85 Cr App R 143 at 151, per Glidewell LJ.
3   *Arrowsmith v Jenkins* [1963] 2 All ER 210, DC.
4   *R v Jones* [1995] 3 All ER 139, CA.
5   *Pugh v Pigden* (1987) 151 JP 644, DC. Also see *Redbridge LBC v Jacques* [1971] 1 All ER 260, DC.

9.81 'Lawful excuse' embraces activities, otherwise lawful in themselves (ie apart from the obstruction), which are a reasonable use of the highway.[1] If the activity is not inherently lawful, the question of whether or not it is a reasonable use (and therefore whether there is a lawful excuse) does not arise.[1]

---

1   *Hirst v Chief Constable of West Yorkshire* (1987) 85 Cr App R 143, DC. Also *Nagy v Weston* [1965] 1 All ER 78 at 80, per Lord Parker CJ.

9.82 In *Nagy v Weston*,[1] Lord Parker CJ, giving the decision of the Divisional Court, held that whether or not a use of the highway which amounts to an obstruction is or is not unreasonable is a question of fact. It depends on all the circumstances of the case, including where it occurs, its duration, its extent and its purpose, and whether there is actual as opposed to a potential obstruction.[1] According to this test, there can be a reasonable use, and therefore a lawful excuse, even though the obstruction does not result from the use of the highway for passage or re-passage, or for purposes reasonably incidental thereto. This was denied in two subsequent cases, *Waite v Taylor*[2] and *Jones v Bescoby*,[3] where it was held that if the obstruction did not so result there could not be a reasonable use of the highway, and that consequently juggling with firesticks on the highway and stopping vehicles at a picket line on the highway were automatically unreasonable uses. However, this stricter approach was expressly disapproved by the Divisional Court in *Hirst v Chief Constable of West Yorkshire*,[4] which affirmed the test in *Nagy v Weston*. In *Hirst*, the Divisional Court held that an obstruction of the highway by animal rights supporters who demonstrated outside a farmer's shop, handing out leaflets and holding banners, could involve a reasonable use of the highway. Because the question of whether it actually did involve such a use on the facts had not been considered, convictions for obstruction were quashed.

The application of the general test of whether or not the accused's use of the highway was unreasonable is illustrated by contrasting *Fabbri v Morris*[5] with *Dwyer v Mansfield*.[6] In *Fabbri v Morris*, the Divisional Court held that conducting a business on premises adjacent to the highway in such a way as to encourage a crowd to develop on the highway was capable of amounting to an unreasonable use of the highway. In this case, the shopkeeper was serving customers through the shop window. On the other hand, in *Dwyer v Mansfield*, a civil case on public nuisance where a queue had formed outside the accused's shop at a time of wartime scarcity, it was held that he was not liable because he was carrying on his business in a normal way and was not doing anything unreasonable.

Two further examples where a use of the highway has been found to be unreasonable are the use of a van, parked in a line of cars in a busy street, to sell hot dogs,[7] and approaches by a club tout to pedestrians on four occasions, on each of which they were forced to step into the roadway.[8]

---

1   [1965] 1 All ER 78, DC; *Cooper v Metropolitan Police Comr* (1985) 82 Cr App R 238, DC.
2   (1985) 149 JP 551, DC.
3   (1987) unreported, DC.
4   (1987) 85 Cr App R 143, DC.
5   [1947] 1 All ER 315, DC.
6   [1946] 2 All ER 247.
7   *Pitcher v Lockett* [1966] Crim LR 283, DC. Also see *Waltham Forest LBC v Mills* [1980] RTR 201, DC.
8   *Cooper v Metropolitan Police Comr* (1985) 82 Cr App R 238, DC.

9.83 Although a person exercising the right to pass or re-pass along the highway may impede the progress of someone else who is also exercising that right, albeit (say) rather faster, the former person does not normally commit the offence of obstructing the highway because his use of it will not be unreasonable in the circumstances. The same is true of a procession.[1] Those taking part are simply exercising their right of passage along the highway en masse. The exercise of that right by those in the procession may, of course, be prohibited by an order under s 13 of the Public Order Act 1986, discussed in paras **6.43–6.53**, in which case there would be an unreasonable use of the highway, but otherwise a procession will not normally be an unreasonable use. Although the primary purpose of those in the procession may be to publicise a particular cause or view, rather than to arrive at a destination, they are nevertheless exercising their right of passage and are doing so in a way which is prima facie a reasonable use of the highway because they are exercising their right of freedom of expression.

This is not to say that the exercise of the right of passage cannot amount to the offence of obstruction of the highway if it is unreasonable. There have been occasions, for example, when motorways have virtually been brought to a halt by lorries or cars driving in line abreast at crawling pace. This unreasonable use of the highway is an obstruction without lawful excuse. In *Norton v Lees*,[2] for example, it was held that the driver of a car, who drove slowly along the crown of the road so that faster vehicles could only overtake at favourable moments, could be convicted of obstructing the highway. Likewise, it is submitted, a procession on the highway will amount to an unreasonable use of it, and be an obstruction without lawful excuse, if it deliberately proceeds at a snail's pace.

---

1   *Lowdens v Keaveney* [1903] 2 IR 82, Irish Div Ct.
2   (1921) 85 JPN 500; on appeal 87 JPN 675, DC.

9.84 It may be that there can be a lawful excuse in circumstances where there is an unreasonable use of the highway. One possible example, referred to in para **9.80**, is where there is a mistaken belief in facts which, if true, would constitute lawful authority. Another example is compliance with a condition imposed on a procession or assembly under s 12 or s 14 of the Public Order Act 1986,[1] which involves an obstruction of the highway. This may amount to a lawful excuse in its own right. Alternatively, it may provide evidence of reasonable use (and be a lawful excuse on that basis).[1] Alternatively, it could be argued, the condition would constitute lawful authority.

---

1   Marston and Tain *Public Order Offences* (1995) p 171.

9.85 The decision in *Hirst v Chief Constable of West Yorkshire*, referred to in para **9.82**, is useful in that it acknowledged that some weight must be attached to the right of free speech.[1] In dealing with whether an obstruction involves reasonable use of the highway, it is important that magistrates pay due regard to right to freedom of expression and of association under Arts 8 and 10 of the ECHR. In *Hubbard v Pitt*,[2] a case involving peaceful picketing on the highway, where the majority of the Court of Appeal granted an interlocutory injunction against the pickets, Lord Denning MR, dissenting, said:[3] '[The courts] should not interfere by interlocutory injunction with the right to demonstrate and protest any more than they interfere with the right of free speech; provided that everything is done peacefully and in good order'. These words were applied to the offence under s 137 of the Highways Act 1980 by Otton J in *Hirst v Chief Constable of West Yorkshire*.[4] His Lordship said that he thought they were of importance when considering whether someone like a demonstrator or picket has committed an offence under s 137 of the 1980 Act.

   Unless the above point is borne firmly in mind, there is danger that the offence will be used as a de facto licensing system over public protest and as a way of banning public processions or assemblies on the highway, or imposing conditions on them, when the requirements of Part II of the Public Order Act 1986 cannot be satisfied. There is also the danger that the fundamental freedoms under the ECHR will be denied by the application of the present offence in cases where it is essentially being used as an instrument of censorship. The police have a particular duty not to use their power to use reasonable force to prevent an offence or the threat of a prosecution for the offence as a weapon against peaceful protest per se; a threat of 'move on or I'll arrest you for obstructing the highway' may well stifle protest, and deprive an individual of the practical benefits of the right to freedom of expression. Many people are deterred by threats of arrest, prosecution or conviction; that the sentence, if convicted, may simply be a binding over or conditional discharge is not sufficient assurance.

---

1   Wallington has argued ('Injunctions and the "right to demonstrate"' [1976] CLJ at 108–109)
     that 'lawful excuse' should be interpreted to cover all demonstrations conducted with due
     regard to the interests of others.
2   [1975] 3 All ER 1, CA.
3   Ibid, at 11.
4   (1987) 85 Cr App R 143 at 152.

General

9.86 Whether there is an obstruction or an unreasonable use is a question of fact, taking into account the considerations referred to above.[1] It follows that the

Divisional Court will not review and overturn a decision that there was or was not an obstruction unless that decision is one which, on the facts found by the magistrates, no reasonable bench could come to.

---

1   *Nagy v Weston* [1965] 1 All ER 78, DC; *Absalom v Martin* [1974] RTR 145, DC.

Trial, punishment and powers

9.87   An offence contrary to s 137 of the 1980 Act is triable summarily only. It is not imprisonable and the maximum fine is one not exceeding level 3 on the standard scale.[1] Where an offence under s 137 is committed in respect of a vehicle, it is a fixed penalty offence under the Road Traffic Offenders Act 1988.[2]

---

1   Highways Act 1980, s 137(1).
2   Road Traffic Offenders Act 1988, Sch 3.

9.88   An offence contrary to s 137 is not an arrestable offence. Obstruction of the highway is, however, one of the general arrest conditions for the purposes of the conditional power of arrest possessed by police under s 25 of PACE. In addition, a particular obstruction may entitle anyone to arrest without warrant under the common law powers to arrest for a breach of the peace, or to use reasonable force under s 3 of the Criminal Law Act 1967 to prevent it.[1]

A constable has power to take reasonable steps to prevent a reasonably apprehended obstruction of the highway, including requiring members of the public to remove themselves or some other obstruction from the highway. For example, a constable can require pickets to move if they would otherwise obstruct lawful passage by other highway-users.[2]

---

1   See *Reed v Wastie* [1972] Crim LR 221, DC.
2   *Kavanagh v Hiscock* [1974] 2 All ER 177, DC.

Obstruction under Town Police Clauses Act 1847[1] and Metropolitan Police Act 1839[2]

9.89   By s 28 of the 1847 Act, anyone who in any street to the obstruction, annoyance or danger of the residents or passengers, by means of any cart, carriage, sledge, truck, or barrow, or any animal, or other means,[3] wilfully interrupts any public crossing or wilfully causes any obstruction[4] in any public footpath or other public thoroughfare commits an offence. Although s 28 does not include 'without lawful authority or excuse', it would be surprising if a court did not interpret wilfully in the same way as 'wilfully' in obstructing a constable,[5] ie as including 'without lawful excuse'. On this basis, an obstruction with lawful authority (which must be a lawful excuse) or reasonable use would not amount to the present offence.

An offence under s 28 is triable summarily only. The maximum punishment is 14 days' imprisonment or a fine not exceeding level 3 on the standard scale.

The offence under s 28 does not apply to Greater London.[1]

---

1   See para **9.18**.

2   See para **9.21**.
3   It may be that 'other means' must be interpreted ejusdem generis the previous list, in which
     case it would not cover obstruction by erecting a stall or by causing a crowd to assemble (see
     Smith and Hogan *Criminal Law* 6th edn (Butterworths, 1983) p 800, citing *Ball v Ward* (1875)
     40 JP 213, DC; *R v Long* (1888) 52 JP 630, DC; *R v Williams* (1891) 55 JP 406, DC).
4   'Obstruction' bears the same meaning as under the Highways Act 1980, s 137, as can be seen
     from the cases cited above.
5   See para **9.67**.

9.90 Section 54, para 6, of the Metropolitan Police Act 1839 provides a similar offence, which applies in the Metropolitan Police district,[1] of wilfully interrupting any public crossing, or wilfully causing any obstruction[2] in any thoroughfare by means of any cart, carriage, sledge, truck or barrow, or any horse or other animal. This offence omits the somewhat otiose reference in s 28 of the 1847 Act to the prohibited conduct being to the obstruction, annoyance or danger of residents or passengers. By a drafting defect the opening words of s 54 require the accused's conduct to be in a thoroughfare or public place. While this is relevant to other offences under s 54, the locus set out in s 54, para 6, is narrower and makes the opening words in s 54 redundant in respect of the present offence. It is submitted that a person is not guilty if he has a lawful excuse, for the reasons given in para **9.89**.

An offence under s 54, para 6, is triable summarily only. It is not imprisonable; the maximum fine is one not exceeding level 2 on the standard scale.

---

1   See para **9.21**, fn 1.
2   'Obstruction' must bear the same meaning as above.

Obstruction of highway: common law offence

9.91 It may be that obstruction of the highway is a common law offence in its own right, but if it does exist its exact scope is uncertain.[1] Alternatively it may be that there is no separate common law offence of obstructing but that any references to it in the case law are to the common law offence of public nuisance which can certainly be committed by an obstruction of the highway.[2] In any event, prosecutions for obstruction are normally brought for the statutory offence under s 137 of the Highways Act 1980.

The importance of all this is that a common law offence is triable only on indictment (unless statute otherwise ordains, which it has not done in this case, although it has in the case of public nuisance[3]) and sentence is at the discretion of the court.[4]

---

1   See ATH Smith *Offences against Public Order* (1987) pp 197–198.
2   See para **9.93**.
3   See para **9.92**.
4   *R v Morris* [1950] 2 All ER 965, CCA, approved in *Verrier v DPP* [1966] 3 All ER 568, HL.

PUBLIC NUISANCE

9.92 Public nuisance, according to Stephen, consists of:

'... an act not warranted[[1]] by law or an omission to discharge a legal duty, which act or omission obstructs or causes inconvenience or damage to the public in the exercise of rights common to all His Majesty's subjects.'[2]

Where an individual suffers particular damage above and beyond that suffered by the community as a whole, that person can maintain an action for damages in tort. Nowadays this is the principal importance of public nuisance. However, public nuisance is also a common law offence, triable either way,[3] and punishable at the discretion of the court on conviction on indictment.[4]

---

1   But see para **9.95**.
2   Stephen *Digest of Criminal Law* 9th edn (1950) p 184. Also see *A-G v PYA Quarries Ltd* [1957] 1 All ER 894 at 902, per Romer LJ; *R v Madden* [1975] 3 All ER 155, CA.
3   Magistrates' Courts Act 1980, s 17(1) and Sch 1.
4   *R v Morris* [1950] 2 All ER 965, CCA, approved by the House of Lords in *Verrier v DPP* [1966] 3 All ER 568, HL. In addition, a relator action for an injunction may be brought by the Attorney-General at the instance of the affected party, or an action for an injunction may be brought at the instance of a local authority exercising its rights under the Local Government Act 1972, s 222, to protect the local community.

9.93 The definition of public nuisance covers a wide range of situations, many of which have nothing to do with public order. In terms of interference with public order, the following situations have, for example, been held capable of being public nuisances: an 'acid house party' or 'rave' that creates considerable noise to the disturbance of the local community;[1] a bomb hoax which causes actual danger to the public or actual risk to the comfort of the public;[2] and obstruction of the highway,[3] which is the most common instance of a public nuisance. These types of public nuisance are also dealt with by specific statutory provisions (including by-laws), and this is true of many other types of public nuisance. Nevertheless, even if there is such a provision, it is likely simply to create a summary offence with an insubstantial penalty, so that even here public nuisance may be the preferred charge.

According to Denning LJ, as he then was, unlike the tort of private nuisance, public nuisance does not require any element of repetition or continuance.[4]

---

1   *R v Shorrock* [1993] 3 All ER 917, CA.
2   *R v Madden* [1975] 3 All ER 155, CA. The Court stated that a 'potential danger' or 'potential risk' was not enough. Given that 'danger' and 'risk' are themselves concerned with the potential of something to occur, it is hard to see what 'potential' adds to 'danger' and 'risk'. Clearly, the Court was not intentionally engaging in tautology. It is submitted that by distinguishing 'actual' and 'potential' it was referring to the fact that a 'danger/risk' might be too remote (in which case it would only be 'potential'). Unfortunately the Court provided no guidance as to the degree of risk required.
3   In *Jacobs v LCC* [1950] AC 361 at 375, Lord Simonds described public nuisance with reference to highways as 'any wrongful act or omission upon or near a highway, whereby the public are prevented from freely, safely and conveniently passing along the highway'.
4   *A-G v PYA Quarries Ltd* [1957] 1 All ER 894 at 909, per Denning LJ.

9.94 Stephen's definition of public nuisance, like other definitions of the term,[1] requires the nuisance to affect all the Queen's subjects. This must not be understood literally, as is shown by reference to *A-G v PYA Quarries Ltd,* where the relevant authorities were considered. Romer LJ stated:

> 'It is . . . clear, in my opinion, that any nuisance is "public" which materially affects the reasonable comfort and convenience of life of a class of Her Majesty's subjects. The sphere of the nuisance may be described generally as the "neighbourhood"; but the

question whether the local community within that sphere comprises a sufficient number of persons to constitute a class of the public is a question of fact in every case. It is not necessary, in my judgement, to prove that every member of the class has been injuriously affected; it is sufficient to show that a representative cross-section of the class has been so affected for an injunction to issue.'[2]

Denning LJ put it rather differently:

'I prefer to look to the reason of the thing and to say that a public nuisance is a nuisance which is so widespread in its range or so indiscriminate in its effect that it would not be reasonable to expect one person to take proceedings on his own responsibility to put a stop to it, but that it should be taken on the responsibility of the community at large.'[3]

As Romer LJ indicated, whether the number of persons affected is sufficient to constitute a class of the public is a question of fact. In answering account may be taken of the cumulative effect of a large number of separate acts aimed at different individuals.[4]

In *A-G v PYA Quarries Ltd*,[5] where blasting operations caused vibrations, splinters and noise that affected the inhabitants of 30 houses and parts of two highways, the nuisance was held to be to the public, whereas in *R v Lloyd*,[6] where there had only been complaints in respect of three houses about noise caused by the accused's conduct, it was held that an indictment for public nuisance could not be sustained. In *R v Johnson*,[7] where the accused had made hundreds of obscene phone calls over a five-year period to at least 13 women in a particular area, it was held that there had been a public nuisance, whereas in *R v Madden*,[8] where a bomb hoax had been telephoned to a factory and had only affected eight security officers there, it was held that they could not be regarded as a class of the public.

---

1   For example, Blackstone 3 *Commentaries* 1st edn (1768) p 216.
2   [1957] 1 All ER 894 at 902.
3   [1957] 1 All ER at 908.
4   *R v Johnson* [1996] 2 Cr App R 434, CA.
5   [1957] 1 All ER 894, CA.
6   (1802) 4 Esp 200.
7   [1996] 2 Cr App R 434, CA.
8   [1975] 3 All ER 155, CA.

9.95 It is not every obstruction or inconvenience to the rights of the public that constitutes a public nuisance. In the passage from his judgment in *A-G v PYA Quarries Ltd* quoted above, Romer LJ spoke in terms of conduct affecting the *reasonable* comfort and convenience of a class of the public. This test of reasonableness is somewhat elastic; it will involve, as a question of fact, issues like the degree of interference with comfort and convenience, its duration and any public benefit or social utility that the interference may have. For example, in the case of an obstruction of the highway, 'If an unreasonable time is occupied in the operation of delivering beer from a brewer's dray into the cellar of a publican, this is certainly a nuisance. A cart or wagon may be unloaded at a gateway; but this must be done with promptness.'[1]

Depending on whether or not they involve an unreasonable interference with the convenience of the public, demonstrations, pickets and other assemblies on or near the highway can constitute a public nuisance. In *R v Clarke (No 2)*,[2] the conviction for incitement to commit a public nuisance of D who had led a crowd through streets in London during a royal visit, in consequence of which one street was wholly blocked, and another partially, was quashed because the judge had failed to direct the jury on the question whether, if there was an obstruction, there had been an unreasonable use of the highway.

Despite the indication to the contrary in Stephen's definition in para **9.92**, it is not necessary that the accused's conduct should be an independently unlawful act; public nuisance is primarily concerned with the effect of the act complained of as opposed to its inherent lawfulness or unlawfulness.[3]

As is indicated by various statements above, there cannot be a public nuisance unless there is an *actual* interference with the reasonable comfort and convenience of a class of the public. In the case of an obstruction of the highway, therefore, there must be an actual (as well as unreasonable) interference with the public's right of passage as a result of D's conduct, whereas in the statutory offence of wilfully obstructing the highway a potential interference can suffice.

---

1   *R v Jones* (1812) 3 Camp 230 at 231, per Lord Ellenborough. See also *Dwyer v Mansfield* [1946] 2 All ER 247; see para **9.82**.
2   [1963] 3 All ER 884, CCA.
3   *Gillingham BC v Medway (Chatham) Dock Co Ltd* [1992] 3 All ER 923, CA.

9.96 Public nuisance is an offence of negligence. It was held in *R v Shorrock*[1] that an accused is guilty if it is proved that he knew or ought to have known that there was a real risk that a nuisance would be the consequence of his conduct.

---

1   [1993] 3 All ER 917, CA.

BY-LAWS UNDER LOCAL GOVERNMENT ACT 1972, s 235

9.97 Section 235(1) empowers the council of a district,[1] the council of a principal area in Wales[2] and a London borough council to make by-laws for the good rule and government of the whole or any part of the district, principal area or borough, as the case may be, and for the prevention and suppression of nuisances therein. The confirming authority in respect of such by-laws is the appropriate Secretary of State; in Wales, the Secretary of State's function is exercisable by him concurrently with the Welsh Assembly.[3] By-laws may not be made under s 235(1) for any purpose as respects any area if provision for that purpose as respects that area is made by, or is or may be made under, any other enactment.[4]

The procedure for the making of a by-law by a local authority under s 235 or under any other enactment is set out in s 236 of the 1972 Act. The terms of s 236 are outside the scope of this book.

The predecessor to s 235 of the 1972 Act was s 251 of the Local Government Act 1933. Despite its repeal, by-laws made under that Act remain in force.[5]

---

1   This will be the unitary authority where one exists. Otherwise it will be the district council.
2   Ie the 11 counties and 11 county boroughs, all of which are unitary authorities, listed in the Local Government (Wales) Act 1994, Sch 1.
3   Local Government Act 1972, s 235(2); Government of Wales Act 1998, s 22(1), and National Assembly for Wales (Transfer of Functions) Order 1999, SI 1999/672.

4   Local Government Act 1972, s 235(3).
5   Ibid, s 272(2).

9.98 Under s 235 of the 1972 Act, and its predecessor, by-laws have been made prohibiting:

– riotous,[1] violent,[1] disorderly, indecent[2] or offensive behaviour in a street or public place;
– indecent, obscene, violent, abusive or profane language in or near a street or other public place to the annoyance of anyone in such street or public place;
– holding or taking part in public discussion or any public meeting, or giving any public address, in a pleasure ground or other open space vested in or maintained by the local authority;
– playing a musical instrument or singing, or making any other noise (eg the use of loud-hailers), in a street or near any house to the annoyance of any inhabitants;
– spitting in the street or other public place;
– dangerous games in the street or other public place;
– nuisances contrary to public decency;
– bill-posting; and
– the distribution of hand-bills.

In addition, such by-laws often restrict the holding of meetings in certain places or require consent to meetings and assemblies. By-laws of some of the types referred to above are open to serious challenge on grounds of incompatibility with the ECHR.

As can be seen, by-laws under s 235 of the 1972 Act can deal with a wide range of activities that can affect public order. The extent to which they do will vary from local authority to local authority. Many by-laws are widespread in their use, although their precise wording may vary from one area to another.

---

1   'Riotous' is not synonymous with 'riot' under the Public Order Act 1986 (see para **3.39**).
     'Riotous' and 'violent' in the present context involve specific acts or threats of physical force
     to persons or property or acts that put others in reasonable apprehension of immediate
     physical harm to themselves or property of which they have present use or control: *Brownlie's
     Law of Public Order and National Security* (1981) p 194, referring to *Scott v Howard* [1912] VLR
     189.
2   For the variable meaning of 'indecent' depending on its context, see paras **9.19** and **9.31**.

9.99 Other statutes empowering a local authority to make by-laws do so for particular purposes. For example, s 35(6) of the Highways Act 1980 authorises the making of by-laws governing the priority and queues in relation to people waiting to board public service vehicles; ss 1 and 10 of the Commons Act 1899 authorise by-laws for the prevention of nuisance and preservation of order on commons; and s 90 of the National Parks and Access to the Countryside Act 1949 and s 41 of the Countryside Act 1968 authorise by-laws for the preservation of order and prevention of damage in national parks and country parks.

Offences against local authority by-laws

9.100 By-laws[1] made by a local authority, whether under s 235 of the 1972 Act or under any other enactment, may provide that contravention of the by-laws is a summary offence punishable with a fine not exceeding such sums as may be fixed by the enactment conferring the by-law-making power, or (if no sum is fixed) not exceeding level 2 on the standard scale.[2] The latter maximum will therefore be applicable in the case of an offence under by-laws made under s 235 or its predecessor. In addition, such by-laws may provide that, in the case of a continuing offence, the person convicted is liable to pay a further fine not exceeding such sum as is fixed by the parent statute, or (if no such sum is fixed) the sum of £5 for each day during which the offence continues after conviction of it.[3]

---

1   By-laws may be proved by certified copies: Local Government Act 1972, s 238.
2   Note that if on 17 July 1978 a by-law specified an amount less than £20 it remains unchanged: Criminal Law Act 1977, s 31(2) and (3). In the case of an offence under a by-law made after 30 April 1984 and before the commencement of the Criminal Justice Act 1988, s 52 (ie 12 October 1988), the maximum fine is construed as the level in the first column of the standard scale corresponding to that amount: Criminal Justice Act 1988, s 52.
3   Local Government Act 1972, s 237.

9.101 Anyone may institute proceedings for breach of a by-law, unless the parent statute restricts the right to prosecute.[1]

A court, including a magistrates' court, can inquire into (and determine) the validity of a by-law if the matter is raised.[2] Like other forms of delegated legislation, a by-law may be invalid if it is ultra vires, ie if it is in excess of the powers conferred by the enabling statute on the rule-making body (substantive ultra vires) or if it is made in breach of a mandatory part of the procedure concerning its making prescribed by that statute (procedural ultra vires). In addition, a by-law is invalid if it is obviously unreasonable,[3] or so uncertain as to have no ascertainable meaning, or so unclear in its effect as to be incapable of certain application in any given situation, or repugnant to the general law (in which cases it is regarded as substantively ultra vires).[4]

If a by-law is partly ultra vires and partly not, because it purports (or its effect is) to deal with matters outside the delegated powers as well as matters within them, it may be valid and enforceable to the extent that it is not ultra vires. It will be valid to that extent if the ultra vires part can be severed. Severance is always possible if the ultra vires part can be removed simply by cutting out the relevant words. If this is not possible, severance may be effected by modifying the text so as to omit the ultra vires aspect of it, provided that this does not change the substantial purpose and effect of the provision as a whole.[5]

The invalidity of a by-law is either challenged directly before the courts on an application for judicial review or raised as a defence to a court action which concerns the application of the by-law. The latter course is not possible if there is a clear Parliamentary intention to the contrary in the Act of Parliament under which the by-law was made.[5] There is no evidence of this in the present statutes referred to above, and by-laws made under s 235 of the 1972 Act, and its predecessor, have, for example, been held invalid in proceedings where their invalidity has been raised as a defence.

---

1   *R v Stewart* [1896] 1 QB 300, DC.
2   *R v Reading Crown Court, ex parte Hutchinson* [1988] 1 All ER 333, DC.
3   The principle of reasonableness must be applied with some liberality to avoid undue interference with locally made decisions: *Kruse v Johnson* [1898] 2 QB 91, DC.
4   See, for example, *Nash v Finlay* (1901) 85 LT 682, DC; *Powell v May* [1946] 1 All ER 444, DC; *Percy v Hall* [1996] 4 All ER 523, CA.

9.102 It must not be forgotten that under s 6(1) of the Human Rights Act 1998 it is unlawful for a public authority to act in a way incompatible with a Convention right; this includes the case where such an authority makes a by-law which is incompatible. Since an 'act' in s 6 includes an omission to act it would seem that it would also be unlawful for a public authority to fail, even if inadvertently, to exercise its power to amend an incompatible by-law, unless the governing statute makes that course impossible.[1]

1   See, further, para **1.16**.

INDEX

References are to paragraph numbers.

Abusive conduct. *See* Threatening, abusive, insulting or disorderly conduct

Accomplices
  affray   3.53
  companies   5.50
  intoxication   3.30
  mental element   3.30
  riot   3.12, 3.19, 3.30
  violent disorder   3.40

Acid house parties. *See* Raves

Admissions   3.32

Adverse inferences   3.25

Adverse occupation   7.136–7.139

Affray   3.51–3.74
  abolition   3.6–3.7
  accomplices   3.53
  arrest without warrant   3.68
  breach of the peace   2.68
  committals   3.66
  convictions
    alternative bases for   3.64
    number of   3.52
  Crown Court   3.71, 3.74
  damage to property   3.54
  defence   3.56
  definition   3.51–3.52
  directions   3.56, 3.72–3.73
  duplicity   3.69–3.70
  either way offences   3.66
  elements of   3.5
  fear of harm   3.52, 3.53, 3.56–3.62
  guidance   3.66
  hypothetical bystander   3.52, 3.53, 3.56–3.62
  intoxication   3.63
  Law Commission   3.6–3.8, 3.52, 3.57, 3.59, 3.65
  magistrates' courts   3.71, 3.74
  mental element   3.63
  number of persons   3.61
  powers of entry   3.68
  private premises   3.53
  prohibited conduct   3.53–3.62
  prosecution   3.65–3.67
  punishment   3.65–3.67
  racially-aggravated public order offences   4.85, 4.87
  reasonableness   3.52, 3.53, 3.56–3.62, 3.68
  riot   3.27, 3.70, 3.73
  searches   3.68
  self-defence   3.56, 3.66
  sentencing   3.67
  summary offences   3.66, 3.71, 3.74
  threats   3.53–3.56, 3.63, 3.65
  trials   3.65–3.67
    indictment, on   3.71–3.73
  use of violence   3.53–3.56, 3.63, 3.65
  verdicts, alternative   3.71–3.74
  violent disorder   3.52, 3.69–3.74
  words   3.55

Age of criminal responsibility   3.19, 3.43, 3.46

Aggravated offences. *See* Aggravated trespass, Racially-aggravated public order offences

Aggravated trespass   7.37–7.66
  adjoining land   7.45–7.46
  animal rights protesters   7.37, 7.42, 7.44–7.45, 7.47, 7.50, 7.52, 7.61, 7.64–7.66
  arrest   7.52, 7.55, 7.64
  badger digging   7.47
  breach of the peace   7.65
  common purpose   7.59–7.60
  defences   7.54, 7.62
  directions to leave land   7.56–7.64, 7.66
    communication   7.60
    duration   7.62, 7.66
    offences   7.62–7.64
    writing   7.60
  disruption   7.50, 7.52, 7.59, 7.65, 7.66
  duplicity   7.38
  European Convention on Human Rights   7.61, 7.62, 7.66
  football matches   7.42
  freedom of assembly and association   7.66

Aggravated trespass – *cont*
  freedom of expression   7.62, 7.66
  highways   7.43
  Human Rights Act 1998   7.61
  hunt saboteurs   7.37, 7.42, 7.44,
    7.47, 7.52, 7.61, 7.64–7.66
  industrial action   7.50
  interpretation   7.43, 7.45, 7.49, 7.52,
    7.57, 7.59
  intimidation   7.51, 7.52, 7.59, 7.66
  land   7.43, 7.45–7.46, 7.57
  licences   7.41
  mental element   7.50–7.53
  necessity   7.54
  obstruction   7.43–7.44, 7.50, 7.52,
    7.59, 7.65
  offences   7.38–7.66
  open air   7.40–7.42
  police powers   7.64, 7.65
  powers of entry   7.64
  prevention of evil   7.54
  prohibited conduct   7.40–7.49
  proportionality   7.66
  punishment   7.55, 7.63
  reasonableness   7.59–7.62, 7.64
  recklessness   7.50
  road protesters   7.37, 7.50, 7.66
  searches   7.64
  seizure   7.60
  sentencing   7.55, 7.63, 7.64
  trials   7.55, 7.63
  vehicles   7.60, 7.62
  warnings   7.61
Alarm. *See* Conduct likely to cause
  harassment, alarm or distress,
  Intentionally causing harassment,
  alarm or distress
Ancient monuments   6.77, 6.86, 6.89,
  6.90
Animal rights protesters
  aggravated trespass   7.37, 7.42, 7.44–
    7.45, 7.47, 7.50, 7.52, 7.61 7.64–7.66
  hunt saboteurs   7.37, 7.42, 7.44,
    7.47, 7.52, 7.61, 7.64–7.66
  offensive weapons   7.64
Anonymous letters   4.32
Anti-social behaviour orders   2.53–2.96
  anti-social manner, acting in an
    2.65–2.74
  appeals   2.86
  applications   2.58–2.61
  background   2.54–2.56
  binding over   2.51, 2.84

  breach of   2.85, 2.88–2.91
  burden of proof   2.80–2.81, 2.89
  civil proceedings   2.53, 2.81, 2.91
  conditions   2.57–2.58
  criminal offences   2.54, 2.80, 2.88,
    2.91
    prosecution for same offence   2.68
  damages   2.56
  defences   2.72
  discharge   2.87
  domestic violence   2.75
  duration of   2.82
  effect of anti-social behaviour   2.75
  either way offences   2.88
  European Convention on Human
    Rights   2.80, 2.85, 2.91
  evaluation   2.91
  evidence   2.81
  further anti-social acts   2.77, 2.83
  guidance   2.53–2.54, 2.82
  harassment, alarm or distress   2.56,
    2.68–2.71, 2.76, 2.90
    lawful conduct causing   2.66
  household, persons in same   2.75
  housing   2.55
  Human Rights Act 1998   2.85
  judicial review   2.86
  local authorities   2.59–2.61
    estates   2.55
  magistrates' courts   2.53, 2.78, 2.86
  necessity for   2.76–2.77
  neighbour disputes   2.54
  pre-commencement conduct   2.62
  procedure   2.79
  prohibitions contained in   2.83–2.85
  racially-aggravated public order
    offences   4.64
  rationale   2.54–2.56
  reasonable acts disregarded   2.72–
    2.74
  reasonable excuse   2.89–2.90
  requirements for   2.62–2.75
  sentencing   2.88
  standard of proof   2.80
  summons   2.79
  variation   2.98
  young offenders   2.78, 2.79
Appeals
  anti-social behaviour orders   2.86
  banning orders   8.35, 8.40
    international   8.46, 8.51, 8.53
  binding over   2.49–2.50
  fear or provocation of violence   4.5
  forfeiture   5.58

Appeals – *cont*
  international football banning
    orders   8.46, 8.51, 8.53
  processions and assemblies   6.94
  recognizances   2.50
  trespassory assemblies   6.86
Armbands   9.4
Arrest
  adverse occupation   7.136
  affray   3.68
  aggravated trespass   7.52, 7.55, 7.64
  arrestable offences   1.2
  assault on the police   9.63
  binding over   2.24, 2.31
  bomb hoaxes   9.29
  breach of the peace   2.7–2.10, 2.17,
    2.24, 3.68, 4.19, 4.60
  churches, etc, disturbances in   9.35
  conduct likely to cause harassment,
    alarm or distress   4.57–4.60
  detention without   2.12–2.13
  drunk and disorderly   9.17
  entering and remaining on
    property   7.135, 7.136
  failure to leave or re-entry on land after
    police direction to leave   7.32,
    7.35
  false or misleading statements   7.126
  fear or provocation of violence
    4.18–4.19
  football banning orders
    domestic   8.37
    international   8.58
  football hooliganism   8.4, 8.29
  general arrest conditions   1.2
  harassment   4.97–4.98
  intentionally causing harassment, alarm
    or distress   4.40
  intimidation and labour relations
    9.49
  meetings, disorderly conduct at
    6.107–6.108, 6.110
  obstruction
    highways   9.88
    police   9.59, 9.67
    public officials   9.71
  political uniforms   9.8–9.9
  processions and assemblies   6.24,
    6.91–6.92
  quasi-military organisations   9.15
  racial hatred   5.19, 5.27
  racially-aggravated public order
    offences   4.86

raves   7.84, 7.86
reasonable suspicion   3.68, 4.18,
  4.57, 6.24, 6.92, 7.32
squatters   7.119–7.120
street offences   9.20
ticket touting   8.65–8.66
unauthorised vehicular campers
  7.107
use of force   1.2, 9.63
warnings   9.69
Assault
  arrest   9.63
  battery   9.61
  breach of the peace   9.69
  evidence   9.62
  football hooliganism   8.26
  mental element   9.64
  obstruction of the police   9.65–9.67
  police   9.58, 9.61–9.71
    execution of his duty, in   9.61–
    9.71
    obstruction   9.65–9.67
    resisting the   9.69
  prohibited conduct   9.62–9.63
  reasonableness   9.63–9.64
  resistance   9.68–9.69
  use of force   9.63–9.64
  wilful obstruction   9.65–9.67
Assemblies. *See* Freedom of assembly and
  association, Processions and
  assemblies, Trespassory assemblies
Associations
  criminal liability   5.50–5.51
  racial hatred   5.24
Attempts   7.117

Badger digging   7.47
Banning orders. *See* Domestic football
  banning orders, International
  football banning orders
Battery   9.61
Besetting   9.42, 9.45
Binding over
  anti-social behaviour orders   2.51,
    2.84
  appeals   2.49–2.50
  arrest   2.24, 2.31
  breach of orders   2.50
  breach of the peace   2.24–2.52
    case stated   2.49
    committals   2.48
    common law   2.35

Binding over – *cont*
    complaints procedure   2.28–2.34
    contempt   2.48
    convictions
        after   2.39
        as   2.26, 2.49
    court's own motion, at   2.35–2.43,
        2.52
    criminal proceedings, as   2.52
    duration of   2.44
    European Convention on Human
        Rights   2.27, 2.51–2.52
    evidence   2.32–2.33, 2.40
    failure to leave or re-entry on land after
        police direction to leave   7.35
    fair trials   2.52
    freedom of expression   2.52
    good behaviour, to be of   2.24–2.52
        meaning of   2.27
    history   2.25
    Law Commission   2.51–2.52
    magistrates' courts   2.24, 2.29–2.33,
        2.39, 2.48–2.50, 2.52
    natural justice   2.43
    own motion, court's   2.35–2.43, 2.52
    peace, to keep the   2.24–2.52
    people against whom order can be
        made   2.38, 2.49
    preventative powers   2.24–2.52
    recognizances   2.24, 2.43–2.48
        appeals   2.50
        breach of   2.50
        refusal to enter into   2.47–2.48,
            2.50, 2.52
    sentencing   2.39, 2.48
    statutory complaints procedure
        2.28–2.34
    summons   2.30
    sureties   2.24, 2.43–2.46, 2.48
    time for making orders   2.39–2.43
    warning   2.43
Bomb hoaxes   9.24–9.29
    arrest   9.28
    false messages   9.28
    interpretation   9.25
    mental element   9.26–9.28
    nuisance   9.24
    offences   9.24–9.28
    placing or dispatching an article
        9.25–9.27
    private places   9.26
    punishment   9.29
    sentencing   9.25, 9.29
    trials   9.29

Boundaries of public order law
    1.1–1.2
Breach of the peace
    aggravated trespass   7.65
    arrest   2.17, 2.24
        detention without   2.12–2.13
        information given on   2.9
        warrant, without   2.7–2.16, 3.68,
            4.19, 4.60
    assault   9.69
    binding over   2.24–2.52
    common law powers   2.2–2.23
    definition   2.4–2.6
    detention
        arrest, without   2.12–2.13
    disturbances   2.4
    England and Wales   2.3
    European Convention on Human
        Rights   2.3, 2.10, 2.14, 2.23
    failure to leave or re-entry on land after
        police direction to leave   7.22,
            7.35
    fear of harm   2.4, 2.8, 2.10, 2.22–
        2.23
    fear or provocation of violence   4.19
    football hooliganism   8.21
    freedom of expression   2.10
    immediacy   2.7, 2.17, 2.20, 2.22
    industrial action   2.17
    lawful conduct   2.6
    legislation   2.2
    meetings
        disorderly conduct, at   6.104
        prohibiting   2.16–2.17
    police   1.5, 2.2–2.23
        assault   9.69
        assisting   2.19
        obstruction   9.57, 9.67
    powers of entry to deal with or
        prevent a   2.14–2.15
    preventive powers   2.2–2.23
        power exercised against   2.21–2.23
    private citizens, exercise of power
        by   2.19
    private premises   2.5, 2.14
        remaining on   2.15
    processions and assemblies   6.1
    provocation   4.102–4.104
    public plays   4.102–4.104
    racial hatred   5.1, 5.8
    raves   7.87
    reasonable belief   2.14, 2.16–2.17,
        2.20–2.23

Breach of the peace – *cont*
  Scotland   2.3
  threatening, abusive, insulting or
     disorderly conduct   4.1, 4.102–
     4.104
  trespassory assemblies   6.70
  use of force   2.18
  violence   2.4
    fear of   2.4, 2.8, 2.22–2.23
Broadcasting
  companies   5.49–5.51
  court reports   5.52
  defences   5.47
  duplicity   5.56
  football matches   5.57
  forfeiture   5.58–5.59
  freedom of expression   5.53
  intention   5.46
  parliamentary reports   5.52
  prosecutions   5.53–5.55
  punishment   5.57
  racial hatred   5.45–5.60
  sentencing   5.57
  threatening, abusive or insulting
     conduct   5.45
  trials   5.57
Burden of proof
  adverse occupation   7.139
  anti-social behaviour orders   2.80–
    2.81, 2.89
  Convention rights   4.38
  dangerous dogs   4.38
  declarations of incompatibility   4.38
  defamation   4.38
  entering and remaining on
     property   7.139
  European Convention on Human
     Rights   4.38
  football banning orders
    domestic   8.34
    international   8.57
  Human Rights Act 1998   4.38
  immoral earnings, living off   4.38
  intentionally causing harassment, alarm
     or distress   4.38
  intimidation and labour relations
    9.46
  obstruction of the highway   9.79
  processions and assemblies   6.23
  riot   3.30
  smuggling   4.38
Burial grounds   9.30–9.36
By-laws   9.97–9.102

Campers. *See* Unauthorised vehicular
  campers
Canada   5.7
Caravan sites. *See also* Gypsies   7.95
Case stated   2.49
Chanting   8.27
Churches, certified places of worship or
  burial grounds, disturbances in
  9.30–9.36
  arrest   9.34
  duplicity   9.30
  European Convention on Human
     Rights   9.36
  freedom of expression   9.36
  indecent behaviour   9.31, 9.32
  interpretation   9.31–9.32
  Law Commission   9.36
  nuisance   9.36
  offences   9.30–9.36
  preachers, molesting   9.33
  punishment   9.34
  reform   9.36
  riotous behaviour   9.31
  sentencing   9.34–9.35
  trials   9.34
  violent behaviour   9.31
Civil proceedings
  anti-social behaviour orders   2.53,
    2.81, 2.91
  failure to leave or re-entry on land after
     police direction to leave   7.21,
    7.29
  harassment   4.89, 4.92–4.96
  remedies   4.92–4.96
Classification of offences   1.9
Clubs
  criminal liability   5.50–5.51
  racial hatred   5.24
Codification   1.3
Collective trespass or nuisance on land. *See*
  also Aggravated trespass, Entering and
  remaining on property, Failure to
  leave or re-entry to land after police
  direction to leave, Raves, Squatters,
  Unauthorised vehicular campers
  7.1–7.140
Commercial premises   7.112
Committals   2.48, 3.66
Common land   7.12
Companies
  accomplices   5.50
  broadcasting   5.49–5.51
  connivance   5.50
  consent   5.50

Companies – *cont*
    criminal liability   5.49–5.51
    directors   5.50
    racial hatred   5.20, 5.49–5.51
Compensation. *See* Damages
Computers   5.33
Conduct likely to cause harassment, alarm
        or distress   4.20
    arrest   4.57–4.60
    behaviour   4.43–4.45, 4.53–4.54
    defences   4.55
    demonstration   4.61
    duplicity   4.56
    European Convention on Human
        Rights   4.63
    freedom of expression   4.54, 4.62
    freedom of peaceful assembly and
        association   4.62
    freedom of thought   4.62
    'hearing or sight' test   4.48–4.51
    immediacy   4.52
    industrial action   4.61
    interpretation   4.46
    letters   4.44
    mental element   4.54
    number of cases   4.61
    'Peeping Toms'   4.45
    police   4.57–4.60, 4.61
    private premises   4.53
    prohibited conduct   4.43–4.53
    punishment   4.56
    reasonableness   4.55
    sentencing   4.42, 4.56
    threatening, abusive, insulting or
        disorderly conduct   4.41–4.62
    trials   4.56
    trivial behaviour   4.20–4.21
    vulnerable persons   4.20
    warnings   4.57, 4.59
    words   4.43–4.45, 4.53–4.54, 4.59
Construction. *See* Interpretation
Contempt
    binding over   2.48
    harassment   4.89, 4.93
    stalking   4.89
Converts   4.75–4.76
Court reports   5.52
Criminal damage. *See* Damage to property
Criminal proceedings. *See also* Either way
        offences, Indictable offences,
        Particular crimes (eg riot), Summary
        offences

anti-social behaviour orders   2.54,
        2.68, 2.81, 2.88, 2.91
    associations   5.50–5.51
    clubs   5.50–5.51
    common law offences   3.2–3.8
    companies   5.49–5.51
    harassment   4.89, 4.92
    intimidation and labour relations
        9.44, 9.47
    possession orders, breach of   7.115
    squatters   7.112
Crown   6.3
Crown Court
    affray   3.71, 3.74
    fear or provocation of violence   4.17
    football banning orders
        domestic   8.31, 8.32, 8.40
        international   8.45, 8.54

Damage to property
    affray   3.54
    failure to leave or re-entry on land after
        police direction to leave   7.17–
        7.20
    racially-aggravated public order
        offences   4.87
    riot   3.27, 3.37
Damages
    anti-social behaviour orders   2.56
    harassment   4.92
    Human Rights Act 1998   1.16
    police fund   3.37–3.38
    riot   3.37–3.38
    time-limits   4.92
Dangerous dogs   4.38
DDP. *See* Director of Public Prosecutions
Declarations of compatibility   1.12–
        1.15, 4.38
Defamation   4.38
Defences
    adverse occupation   7.139
    affray   3.56
    aggravated trespass   7.54, 7.62
    anti-social behaviour orders   2.72
    broadcasting   5.47
    conduct likely to cause harassment,
        alarm or distress   4.55
    crowd safety   8.3
    entering and remaining on
        property   7.139
    failure to leave or re-entry on land after
        police direction to leave   7.30

Defences – *cont*
  intentionally causing harassment, alarm
    or distress   4.36–4.38
  intimidation and labour relations
    9.46
  obstruction of the highway   9.80
  processions and assemblies   6.21–
    6.23
  racial hatred   5.10, 5.43
  riot   3.17
  unauthorised vehicular campers
    7.105
Demonstrations. *See* Processions and
  assemblies
Destruction of vehicles   7.34
Diplomatic premises   7.140
Director of Public Prosecutions   3.34
Directors   5.50
Discretion
  failure to leave or re-entry on land after
    police direction to leave   7.21
  margin of appreciation   1.25–1.26
  police   1.5, 1.6, 7.21
  public authorities   1.25–1.26
Discrimination   1.27
Disorderly conduct. *See* Threatening,
  abusive, insulting or disorderly
  conduct
Displays
  fear or provocation of violence   4.7
  intentionally causing harassment, alarm
    or distress   4.32
  racial hatred   5.15–5.19, 5.21–5.22
Disposal of vehicles   7.34
Distress. *See* Conduct likely to cause
  harassment, alarm or distress,
  Intentionally causing harassment,
  alarm or distress
Disturbances   2.6
Dogs   4.38, 7.65
Domestic disputes   4.33
Domestic football banning orders
  appeals   8.35, 8.40
  arrest   8.37
  breach of   8.42–8.43
  burden of proof   8.34
  Crown Court   8.31, 8.32, 8.40
  declarations of violence   8.35
  designated football matches   8.35
  duration of orders   8.39
  football   5.57, 8.23, 8.30–8.43
  interpretation   8.32
  journeys to and from matches   8.35
  magistrates' courts   8.31, 8.40

  notice   8.36
  obstruction   8.37
  offences   8.35
  photographs   8.37–8.38
  police   8.37
  reasonableness   8.34
  Secretary of State   8.31
  sentencing   8.42
  termination, applications for   8.41
Domestic violence   2.75
Drilling   9.16
Driving   9.56–9.57
Drugs. *See* Intoxication
Drunk and disorderly   9.17
Drunkenness. *See* Drunk and disorderly,
  Intoxication
Duplicity
  affray   3.69–3.70
  aggravated trespass   7.38
  broadcasting   5.56
  churches, disturbances in   9.30
  conduct likely to cause harassment,
    alarm or distress   4.56
  failure to leave or re-entry on land after
    police direction to leave   7.25
  fear or provocation of violence   4.17
  intimidation and labour relations
    9.38
  obstruction of the police   9.50
  racial hatred   5.13, 5.16, 5.60
  riot   3.70
  violent disorder   3.69–3.70
Duress
  riot   3.19
  violent disorder   3.43, 3.46

Either way offences   1.9
  affray   3.66
  anti-social behaviour orders   2.88
  crowd safety   8.3
  football hooliganism   8.3
  harassment   4.95
  nuisance   9.92
Election meetings, disorderly conduct
  at   6.109–6.110
Entering and remaining on property
  7.127–7.140
  adverse occupation   7.136–7.139
  arrest   7.135, 7.136
  burden of proof   7.139
  defences   7.139
  diplomatic premises   7.140

Entering and remaining on property –
      cont
   displaced residential occupiers
         7.133, 7.136, 7.137
   interpretation   7.129, 7.133
   lawful authority, without   7.132,
         7.134
   mental element   7.131, 7.137
   occupied premises   7.130–7.133
   offences   7.127–7.135, 7.140
   prohibited conduct   7.129–7.130,
         7.137
   protected intending occupiers
         7.133, 7.136, 7.137
   re-entry   7.132
   sentencing   7.127, 7.140
   squatters   7.127, 7.130, 7.132–7.133,
         7.136
   tenants   7.133
   violence for securing entry   7.128–
         7.135
Entry. *See* Powers of entry
European Convention on Human Rights
      1950. *See also* Human Rights Act
      1998   1.10–1.27
   aggravated trespass   7.61, 7.62, 7.66
   anti-social behaviour orders   2.80,
         2.85, 2.91
   binding over   2.27, 2.51–2.52
   breach of the peace   2.3, 2.10, 2.14,
         2.23
   broadcasting   5.60
   burden of proof   4.38
   churches, disturbances in   9.36
   codification   1.3
   conduct likely to cause harassment,
         alarm or distress   4.62
   Convention rights   1.14–1.15,
         1.17–1.27
      application of   1.18–1.27
      democratic society, necessary in
            1.23–1.26
      interference with   1.20, 1.22–1.24,
            2.10
      lawfulness of   1.21
      legitimate aim of interference
            1.22–1.24
   discrimination   1.27
   European Court of Human Rights
         1.18
   failure to leave or re-entry on land after
         police direction to leave   7.36

fair trials   2.52
   family life, right to   7.36, 7.110
   fear or provocation of violence   4.5
   freedom of assembly and
         association   4.62, 4.91, 6.9, 6.42,
         6.89, 7.36, 7.66, 7.85–7.86, 9.85
   freedom of expression   2.10, 2.52,
         4.5, 4.62, 4.91, 5.13, 5.60, 7.62,
         7.66, 9.36, 9.85
   freedom of thought   4.62
   harassment   4.91
   home life, right to   7.110
   impact of   1.7
   individual petition   1.18
   intentionally causing harassment, alarm
         or distress   4.36, 4.38
   international football banning
         orders   8.47, 8.57
   interpretation   1.19–1.20
   margin of appreciation   1.25–1.26
   nuisance   9.98, 9.102
   obstruction of the highway   9.79,
         9.85
   police   1.5
   presumption of innocence   4.38,
         9.79
   privacy   5.16, 7.36, 7.110
   processions and assemblies   6.9,
         6.42, 6.53
   proportionality   1.24, 5.60
   public authorities   9.102
   racial hatred   5.13, 5.16, 5.60
   raves   7.85–7.86, 7.89
   seizure   7.33, 7.89
   trespassory assemblies   6.77, 6.89,
         6.90
   unauthorised vehicular campers
         7.110–7.111
Evidence. *See also* Burden of proof,
      Standard of proof
   assault on the police   9.62
   binding over   2.32–2.33, 2.40
   intentionally causing harassment, alarm
         or distress   4.31, 4.38
   failure to leave or re-entry on land after
         police direction to leave   7.21,
         7.27
   obstruction of the police   9.51–9.52,
         9.60
   racially-aggravated public order
         offences   4.79

Failure to leave or re-entry to land after
   police direction to leave   7.2–7.36
  agricultural buildings   7.13
  ancient monuments   7.13
  arrest   7.32, 7.35
  binding over   7.35
  boundaries of land   7.28
  breach of the peace   7.22, 7.35–7.36
  civil law   7.21, 7.29
  common land   7.12
  common purpose   7.15, 7.21
  damage to property   7.17–7.21
  deadlines   7.25
  defences   7.30
  directions
    back up   7.24
    communication of   7.23
    guidance   7.23
    making of   7.21–7.24
    records of   7.23
    seizure   7.33–7.34
    vagueness   7.29
    who may give   7.5–7.6, 7.23
    writing, in   7.23
  discretion   7.21
  duplicity   7.25
  European Convention on Human
    Rights   7.33, 7.36
  evidence   7.27
  family life, right to   7.36
  freedom of assembly and
    association   7.36
  gypsies   7.4, 7.20
  highways   7.14
  interpretation   7.13–7.15, 7.18–7.20,
    7.24, 7.26, 7.28
  judicial review   7.21
  'land'   7.13–7.14
  licence, termination of   7.16
  mass trespasses   7.2–7.3
  mental element   7.29
  need   7.35–7.36
  New Age Travellers   7.3
  number of trespassers   7.8–7.14
  obstruction   7.14, 7.35, 9.70
  occupiers   7.16
  offences   7.2, 7.25–7.32
  possession of vehicles   7.17–7.20
  possession orders   7.35
  privacy   7.36
  prohibited conduct   7.26–7.28
  punishment   7.31
  reasonableness   7.7, 7.8–7.10, 7.13,
    7.15, 7.17–7.30

  re-entry   7.27–7.28, 7.30
  removal notices   7.34
  requests to leave   7.16
  road protesters   9.70
  seizure   7.33–7.34
  sentencing   7.31
  statistics   7.35
  tenants whose lease has expired   7.9
  threats   7.17–7.20
  trials   7.31
  unauthorised vehicular campers
    7.14, 7.21
  use of force   7.35
  vehicles
    disposal   7.34
    number of   7.20
    possession of   7.17–7.20
    retention   7.34
    seizure   7.33–7.34
Fair trials   2.52
False messages   9.28
False or misleading statements
  arrest   7.126
  interim possession orders   7.121–
    7.126
  mental element   7.124
  prohibited conduct   7.122–7.123
  punishment   7.126
  recklessness   7.124
  sentencing   7.126
  squatters   7.121–7.126
  trials   7.126
Family life, right to
  European Convention on Human
    Rights   7.36, 7.110
  failure to leave or re-entry on land after
    police direction to leave   7.36
  unauthorised vehicular campers
    7.110
Fear of harm. *See also* Fear or provocation
  of violence
  affray   3.52, 3.53, 3.56–3.62
  breach of the peace   2.4, 2.8, 2.10,
    2.22–2.23
  harassment   4.95
  obstruction of the highway   9.75
  riot   3.26–3.28
  unlawful assembly   3.4
  violent disorder   3.40–3.41
Fear or provocation of violence
  affray   4.3
  appeals   4.5
  arrest   4.18–4.19
  behaviour   4.6, 4.8, 4.11, 4.13

Fear or provocation of violence – *cont*
  breach of peace   4.19
  Crown Court   4.18
  distribution or display of writing   4.7
  duplicity   4.17
  European Convention on Human
    Rights   4.5
  freedom of expression   4.5
  homes   4.10
  homosexual conduct   4.8
  Human Rights Act 1998   4.5
  immediacy   4.13–4.15
  interpretation   4.5, 4.8, 4.10, 4.13
  intoxication   4.12
  magistrates' court   4.17
  mental element   4.11–4.16
  police powers   4.18–4.19
  powers of entry   4.18
  private places   4.9–4.10
  prosecution   4.17
  punishment   4.17
  searches   4.18
  sentencing   4.17
  summary offences   4.3, 4.17
  threatening, abusive, insulting or
    disorderly conduct   4.2–4.19
  towards or to another   4.8
  trials   4.17
  use of force   4.18
  violence
    justified   4.13
    likely to cause   4.15–4.16
  violent disorder   4.3
  vulnerable persons   4.20
  words   4.6, 4.11, 4.13
Films   5.17, 5.33
Fireworks   8.16–8.23
Following people   9.40, 9.43
Football hooliganism   8.1–8.66
  affray   8.26
  aggravated trespass   7.42
  alcohol on coaches, trains etc
    8.5–8.6, 8.10–8.20
  arrest   8.4, 8.29
  assault   8.26
  breach of the peace   8.21
  broadcasting   5.57
  chanting   8.27
  containers   8.20, 8.22
  covert operations   8.1
  designated sporting events   8.7–8.9,
    8.16–8.23, 8.25
    drunkenness at   8.23

    duration of   8.18
    possession of alcohol at   8.19–8.22
  domestic football banning orders
    5.57, 8.23, 8.30–8.58
  either way offences   8.3
  fireworks   8.16–8.23
  international football banning
    orders   8.23, 8.44–8.58
  interpretation   8.6–8.9, 8.11–8.12,
    8.17–8.21, 8.26–8.27
  intoxication   8.2, 8.5–8.6, 8.10–8.20
  lawful authority   8.21, 8.28
  licences   8.3
  mental element   8.12
  missiles   8.20, 8.26
  national membership schemes   8.3
  offences   8.13, 8.19, 8.21–8.29
  pitch invasion   8.28
  police   8.1, 8.4, 8.15, 8.19–8.22, 8.24
  possession   8.12
  powers of entry   8.24
  punishment   8.29
  racial hatred   5.61, 8.27
  safety   8.3
  Scotland   8.9
  searches   8.15, 8.24
  seating   8.3
  sentencing   8.11–8.12, 8.19, 8.23,
    8.29
  spectators   8.3
  statutory provisions   8.2–8.3
  throwing objects   8.26
  trials   8.29
  use of force   8.15
  vehicles   8.5–8.6, 8.10–8.20
    drunkenness on   8.13
  violence   8.26
  violent disorder   8,26
Football ticket touting   8.59–8.66
Forfeiture
  appeals   5.58
  broadcasting   5.58–5.59
  claims, determining   7.91
  disposal of   7.92
  magistrates' courts   7.90–7.92
  racial hatred   5.58–5.59
  raves   7.90–7.92
  seizure   7.34, 7.90–7.92
  sentencing   5.58–5.59, 7.92
  sound equipment   7.90–7.92
  vehicles   7.34
France   4.65
Freedom of assembly and association
  aggravated trespass   7.66

Freedom of assembly and association –
cont
conduct likely to cause harassment,
alarm or distress 4.62
European Convention on Human
Rights 4.62, 4.91, 6.9, 6.42,
6.89, 7.36, 7.66, 7.85–7.86, 9.85
failure to leave or re-entry on land after
police direction to leave 7.32–
7.36
harassment 4.91
obstruction of the highway 9.85
processions and assemblies 6.1, 6.4,
6.9, 6.42, 6.69
racial hatred 5.2, 5.13, 5.14
rave 7.85–7.86
trespassory assemblies 6.69, 6.89,
6.90
Freedom of expression
aggravated trespass 7.62, 7.66
binding over 2.52
breach of the peace 2.10
broadcasting 5.53
churches, disturbances in 9.36
conduct likely to cause harassment,
alarm or distress 4.54, 4.62
European Convention on Human
Rights 2.10, 2.52, 4.5, 4.62,
4.91, 5.13, 5.60, 7.62, 7.66, 9.36,
9.85
fear or provocation of violence 4.5
harassment 4.91
intentionally causing harassment, alarm
or distress 4.40
obstruction of the highway 9.85
processions and assemblies 6.1, 6.4,
6.16, 6.42, 6.69
proportionality 5.60
trespassory assemblies 6.69, 6.89
Freedom of movement 8.47
Freedom of thought 4.62
Funerals 6.10

Germany 4.65
Graveyards, disturbances in 9.30–9.36
Gypsies
abolition of duty to provide sites for
7.93–7.94, 7.110
failure to leave or re-entry on land after
police direction to leave 7.4,
7.20
planning permission 7.94, 7.110

unauthorised vehicular campers
7.93–7.95, 7.110
vehicles 7.20

Harassment. *See also* Conduct likely to
cause harassment, alarm or distress,
Intentionally causing harassment,
alarm or distress
anti-social behaviour orders 2.56,
2.66, 2.68–2.71, 2.76, 2.90
lawful conduct causing 2.66
arrest 4.98
civil proceedings 4.89, 4.92–4.96
contempt 4.89, 4.93
course of conduct 4.90–4.91, 4.94–
4.95
criminal law 4.89, 4.92
damages 4.92
demonstrations 4.91
either way offences 4.95
European Convention on Human
Rights 4.91
fear of harm 4.95
freedom of assembly and
association 4.91
freedom of expression 4.91
injunctions 4.89, 4.91, 4.92, 4.93
offences 4.94–4.96
persistence 4.20
prohibition of 4.90–4.91
protection from 4.89–4.101
punishment 4.98
racial hatred 4.22, 5.13, 5.61
racially-aggravated public order
offences 4.64, 4.97–4.101
reasonableness 4.90
remedies 4.92–4.96
restraining orders 4.96, 4.99
sentencing 4.93–4.96, 4.98
stalking 4.89
standard of proof 4.92
summary offences 4.95, 4.101
threatening, abusive, insulting or
disorderly conduct 4.89–4.101
time-limits 4.92
trials 4.98
indictment, on 4.95, 4.100
verdicts, alternative 4.100–4.101
Hiding property 9.41
Highways. *See also* Obstruction of the
highway
aggravated trespass 7.43

Highways – *cont*
    failure to leave or re-entry on land after
        police direction to leave   7.14
    meetings, disorderly conduct at
        6.106
    street offences   9.18–9.23
    trespassory assemblies   6.87–6.88
    unauthorised vehicular campers
        7.97
Hoaxes. *See* Bomb hoaxes
Homes. *See* Households and homes
Homosexual conduct   4.8
Households and homes
    anti-social behaviour orders   2.75
    European Convention on Human
        Rights   7.110
    fear or provocation of violence   4.10
    unauthorised vehicular campers
        7.110
Housing
    anti-social behaviour orders   2.55
    local authority   2.55
Human rights. *See* European Convention
    on Human Rights, Human Rights Act
    1998
Human Rights Act 1998   1.3, 1.10–1.27
    aggravated trespass   7.61
    burden of proof   4.38
    by-laws   9.102
    Convention rights   1.14–1.15, 1.17–
        1.28
        application of   1.18–1.27
    damages   1.16
    declarations of incompatibility
        1.12–1.15, 4.38
    entry into force   1.11
    fear or provocation of violence   4.5
    impact of   1.7, 1.12–1.16
    interpretation   1.14
    judges' role   1.13
    nuisance   9.102
    parliamentary sovereignty   1.12
    precedent   1.14
    public authorities   1.16
    unlawful actions   1.16
    'victim-rule'   1.16
Hunt saboteurs
    aggravated trespass   7.37, 7.42, 7.44,
        7.47, 7.52, 7.61, 7.64–7.66
    trespass by hunt   7.65
Hypothetical bystander test
    affray   3.52, 3.53, 3.56–3.62
    riot   3.26–3.28, 3.31
    violent disorder   3.40–3.41

Immoral earnings, living off   4.38
Impact of public order law   1.6–1.8
Incitement   6.41, 6.52
Indecent behaviour   9.31
Independent Parades Commission
    6.26, 6.48
Indictable offences. *See also* Trials on
    indictment   1.9, 3.1
    riot   3.35
Industrial action
    aggravated trespass   7.50
    breach of the peace   2.17
    conduct likely to cause harassment,
        alarm or distress   4.61
    immunities   9.44, 9.47
    intimidation   9.37–9.41
    nuisance   9.95
    obstruction of the highway   9.76
    processions and assemblies   6.59
    riot   3.21
    trespassory assemblies   6.72
    violent disorder   3.44
Inferences. *See* Adverse inferences
Injunctions
    breach of   4.93
    harassment   4.89, 4.91, 4.92, 4.93
    stalking   4.89
Insanity
    riot   3.19
    violent disorder   3.43, 3.46
Insulting conduct. *See* Threatening,
    abusive, insulting or disorderly
    conduct
Intentionally causing harassment, alarm or
    distress
    'alarm'   4.29
    arrest   4.40
    behaviour   4.26
    burden of proof   4.38
    causation   4.27–4.31
    coverage   4.21–4.22
    defences   4.36–4.38
    displays   4.32–4.33
    'distress'   4.30
    domestic disputes   4.33
    European Convention on Human
        Rights   4.36, 4.38
    evidence   4.31, 4.38
    freedom of expression   4.40
    'harassment'   4.28
    Human Rights Act 1998   4.38
    interpretation   4.23–4.24, 4.28–4.32,
        4.38
    intoxication   4.35

Intentionally causing harassment, alarm or
    distress – *cont*
  leaflets   4.25, 4.32
  letters   4.25
    anonymous   4.32
  mental element   4.34–4.35
  private premises   4.32–4.33
  processions and assemblies   4.37,
    4.40
  prohibited conduct   4.23–4.33
    isolated   4.31
    reasonableness   4.36–4.38
  punishment   4.38
  reasonableness   4.36–4.38
  representations   4.25
  sentencing   4.39
  telephone calls   4.33
  threatening, abusive, insulting or
    disorderly conduct   4.22–4.40
  towards or to another person   4.26,
    4.35
  trials   4.39
  warrants   4.40
  words   4.26
Interim possession orders
  applications for   7.114
  documents   7.114
  false or misleading information
    7.121–7.126
  form of   7.114
  scope   7.114
  service   7.114
  squatters   7.112–7.126
  time for hearing   7.114
International football banning orders
  appeals   8.46, 8.51, 8.53
  arrest   8.58
  breach of   8.55–8.57
  conditions   8.47, 8.55
  Crown Court   8.45, 8.54
  designated football matches   8.44
  duration of   8.49
  effect of   8.47
  European Convention on Human
    Rights   8.47, 8.57
  evidence   8.57
  exemptions   8.51
  Football Banning Orders Authority
    8.48
  football hooliganism   8.44–8.58
  freedom of movement   8.47
  imprisonment, during   8.47, 8.48
  International Covenant on Civil and
    Political Rights   8.47

interpretation   8.44, 8.46, 8.48
  magistrates' courts   8.46, 8.54
  notice   8.48
  offences   8.45–8.46
  Orders in Council   8.46
  police   8.47, 8.50
  procedure   8.46
  reasonableness   8.45, 8.56–8.57
  reporting procedure   8.50
  Secretary of State   8.48
  sentencing   8.50, 8.52, 8.55
  termination of   8.54
  time for making   8.45–8.47
International Covenant on Civil and
    Political Rights   8.47
Interpretation
  aggravated trespass   7.43, 7.45, 7.49,
    7.52, 7.57, 7.59
  alarm   4.29
  assembly   6.72
  associations   9.6
  besetting   9.42
  bomb hoaxes   9.25
  buildings   7.114
  causes   8.11
  churches, etc, disturbances in   9.31–
    9.32
  churchyards   9.32
  colour   4.69
  damage   7.18
  designated football matches   8.44,
    8.62
  designated sporting event   8.7, 8.17
  disorderly   9.17
  distress   4.30
  distributing   5.21
  drunk   9.17
  enforcing authority   8.48
  engaging   7.49
  entering and remaining on
    property   7.129
  ethnic origins   4.71
  European Convention on Human
    Rights   1.19–1.20
  failure to leave or re-entry on land after
    police direction to leave   7.13–
    7.15, 7.18–7.20, 7.24, 7.26, 7.28
  fear or provocation of violence   4.5,
    4.8, 4.10, 4.13
  football banning orders
    domestic   8.32
    international   8.44, 8.46, 8.48
  football hooliganism   8.6–8.9, 8.11–
    8.12, 8.17–8.21, 8.26–8.27

Interpretation – *cont*
  harassment   4.28
  highways   7.97, 9.74
  Human Rights Act 1998   1.14
  indecent behaviour   9.31
  intentionally causing harassment, alarm
       or distress   4.23–4.24, 4.28–4.32,
       4.38
  intimidation and labour relations
       9.39–9.40, 9.42–9.44
  land   7.13–7.14, 7.43, 7.57, 7.72, 7.82
  lawful activity   7.57
  lawful authority   8.21
  meetings   9.3
  music   7.75
  national origins   4.70
  nationality   4.69
  night   7.76
  obscenity   9.19
  obstruction   9.89
    highway   9.74, 9.78
    police   9.67
  occupiers   7.97
  organising   6.38, 6.68
  passengers   9.19
  permits   8.11
  persistently follows   9.40
  political   9.6
  political uniforms   9.3–9.6
  possession   8.12
  premises   8.32
  processions and assemblies   6.5–6.6,
       6.27–6.32, 6.38, 6.57–6.59, 6.68
  profane   9.19
  public assembly   6.57–6.59
  public places   8.63, 9.3, 9.17
  publishing   5.21–5.22
  race   4.69
  racial groups   4.68–4.73, 5.6
  racial hatred   5.4, 5.14, 5.17, 5.21–
       5.24, 5.33
  racially aggravated public order
       offences   4.68–4.80, 4.82
  raves   7.68–7.78, 7.82, 7.86
  representations   5.17
  residents   9.19
  residing   7.15, 7.99
  riotous   9.31
  roads   9.74
  section of the public   5.24
  serious damage   6.29, 6.77
  serious public disorder   6.29
  significant damage   6.77
  squatters   7.114

  ticket touting   8.61–8.63
  trespassory assemblies   6.72, 6.77,
       6.82
  unauthorised vehicular campers
       7.97–7.102
  uniforms   9.5
  vehicle   7.20, 7.100
  violence   7.129, 8.26, 9.31
  watching   9.42
  wearing   9.4
  wilful   9.67, 9.78, 9.89
  written material   5.17, 5.25
  wrongfully   9.44
Intimidation. *See also* Intimidation and
     labour relations
  aggravated trespass   7.51, 7.52, 7.59,
       7.66
  public processions and assemblies
       6.31–6.33
Intimidation and labour relations
     9.37–9.49
  arrest   9.49
  burden of proof   9.46
  contracts, threats to break   9.39
  criminal liability   9.44, 9.47
  defences   9.46
  duplicity   9.38
  following   9.40, 9.43
    disorderly manner, in   9.43
  hiding property   9.41
  immunities   9.44, 9.47
  interpretation   9.39–9.40, 9.42–9.44
  lawful authority   9.46–9.47
  mental element   9.45
  persistently following a person   9.40
  pickets   9.39, 9.47
    code of practice   9.47
  prohibited conduct   9.38–9.44
  punishment   9.48
  sentencing   9.48
  statutory provisions   9.37
  threats   9.39
  trials   9.48
  violence   9.39
  watching or besetting   9.42, 9.45
  wrongful conduct   9.44
Intoxication
  accomplices   3.30
  common purpose   3.30
  drunk and disorderly   9.17
  fear or provocation of violence   4.12
  football hooliganism   8.2, 8.5–8.6,
       8.10–8.20

Intoxication – *cont*
  intentionally causing harassment, alarm
      or distress   4.35
  mental element   3.30, 3.45, 3.63,
      4.34–4.35
  riot   3.30
  self-induced   3.30, 4.12, 4.35
  vehicles   8.13
  violent disorder   3.45

Judges
  binding over   2.36
  Human Rights Act 1998   1.13
  role of   1.13
Judicial review
  anti-social behaviour orders   2.86
  delay   6.98
  failure to leave or re-entry on land after
      police direction to leave   7.21
  leave   6.98
  local authorities   6.99
  processions and assemblies   6.95–
      6.99, 6.103
  ultra vires   6.96
  Wednesbury unreasonableness   6.97
Juveniles. *See* Young offenders

'Knee-jerk' changes to law   1.2, 1.10

Labour relations. *See* Industrial action,
    Intimidation and labour relations
Law Commission
  affray   3.6–3.8, 3.52, 3.57, 3.59, 3.65
  binding over   2.51–2.52
  churches, etc, disturbances in   9.36
  riot   3.6–3.8, 3.34
  rout   3.6–3.8
  unlawful assembly   3.6–3.8
Leaflets   4.32
Letters
  anonymous   4.32
  conduct likely to cause harassment,
      alarm or distress   4.44
  intentionally causing harassment, alarm
      or distress   4.25, 4.32
  malicious communications   4.32
Licences
  aggravated trespass   7.41
  failure to leave or re-entry on land after
      police direction to leave   7.16
  football hooliganism   8.3

raves   7.67, 7.69
Local authorities
  anti-social behaviour orders   2.55,
      2.59–2.61
  by-laws   9.97–9.102
  gypsies   7.94–7.94
  housing   2.55
  judicial review   6.99
  nuisance   9.97–9.102
  processions and assemblies   6.3,
      6.46–6.49, 6.55, 6.99, 6.102
  unauthorised vehicular campers   7.4,
      7.21, 7.93, 7.104, 7.107–7.108, 7.110

Magistrates' courts
  affray   3.71, 3.74
  anti-social behaviour orders   2.53,
      2.78, 2.86
  binding over   2.24, 2.29–2.33, 2.39,
      2.48–2.50, 2.52
  dogs   7.65
  fear or provocation of violence   4.17
  fines   1.9
  football banning orders
    domestic   8.31, 8.40
    international   8.46, 8.54
  forfeiture   7.90–7.92
  obstruction of the police   9.51
  unauthorised vehicular campers
      7.95, 7.107
  violent disorder   3.74
  young offenders   2.78
Malicious communications   4.32
Margin of appreciation
  discretion   1.25–1.26
  European Convention on Human
      Rights   1.25–1.26
  public authorities   1.25–1.26
  Wednesbury unreasonableness   1.26
Meetings
  arrest   6.107–6.108, 6.110
  breach of the peace   2.16–2.17,
      6.104
  disorderly conduct   6.104–6.106
  elections   6.109–6.110
  highways   6.106
  interpretation   6.106, 9.3
  nuisance   9.98
  police   6.107–6.108, 6.110
  political uniforms   9.3
  preventing   2.16–2.17
  processions and assemblies   6.55,
      6.104–6.110

Meetings – *cont*
  public   6.105–6.106, 6.109
  sentencing   6.105, 6.107, 6.109
  summary offences   6.105, 6.107,
    6.110
  threatening, abusive, insulting or
    disorderly conduct   4.105
  trespassory assemblies   6.69
Mens rea. See Mental element
Mental element
  accomplices   3.30
  adverse occupation   7.138
  affray   3.63
  aggravated trespass   7.50–7.53
  assault on the police   9.64
  bomb hoaxes   9.26–9.28
  conduct likely to cause harassment,
    alarm or distress   3.54
  entering and remaining on
    property   7.131, 7.138
  failure to leave or re-entry on land after
    police direction to leave   7.29
  false or misleading statements   7.124
  fear or provocation of violence
    4.11–4.16
  football hooliganism   8.12
  intentionally causing harassment, alarm
    or distress   4.34–4.34
  intimidation and labour relations
    9.45
  intoxication   3.30, 3.45, 3.63, 4.35
  obstruction of the highway   9.78
  possession   8.12
  processions and assemblies   6.20
  racial hatred   5.18, 5.26, 5.31, 5.36–
    5.37, 5.43
  riot   3.29–3.32
  squatters   7.118
  ticket touting   8.64
  violent disorder   3.43, 3.45
Military organisations. *See* Quasi-military
  organisations
Missiles   8.20, 8.26

Nationality   4.69
Natural justice   2.43
Necessity   7.54
Negligence   9.96
Neighbour disputes   2.54
New Age Travellers
  failure to leave or re-entry on land after
    police direction to leave   7.3

  unauthorised vehicular campers
    7.93
Noise   7.73, 7.75–7.77
Northern Ireland
  Independent Parades Commission
    6.26, 6.48
  processions and assemblies   6.26,
    6.48
  racial hatred   5.7
Nuisance. *See also* Collective trespass or
  nuisance on land
  bomb hoaxes   9.24
  by-laws   9.97–9.102
    validity of   9.101
  churches, etc, disturbances in   9.35
  common law   9.92
  Convention rights   9.102
  either way offences   9.92
  European Convention on Human
    Rights   9.98
  interpretation   9.94
  local authorities   9.97–9.101
  meetings   9.98
  negligence   9.96
  obscene phone calls   9.94
  obstruction on the highway   9.95
  offences   9.100–9.102
  processions and assemblies   9.95
  prosecutions   9.101
  public   9.92–9.96
  raves   7.73, 7.82
  reasonableness   9.95
  sentencing   9.100
  summary offences   9.93
  trespassory assemblies   6.86

Obscene phone calls   9.94
Obscenity   9.19, 9.21
Obstruction. *See also* Obstruction of the
  highway, Obstruction of the
  police   9.89–9.91
  aggravated trespass   7.43–7.44, 7.50,
    7.52, 7.59, 7.65
  arrest   9.71
  failure to leave or re-entry on land after
    police direction to leave   7.14,
    7.35
  interpretation   9.89
  lawful excuse, without   9.89–9.90
  powers of entry   9.70
  public officials   9.70–9.71
  searches   9.71
  sentencing   9.70, 9.90

Obstruction – *cont*
    trespassory assemblies   6.87
    unauthorised vehicular campers
        7.109
    wilful   9.89
Obstruction of the highway   9.72–9.89
    arrest   9.88
    authorisation   9.80
    burden of proof   9.79
    common law   9.74, 9.91
    de minimis obstruction   9.75, 9.77
    defences   9.80
    European Convention on Human
        Rights   9.79, 9.85
    failure to leave or re-entry on land after
        police direction to leave   7.14
    fear of harm   9.75
    freedom of assembly and
        association   9.85
    freedom of expression   9.85
    industrial action   9.76
    injunctions   9.85
    interpretation   9.74, 9.78
    lawful authority or excuse, without
        9.79–9.85
    mental element   9.78
    nuisance   9.95
    obstruction of the police   9.78
    omissions   9.76
    processions   9.83
    prohibited conduct   9.74
    reasonableness   9.81–9.82, 9.84–9.86
    sentencing   9.87–9.88, 9.91
    summary offences   9.73, 9.79
    trials   9.87–9.88
        indictment, on   9.91
Obstruction of the police   9.50–9.61
    arrest   9.59, 9.67
    banning orders   8.37
    breach of the peace   9.57, 9.67
    common law   9.54–9.55, 9.57
    drivers   9.56–9.57
    duplicity   9.50
    evidence   9.51–9.52, 9.60
    execution of his duty, in the   9.51–
        9.52, 9.65
    failure to comply with instructions
        9.55, 9.67
    failure to leave or re-entry on land after
        police direction to leave   7.14
    interpretation   9.67
    lawful conduct of police officers
        9.53, 9.56–9.60
    legal duty, persons under a   9.67
    magistrates' court   9.51
    offences   9.50–9.51
    private premises   9.58
    questions, refusal to answer   9.67
    resisting a constable   9.68
    use of force   9.58
    warnings   9.66
    wilful   9.65–9.67
Offensive weapons   7.64

Parliament
    processions and assemblies   6.101
    racial hatred   5.52
    reports   5.52
Parliamentary sovereignty   1.12
Passengers   9.19
'Peeping Toms'   4.45
Pickets. *See* Industrial action
Pirate traders   7.112
Pitch invasions   8.28
Planning
    gypsies   7.94, 7.110
    unauthorised vehicular campers
        7.94, 7.110
Police. *See also* Arrest, Obstruction of the
        police
    assault   9.58, 9.61–9.71
    assisting   2.19
    breach of the peace   1.5, 2.2–2.23
    conduct likely to cause harassment,
        alarm or distress   4.57–4.60,
        4.61
    damages   3.37–3.38
    delegation   6.93–6.99
    discretion   1.5, 1.6, 7.21
    European Convention on Human
        Rights   1.5
    eviction   7.115
    execution of his duty, acting in
        9.51–9.71
    failure to leave or re-entry on land after
        police direction to leave   7.2–
        7.36
    fear or provocation of violence
        4.18–4.19
    football banning orders
        domestic   8.37
        international   8.47, 8.50
    football hooliganism   8.1, 8.4, 8.15,
        8.24
    fund   3.37–3.38
    meetings, disorderly conduct at
        6.107–6.108, 6.110

Police – *cont*
  orders from, obeying   1.5
  powers of entry   1.2
  processions and assemblies   6.17,
      6.25–6.48, 6.55–6.56, 6.60–6.65,
      6.70, 6.92, 6.100–6.103
  quasi-military organisations   9.12
  questions, refusal to answer   9.67
  raves   7.67, 7.80–7.83, 7.86–7.89
  resisting the   9.68–9.69
  riot   3.37–3.38, 4.18
  role of   1.4–1.5
  searches   1.2, 4.18
  squatters   7.115, 7.120
  trespassory assemblies   6.70–6.71,
      6.74, 6.78–6.79, 6.86, 6.90
  unauthorised vehicular campers
      7.95
Political uniforms   9.1–9.10
  armbands   9.4
  arrest   9.8–9.9
  interpretation   9.3–9.6
  meetings   9.3
  offences   9.3, 9.6, 9.8, 9.10
  powers of entry   9.9
  proscribed organisations   9.10
  prosecutions   9.8
  quasi-military organisations   9.10
  searches   9.9
  seizure   9.4
  sentencing   9.8–9.10
Possession. *See also* Interim possession
      orders
  alcohol   8.12
  failure to leave or re-entry on land after
      police direction to leave   7.17–
      7.20
  fireworks   8.21
  football hooliganism   8.12
  interpretation   8.12
  mental element   8.12
  orders   7.95, 7.112, 9.70
    breach   7.115
    criminal offences   7.115
  racial hatred   5.33–5.39
  unauthorised vehicular campers
      7.95
  vehicles   7.17–7.20
Powers of entry
  aggravated trespass   7.64
  breach of the peace   2.14–2.15
  fear or provocation of violence   4.18
  football hooliganism   8.24
  obstruction   9.71

political uniforms   9.9
  racial hatred   5.27, 5.39
  raves   7.87
  squatters   7.120
  use of force   1.2, 4.18
Precedent   1.14
Presumption of innocence   4.38, 9.79
Preventative powers   2.1–2.91
  anti-social behaviour orders   2.53–
      2.91
  binding over   2.24–2.52
  breach of the peace   2.2–2.23
Privacy
  European Convention on Human
      Rights   5.16, 7.36, 7.110
  failure to leave or re-entry on land after
      police direction to leave   7.36
  racial hatred   5.16
  unauthorised vehicular campers
      7.110
Private premises
  affray   3.53
  bomb hoaxes   9.24
  breach of the peace   2.5, 2.14–2.15
  conduct likely to cause harassment,
      alarm or distress   4.53
  fear or provocation of violence
      4.9–4.10
  intentionally causing harassment, alarm
      or distress   4.32–4.33
  obstruction of the police   9.58
  processions and assemblies   6.5, 6.58
  racial hatred   5.16, 5.30
  riot   3.11, 3.28
  violent disorder   3.41
Private prosecutions   3.34
Processions and assemblies. *See also*
      Trespassory assembly   6.1–6.110
  advance notice   6.1, 6.7–6.24, 6.38
    bans   6.49
    contents   6.17
    delivery   6.12–6.16
    exemptions   6.10, 6.18
    immunity   6.16
    judicial review   6.98
    offences   6.18–6.23
    person who must give   6.11
    reasonably practicable   6.9, 6.13–
        6.15, 6.46
    when notice must be given   6.9
    written   6.9, 6.35
  appeals   6.94
  arrest   6.24, 6.91–6.92

Processions and assemblies – *cont*
 bans 6.1–6.2, 6.43–6.53
  appeals 6.94
  applications 6.47
  challenging 6.94–6.99
  class 6.51
  duration of 6.51
  judicial review 6.95–6.99
  notice 6.49
  offences 6.52
  procedure 6.45–6.48
  terms 6.50–6.51
 breach of the peace 6.1
 burden of proof 6.23
 class of 6.50
 common purpose 6.6
 commonly held 6.10
 conditions 6.1–6.2, 6.25–6.42
  appeals 6.94
  challenging 6.94–6.99
  example 6.66
  formal imposition 6.67
  grounds 6.28–6.32, 6.43, 6.59
  judicial review 6.95–6.99
  offences 6.37–6.41
  persons who can impose 6.26–
   6.27, 6.60–6.61
  public assemblies, on 6.54–6.68
  refusal to impose 6.99
  types 6.62–6.67
 conduct likely to cause harassment,
   alarm or distress 4.61
 Crown 6.3
 defences 6.21–6.23
 European Convention on Human
   Rights 6.9, 6.42, 6.53
 exempt 6.10, 6.18
 freedom of assembly and
   association 6.1, 6.4, 6.9, 6.42,
   6.69
 freedom of expression 6.1, 6.4, 6.16,
   6.42, 6.69
 funerals 6.10
 harassment 4.91
 incitement 6.41, 6.52
 Independent Parades Commission
   6.26, 6.48
 industrial action 6.59
 intentionally causing harassment, alarm
   or distress 4.37, 4.40
 interpretation 6.5–6.6, 6.27–6.32,
   6.38, 6.57–6.59, 6.68
 intimidation 6.31–6.34
 judicial review 6.95–6.99, 6.103

 local authorities 6.3, 6.46–6.49, 6.55,
   6.99, 6.102
 meetings 6.55, 6.104–6.110
 mental element 6.20
 Northern Ireland 6.26, 6.48
 number of persons 6.57–6.58, 6.63,
   6.68
 obstruction of the highway 9.83
 offences 6.18–6.23, 6.37–6.41, 6.52,
   6.68
 organisers 6.38, 6.52, 6.68
 Parliament 6.101
 permits 6.7
 police 6.2, 6.7–6.8, 6.11, 6.17, 6.25–
   6.48, 6.55–6.56, 6.60–6.65, 6.70,
   6.92, 6.100–6.103
  delegation of powers 6.93–6.99
  presence at the scene 6.27
 political 6.10
 private premises 6.5, 6.58
 procedure 6.35–6.36, 6.45–6.48
 prohibited conduct 6.19–6.20
 prohibition 6.1–6.2, 6.43–6.53,
   6.69–6.70
 public access 6.5
 public assemblies 6.54–6.68
  conditions 6.54–6.68
  definition 6.57–6.59
  offences 6.68
  trespass 6.69–6.90
 'public processions' 6.5–6.6
 reasonableness 6.21, 6.28–6.31,
   6.45–6.47, 6.61, 6.70
 roadblocks 6.100
 routes, regulation of 6.100–6.103
 sentencing 6.18, 6.37, 6.39, 6.41,
   6.52, 6.100
 serious disruption 6.30
 serious public disorder/serious
   damage 6.29
 spontaneous 6.9, 6.18
 statutory bodies 6.3
 statutory powers 6.2
 summary offences 6.2
 violent disorder 3.40
Profanity 9.19, 9.21
Proof. *See* Burden of proof, Standard of
   proof
Property damage. *See* Damage to property
Proportionality
 aggravated trespass 7.66
 European Convention on Human
   Rights 1.24, 5.60
 freedom of expression 5.60

Proscribed organisations. *See* Quasi-
    military organisations
Prosecutions. *See also* Director of Public
    Prosecutions, Private
    prosecutions   1.6
  affray   3.65–3.67
  Attorney-General   5.53, 5.55
  broadcasting   5.53–5.55
  fear or provocation of violence   4.17
  nuisance   9.101
  political uniforms   9.8
  quasi-military organisations   9.14
  racial hatred   5.3, 5.19, 5.27, 5.53–
    5.55
  racially-aggravated public order
    offences   4.88
  riot   3.34–3.36
  violent disorder   3.50
Provocation
  breach of the peace   4.102–4.104
  fear or provocation of violence
    4.2–4.19
  public plays   4.102–4.104
Public authorities. *See also* Local
    authorities
  discretion   1.25–1.26
  European Convention on Human
    Rights   9.102
  Human Rights Act 1998   1.16
  margin of appreciation   1.25–1.26
  Parliament, as   1.16
Public nuisance   9.92–9.96
Public plays   4.102–4.104, 5.40–5.44
Publications   5.20–5.27, 5.33–5.37
Punishment. *See also* Sentencing   1.9
  affray   3.65–3.67
  aggravated trespass   7.55, 7.63
  bomb hoaxes   9.29
  broadcasting   5.57
  churches, etc, disturbances in   9.34
  conduct likely to cause harassment,
    alarm or distress   4.56
  failure to leave or re-entry on land after
    police direction to leave   7.31
  false or misleading statements   7.126
  fear or provocation of violence   4.17
  football hooliganism   8.29
  harassment   4.97–4.98
  intentionally causing harassment, alarm
    or distress   4.39
  intimidation and labour relations
    9.48
  obstruction of the highway   9.87–
    9.88

racial hatred   5.19, 5.27, 5.57
racially-aggravated public order
    offences   4.83
riot   3.34–3.36
squatters   7.119–7.120
ticket touting   8.65–8.66
unauthorised vehicular campers
    7.106, 7.109
violent disorder   3.50

Quasi-military organisations
  arrest   9.15
  drilling   9.16
  offences   9.11, 9.13, 9.15
  police   9.12
  political objects   9.12
  political uniforms   9.10
  prohibition of   9.11–9.16
  prosecution   9.14
  searches   9.15
  security firms   9.12
  seizure   9.15
  sentencing   9.14, 9.15
  stewards   9.11
  use of force   9.12
  vigilantes   9.12

Racial hatred   5.1–5.61
  abuse   5.1
  arrest   5.19, 5.27
  associations   5.24
  behaviour   5.15–5.19
  breach of the peace   5.1, 5.8
  broadcasting   5.45–5.60
  Canada   5.7
  chanting   8.27
  clubs   5.24
  common features of offences
    5.4–5.7
  companies   5.20, 5.49–5.51
  computers   5.33
  court reports   5.52
  defences   5.10, 5.43
  displays   5.15–5.19, 5.21–5.22
  distributing   5.20–5.27, 5.30–5.37
  duplicity   5.56
  European Convention on Human
    Rights   5.13, 5.16, 5.60
  films   5.17, 5.34
  football matches   5.61, 8.27
  forfeiture   5.58–5.59

Racial hatred – *cont*

freedom of expression 5.2, 5.13, 5.14

harassment 4.22, 5.13, 5.61

intention 5.8–5.12

international football banning orders 8.56

interpretation 5.4, 5.14, 5.17, 5.21–5.24, 5.34

likely to cause 5.8–5.12

mental element 5.18, 5.26, 5.31, 5.36–5.37, 5.43

Northern Ireland 5.7

parliamentary reports 5.52

possession of racially inflammatory material 5.33–5.39

powers of entry 5.27, 5.39

prohibited conduct 5.16–5.17

privacy 5.16

private places 5.16, 5.30

prohibited conduct 5.21–5.25

prosecutions 5.3, 5.19, 5.27, 5.53–5.55

public plays 5.40–5.44

publication 5.20–5.27, 5.33–5.37

punishment 5.19, 5.27, 5.57

racial groups 5.4–5.6, 5.9, 5.14

recordings 5.28–5.31

religious groups 5.5

representations 5.17, 5.25

searches 5.27, 5.39

tape recordings 5.28

threatening, abusive or insulting conduct 5.2–5.3, 5.13–5.14, 5.20, 5.26, 5.29, 5.34

trials 5.19, 5.27, 5.57

use of force 5.40

videos 5.17, 5.28, 5.30

violent disorder 3.40

words 5.5, 5.14–5.19

written material 5.17, 5.25

Racially-aggravated public order offences

affray 4.85, 4.87

anti-social behaviour orders 4.64

arrest 4.86

converts 4.75–4.76

damage to property 4.87

ethnic origins 4.71

evidence 4.79

France 4.65

Germany 4.65

harassment 4.64, 4.97–4.101

interpretation 4.68–4.80, 4.82

language groups 4.73

'membership' 4.76

motivation 4.79–4.80

national origins 4.70

nationality 4.69

offences 4.81–4.88

prosecutions 4.88

punishment 4.83

racial groups 4.75, 4.77–4.78

definition of 4.68–4.73

racial hostility 4.74, 4.77–4.80

racial incidents 4.63

religious groups 4.72

riot 4.87

sentencing 4.65, 4.83, 4.87–4.88

statistics 4.63

summary offences 3.84

threatening, abusive, insulting or disorderly conduct 4.63–4.88

trials 4.83

indictment, on 4.84

United States 4.65

verdicts, alternative 4.84–4.85, 4.87

violent disorder 4.85, 4.87

Raves 7.67–7.92

amplified music 7.75–7.76, 7.79

arrest 7.84, 7.86

breach of the peace 7.67

conditions 7.69

definition 7.68–7.78

directions to leave 7.80–7.83, 7.86, 7.88

communication 7.82

grounds 7.81

who can make 7.80

writing, in 7.82

duration of 7.79–7.82

European Convention on Human Rights 7.85–7.86, 7.89

forfeiture 7.90–7.92

freedom of assembly and association 7.85–7.86

guidance 7.82

interpretation 7.68–7.78, 7.82, 7.86

licences 7.67, 7.69

night, during the 7.76

noise 7.73, 7.75–7.77

nuisance 7.73, 7.82

number of people 7.70, 7.74

occupiers 7.82

offences 7.83–7.84

open air 7.72–7.73

place 7.72–7.73

police powers 7.67, 7.80–7.83, 7.86–7.89

Raves – *cont*
    powers of entry   7.87
    proceeding, power to stop persons
        7.86–7.89
    reasonableness   7.81, 7.83
    re-entry   7.83
    seizure   7.88–7.92
    sentencing   7.83, 7.86
    serious distress   7.77–7.79
    sound equipment   7.88–7.92
    spontaneous gatherings   7.74
    vehicles   7.88–7.89
Reasonableness. *See also Wednesbury*
        unreasonableness
    affray   3.52, 3.53, 3.56–3.62, 3.68
    aggravated trespass   7.59–7.62, 7.64
    anti-social behaviour orders   2.72–
        2.74
    arrest   3.68
    banning orders (football)   8.34
        international   8.45, 8.56, 8.57
    breach of the peace   2.14, 2.16–2.17,
        2.20–2.23
    conduct likely to cause harassment,
        alarm or distress   4.55
    failure to leave or re-entry on land after
        police direction to leave   7.7,
        7.8–7.10, 7.13, 7.15, 7.17–7.30
    hypothetical bystander   3.26–3.28,
        3.31
    intentionally causing harassment, alarm
        or distress   4.36, 4.37–4.38
    international football banning
        orders   8.45, 8.56, 8.57
    nuisance   9.95
    obstruction of the highway   9.81–
        9.82, 9.84–9.86
    processions and assemblies   6.21,
        6.28–6.31, 6.45–6.47, 6.61, 6.70
    raves   7.81, 7.83
    riot   3.26–3.29, 3.31
    trespassory assemblies   6.84
    unauthorised vehicular campers
        7.101, 7.103, 7.104
    use of force   2.18
    violent disorder   3.40–3.41
Recklessness
    aggravated trespass   7.50
    Caldwell   7.124
    false or misleading statements   7.124
    riot   3.29
Recognizances   2.24, 2.43–2.48
    appeals   2.50

    binding over   2.24, 2.43–2.48,
        2.50, 2.52
    breach of   2.50
    forfeiture   2.50
    refusal to enter into   2.47–2.48, 2.50,
        2.52
    sureties   2.24, 2.43–2.46, 2.48
Recordings
    films   5.17
    racial hatred   5.28–5.31
    videos   5.17, 5.28, 5.30
Religious groups
    racial hatred   5.5
    racially-aggravated public order
        offences   4.72
Remedies. *See also* Damages, Forfeiture,
        Injunctions
    harassment   4.92–4.96
    racially inflammatory material   5.58
    removal orders   7.34, 7.95, 7.101–
        7.109
    restraining orders   4.96, 4.99
Removal
    failure to leave or re-entry on land after
        police direction to leave   7.34
    local authorities   7.107
    seizure   7.34
    unauthorised vehicular campers
        7.95, 7.101–7.102, 7.104, 7.107–
        7.109
    vehicles   7.101–7.102, 7.107–7.109
Residents   9.19
Resisting the police   9.68–9.69
Restraining orders
    breach   4.96
    harassment   4.96, 4.99
    sentencing   4.96
Riot   3.9–3.39
    abolition   3.6–3.9
    accomplices   3.12, 3.19, 3.30
    admissions   3.32
    adverse inferences   3.25
    affray   3.70, 3.73
    age of criminal responsibility   3.19
    boundaries   3.12
    burden of proof   3.30
    churches, etc, disturbances in   9.31
    common law   3.2, 3.4
    common purpose   3.4, 3.20–3.25,
        3.29–3.30
    convictions, alternative bases for
        3.33
    damage to property   3.27, 3.37
    damages   3.37–3.38

Riot – *cont*
   defences   3.17
   Director of Public Prosecutions   3.34
   duplicity   3.70
   duress   3.19
   elements of offence   3.2–3.3
   fear of harm   3.26–3.28
   hypothetical bystander   3.26–3.28, 3.31
   indictable offences   3.35
   industrial action   3.21
   insanity   3.19
   intoxication   3.30
   Law Commission   3.6–3.8, 3.34
   mental element   3.29–3.32
   motives   3.25
   number of people   3.9–3.10, 3.18–3.20
   police fund   3.37–3.38
   private premises   3.11, 3.28
   private prosecutions   3.34
   prohibited conduct   3.10–3.28
   prosecution   3.34–3.36
   punishment   3.34–3.36
   racially-aggravated public order offences   4.87
   reasonableness   3.29
   recklessness   3.29
   self-defence   3.17, 3.19
   sentencing   3.35, 3.50
   statutory   3.7, 3.39
   threats   3.12–3.13, 3.16, 3.19, 3.21–3.24
   trials   3.34–3.36
   unlawful assembly   3.4
   use of force   3.17, 3.19
   violence   3.10, 3.12–3.17
      definition   3.14–3.17
      unlawful   3.17, 3.19, 3.31
      use of   3.21–3.24, 3.29–3.30
   violent disorder   3.43, 3.50
   words   3.21
Roadblocks   6.100
Road protesters
   aggravated trespass   7.37, 7.50, 7.66
   eviction   9.70
   obstruction   9.70
Rout   3.3
   abolition   3.6–3.7
   Law Commission   3.6–3.8
Route regulation   6.100–6.103

Scotland
   breach of the peace   2.3
   football hooliganism   8.9
Searches
   aggravated trespass   7.64
   fear or provocation of violence   4.18
   football hooliganism   8.15, 8.24
   obstruction   9.71
   offensive weapons   7.84
   police   1.2, 4.18
   political uniforms   9.9
   quasi-military organisations   9.15
   racial hatred   5.27, 5.38
   squatters   7.120
   stop and search   8.24
   use of force   1.2
Security firms   9.12
Seizure
   aggravated trespass   7.60
   charges   7.34
   European Convention on Human Rights   7.33, 7.89
   failure to leave or re-entry on land after police direction to leave   7.33–7.34
   forfeiture   7.34, 7.90–7.92
   political uniforms   9.4
   quasi-military organisations   9.15
   raves   7.88–7.92
   removal notices   7.34
   sound equipment   7.88–7.89
   unauthorised vehicular campers   7.111
   vehicles   7.33–7.34, 7.88–7.89
Self-defence
   affray   3.56, 3.66
   riot   3.17
Sentencing
   affray   3.67
   anti-social behaviour orders   2.88
   binding over   2.39, 2.48
   bomb hoaxes   9.29
   broadcasting   5.57
   churches, etc, disturbances in   9.34, 9.35
   conduct likely to cause harassment, alarm or distress   4.42, 4.56
   diplomatic premises   7.140
   entering and remaining on property   7.127, 7.140
   failure to leave or re-entry on land after police direction to leave   7.31
   false or misleading statements   7.126
   fear or provocation of violence   4.17

Sentencing – *cont*
  football banning orders
    domestic   8.42
    international   8.50, 8.53, 8.56
  football hooliganism   8.11–8.12,
    8.19, 8.23, 8.29
  forfeiture   5.58–5.59, 7.92
  harassment   4.93–4.96, 4.98
  intentionally causing harassment, alarm
    or distress   4.39
  international banning orders   8.50,
    8.53, 8.56
  intimidation and labour relations
    9.48
  meetings, disorderly conduct at
    6.105, 6.109
  nuisance   9.100
  obstruction   9.70
    highways   9.87–9.88, 9.90, 9.91
  offensive weapons   7.64
  processions and assemblies   6.18,
    6.37, 6.39, 6.41, 6.52, 6.100
  public plays   4.102
  quasi-military organisations   9.14,
    9.16
  racially-aggravated public order
    offences   4.65, 4.83, 4.88
  raves   7.83, 7.86
  resisting the police   9.70
  restraining orders   4.96
  riot   3.35, 3.50
  squatters   7.119
  street offences   9.20, 9.21
  ticket touting   8.65
  trespassory assemblies   6.84
  unauthorised vehicular campers
    7.99, 7.106, 7.109
  violent disorder   3.50
Smuggling   4.38
Sound equipment   7.88–7.92
Squatters   7.112–7.126
  arrest   7.119–7.120, 7.126
  attempts   7.117
  commercial premises   7.112
  criminal law   7.112, 7.115
  entering and remaining on
    property   7.127, 7.130, 7.132–
    7.133, 7.136
  eviction   7.115
  false or misleading information
    7.121–7.126
  interim possession orders   7.112–
    7.126
    applications for   7.114

    documents   7.114
    false or misleading information
      7.121–7.126
    form of   7.114
    scope   7.114
    service   7.114
    time for hearing   7.114
  interpretation   7.114
  mental element   7.118, 7.124–7.125
  occupiers   7.112
  offences   7.115, 7.116–7.117
  pirate traders   7.112
  police   7.115
  possession orders   7.112, 7.116–
    7.126
    breach   7.115
    enforcement   7.115
    interim   7.112–7.116
  powers of entry   7.120
  prohibited conduct   7.122–7.123
  punishment   7.119–7.120, 7.126
  recklessness   7.124
  searches   7.120
  sentencing   7.119
  trespass or re-entering as trespasser
    7.116–7.126
  trials   7.119–7.120, 7.126
Stalking   4.89
Standard of proof
  anti-social behaviour orders   2.80
  harassment   4.92
Stop and search   8.24
Street offences   9.18–9.23
Summary offences   1.9
  affray   3.66, 3.71, 3.74
  fear or provocation of violence   4.17
  harassment   4.95, 4.101
  meetings, disorderly conduct at
    6.105, 6.107
  nuisance   9.93
  obstruction of the highway   9.73,
    9.79
  processions and assemblies   6.2
  racially-aggravated public order
    offences   4.84
  unauthorised vehicular campers
    7.107
  verdicts, alternative   3.74
Summons
  binding over   2.30
  service   7.107
  unauthorised vehicular campers
    7.107

Sureties
  binding over   2.24, 2.43–2.46,
    2.48
  recognizances   2.24, 2.43–2.46, 2.48

Tape-recordings   5.28
Telephone calls
  intentionally causing harassment, alarm
    or distress   4.33
  obscene   9.94
Tenants
  entering and remaining on
    property   7.133
  failure to leave or re-entry on land after
    police direction to leave   7.9
Theatres   4.102–4.104, 5.39–5.44
Threatening, abusive, insulting or
    disorderly conduct   4.1–4.21
  breach of the peace   4.1
  provocation to cause, by showing a
    public play   4.102–4.104
  broadcasting   5.45
  fear or provocation of violence
    4.2–4.19
  harassment, alarm or distress,
    conduct likely to cause   4.41–4.62
  intentionally causing   4.22–4.40
  protection from harassment
    4.89–4.101
  meetings   4.105
  protection from harassment   4.89–
    4.101
  racial hatred   5.2–5.3, 5.13–5.14,
    5.20, 5.26, 5.29, 5.34
  racially-aggravated public order
    offences   4.63–4.88
  related offences   4.105
Threats. *See also* Threatening, abusive,
    insulting or disorderly conduct
  affray   3.53–3.56, 3.63, 3.65
  contract breaking   9.39
  failure to leave or re-entry on land after
    police direction to leave   7.17–
    7.20
  intimidation and labour relations
    9.39
  riot   3.12–3.13, 3.16, 3.19, 3.21–3.24
  violent disorder   3.42–3.46
Throwing objects   8.26
Ticket touting
  access to public   8.63
  arrest   8.65–8.66
  designated football matches   8.62

  football   8.59–8.66
  interpretation   8.61–8.63
  mental element   8.64
  offences   8.59–8.63
  place of commission   8.63
  prohibited conduct   8.60–8.63
  punishment   8.65–8.66
  sentencing   8.65
  sporting events besides football   8.59
  trials   8.65–8.66
  unauthorised persons   8.61
Time-limits
  damages   4.92
  harassment   4.92
Trespass. *See* Collective trespass or
  nuisance on land, Trespassory
  assemblies
Trespassory assemblies
  advance notice   6.71
  ancient monuments   6.77, 6.86, 6.89,
    6.90
  appeals   6.86
  bans   6.69–6.90
    duration   6.83
    procedure   6.78–6.80
    terms of   6.82–6.83
    writing, in   6.81
  breach of the peace   6.70
  European Convention on Human
    Rights   6.77, 6.89, 6.90
  freedom of assembly and
    association   6.69, 6.89, 6.90
  freedom of expression   6.69, 6.89
  highways   6.87–6.88
  industrial action   6.72
  interpretation   6.72, 6.77, 6.82
  meetings   6.69
  nuisance   6.86
  obstruction   6.87
  offences   6.84–6.90
  permission
    excess of   6.74
    lack of   6.74
  police   6.70–6.71, 6.74, 6.78–6.79,
    6.86, 6.90
  power to stop people proceeding
    with   6.90
  procedure   6.78–6.80
  prohibition of   6.69–6.90
  public access   6.73, 6.86
  reasonableness   6.74, 6.76–6.77,
    6.88, 6.90
  sentencing   6.84

Trespassory assemblies – *cont*
  serious disruption or damage   6.75–
    6.77
  types of   6.72–6.73
Trials. *See also* Trials on indictment
  1.9
  affray   3.65–3.67
  aggravated trespass   7.55, 7.63
  bomb hoaxes   9.29
  broadcasting   5.57
  churches, etc, disturbances in   9.34
  conduct likely to cause harassment,
    alarm or distress   4.56
  failure to leave or re-entry on land after
    police direction to leave   7.31
  fair   2.52
  false or misleading statements   7.126
  fear or provocation of violence   4.17
  football hooliganism   8.27
  harassment   4.98–4.99
  intentionally causing harassment, alarm
    or distress   4.39
  intimidation and labour relations
    9.48
  obstruction of the highway   9.87–
    9.88
  racial hatred   5.19, 5.27, 5.57
  racially-aggravated public order
    offences   4.83
  riot   3.34–3.36
  sentencing   8.65–8.66
  squatters   7.119–7.120
  unauthorised vehicular campers
    7.106
  violent disorder   3.50
Trials on indictment
  affray   3.71–3.73
  harassment   4.95, 4.100
  obstruction on the highway   9.91
  racially-aggravated public order
    offences   4.84
  violent disorder   3.71
Trivial behaviour   4.20–4.21

Unauthorised vehicular campers
  7.93–7.111
  arrest   7.107
  caravan sites   7.95
  consent   7.97
  defences   7.105
  directions to leave   7.96–7.104
    local authorities   7.101

  notice   7.103
  offences   7.104–7.106
  European Convention on Human
    Rights   7.110–7.111
  failure to leave or re-entry on land after
    police direction to leave   7.14,
    7.21
  family life, right to   7.110
  guidance   7.101
  gypsies   7.95
    abolition of duty to provide sites
      for   7.93–7.94, 7.110
  highways   7.97
  home, right to   7.110
  interpretation   7.97–7.102
  local authorities   7.4, 7.21, 7.93–
    7.104, 7.107–7.108, 7.110
  magistrates' courts   7.95, 7.107
  New Age Travellers   7.93
  number of persons   7.98
  obstruction   7.109
  occupiers   7.97
  offences   7.104–7.106
  planning permission   7.94, 7.110
  police   7.95
  possession orders   7.95
  privacy   7.110
  punishment   7.106, 7.109
  re-entry   7.102, 7.104
  reasonableness   7.101, 7.103, 7.104
  removal orders   7.95, 7.101–7.102,
    7.104, 7.107–7.109
  residence   7.99
  seizure   7.111
  sentencing   7.99, 7.106, 7.109
  summons   7.107
  trials   7.106
  vehicles   7.99–7.100, 7.102, 7.104,
    7.107–7.109
Uniforms. *See* Political uniforms
United States   4.65
Unlawful assembly
  abolition   3.6–3.7
  common law   3.4
  Law Commission   3.6–3.8
  riot   3.4
  violence, fear of   3.4
Unreasonableness. *See Wednesbury*
  unreasonableness
Use of force
  arrest   1.2, 9.63
  assault on the police   9.63, 9,64
  breach of the peace   2.18

Use of force – *cont*
   failure to leave or re-entry on land after
      police direction to leave   7.35
   football hooliganism   8.15
   obstruction of the police   9.59
   powers of entry   1.2
   quasi-military organisations   9.12
   racial hatred   5.38
   reasonableness   2.18
   riot   3.17, 3.19
   searches   1.2

Vehicles. *See also* Unauthorised vehicular
      campers
   aggravated trespass   7.60, 7.62
   alcohol carried on   8.10–8.20
   failure to leave or re-entry on land after
      police direction to leave   7.17–
      7.20, 7.33–7.34
   destruction   7.34
   disposal   7.34
   football hooliganism   8.5–8.6, 8.10–
      8.20
   forfeiture   7.34
   gypsies   7.20
   interpretation   7.20, 7.100
   intoxication   8.13
   possession   7.17–7.20
   raves   7.88–7.89
   removal   7.101–7.102, 7.107–7.109
   seizure   7.33–7.34, 7.88–7.89
   unauthorised vehicular campers
      7.99–7.100, 7.102, 7.104, 7.107–
      7.109
Vehicular campers. *See* Unauthorised
      vehicular campers
Verdicts
   affray   3.71–3.74
   alternative   3.71–3.74, 4.84, 4.87,
      4.100–4.101
   harassment   4.100–4.101
   racially-aggravated public order
      offences   4.84
   summary offences   3.74, 4.86
Videos   5.17, 5.28, 5.30, 5.34
Vigilantes   9.12
Violence. *See also* Domestic violence, Fear
      or provocation of violence, Violent
      disorder
   breach of the peace   2.4, 2.8,
      2.22–2.23
   churches, etc, disturbances in   9.31
      entering and remaining on
         property   7.128–7.135
      football hooliganism   8.26
      interpretation   7.129, 8.26, 9.31
      riot   3.10, 3.12–3.17
         definition of violence   3.14–3.17
         unlawful   3.17, 3.19, 3.31
         use of   3.21–3.24, 3.29–3.30
      unlawful assembly   3.4
Violent disorder   3.40–3.49
   accomplices   3.40
   acquittals of all but one or two
      3.46–3.48
   affray   3.52, 3.69–3.74
   age of criminal responsibility   3.43,
      3.46
   common purpose   3.44
   convictions
      alternative bases for   3.49
      number of   3.40
   directions   3.48–3.49
   duplicity   3.69–3.70
   duress   3.43, 3.46
   fear of harm   3.40–3.41
   hypothetical bystander test   3.40–
      3.41
   industrial action   3.44
   insanity   3.43, 3.46
   intoxication   3.45
   magistrates' courts   3.74
   mental element   3.43, 3.45, 3.46
   number of persons   3.42–3.43
   private premises   3.41
   processions and assemblies   3.40
   prohibited conduct   3.41–3.44
   prosecution   3.50
   punishment   3.50
   racial hatred   3.40
   racially-aggravated public order
      offences   4.85, 4.87
   research   3.40
   riot   3.43, 3.50
   sentencing   3.50
   threats   3.42–3.46
   trials   3.50
      indictment, on   3.71
   use of violence   3.42–3.46
   words   3.40

Warnings
   aggravated trespass   7.61
   arrest   9.69

Warnings – *cont*
  conduct likely to cause harassment,
    alarm or distress   4.57, 4.59
  obstruction of the police   9.66
Watching and besetting   9.42, 9.45
Wednesbury unreasonableness
  judicial review   6.97
  margin of appreciation   1.26
Words. *See also* Threats
  affray   3.55
  conduct likely to cause harassment,
    alarm or distress   4.43–4.45,
    4.53–4.54, 4.59
  fear or provocation of violence   4.6,
    4.11, 4.13

intentionally causing harassment, alarm
    or distress   4.26
racial hatred   5.5, 5.14–5.19
riot   3.21
violent disorder   3.40

Young offenders. *See also* Age of criminal
    responsibility
  anti-social behaviour orders   2.78,
    2.79
  magistrates' courts   2.78
  welfare of the child   2.78
  youth offending teams   2.78